Walnut Pickles
❖　and　❖
Watermelon Cake

GREAT LAKES BOOKS

Philip P. Mason, Editor
Walter P. Reuther Library, Wayne State University

Dr. Charles K. Hyde, Associate Editor
Department of History, Wayne State University

Advisory Editors

*Rainy day fun in the kitchen while mother is away
(Townsend, 1894).*

Walnut Pickles
❖ and ❖
Watermelon Cake

A CENTURY OF
MICHIGAN COOKING

Larry B. Massie and Priscilla Massie

⚞ WAYNE STATE UNIVERSITY PRESS
DETROIT   1990

94 93 92 91 90   5 4 3 2

Library of Congress Cataloging-in-Publication Data
Massie, Larry B., 1947–
    Walnut pickles and watermelon cake : a century of Michigan cooking
/ by Larry B. Massie and Priscilla Massie.
        p.   cm. —(Great Lakes books)
    Bibliography: p.
    Includes index.
    ISBN 0-8143-1939-4
    1. Cookery—Michigan.   I. Massie, Priscilla, 1955–
II. Title.   III. Series.
TX715.M19   1990
641.59774—dc20   89-16448
                                                          CIP

Acknowledgments

We would like to thank Al Beet for his masterful photographic processing and Betty L. Fouch for her humor and help in proofreading.

*For Dr. Albert Castel, friend, scholar, and gourmet,
with whom we have shared many a memorable meal*

We may live without poetry, music and art.
    We may live without conscience,
We may live without heart;
    We may live without friends,
We may live without books,
    But civilized man cannot live without cooks.

He may live without books,
    What is knowledge but grieving?
He may live without hope,
    What is hope but deceiving?
He may live without love,
    What is passion but pining?
But where is the man that can live without dining?
                    (Kalamazoo, 1906)

Contents

Introduction

This is a cookbook for people who long for a warm country kitchen filled with the magic aroma of freshly baked bread, rich stew bubbling on the back burner, and wood smoke. It's for people who enjoy the feel of old kitchen utensils worn thin through generations of use. It's for those who remember their grandma's incomparable coleslaw, chicken and dumplings, raspberry jam, or pumpkin pie. It's for those who'd like to try Hannah Barlow's Boiled Dinner, Elvira's Muffins, and Fanny's Molasses Cake. It's for those who don't like to buy everything prepackaged and ready to eat, who would like to experiment with bread made from scratch, pear honey, potato candy, spruce beer, and rhubarb wine. It's for those who wouldn't be afraid to serve guests bubble and squeak, squash soup, sailor's duff, blushing bunny, peanut sausage, shoepack pie, painted ladies, gooseberry fool, toad in the puddle, or toad in the hole.

But most of all this collection is for those native born or adoptive Michiganians who love their state, its beauty, its ethnic and cultural traditions, its history, and its culinary heritage.

The story behind this book can be traced back to two seven-year-old children. When Larry was seven, he got his hands on a box of old books. He was fascinated with their quaint texts and strange old bindings. He learned to savor the very smell of ancient leather and paper browned with age. As he grew older his affection for old books ripened into a passion, and no matter what else he needed to do for a living, he knew the most important thing was to collect books. He gradually became a specialist in Michigan history.

There was also a seven-year-old Michigan girl named Priscilla who began to learn to cook each day after school. Fascinated with the mysteries of the kitchen, she helped the family housekeeper prepare dinner. Her first solo effort, an orange cake with orange frosting, was memorable. She had omitted some vital ingredient, and the cake crumbled apart. Nevertheless she patched it back together with toothpicks, frosted it, and served it at a dinner party. Guests cautiously chewed prickly mouthfuls, but their gracious compliments thrilled her little heart. Under the housekeeper's expert guidance, Priscilla grew more skillful, much to the pleasure of her five hungry brothers and sister. By the time Priscilla had grown to womanhood she had become an accomplished cook, eager to please those she loved with culinary creations.

We married and moved into an old one-room schoolhouse located in the midst of the Allegan State Forest. Crowded within the main part of the structure is our collection of thirty thousand books. Thirteen-feet-high bookshelves surround all sides of a vast room. More bookshelves in the center of the room support a loft where Larry studies and writes about Michigan history.

In an attached room lies Priscilla's domain. She does what she does best at a "Hoosier cabinet" built in 1910 in Niles, Michigan. It is flanked on one side by a General Electric "monitor top" refrigerator made in 1932 and on the other by an electric range of a similar vintage. Antique kitchen utensils, cast-iron "Griswold" pots and pans, and other domestic artifacts hang everywhere. A round oak table and chairs stand in the center of the room opposite an ornate oak buffet built in Hastings in 1905. We love history so much that we have surrounded ourselves with period household furnishings. Priscilla cooks with antique utensils, and we dine on vintage tableware.

As we made periodic forays to antiquarian bookshops, book sales, and auctions in quest of yet more old books, Priscilla began to collect in her specialty—old Michigan cookbooks. She succeeded in locating more than one hundred titles published in Michigan before World War II. Some were large hardbound tomes, but many others were fragile pamphlets published as fund-raisers by church guilds, ladies' libraries, and other women's groups.

The books themselves command interest as

artifacts from the past. Cookbooks, like children's books, are generally read to pieces because of the nature of their use—that is, spread open on the kitchen counter at peril from any number of wet and sticky ingredients. For an ephemeral pamphlet published by a small organization in a limited printing to have survived the vicissitudes of time is a miracle in itself. Some early cookbooks command bibliographic interest as rare Michigan imprints.

Often Michigan cookbooks contain advertisements for local firms and manufacturers. Such advertisements are an important source for the business history of Michigan. They can also provide clues to the publication date of cookbooks that often lack a traditional imprint. Despite their value in terms of printing history and business advertisements, Michigan cookbooks have been largely ignored by those institutions charged with preserving Michigan history. Even major collections like the State Library in Lansing contain very few Michigan cookbooks.

But the prime value of these scarce publications is the recipes they contain. Good cooking, then as now, was a mixture of native aptitude, experience, proper ingredients, and a good recipe. Contributors shared their prize recipes, perhaps passed down from mother to daughter or developed through half a century of experimentation. Certainly not every recipe can be considered good by modern standards. Individual tastes vary, and not every cook was as skillful in describing her culinary techniques as she was in turning out the finished dish. An interesting recipe for steak pie, for example, yielded an unappetizing gummy mixture that even our border collie refused to touch.

While the idiosyncrasies of individual cooks and their recipes pose some problems, another set of difficulties results from changing ideals as to what constitutes good eating. What the generation of the 1890s found mouth-watering might shock modern palates. Early recipes, for example, routinely called for more salt than the average person would tolerate today. Then too, Victorian diners seemed to relish more vinegary dishes. It was the golden age of pickling, with everything from lemons to walnuts fair prey for the vinegar jar. Such unlikely ingredients as cherries, gooseberries, lemons, and mushrooms were also turned to catsup.

In addition to the evolution of eating preferences, early recipes also chart Michigan's social history. Recipes for game dishes, including sturgeon, passenger pigeon, opossum, bear, raccoon, squirrel, and venison capture the pioneer experience. Techniques for baking bread without the benefit of yeast testify to the deprivations and in-

ventiveness of frontier times. The many New Englanders who pioneered in Michigan brought with them a fondness for certain types of food, like oysters, which were more available in their area of origin. Some recipes also document tra⁻ planted folk beliefs like the old New England custom of making sauerkraut "early in the light of the moon."

The variety of ethnic groups that peopled the peninsulas contributed colorful specialities to Michigan's menu. Long after memories of the "old country" had faded, Cornish pasties, Dutch wine soup and hutspot, Danish aebelskiver, and Scottish haggis continued to make Michigan eating a unique experience. In the 1880s, a missionary who had spent forty years in India contributed authentic recipes for chicken curry and other Indian specialities to Dr. Chase's Ann Arbor compendium. In 1898 a woman from Menominee submitted a recipe for chutney, an East Indian relish. By 1917 a Grand Rapids cook could proudly pass on her favorite recipe for "Michigan tomales." While the boiling-pot theory of ethnic assimilation might not have been operating smoothly throughout American society, in Michigan kitchens it was bubbling nicely.

The pages of Michigan's history contain many success stories of locales that capitalized on geographic factors or entrepreneurial daring to win national laurels for their products. Cookbooks printed in these areas capture their claim to fame in a culinary sense. Kalamazoo cooks celebrated their city's renown as the celery center of the world with many recipes using that crunchy vegetable. Battle Creek promoted its title as "Cereal City" with distinctive recipes containing Kellogg's and Post's famous breakfast foods as well as a host of strange-sounding and long-forgotten local cereals. And what could be more appropriate than a turn-of-the-century recipe for cherry cake from Traverse City, Michigan's cherry capital?

Pages yellowed with age and not infrequently stained with ancient kitchen spills preserve little-known details of early domestic life. It can be a treasure hunt to leaf through these pages in search of lost bits of culinary lore, unique Michigan recipes, and mention of forgotten utensils. One recipe calls for a piece of butter the size of a hickory nut, another makes it the size of a butternut, and yet another measures liquids by the egg shell. One contributor discusses the merits of a hair sieve or the indispensable splints from a corn broom. Reference to cast-iron spiders, potato jammers, celery holders, aebelskiver pans, and other utensils found now only in antique shops evoke nostalgic images of ancestral kitchens.

The human element breathes life into many

recipes, transforming them from cookery formulas into warm messages from the past. Some are indelibly imprinted with the personality of the contributor. A cook with a sense of humor tells us "a cherry can be as sour as a deacon with a bunion." Another didactic matron states, "Do not think that it will be just as good if the flour and sugar are not sifted three times, for it will not!" Sometimes cookbooks document a thinly veiled rivalry between competing cooks. Two "never-fail" recipes for the same dish that contain totally different instructions, for example, might appear on the same page. Some recipes approach the poetic in their wording: "Make a puff paste and line your pattie pans." A special thrill comes from discovering recipes signed by the wives of state governors, city founders, famous authors, and other personalities from Michigan history.

For these and many other reasons, we have found the collecting and sampling of Michigan recipes a fascinating experience, an adventure we want to share with you. Apart from an occasional flop, most historic recipes yield some mighty tasty victuals. We've included more than thirteen hundred recipes from Michigan's past in this volume. They date from the 1820s through the end of World War II. We've tried to cover the gamut of traditional dishes from all sections of the state.

We've also included Priscilla's suggestions for modernizing some of the recipes she has tried. For the most part, however, we have left for you the adventure of trying these historic Michigan recipes. However, by referring to the Measuring Tables, Oven Temperatures, Hints, and Suggestions chapter, you can convert archaic measurements (drachms, gills, etc.) to modern equivalents. All the recipes have been copied verbatim. We have retained variant spellings and styles to preserve the appeal of the originals. We have annotated some selections with information about contributors, early cooking techniques, and some esoteric utensils and ingredients.

We've also included the names of the original contributors when known and hope some of you will enjoy discovering an ancestor's favorite recipe. The date and city of publication code after each recipe refers to the cookbook that recipe was gleaned from. A list of all the cookbooks used, with full bibliographic information supplied, is in the Sources section at the end of the volume. We have interspersed the recipes with illustrations of period kitchen scenes and vintage utensils taken from Michigan cookbooks and related works.

We hope you enjoy as much as we have learning about, experimenting with, and, most importantly, sampling our state's colorful culinary heritage.

Snacks

Victorians, who usually devoured three hearty meals a day, had little shift with the light snacks and hors d'oeuvres that have become fashionable today. The typical seven-course dinner served on special occasions, however, might include a number of dishes appropriate for appetizers. Afternoon teas became fashionable particularly with ladies' church and social organizations during the 1880s. Desserts were the usual refreshments served at such events, but some cooks developed meat, cheese, or egg specialties.

Early cookbooks rarely devote much space to appetizers and canapes, but we have garnered the following lighter dishes that can be enjoyed as snacks for parties and social occasions. Many recipes originally intended as sandwich fillings work nicely as a vegetable dip or spread for crackers. Victorian technology decreed that most of these dainties be prepared just prior to consumption, but we have found that most recipes can be made ahead of time, refrigerated or frozen, and warmed when needed in a conventional or microwave oven.

Appetizers

Roll regular pastry to the usual thickness. Cut it into two or two and a half inch squares. Spread the pastry with cream cheese beaten until it is fluffy and seasoned with a speck of onion juice. In the center of each square place a plump meaty stuffed olive. Pull the ends of dough together over the olive and pinch them tightly to hold them in place. Just before serving time, fry in hot, deep fat. Drain on paper and serve at once.

Mrs. Robert Farmer
(Kalamazoo, 1941)

Baked Bean Sandwich

Mash cold baked beans to a paste, season with onion juice, a little mustard, add some finely chopped celery and parsley and spread between buttered bread, either brown or white.

(Kalamazoo, 1899)

The Ladies of the First Presbyterian Church of Kalamazoo published their 198-page cookbook, well enlivened with local advertisements, in 1899. In launching the volume upon the "popular wave of innumerable cookbooks, professional, sectional and ecclesiastical already flooding the land," they took care to claim for it "only such merits as belong to the tried and true." Furthermore, many of the recipes had been handed down within families for generations, "gathered from the experience of those closely associated with the community from its earliest days, some of whom toiled in the past with loving heart, and hand now stilled to make the home and table complete in every detail." Could anyone say no to a baked bean sandwich served with such nostalgic emotion?

Beefsteak Fingers

Take about 2 lbs. tender, juicy steak and lay it in a stew pan. Sprinkle over it a little salt and pepper, a large onion chopped fine, 1 tablespoon minced celery; cover with equal quantities of vinegar and water, stew gently with the pan closely covered for ½ hour. When cold cut the meat into strips about 3 inches long and 1 wide, dip into beaten egg, then into a mixture of bread crumbs, minced onion, parsley and celery, fry in boiling lard. Place

The Simpson, Hall, Miller and Company's "electro plated" covered bowl sold for eight dollars in 1872 (Wallingford, 1872).

a bed of well mashed potatoes on a hot dish, arrange the meat tastefully on this and serve.

Mrs. E. M. Coppens, Grand Rapids
(Muskegon, 1890)

We eschewed the bed of potatoes and found beefsteak fingers a nice finger food. Round steak works well, and we added celery seed and onion powder to the egg mixture.

This recipe appears in the *Muskegon Cook Book* published in 1890. The Ladies Aid Society of the First Baptist Church compiled the recipes, taking care to observe "total abstinence" in their selections. They sold the volumes for one dollar each, and donated the profits to the church building fund. In return for their dollar, more than an average ten-hour-day's wage for women factory workers in 1890, patrons were assured that not only had each recipe been tested by the lady to whom it was subscribed but also that the instructions would enable "any ordinarily capable housewife" to prepare a delicious dish.

Blushing Bunny

1 lb. cheese	*1 teaspoon mustard*
1 can tomato soup	*Salt and pepper*
2 eggs	*Paprika*
	Worcestershire sauce

Beat yolks; add soup and mix; add seasoning then heat and add melted cheese. When hot, add stiffly beaten egg whites and beat until fluffy. Serve on toast or crackers.

(Grayling, 1937)

Sharp cheese is preferable but almost any variety works. We served this in a chafing dish as a fondue at a Valentine's Day party. Using toothpicks, guests dipped bite-sized pieces of toasted bread until the bunny was all gone.

Bonchees

Make a puff paste and line your pattie-pans. Bake. Fill with any kind of highly seasoned chopped meat.

(Kalamazoo, 1899)

This simple alliterative recipe approaches the poetic. Directions for puff paste can be found in the dessert section. Pattie-pans are any type of muffin or cupcake pan.

Canopees

Take a stale square loaf of bread and cut into very thick squares and scoop the inside out. This is a delicate piece of work but if careful one can do it, leaving a round space inside. Take 1 egg and ½ an egg shell of milk, a little salt. Dip the shells [of bread] in the mixture then drain them and drop in hot lard until a delicate brown. Fill them with chicken or veal minced and cooked with a dressing. Add a sprig of parsley.

(Kalamazoo, 1899)

Crack your egg carefully or it will not make a very good measuring cup. Actually, ½ of a large egg shell of milk equals ⅛ of a cup of milk.

Stuffed Celery

One pound fresh cheese, juice of 1 lemon, cream with a fork after adding juice of lemon and a dash of red pepper; when cheese is soft take 3 small stalks of celery, folding them together and fill with the mixture; tie stalks with baby ribbon—delicious.

(Battle Creek, 1903)

Stuffed Celery

Mix cream cheese with enough cream to moisten it, season with salt and pepper, chop 8 olives and ½ pound English walnuts and mix with cheese. Select short wide pieces of celery, trim off most of the leaves, and fill with cheese mixture.

(Higgins Lake, 1920)

Stuffed Celery

Wash and scrape celery, rub cream cheese until soft and creamy with a little cream or milk. Add some pimento, cut fine and mix with mayonnaise. Press smoothly into celery stalks.

Mrs. George E. Miller
(Kalamazoo, 1921)

Take your pick from three historic recipes for that old stand-by stuffed celery. We lean toward the 1921 Kalamazoo recipe. In the early part of this century, Kalamazoo proudly promoted its nickname, "the Celery City," in celebration of its status as the world's largest producer of the crunchy vegetable. Dutch immigrants had transformed the swampy mucklands bypassed by other settlers into lush celery beds during the late nineteenth century. Using a specialized technology adopted from the old country, they grew a large, creamy white variety of celery. Unfortunately, Kalamazoo celery fell victim to a blight in the 1930s and competition from California-grown Pascal celery.

Cheese Balls

One pint grated cheese, 1 sprinkle cayenne pepper, ½ teaspoon salt, whites of 2 eggs well beaten, mix thoroughly and roll in balls the size of a large marble. Roll in bread crumbs, then in egg, then in crumbs, fry in basket in hot lard. To be served hot with salad.

Bertha Ashby
(Kalamazoo, 1899)

These delicious appetizers, which puff up hollow in the middle, can be served hot or cold. Use the remaining egg yolks to roll the cheese balls in and cook in a deep fryer for one minute at 400°. One batch yields about two dozen cheese balls.

Cheese Balls

Grate enough cream cheese to fill 1 cup, add ½ cup of sifted bread crumbs, 1 tablespoon of melted butter, a few drops of onion juice, ½ teaspoon of made mustard and one egg well-beaten. Shape into

This happy family prepares to enjoy a hearty meal. But where's Papa? (Cleveland, 1894).

small balls, coat them with finest bread crumbs and drop in hot lard.

(Battle Creek, 1903)

Cheese Bundles

Take neat strips of cheese half an inch thick. Roll each one carefully in a thin slice of dried beef (without freshening), lay on well buttered slices of toast. Bake in hot oven 5 to 8 minutes until cheese melts. Garnish with parsley and sweet or dill pickle.

(Higgins Lake, 1920)

Cheese Canape

½ cup grated cheese
4 tablespoons mayon-
naise

1 teaspoon grated
onion
4 tablespoons finely
minced parsley

All mixed together. Place on circle of bread upon which a ring of freshly chilled tomato has been placed. Dust with paprika.

(Grand Rapids, 1935)

We found that a dash of cayenne pepper and 2 tablespoons of sour cream improved the mixture.

Cheese and Celery Sandwich

Whip a gill of thick sweet cream, add grated cheese to make a thick paste. Spread on buttered bread and cover thickly with finely chopped white celery.

Margaret Waite
(Kalamazoo, 1899)

This also makes a good dip for vegetables or can be spread on cocktail rye.

Cheese Puffs—To Serve with Salad

Two tablespoons butter, 4 tablespoons flour, 4 tablespoons grated cheese, 1 cup water, ½ teaspoon salt, little cayenne pepper, 2 eggs. Put butter and water on stove, mix cheese, flour, salt and pepper and stir into water. Cook for three minutes, stirring all the time. Let this mixture get cold, then add eggs one at a time. Beat this batter 5 minutes, and drop in teaspoonfuls on buttered pan, bake in moderate oven 20 minutes. Serve hot.

Mrs. L. B. Kendall
(Kalamazoo, 1899)

Contrary to its name, the batch we prepared turned out to be more of a cheese wafer, but they are very good.

Cheese Relish

One small jar of cheese, 1 c. English walnut meats, 6 olives, 1 small pepper, red or green; chop together and mix with cheese; add 3 tbsp. salad dressing. Form in balls and arrange in nests of lettuce leaves.

Mrs. Herbert Smith
(Kalamazoo, 1921)

Cheese Salad

Odd bits of cheese to the amount of a pound. Grated, one hard-boiled egg. One teaspoonful of cayenne pepper, one of salt, one of white sugar, one of made mustard, one tablespoonful of vinegar, one of salad oil or melted butter. Rub the yolk of the egg to a paste with the oil or butter, adding in order the salt, pepper, sugar, mustard, and lastly the cheese. Work all well together before putting in the vinegar. These mixtures bear a marvelous resemblance in taste to a deviled crab, and make a very good impromptu relish to eat with crackers and butter. This is still better if you can add a cupful of cold minced chicken.

Helen Brown, Hudson
(Chicago, 1896)

Cheese Straws

Three tablespoons flour, 1 of bread crumbs, pinch of salt, little red pepper, 4 tablespoons grated cheese, yolk of 1 egg, 1 tablespoon water, knead with fingers very hard, roll out. Cut in narrow strips like straws, bake on greased manila paper.

Mrs. Sawnders
(Kalamazoo, 1899)

Using swiss, cheddar, smoked, or pepper cheese, this makes a tasty snack that can be frozen and reheated.

Cheese and Walnut Sandwich

One-half pound cheese, ¼ pound English walnuts, saltspoon salt, mix with mayonnaise dressing until soft enough to spread between two slices of buttered bread.

Edna May White
(Kalamazoo, 1899)

A saltspoon of salt is equal to a "pinch" of salt or a quarter of a teaspoon of salt. We would spice to taste.

Chicken Finger Sandwiches

Mince cold cooked chicken very fine; moisten with enough boiled salad dressing to roll in size of finger; season with minced celery and onion. Cover with thin baking powder biscuit crust, pinch ends together, brush with beaten egg. Bake in oven.

(Detroit, 1915)

The Woman's Association of the Brewster Congregational Church, located at the corner of Warren and Trumbull Avenues in Detroit, included this recipe in their Book of Recipes published ca. 1915. They prefaced their compilation:

Some women are loved
Because of good looks,

But everyone loves
The women who cooks. . . .

Ordinary mayonnaise serves as boiled salad dressing, and we found celery seed and onion powder better than the minced celery and onion called for. The biscuit recipe is:

1 cup flour   *1 tsp baking powder*
½ cup butter   *½ cup milk*

Roll out very thin.

Pressed Chicken

Cook a fowl until the meat will slip from the bones, season with salt, skim from the liquor, pick out all the bones and skin, chop a little, add 1 cup of bread or cracker crumbs, ½ grated nutmeg, salt and pepper to taste, boil the liquor down to 1 pint, stir all together and pack in a dish to cool. It is nice to use tumblers for this as the round slices garnished with slices of hard boiled eggs make an attractive tea dish.

Helen Coddington
(Union City, 1902)

This romantic wicker picnic basket featured a built-in table setting for two (Grand Rapids, 1890).

We tried this with turkey left over from Christmas. We added a package of gelatin to the mixture. Make sure to oil the tumblers lightly before packing them. The nutmeg gives this a special taste. Ann Arbor *bon vivant*, Dr. Chase, preferred the following variation.

Italian Cheese, or to Prepare Veal, Chicken, Turkey, etc., for Picnics

Take a 4 or 5 lb. piece of veal, boil it perfectly tender, then remove all the bones, and chop the meat fine; add a grated nutmeg, as much cloves, allspice, pepper and salt to suit; strain the liquor in which it was boiled, and mix all together, put over the fire and simmer till the liquor, on cooling a little of it, will jelly; then put in molds or bowls till the next day, when it may be sliced for sandwiches for the picnic or for company tea. Chicken or turkey may be done in the same way. If you like you can line the molds, or bowls, with hard-boiled eggs, sliced, which adds to its appearance as well as its richness.

(Ann Arbor, 1884)

Liver and Bacon Balls

One cup of boiled calf's liver, one-half cup bacon, mince very fine, add one-half saltspoon pepper, form into balls or small cakes, dip in egg, then in bread crumbs, and fry in hot fat; serve garnished with parsley.

Mrs. Elizabeth Waldo, Charlotte
(Chicago, 1896)

Margarites

Gather together any remains of cold meat there may be on hand. Free them from skin, bones and gristle, and season appropriately. Mince the meat very fine, moisten it with beaten egg or soup stock and form into tiny balls. Enclose each of these in a round of good pastry rolled very thin, pinching the edges closely together to form a complete covering for the meat. Brush the pastry over with beaten eggs and fry in plenty of boiling fat. When colored a nice brown remove, drain, and serve on a folded napkin garnished with fried or fresh parsley.

Mrs. E. M. Coppens
(Muskegon, 1890)

We tried this with ground beef. Precook small meatballs in the oven, drain the meatballs, then wrap them in pastry. We used Professor Blot's recipe for pie crust that appears in the pastry section (see page 257). Deep fry the margarites for 2½ minutes at 400°. These can also be prepared well ahead of time, frozen, and warmed in the oven before use. They have made quite a hit at parties.

Mock Pate de Foie Gras

Place four pieces of salt pork in a kettle (Scotch basin), and after it has cooked crisp put on it a well washed and trimmed calf's liver, with about 8 cloves, 8 bay leaves, and an onion sliced. Pour over boiling water, or better, hot beef stock, and cook slowly, well covered, 2 hours, then take out, chop fine, and add one cup butter, juice of half a lemon, a little nutmeg, paprika and salt, if the pork has not made it salt enough. Mesh fine with wooden spoon, add the strained gravy left in kettle, and pack in mould to slice when cold.

Margaret Parkhurst Mowry
(Coldwater, 1907)

When we first attempted this dish, following the recipe precisely, it turned out too salty. This is always a problem when salt pork is used. Judging from the usual quantities of salt in early recipes, we believe our ancestors craved salt more than we do today. Perhaps we get more salt in our diet through prepackaged foods. Also, they were not aware of the harmful effects of too much salt.

We find that bacon could be substituted for salt pork in early recipes. It provides the grease and pork flavor without the extreme saltiness. For this recipe we also added one envelope of unflavored gelatin, which helped the paté to congeal. Be sure to trim all fat from the liver. After cooking, the liver can be mashed as you would potatoes, but it achieves a smoother consistency if mixed in a blender or food processor. Our guests who enjoy paté thought this an excellent version.

Nut Balls

Mix smoothly 1 cup grated cheese, 1 cup ground peanuts, 1 tablespoon orange juice or sufficient of latter to moisten the mixture so that it can be formed into balls the size of a hickory nut.

Marie Clark
(Kalamazoo, 1899)

This easily prepared treat can be made days ahead of time. We used three tablespoons of frozen orange juice concentrate, dry roasted, unsalted peanuts ground in an electric blender, and a medium sharp cheddar cheese.

For another version, we tried crunchy peanut butter, the juice of one medium orange, and a teaspoon of grated orange rind. This turned out moister and seemed more appealing. Chill for four hours and thrust a toothpick in each ball for easier handling.

Sozijzen

Five cups flour sifted with 2 heaping teaspoonfuls Royal baking powder; 1 level teaspoonful salt; 1 level tablespoonful sugar; 2 eggs, beaten; 1 large cup lard, and as much milk as would make a light dough. Do not make stiff dough. Get special made pork sausage. Make little rolls of it and cut dough size of rolls wanted. Spread with white of egg to brown.

Mrs. J. Van Putten, Sr.
(Holland, 1925)

This traditional Dutch recipe, which is sometimes called "pigs in a blanket," appeared in *Holland's Choicest Cooking Recipes*, published in 1924. Serve these as hors d'oeuvres with a bowl of hot mustard for dipping, and there won't be many left when the guests depart.

Vanities—To Serve with Salads

One egg, a little salt, beat very light, add enough flour to roll, using just as little as possible, roll out as thin as paper, you cannot get them too thin. Cut in fancy shapes and drop in hot lard until they are a delicate brown. Sprinkle while hot with salt.

(Kalamazoo, 1899)

Walnut Croquettes

(These are fine and make an excellent substitute for meat.)

One cup chopped or ground English walnuts

One cup mashed potatoes

One-half teaspoon salt

One cup bread crumbs

Yolks of three eggs, well beaten

One teaspoon grated onion

Mix together thoroughly, shape into any desired form and bake in a moderate oven twenty to thirty minutes.

(Hammond, 1913)

Helen Ferris, wife of Michigan governor Woodbridge N. Ferris, contributed this recipe to the *Economy Administration Cook Book*. It was published in 1913 to promote President Woodrow Wilson's campaign theme of economy in government and in the home. Helen F. Gillespie of Fulton, NY, became Mrs. Ferris in 1873. In 1884 she assisted her husband in organizing the Ferris Industrial School in Big Rapids, which later became Ferris State College. She also taught at the institute until 1901. Woodbridge Ferris served as governor of Michigan from 1913 to 1917 and was elected to the U.S. Senate in 1922. Mrs. Ferris established a reputation as an excellent cook and hostess.

English walnuts meats are much easier to procure, but for a more genuinely Michigan recipe try black walnuts. It's very time consuming to gather, age, and crack them, but the taste is worth the work. We shaped the mixture into small balls, brushed each lightly with egg white, and baked them at 300° for 20 minutes. Served with a toothpick inserted, they proved very rich and filling. For a zippier version, add a teaspoon of curry powder.

Sandwich Spread

A new way to make sandwiches is to boil a few pounds of nice ham; chop very fine while yet warm, fat and lean together, with an equal quantity of lean veal boiled or roasted; rub dry mustard through the mass in proportion to suit the taste, also a pinch of cayenne pepper; a single clove of garlic chopped with the meat vastly improves it; add as much sweet butter as you would use to spread on bread sandwiches; mix well; have some nice light soda and sour milk biscuit, cold; cut in two and spread the mixture between, or use muffins if you have them. These are very nice for a picnic or festival table, and not half the work of those made in the old way, as it saves you buttering the bread, slicing the ham and spreading the mustard, and you will find that twice the number will be eaten than if made in the old way.

(Ann Arbor, 1884)

Dr. Alvin Chase of Ann Arbor sported a beard nearly as long as his voluminous cookbook (Ann Arbor, 1884).

Colorful Dr. Alvin Wood Chase, merchant, physician, author, publisher, culinary expert, and raconteur extraordinaire, included this sandwich recipe in his *Third, Last and Complete Receipt Book and Household Physician,* first published in 1884. He dedicated the volume to the "twelve hundred thousand families" who had purchased his previous two compendiums. Born in Cayuga County, NY, in 1817, Chase received his early education in a log schoolhouse near Buffalo. At age seventeen, he immigrated to the Maumee River area, married Martha Shutts in 1841, and bounced around the Midwest seeking his fortune. In 1856 he landed in Ann Arbor, attended medical lectures at the University of Michigan, and ultimately received a diploma from the Eclectic Institute of Cincinnati. Eclectic practitioners combined the precepts of homeopathic physicians, who dispensed small doses of drugs that produced in a healthy person reactions similar to that of the disease, and allopathic physicians, who dosed patients with drugs that had the opposite effect.

Not only was Chase eclectic in his medical philosophy, but his own career combined a variety of rather diverse occupations. He operated a grocery store for a number of years, served Ann Arbor residents as a physician, and founded a large publishing house that ultimately gave employment to fifty typesetters, printers, and binders. Like so many nineteenth-century entrepreneurs, Chase never seemed able to shake his wanderlust and in his many travels collected recipes and cooking techniques, medicines for people and animals, as well as a distinctive philosophy for living. Chase's forte, an affable personality, brought him success in obtaining valuable recipes. Around 1860 Chase published his first slim pamphlet of recipes. By 1867 the volume had gone through forty-five editions and swelled to embrace "departments" offering special advice to merchants and grocers, saloon keepers, medical practitioners, harness makers, painters, blacksmiths, tinners, gunsmiths, farriers, barbers, cooks, etc. In 1873 he compiled *Dr. Chase's Family Physician, Farrier, Bee-Keeper, and Second Receipt Book.* Two months before his death in 1884, he completed his *magnum opus,* based on over fifty years of collecting and experimenting. He had become rich through his popular guides but fell on financial reverses in the 1870s. He left his manuscript as the only legacy to his family. The volume went through scores of editions, remaining in print into the 1920s.

Banana Sandwich

Butter thin slices of bread and spread with mayonnaise dressing and thin slices of banana.

Margaret Waite
(Kalamazoo, 1899)

A few decades earlier, bananas were scarcely known in Michigan, but by 1899 rapid railroad transportation provided exotic fruits and vegetables at affordable prices. Oranges, for example, once so costly and rare as to constitute the one and only Christmas gift for many Victorian children, had become integrated into everyday life.

Cottage Cheese Sandwiches

One cup cottage cheese, ½ cup chopped cucumber, 1 tablespoon chopped onion, 1 tablespoon chopped parsley, ½ cup chopped pickle, 1 teaspoon salt, ¼ teaspoon Quaker celery salt, ¼ teaspoon paprika, 3 tablespoon thick Quaker salad dressing. Mix all together to form soft paste and spread on graham bread.

(Lansing, 1923)

The cottage cheese should be drained first. This also makes a good stuffing for celery stalks.

The Lansing Ladies, members of Arbutus Chapter No. 45 Order of the Eastern Star, who included this recipe in their 1923 cookbook also offered a bit of poetic advice:

He who eats what's cooked our way,
Will live to eat some other day

Two years earlier, Kalamazoo members of the Corinthian Chapter No. 123 Order of the Eastern Star had prefaced their cookbook:

Now the secret of being
An excellent cook
Lies in possession
Of a reliable book.

The Kalamazoo ladies also included an alternative version of the Cottage Cheese Sandwich.

Cottage Cheese Sandwich

Take cottage cheese and moisten with thick cream, add chopped nuts and a few drops of onion juice. Cottage cheese moistened with cream and some finely shredded pineapple makes a nice sweet sandwich.

(Kalamazoo, 1921)

French Sandwiches

Remove the skin from sardines and pick them up fine, add to them some finely chopped ham and some chopped pickle, mix all with mayonnaise dressing and spread between thin slices of bread and butter.

Mrs. E. G. Gregory
(Grand Rapids, 1890)

Ginger Sandwiches

Thin slices of nut bread, buttered. Filling made of fig paste, finely chopped Canton ginger and whipped cream.

(Charlotte, 1909)

Hot Weather Dutch Sandwich

Cut bread thin, spread with butter and prepared mustard. Cover this with thin slices of onion, then onto this put thin slices of dill pickle and cover with other slice.

Mrs. Edith Walrath
(Sunfield, 1915)

Neither of these sandwiches is recommended for romantic spring picnics.

Nasturtium Sandwich

Cut bread in round slices with biscuit cutter, spread with a little butter, press on a Nasturtium leaf, leaving the edges to protrude. Cover with a little mayonnaise dressing, place another slice of bread, press together.

Mrs. Marion Crooks
(Kalamazoo, 1899)

Nasturtium creations turn up frequently in turn-of-the-century cookbooks. Having known nasturtium only as a houseplant we thought such recipes peculiar. We consulted the works of Liberty Hyde Baily, South Haven's native son and still regarded as America's leading horticulturist. There we found that nasturtium is also a synonym for cress, a common garden plant also called pepper grass (*Lepidium sativum*). The house plant is a different genus and probably not edible.

Olive Sandwiches

Scald stone and chop to a fine pulp one dozen large olives. Drain as dry as possible, mix with ½ a cup of mayonnaise dressing and use as filling between thin slices of white bread.

Mrs. George McDonald
(Kalamazoo, 1906)

Onion Sandwich

Cut Spanish onions into thin slices, dip in vinegar and sprinkle with salt and pepper. Lay these upon a thin slice of bread and butter, pour over it a little tomato catsup and cover with another slice of bread and butter.

Anna Goodale
(Kalamazoo, 1899)

Peanut Sandwich

One pint freshly roasted peanuts, chopped fine. Add sufficient salad dressing to enable you to spread the mixture between thin slices of buttered bread.

Mrs. D. T. Jones
(Kalamazoo, 1899)

Prussian Sandwich

Spread wafers with thin slices of cream cheese; cover with chopped olives, mixed with mayonnaise. Place a wafer over each and press together.

Mrs. F. Pagenstecher
(Kalamazoo, 1906)

Edith Pagenstecher contributed this recipe to the cookbook compiled by the Ladies of Kalamazoo's St. Luke's Church in 1906. She undoubtedly named her specialty in honor of husband Felix, first generation son of a German immigrant. He earned local fame as an executive of several Kalamazoo paper mills.

Shrimp Nut Sandwich

One cup shrimps picked fine, 2 hard boiled eggs chopped very fine, ½ cup walnut meats, 1 cup salad dressing. Add nut meats just before using. Minced chicken may be substituted for the shrimp.

Mrs. August Schneidt
(Muskegon, 1912)

We tried this using one 6-ounce can of shrimp and ¼ cup of walnuts, and it turned out very tasty. We served it on crackers.

Sweet Chocolate Sandwiches

Two squares chocolate, 2 tbsp. butter, 1 c. powdered sugar, 3 tbsp. cream, ⅔ c. finely chopped nuts, slices of butter, white bread. Melt chocolate over gentle heat, add butter, sugar and cream, then cook 5 m. over hot water, add nuts and mix. Cool slightly before spreading between the slices of buttered bread.

Mrs. Margaret Spoor
(Kalamazoo, 1921)

Toasted Mushroom Sandwiches

Skin 1 pound mushrooms. Chop and cook 3 minutes in 3 tablespoons butter. Add ½ cup of flour, stir and add ¾ cup of thin cream. Bring to boiling point. Season with salt and pepper. Cool and spread between thin slices of bread cut in rounds. Toast until a delicate brown. Serve hot.

Mrs. Morris Cassard
(Grand Rapids, 1935)

Vegetable Sandwich

12 large lettuce leaves
  chopped fine
1 large sweet pepper

1 large cucumber
  chopped and
  drained
1 large tomato
  chopped and
  drained

Mix ingredients with dressing. Spread bread with butter substitute and fill. Ground olives may be used with the filling.

(Berrien Springs, 1941)

Mildred G. Whitfield, Maria Hornbacher, and Ruth Pearson included this recipe in their vegetarian cookbook published in Berrien Springs in 1941. It is no coincidence that the volume bears a Berrien Springs imprint. The Seventh Day Adventist Church, which maintained its world headquarters in Battle Creek from 1855 to 1902 adopted vegetarianism as one of its tenets in the early 1860s. Andrews University in Berrien Springs, founded as Immanuel Missionary College in 1901, continues as one of the church's leading training centers.

Wine Sandwich

Two cups raisins, stoned, 1 cup Brazil nuts, chopped very fine, mix with 2 tablespoons sherry wine. Serve between slices of brown bread.

Mrs. F. A. Taylor
(Kalamazoo, 1899)

Too many of Katherine Taylor's sandwiches and more than the raisins could be stoned.

Stews, Soups, and Salads

STEWS and SOUPS

From the days of the first French explorers and missionaries, soups and stews have been staple elements in the Michigan diet. Some recipes may have been derived from Potawatomie, Chippewa, or Ottawa stew pots. Pioneer homesteaders fanned out across southern Michigan in the 1820s and 1830s and brought other nutritious soup recipes from New England and New York. When cast-iron wood stoves supplanted fireplaces in the 1850s, the fragrant smell of bubbling soup slowly cooking on the back of the range made many a Michigan kitchen unforgettable. It is rare to find a historic Michigan cookbook that does not include a full complement of soups and stews. Since soups are among some of our favorite dishes, it was enjoyable to garner the following particularly interesting examples.

In the late 1870s and early 1880s, the *Detroit Free Press* ran a feature called "The Household," which printed recipes and useful suggestions for domestic improvements contributed by subscribers. In 1881 Mary Perrin Goff edited a 644-page compilation of the best of the series. Mrs. Goff offered practical advice for the inexperienced soup maker.

Soup

The basis of all good soups is the juice of meat. This may be made by boiling the cracked joints of uncooked beef, veal or mutton; to these may be added the cracked bones of cooked game or underdone beef or mutton, but for juices and nourishment depend upon the juices of the uncooked

Hung on the "crane" over a fire, the bulged kettle was sometimes the only cooking implement in pioneer Michigan households (Grand Rapids, 1890).

meat, the rest being only added for flavoring. To extract the juices, cut the meat into small pieces, break the bone the whole length, put into cold water, without salt, and let heat very slowly. When it once comes to a boil, let it be well skimmed, and then put the pot where it will simmer slowly until the meat is thoroughly done and freed from the juices, keeping the pot closely covered the while. The next day, when the soup is cold, remove the fat, which will harden on top of the soup. All soups are better for being made one day before using, and the next day put on the stove and the vegetables added.

This is the basis of almost all gravy soups,

which are called by the name of the vegetables that are put into them: carrots, turnips, onions, celery, and a few leaves of cabbage, make what is called spring soup; to this is a pint of green peas, or asparagus, or French beans cut into pieces, or a cabbage lettuce, is an improvement. With rice, Scotch barley, or vermicelli, maccaroni or celery, cut into lengths, it will be the soup usually called by those names. Or turnips scooped, round or young onions, will give a clear turnip or onion soup. The roots and vegetables used must be boiled first, or they will impregnate the soup with too strong a flavor. Seasoning for those soups is the same, viz., salt, and a very little cayenne pepper.

Caramel (which is only a fancy name for burned sugar) eggs, and slices of bread, fried to a crisp in butter, are also sometimes added, and impart a savory relish to the soup.

To make soup attractive, therefore palatable, always strain it before sending to the table. Do not uncover until ready to ladle out the soup and be sure to have the soup plates heated beforehand.

(Detroit, 1881)

Flamboyant and outspoken Dr. Chase of Ann Arbor had his own ideas concerning the necessity of filtering soups. We think most modern nutritionists would side with the good doctor.

Straining and Filtering not at all Necessary

The fancy "Cook-Books" talk about straining soups, and some even of filtering through a hair sieve after straining. The straining will remove fully one-half of the nourishing properties used, but if "style is preferable" to the strength which would otherwise be obtained from the thicker parts of the soup, by all means both strain and filter them. One point more, and I am done with the general ideas of soup-making—it is this: for healthy people it is not essential to trim off the fat from soup meats, nor the oily particles from the top of soups; but for invalids both these must be done, either by making the day before and removing the fat when cold from

the top, or by dipping off as much as possible while hot.

(Ann Arbor, 1884)

Almond Soup

One quart sweet milk, 1 heaping tablespoon flour, 1 heaping tablespoon butter, ½ pint of blanched, browned and ground almonds. Melt butter, add flour, then milk (cooking in double boiler). When this begins to thicken, add almonds. Serve with bread sticks.

Mrs. Jack Penoyer
(Higgins Lake, 1920)

Culinary columns have been a popular feature in many newspapers and journals. Old cookbooks frequently bulge with recipes clipped from such sources, but because of the ephemeral nature of the original publications, most were destined to be lost. Occasionally, however, compilations taken from periodicals appeared in book form. During a six-month period beginning in November 1934, some 8,000 women from Kalamazoo and nearby communities submitted their favorite recipes to the weekly "recipe page" of the *Kalamazoo Gazette*. When the contest ended the *Gazette* published more than 400 of the prize-winning recipes in pamphlet form, including Mrs. George Fiestemal's favorite stew recipe.

Arabian Stew

6 pork chops	3 cups hot water
6 tbsp. raw rice	1 green pepper
1 large onion	6 tbsp. tomato soup

Salt and pepper to taste. Sear chops on each side. On each chop place 1 tbsp. rice, 1 slice of onion and 1 tbsp. tomato soup. Add salt, pepper and water. Cover well and bake in moderate oven (350 degrees) one and one-half hours. Add 1 green pepper, sliced, 10 minutes before serving.

Mrs. Geo. Fiestemal, Paw Paw
(Kalamazoo, 1935)

Bean Soup

As I look upon bean soup as the *best* of old soups, I will give a receipt taken from "A Book of the Sea," which, having had it made several times, I can say it can be depended upon. And when I say it was given by a sailor, the phraseology needs no further explanation. He says:

"The fact is, that bean soup at sea is such a stand-by that the sailor-man on shore sometimes gets quite mad when it's offered him, and still, bean soup is a mighty good thing, and all according to the way you make it. Now, you get a lot of swells on board, and make 'em soup, and call it *haricot* (in England, this name is still used for beans) and not beans, which is vulgar, and if you know how to turn it out, they will take three platefuls.

"First, you get a *pint and a half* of good sound beans—I don't think there is much difference in beans, whether they are *big* or *little*—and pick 'em over and stand them for an hour in a bowl of cold water. Take three pounds of meat or a shin-bone, and put the beef in 4 quarts of cold water, and let it boil. Fry an onion and put that in, with say 6 white cloves and a dozen peppers (the small cayenne peppers, the same that are used in making pepper sauce), and some parsley, with a tablespoon of salt. Let it boil for two hours, and you keep skimming. As fast as the water boils away, you keep adding a little hot water. When the concern is cooked, take a colander and strain your soup through it, mashing up the beans and keeping out the meat and the bean shin. If you want to be superfine, you can hard boil an egg, and slice white and yellow through, and put them in the tureen; likewise some slices of lemon. Bits of toast don't go bad with it. If you happen to be cruising south just you use, instead of the New England bean, the Georgia or South California cow-pea."

Remarks—The author never had any soup he liked better than this, although the following is very nice.

(Ann Arbor, 1884)

Bean Soup with Cream or Milk

Take 1 pt. of beans, parboil and drain off the water, adding fresh. Never put cold water upon beans which have been once heated, as it hardens them—boil until perfectly tender, season with pepper and salt, and a piece of butter the size of a walnut, or more if preferred; when done skim out half the beans, leaving the broth with the remaining half in the kettle, now add a teacup of sweet cream or good milk, a dozen or more of crackers broken up, let it come to a boil, and you have a dish good enough to offer a king.

(Ann Arbor, 1884)

Black Bean Soup

One pint black beans, 4 quarts cold water; 2 tablespoons chopped onion; 2 stalks celery or ¼ teaspoon celery salt; 3 teaspoons salt; ½ teaspoon pepper; ¼ teaspoon mustard, cayenne, 4 tablespoons butter, 4 tablespoons flour; 2 hard boiled eggs, 1 lemon. Soak the beans in cold water over night; drain and add fresh water, (cold). Brown the onion in 1 tablespoon butter and add to the beans with celery broken in pieces; simmer until beans are soft, adding more water as it boils away to keep the quantity about 4 quarts; rub through sieve and reheat to boiling point. Mix flour, salt, pepper, mustard, cayenne with remaining butter heated to bubbling; add these to strained liquid and simmer for a short time. Place sliced eggs and lemon in a tureen and strain soup over them.

Mrs. A. Montgomery
(Detroit, 1915)

Brunswick Stew

Two chickens, whole, nine quarts of water; boil till tender, take out skin and bones, chop fine and return to kettle, adding six potatoes previously soaked an hour in cold water and chopped very fine, also one pint of sweet corn, one quart of tomatoes; boil two hours. Before dishing, add two hard-boiled eggs chopped fine, and one in slices, a piece of butter the size of a hen's egg, fourteen hard crackers, a little salt, very little red pepper, and three teaspoonfuls of Worcestershire sauce. To be served like soup.

(Detroit, 1878)

This is definitely a Michigan version of the famous Georgian delicacy. This cousin of chili con carne may have lost some of its popularity for when we visited Brunswick, Georgia, in 1984, the original home of Brunswick Stew, we had difficulty in even locating a restaurant that served it. Southern recipes usually call for squirrel or a mixture of pork and chicken. This Michigan recipe compares favorable with the Georgian variety, but we recommend that you skin and remove the fat from the chicken before boiling.

Camp Custer Stew

4 large potatoes
4 large onions
1 pound hamburger

1 can Campbell's
 soup, tomato

Salt, pepper, butter. Bake 2 hours.

Mrs. Clarence Baker
(Parchment, 1926)

In mid-1917, the federal government began converting a 10,000-acre tract west of Battle Creek into Camp Custer. Throughout World War I, Camp Custer, named after General George Armstrong Custer from Monroe, served as a major Midwestern army training station. By 1926 when the Parchment Parent-Teacher Association included this recipe in their *Parchment Cook Book*, a Citizens Army Training Corps practiced military tactics at Camp Custer in preparation for the next war. During the depression, the base became a CCC staging ground. When World War II broke out, the post, rechristened Fort Custer, again functioned as an induction and training center for the next generation of recruits.

This simple but hearty recipe is easily prepared in a crock pot. We found that the addition of diced celery improves the flavor. The fact that a can of "Campbell's soup" is called for illustrates the success of that company in promoting their product, as well as the emergence of a general acceptance of prepared foods to facilitate cooking.

Carrot Cream Soup

Wash, scrape and cut in slices enough carrots to fill a pint bowl; boil in a quart of boiling water slightly salted till soft enough to rub through a sieve with the potato-masher. Mix together in a thick saucepan two tablespoonfuls each of flour and butter, stirring with wooden spoon till they begin to bubble together. Gradually stir into this a quart of hot milk and the carrot pulp; add hot water to make two quarts of soup. Add a small teaspoon of salt and a pinch of cayenne pepper.

Mrs. W. Birchby, Holland
(Chicago, 1896)

Eight carrots filled a pint-sized bowl. Rather than "rubbing them through a sieve," we mashed the cooked carrots like potatoes and used the carrot water in the recipe. The original recipe made a very thin broth so we added eight more mashed carrots. This yielded a tasty soup, embellished by sprinkling a little crushed dill weed over each bowl before serving.

Celery Soup

One quart celery cut fine; boil several hours, using the leaves and roots if you wish it strong. Strain. Boil 1 quart new milk in a double boiler with 2 slices of onion, add 2 tablespoons flour and 3 tablespoons butter creamed together, salt and pepper to taste. Remove the onion and add the celery juice. One cup cream added last before serving.

Mrs. N. H. Stewart
(Kalamazoo, 1899)

Fannie Stewart, wife of a prominent Kalamazoo attorney, contributed this recipe to the cookbook compiled by the Ladies of the First Presbyterian Church located in the "Celery City." The celery can be left in if you like more texture to your soup. The addition of diced leftover chicken or ham is also good.

Chestnut Soup

Use the large Italian chestnuts. Drop into boiling water, and cook in the shells from one to three quarters of an hour, then place in a hot oven, and bake for ten or fifteen minutes. The length of time required will depend upon the age of the chestnuts. They should be tender and mealy when done. Shell, and press them through a colander, add boiling water to make the soup of a proper consistency, salt to taste, and season with nuttolene.

(Battle Creek, 1910)

Ella Eaton Kellogg included this recipe in her *Science in the Kitchen*, "a scientific treatise on food substances and their dietic properties." The volume was first published in Battle Creek in 1892, but this recipe comes from the revised and enlarged edition of 1910. Ella's husband, Dr. John Harvey Kellogg, colorful proprietor of the famous health spa, the Battle Creek Sanitarium, experimented long and hard to develop vegetarian health foods palatable to guests at the "San." In the process, he invented granola, peanut butter, and in conjunction with his brother, William Keith Kellogg, corn flakes. Ella's cookbook, which helped promote the concept of healthful vegetarian cuisine, included recipes using a host of strange sounding meat substitutes invented by her husband including savita, protose, and nuttolene. Most are no longer available, at least by those names.

Chicken Soup

Two young fowls, or one full-grown; half pound pickled ham or pork; one gallon water; cut the fowls in pieces, put into the pot with the ham or pork, and one quart of water, or enough to cover them; stew for an hour, or until you can cut easily into the breast; take out the breasts, leaving the rest of the meat in the pot, and add the remainder of the water, boiling hot; keep the soup stirring slowly while you chop up the breasts; rub the yolks of four hard-boiled eggs smooth, moistening to a paste with a few spoonfuls of soup; mix with these a handful of fine bread crumbs and the chopped meat, and make it into small balls. When the soup has boiled in all two-and-a-half hours, if the chicken

be reduced to shreds, strain the meat and bones; season with salt, pepper, and a bunch of parsley; drop in the balls of force-meat, and after boiling ten minutes incorporate the ingredients thoroughly; add, a little at a time, one pint of rich milk thickened with a little flour; boil up once and serve.

(Detroit, 1881)

The preparation of chili con carne has become an American folk art with regional cooks devising unique recipes. Nevertheless it is uncommon to find chili con carne in pre-World War II Michigan cookbooks. Here are two exceptions, variations from Kalamazoo and Grayling.

Chili Con Carne

One lb. hamburg, ½ can pimentoes, cut fine; 2 large onions, cut fine; 1 c. diced celery, 1 tsp sugar, 1 pt. tomatoes, 1 pkg. spaghetti, cooked in boiling salted water. When spaghetti is tender, drain off water; add hamburg, celery, tomatoes, pimentoes, onions, sugar. Cook slowly until meat is done. Add salt and pepper to taste.

Mrs. J. H. Shirley
(Kalamazoo, 1921)

Chili Con Carne

One lb. roundsteak cut up in very small cubes. Fry in butter slowly until tender. Fry chopped onions in butter till done. Put together in a kettle and add 1 can mushrooms and a few sliced stuffed olives, 1 can kidney beans, about two pimentos cut up fine. Salt, pepper, cayenne. Thicken with flour and water thickening. Serve on lettuce leaf with buttered roll.

Mrs. Esbern Hanson
(Grayling, 1937)

Clam Chowder

One can minced clams, 2 medium sized potatoes, 1 stalk celery, small onion, small can tomato soup, 3 slices bacon. Cut bacon in cubes, also onions; fry bacon. Add clams and juice, onions and bacon, tomatoes, 1 pt. milk. Thicken as you would like for soup.

Mrs. Chas. Doyle
(Hastings, 1921)

Substitute bacon for salt pork for the following two recipes or they will be too salty for modern tastes.

Chowder

Slice six large onions and fry in the gravy of fried salt pork; cut five pounds of bass or cod into strips about three inches long and one inch thick and line the bottom of a pot with them; scatter in a few slices of onions, a little salt, half a dozen whole black peppers, one or two cloves, a pinch of thyme and one of parsley, a tablespoonful of tomato or mushroom catsup and six oysters, then a layer of oyster crackers buttered thickly and well soaked in milk, another layer of fish, onions, seasoning, and so on until all are used up; cover with water, boil slowly for an hour and pour out. Serve with capers and sliced lemon. A cup of oyster liquor added to the chowder while boiling improves it.

(Detroit, 1881)

Clam Soup

Cut salt pork into very small squares and fry light brown; add one large or two small onions cut very fine, and cook about ten minutes; add two quarts of water and one quart of raw potatoes sliced; let it boil, then add one quart of clams. Mix one tablespoonful of flour and water, add to it one pint of milk, pour into the soup and let it boil about five minutes. Add butter, pepper and salt to taste. Worcestershire sauce may be added if liked.

(Detroit, 1881)

Consomme

Twelve pounds beef (any part) 4 or 5 bones and 2 or 3 lbs pork rinds. ½ oz. white peppers, ½ oz.

celery seeds, 1 oz. salt, 2 carrots cut up, 2 tablespoonfuls thyme and savory, leaf herbs: fresh celery may be used instead of celery seeds. Put the bones into the bottom of a soup kettle, then the meat cut small with which has been mixed the rinds, vegetables and herbs and add 12 qts. cold water, let it boil very slowly 1 hour, then stir and set where it will boil well for 4 or 5 hours more. Keep well covered and the steam in. When done and while hot, strain through a coarse strainer, press all the liquid from the meat-fibre, and let stand in a very cold place until next day. Then take every particle of fat off, cut the jelly out freeing it from the worst of the sediment. Then just melt the jelly in the kettle and stir well in the whites of 4 eggs well beaten, also put in the shells, boil up quickly and when the scum divides pour into a jelly bag or through a fine, closely woven cloth. If it does not run perfectly clear return it to the bag or cloth. The bag should be put into boiling water and wrung out before using. Keep the kettle covered while boiling, open while clarifying.

Harry Fox
(Muskegon, 1890)

With the exception of some compendiums compiled by male authors, it is unusual to find recipes submitted by men in older cookbooks. But Harry Fox contributed some of the best and most detailed recipes found in the *Muskegon Cook Book,* published by the Ladies Society of the First Baptist Church in 1890.

Corn Soup

One can sweet corn, 1 quart boiling water, 1 quart milk, three tablespoons butter rolled in 1 tablespoon flour, 2 eggs, pepper and salt and 1 tablespoon tomato catsup. Drain the corn and chop very fine, put it in an Agate milk boiler, pour on it the boiling water and cook steadily for 1 hour; rub through a cullender to take out all the husks. Return it to the fire, season with salt and pepper, and boil gently for 3 minutes, then stir in the butter and flour. Have ready the boiling milk, mix with the beaten eggs, and pour all into the soup; simmer 1 minute, stirring all the while. Take off the fire and add the catsup, when it will be ready to serve.

(Grand Rapids, 1890)

An "agate" milk boiler prevented milk from scalding (Grand Rapids, 1890).

In 1890, H. Leonard's Sons and Company, a prominent Grand Rapids firm specializing in china, glass, silverware, and household furnishing, issued the *Grand Rapids Cook Book*, first compiled by the Ladies of the Congregational Church in 1871 and updated with "many new and valuable recipes contributed by the ladies of Grand Rapids." Three-quarters of the 267-page book actually consisted of a company catalog. Lavishly illustrated with line engravings, the rare volume comprises a virtual encyclopedia of late Victorian kitchen and serving utensils.

Herman Leonard founded the firm when he built a one-story wooden store on Monroe Street in 1845. By 1887 an ornate stone structure in the fashionable Queen Anne style offered four floors of salesrooms as well as "a ladies' toilet room on the second floor." H. Leonard's Sons and Company also operated a large home furnishing's outlet at the corner of Fulton and Spring Streets as well as the Grand Rapids Refrigerator Company, manufacturer of the "Leonard Cleanable Refrigerator."

Cream of Cauliflower Soup

Heat 1 pint of chicken or veal stock; 1 pint milk, and ½ cup sweet cream. When boiling, thicken with 1 tablespoonful of flour, add salt and pepper to taste. Cook ½ of a cauliflower in salted water ½ hour; cut off the little flowerets, using none of the stalk. Put in enough to thicken the broth.

Mrs. Elmer England
(Flint, 1912)

Whipping cream works nicely as sweet cream.

Cream of Chestnut

Scald and peel chestnuts to make 1 pint. Cook in 1 quart water until soft, then put through a sieve. Add 1 cup soy-bean milk, and 1 cup water. Let cook two minutes and serve. Chestnuts and mushrooms may be combined and creamed.

(Berrien Springs, 1941)

Unfortunately, a fungus bark disease wiped out the once-prevalent American chestnut trees during the early twentieth century. The chestnuts available on the market now are all European varieties. They are larger but not quite as tasty as the American chestnuts, according to old timers.

Cream of Spinach Soup

Make thin cream sauce of 1 tablespoon butter (melted) and 2 tablespoons flour mixed together

This was one of many china patterns available in the fashionable Grand Rapids department store H. Leonard's Sons and Company in 1890 (Grand Rapids, 1890).

and add to 1 quart milk. Bring to boiling point and add ¼ cup chopped, cooked spinach, pepper and salt to taste. A little finely cut parsley may be added if desired.

Mrs. Van der Noot
(Detroit, 1915)

Jellied Cucumber Soup

(As used in China)

2 cups of chicken stock	4 tablespoons of sherry
2 medium sized cucumbers	Salt and pepper
	¼ cup of heavy cream

Peel and grate cucumbers and squeeze through a cheese cloth. Combine with other ingredients, excepting the cream. Bring to a boil, add cream, and jelly.

Mrs. Homer Pace Ford
(Grand Rapids, 1935)

Mrs. Homer Pace Ford of Grand Rapids, an energetic world traveler, contributed a number of exotic recipes gathered during her journeys to the *Cathedral League Cook Book* put out by the Ladies of St. Mark's Church in Grand Rapids in 1935.

Egg Soup

Mix 1 egg with flour until fine like corn meal and sift into soup stock as you would corn meal. Just befor taking up add a raw egg well beaten, and season to taste.

(Charlotte, 1909)

Fish Chowder

Have a deep iron kettle ready. Fresh cod or haddock are best for chowder. Cut into 2 inch slices. Fry some slices of salt pork in kettle. Take out, chop fine, leaving fat, put a layer of fish in this fat; then a layer of split Boston crackers, then some bits of pork; some thick slices of potatoes (peeled), and some chopped onion and pepper. Then another

layer of fish, with a repetition of the other articles. Cover with boiling water, and boil ½ hour. Skim out in the dish in which it is to be served, thicken the gravy with flour, boil up and pour over chowder.

Mrs. I. F. Hopkins
(Muskegon, 1890)

"Gronkaal" Soup

Two pounds lean salt pork or salt mutton boiled until nearly done. Then add to this six large potatoes, diced, and about two cupsful of kale; a little green onion, and about a cupful of cabbage; all chopped fine. Let boil until potatoes are done. Diced carrots may also be added if desired.

Mrs. Hansine Hanson
(Grayling, 1937)

Grayling, originally a railroad town platted in 1874, drew its name from the once-prevalent Michigan game species that was fished to near extinction in the late nineteenth century. In the 1870s Scandinavians migrated to the region where they found work as lumberjacks. The Hanson family, prominent timber operators, later donated 18,000 acres of land as a Michigan National Guard training camp. Mrs. Hansine Hanson contributed the recipe for "Gronkaal" soup, a Scandinavian specialty, to the *Grayling Cook Book* published in 1937.

Gumbo

One-half pound breakfast bacon cut in small pieces and fry very brown. Brown 1 cup of flour, 1 large onion cut in small pieces, 1 small can corn, 1 can tomatoes and okra—Brown all ingredients together. 1 can shrimp (chicken or veal may be used). Add water until you have about 1 gallon of mixture. Let simmer five hours, season highly, serve with rice.

Mrs. John L. Jackson
(Higgins Lake, 1920)

Gumbo Soup

Put on half a peck of tomatoes in a porcelain kettle and let them stew; have half a peck of ochra

This enameled porcelain soup tureen in the "sylvan" pattern sold for $1.78 in 1890 (Grand Rapids, 1890).

cut in fine shreds; put them with thyme, parsley and an onion cut fine, into the tomatoes and let them cook until quite tender. Fricassee a chicken in ham gravy; then take yolks of four eggs, a little vinegar, the juice of one lemon and season to taste, beating the eggs into the vinegar; pour this over the chicken, and put all then into the tomatoes, letting the kettle be nearly filled with water. Boil all together four or five hours.

(Detroit, 1881)

Holland Stew

Take any kind of leftover meat (beef or veal is best), cut in small pieces and put on to simmer. Take two or three large onions, slice thin and fry brown but do not burn. Now pour meat and juice in pan containing the onion and add just enough vinegar to sour it a little. A sliced pickle may be added. One tablespoonful sugar, ¼ tablespoonful each of cinnamon and cloves. Thicken a little with flour.

Mrs. M. A. Hopper
(Manistee, 1929)

Priscilla's mother's maiden name is Clancy and her paternal grandmother was a McCarthy. Needless to say, she was raised to take strong pride in her Irish heritage. Consequently we are pleased to include the following variations of Irish stew.

Irish Stew

Mutton cutlets, or chops, 2 lbs.; potatoes, 4 lbs., or enough for the family; 1 onion; pepper and salt. Directions—Cut the chops into small pieces, cracking the bones, if any; peel and slice the potatoes; shred, or chop the onion finely; butter the bottom of a stew pan, and place a layer of the sliced potatoes over the bottom, with a proper proportion of the onion upon them, and season each layer with salt, and a very little pepper; then a layer of the chops, etc., until all are in; then put on 1 pt. of cold water, cover the pan and simmer 2 hours, or until done. Serve hot, and keep hot as long as dinner lasts, by keeping the tureen covered.

Remarks—Notwithstanding this is called an Irish stew, if it is done nicely it is quite good enough for an American. It is a very popular dish at hotels and boarding houses, and any kind of cold meats, not too fat, may be utilized in this way, remembering that if made of cooked meats, only about half the time will be required, enough only to cook the potatoes.

(Ann Arbor, 1884)

Irish Stew from Left-Over Steak and Potatoes

Cut the leftover steak and potatoes into squares of half an inch. Stew the steak in a covered stew-pan until very tender; cut an onion, and add the potatoes with a little of the left-over gravy from the steak; season with pepper, and a little salt if needed, thyme and summer savory.

Remarks—Be certain to have just enough juices of the stew left, as a gravy, *i.e.*, do not cook it too dry, and it will be fit for a king. At least, the author first found a dish of it good enough for him, seasoned as above, at Florence, Kan. Try it if you like a good thing, and can get the thyme and savory. The only fault I ever found, or heard about it, was "I want a little more of that stew."

(Ann Arbor, 1884)

Irish Stew with Dumplings

Cut 1½ lb. beef or mutton (or both) in cubes. Try out suet in frying pan and saute meat, which has been dredged in flour, until it is well seared. Cover meat with boiling water and boil fast 3 minutes, then lower temperature; boil ¾ or 1 hour. Add carrots, onion and turnips (about 2 cups altogether) and 3 or 4 potatoes, cut small and boil until vegetables are cooked.

Recipe for Dumplings
(Will never fail to be light)

Two cups sifted flour; 4 teaspoons baking powder; ½ teaspoon salt; 2 teaspoons butter; ¾ cup milk. Sift dry ingredients. Work in butter with tips of fingers or knife, then add milk. More milk may be necessary. Drop from spoon into stew, which must be kept boiling and cook exactly 12 minutes.

Mrs. Wm. Ryan
(Detroit, 1915)

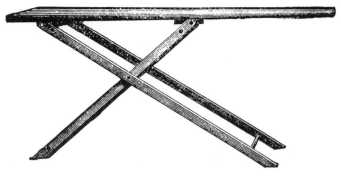

The instrument of torture that inspired Ironing Day Soup (Grand Rapids, 1890).

Irish Stew with Dumplings

Ingredients—2 pounds forequarter lamb; 1 onion; 2 quarts boiling water; 1 carrot; 2 teaspoonfuls salt; small white turnip; ⅛ teaspoonful pepper; 4 potatoes; 4 tablespoonfuls flour. Preparation—Cut meat in small pieces, trim off most of fat; cover with boiling water and simmer for one hour; add salt and pepper, onion, carrot and turnip cut in small cubes and cook one hour. Pare and slice potatoes, add to stew, and cook twenty minutes; thicken with flour mixed to a paste with cold water; add dumplings, cover, and cook twelve minutes.

Mrs. C. D. Deuel, Centerville
(Homer, 1925)

Several irons were kept hot on the stove top. When the iron being used cooled, another was picked up with a quick-release handle (Grand Rapids, 1890).

Ironing Day Soup

Two pounds round steak, 1 can tomatoes, 1 onion, 6 cloves; put all in a kettle with 4 qts. cold water, add salt to taste. Boil all day, at night put through a colander. Next day warm and add a little thickening to make as thick as cream.

Mrs. Frank Wood
(Muskegon, 1890)

Monday, the traditional wash day in Victorian households, was followed by ironing day on Tuesday. This easily prepared soup could bubble on the back burner of the kitchen range all day as the front burners heated massive copper boilers filled with wash water. Days spent hand-scrubbing and ironing with heavy cast-iron sad irons left little time for preparation of more elaborate meals.

Kalamazoo Special Stew
(With canned celery)
(To can celery in fall)

Wash and cut big bunches of celery in inch pieces. To one qt. add 1 or 2 onions cut. ½ green pepper and if liked a bit of garlic. Salt to taste.

Add enough cooked tomatoes to cover celery and cook until tender not mushy. Put boiling hot in mason jars and seal. Will keep indefinitely. Used for chop suey and vegetable soup. An average family can use 25 qts. in year.

Kalamazoo Celery Stew

Cut 1 lb. veal and 1 lb. pork or any preferred meat, round steak can be used in inch pieces. Dredge thoroughly in flour. Brown in butter. Add 1 qt. canned celery. Cover, and stew slowly until meat is tender. If meat is tough cook awhile before adding celery. Thicken more if necessary. Serve with boiled rice or noodles. Out of town guests ask for celery stew.

Mrs. John Butine
(Kalamazoo, 1935)

Out-of-town guests might well have asked for celery stew. During the 1930s it was impossible to get in or out of Kalamazoo by automobile or train without encountering children hawking huge stalks of Kalamazoo celery on every street corner.

Lamb Bouillon

Add to the liquor in which a leg of lamb has been boiled, a small whole onion, a few cloves, a small bay leaf, season with salt and paprika to taste. Serve in cups with small piece of lemon. Remove onion and spices before serving.

(Charlotte, 1909)

Lenten Soup

Prepare three carrots, three turnips and three onions by scraping, peeling and washing. Slice them and fry them a golden brown in fresh lard or dripping. Cut up a head of celery and put in and fry a few moments also. Add to this two cloves, one teaspoonful of salt, one-half teaspoonful of pepper, a little parsley and a little grated nutmeg. Cover this with nearly three quarts of water and simmer three hours. This may be used instead of broth in the Lenten season.

Mrs. Wilson, Hudson
(Chicago, 1896)

Lettuce Soup

One pound mutton, one onion, two cloves and a bay leaf cooked slowly in water two hours. Cool and remove fat. Melt one large tablespoon butter, stir in one large tablespoon flour. Pour the hot broth slowly into this, and while boiling chop ten or twelve good-sized lettuce leaves and one onion quite fine, add to soup and boil five minutes. When ready to serve add salt and pepper to taste and yolk of one egg stirred into a cup of cream or rich milk. Stir a minute or two and serve.

Nita Coit Allee
(Detroit, 1923)

Lobster Soup

One large lobster or two small ones; pick all the meat from the shell and chop fine; scald one quart of milk and one pint of water; then add the lobster, one pound of butter, a tablespoonful of flour, and salt and red pepper to taste. Boil ten minutes and serve hot.

(Detroit, 1881)

Mulligatawny Soup

One lean soup bone, one lemon, rind and juice, one pint tomatoes, two onions, one turnip, one carrot, one bunch parsley, one stalk celery, ¼ teaspoon cloves, dash of nutmeg, two tablespoons browned sugar, 3 or 4 dice of salt pork, 1 small beet (to give color) salt and pepper to taste. Simmer until vegetables and meat are well done, strain.

Annie Carpenter
(Union City, 1902)

Annie Carpenter contributed this interesting sounding and tasting soup to the *Union City Cook Book* compiled by the Ladies of the First Congregational Church there in 1902. Local clothier, George F. Minto, advertised that while the book "provides most completely for the inner man, his stock would superbly take care of the outer man."

Mushroom Soup
(For six persons)

One pound mush-
rooms, peel, and

One-third teaspoon
pepper

*wipe and cut in
small pieces*
One teaspoon salt

*One piece butter size
of pecan nut*
One pint water

Stew gently two hours, then add one quart milk; heat it again and thicken with two level tablespoons butter and one of flour. Add one-half pint whipped cream when ready to serve.

(Hammond, 1913)

Mrs. Edwin Forrest Sweet of Grand Rapids contributed this recipe to *The Economy Administration Cook Book*. Woodrow Wilson based his successful 1912 presidential campaign on the "subject of economy from every stand point, not only in the national government, but in the home." This 700-page cookbook provided recipes submitted by the wives of governors, congressmen, cabinet officials, and democratic supporters that "reduced meal costs without losing food values." We found this to be a rich and delicious recipe. Be sure to not let the soup boil after you have added the milk.

Mock Oyster Soup

Two-thirds cup of codfish shredded, two cups tomatoes, two cups hot water, boil 20 minutes. Strain, add one cup rich milk, tablespoon of butter, 8 crackers rolled fine, season with salt and pepper.

Annie Carpenter
(Union City, 1902)

Mock Turtle Soup

One quart of black beans soaked over night, boiled until soft and mashed through a colander; have ready two quarts of soup made of beef bones, add the beans, and boil about an hour; have in the tureen two hard boiled eggs cut up, and slices of lemon, half teaspoonful brown sugar, a pinch of powdered cloves, cinnamon, black pepper and salt; a tablespoonful of tarragon vinegar and six blades of mace, and a half dozen force-meat balls.

(Detroit, 1879)

Forcemeat is various compounds used to stuff fowls, fish, pigs, tomatoes, eggplants or in this case added to soup. Some forcemeats are composed principally of ground veal, beef, chicken or bacon with herbs and seasonings, bread crumbs, butter, eggs, etc. Fish forcemeat is fish eggs, butter seasonings and bread crumbs. Forcemeat for egg plants, cucumbers and tomatoes consist of the removed interiors mixed with minced onions, bread crumbs and butter.

Mutton Soup

Boil a leg of mutton three hours, season with salt and pepper, add a teaspoonful summer savory; make a batter of one egg, two tablespoonsful milk, two of flour, all well beaten together; drop this batter into the soup with a spoon and boil three minutes.

(Detroit, 1881)

Noodle Soup

To ½ egg-shell of water and 2 eggs add as much flour as can possibly be worked well. Mix until all is smooth, cut in two or three pieces, roll out as thin as paper and lay on a cloth to dry partly. Roll the sheet in a roll and cut as thin as possible. Shake out well and dry thoroughly. Have your soup stock well strained and when boiling add the noodles, not very many, as they thicken. Boil about five minutes, then serve. Chop fine 3 medium-sized potatoes and 2 onions and add to stock.

A Friend
(Kalamazoo, 1906)

Noodle Soup—Bertha's

Beat thoroughly together 2 eggs, and add ½ teaspoon sweet milk, add a little salt and flour sufficient to make thick enough to roll out. Take out on moulding board and knead until a little porous when you cut off a slice. Roll out on board (with rolling pin) until very thin; let dry a little, then roll it up like jelly cake and cut in little shreds with a sharp knife; when all cut up, shake them apart with your fingers, and place on plates to dry. (You can make these a day or two before using, if you like). Make beef soup, or chicken soup, by taking a good beef bone or a chicken cut in small pieces, put in a kettle and pour over it cold water, cooking it until all the juices of the meat and bones are extracted, strain this and season with salt and pepper. Let this get cold, and skim off the grease which when cold will rise to the top. (It is well to make the soup stock the day before you wish to use it.) Pour the soup in the kettle, and let come to a boil. Pour hot water over the noodles, salt a little, and let them just come to a boil. Skim out in the soup tureen, and pour over them the soup.

(Ann Arbor, 1872)

Dr. Chase never mentioned who Bertha was but we can testify that she made a good noodle soup. If you have the time to try any of these variations, you will never go back to canned noodle soup.

Noodle Soup

Two eggs mixed with flour, and a little salt; roll it out like pie crust, only make it thin as possible; set it away till dried a little; when ready for soup roll

A soup ladle in the "oval" pattern popular in 1872 (Wallingford, 1872).

the crust all up with the hands and cut it into very thin slices from the end, which pull out so they seem like a string. Have some water with milk, pepper, salt and butter heating, or chicken soup, into which drop the strings of noodle; then let them boil up about five minutes, when they will be done. A nice addition is green corn off the cob, boiled up in the milk.

(Detroit, 1881)

Onion Soup

Put into saucepan butter the size of a hickory nut, when very hot add 3 or 4 large onions sliced thin. Stir and cook until red but be careful not to burn them; add ½ cup of flour and stir. Pour in 1 pt. boiling water, add pepper and salt, mix well and let boil a minute. Set back until almost ready to serve then add 1 qt. boiling milk and 2 or 3 mashed potatoes. Put a little of the soup to potatoes till all are smoothly mixed. Let simmer a few minutes, put piece of toast in bottom of tureen and serve hot. Leave out potatoes if you choose.

Mrs. Bascomb
(Muskegon, 1890)

If you are not familiar with a hickory nut, the shagbark hickory tree in our front yard produces nuts about ¾ of an inch in diameter. This would equal approximately one teaspoon of butter.

Orange Bouillon

The juice from enough ripe oranges to make 1 quart of solid juice. Heat to boiling point, add 1 tablespoonful of dissolved corn starch, cook till creamy; add small dash of salt. Cool, then add 1 teaspoonful orange flower water, 1 of orange curacoa. Serve in crystal soup bowls with wafers.

Mrs. Conklin
(Flint, 1912)

Ox-Tail Soup

Two ox-tails, two slices of ham, one ounce of butter, two carrots, two turnips, three onions, one leek, one head of celery or celery salt, one bunch of savory herbs, pepper, a tablespoon of salt, 2 tablespoons of catsup, one-half glass of port wine, three quarts of water.

Cut up the tails, separating them at the joints; wash them, and put them in a stewpan with the butter. Cut the vegetables in slices and add them with the herbs. Put in one-half pint of water, and stir it over a quick fire till the juices are drawn. Fill up the stewpan with water, and when boiling, add the salt. Skim well, and simmer very gently for four hours, or until the tails are tender. Take them out, skim and strain the soup, thicken with flour, and flavor with the catsup and port wine. Put back the tails, simmer for 5 minutes and serve.

Another way to make an appetizing ox-tail soup. You should begin to make it the day before you wish to eat the soup. Take two tails, wash clean, and put in a kettle with nearly a gallon of cold water; add a small handful of salt or celery salt; when the meat is well cooked, take out the bones. Let this stand in a cool room, covered, and next day, about an hour and a half before dinner, skim off the crust or cake of fat which has risen to the top. Add a little onion, carrot or any vegetable you choose, chopping them fine first; summer savory may also be added.

(Vermontville, 1906)

Our boys made faces when we told them they were having ox-tail soup, but they soon cleaned their bowls and asked for seconds. For our soup, we used the following quantities and deviations:

1 teaspoon chives	*2 beef bouillon cubes*
1 tablespoon onion powder or one onion diced	*½ teaspoon pepper*
	1 cup burgundy wine
	1½ pounds ox-tail
¼ teaspoon garlic	*1 cup diced ham*
1 teaspoon tarragon	*3 quarts water*

We used no salt in our variation.

Oyster Bouillon

Wash and chop fine 50 oysters, cook in double boiler, closely covered, one hour; add one pint water, one teaspoonful of celery seed; strain through two thicknesses of cheesecloth, reheat,

As this advertisement suggests, the introduction of gas ranges made life much easier for the twentieth-century cook (Charlotte, 1909).

add one tablespoonful salt and pepper and serve in cups.

(Union City, 1902)

Oyster Soup

Drain the liquor from the oysters through a colander. Put the liquor over the fire with half as much water, salt, pepper and a large tablespoonful of butter for each quart of soup. Let it boil up well and put in the oysters. Heat slowly, and as they "ruffle," which should be about five minutes after they reach the boil, strain off the soup. Have in another vessel as much boiling milk as there was oyster liquor. Pour the oysters into a tureen, put a large spoonful of butter upon them; when it melts entirely turn in the milk. Stir in well, add the hot soup, cover, and serve with cabbage and crackers crisped in the oven. Half a pint of rich cream is a great improvement and may be used instead of the butter.

(Detroit, 1881)

Parsnip Stew

First take and clean your parsnips thoroughly, cut them lengthwise and quarter them; have ready some nice salt pork, and place it in the bottom of a flat-bottomed kettle, and fry brown; when done, remove from the kettle, take the parsnips and lay them evenly on the bottom of the kettle, using half of them; take the pork scraps and lay them on the parsnips; put on the remainder of them, and season with salt, pepper and a sprig of thyme; then put on water enough to cover them. When nearly done, have ready some dumplings the size of a tea biscuit, put in and cover closely; let them cook fifteen minutes without removing the cover.

(Detroit, 1881)

Dutch Style Pea Soup

3 cups whole green peas	1½ tablespoons salt
1½ lbs. spare ribs	3 large onions
	6 small potatoes

Soak peas overnight in rainwater if possible. Wash peas and parboil for 10 minutes in enough rainwater to cover. Drain, add 1 gallon hot rainwater which has been strained through a cheese cloth to the peas. Cook for ½ hour and add salt and spare-ribs which have been scalded and cut in small pieces. Cook about ½ hour or until meat is almost done then add potatoes cut in very small cubes and sliced onions. Cook ½ hour longer. Have a slower fire the last ½ hour, because it will burn easily after the potatoes are added. More water may be added if the soup seems too thick. Pig hock, or small pork sausages may be used instead of the spare-ribs.
This is a great favorite with men.

Mrs. John Zomer
(Kalamazoo, 1935)

If it's not convenient for you to catch rainwater, nature's answer to the "Culligan man," distilled water should produce whatever special effect Mrs. Zomer desired. Actually in these days of acid rain, distilled water would probably be safer.

Peanut Butter Soup

Boil a little celery and onion in the amount of milk desired. Dissolve four tablespoons of peanut butter and add a large lump of butter, red pepper and salt. Thicken if desired.

(Higgins Lake, 1920)

Peanut and Tomato Soup

Ingredients—1½ cups stewed and strained tomatoes; ¾ teaspoonful salt; ½ cup peanut butter; ¼ teaspoonful paprika; 2½ cups boiling water. Preparation—Add tomatoes gradually to peanut butter, when smooth add seasonings and water. Simmer ten minutes, and serve with croutons. Well seasoned soup stock may be substituted for the water. If so, use less salt.

Mrs. C. D. Deuel, Centerville
(Homer, 1925)

Pimento Bisque
(to be served in bouillon cups)

Cook ½ cup rice with 3 pints of chicken stock in double boiler until rice is tender, then rub through a sieve and add 5 canned pimentoes, also rubbed through a sieve. Add 1 teaspoon of salt, bring to the boiling point and add the yolk of 1 egg slightly beaten and diluted with ½ cup of cream.

(Higgins Lake, 1920)

Salmon Soup

One can salmon picked to pieces, 1 quart boiling milk, 1 quart boiling water, salt, pepper, butter to suite taste.

(Vermontville, 1906)

Squash Soup

When summer squash first appear in the markets, they are expensive, but only a small one will be needed for Squash Soup. Prepare and cut into dice two cups of summer squash. Add one onion chopped fine and cook in three cups of boiling water until the squash is tender. Mash the squash slightly and add one cup of top milk. Thicken with two tablespoons of flour mixed with three tablespoons melted fat, while stirring constantly. Season with one teaspoon salt and one-eighth teaspoon white pepper. Serve very hot, garnish with whipped cream. Serves six.

(Detroit, 1935)

Swiss Soup

A pint of white turnip cut into dice, boil tender in a little water. When tender add three pints sliced potatoes. Let boil to the consistency of mush, adding a little water if necessary. When done drain and rub through a colander, add one and one-half pint milk and a cup of thin cream. Season to taste. If too thick add a little hot water.

Mrs. Margaret Powers
(Coldwater, 1907)

Tomato Soup

One qt. can tomatoes, or an equal quantity of ripe tomatoes, boiled well in 2 qts. of water rub through a sieve, add ½ cup butter, 1 teaspoon of sugar, salt and pepper to taste. Let all come to a boil and thicken with flour until the proper consistency, serve with dice made by cutting stale bread into small squares and frying in hot butter until quite brown.

Mrs. Fred Nims
(Muskegon, 1890)

Green Turtle Soup

One turtle, two onions, a bunch of sweet herbs, juice of one lemon, five quarts of water, a glass of Madeira.

(Vermontville, 1906)

Vegetable Jam or Soup

One peck ripe tomatoes chopped very fine (peel), ½ peck onions run through food chopper, 12 large carrots run through food chopper, 2 heads medium-sized cabbage chopped very fine, 3 to 5 stalks celery, cut very fine with knife, 1 bunch parsley cut fine. Boil 1 doz. ears of corn cooked 10 m., then cut from cob. Mix all together, add ½ c. salt for each gal. Cook 3 hours, seal hot the same as fruit. Cook soup meat and add broth to 1 qt. of jam to water. Also add potatoes to taste.

Mrs. Beach
(Kalamazoo, 1921)

Vegetable Soup

One cup of cabbage; 1 cup of onion; 2 cups of celery; 2 cups of turnips; 2 cups of carrots; 1 cup of tomato or puree; 2 tablespoonfuls butter; one teaspoon salt and 2 teaspoonfuls sugar. Dice the vegetables and cook preferably in a double boiler.

Mrs. J. T. Cook, Albion
(Homer, 1925)

Wijn Soep (Wine Soup)

1 cup Barley	*1 Cinnamon Stick*
3 quarts Water	*1 pint Grape or Sherry*
1 cup Sugar	*Wine*
¼ cup Citron	*1 cup Small Raisins*

Soak scant cup of barley in water overnight. Boil for one hour, then add raisins, sugar, citron and cinnamon stick. Boil 30 minutes longer. Add grape or

This handy spoon rack, advertised in 1872, featured a bell for summoning servants (Wallingford, 1872).

Sherry wine. Boil a little longer. If too thick add more water.

(Holland, 1936)

Reverend Albertus Van Raalte led a party of religiously oppressed and destitute countrymen from the Netherlands to Michigan in 1847. They founded what was to be a Zion in the wilderness of southern Ottawa County. Those hard-working Calvinists who survived the early days of starvation and disease were soon joined by hundreds of other Dutch immigrants. Despite a fire that destroyed most of the city in 1871, Holland prospered. Long an enclave of Dutch culture, Holland annually celebrates its heritage during the week-long Tulip Festival in May. This authentic Dutch recipe comes from the *Hollandsche Kookerij Boek* published in Holland in 1936.

Browning for Soups

Put 3 tablespoonfuls of brown sugar and 1 tablespoonful of butter in a small frying pan and set over the fire; stir constantly until of a bright brown color and smells slightly burned; add ½ pint of water, boil and skim; when cold, bottle to color soups.

(Union City, 1902)

SALADS

The lush salads created from the many vegetables that we now routinely enjoy throughout the year were unavailable to most nineteenth-century Michigan diners except during particular growing seasons. The springtime, when succulent wild greens flourished, was a favorite salad season. Pioneers and later residents also relished salads in the spring as a tonic for the winter's dearth of green vegetables. The twentieth century saw the widespread implementation of refrigerated railroad cars. Gradually out-of-season vegetables, available to shoppers at an affordable price, made salads more commonplace throughout the year. Earlier, Michigan cooks ingeniously devised salads that made up in originality what they lacked in variety.

Salads

Salads are the most delicious of all vegetable dishes, and are good appetizers, especially in warm weather. The vegetables used for salads are: Lettuce, cabbage, boiled asparagus, boiled cauliflowers, celery, water-cress, onions, etc. Prepare these carefully by washing in ice-cold water, cleaning thoroughly from all dirt or foreign substances, drying carefully in a towel, avoiding as much as possible crushing or breaking the leaves, as it causes them to wilt, and then shredding with the fingers instead of using a knife. Always avoid using a knife on any kind of salad, as it blackens and destroys the crispness and freshness of the vegetable. Lettuce is often served with the leaves entire, except the leaves are broken from the center stalk, and the stalk reserved for garnishing; serve the lettuce on ice without dressing, and let it be prepared by the one served, or if dressing is preferred, use one-third as much oil as vinegar; pepper and salt at discretion, mustard if liked; pile in a salad bowl; sprinkle with powdered sugar, and pour the rest of the ingredients mixed together over the salad. Toss up with a silver fork to mix all well.

If eggs are used, boil them hard and powder them, by mashing with the back of a silver spoon; add the seasoning, then the oil, a few drops at a time, and lastly and gradually the vinegar. A celebrated caterer says the dressing of a salad should be saturated with oil, and seasoned with pepper and salt, before the vinegar is added; it results from this process that there can never be too much vinegar, for, from the specific gravity of the vinegar compared with the oil, what is more than useful will fall to the bottom of the bowl; the salt should not be dissolved in the vinegar, but in the oil, by which means it is more equally distributed throughout the salad. Always use the freshest olive salad oil; cream or melted butter is a good substitute if the salad oil cannot be procured, or even pure meat drippings, but if these are used, they should be added the last of all.

For chicken or potato salads, prepare the dressing, pour it over the dish prepared, garnish the top with slices of cold boiled egg or lemon, and finish the edge of dish with sprigs of celery, and set away until needed. Salads should not be prepared more than two hours before eating, and should be left in the ice-box until the meal is ready to serve. Lettuce, cabbage, celery and all vegetables used for salads, should be left in ice water for several hours before using. Vegetable salads should be stirred as little as possible in order that their freshness may be preserved until ready to serve.

To fringe celery stalks for chicken, meat, or salad garnishes, cut the stalks into two-inch lengths; stick plenty of coarse needles into a cork; draw half of the stalk of celery through the needles; when done lay in a cold place to curl. Stir salads with a wooden fork or spoon.

(Detroit, 1881)

Asparagus Salad

After having washed and scraped asparagus, boil soft in salt water, drain off water, add pepper, salt and strong cider vinegar, and then cool. Before serving, arrange asparagus so that heads will all lie in center of dish; mix the vinegar in which it was put, after removing from the fire, with good olive oil or melted butter, and pour over the asparagus.

(Detroit, 1881)

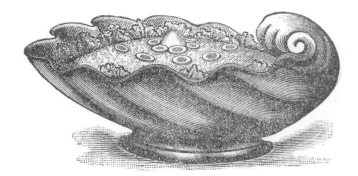

Banana Salad

Slice the fruit with a silver knife, place in a glass dish, each layer alternately with one of finely cracked ice and pulverized sugar. Over this is poured a dressing of orange juice sweetened and flavored with vanilla. Set it on ice for two hours before serving.

(Muskegon, 1890)

Bird's Nest Salad

Boil hard 15 eggs. When cold remove yolks, mix to a smooth paste with ½ cup cream, 3 teaspoons cheese, a little cayenne pepper and salt. Roll and shape like a small bird's egg. Cut the whites into long narrow strips, arrange on a lettuce leaf as nearly as possible like a bird's nest. Place 4 of the eggs in each nest.

Mrs. H. O. Statler
(Kalamazoo, 1899)

Breakfast Salad

Scald two ripe tomatoes, peel them in cold water or fine ice to become cold; drain and slice. Peel and slice one cucumber, very thin; line a salad bowl with lettuce leaves, add the tomatoes and cucumber, a teaspoon of minced parsley, with a few blades of chives, if possible add a few tarragon leaves. Pour over all a plain dressing of olive oil, vinegar, salt and pepper.

(Greenville, 1910)

Few today would think of serving a vegetable salad for breakfast, but in 1910 breakfast was a much more robust meal.

Cabbage Salad

One small head of cabbage, chopped fine or cut into shreds, one cup of boiling milk, three-fourths of a cup of vinegar, one tablespoonful of butter, one tablespoonful of white sugar, two eggs well beaten, one teaspoonful essence of celery, pepper and salt. Heat milk and vinegar in separate vessels. To the boiling vinegar add butter, sugar and seasoning, lastly the chopped cabbage. Heat to scalding, but do not let it boil. Stir the beaten eggs into the hot milk. Cook one minute together after they begin to boil. Turn the hot cabbage into a bowl; pour the mixture over it; toss up and about until all the ingredients are well mixed. Cover and set in a very cold place for several hours.

(Detroit, 1881)

Celery Salad

One-half head of cabbage, three bunches of celery, both chopped fine. Take one cup of vinegar, a lump of butter the size of an egg, yolks of two eggs, well beaten; one teaspoonful of salt, same of mustard, a pinch of cayenne pepper, one teaspoonful of sugar. Mix these well and put over the fire and stir until like thick cream. When cold add two tablespoonfuls of thick, sweet cream. If not moist enough, add a little cold vinegar.

(Detroit, 1881)

Celery Victor

Make a good stock from veal bones and spices. Clean and wash celery hearts thoroughly. Boil in strained stock 45 minutes to 1 hour. Let cool in stock. When cool place in a deep dish and pour over a dressing of crushed white pepper, a little salt, ol-

ive oil, and a little Tarragon vinegar. Let stand 3 to 4 hours. Serve with water cress.

Mrs. L. J. Schermerhorn
(Grand Rapids, 1935)

Cherry Salad

Marinate as many hazelnuts as cherries with plenty of oil, half as much lemon juice as oil, and a little salt, one or two hours. Put a nut in the place of the stone in the cherries. Sprinkle with oil and a very little lemon juice and serve in lettuce nests.

Dorothy Rice
(Higgins Lake, 1920)

Chestnut Salad

Boil and shell chestnuts, cut in small pieces and add ½ as much celery. Serve with mayonnaise dressing.

(Kalamazoo, 1899)

Crab Salad

1 can of crab meat	1 can of tomato soup
Add garlic and	
lemon juice	

Dissolve two tablespoons of gelatine and add to hot tomato soup. Add crab meat and pour in ring mold. Fill mold with halved devilled eggs or cottage cheese garnished with sliced stuffed olives.

Mrs. Geo. L. Erwin
(Grand Rapids, 1935)

Dandelion Salad

Serve the tender young leaves which have blanched under leaves or boards. If one grows dandelions in the garden, lay boards over them for a few days to whiten the leaves. French dressing is used.

A good salad is made with tender dandelions shredded and placed alternately with layers of hot boiled potatoes in a dish. Fry finely minced bacon until crisp, being careful not to scorch. Add vinegar to drippings while hot, pour over salad which has been seasoned and garnish with hard boiled eggs sliced. Endive or head lettuce may be used in place of dandelions.

(Hastings, 1921)

The process by which dandelion leaves are rendered more tender, blanching, was also practiced by Kalamazoo celery growers who placed boards over rows of celery prior to harvesting.

Dutch Lettuce

Shred one pound leaf lettuce, add two mashed potatoes. Cut 3 strips bacon in cubes and fry until brown. Add ½ cup vinegar and pour over lettuce. Garnish with hard boiled eggs.

(Holland, 1936)

Kalamazoo's first party of Dutch settlers arrived in 1851. Paulus den Bleyker, a cultivated and wealthy immigrant from Holland, purchased a farm adjoining the city from ex-governor Epaphroditus Ransom, which he platted into a subdivision. Throughout the last half of the nineteenth century, other Hollanders immigrated to Kalamazoo to established celery farms and work in the city's burgeoning paper mills. Citizen of Dutch heritage formed a conservative, religious, and hard-working core of Kalamazoo citizens.

This traditional Dutch salad recipe appeared in the *Book of Recipes,* published by the Kalamazoo Chapter of the Eastern Star in 1921. This dish is similar to German potato salad. We use dill pickle juice instead of vinegar for an interesting variation.

Dutch Salad

Pare 6 or 8 large potatoes and boil till done, and slice thin while hot, peel and cut up 3 large onions into small bits and mix with potatoes, 1 c. of bacon cut fine and fried a light brown. Skim cut meat and

to the fat add 3 tbsp. vinegar. Pour this with the bits of bacon over the potatoes. Mix lightly; eat while hot.

K. G.
(Kalamazoo, 1921)

Egg or Fish Salad

Take cooked potatoes and slice very thin; add to them three hard-boiled eggs, also sliced thin; chop one small, fresh onion. In a glass bowl or salad, dish put a layer of potatoes, then a layer of eggs, and sprinkle over them a little chopped onion, salt and pepper. For dressing, take the yolk of a raw egg and stir into it half teaspoonful of made mustard. Beat into it, drop by drop, three tablespoonfuls of sweet cream; add one tablespoonful of strong vinegar and the white of the egg beaten to a stiff froth. If needed for supper make at noontime. Flakes of cold boiled salmon, cod or halibut, substituted for the eggs, or added with them, will make a fish salad.

(Detroit, 1881)

Italian Salad

Green peas, string beans, carrots, turnips, cooked and diced. Beets and potatoes may also be used and cut into fancy shapes. Add finely minced olives and parsley to diced vegetables. Macerate with French dressing. Garnish with lettuce and fancy shaped vegetables.

(Hastings, 1921)

Monte Carlo Salad

Two lbs. roast beef or round steak, cooked ½ lb. bacon, fried crisp; 4 c. cold boiled potatoes, diced; 2 large onions, chopped; 2 c. celery, chopped; 3 large tomatoes, chopped; 1 bunch radishes, sliced. Mix all together, add salt and pepper to taste. Pour over following dressing: ½ c. catsup,

4 tbsp. olive oil, 1 raw egg, vinegar to taste. Beat egg and add other ingredients.

Mrs. J. B. Dodge
(Kalamazoo, 1921)

Orange Salad

On each salad plate lay a crisp lettuce leaf, peel and quarter oranges, slice a generous layer on each loaf, cover with broken English walnut meats and pour over any nice salad dressing.

Mrs. Cooper, Bay City
(Union City, 1902)

This is a favorite with children. We use the fruit dressing contributed by Mrs. Clark of Grand Rapids that appears at the end of this section (see page 52).

Oyster Salad

One qt. of oysters steamed till plump, throw them into cold water. Four heads celery cut with a knife, cut the oysters in halves and mix with celery; salt slightly. Dressing—Beat well 4 eggs, add 1 teaspoon mixed mustard, 1 teaspoon cornstarch, ½ cup good strong vinegar, cook over steam until thick, add piece of butter size of an egg. Wine glass cream added when cold.

Mrs. W. W. Barcus
(Muskegon, 1890)

Pea Salad

Chop 1 cucumber, chop 1 large sour pickle, chop 1 onion, chop 1 head celery, chop 3 hard boiled eggs. Add 1 can of peas. Pour salad dressing over all.

B. B.
(Kalamazoo, 1921)

Potato salad, like chili con carne, is an American folk art form. Regional, ethnic, and seasonal variations result in hundreds of different recipes.

Most people agree, however, that nobody's potato salad tastes as good as their mother's. Potato salad recipes could fill a book by themselves. We've included fifteen variations of this summertime favorite.

Potato Salad

Can be made a delicious and rather complicated dish, like "the beggars' stone soup." Take six boiled potatoes steaming from the pot, cut them in slices, pepper and salt a little, lay over a shadow of very thinly sliced onion, a sprig of parsley or so cut very fine, some olives cut fine or left whole, as garnishes, two or three red beets sliced like the potatoes, some scraps of red herring or sardines, a cucumber pickle or two cut into small dice, and some pickled French beans. Over this pour French Dressing for a salad.

(Detroit, 1881)

Potato Salad

Slice several cold boiled potatoes with one large onion; season with salt and pepper. The dressing—Take yolks of three hard-boiled eggs (slice the whites with the potatoes), stir them to a cream, beat in two teaspoonfuls of sugar, one of made mustard, one of white mustard seed, two tablespoonfuls of salad oil, and one-half teacup of vinegar. This should be of the consistency of cream. Pour over the salad and set on the ice till served.

(Detroit, 1881)

American Potato Salad

Take as many cold potatoes, boiled with the skins on, and peeled while hot, as may be required. Cut into small pieces, half the size of a hickory-nut, add one tablespoonful of grated onion. Cover them with mayonnaise dressing and set on ice. Or slice cold potatoes—not too thin—and young onions—

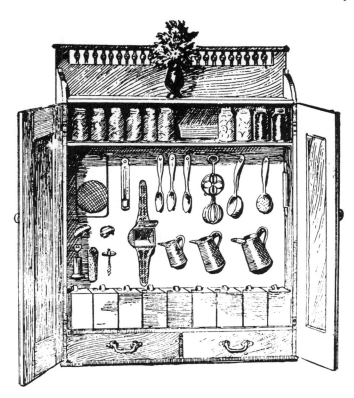

Ella Kellogg of Battle Creek called this kitchen wall cabinet a "multum in parvo of convenience" (Battle Creek, 1910).

one-third onions—and pour over them "a simple salad dressing."

(Detroit, 1881)

French Potato Salad

The potatoes are first put into cold water in their jackets, with a good teaspoonful of salt added to a dozen potatoes. They are then allowed to boil up, and afterward left to simmer gently until quite tender. When cold they are peeled and cut up into rounds as thin as possible, which are laid in a dish, well seasoned with salt and pepper, sprinkled with plenty of finely-chopped parsley, and then saturated with oil and vinegar. In other salads, vinegar is used in about the proportion of one to four of oil; but potatoes require a great deal more—in fact, an almost equal quantity of each, not less in any case than three spoonfuls of vinegar to four of oil. Those who like the flavor will find thinly sliced onions, either spring or Spanish, or a very small piece of

garlic, finely shred, a great improvement to the salad.

(Detroit, 1881)

German Potato Salad

Take as many potatoes as liked and boil them in their jackets until done; when partly cold, slice them up and add sliced onions to the taste, with pepper, salt, vinegar and salad oil, or roast beef drippings if you have no salad oil. Be sure and have the potatoes warm enough, and don't put too much vinegar to them, only enough to wet them through. Winter lettuce chopped with the onions, makes potato salad very much nicer, and the dish is made very attractive by being garnished with it.

(Detroit, 1881)

Potato Salad

A potato salad is easily prepared, and very nice alone; but if you have any cold fish, as called for in this recipe, it gives an additional relish. If you have no cold potatoes, boil or steam a dozen with their jackets on; when done peel and let stand till entirely cold; then slice them ¼ inch thick; mix with some flakes of cold boiled fish (halibut, cod or salmon) and pour over them a salad dressing made with 6 table-spoonfuls of melted butter or salad oil, 6 table-spoonfuls of cream or milk, 1 table-spoonful of salt, ½ the quantity of pepper and 1 tea-spoonful of ground mustard. Into this mix 1 cupful of vinegar. Boil well, then add 3 raw eggs, beaten to a foam; remove directly from the fire and stir for 5 minutes; when thoroughly cold turn over the salad. Garnish with slices of pickled cucumber, cold beet, hard boiled eggs, celery or parsley.

Remarks—It strikes the author that if there is no cold fish on hand that a sprinkling of cold chopped turnips would do remarkably well, for variety's sake, to mix with the potatoes. They make a nice dish mashed with potatoes, for dinner, why not in a salad also.

(Ann Arbor, 1884)

Hot Potato Salad

Boil potatoes, cut in dice, and while hot add the dressing and ½ cup onion cut fine. Dressing, ½ cup vinegar, 4 spoons water, a little red pepper. Cook with flour enough to thicken to the consistency of cream.

Mrs. Lorenzo Bixby
(Kalamazoo, 1899)

Potato Salad

One egg beaten well, ½ cup each of sugar, vinegar and hot water and butter; onions to taste and 1 quart of mashed potatoes.

(Vermontville, 1906)

Potato Salad

Boil six large potatoes, chop a coffee-cupful of celery very fine, using only the white stalks. Fill the salad bowl with alternate layers of potato, sliced very thin, the chopped celery and dressing. To make the dressing, take 3 eggs, 1 tablespoon each of sugar, oil and salt, a scant tablespoonful of mustard, a cup of milk and 1 of vinegar. Stir oil, salt, mustard and sugar in a bowl until smooth, add the eggs and beat well; then add the vinegar and finally the milk. Put the bowl in a basin of boiling water and cook until it thickens like custard.

Miss Marie Jones
(Kalamazoo, 1906)

Potato Salad

Boil potatoes and let stand in ice box until cold and firm. Dice cucumbers, radishes and onion and season with salt and paprika; fry bacon crisp and cut into small strips; put these ingredients, lightly mixed into salad bowl. To thin salad dressing use 2 tablespoons clear bacon drippings, beat well and pour over salad in bowl. Garnish bowl and cover top with hard boiled egg that has been put through potato ricer.

Carrie Guerne, Kalamazoo
(Charlotte, 1909)

Potato Salad

Chop three or four left-over Irish potatoes, or else cut them into dice. Add to them one-half cup of chopped protose, one stalk of celery finely minced, and enough onion and salt to give a delicate flavor. Chopped egg yolks may be used if desired. Over this squeeze the juice of one lemon and allow it to stand in a cool place while preparing the following dressing: Mix together the yolks of two eggs, three tablespoonfuls of lemon juice, two tablespoonfuls of water, one-fourth tablespoonful of salt, two tablespoonfuls of nuttol or olive oil. Put in the inner cup of a double boiler, and cook slowly, stirring carefully until slightly thickened. Remove from the fire and cool at once. Add a little sugar if desired. When cold, mix with the potato; allow it to stand for at least one hour, and serve on a lettuce leaf and garnish with sliced egg yolks which have been steamed or with cooked beets cut into fancy shapes.

(Battle Creek, 1910)

See page 30 for an explanation of protose and nuttol, or nuttolene.

Hungarian Potato Salad

Take small potatoes, boil, and peel while warm. Slice very thin. To every pint of potatoes mince one small onion, one pickled beet, one fresh cucumber sliced, a Dutch herring, four sardines, and a spoonful of minced cold ham. Mix all thoroughly and pour over a teacup of vinegar. Garnish with walnut pickles.

(Greenville, 1910)

A ubiquitous Victorian table piece, the condiment set contained bottles for vinegar, oil, mustard, salt, and pepper (Wallingford, 1872).

Potato Salad

Boil ten medium sized potatoes and when cold cut into dice. Cut into dice one large cucumber and allow same to drain about an hour. Drain one can of small salad peas. Cut into small pieces one medium sized onion and two stalks of celery. Mix all in large bowl with salt, paprika and Mayonnaise dressing. Boil four eggs for twenty minutes. Chop whites up finely and use for garnishing salad; also powder yolks with a fork for garnish. This will serve twelve.

(Higgins Lake, 1920)

Potato Salad

Six medium potatoes boiled with skins, slice thin when cold; Spanish onion chopped fine, ½ lb. lettuce shredded. Dressing—One-quarter pound

bacon, dice and fry but do not brown. Add ⅓ cup vinegar in which has been dissolved teaspoon salt; ½ teaspoon pepper, 1 teaspoon dry mustard. Toss all together.

(Hastings, 1921)

Sweet Potato Salad

3 cups thinly sliced sweet potato	*Salt—pepper—paprika*
½ cup sliced celery	*Boiled dressing*
½ cup broken nut meats	

Mix with fork, tossing lightly.

Mrs. R. O. Turner
(Kalamazoo, 1941)

Shamrock Salad

Stuff sweet green peppers with cottage cheese mixed with a few chopped nuts and a pinch of onion, salt and a little olive oil. Pack peppers firmly and place in refrigerator until ready to serve. Arrange on tender lettuce leaves in thin slices which will be found to form a perfect shamrock. Either French or Mayonnaise dressing may be served with this. Two peppers will serve eight people.

Another pack for these peppers may be made with ¼ pound Kraft pimento cheese, 5 tablespoonfuls cream, 1 teaspoonful gelatine, 1 tablespoonful cold water, salt, pepper. Soften gelatine in cold water and dissolve over hot water. Add this to cheese which has been rubbed through grater and made smooth and moist with cream. Stuff peppers with mixture and place on ice.

(Fennville, 1924)

St. Patrick's Day always called for a big celebration in Priscilla's family, and the "divil" away with anybody wearing orange. What better way to begin a nice corned beef dinner than with a shamrock salad.

Spaghetti Salad

One cup spaghetti cooked; should measure cup before cooked, 4 hard boiled eggs; 1 cup chopped celery. Dressing: Yolks of 2 eggs; 3 tablespoons melted butter; 3 tablespoons sugar; 1 teaspoon prepared mustard; ½ cup hot vinegar; 1 teaspoon salt; a pinch of red pepper. When dressing is cold mix with an equal amount of sweet cream, and mix with salad.

Mrs. Cora Hildinger
(Sunfield, 1915)

Mrs. Cora Hildinger contributed this unusual recipe to the cookbook compiled by the Ladies of the Sunfield Eastern Star in 1915. The slim pamphlet was published locally in this small, northern Eaton County community. Mrs. E. D. Mapes, a local grocer who fancied herself a poet, dashed off an advertisement in verse:

We have sugar, molasses, baking powder, and
    spices,
Flour, and extracts, and raisins—that are nice
You'll need many other things, we cannot mention
    all,
Don't be bashful, "Just give us a call"
Phone No. 73

Before the advent of the revolutionary self-serve market, shoppers were waited on at a service counter (Chicago, 1909).

Tomato Salad

Take 6 large tomatoes and put on ice, wash and drain lettuce leaves and form into little nests on a dish; when ready to serve, cut the tomatoes into large dice, and place a large spoonful in each nest, serve immediately with the following dressing: Yolks of 4 beaten eggs, ½ cup of vinegar heated with 1 tablespoon sugar, 1 teaspoon mustard, salt and pepper; pour in the egg when hot and cook carefully until thick, remove from stove and add ½ cup melted butter, place on ice, and when ready to use thin with cream.

Mrs. E. M. Coppens, Grand Rapids
(Muskegon, 1890)

Tomato Salad

One and one-half pints of canned tomatoes, one-half box of Knox's gelatine dissolved in one-half cupful of water, one teaspoonful of sugar, a little salt. Cook the tomatoes and put them through the colander, add the gelatine, mix and pour into a round mould, set on ice to harden. Serve in slices with lettuce leaves and mayonnaise, or other dressing, as preferred.

Mrs. Wm. Armstrong, Menominee
(Chicago, 1898)

Vegetable Salad

Take new potatoes and young beets; boil until done in separate kettles, then slice into the dish in which they are to be put on the table; first put a layer of potatoes, sprinkled with pepper and salt and little lumps of butter, then a layer of beets, treated in the same way, and so on until the dish is full, then pour over all a very little sweet cream or milk, or vinegar, if preferred.

(Detroit, 1881)

A Wholesome Summer Salad

Cut up a pound of beef into thin slices, and half a pound of white, fresh lettuce; put in a salad bowl, season with a teaspoonful of salt, half that quantity of pepper, two tablespoonfuls of vinegar, and four of good salad oil. Stir all together lightly with a fork and spoon, and when well mixed it is ready to serve.

(Detroit, 1881)

Salad Dressings

Mrs. Rorer of Kalamazoo set down her rather dogmatic rules for the use of salad dressings in 1899.

Salad Dressing

There are 2 kinds of salad dressing used, Mayonnaise and French dressing.

A good rule to remember is that all meat and fish salads should be served with Mayonnaise dressing and all vegetable salads with French dressing. The two exceptions are tomatoes and celery, which are equally good when served with Mayonnaise dressing.

Mrs. Rorer
(Kalamazoo, 1899)

Celery Seed Dressing

Put in quart can
1 tsp. salt
little pepper
1 tsp. wet mustard
⅝ cup sugar

1 tbsp. grated onion
1 cup mineral oil
½ cup vinegar
1 tbsp. celery seed

Put cover on can and shake good for 15 or 20 minutes. Swell on green salad.

Mae De Leeuw
(Kalamazoo, 1945)

Cream Salad Dressing, in Place of Mayonnaise, or Salad Oil

Rub the yolks of 2 hard boiled eggs through a sieve, 1 dessert-spoonful of dry mustard, 1 table-spoonful of butter, 1 tea-spoonful of salt, ½ pt. of cream: either juice of 1 lemon or 2 table-spoonfuls of vinegar, and as much cayenne pepper as can be taken up on the blade of a small penknife. This is a good substitute for mayonnaise for those who like myself, do not like oil, for any dish of vegetables, chicken, or upon meats, at dinner or tea.

(Ann Arbor, 1884)

Delia's Salad Dressing No. 1 (Excellent)

Rub smooth the yolk of 1 hard boiled egg, beat the yolks of two raw eggs and add to the other, drop in this a small bottle of olive oil, a drop at a time, beating constantly (to prevent its separating), 2 saltspoons salt, mustard and cayenne pepper to taste, vinegar, a few drops at a time, and a little lemon juice, little sugar; beat it thoroughly and put in a cold place to thicken. It should be about as thick as good rich cream. This dressing will keep for weeks in a cool place.

(Ann Arbor, 1872)

Two saltspoons are equivalent to ½ teaspoon. Since Dr. Chase failed to identify the size of the small bottle of olive oil, we experimented to find that 5 tablespoons were sufficient. Salad oil can be substituted for olive oil. We added 2 tablespoons of vinegar, ½ teaspoon of lemon juice, ½ teaspoon of sugar, and mustard and cayenne pepper to taste. This is a delicious dressing for a fresh lettuce or spinach salad.

The diminutive saltspoon holds only ¼ of a teaspoon.

Diet Salad Dressing

2 tablespoons vinegar
A pinch of salt and pa-
  prika
1/4 teaspoons dry mus-
  tard

1 teaspoon chives
  chopped fine
1 teaspoon tomato
  catsup or Worces-
  tershire sauce

Rub the salad bowl with an onion.

(Higgins Lake, 1920)

Economy Salad Dressing

Four tbsp. butter, 4 tbsp. sugar, 1 tsp. salt, 2 tbsp. flour, 1 tbsp. mustard (dry), 1 c. milk, 1 c. vinegar, 3 eggs, separated; pinch red pepper. Melt butter in double boiler, add sugar, flour, mustard and salt, blended together; beat yolks and add to the milk, then add to the other ingredients in the double boiler; when it begins to thicken, gradually add vinegar, stirring all the time; cook until thick; when cold add the beaten whites; 1/2 c. olive oil may be added if desired, but not necessary.

Mrs. William Shakespeare
(Kalamazoo, 1921)

Lydia A. Shakespeare, wife of Kalamazoo attorney and Civil War hero William Shakespeare, contributed her favorite salad dressing to a Kalamazoo Eastern Star cookbook published in 1921. Her son, William Shakespeare, Jr., founded the world-famous fishing tackle firm that bore his name.

French Dressing for a Salad

Put into three tablespoonfuls of the purest salad oil a heaping saltspoon or level teaspoonful of salt, one even teaspoonful of scraped onion, one tablespoonful of vinegar, one teaspoonful of tarragon or pepper vinegar. Beat for a few moments with a fork, and pour over a vegetable salad.

(Detroit, 1878)

We found this recipe too salty and reduced the quantity called for by one-half.

Fruit Dressing

1 cup of sugar
1 cup of water
Juice of 1 orange

Juice of 1 lemon
1 1/2 tablespoons corn-
  starch

Cook in a double boiler 10 or 12 minutes. Cool and when ready to serve add whipped cream.

Mrs. C. S. Clark
(Grand Rapids, 1935)

This proved to be an easily prepared and tasty dressing. We recommend that you dissolve the sugar in 3/4 cup of water, add the fruit juices, and cook for 5 minutes. Then dissolve the cornstarch in 1/4 cup of water, fold it into mixture, and cook an additional 7 minutes.

French Dressing

Six tablespoons oil, 1/2 teaspoon salt, dash Quaker paprika, 2 tablespoons vinegar.

Helena A. Breda
(Lansing, 1923)

Golden Dressing

One-third cup sugar, 1/4 cup lemon juice, 1/4 cup pineapple, apple or other light colored fruit juice, 2 eggs. Beat the eggs, sufficiently to blend the yolks and whites but not foamy, add the lemon juice, the pineapple or other juice and the sugar. Cook in double boiler, stirring constantly, until thickened. Excellent for fruit salad.

Genevra S. Ablett
(Lansing, 1923)

Golden Salad Dressing

One-fourth c. pineapple juice, 1/4 c. orange juice, 2 tbsp. lemon juice, 1/8 tsp. salt, yolks of 2 eggs, 1/3 c. sugar, whites of 2 eggs. Heat in double boiler pineapple, orange and lemon juice, also salt. Beat yolks of eggs very light adding gradually half of sugar, add to mixture in double boiler stirring constantly till thick and smooth. Beats whites of eggs until stiff, add remaining sugar and combine with first mixture just before removing from fire.

Mrs. A. M. Todd
(Kalamazoo, 1921)

Iroquois Salad Dressing

1 tablespoon chopped pimento	½ tablespoon chives
1 tablespoon chopped green peppers	¼ tablespoon paprika
2 tablespoons boiled egg	½ pint French dressing
	4 tablespoons catsup
	1 tablespoon tarragon

(Higgins Lake, 1920)

Mayonnaise, Real, or French Dressing for Salads

Yolks of 2 or 3 eggs, 1 lemon, salad oil, 1 teaspoonful each of pepper, salt, and brown or moist sugar. Directions—Mix the yolks of the eggs raw with the pepper, salt and sugar (a wooden spoon is said to be best to work it with); then begin to work in, little by little, the salad oil (the author thinks not above 1 table-spoonful for each yolk used—the amount was not given by Warne's Model Cookery (English), from which I quote, but left to depend upon its creaming with the lemon juice), mixing so thoroughly that it may appear a perfect cream. Keep by your side the lemon, cut in two. As soon as the oil and eggs begin to mix, squeeze in some of the lemon juice, adding more oil, drop by drop, (little by little, as above mentioned, I think best, as drop by drop, unless you have a helper to drop it, would be too slow for Americans), then more lemon juice, till all is finished. Let it be a perfect cream before you use it, and mix in a cool place.

Remarks—I have no doubt the mixing in a cool place will be an important point in keeping the oil less "greasy," as we say. In case the lemon juice is not acid enough to make all of a creamy consistence, add by degrees stirring all the time, as much good vinegar as will accomplish it. It is generally used for chicken, but may be used on anything used for salad, by those who prefer the oil, in place of butter or cream. It is simple and easily made.

(Ann Arbor, 1884)

Roquefort Cheese Dressing

Two-thirds c. olive oil, ⅛ tsp. salt, ⅓ c. vinegar, ¼ lb. Roquefort cheese, ¼ tsp. paprika, ½ tsp. Worcestershire sauce. Blend together cheese and oil, seasonings and vinegar; stir until creamy. Serve on endive, romaine or lettuce salad.

(Kalamazoo, 1921)

Russian Dressing

First a rich stiff mayonnaise using both Tarragon and cider vinegar in mixing. Then equal portions of parsley, chives and chervil minced. Then minced red and green sweet peppers and last of all stir in whipped sour cream.

(Higgins Lake, 1920)

Tuna Fish Salad Dressing

One half teaspoon dry mustard, 2 teaspoons sugar, yolks of 2 eggs, 1 heaping tablespoon flour, ½ cup vinegar, ½ cup water, butter. Cook until thick, thin with milk or cream. 1 can tuna fish, 1 cup chopped cabbage or celery. Mix with dressing.

Mrs. J. P. Boerman
(Kalamazoo, 1920)

Pickles and Preserves

Pickling, actually a process of preserving food, was widely practiced by Victorian cooks. They pickled every conceivable fruit and vegetable. Young homemakers were judged by their ability to produce a tasty pickle; mothers carefully handed down from one generation to the next their prize pickle recipes. Pickles, relishes, and strong condiments were a mainstay of most meals. Special occasions might feature six or more vinegary creations. In the 1830s, health reformers such as Sylvester Graham and later Battle Creek's John Harvey Kellogg railed against the pernicious effects on the digestive system of too much vinegar and spices. But most Victorians were willing to accept a little dyspepsia, what they called indigestion, rather than give up their pickles. Compared to the few standardized varieties now available, theirs was truly the golden age of pickles.

The expression on this woman's face indicates that she is dipping vinegar (New York, 1908).

PICKLES

Sour and Sweet

When making pickles use good, sharp vinegar, or the pickles will be insipid. Keep them from the air and see that they are well covered with the vinegar. Boil in a porcelain kettle; never in brass or metal. Parboil the pickles first, then let them get perfectly cold, and pour on the scalding hot vinegar. A small lump of alum dissolved and added to the vinegar when scalding the first time makes them crisp and green. To make them sharp and crisp they should be parboiled in one vinegar, and then a second vinegar poured over them when ready to put in the crock. Keep in a dry, cool place, either in stone or glass. If put away in stone jars, put a plate or saucer over them so as to keep the pickles under vinegar. If white specks appear on the vinegar, drain off and scald, adding a handful of sugar to each gallon of vinegar.

Most people prefer their pickles highly spiced; cloves and cinnamon put in bags are good for this, also bits of horseradish and red or green peppers. The horseradish helps to preserve the life of the vinegar, but if it will after this persist in losing its strength, pour off the old and replace by new, poured over the pickles scalding hot. Ginger is the most healthy of all spices, cloves are the strongest, after these allspice and cinnamon. Proportion these or the pickles will be black in color and too hot for the palate. Mustard seed is also an improve-

54

ment. Never put up pickles in anything that has held grease, or do not let them freeze; if they do they will be entirely spoiled.

Sweet pickles may be made of any fruit that can be preserved, including the rind of ripe cucumbers or melons. The proportions of sugar to vinegar is three pints to a quart. Make into a syrup and pour over the ripe fruit. With some fruits it is necessary that they may be scalded or steamed; with others it is not. Very ripe peaches or plums do not need steaming, but pears, apples, cucumber and melon rinds are better steamed and the hot vinegar syrup afterward poured over them. With these it is also necessary the spices should be put in bags or the fruit will be much discolored. Crabapples make particularly good pickles, though many seem to think only of making them into jelly or preserves.

In making pickles use none but the best cider vinegar. The vinegar should always be two inches or more above the vegetables, as it is sure to shrink, and if the vegetables are not thoroughly immersed in pickle they will not keep. They should be examined every month or two and soft pieces removed. If there is much tendency to soften, it is advisable to strain off the vinegar, add to each gallon a cup of sugar, boil it and return it to the pickle jar while hot. The occasional addition of a little sugar keeps pickles good and improves them. Spices in pickles should be used whole, slightly bruised, but preferably not ground; if ground they should be tied up in thin muslin bags. Most pickles, if well kept, improve with age by the vinegar losing its raw taste and the flavor of the spices improving and blending.

To strengthen weak vinegar, if in pickles, turn it off, heat it scalding hot, put it on the pickles and when lukewarm put in a small piece of alum the size of a filbert and a brown paper four inches square wet with molasses. If it does not grow sharp in two weeks it is past recovery and must be thrown away. If in winter, freeze it and remove the ice on the surface, for the water alone freezes, leaving the vinegar.

To keep up a constant supply of vinegar: Before the barrel is quite out, fill the barrel with one gallon of molasses to every eleven gallons of soft water. This mixture will become good vinegar in about three weeks. If the barrels stand on end, there must be a hole made in the top, protected with gauze to keep out insects. If standing on the side, the bung-hole must be left open and similarly protected.

A simple method of pickling is to merely put the

No. 102 Pickle.
Double Plate. With Fork. Price
each........ .... 1 45

Who could resist a gherkin passed in such an elegant castor? (Wallingford, 1872).

articles into cold vinegar. This cold vinegar should be used for those that do not require the addition of spice, and such as do not require to be softened by heat, such as capsicums, chillies, nasturtiums, button onions, radish pods, horseradish, garlic and eschalots. Half fill the jars with best vinegar, fill them up with the vegetables, and tie down immediately with bladder. These are much better if pickled quite fresh and all of a size. The onions should be dropped in the vinegar as fast as peeled; this secures their color. The horseradish should be scraped a little outside and cut up in rounds half an inch deep. Barberries for garnish; gather fine full bunches before they are quite ripe, pick away all bits of stalk and leaf and injuried berries and drop them in cold vinegar; they may be kept in salt and water, changing the brine whenever it begins to ferment, but the vinegar is best.

To put up cucumbers in brine: Leave at least an inch of stem to cucumbers and wash well in cold water. Make a brine of salt and water strong enough to bear an egg; put the cucumbers in this as they are gathered each day from the vines. Cut a board so as to fit inside of the barrel; bore holes here and there through it, and put this board on the cucumbers with a weight sufficient to keep it down. Each day take off the scum which arises. When wanted for use take out what is necessary and soak them two or three days, or until the salt is out of them, and then pour boiling spiced vinegar over them. A red pepper or two is an improvement if one likes hot pickles.

To harden them after they are taken out of the brine, take a lump of alum and a horseradish cut in strips; put this in the vinegar and it will make them hard and crisp. When you wish to make a few cucumber pickles quick, take good cider vinegar; heat it boiling hot and pour it over them. When cool, they are ready for use.

(Detroit, 1881)

Cassia Bud Pickles

One peck pickles (small dill size) cut in half lengthwise. Add one pound coarse salt, cover with water. Let stand five days. Then for five days freshen with cold water every day. Drain. Then put pickles in kettle and put on one quart of vinegar and one and one-half ounces of lump alum and enough water to cover. Boil slowly one hour. Drain. Put pickles in crock. Then take one quart vinegar, 2½ pounds white sugar, 2½ pounds brown sugar, 1½ ounces allspice and 1½ ounces of cassia buds. Boil this up and pour over pickles. Put on a plate with a stone and cover with paper.

Mrs. George G. Oetman, Hamilton
(Allegan, 1938)

Cassia buds, from the cinnamon shrub, is a spice rarely used now and might be difficult to find. It was offered in the 1901 Sears, Roebuck & Co. catalog at 37 cents per pound. We substituted 1½ ounces of cinnamon for the cassia buds.

Pickling Cucumbers

Pick each morning; stand in weak brine 3 or 4 days, putting in mustard pods and horseradish leaves to keep them green. Then take out and drain, covering with vinegar for a week; at which time take out and drain again, putting into new vinegar, adding mustard seed, ginger root, cloves, pepper and red pepper pods, of each about 1 or 2 oz.; or to suit different tastes, for each barrel.

The pickles will be nice and brittle, and pass muster at any man's table, or market. And if it was generally known that the greenness of pickles was caused by the action of the vinegar on the copper kettle, producing a *poison*, (verdigris,) in which they are directed to be scalded, I think no one would wish to have a nice *looking* pickle at the expense of HEALTH; if they do, they can continue the bad practice of thus scalding; if not, just put your vinegar on cold, and add your red peppers, or cayennes, cloves, and other spices, as desired; but the vinegar must be changed once, as the large amount of water in the cucumber reduces the vinegar so much that this change is absolutely necessary; and if they should seem to lose their sharp taste again, just add a little molasses, or spirit, and all will be right.

(Ann Arbor, 1864)

Cucumber Pickles

For ½ bushel small cucumbers make a brine of cold water and salt strong enough to bear up an egg, heat boiling hot and pour over the cucumbers, cover and let them stand 24 hours. Drain and wipe them dry. Scald a weak vinegar and pour over them, let them stand 24 or 48 hours, drain and wipe them again and to fresh vinegar enough to cover add 3 quarts brown sugar, 3 large green peppers, ½ pint white mustard seed, 6 cents worth ginger root and stick cinnamon, 3 cents worth whole cloves and allspice, a heaping tablespoon celery seed and alum the size of a butternut. Scald sugar, alum and vinegar together thoroughly and skim before adding peppers, which must be cut open, and spices which should be put in a thin bag. Pour vinegar boiling hot over cucumbers, cover and let stand for 2 weeks, then put in glass cans.

Julia H. Snook
(Kalamazoo, 1899)

Julia Snook's recipe demonstrates the amount of fastidious labor necessary to produce a good pickle. Her directions as to making a brine strong enough to bear up an egg made common sense and were easier to remember than specific quantities. Alum the size of a butternut, essentially an elongated walnut, is easier to follow than "6 cents worth of ginger root and stick cinnamon." According to a 1901 Sears, Roebuck & Co. catalog, whole allspice, ginger, and cinnamon sold for 18 cents a pound and cloves cost 13 cents a pound. A little money bought a lot of spices back then.

Delicious Pickle for 400 Small Cucumbers

Two gallons best cider vinegar, 6 oz. ground yellow mustard, ¼ lb. whole cloves, ¼ lb. allspice, ¼ lb. turmeric powder, 1 oz. mace, 2 grated nutmegs, 1 oz. red pepper, ½ lb. celery seed, ¾ lb. white mustard seed, ¾ lb. ground black pepper, 5 lbs. brown sugar; soak cucumbers in salt and cold water 24 hours, drain and wipe dry, pack in stone jar; mix all the spices, sugar and vinegar in a separate dish, mixing thoroughly and pour on cucumbers cold, cover closely. This receipt can be divided for a smaller number of pickles; the same vinegar and spices for 3 years with good results.

Mrs. E. G. Carel
(Greenville, 1915)

Danish Pickles

1 bu. large ripe cucumbers	12 little red peppers in each jar
2 gals. white vinegar	½ cup black and white pepper
1 pt. little onions	15 bay leaves
½ cup mustard seed	11 cups sugar

Peel cucumbers, half and scrape out seeds; put in crock with coarse salt; let stand over night. In the morning, let drain for 2 hours; wipe with cloth. Put them in a few at a time in boiling vinegar; let heat through; put in crocks, sprinkle a few little onions and red peppers; then pour over them 6 quarts of boiling vinegar with the sugar and spices in it.

Mrs. Victor Salling
(Grayling, 1937)

Dutch Pickles

One peck large cucumbers, 1 doz. onions, cut up and soak in salt water over night, in the morning drain and cook in the following pickle: 1 qt. vinegar, 1 c. brown sugar, 1 tbsp. mixed spices, 1 tsp. mustard seed, 1 tsp. black pepper, a pinch of red pepper.

Mrs. Ezra Smith
(Kalamazoo, 1921)

German Pickles

Take two or three dozen pickles (good sized ones), half a peck of small grape leaves and some dill; wash the pickles and leaves; take a small jar and lay in the bottom of it a layer of leaves and then of pickles, and a little dill; lay in alternate layers; make a salt water brine of very warm water, enough to cover the pickles; do not make it too salty; put a plate in the jar, and lay on it a heavy stone. In about a week the pickles will be sour.

(Detroit, 1881)

Liberty Pickles

Put 2 gallons of pickles in crock, cover with one gallon of hot water and 1 pint of salt.

Stir every day. Let stand one week. Then drain and put on one gallon of fresh hot water and let stand 24 hours.

Then drain and put in one gallon of hot water and 2 tablespoons of alum; let stand 24 more hours. Then drain. Then cut all pickles in half and make syrup of:

2½ qt. vinegar
8 cups sugar
2 tsp. celery seed

5¢ worth of cinnamon bark
(a few mixed spices if you like)

Bring this to a boil and pour over pickles. Next morning pour off syrup and bring to boil again and put on pickles. Do this for 3 mornings and on 4th morning put pickles in cans, heat syrup and pour on pickles while hot. Can and seal.

(Kalamazoo, 1945)

Kalamazoo Navy Mothers uplifted the homefront spirit with this recipe for Liberty Pickles in 1945. Many commodities took on patriotic names in war time. During World War I, German silver became liberty nickel, sauerkraut became liberty cabbage, and the Kent County village of Berlin was renamed Marne. We used 3 ounces of stick cinnamon instead of 5 cents worth of cinnamon bark.

Mostered Komkommers
(Mustard Cucumbers)

1 gallon Vinegar
1 cup Brown Sugar
4 quarts Small Cucumbers

1 cup Ground Mustard
1 cup Salt

Mix cold vinegar with other ingredients and put in sterilized crock. Wash and dry cucumbers and put in mixture.

(Holland, 1936)

Presbyterian Sweet Pickle

Take 3 dozen medium sized cucumber pickles that have been in vinegar, 2 pounds seeded raisins, 1 quart vinegar, 3 pounds brown sugar, a little cinnamon, nearly 1 ounce mace. Let it boil down some, then drop in the cucumbers, which must be cut into inch pieces. Let it boil until the cucumbers are tender, take off and when it cools stir in enough white mustard seed to mix all through.

Caroline Abbot Stanley
(Kalamazoo, 1899)

Caroline Abbot Stanley submitted her special recipe for Presbyterian Sweet Pickles to the cookbook compiled by the Ladies of Kalamazoo's First Presbyterian Church in 1899. Following graduation from the Kalamazoo Training School in 1879, she stayed on to become a critic, teacher, and ultimately principal. In 1896 she resigned her position to devote full time to literary work. She published *Order No. 11* in 1904 and *A Modern Madonna* in 1906, popular novels of the period.

Pyper Pickles

Salt pickles down dry for ten days, soak in fresh water one day; pour off water, place in porcelain kettle, cover with water and vinegar and add one teaspoonful pulverized alum; set over night on a stove which had fire in it during the day; wash and put in a jar with cloves, allspice, pepper, horseradish, onions or garlic; boil fresh vinegar and pour over all. Ready for use in two weeks.

(Detroit, 1881)

Smart Weed Pickles

Make a brine strong enough to hold up an egg. Wash cucumbers. Heat brine hot and pour over the pickles. Let stand 24 hours. Pour off brine, heat hot and pour over pickles again. Repeat this the third morning. Then the fourth morning pour off brine and cover pickles with clear boiling water and let stand 24 hours. Then put horseradish root in the bottom of jar and pack pickles in, putting pieces of horseradish root through them.

To each gallon of pickles add vinegar to cover and one pound brown sugar, one ounce cinnamon bark, one ounce whole allspice, one ounce ground mustard, level tablespoon alum and handful smart weed leaves (the smarty kind with the white flowers). Heat vinegar and other ingredients boiling hot. Then pour over pickles and put on a light weight. They will be ready for use in a few days. Tie allspice in a sack to keep from making pickles dark.

Miss Nellie Turrell, Fennville
(Allegan, 1938)

Smart weed, *Persicaria hydropiper*, sometimes called the water pepper, commonly grows in Michigan swamps. But if you don't want to go to the trouble of identifying and finding smart weed, substitute crushed hot red pepper.

MIXED PICKLES

Stuffed Cucumbers

Wash 15 cucumbers, 5 inches long and 2 inches thick. Put in brine for 3 days, then put in cold water for 3 hours. Cut off one end, scoop out and fill with ½ head of cabbage, ½ head of celery, 2 red peppers, 8 onions, all chopped fine and 4 ounces mixed spices in a bag. Make syrup of 4 quarts vinegar and 7 pounds light brown sugar. Stuff cucumbers and sew on ends and boil in the syrup until tender. Put in jar and cover with syrup.

Mrs. Martha Hay Ayers
(Higgins Lake, 1920)

English Mixed Pickles

One-half peck of small, green tomatoes, three dozen small cucumbers, two heads of cauliflower, one-half peck of tender string beans, six bunches of celery, six green peppers, and a quart of small, white onions. Chop the vegetables quite fine, sprinkle with salt, and let stand over night; to six or seven quarts of vinegar add one ounce each of ground cloves, allspice and pepper, two ounces of turmeric and four ounces of mustard seed; let the vinegar and spices come to a boil, put in the vegetables and scald until tender and a little yellow.

(Detroit, 1881)

French Pickles

Slice a peck of green tomatoes and six large onions, half pint salt, two pounds brown sugar, half pound white mustard seed, two tablespoonfuls each of ground allspice, cloves, cinnamon, ginger, mustard, one teaspoonful red pepper, five quarts vinegar, two of water. Sprinkle salt over the tomatoes and onions; let stand over night, drain in the morning; add the water and one quart vinegar. Boil the tomatoes and onions twenty minutes and drain, boil the four quarts of vinegar with the other ingredients fifteen minutes; put in jars, pour over the hot dressing, seal and keep in a cool dry place.

(Detroit, 1881)

Hodge Podge

Slice one peck of green tomatoes, sprinkle lightly with salt and let it stand two hours, then drain off the liquid and throw it away, and to the tomatoes add the following ingredients: Half a gallon good vinegar, one dozen large onions (sliced), four large pods of green pepper (minced fine), half pound of white mustard seed, quarter pound black mustard seed, and one teaspoonful each of cloves, mace, ginger, black pepper, cinnamon, and celery seed. It is best to put this pickle up in small jars and seal. It is ready for use as soon as made.

(Detroit, 1881)

Last of the Garden

Two or 3 cauliflowers; 1 gallon cabbage; ½ gallon green tomatoes; ½ gallon of cooked corn; ½ gallon large cucumbers, chopped; 1 quart cooked lima beans; ½ dozen carrots; 1 dozen onions; 6 dozen small cucumbers, which have stood in salt water a short time; 1 doz. sweet peppers; 1 gallon vinegar; salt; 2 pounds brown sugar; ½ pound mustard seed. Chop cauliflower, cabbage, green tomatoes, large cucumbers, carrots, onions, and peppers. Mix with other ingredients and cook until soft. Can up while hot.

Mrs. Cora Hildinger
(Sunfield, 1915)

The careful art of canning took lots of patience and lots of coal in 1908 (New York, 1908).

Picklette

Take four large, firm cabbages chopped fine, one quart onions chopped, two quarts vinegar, or enough to cover the cabbage, two pounds brown sugar, two tablespoonfuls each of ground mustard, black pepper, cinnamon, turmeric and celery seed, one tablespoonful each of allspice, mace and alum, pulverized; pack the cabbage and onions in alternate layers, with a little salt between them; let it stand twenty-four hours; then scald the vinegar, sugar and spices together and pour over the cabbage and onions after draining them well; do this three mornings in succession and on the fourth put all over the fire and boil five minutes; put in jars and keep cool.

(Detroit, 1881)

Ragan Pickle

Two gallons of cabbage, sliced fine; one gallon of chopped green tomatoes; twelve onions, also chopped; one gallon best vinegar; one pound brown sugar; one tablespoonful of black pepper; half an ounce turmeric powder, one ounce celery seed; one tablespoonful ground allspice; one teaspoonful ground cloves; one-quarter pound white mustard; one gill of salt. Boil all together, stirring well, for two hours. Take from the fire, and add the spices; then put in air-tight jars. Set in a cool, dry place, and this delicious pickle will keep all winter.

(Detroit, 1881)

PICKLED FRUITS, VEGETABLES, and NUTS

Pickled Apples

For 1 pk. of sweet apples take 3 lbs. sugar, 2 qts. vinegar, ½ oz. cinnamon, ½ oz. cloves; pare the apples leaving them whole, boil in part of the vinegar and sugar until you can put a fork through them. Take them out, heat the remainder of the vinegar and sugar and pour over them. Have care that you do not boil them too long or they will break.

(Muskegon, 1890)

Pickled Artichokes

Boil your artichokes in strong salt and water for two or three minutes; lay on a hair sieve to drain; when cold lay in narrow-topped jars. Take as much white wine vinegar as will cover the artichokes and boil with it a blade or two of mace, some root ginger and a nutmeg grated fine. Pour it on hot, seal and put away for use.

(Detroit, 1881)

It doesn't seem very hygenic, but Victorian cooks used a hair sieve to drain foods. It consisted of a frame covered with hair cloth, a stiff material made from camel or horse hair. Feel free to use a colander, fine sieve, or cheesecloth in your kitchen.

Beet Pickle

1 qt. of raw cabbage, chopped fine	1 tablespoonful of salt
1 qt. of boiled beets, chopped fine	1 teaspoonful of black pepper
1 qt. of celery, chopped fine	¼ teaspoonful of red pepper
2 cups of sugar	1 teacup of grated horseradish

Put in cans, and cover with cold vinegar; seal.

Mrs. J. A. Newell
(Kalamazoo, 1906)

Pickled Butternuts or Walnuts

Gather them when soft enough to be pierced with a pin. Lay them in strong brine for five days changing this twice in the meantime. Drain and wipe dry; pierce each by running a large darning-needle through it, and lay them in cold water for six hours. To each gallon of vinegar allow one cup of sugar, three dozen each of whole cloves and black pepper corns, half as much allspice and a dozen blades of mace. Boil five minutes; pack the nuts in small jars and cover with the scalding vinegar. Repeat this twice within a week; tie up and set away. Good to eat in a month.

(Detroit, 1881)

The concept of pickling walnuts or butternuts (an elongated cousin to the walnut) has fascinated us for many years. But we never remembered to harvest unripe walnuts until too late—that is, until late July of 1988. It took a long stick and plenty of energy to get enough black walnuts, ½ inch in diameter, for our experiment.

We followed the recipe precisely. Six weeks later we thought they should be pickled enough to sample. Although the recipe does not so state, the green outer husk of the nut should be pared away before they are eaten. The pickled walnuts tasted strong and vinegary, not like ordinary cucumber pickles. During a historic cooking demonstration later that fall, we passed around a plate of pickled walnuts. Everybody in the audience daringly sampled a nut—most made wry faces, a few coughed, and some said they liked them.

Butternut Pickles

Gather the green butternuts soon after the first of July, or when they can be pierced with a needle. They must not be too hard and yet if too young will go to pieces. Pierce each with a darning needle. Drop into a stone jar containing a strong brine. Leave two or three weeks, changing the brine once a week. Pour over scalding hot. Some day when you have plenty of time, put on rubber gloves and rub the fuzz off of each butternut. Freshen in water a day, or two, then pour over them cold vinegar. Leave until a convenient season, even weeks. Boil the last vinegar with some allspice, cloves and whole black peppers. They need less flavoring than other pickles, the natural flavor of the nut being so very delicious that they require little other than their own flavor.

Mrs. Allan M. Stearns
(Kalamazoo, 1906)

This turn-of-the-century housekeeper displays a complete complement of canning accessories, including a portable kerosene lamp stove (Battle Creek, 1910).

Pickled Cauliflower, No. 2

These should be sliced and salted for 2 or 3 days, then drained and spread upon a dry cloth before the fire for 24 hours; after which they are put into a jar, and covered with spiced vinegar.

(Detroit, 1890)

Celery Pickles

Select cucumbers about 3 inches long, cut celery in pieces same length and cut in strips, quarter pickles lengthwise, soak both in ice water 3 hours. To 1 qt. white vinegar add 1 c. gran. sugar, ½ c. salt, bring to boil. Place in bottom of fruit jar several slices of onion and 1 tsp. white mustard seed; fill jar with pickles and celery, cover with boiling vinegar and seal. If vinegar is too strong dilute with 1 c. water to 1 qt. vinegar. These pickles are ready to eat in 3 weeks.

Mrs. Howard M. Jordan
(Kalamazoo, 1921)

They did just about anything you can imagine with celery in Kalamazoo. Nicknamed "Celery City," at the turn of the century it was the world's leading producer of the vegetable. Samuel Dunkley, a local inventor, marketed celery pickles, canned celery, celery salad, celery mustard, celery pepper, and celeryade drops, a medicinal lozenge. Consumer acceptance was disappointing, but he later made a fortune out of his patented mechanical cherry pitter. Other Kalamazoo entrepreneurs took advantage of celery's folk reputation as an aphrodisiac to bottle shelves of patent medicine concoctions guaranteed to restore "lost manhood."

Cherry Olives

Fill quart cans with ripe cherries, leaving on the stems, and add 2 tablespoonfuls salt. Fill can one-half full of vinegar and the rest water. Seal.

(Fennville, 1924)

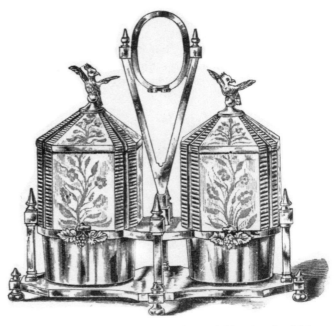

This silver-plated and etched glass pickle stand sold for seventeen dollars in 1872 (Wallingford, 1872).

Pickled Grapes

Take grapes fresh from the stems without breaking, and put them in a jar. For 7 pounds of grapes take 1 quart vinegar, 3 pounds sugar, 1 tablespoon whole cloves and the same of cinnamon bark, boil all together a few minutes, then let it cool until you can bear your finger in it, pour over the grapes, turn a plate over them, set them in a cool cellar and they are done. Do not cook the grapes nor heat the pickle over. If properly prepared will keep a year, and be as plump and fresh as when picked from the vines.

Mrs. J. H. McCall
(Kalamazoo, 1899)

Pickled Lemons

Take 8 thick-skinned lemons, ½ pound fine salt, 2 quarts vinegar, ¼ ounce each of cloves, nutmeg, mace, and cayenne, 2 ounces mustard seed; 1 small onion. Put all this in a muslin bag, the whole to be put in a tight, covered jar. Set in a kettle of boiling water and let it remain till the lemons are tender. It is better to keep them three months before using.

(Detroit, 1890)

Sounds horrible, doesn't it!

Pickled Mangoes

Cut a round piece out of the top of small round musk melons and extract the seeds. Then tie the pieces on again with a thread and put in a strong brine for ten days. Drain and wipe, put them into a kettle with nice leaves under and over them, adding a small piece of alum and put over a slow fire to green, keeping them tightly covered. To fill, make a dressing of scraped horseradish, white mustard seed, mace, nutmeg pounded, green ginger cut small, pepper, turmeric and sweet oil. Fill the mangoes with this mixture, putting a small clove of garlic into each one of them, replacing the pieces at the opening and sewing them in with strong thread. Put into stone jars and pour boiling vinegar over them.

(Detroit, 1881)

A mango to a nineteenth-century Michigan cook meant muskmelon rather than the tropical fruit known today.

Peach Mangoes

Take sound, ripe, free-stone peaches, rub off the fur, split them open, take out the pits; have ready some finely chopped tomatoes and cabbage, grated horse-radish and mustard seed; fill the vacancy in the peach, then place them together and tie with a string; place in a jar and fill up with hot spiced vinegar.

(Detroit, 1890)

To Pickle Mushrooms

Select a number of small, sound, pasture mushrooms, as nearly as possible alike in size;

throw them for a few minutes into cold water; then drain them; cut off the stalks, and gently rub off the outer skin with a moist flannel dipped in salt; then boil the vinegar, adding to each quart 2 ounces salt, ½ nutmeg sliced, 1 drachm mace, and 1 ounce white pepper-corns; put the mushrooms into the vinegar for 10 minutes over the fire; then pour the whole into small jars, taking care that the spices are equally divided; let them stand a day, then cover them.

Another Method

In pickling mushrooms, take the buttons only, and while they are quite close, cut the stem off even with the gills, and rub them quite clean. Lay them in salt and water for 48 hours, and then add pepper and vinegar, in which black pepper and a little mace have been boiled. The vinegar must be applied cold. So pickled they will keep for years.

(Detroit, 1890)

One drachm is ⅛ of an ounce.

Musk Melon Pickles

Take them when just ripe; pare and slice about an inch and a half thick; put them in alum water one night; take out and drain well; allow three pounds sugar to three pints vinegar; boil well and skim; pour over the melons; pour off the syrup and heat and pour back nine mornings, the last time add cinnamon and cloves to suit the taste; boil the syrup down till just enough to cover the pickles.

(Detroit, 1881)

Pickled Nutmeg Muskmelons

Half ripe melons washed and pared, seeds removed, and cut in 4 or 6 pieces. Lay them in stone jars and cover with vinegar 24 hours; take them out and to each qt. of fresh vinegar add 3 lbs. brown sugar. For 12 melons take 3 oz. of cinnamon, 2 oz. cloves, and 2 oz. allspice; boil the sugar and spices in the vinegar, skim well, then put in the melons and boil 20 minutes. Let the syrup boil a few

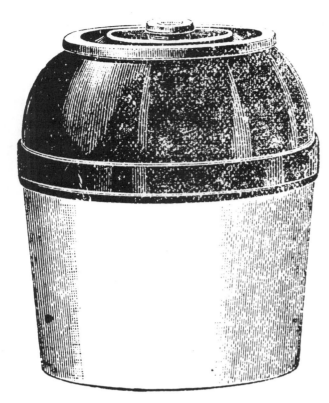

Crockery preserve jars are highly prized collector's items today (Grand Rapids, 1890).

minutes after taking them out, then pour the hot vinegar over them.

Mrs. Trott
(Muskegon, 1890)

Pickled Nasturtiums

Soak for 3 days in strong salt and water; then strain and pour boiling vinegar over them, omitting the spice. Vinegar for any pickle should never be allowed to boil over 1 minute.

(Detroit, 1890)

Nasturtium is a synonym for garden cress.

Pickled Onions

Small silver-skinned onions; remove outer skin so that each one is white and clean; put them into brine that will float an egg for 3 days; bring vinegar to a boiling point, add a little mace and whole red peppers and pour hot over the onions, well drained from the brine.

(Detroit, 1890)

The onions stay in the brine for three days, not the floating egg.

Pickled Onions

Peel small onions till white; cook in strong salt water for a few minutes; put in glass jars; pour over them hot spice vinegar. Cover close; keep in dark place.

Mrs. McAfee
(Flint, 1912)

Peach Pickle

Select any variety of peaches you like best, rub them well and stick into them 3 or 4 whole cloves, according to size, put the peaches into steamer and steam until you can prick them easily with a broom splint. Make the syrup in the proportion of 1 quart best cider vinegar to 3 pints sugar and 2 ounces whole cinnamon. After the syrup boils well skim it, and drop the peaches from the steamer into it, just a few minutes, 5 or 10, and put in your jars or cans, and fill with the syrup. All that is necessary to keep sweet pickles is to have enough syrup to cover, and keep the fruit well under. Be careful and not cook the peaches too much.

Mrs. J. H. McCall
(Kalamazoo, 1899)

Splints from corn brooms made handy, albeit unhygenic, tools in early Michigan kitchens.

Stuffed Peppers

Get large bell peppers, cut around the stem, remove it and the seeds, soak well in fresh water over night. For the stuffing use 2 quarts chopped cabbage, 1 cupful of white mustard seed, 1 cupful of grated horseradish: fill each pepper with some of this mixture, and with each put in a small onion and a little cucumber, tie or sew the stem on again, put the filled peppers in a jar and cover with cold vinegar.

(Muskegon, 1890)

Pickled Purple Cabbage

Quarter them, put them in a keg and sprinkle over them a great deal of salt; let them stand 5 or 6 days; to gal. of vinegar, 1 oz. mace, peppercorns, cinnamon, cloves and allspice; heat the vinegar hot, put in a little alum and turn on, leave the salt on cabbage turn 6 or 7 times.

(Grand Rapids, 1890)

This recipe would have been made in a covered crock stored most likely in the cellar. After the hot vinegar and spices have been poured onto the cabbage, the cabbage was to be stirred or "turned" 6 or 7 times before being used, in other words a week.

Strawberry Pickles

Pickles made of the large garden strawberries are a novelty, and are highly esteemed. Put the fresh berries in a jar, a layer in the bottom first with cinnamon and cloves scattered over them, then put another layer of berries and continue in this way until the jar is nearly full; then pour over them a syrup made of 2 cups vinegar and about 3 cups sugar; heat this to the boiling point, and then pour it into the jar. Let it stand from one morning until the next; then set the jar into a kettle of water and let them boil slowly for nearly 1 hour. If you are careful to let them cook slowly, and do not break them when stirring, the berries will keep their shape perfectly. If canned they are sure to be fresh and delicious when wanted.

(Detroit, 1890)

Wild strawberries grew plentifully on Michigan oak openings and prairies. Early travelers raved about their beauty and taste. Pioneers who traveled across Michigan in the 1830s wrote of their wagon wheels being stained red by fields of strawberries.

Pickled Turnips

Wash them clean before boiling; do not pare them. If the rind is broken the juice escapes. When cooked take off the outside, slice them like beets and pour hot spiced vinegar over them. They are to be eaten while newly cooked and warm, and are as good as pickled beets.

(Detroit, 1881)

Water Melon Rind Pickles

Pare them; cut up the inside rind in small squares; then boil in weak ginger water until tender; make a syrup of sugar and vinegar spiced with cloves and cinnamon, and pour on hot three successive mornings. Musk melon rinds may be pickled in the same way.

(Detroit, 1881)

Watermelon Pickles

Pare off the green outside, and cut out the pink inside, slicing the white part into thick strips. Weigh 8 lbs., and put in kettle, pouring over it 1 gal. of water in which 1 oz. alum has been dissolved. Stand on hot part of stove for 3 hours. Then place in ice water for half an hour. Take 4 lbs. of white sugar, 1 qt. vinegar, and a large cupful of mixed spices, such as whole cloves, allspice, cassia buds, stick cinnamon, and green ginger root tied in cheese cloth bags. Boil 3 minutes. Skim, cool a little, and drop in rinds. Simmer gently a half hour or till clear and tender; put in jars. Boil down syrup and pour it over.

Juliet Sebring Hunter
(Kalamazoo, 1906)

RELISHES

Apple Relish

Three and one-half pounds of apples (6½ cups when chopped), 1 lb. raisins, 1 c. vinegar, 3½ c. sugar, 1 orange, ½ tsp. powdered cloves, 1 tsp. powdered cinnamon. Core apples, may be peeled or not; put apples and rind and pulp of orange through food chopper. Add vinegar, sugar, raisins and spices. Cook slowly for half an hour. This makes an excellent relish for meats, or if cooked thicker may be used as a filling or spread.

Minnie M. Engel
(Kalamazoo, 1921)

Carrot Relish

1 cup chopped carrots
2 cups boiling water
1 cup sugar
½ lemon (juice and rind)

Cook carrot with boiling water till tender, then add sugar and lemon, boiling all till thick like honey and put in glasses.

Jennie Pixley
(Grand Rapids, 1917)

Celery Relish

Two qt. celery or 6 bunches, 3 qt. cabbage or 2 large heads, 1 qt. onions. Chop all this fine and cover with salt water for 2 days. Drain well and put on stove with 1½ qt. vinegar, ¼ lb. mustard, 4 c. brown sugar, 1 tbsp. flour, 1 tbsp. turmeric powder. Boil 20 m., then add 3 well beaten eggs, before taking from fire. Add more salt and sugar if needed.

Mrs. O. Garline
(Kalamazoo, 1921)

Chutney

Cut two quarts of green tomatoes in slices, take out the seeds, sprinkle with three tablespoonfuls of salt; let stand over night and drain through colander; put in porcelain kettle, add two quarts of sour apples chopped fine, two green peppers chopped, one pound of raisins seeded and chopped, two pints of cider vinegar; simmer two hours, then add one pound of brown sugar, one pint of lemon juice, three tablespoonfuls of mustard seed, two tablespoonfuls each of ginger and salt, a little cayenne; cook slowly another hour; seal hot.

Mrs. H. P. Bird, Menominee
(Chicago, 1898)

Recipes by cooks from Michigan's Upper Peninsula have been difficult to find. Mrs. Mary Ellis of Peshtigo, Wisconsin, put together an excellent cookbook containing more than four thousand recipes in 1898. Fortunately she included a number of recipes submitted by cooks residing in the U.P., including this Americanized East Indian relish.

Corn Relish

One dozen ears of corn (cut off cob), mix with 1 large head of cabbage (chopped fine).

6 onions
6 green peppers
½ gallon of vinegar
¼ pound of mustard
4 tablespoons salt
3 cups sugar

Let vinegar come to a boil, dissolve mustard in a little cold vinegar, pour all together and boil 30 minutes and seal while hot.

Mrs. Wm. Vyn
(Grand Rapids, 1917)

Dresden Relish

3 heads cabbage
8 green mangoes
8 red mangoes
8 yellow mangoes
8 large onions

Grind all in the food chopper. Put in weak salt water and let stand over night. In the morning squeeze out and add—

1 tablespoon white
     mustard seed   3 pints vinegar
1 tablespoon celery   2 pints of sugar
     seed

Mix all of this together well; put in cans and seal, all cold. This is fine.

Mrs. J. Kindleberger
(Parchment, 1926)

Jacob Kindelberger, who emigrated to the United States with his family from Alsace-Lorraine, led a Horatio Alger-type, rags-to-riches early life. He went to work in a paper-mill rag sorting room at the age of ten and struggled to gain an education. In 1909 he founded the Kalamazoo Vegetable Parchment paper mill in an old sugar beet factory located on the Kalamazoo River, north of the city. A company town, known as Parchment, grew up around this famous factory, which produced one of America's first water-impervious papers suitable for food packaging. In 1926 Lucy Kindelberger submitted her recipe for Dresden Relish to the *Parchment Cook Book*, compiled by the Parent-Teacher Association of the community her husband had created.

Chili Sauce

One peck of ripe tomatoes, boiled one hour, add one-half cupful of salt, one quart of vinegar, one ounce of whole cloves, one ounce of cinnamon, one ounce of allspice, one ounce of mustard seed, one quart of onions chopped, a little celery, a little horse radish, one-half pound of sugar, six red peppers chopped (ground cloves may be used) boil slowly; strain if preferred.

E. L. Ellis, Nahma
(Chicago, 1898)

Nahma, named for the Chippewa word for sturgeon, is a small community east of Escanaba on Lake Michigan's Big Bay De Noc.

CATSUPS

Today when we say pass the catsup, we expect a thick, spicy tomato sauce, but early Michigan cooks made catsup out of just about anything that came their way.

Cherry Catsup

One pint of pure cherry juice, half a pound of sugar, a teaspoonful each of ground cloves and cinnamon. Boil to a thick syrup and bottle.

(Detroit, 1881)

Cucumber Catsup

Take medium sized cucumbers grate and press out juice thoroughly, add vinegar to make it of the consistency of catsup, season with salt and pepper to taste, seal.

(Kalamazoo, 1899)

Cucumber Catsup

Take green cucumbers, as you like them for the table, peel them and let them lie in salt water a short time. If large, cut in two and scrape out the seeds, grate on a coarse grater. For every dozen cucumbers grate one good-sized onion. After all is grated pour off the water which has collected, measure it and for as much water as you pour off add the best cider vinegar. Season with pepper and salt to your taste. Should the vinegar be too sharp dilute with the cucumber water; if it is too thin use less vinegar. Put in jars like fruit—no heating required.

(Detroit, 1881)

Currant Catsup

When making currant jelly wash the pulp and seeds and strain, add sugar, small quantity of vinegar and cinnamon and cloves; boil until thick enough. Cannot give amount of anything as one cannot tell richness of juice from rinsed pulp. Very good with any kind of cold meat, especially lamb.

Mrs. Higbie
(Flint, 1912)

Gooseberry Catsup

Nine lbs. gooseberries, 6 lbs. brown sugar, put on the fruit and sugar, with a gill of water, and boil slowly for three hours, stirring constantly, 1 qt. good vinegar and boil ½ hour, then add ½ teacupful of cloves, and the same of allspice, just as you are taking it off. Bottle while hot and seal. It will keep for years. Plums and cherries are also done in the same way.

Mrs. F. M. Chamberlain
(Grand Rapids, 1890)

Gooseberry Catsup

Five pints of vinegar, four pounds of green gooseberries, one-half pound of brown sugar, one-half pound of raisins, one-quarter pound of currants, one-quarter pound of common salt, two ounces of mustard, two ounces of onions, one-half ounce chillies; one-half ounce allspice, one-half ounce ground ginger, one-half ounce of ground mace, one-half ounce ground turmeric, one nutmeg. Boil the vinegar, currants, onions, gooseberries and chillies till quite soft; then pour through a fine sieve on the remaining ingredients.

(Detroit, 1881)

Grape Catsup

Nine pounds of grapes and six pounds of brown sugar. Boil the grapes until soft; rub through colander; add sugar and boil until quite thick, then add three pints of vinegar, one tablespoonful each of cloves, cinnamon, allspice and black pepper.

(Detroit, 1881)

Lemon Catsup

One pound and a quarter of salt, quarter of a pound of ground mustard, one ounce each of mace, nutmeg, cayenne and allspice, one gallon of cider vinegar, eight or nine garlic cloves, fifteen large lemons. Slice the lemons; add the other ingredients; let simmer from twenty to thirty minutes; place in a covered jar; stir every day for seven or eight weeks, strain, then bottle, cork and seal.

(Detroit, 1881)

How would you like to get up early every morning for seven or eight weeks to stir the lemon catsup?

Mushroom Catsup

Break the mushrooms in small pieces, place alternately in an earthen dish, a layer of mushrooms and then one of salt, let stand 24 hours, then mash and strain. To every quart of this liquor, add 1 ounce pepper corns, ¼ ounce whole allspice, ½ ounce sliced ginger root, 1 dozen whole cloves and 3 blades of mace, boil ¾ of an hour. Take from fire and cool, strain, bottle and seal.

(Kalamazoo, 1899)

Red-Pepper Catsup

Cut up red peppers and place them in a preserving kettle until it is full; then cover with the best cider vinegar and boil until the peppers have dropped to pieces. After removing from the fire, as soon as the sauce is cool enough, rub it through a wire sieve. It is much better without salt or any other condiments, and is of a beautiful scarlet color, and so thick that it must be put for use in large-mouthed bottles or jars. This will keep fresh for years. It should boil slowly for at least four hours.

(Detroit, 1881)

Tomato Catsup

Take a bushel of ripe tomatoes; rub them with a damp cloth; cut out the hearts and place them over a fire with two heaping handfuls of peach leaves, one dozen large onions (cut in small pieces) and one quart of water; boil until soft and strain through a coarse sieve; it will take about two hours to boil soft enough. Put the liquid in the boiler again over the fire, adding a half gallon of strong vinegar. Have ready two ounces ground allspice, two ounces ground black pepper, two ounces cayenne pepper, two ounces mustard and, if preferred, two ounces celery seed, one ounce ground cloves, two grated nutmegs, two pounds brown sugar and one pint of salt; mix the ingredients thoroughly before putting them in the boiler. Boil two hours and when cool put in bottles, cork, seal and keep in a cool place.

(Detroit, 1881)

Tomato Mustard

One peck of ripe tomatoes; boil with two onions, six red peppers, four cloves of garlic, for one hour, then add a half pint or half pound of salt, three tablespoonfuls of black pepper, half ounce ginger, half ounce allspice, half ounce of mace, half ounce of cloves, then boil again for one hour longer, and when cold add one pint of vinegar and a quarter pound of mustard, and if you like it very hot, a tablespoonful of cayenne.

(Detroit, 1881)

Walnut Catsup

Take the fresh, green shell from 200 walnuts when they are ripe enough to shell; lay them in a deep pan, sprinkling each layer with salt, let them stand a week, stirring them each day with a wooden

spoon; then strain through a sieve and measure the liquid into a sauce-pan and to each pint of liquor add ¼ ounce bruised ginger, ¼ ounce mace, and a small piece of garlic. Boil these together 20 minutes, set to cool and bottle for use.

(Detroit, 1890)

Vinegar

Three gallons of rain water, one quart of molasses, one pint of yeast. Set in a warm place where it will be exposed to the air. Can be used in three weeks.

(Battle Creek, 1890)

Home-Made Table Vinegar

Put in an open cask 4 gallons warm rain-water, 1 gallon common molasses, and 2 quarts yeast; cover the top with thin muslin and leave it in the sun, covering it up at night and when it rains. In 3 or 4 weeks it will be good vinegar. If cider can be used in place of rain-water the vinegar will make much sooner—will not take over a week to make very sharp vinegar. Excellent for pickling purposes.

(Detroit, 1890)

Instead of going to the trouble of collecting rain water, we are sure distilled water would work just fine.

Cheap Vinegar

Have some good cider vinegar in a keg to start with. Save all skimmings, currants, pieces of fruit, etc., left after making jelly; put all together in a stone jar, cover with soft water that has been boiled, and let stand several days. Also save apple peelings, boil them up well in a porcelain kettle, and drain off this liquid into another stone jar; now drain the first jar into the second, and add any remnants of jelly or fruit syrups, the rinsings of the molasses jug, etc., and then if not sweet enough put in some brown sugar or molasses; pour the clear part of the liquid into the vinegar keg and keep in a warm place. Give the air free access, but keep out the dust with a thin cloth.

(Detroit, 1890)

Clover Vinegar

Put 1 large bowl of molasses in a crock, and pour over it 9 bowls boiling rain-water; let stand until milk-warm, put in 2 quarts clover blossoms, and 2 cups baker's yeast; let this stand 2 weeks and strain through a towel. Nothing will mold in it.

(Detroit, 1890)

Horse-Radish Vinegar

Put into a jar, four ounces of grated horse-radish, a teaspoonful of cayenne, two of salt, the same of mustard. Pour over them a quart of boiling vinegar. Let it stand near the fire for two weeks; then boil, strain and bottle. Excellent for salads, cold meats, etc.

(Battle Creek, 1890)

Mint Vinegar

Put into a wide-mouthed bottle enough fresh, clean peppermint, spearmint, or garden parsley leaves to fill it loosely; fill up with good vinegar, stop closely, leave on for 2 or 3 weeks, pour off into

Victorian cooks used so much vinegar that they bought it by the barrel (Polk, 1881).

another bottle, and keep well corked for use. This is excellent for cold meats, soups and bread-dressings for roasts; when mints can not be obtained, celery seed is used in the same way.

(Detroit, 1890)

Orange Vinegar

Peel 5 or 6 fresh oranges, press the juice out in a tall glass and let it stand covered to clarify. Free the rinds from the white part, pound them to a paste and pour 1 gallon of good vinegar over it. Let it stand a few days, then pour off the vinegar, mix it with the clear juice, filter and bottle.

(Detroit, 1890)

Pepper Vinegar

Fill a quart bottle or jar with small peppers, either green or ripe; put in two tablespoonfuls of sugar and fill with good cider vinegar. Invaluable in seasoning sauces, and good to eat with fish or meat.

(Detroit, 1878)

Tarragon Vinegar

Gather the tarragon just before it blossoms, strip it from the larger stalks and put it into small stone jars or wide-necked bottles; and in doing this twist the branches, bruising the leaves; pour over it vinegar enough to cover; let it stand 2 months or longer, pour off, strain, and put into small dry bottles, cork well and use as sauce for meats.

(Detroit, 1890)

Curry Powder

One of the finest condiments ever prepared, and this is one of the best recipes. Six ounces turmeric, 8 ounces coriander seed, 4 ounces black pepper, 2 ounces fenugreek, ½ ounce cayenne pepper, 2 ounces ginger, ½ ounce cumin seed, all ground fine and bottled for use.

(Detroit, 1890)

Hot Spice

Hot spice is the name given by a cook of a past generation for a delicious adjunct to gravies, steaks, chops, and soups. Take 3 drachms each of ginger, black pepper and cinnamon, 7 cloves, 1 ounce each of mace, cayenne, grated nutmeg and white pepper; pound these together, mix till well blended, and then put it in a perfectly clean, dry bottle for use.

(Detroit, 1890)

Nasturtium Seed

Take the green seed after the flower has dried off, lay it in salt and water two days, in cold water one day; pack in bottles and cover with scalding vinegar, seasoned with mace and white peppercorns, and sweetened slightly with white sugar. Cork and set away four weeks before you use them. A good substitute for capers.

(Detroit, 1881)

See the note about nasturtiums on page 24.

Jams, Jellies, and Marmalades

Victorian diners filled in the chinks around their hearty meals with myriad pickles, relishes, and spicy sauces, but the breakfast table groaned with jams, jellies, and marmalades.

Jams and Jellies

The fruit must be picked when just ripened, as when too old, it will not form jelly. Look over the fruit, and then put stems and all in a porcelain-lined kettle, or they may be put in a brass or tin kettle, if scoured very bright, and the fruit removed immediately after it is taken from the fire. Use the best refined or granulated sugar, taking care that it has not a bluish tinge; for jelly from bluish-white sugars does not harden well.

If two fruits are combined for jams or jellies, the flavor is much enhanced, as raspberries and currants. To extract the juice, crush a little of the fruit and put all together in the kettle, but add no water. As it heats, mash with a potato-masher, and, when hot, strain through a jelly-bag. Let all run off that will before squeezing the bag. It will be a little clearer than the squeezed juice. To every pint of this juice add one pound of sugar. Boil the juice twenty-five minutes; add the sugar and boil for five more; put up in glasses. Crab-apple, quince, grapes, etc., are all made in the same way. Allow a teacup of water to a pound of fruit; boil till very tender: then stain through a cloth, and treat as currant jelly. Cherries will not jelly without gelatine, and grapes are sometimes troublesome. Where gelatine is needed, allow a package to two quarts of juice.

For jams the syrup is made as above. Use raspberries, strawberries, or any small fruit, and thoroughly bruise before cooking, as this prevents it from becoming hard. Boil fifteen or twenty minutes before adding the sugar, and then boil half an hour longer. Jams require constant stirring with a wooden spoon, and the closest attention, as they are easily burned, and if in the slightest degree, the flavor is destroyed. Put up in small jars, of either glass or stone, and seal or secure like canned fruits or jellies.

Jelly should be examined toward the end of summer, and if there are any signs of fermentation, reboil. Jelly needs looking after more closely in damp, rainy weather than in dry. If troubled with jelly getting moldy, cover the glasses with buttered paper pressed down closely to the jelly, and paste as usual. To test jelly, drop a little in a glass of very cold water, and if it immediately falls to the bottom, it is done; or drop it on a saucer and set it on ice, and if it does not spread but remains rounded, it is done. A very little butter rubbed with a cloth on the outside of jelly glasses or cans, will enable one to pour in the boiling fruit without breaking the cans. If jelly is not firm let it stand in the hot sun for a few days covered with thin cloth, or window glass. Jellies and jams should be covered with paper dipped in the purest salad oil, and fine tissue paper stretched over the top, cut about two inches larger, and brushed with whites of an egg; then, when dry, they will be perfectly hard and air-tight. They should then be set away in a dry, cool and dark place.

(Detroit, 1881)

Apple Jam

Peel and core the apples, cut in thin slices and put them in a preserving kettle with three-quarters of a pound of white sugar to every pound of fruit: add (tied up with a piece of muslin) a few cloves, a small piece of ginger and a thin rind of lemon; stir on a quick fire for half an hour.

(Detroit, 1881)

Apricot Jam

Pare the apricots, which should be ripe, as thinly as possible; break them in half and remove the stones, weigh the fruit, and to every pound allow the same proportion of loaf sugar; roll the sugar fine, strew it over the apricots, which should be placed on dishes, and let them remain for twelve hours, then put the sugar or fruit into a preserving pan, let them simmer very gently until clear, take out the pieces of apricots singly as they become clear, and as fast as the scum arises carefully remove it; put the apricots in small jars, pour over them the syrup, and put up the same as jelly.

(Detroit, 1881)

Whereas we simply measure the correct quantity of granulated sugar, nineteenth-century cooks needed to first break up with a mallet the hard loaf in which sugar came and then, using a rolling pin, pulverize it for use.

Blackberry Jam

To each pound of fruit add three-fourths of a pound of sugar; then put together and boil from one-half to three-fourths of an hour.

(Detroit, 1881)

Cherry Jam

To every pound of fruit, weighed before stoning, allow one-half pound of sugar; to every six pounds of fruit allow one pint of red currant juice, and to every pint of juice one pound of sugar. Weigh the fruit before stoning, and allow half the weight of sugar; stone the cherries and boil them in a preserving pan until nearly all the juice is dried up; then add the sugar, which should be crushed to

powder, and the currant juice, allowing one pint to one pound of sugar.

(Detroit, 1881)

White or Red Currant Jam

Pick the fruit very nicely, and allow an equal quantity of purely powdered loaf sugar; put a layer of each alternately into a preserving pan, and boil for ten minutes; or they may be boiled the same length of time in sugar previously clarified and boiled like candy.

(Detroit, 1881)

Gooseberry Jam

Take what quantity you please of red, rough, ripe gooseberries, take half the quantity of lump sugar; boil them together for half an hour or more, if necessary.

(Detroit, 1881)

Grape Jam

Boil ripe grapes to a soft pulp (about one hour and a half will do) and strain through a sieve; weigh them and to every pound of fruit allow three quarters of a pound of sugar; boil together twenty minutes, stir and strain.

(Detroit, 1881)

Green Gage Jam

To every pound of fruit weighed before being stoned, allow three-fourths of a pound of lump sugar. Divide the green gages, take out the stones, and put them into a preserving pan; bring the fruit to a boil, then add the sugar, and keep stirring it over a gentle fire until it is melted; remove the scum as it rises, and just before the jam is done, boil it rapidly for five minutes.

(Detroit, 1881)

Greengages comprise several varieties of high-quality greenish-yellow plums.

Peach Jam

Gather the peaches when quite ripe, peel and stone them, put them in a preserving pan, mash them over the fire till hot; rub them through a sieve and add to a pound of pulp the same weight of pounded loaf sugar, and half an ounce of bitter almonds, blanched and pounded; let it boil ten or twelve minutes. Stir and skim it well.

(Detroit, 1881)

Raspberry Jam

Three-quarters of a pound of sugar to each pound of fruit; put the fruit on alone or with the addition of half a pint of currant juice to every four pounds of fruit; boil half an hour, mashing and stirring well; add the sugar, and cook twenty minutes more. Blackberry jam is very good made as above, omitting the currant juice.

(Detroit, 1881)

Strawberry Jam

To every pound of fruit allow three-fourths pound of sugar, one pint of red currant juice to every four pounds of strawberries. Boil the currant juice with the strawberries for half an hour, stirring all the time; add the sugar and boil twenty minutes more, skimming carefully. The currant juice may be omitted, but it improves the jam.

(Detroit, 1881)

General Rules for Making Jelly

Always make in porcelain kettle. Use refined or granulated sugar. Do not have fruit, especially grapes or currant, over-ripe. Make not over two or three pints of jelly at a time. As a general rule allow equal measure of juice and sugar. Boil juice rapidly ten minutes, skim and add sugar, boil ten minutes longer. To test jelly, drop a little in a glass of very cold water and if it immediately falls to the bottom, it is done.

(Vermontville, 1906)

Jellies

Every fancy you consult,
consult your purse.
—Franklin

Jellies are best made from the bones, legs and tendons of poultry, by cooking them 8 to 10 hours in water, or until all the solid portions are cooked into bits, then strain off the liquor through a colander, pressing out all the juice; set this liquor away, and when solid, which will be the next day, remove all the fat you can with a knife, pour a pint of boiling water over the jelly turning it off quickly, and with a cloth absorb all the grease. Cut the sediment from the bottom, place on the stove, and when melted strain through a cashmere flannel bag, but do not squeeze at all. Return to the bag and strain the second, perhaps the third time, and your jelly will be clear, which you can flavor as you desire. If you use isinglass, the Russian is the best though more expensive. For flavoring jellies it is better to use the juice of any kind of fruit except currants which are too acid.

(Muskegon, 1890)

Now you know what to do if you don't have packaged gelatin available. It seems like a lot of work, but a 2-ounce package of Cox's gelatin retailed for 14 cents at the turn of the century. Women factory workers might earn as little as 75 cents per 10-hour work day at this time.

Culinary isinglass, not to be confused with the thin translucent sheets of mica commonly used on the doors of early wood stoves, was a preparation made from the air bladder of sturgeon. It was widely used in nineteenth-century cooking for jellies. Gelatin when first marketed commercially was sold as isinglass.

Apple Jelly

Peel and core a quantity of apples and then stew them until there are no lumps in the mass, strain through a coarse sieve, pressing them all through with the hand. Throw out all tough or woody bits, or the remains of dry bruised places before refilling the sieve. Then take a tin cup and measure the cooked apples, and to every four cups of apples add one cup of fine, dry sugar. Boil until it makes a stiff jam; put in bowls and jars and set away in a cool dry place. Peach butter of dried peaches can be made in this way, only to every three cups of the peach sauce add one cup of sugar.

Or, take tart juicy apples, cut in pieces, core them if at all defective; add water to just cover them; stew gently till tender; turn into a bag or strainer of cloth; let drain over night, or for several hours; then put back on the stove, heat and skim; add three-fourths pint of sugar to a pint of juice; boil about ten minutes; seal up like jelly.

(Detroit, 1881)

Apple Jelly

Cut nice tart apples in quarters, but unless wormy, do not peel or core. Put into a porcelain kettle with a cup of water for each six pounds of fruit, and simmer very slowly until the apples are thoroughly cooked. Turn into a jelly-bag, and drain off the juice. If very tart, allow three fourths of a pound of sugar to each pint of juice. If sub-acid, one half pound will be sufficient. Put the sugar into the oven to heat. Clean the kettle, and boil the juice therein twenty minutes after it begins to boil thoroughly. Add the sugar, stirring until well dissolved, let it boil up once again, and remove from the fire. The juice of one lemon may be used with the apples, and a few bits of lemon rind, the yellow portion only, cooked with them to give them a flavor, if

liked. One third cranberry juice makes a pleasing combination.

(Battle Creek, 1910)

Apple Jelly without Sugar

Select juicy, white fleshed, sub-acid fruit, perfectly sound and mature, but not mellow. The snow apple is one of the best varieties for this purpose. Wash well, slice, and core without removing the skins, and cook as directed in the preceding recipe. Drain off the juice, and if a very clear jelly is desired, filter it through a piece of cheese cloth previously wrung out of hot water. Boil the juice—rapidly at first, but more gently as it becomes thickened—until of the desired consistency. The time required will vary with the quantity of juice, the shallowness of the dish in which it is boiled, and the heat employed. One hour at least, will be required for one or two quarts of juice. When the juice has become considerably evaporated, test it frequently by dipping a few drops on a plate to cool; and when it jellies sufficiently, remove at once from the fire. A much larger quantity of juice will be needed for jelly prepared in this manner than when sugar is used, about two quarts of juice being required for one half pint of jelly. Such jelly, however, has a most delicious flavor, and is excellent served with grains. Diluted with water, it forms a most pleasing beverage.

(Battle Creek, 1910)

Astrakhan Jelly

Take Astrakhan apples, wash them, quarter and core, but do not pare them. Cook until soft with one tumbler of water in a granite pan. Do this at evening; then put the apples in jelly bag and suspend over earthen dish, and let them drain all night; do not squeeze the bag if you want your jelly clear. To one pint of juice add one pound of granulated sugar; boil twenty minutes; then pour in jelly bowls or glasses. After a day or two pour melted paraffin over the top and seal.

Mrs. B. G. Wilbur, Hillsdale
(Chicago, 1896)

Berry and Currant Jellies

Express the juice. For strawberries, red raspberries, and currants, allow three fourths of a pound of sugar to a pint of juice. Black raspberries, if used alone, need less sugar. Strawberry and black raspberry juice make better jelly if a little lemon juice is used. The juice of one lemon to each pint of fruit juice will be needed for black raspberries. Two parts red or black raspberries with one part currants, make a better jelly than either alone. Boil the juice of strawberries, red raspberries, and currants twenty minutes, add the sugar, and finish. Black raspberry juice is much thicker, and requires less boiling.

(Battle Creek, 1910)

Pig or Calves' Foot Jelly

Take the feet, strike them against a hard substance to get the hoof off, and then put them in clean water without salt, and let them remain so three days, changing water night and morning. On the fourth day take out early and have ready on the fire a pot of water; put the feet in and boil hard for three or four hours, filling up the pot with boiling water as fast as it boils down. About a half hour before it is done, allow the water to boil down to the quantity of jelly you wish to make. When done the meat will fall from the bones when touched with a fork; it must then be all lifted out, and strain the liquor in bowls, and set in a cool place until the next morning; then skim off all the grease upon the jelly and sides of the bowls, else the jelly will be dark. Now put the jelly on to boil, and when it boils up pour in one large cup of whisky, one pound of sugar, one tablespoonful each of cinnamon and mace, and flavor with lemon or orange peel. Let it continue to boil fifteen minutes. Pour in a cup of water; take it off; let it set five minutes; return it to the fire and let it again come to a boil. Have ready your jelly bag, pour it back and forth as fast as it drips out, the oftener the clearer the jelly will be. Finally, hang it up and let drip slowly.

(Detroit, 1881)

Calf's Foot Jelly

Four feet boiled in 4 qts. of water until reduced to 1 qt., let it cool, remove all fat and dregs. Warm the jelly over a slow fire and add ½ pint water, the juice and grated rind of 3 lemons, a stick of cinnamon and whites of 6 eggs, beaten. Sweeten and boil 15 minutes, strain through a flannel bag.

(Muskegon, 1890)

Cherry Jelly

Jelly may be prepared from cherries by using with the juice of the cherries an equal quantity of apple juice, which gives an additional amount of pectose to the juice and does not perceptibly change the flavor.

(Battle Creek, 1910)

Coffee Jelly

Half box of Cox's gelatine soaked half an hour in a half a tea cup of cold water, one quart of strong coffee, made as for the table and sweetened to taste; add the dissolved gelatine to the hot coffee, stir well, strain into a mold rinsed with cold water just before using set on ice or in very cool place, and serve with whipped cream. This jelly is very pretty formed in a circular mold with a tube in the center; when turned out fill the space in the center with whipped cream heaped up a little.

Mrs. J. W. Milliken
(Traverse City, 1900)

In 1885 the *Traverse City Herald* published and distributed as a premium to subscribers a small cookbook containing recipes furnished by "practical housekeepers" of the city. The third edition published in 1900 as *The Herald Century Cook Book* had grown to a 120-page volume sensibly bound in oilcloth. Mrs. J. W. Milliken, wife of the proprietor of a fashionable dry goods store on Front Street and ancestor of former Michigan governor William Milliken, contributed her favorite recipe for coffee jelly. Cox's gelatine came in a 2-ounce package.

Crabapple Jelly

Cut the apples into quarters, cover with water, and boil till tender. Strain through a flannel bag over night. For 1 pt. of juice, take 1 pt. of sugar. Boil juice 20 minutes, then add sugar which has been heated in oven. Boil until it begins to jelly. Skim constantly.

Quince and peach jelly can be made same as crab apple jelly.

(Kalamazoo, 1906)

Cranberry Jelly

Scald the berries and express the juice as for other jellies. Measure the juice, and allow three fourths of a pound of sugar to one of juice. Boil twenty minutes, add the sugar hot, and finish as directed for other jellies.

(Battle Creek, 1910)

Currant Jelly. Never Fails

Wash and weigh your currants, leaving them on the stems. Then crush the currants, and put into the preserving kettle with one pint of cold water. When they begin to boil, let them boil at least twenty minutes, stirring them so they won't burn. Let drain over night. In the morning, pour the juice into a preserving kettle, and let it boil thoroughly for three or four minutes, then add half as many pounds of granulated sugar as you had pounds of fruit when weighed. For instance, if you had twelve pounds of fruit, use six pounds of sugar, and as soon as sugar is dissolved, pour into glasses. Always warm the sugar before adding it to the juice.

Mrs. A. C. Wortley
(Kalamazoo, 1906)

Uncooked Currant Jelly

To one pint of currant juice add one pound of granulated sugar, stir the juice very slowly into the sugar until the sugar is dissolved, then let it stand twenty-four hours and it will be stiff jelly. Tie it with paper dipped in brandy, and set it in the sun. Half a bushel of currants makes twenty-two and one-half pint glasses of jelly.

(Detroit, 1881)

Elderberry and Apple Jelly

Place 4 pounds of elderberries in a preserving kettle with 4 cups of cold water and let them simmer for an hour. Quarter and core without paring 4 pounds of apples. Mix them with the elderberries at the end of the hour and cook the fruit until the apples begin to break. Strain and measure the resulting juice into another preserving kettle. Add to each pint a pound of sugar, boil gently until the jelly stiffens when tested.

Mrs. J. Johnson
(Kalamazoo, 1920)

Orange Jelly

Express the juice of rather tart oranges, and use with it an equal quantity of the juice of sub-acid apples, prepared in the manner directed for apple jelly. For each pint of the mixed juice, use one half pound of sugar and proceed as for other jellies.

(Battle Creek, 1910)

Peach Jelly

Stone, pare, and slice the peaches, and steam them in a double boiler. Express the juice, and add for each pint of peach juice the juice of one lemon. Measure the juice and sugar, using three fourths of a pound of sugar for each pint of juice, and proceed as already directed. Jelly prepared from peaches will not be so firm as many fruit jellies, owing to the small amount of pectose contained in their composition.

A mixture of apples and peaches, in the proportion of one third of the former to two thirds of the latter, makes a firmer jelly than peaches alone. The apples should be pared and cored, so that their flavor will not interfere with that of the peaches.

(Battle Creek, 1910)

Pie Plant Jelly

Pick the pie plant and wash, but do not peel it, cut in strips, put in the kettle; add enough water to cook until soft, strain the juice off and weigh; add sugar pound for pound; cook ten minutes, or as thick as desired.

(Detroit, 1881)

Pie plant is the old-fashioned term for rhubarb.

Pine Apple Jelly

Take one pine apple, or one can of pine apples, and cut very fine, and boil ten minutes in a pint of water which has half a box of gelatine dissolved in it; add the juice of a lemon and sugar to your taste; turn into a mold, and set in a cool place twenty-four hours.

(Detroit, 1881)

Plum Jelly

Pour boiling water over the plums sufficient to cover them. Pour off the water immediately and drain. Then put the plums in a preserving kettle with boiling water enough to cover them again, and boil until they begin to open and some of the juice is extracted; pour off the liquid and strain it; to each pint of juice add one pound of white sugar; return to the kettle and boil from twenty to thirty minutes, as it may require. The plums may be used for sauce

or pies and are as good as though they had not gone through the above operation.

(Detroit, 1881)

Wild Plum Jelly

Fill your preserving kettle with the plums, and cover them with water; let come to a boil, and as soon as they begin to burst drain off the water and throw it away (it is not fit for use on account of its extreme bitterness); fill up your kettle again with water, and let boil till the plums have cooked to pieces; drain off, and to every pint add one-half pint of sugar and cook until it jells.

For jam, take the pulp left after you drained off the water for your jelly, and for every pound add a pound of sweetening, equal proportion of sugar and molasses, or all sugar, if preferred, and cook until reduced to a jam. This makes a most delightful tart for winter.

(Detroit, 1881)

Quince Jelly

Peel, cut up and core some fine ripe quinces; put them in sufficient cold water to cover them and stew gently till soft, but not red. Strain the juice without pressure, weigh, and to every pound of juice allow one pound of crushed sugar; boil the juice twenty minutes, add the sugar and boil again until it jellies—about a quarter of an hour; stir and skim well all the time; strain through thin cloth into your jelly glasses and when cold cover it. The remainder of the fruit can be made into marmalade with three-quarters of a pound of sugar and a quarter of a pound of juicy apples to every pound of quinces, or it can be made into pies or tarts.

(Detroit, 1881)

Quince Jelly

Clean thoroughly good sound fruit, and slice thin. Put into a double boiler with one cup of water for each five pounds of fruit, and cook until softened. Express the juice, and proceed as with other jellies, allowing three fourths of a pound of sugar to each pint of juice. Tart or sweet apples may be used with quinces, in equal proportions, and make a jelly of more pleasant flavor than quinces used alone. The seeds of quinces contain considerable gelatinous substance, and should be cooked with the quince for jelly making.

(Battle Creek, 1910)

Strawberry Jelly

Take small berries, do not stem them, but strain through a cloth or jelly strainer; put the juice on the stove, and boil twenty minutes. Then measure a pint of juice and a pint and a third of sugar, set on and boil from fifteen to twenty minutes longer. Let it drop off the spoon; when it drops off thick and heavy it will jelly. Then take it off and fill the glasses, having previously dipped them in cold water, so that the jelly will turn out nicely.

(Detroit, 1881)

Wine Jelly

One package Cox's gelatine. Add juice of 3 lemons and rind of one. Pour over 1 pint of cold water, and let stand an hour. Then add 2 ½ pints boiling water, 1 pint wine, 2 lbs. white sugar, and a few sticks of cinnamon. Boil up, once, and strain through old linen.

Mrs. Chas. A. Peck
(Kalamazoo, 1906)

Many housewives sold their old linen to the rag man who made his rounds up and down the streets of Kalamazoo shouting "Rags! Rags!" Mary Peck, wife of prominent local "investor," Charles A. Peck, saved hers for straining wine jelly.

Preserves and Marmalades

One great defect in preserving fruits is overboiling; of course they must be done through, but strawberries and the small fruits, such as raspberries, are spoiled if more than slightly cooked. Over sugaring is quite as great a defect as overboiling. Pound for pound of sugar to fruit is hardly a good rule to go by, because it differs so entirely in sweetness. For currants and plums this amount may be used, but for other fruits the sweetness becomes cloying. A fair rule in preserving sliced or whole fruit is to make a syrup of one and one-half pounds of sugar to one of water, which in volume should be once and a half more than that of the fruit.

The following tables gives the time or number of minutes that each kind of fruit should be boiled; Boil cherries moderately five minutes; boil raspberries moderately six minutes; boil blackberries moderately six minutes; boil plums moderately ten minutes; boil strawberries moderately eight minutes; boil whortleberries five minutes; boil pie plant, sliced, ten minutes; boil small sour pears, whole, thirty minutes; boil Bartlett pairs, in halves, twenty minutes; boil peaches, in halves, eight minutes; boil peaches, whole, fifteen minutes; boil pineapples, sliced half an inch thick, fifteen minutes; boil Siberian or crab apples, whole, twenty-five minutes; boil sour apples, quartered, ten minutes; boil ripe currants six minutes; boil wild grapes ten minutes; boil tomatoes twenty minutes. The amount of sugar to a quart jar should be—For cherries, six ounces; for raspberries, four ounces; for Lawton blackberries, six ounces; for field blackberries, six ounces; for strawberries, eight ounces; for whortleberries, four ounces; for quinces, ten ounces; for small sour pears, whole, eight ounces; for wild grapes, eight ounces; for peaches, four ounces; for Bartlett pears, six ounces; for pineapples, six ounces; for Siberian or crab apples, eight ounces; for pie plant, ten ounces; for sour apples, quartered, six ounces; for ripe currants, eight ounces; for plums, eight ounces.

When fruit which is white and clear in color is wanted as a preserve, such as quinces or pears, the whole operation must be carried on as rapidly as possible. Everything must be ready. Just as soon as the fruit is pared or sliced it must at once be cooked. The contents in a jar cannot be too hot. A very easy method of doing this is to place the clean jars, when empty, in a vessel of water which is kept on the full boil while the fruit is being introduced into these jars from the preserving kettle. To take the hot fruit from one vessel to the other without this precaution is to run a useless risk. Take out the jar from the boiling water containing the preserve just as rapidly as possible, and when it is piping hot screw on the lid. Many think that a crust of mold found on the top of a preserve does no harm, as it can be removed. Moldy preserves are not always ruined, but it gives a bad taste to the preserves. A sure prevention of mold is to take white of an egg and wet slightly both sides of a piece of letter paper, sufficiently large to cover over the top of the preserves snugly.

Plums and fruit of which the skin is liable to be broken do better to be put in little jars, with their weight of sugar, and the jars set in a kettle of boiling water till the fruit is done. See that the water is not high enough to boil into the jars. When you put preserves in jars lay a white paper, thoroughly wet with brandy, flat upon the surface of the preserves, and cover them carefully from the air. If they begin to mold scald them by setting them in the oven till boiling hot. Glass is much better than earthen ware for preserves; they are not half as apt to ferment.

In making marmalades, if put up in small quantities and for immediate use, three-quarters of a pound of sugar to one pound of fruit is sufficient; but if desirable to keep them longer, a pound of sugar to a pound of fruit is a better proportion. As in preserves, the best sugar should be used. Put up in tumblers or small jars.

(Detroit, 1881)

Dr. Ransom Sabin, who had spent "many long, long years in the active practice of medicine," codified the wisdom he had learned while so doing into a 480-page book published in Battle Creek, in 1890. Sabin's *The Home Treasure*, "a guide to health, wealth and happiness," contained home, medical, culinary, farriery and miscellaneous departments. In the course of his practice, Dr. Sabin "had been brought in contact with all phases of humanity, with its endless wants and necessities, and its ever varying conditions." He wrote his guide to better those conditions. Sabin offered practical common-sense advice on many subjects, and while we are chiefly concerned with culinary suggestions such as the following on canning and preserving, we want to share some of his remarks on the subject of "domestic quarrels."

Suppose the wife does have a little conversation with John Jones, or the husband speaks to Sarah Filkins, what of it? This is a social world; let people talk and be friendly. In all purity, let all be sociable, kind, and pleasant. Suppose the bread is burned a little, or the fire-wood is wet and green, will scolding about it help the matter? Suppose the wife has the toothache, or the husband has a sliver in his thumb, what of it? Is quarreling the right kind of medicine? Suppose the wife has dinner a little late, or does not want to milk the cow, or the husband is out late and comes home with the odor of tobacco about him, what of it? Quarreling is not the panacea for these ailments. Suppose one eats too much, and another not enough; suppose the drought kills one crop, and the frost another; what of all these troubles? Quarreling will never mend them. Suppose the wife lent Mrs. Piper some pepper; suppose the husband let Sam Houston take a horse; what of it?

Canning and Preserving

Canned fruit, besides being much more healthful, is much cheaper than preserves or pickles. In both canning and preserving, a porcelain kettle should be used. In the absence of that, a stone milk crock or a bright tin pan will do. Should your porcelain kettle become brown with use, boil peeled potatoes in it, and it will become as white as new.

Fruit will keep just as well without sugar. In canning juicy fruits, it is better to add no water, but steam the fruit over a kettle of water, setting it on the stove to boil a minute just before canning. In canning small fruits, the first ripening should be used, as they are not so apt to be soured or sunburned.

After the canning is done, the remaining syrup can be used for jelly, but it is not so apt to harden.

In using "Mason" or self-sealing jars, which are best, great care must be used. The fruit will keep indefinitely if the work is properly done. Have a kettle or large pan of almost boiling water on the stove beside the preserving kettle, and also a small dipper full of hot water. *Plunge* a jar into the hot water, having the water strike the inside and outside at the same time. If you set it down instead, it will surely break. Put cover and rubber into the dipper. Pour every drop of water out of the can into the kettle. Set it back into the hot water, and fill with hot fruit from the preserving kettle. Fill up to the brim with hot syrup. Put on the rubber, being sure it lays down all around, and screw on the cover as tight as possible. Fruit should not be put away for a day or two, but left where the covers can be tightened occasionally. Observe carefully whether there is any escaping of air as you tighten the covers. If there is, the fruit must be reheated. It should be put away in a cool dry place where there is little light.

Jellies and jams should be put in tumblers or

bowls. Powdered sugar sprinkled over the top prevents molding. Or, a paper cut to fit the top, and wet in brandy, may be used. A second paper should in either case be pasted over the glass. Jelly keeps much better in this way. If it does not seem hard as it should be the day after making, set in the sun for several hours; it will help it greatly.

The general rule for preserves is a pound of sugar to a pound of fruit. It may be varied to suit the taste, using less sugar if desired. White crushed sugar is much the nicest for all preserving.

(Battle Creek, 1890)

Hints About Making Preserves

It is not generally known that boiling fruit a long time, and skimming it well, without sugar and without a cover to the preserve pan is an economical way, because the bulk of the scum rises from the fruit, and not from the sugar, if the latter is good; and boiling it without a cover, allowing the evaporation of all the watery particles, the preserves keep firm and well flavored. The proportions are ¾ lb. of sugar to 1 lb. of fruit. Jams made in this way of currants, strawberries, and raspberries are excellent.

(Muskegon, 1890)

Barberry Preserves

Few are aware that barberries preserved in common molasses are very good for common use. Boil the molasses, skim it, throw in the barberries and simmer until they are soft. If you wish to lay by a few for sickness, preserve them in sugar. Melt the sugar, skim it, throw in the barberries; when done soft, take them out and throw in others. For preserving, the sugar should be melted over a fire moderate enough not to scorch it. When melted it should be skimmed clean and fruit dropped in, to simmer until it is soft.

(Detroit, 1881)

Barberry shrubs, once commonly used as hedges, are quite a useful plant. The red berries of the species *Berberis vulgaris* can be made into preserves and were formerly used medicinally as a fever remedy. The bark also yields a yellow dye.

Cantalope Rind Preserves

Keep the rinds of cantelopes or watermelons in strong brine until you wish to preserve them; then boil in fresh water until the salt is removed. Soak or boil a short time in weak alum water, then boil again in fresh water until there is no taste of alum left. Make a rich syrup of two pounds of white sugar to each of rind. When the syrup has boiled until well clarified, drop the rind in, and boil an hour. Lemon flavoring may be added and a few drops of citric acid to prevent sugaring.

(Detroit, 1881)

Brandied Cherries or Berries

Make a syrup of 1 pound sugar and ½ gill water for each 2 pounds fruit; heat to boiling, stirring to prevent burning, and pour over the fruit while warm—not hot; let them stand together 1 hour; put all into a preserving-kettle, and heat slowly; boil 5 minutes, take out the fruit with a perforated skimmer, and boil the syrup 20 minutes; add 1 pint brandy for each 5 pounds fruit. Pour over the berries hot, and seal.

(Detroit, 1890)

Home Made Maraschino Cherries

Stone the desired amount of cherries, then soak them for 24 hours in a weak vinegar, which is to make them firm; drain, measure and allow an equal amount of granulated sugar, mix thoroughly, and keep in a covered crock or deep earthenware dish for one week, stirring every day. Seal in glass jars and let stand at least a month before using.

One-third vinegar and ⅔ water is a good proportion to soak cherries in.

Mrs. L. D. Hall
(Kalamazoo, 1921)

Spice Cherries

To 12 lbs. fruit, 6 lbs. sugar, 1 pt. vinegar, 3 tablespoons cinnamon, 2 each of allspice and cloves, tie spices in a thin cloth, put syrup on stove and heat until sugar is dissolved, then add fruit and boil slowly ½ hour, then seal.

Mrs. J. E. Montgomery
(Muskegon, 1890)

Cherry Sunshine

One pint of sugar to quart of cherries. Boil from 5 to 8 minutes, pour in tumblers and set in the sun for 3 days.

(Vermontville, 1906)

The Buckeye Publishing Company of Minneapolis, Minnesota, published a revised and enlarged edition of *Buckeye Cookery* in 1881, compiled "from the choicest bits of the best experience of hundreds who have long traveled the daily round of household duties, not reluctantly like drudges, but lovingly, with heart and hand fully enlisted in the work." The publishers had the good sense to include a number of examples by Michigan cooks including the following recipe.

Canned Currants

Look them over carefully, stem and weigh them, allowing a pound of sugar to every one of fruit; put them in a kettle, cover, and leave them to heat slowly and stew gently for twenty or thirty minutes; then add the sugar, and shake the kettle occasionally to make it mix with the fruit; do not allow it to boil, but keep as hot as possible until the sugar is dissolved, then pour it in cans and secure the covers at once. White currants are beautiful preserved in this way.

Mrs. Wm. Patrick, Midland
(Minneapolis, 1881)

Spiced Gooseberries

Five pounds gooseberries, 4 pounds brown sugar, 1 pint of vinegar, 2 tablespoonfuls ground cloves, 2 tablespoonfuls ground cinnamon. Boil two hours. Watch carefully the last hour and stir often to prevent burning.

(Kalamazoo, 1920)

Grapes Preserved with Honey

Take seven pounds of sour grapes on the stem, and pack snugly, without breaking, in a stone jar. Make a syrup of four pounds of honey, one pint of vinegar, and spices to suit. Boil together for twenty minutes, and turn boiling hot over the grapes. Seal immediately. They will keep for years.

Apples, peaches and plums may be preserved in the same way.

(Battle Creek, 1890)

Heavenly Hash

Five lbs. red currants or cherries, 5 lbs. granulated sugar, 3 oranges cut in small pieces, 1 orange rind shredded, 2 lbs. seeded raisins, 1 lb. figs. Put all ingredients into a granite kettle and boil until thick, stirring often. When done put into jelly cups or cans. This is delicious and will keep indefinitely.

Monday Study Club, Boyne City
(Charlotte, 1909)

The granite kettle referred to was actually granite ware, a popular type of kitchen ware available in pots, pans, pie plates, muffin pans, etc. It was composed of iron coated with enamel that resembled granite or marble porphyry in a wide variety of colors.

Lemon Conserve

One pound powdered white sugar, quarter pound fresh butter, six eggs, leaving out the whites

An "agate" iron coffee pot (Grand Rapids, 1890).

of two, adding the juice and grated rind of three fine lemons. Put all into a saucepan; stir the whole gently over a slow fire until it gets thick as honey. A delicious spread for bread, biscuit or rolls.

(Detroit, 1881)

Pasadena Orange Marmalade

Six large naval oranges, 2 lemons. Wash and slice fruit thin and remove seeds. Add 3 pints of water to each pound fruit. Let stand 24 hours. Then boil 1 hour. Then cool and for every pound of this mixture add 1 quart of sugar and boil another hour. This will make 20 glasses. To keep a long time seal.

E. S., Benton Harbor
(Freeport, IL, 1915)

This recipe contributed by a Benton Harbor cook to a promotional cookbook put out by a Freeport, Illinois, spice and medicinal preparation manufacturer, Fuss-McNess Co., in 1915 carries a little-known Michigan significance. The southern California city of Pasadena was named by a Michigan Indian missionary who had never even been to the West Coast. Rev. George N. Smith, founded a Congregational mission to the Ottawas at Old Wing Mission in northern Allegan County in 1839. In 1846 when Albertus Van Raalte founded the town of Holland nearby, difficulties arose between the Ottawas and the Dutch colonists. Smith relocated his mission to the Leelanau Peninsula, near Northport, in 1848 and for many years taught the Ottawa, who followed him there, and the native Chippewa.

In the 1870s a colony of Hoosiers migrated to southern California. They formed a committee to name their settlement in 1875. One of the committee members wrote to Rev. Smith asking him to translate into Chippewa the phrase "Crown of the Valley." Smith sent four variant translations all ending in "Pa-sa-de-na" and, despite the fact that neither Smith nor the Chippewa tribe had ever roamed within 2,000 miles of the site, the committee voted 17 to 4 for the melodious new appellation.

Brandied Peaches

Fifteen pounds of peaches, after they are peeled; seven pounds of sugar. Put a layer of peaches in a stone crock and then a layer of sugar, alternately, until all are used. Over this pour one quart of alcohol; cover with a plate and put a heavy weight on it; cover the crock with a thick cloth and a tight cover and place it on the back part of the stove and cook slowly for four hours; allow it to cool before opening; then put away in glass cans.

Mrs. John Emery, Muskegon
(Chicago, 1898)

Pickle Peaches

| 5 lbs. of peaches | ½ pint vinegar |
| 3 lbs. granulated sugar | 1 oz. cassia buds |

Stick cassia buds into peaches. Make a good syrup with sugar and vinegar. Put fruit into hot syrup, and cook until tender. Place peaches in jar and pour over them the hot syrup.

Florence Myers
(Kalamazoo, 1906)

Pickled Peaches, Baked

Rub the fuzz off the peaches, and put 2 cloves in each one. Take a stone jar, and put in a layer of sugar and one of peaches, alternating, till the jar is nearly full, and every crevice is filled with sugar; put a layer of sugar on top, then add ½ pint of vinegar. Put in a moderate oven and bake 3 hours.

Ella Lewis
(Kalamazoo, 1906)

Brandied Peaches

Peel, halve and weigh peaches. To every pound of peaches, take ¾ lb. of granulated sugar. Dissolve sugar in water, and boil until syrup hairs; put in peaches, and cook until clear and tender. Skim out peaches, and place in quart cans, filling cans two-thirds full, and cover, while boiling down syrup. When syrup has boiled until thick, add 1 cup of French brandy for each quart can of peaches; remove from fire immediately, and pour over peaches. Seal can at once. It is better not to cook more than enough peaches to fill two cans at one time. This is not too much brandy.

Mrs. Hutson B. Colman
(Kalamazoo, 1906)

Ginger Pears

Slice and add to a large panful of quartered pears, 3 large lemons and ½ box preserved ginger and 4 pounds granulated sugar. Cook until clear and the syrup is of desired thickness. Seal while hot.

Mrs. M. Z., Waldron
(Freeport, IL, 1915)

Ginger Pears

Pare, core and chop fine 4 lbs. of green pears, 4 lbs. of sugar, 4 lemons, rinds of 2 chopped fine, pulp of all, 2 ounces preserved ginger root, cook until clear (about 2 hours). To be used in place of jelly.

Eleanor Thompson, Northville
(Charlotte, 1909)

Pear Honey

Peel and core ripe pears. Grind in meat chopper. Measure pulp and add an equal amount of granulated sugar. Boil up quickly. Seal in sterilized jars.

(Detroit, 1935)

Plum Cheese

Boil plums in sufficient water to prevent burning; then wash and strain; to every pound of pulp add half a pound of clear brown sugar; cook as you would jam, stirring to prevent burning. It can be cut in slices, and is a nice addition for lunch.

(Detroit, 1881)

Quince Honey

Pare and grate 5 nice quinces, 5 pounds sugar to 1 pint boiling water. Stir over fire until dissolved, add the grated quinces. Cook fifteen minutes; pour into glasses. Cover when cold.

(Vermontville, 1906)

Razzle Dazzle

One quart cherries pitted, 1 quart currants, 1 quart red raspberries, 1 quart gooseberries. Put gooseberries at the bottom of the kettle, cherries next, currants next and red raspberries on top. To every pound of fruit add ¾ pounds of sugar and boil until it jellies.

Mrs. William Moerdyke
(Kalamazoo, 1920)

Strawberry Sun Preserves

One pint fruit, 1 pint sugar. Boil ten minutes, spread on plates and set in sun one day.

(Vermontville, 1906)

Tomato Marmalade

6 lbs. ripe tomatoes
3 lbs. of sugar
3 lemons, juice, peel and pulp and chop fine

2 oz. white ginger root, broken in small pieces

Cook slowly until thick. Cut out the hard center of tomato, and remove the skin before weighing.

Mrs. F. W. Myers
(Kalamazoo, 1906)

Preserved Water-Melon in Place of Citron, for Cakes

The harder part of water-melon, next to the skin, made into preserves with sugar, equal weights; cooking down the syrup rather more than for common use, causes it to granulate, like citron, which is kept for sale.

This chopped fine, as citron, makes an excellent substitute for that article; and for very much less cost. Call in the neighbors, to help eat about a dozen good sized melons, and you have outside enough for the experiment; and if the Doctor is near he will help without a fee. They are nice, also, in mince-pies in place of raisins.

(Ann Arbor, 1864)

Dr. Chase must have been very fond of water-melon.

Making Fine Butter

To make fine butter you must have fine milk; the making of fine butter must begin with the cows. They will give just as they receive. Good food and good care will give good milk, poor food and careless keeping will give poor milk, and the result will be poor butter; but it often happens poor butter is made of good milk, and to avoid this observe the following simple rules:

1st. Set the milk in the pans as near its natural heat as possible, 98°, if the room is very cold; if not very cold, set the milk 85° to 90°.

2d. Don't let it stand too long before the cream is taken off—24 hours in a cool place.

"Beside the churn a maiden stands, / Nimble and naked her arms and hands," wrote Benjamin F. Taylor, who was a pioneer Michigan schoolteacher (Chicago, 1877).

3d. Don't gather cream too long before it is churned; 3 days is long enough.

4th. Heat the cream and keep it in a warm place for 24 hours to ripen before being churned.

5th. Heat the churn with warm water before putting the cream in it, and see that the cream is at its proper heat. What is a proper heat to churn at? Every one must find out by experiments what suits their own cream; as a general rule in winter about 64°. But see that the temperature is kept at that all the time of churning until the butter is coming. Then it can be cooled down gradually till the churning is finished.

6th. About coloring butter: Put all the color you can in the milk through the cow's feed and she will color the butter better than you can; but to supplement what she cannot do, use a little annatto diluted with water; put into the churn when you begin to churn; use no more than what will give the butter a bright, white, oatstraw color.

7th. Give the butter no more working than to press the milk clean out of it; a wash or two with brine does not hurt it when in a granulated state; when the brine runs off perfectly clear, stop working it.

8th. Do not spoil it with salt; use fine dairy salt, ½ ounce to 1 pound; weigh both butter and salt—do not guess. This quantity is sufficient for winter butter, which enters into immediate consumption. Use ¾ to 1 ounce per pound in summer.

9th. If put up in pound rolls do it neatly, smoothly and all in one shape, with a nice white cloth around each roll.

10th. If put in crocks be sure to pack it down solid; dress the top and cover it from the air till it is taken to the market.

(Detroit, 1890)

Annatto is a yellowish red dye made from the pulp surrounding the seeds of a Caribbean tree.

Apple Butter

One bushel sour apples pared and quartered. 8 lbs. brown sugar, 12 qts. water, 1 oz. each of cloves, cinnamon and allspice, 1 teaspoonful ground sassafras. Boil in large boiler until the water is all boiled out; it will take about 6 hours. Stir often to keep from burning.

Mrs. C. E. Moore
(Muskegon, 1890)

Lemon Butter

Two lemons, 4 eggs, 2 cups of sugar and 1 teaspoon of butter, the grated rind of 1 and juice of 2 lemons. Beat well and boil, stirring constantly until it reaches the consistency of honey.

(Muskegon, 1890)

Pumpkin Butter, as Made in the North Woods

Take out the seeds of 1 pumpkin, cut it in small pieces and boil it soft; take 3 other pumpkins, cut them in pieces and boil them soft; put them in a

This covered butter dish featured a compartment for ice to keep the butter cool (Wallingford, 1872).

coarse bag and press out the juice; add the juice to the first pumpkin and let it boil 10 hours or more to become the thickness of butter; stir often. If the pumpkins are frozen the juice will come out much easier.

Remarks—All I have to guide me as to the "North Woods" manner of making is that on the back of the slip cut from some newspaper; there was the date of the paper—Feb. 7, 1880,—also "Sleighing fair," and "Loggers feel better," therefore, to know that "loggers felt better," they must have that class of persons among them; and hence it was from some northern paper, where loggers in the winter do congregate. It will make a good butter if boiled carefully to avoid burning. I should say boil the juice at least half away before putting in the nicely cut pieces of the 1 pumpkin, boiling it soft in the juice of 3 other ones, after its reduction one-half. It makes a very good substitute for cow's butter, and for apple butter, too. But I must say if I used frozen pumpkins to obtain the juice from, I should not want the one frozen that was to be cut up to make the butter of. I think it would not be as good if frozen. If any of these butters are too sour add good brown sugar to make it sweet enough to suit the taste.

(Ann Arbor, 1884)

Tomato Butter

To every seven pounds of firm ripe tomatoes, pared and sliced, add three pounds sugar, a scant pint of vinegar, one ounce powdered cinnamon and half an ounce of whole cloves. Boil slowly three hours.

(Grandville, 1920)

Honeys

Artificial Cuba Honey—Good brown sugar 10 lbs; water 1 qt.; old bee bread honey in the comb 2 lbs; cream of tartar 1 tea-spoon; gum arabic 1 oz.; oil of peppermint 3 drops; oil of rose 2 drops. Mix and boil 2 or 3 minutes and have ready 1 qt. more

of water in which an egg is put well beat up; pour it in, and as it begins to boil, skim well, remove from the fire, and when a little cool, add 2 lbs. of nice bees' honey, and strain.

This is really a nice article, looking and tasting like honey. It has been shipped in large quantities under the name of "Cuba Honey." It will keep any length of time as nice and fresh as when first made, if sealed up. Some persons use a table-spoon of slippery elm bark in this amount, but it will ferment in warm weather, and rise to the top, requiring to be skimmed off. If it is to be used only for eating purposes, the cream-of-tartar and gum arabic may be left out, also the old bee-bread honey, substituting for it another pound of nice honey.

Domestic Honey—Coffee sugar 10 lbs.; water 3 lbs.; cream of tartar 2 ozs.; strong vinegar 2 table-spoons: the white of 1 egg well beaten; bees' honey ½ lb.; Lubin's extract of honeysuckle 10 drops.

First put the sugar and water into a suitable kettle and place upon the fire; and when luke-warm stir in the cream of tartar, and vinegar; then continue to add the egg; and when the sugar is nearly melted put in the honey and stir until it comes to a boil, take it off, let it stand a few minutes, then strain, adding the extract of honeysuckle last, let

Wooden butter molds used by home butter makers to produce a uniformly sized block also imprinted a decorative design on the butter (Grand Rapids, 1890).

stand over night, and it is ready for use. This resembles candied honey, and is a nice thing.

(Ann Arbor, 1864)

Bee-bread is raw pollen stored within some sections of the honeycomb. Young bees live on a mixture of pollen and honey. In the old days when bees were killed by sulphur to get their honey, such pollen was often found mixed up with the honey. It has somewhat of a "bready" taste, hence its name. By the late nineteenth century, more sophisticated apiary techniques, including the use of honey extractors and section boxes, largely eliminated the occurrence of bee-bread in commercial honey.

Eggs and Cheese

EGGS

Eggs

To test the freshness of eggs:

A fresh egg when placed in a glass of water will drop to the bottom. A stale egg will rise to the top of the water.

Try to cook eggs just below the boiling point of water.

Boiling eggs destroys much of their food value and makes them tough and difficult to digest.

(Detroit, 1935)

Putting Down Eggs in Water Glass

One part of water glass to ten parts of water.

Use only strictly fresh eggs as the water glass will preserve the eggs in exactly the state of freshness in which they are at the time they are put down.

Boil the water and allow to cool. Add to the water glass, which may be purchased at the drug store. Stir the water into the water glass thoroughly. Place eggs in layers in a stone crock and pour over the liquid, covering the eggs well. Place an old dish on top of the eggs to weigh them down. Keep in a cool place.

When eggs are wanted for use, take them out of the liquid and wash them in fresh water. New eggs may be added from time to time. The eggs must always be under the liquid or they will spoil.

(Detroit, 1935)

Water glass is a substance usually consisting of sodium silicate but sometimes potassium silicate. When dissolved in water it makes a syrupy liquid. It is also called soluble glass.

Milk and Tomato Bisque with Eggs

Place 1½ cupfuls of milk, ½ cupful of water and 1 tsp. of oil in upper part of a double boiler, beat 1 egg lightly and add to the mixture, stirring constantly; cook until quite thick; heat 1 c. of strained tomato juice and add 1 egg beaten lightly; cook until the mixture is thick; gradually add the tomato to the custard, stirring constantly; season with salt, pepper and paprika; sprinkle with grated cheese over the top when served; serve with croutons of toasted crackers.

Lola A. Sales
(Kalamazoo, 1921)

Breakfast Dish

Take about half a pound dried beef, first sliced thin, then pulled in small pieces. Have a quart of milk boiling, into which put the beef with a good piece of butter and a little pepper. When it comes to a boil thicken with a little flour; then toast bread, a slice for each member of family, and poach in hot water an equal number of eggs; place one on each slice of toast; put all on a large platter and pour over the above dressing and send to the table hot; lean ham may be used in place of the beef.

(Detroit, 1881)

Chinese Eggs

Make a cream sauce, have ready six hard boiled eggs cut into quarters, when the sauce is hot season and add the eggs, let stand a minute covered, then sprinkle over one tablespoonful of finely chopped parsley and serve.

Mrs. W. Rea, Menominee
(Chicago, 1898)

In the 1890s the *Chicago Record,* the Windy City's leading morning newspaper, offered prizes for the best original recipes. More than 10,000 women, "scattered from ocean to ocean, and from the great lakes to the Gulf of Mexico," submitted manuscripts. In 1896 the *Chicago Record* codified "the cream" of these recipes into a 600-page cookbook. It provided recipes for daily menus that would "furnish a great variety of pleasing and nutritious meals, daintily served" and enable a family of five to stay within a annual food budget of $500.00. This guide for frugality included a variety of recipes by Michigan cooks including the following from Hillsdale. The dish probably earned its name in honor of the 500th anniversary of Columbus's discovery of America which the country celebrated in gala form, albeit a year late, at Chicago in 1893.

Columbus Eggs

Peel the shells from ten hard-boiled eggs, and cut each egg in two through the center, cutting off a small piece from one end, so that they will stand on end. Pulverize the yolks and mix with two table-spoonfuls of cold lean ham, chopped fine; moisten with three tablespoonfuls of vinegar and season with one saltspoonful of salt and one teaspoon of mustard and a good pinch of pepper. Mix smooth and fill the empty whites, being careful not to break

them, and press the two halves together. The filling which remains over may be made into a dressing by adding a little more vinegar and pouring over the eggs.

Mrs. B. G. Wilbur, Hillsdale
(Chicago, 1896)

Scrambled Eggs and Corn

½ pound diced bacon	*¼ cup milk*
1 can corn	*½ t salt*
6 eggs	*½ t pepper*

Brown the bacon; add corn. Beat eggs and add rest of ingredients. When eggs are cooked put on buttered toast. Serves six people.

Evelyn Schwartz, Hopkins
(Allegan, 1938)

Egg Croquettes

The eggs for croquettes should be boiled for 10 minutes and the whites and yolks pressed together through a potato press or chopped very fine. For 6 croquettes allow 6 eggs.

One-half pint milk, 1 tablespoon butter, 2 tablespoons flour, 1 tablespoon chopped parsley, 10 drops onion juice, 1 level teaspoon salt, 1 salt-spoon pepper. Put milk over the fire, rub butter and flour together, add it to the milk, cook till a smooth paste, add all seasoning to the chopped eggs, mix with cream sauce and turn out to cool. Form into cylinders, dip in egg and bread crumbs and fry in smoking hot fat. Serve with mushroom sauce.

Mrs. Wm. C. Hoyt
(Kalamazoo, 1899)

Curried Eggs

2 tablespoonfuls of *butter*	*½ pint veal or chicken* *stock*
2 small onions	*6 hard-boiled eggs*

*2 dessertspoonfuls
curry powder*

*2 tablespoonfuls
cream*

2 tablespoonfuls flour

Mince the onions; put them and the butter into the Chafing Dish and cook until they are brown. Stir in the curry powder. Mix well and add the flour, stirring quickly all the time; then add the stock or a tablespoonful of fluid beef dissolved in boiling water. When the mixture has simmered for ten minutes add the cream and eggs. Serve them hot.

(Grand Rapids, 1917)

Use beef bouillon instead of fluid beef.

Deviled Eggs

One-fourth lb. grated cheese. Butter a baking dish, spread the cheese in the bottom with bits of butter and sprinkle with a dash of salt and pinch of paprika. Break 6 eggs one at a time over the cheese, being careful not to break the yolks. Stir into half a cup of cream 1 teaspoon of mixed mustard and pour over eggs. Set in a hot oven for 15 minutes and serve.

Mrs. Wm. Rose, Grand Haven
(Charlotte, 1909)

This easily prepared and tasty dish similar to quiche is excellent for Sunday brunch. We baked it in a glass casserole dish at 400° for 35 minutes. We also experimented by adding chives, celery seed, and ham or bacon.

Escaloped Eggs

Chop very fine some ham (or any cold meat) and add fine bread crumbs, pepper and salt and some melted butter; moisten with milk to a soft paste, and half fill patty pans with the mixture, break an egg carefully upon the top of each, sprinkle finely powdered cracker crumbs over all and dust on salt and pepper. Bake about eight minutes. Eat hot.

(Ann Arbor, 1872)

Egg Florentine

Fill the bottom of a baking dish with creamed spinach. Break enough eggs over this to cover. Over the eggs place a thick layer of cheese sauce. Place in oven until eggs are firm.

Bessie Ketcham Gaylord
(Higgins Lake, 1920)

This makes a gustatory entrée using either creamed or fresh spinach. If you prefer fresh spinach, wash and drain but allow a little water to cling to the leaves. Be sure to grease the baking dish, add the eggs and cheese sauce and bake at 375° for 30 minutes.

To Fry—Extra Nice

Three eggs; flour 1 table-spoon milk 1 cup.
Beat the eggs and flour together, then stir in the milk. Have a skillet with a proper amount of butter in it, made hot, for frying this mixture; then pour it in, and when one side is done brown, turn it over, cooking rather slowly; if a larger quantity is needed, it will require a little salt stirred in, but for this amount, the salt in the butter in which you fry it, seasons it very nicely.

(Ann Arbor, 1864)

Lemon Toast

Take the yolks of six eggs, beat well, and add three cups of sweet milk; take bread, not too stale, and cut into slices; dip them into the milk and eggs, and fry in butter to a delicate brown; take the whites of the six eggs and beat to a froth; add a large cup white sugar and two cups of boiling water, and the juice of two lemons; serve over the toast as a sauce, and you will have a delicious supper dish.

(Detroit, 1881)

For modern eating habits, we recommend this version of french toast as a breakfast treat.

Eggs, Newport Style

Take one pint of bread crumbs and soak in one pint of milk. Beat eight eggs very light and stir with the soaked crumbs, beating five minutes. Have ready a saucepan, in which are two tablespoonfuls of butter, thoroughly hot, but not scorching: pour in the mixture, season with a dash of pepper and three-quarters of a teaspoon of salt as the mass is opened and stirred with the scrambling, which should be done quickly with the point of a knife for three minutes, or until thoroughly hot. Serve on hot platter with squares of buttered toast.

Mrs. B. G. Wilbur, Hillsdale
(Chicago, 1896)

Plain Omelet

Beat the yolks of three eggs to a cream and beat the whites to a stiff froth. Add to the yolks three tablespoonfuls of milk or cream, one tablespoonful of finely grated bread crumbs, and season lightly with salt; lastly, fold, not stir, the whites lightly in. An omelet pan is the best utensil for cooking, but if that is not to be had, an earthen-ware pudding dish which will stand the heat is good; an iron spider will do, but a larger omelet would need to be prepared. A tin saucepan is apt to cook the omelet so rapidly as to burn it in spots. Whatever the utensil used, it should be hot, the fire clear and steady, and all in readiness by the time the eggs are beaten.

Oil the dish well and gently pour in the omelet mixture; cover, and place the pan on the range where the heat will be continuous. Do not stir, but carefully, as the egg sets, lift the omelet occasionally by slipping a broad-bladed knife under it, or with a fork by dipping in here and there. It should cook quickly, but not so quickly as to burn. From three to five minutes will generally be ample time. When the middle of the omelet is set, it may be put into a hot oven to dry the top. As soon as the center is dry, it should be removed immediately, as it will be hard and indigestible if overdone. To dish, loosen from the pan by running a knife under it, lay a hot platter, bottom upward, over the pan, and invert the latter so as to shake out the omelet gently, browned side uppermost; or if preferred, double one part over the other before dishing. Serve at once, or it will fall.

An omelet of three eggs is sufficient for two or three persons; if more is desired, a second omelet of three eggs may be made. Larger ones are not so light nor so easily prepared. The dish used should be reserved for that purpose alone, and should be kept as smooth and dry as possible. It is better to keep it clean by wiping with a coarse towel than by washing, if the omelet comes from the pan perfectly whole and leaving no fragments behind.

(Battle Creek, 1910)

Spider is a term, uncommon in modern usage, for a long-handled cast iron or steel fry pan. In pioneer days, housewives used an earlier model that had long legs so that it could be used in the hearth.

Foam Omelet

Prepare as above, leaving out the white of one egg, which must be beaten to a stiff froth and spread over the top of the omelet after it is well set. Let this white just heat through by the time the omelet is done. Fold the omelet together, and dish. The whites will burst out around the edges like a border of foam.

(Battle Creek, 1910)

Baked Omelet

Four eggs, whites and yolks beaten separately. Add to yolks 1 teacup sweet milk, 1 tablespoon flour, ½ teaspoon salt, pepper to taste, and lastly the whites of eggs beaten very stiff. Have a skillet as hot as can be without scorching butter, put in 1

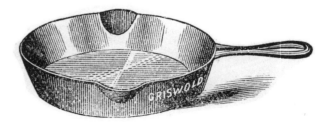

The Griswold Manufacturing Company of Erie, Pennsylvania, made quality cast-iron skillets for more than fifty years until the plant closed during the Depression (Grand Rapids, 1890).

tablespoon butter and pour in the omelet, which should at once begin to cook. Then place in hot oven and bake until a golden brown.

(Kalamazoo, 1899)

Fancy Omelets

Various fancy omelets may be made by adding other ingredients and preparing the same as for plain omelets. Two or three tablespoonfuls of orange juice instead of milk, with a little grated rind for flavor and three tablespoonfuls of sugar, may be combined with the eggs and called an orange omelet.

A little cold cauliflower or cooked asparagus chopped very fine and mixed in when the omelet is ready for the pan, may be denominated a vegetable omelet.

(Battle Creek, 1910)

Pineapple Omelet (new)

Beat five eggs and five tablespoons of cold water together in a bowl; when light add two tablespoons of sugar, one-half teaspoon salt; pour into flat spider, and as it cooks gently lift in places with a four-tined fork till cooked. Shred fine five or six slices of fresh pineapple, adding sugar to taste. After the omelet is removed to hot platter, place upon it the shredded pineapple and fold over and serve. Delicious.

Mrs. R. W. Boyd, Adrian
(Chicago, 1896)

Tomato Omelet

One cup cooked tomatoes, 1 cup bread crumbs, 2 eggs, salt and pepper. Put 1 tablespoon butter in spider, heat and turn in eggs. When set turn in the tomatoes, bread and seasoning. Have tomatoes and bread hot when put in. Turn over like omelet, and roll on to a platter.

Mrs. T. Sherwood
(Kalamazoo, 1899)

Ox Eyes

Cut a stale loaf of baker's bread into 6 square pieces. With a spoon dig out a well in each square, butter well inside and out and place a small piece of butter in each well; break an egg in this and lastly put a teaspoon milk or cream on top of egg; season with salt and pepper. Place in a baking pan and bake in a quick oven until the eggs are cooked.

Mrs. Ruth Dickinson
(Kalamazoo, 1899)

Well in advance of the meal announce to guests that you are serving ox eyes. It makes for interesting repartee.

Pickled Eggs

Sixteen eggs, one quart of vinegar, one-half ounce of black pepper, one-half ounce of Jamaica pepper, one-half ounce of ginger; boil the eggs twelve minutes; dip in cold water and take off the shell; put the vinegar with the pepper and vinegar into a stew pan and simmer ten minutes; place the eggs in a jar, pour over the seasoned vinegar boiling hot, and when cold tie them down with a bladder to exclude the air; ready for use in a month.

(Detroit, 1881)

If you don't have a bladder handy, feel free to use waxed paper or plastic wrap under the jar lid. We found these eggs to have a strong and interesting taste, but a very unappetizing brown appearance. The Jamaican pepper is allspice.

Paris Eggs

Boil 6 eggs hard. When cool remove shells, cut in two, take out the yolks and put them in a bowl with the juice of one onion, a pinch of red pepper, saltspoon of salt, and ½ cup cream. Mix thoroughly into a smooth paste, then return to the whites and stand them in the bottom of a small pudding dish. Pour cream sauce over them and bake 20 minutes.

Mrs. Dan F. Bradley
(Grand Rapids, 1902)

Eggs

Boil the eggs hard, remove the shells and cover the eggs with vinegar, in which blood beets have been pickled. For a picnic these make a very pretty, as well as an appetizing dish.

(Battle Creek, 1890)

Poached Eggs with Creamed Celery

Arrange carefully poached eggs neatly on rounds of hot buttered toast; fill in the center of the dish with a pint of celery cut into inch lengths and cooked in boiling water until tender, then stirred into a cupful of cream sauce; serve very hot. This is a light and nourishing breakfast dish.

(Lansing, 1901)

The ladies of Lansing's Pilgrim Congregational Church compiled a revised and enlarged edition of their *Pilgrim Cook Book* in 1901. The 160-page, oil-cloth covered volume, emblazoned with a pilgrim lass en route to church, sold for 25 cents. The title page assured purchasers that:

There's a maid and there's an art,
To which the world is looking;
The nearest art unto the heart—
The good old art of cooking.

Eggs Poached in Milk

Put a sauce pan into a dish of boiling water, and pour into pan enough milk to cover the eggs, have water and milk boiling hot and prepare pieces of nicely toasted bread. Drop the eggs into the hot milk and cook as much as you like best: lift them from the milk with a spoon and place on the toast.

Victorians had specialized table pieces for practically everything, including a silver-plated soft-boiled egg set (Wallingford, 1872).

Season the milk and pour over the toast and eggs. A fine dish for breakfast.

Mrs. Firman
(Muskegon, 1890)

Eggs Poached in Tomatoes

Take a pint of stewed tomatoes, cooked until they are homogeneous or which have been rubbed through a colander; season with salt if desired, and heat. When just beginning to boil, slip in gently a half dozen eggs, the shells of which have been so carefully broken that the yolks are intact. Keep the tomato just below the boiling point until the eggs are cooked. Lift the whites carefully with a fork as they cook, until they are firm, then prick them and let the yellow mix with the tomato and the whites. The whole should be quite soft when done, but showing the red of the tomatoes and the white and yellow of the eggs quite distinctly. Serve on toast. If the flavor is agreeable, a little onion minced very finely may be cooked with the tomatoes.

(Battle Creek, 1910)

Eggs Shirred in Tomatoes

Cut out circular pieces from the stem ends of several tomatoes and remove part of the pulp; season with salt and pepper, also with onion juice and chopped parsley if agreeable; break an egg into each tomato and cook in a slow oven until the egg is set; serve on rounds of hot buttered toast.

(Lansing, 1901)

This attractive dish is especially good when luscious, home-grown Michigan tomatoes are in season. Bake for 45 minutes at 250°.

Scotch Ham and Eggs

Cut ham as thin as paper, bake in hot oven, watch and turn all the time. Boil eggs 4 minutes, put in cold water long enough to peel, then put in the ham gravy on the stove long enough to beat through, turn and do not let them get brown. Serve ham on platter and eggs around with parsley, also the gravy.

(Higgins Lake, 1920)

Larry's father, Wallace Massie, a full-blooded Scot, is the only person we know who can cut ham as thin as paper, and routinely does so.

Scotch Eggs—Cheese Sauce

Boil hard desired number of eggs; cut in halves, remove yolks, mash, season, using little mustard. Refill whites, press halves together firmly, roll in flour to dry. Cover entirely with well-seasoned sausage meat. Roll in crumbs, egg and crumbs, and fry carefully in deep fat. Drain, place on rounds of toast, surround with cream cheese seasoned with tomato catsup.

(Grayling, 1937)

Tradition has it that this dish was invented by an Englishman and so named because thrifty Scots are famous for stretching the meat bill.

Eggs à la Suisse

Spread a baking dish with 2 ounces of butter cover with a thick grating of cheese, break 8 eggs on the cheese being careful not to break the yolks, season with salt and red pepper, pour 3 tablespoonfuls of cream over them, cover with two ounces (or two heaping tablespoonfuls) of grated cheese; bake in a moderate oven 15 minutes.

Mrs. E. H. Page
(Union City, 1902)

Spinach Nests

Cook spinach and chop fine, season well with salt, pepper and plenty of butter, put in glass pie dish with more butter. Make nests all around and drop raw eggs in nests, put in oven and bake eggs.

(Higgins Lake, 1920)

Whirled Eggs

Have a small kettle of water heated almost to boiling, and with a wooden spoon, stir it rapidly round and round in the same direction until a miniature whirlpool is produced. Have ready some eggs broken in separate cups, and drop them carefully one at a time into the whirling water, the stirring of which must be kept up until the egg is a soft round ball. Remove with a skimmer, and serve on cream toast.

(Battle Creek, 1910)

Eggs with White Sauce

Cook eggs until hard, pour off hot water and dip in cold water to remove shell easily, cut lengthwise and arrange on platter with white side up; prepare a sauce as follows; one tablespoonful butter, one tablespoonful flour, melting together; then add a cup or more of milk, season with salt and pepper and a teaspoon vinegar added after milk has boiled; then chop parsley and add to sauce; pour all over eggs and serve.

Mrs. Edna Briggs
(Grand Rapids, 1917)

Egg Sauce

Chop six hard cooked eggs and mix with one cup cream. Heat in a double boiler, add one tablespoon butter, pinch of salt and a little paprika. Cook for ten minutes. Remove from flame, add a little chopped parsley and serve hot over asparagus, brussels sprouts or fish.

(Detroit, 1935)

CHEESE

How to Improve the Taste of Cheese

Buy a large whole Swiss cheese. (In Wisconsin they make them equal to the imported article.) Bore on the flat side eight half inch augur holes down to within one inch of the other side. Fill these augur holes with a good white wine and cork the holes. Then put the cheese away in a good keeping place for two or three weeks and the cheese will be ready for use.

Under this treatment, it will be moist; will keep fresh, and will be found to have a delicious taste.

F. T. Lodge
(Marine City, 1923)

Scalloped Cheese Bread

Four slices buttered bread, ¾ c. grated cheese, 2 beaten eggs, 2 c. milk, salt, pepper. Place slices of bread in buttered pudding dish, cover these with grated cheese. Beat the eggs, add milk, salt and pepper. Pour this mixture over bread and bake in a hot oven.

Mrs. Kathryn Sheldin
(Kalamazoo, 1921)

Canada Cheese

Two tablespoons butter, 4 tablespoons bread crumbs, ½ lb. cheese, 1 cup sour milk, 8 eggs. Cut up cheese and butter and put them into a bowl with the bread crumbs, pour on the milk scalding hot, add the yolks well beaten, pinch of salt; mix well together, cover, and place on back of range, stirring occasionally till all is dissolved, then add the whites beaten to a froth; put all in a buttered pie plate and bake in a quick oven about 20 minutes. Serve immediately.

E. C. L.
(Grand Rapids, 1890)

We substituted sour cream for sour milk and baked for 20 minutes at 400°. It was a delicious dish reminiscent of cheese soufflé.

Damson Cheese

Take twelve pounds of damsons and put them into the oven; when they are soft take out the stones, crack them and then blanch the kernels, then add three and a half pounds of lump sugar; boil the plums about three hours; wet the molds before using them. Weigh the damsons after they are put into the molds.

(Detroit, 1881)

Damsons are a variety of plum. Damson cheese is an old English recipe. The stones or pits have a kernel inside which has an almond-like flavor. The cheese should not be eaten for six months and is good for up to two years. We recommend the use of canning jars instead of molds. It can be served as a dessert or dissolved for tarts and cakes. It has the consistency of marmalade if set with gelatine. To "weigh" the damsons is to place a heavy weight on the mold.

Cottage Cheese

This dish is usually prepared from milk which has curdled from lack of proper care, or from long standing exposed to the air, and which is thus in some degree decomposing. But the fact that the casein of milk is coagulated by the use of acids makes it possible to prepare this dish in a more wholesome manner without waiting for decomposition of the milk. Add to each four quarts of milk one cupful of lemon juice; let it stand until coagulated, then heat slowly, but do not boil, until the curd has entirely separated from the whey. Turn the whole into a colander lined with a square of clean cheese cloth, and drain off the whey. Add to the curd a little salt and cream, mix all together with a spoon or the hands, and form into cakes or balls for the table. The use of lemon gives a delicious flavor, which may be intensified, if desired, by using a trifle of the grated yellow rind.

(Battle Creek, 1910)

Cottage Cheese Pie

One and one-half cups cottage cheese, ½ cup sugar, 3 eggs, 2 tablespoonfuls cream, juice and grated rind of 1 lemon, 1 teaspoonful butter, press cheese through colander, add well beaten eggs and the other ingredients; stir till smooth, bake in 1 crust in quick oven 30 minutes.

Mrs. A. R. Barrett
(Union City, 1902)

Hungarian Cottage Cheese Pie

Pie Crust:

1 cup flour dipped from sack	½ cup lard
	4 tbsps. cold water
1 tsp. salt	2 tsps. butter

Sift flour with salt. Blend lard with flour, add water and mix thoroughly. Divide in two parts. Roll out part for lower crust. Roll the remaining part and dot with butter, fold, and roll again for upper crust.

Pie Filling:

2 cups cottage cheese	1 tsp. cinnamon
	½ cup sugar
2 eggs	¼ tsp. salt
⅓ cup raisins	

Place cheese in dish; break in eggs without beating; add raisins, cinnamon, sugar and salt. Mix all together and put in pastry lined pie plate. Put on upper crust and bake 30 to 45 minutes in moderate oven.

Mrs. Ellen W. A. Smallridge
(Kalamazoo, 1935)

Italian Gnocchi

¼ cup butter	2 eggs
¼ cup flour	1 cup grated cheese
¼ cup cornstarch	¼ teaspoon salt
2 cups milk	

Melt the butter and add the flour, cornstarch and salt. Stir in the milk and boil all together for five minutes, stirring continually to keep smooth.

Add the beaten egg, the salt and the grated cheese. Cook for a minute and turn into a low greased pan to cool.

Cut into small rounds with a cookie cutter, about one and one-half inches across. Arrange in a flat glass baking dish; sprinkle with grated cheese and brown in a hot oven.

(Detroit, 1935)

Cheese Loaf

½ pkg. noodles, cooked	¼ lb. cheese
	3 eggs (or 2)
½ cup milk	Seasoning

Mix together, adding well-beaten whites last. Bake at 300° an hour. Serve with sauce.

Sauce

I. Make a cream sauce adding tuna, pimientoes and peas, if desired.

II. Make a cream sauce and add chicken and mushrooms.

Mrs. J. W. Spalsbury
(Kalamazoo, 1941)

Pimento and Cheese

1 cup sweet milk
1 tablespoon flour,
   cook and add 1 tea-
   spoon salt

Pinch cayenne pepper
½ pound cream
   cheese

When thick, add 1 can of pimentoes (cut up).

Mrs. Lussenden
(Grand Rapids, 1917)

Playthings for the Palate—
Post Tavern Ramequins

One-half pound of grated cheese, 1 tablespoon grated horseradish, ½ ounce butter, 1 beaten egg; incorporate into balls, serve on lettuce leaf and pierce, a la porcupine, with julienne truffles.

(Battle Creek, 1903)

Following a brief stay at Dr. John Harvey Kellogg's fashionable Battle Creek Sanitarium where he was exposed to some of the health foods invented by Kellogg, Charles W. Post set up his own modest firm in 1894 to manufacture a coffee substitute. He rather immodestly named it Postum. By 1901 the "grandfather of modern advertising" had become a millionaire and incidentally inspired a Battle Creek breakfast-food boom that saw the birth and rapid demise of more than eighty strange-sounding breakfast foods. In 1901 Post financed the Post Tavern, a luxurious six-story hotel located on the southwest corner of West Michigan Ave. and McCamly Street. Generations of travelers fondly remembered a special stay at the plush hostelry.

Welsh Rarebit

Place two tablespoonfuls of butter in the pan, when melted add one-half pound of cheese, grated or cut fine, and a dash of cayenne, when the cheese is nearly melted add gradually one-half cupful of cream or milk, then the beaten yolks of two eggs; stir constantly, and when smooth, serve at once on toast or sweet crackers. This will serve six or eight persons.

Mrs. Wm. Rae, Menominee
(Chicago, 1898)

Olive Rarebit

One tablespoon butter, 1 cup grated cheese, ¼ cup milk, water or cider, 1 egg (beaten), ½ teaspoon salt, paprika, 6 large olives (chopped). Melted butter, add cheese when partly melted, add milk, water or cider. Cook until smooth. Add other ingredients.

Dorothy Rice
(Higgins Lake, 1920)

Cheese Torte

Mix well together the following: One package Holland Rusk or (Zwieback) rolled fine, with 1 teaspoon cinnamon; ½ cup sugar; ¼ cup butter. Line a deep pie pan with this mixture well on the sides of the pan, and fill with the following: One pound cottage cheese; 2 eggs, ½ cup sugar, 1 teaspoon vanilla; 1 tablespoonful flour; pinch of salt. Reserve a cup of the rusk mixture and spread over filling before baking. Bake slowly.

Harrison W. Hinds
(Marine City, 1923)

Nut Cheese

1 cup peanut butter
2 cups cold water

½ cup gluten flour
1½ teaspoons salt

Stir the nut-butter smooth with water, adding the water a little at a time. Stir in the flour and salt, and put into a tin can that has a tight-fitting cover, and steam or boil from three to five hours.

(Berrien Springs, 1941)

Home-Made Cream Cheese

As rennet is the principal agent in making cheese, that should be provided first. If rennet extract can be obtained, that will be the best, because it is always pure and sweet, and uniform in strength, and comes with directions for using. But if it cannot be had, rennet may be prepared by steeping a good clean and sweet rennet in a weak brine at least 2 days in advance, and giving it a half dozen or so good rubbings before using. No definite amount can be given as to how much you should use of this for any given quantity of milk on account of its varying strength (2 inches square of good rennet is sufficient to make 50 or 60 pounds cheese), but rennet enough should be thoroughly stirred in to make coagulation begin in 12 or 15 minutes.

The next essential is some kind of press. Any man can make one. A draining-box is also needed, with a slat division across it and open at one end, or a basket might be substituted, though it is not nearly so good, and a hoop in which the curd will be pressed. Annatto is used for coloring by those who do not think it injurious; if you wish it, a piece the size of a hickory-nut dissolved in 1 cup hot water is sufficient for 6 or 8 gallons milk.

Keep the night's milk cool and, in the morning, skim, put the cream in the strainer, and strain the morning's milk, which is warm, through it to dissolve the cream and add to the night's milk.

A thermometer will be wanted. Some convenience for heating a mess of milk so it will not get scorched must be devised. For a few cows this may be done on the kitchen stove or range, with a tin pan large enough to hold the mess to be heated set in, or over, a pan or kettle containing water, or, by setting a tin-pail of hot water in the milk; heat to 80° or 85°, and add the rennet. It should coagulate in from 30 to 35 minutes; then stand 40 minutes, and cut the curd; then stand about the same length of time before heating up the whey; when the heat has been raising about 10 minutes, commence working gradually, till it gets to 100°. Work it up with clean hands to keep the curd from sticking together, until it will cleave apart; then let the fire go down, and let it stand till the whey becomes a sickish sweet, then drain off the whey.

If the cheese is wanted for immediate use, salt at the rate of ½ pound to 25 pounds of curd should be evenly mingled with the curd. If to be kept long, ½ pound salt to 15 or 16 of curd may be used.

Wring out a square of strong domestic (¾ yard), in whey, put over the hoop, and put the curd in, pressing down evenly with the hand. Put on the top and put to press. Begin slowly and gradually increase the pressure. Leave in the press all night. Next morning turn and press again; the next day rub with melted butter, and put in a cool, dry room to cure, turning frequently.

(Detroit, 1890)

The curd is separated from the milk usually using rennet or pepsin, a coagulating agent. Rennet is the lining of the fourth stomach of a ruminant, usually a calf. "Strong domestic" is cheese cloth, a loosely woven cloth used in pressing the cheese.

Vegetables, Nuts, Grains, and Pasta

Vegetables

Always boil vegetables in soft water, if you can procure it; if not, put a teaspoonful or more of carbonate of soda in it to render it so. The water should be freshly drawn, and should be put over the fire only in time to reach the boiling point before the time for putting in vegetables, as standing and long boiling frees the gases and renders the water insipid. The fresher all vegetables are the more wholesome. Take care to wash and cleanse them from dust and other impurities, before putting them into the pot or pan; they should be thoroughly cleansed, for which purpose it will be necessary to open the leaves of all greens.

It is best to boil vegetables, if possible, by themselves. The quicker they boil the greener they will be. When vegetables are quite fresh gathered, they require much less boiling than those that have been kept. Strong scented vegetables ought to be kept apart. If onions, leeks and celery, are laid among such delicate vegetables as cauliflowers, they will spoil in a very short time. In boiling vegetables, if they sink they are generally done enough, if the water has been kept constantly boiling. When done, take them up immediately, and thoroughly drain. If vegetables are a minute too long over the fire, they lose all their beauty and flavor. If not thoroughly boiled tender, they are tremendously indigestible; and much more troublesome during their residence in the stomach, than underdone meats.

Vegetables are in greatest perfection, when in greatest plenty, and they are only in greatest plenty when in full season. All vegetables are best when they are so cheap as to enable the artisan to eat them. Very early peas, or very early potatoes—that is, peas or potatoes raised by artificial means— may be valued as great rarities, but for nothing else. The same thing may be asserted of nearly all other vegetables; early rhubarb is perhaps an exception. All vegetables should be ripe; that is, ripe as vegetables; otherwise, like fruits, they are bad tasting or unwholesome.

With regard to the quality of vegetables, the middle size are to be preferred to the very large. Green vegetables, such as cabbages, cauliflowers; etc., should be eaten fresh, before the life is out of them. When once dead, they are good for nothing but to throw away.

Greens, roots, salads, etc., etc., when they have lost their freshness by long keeping, may be refreshed a little by putting them in cold spring water for an hour or two before they are dressed; but this process will not make them equal to those which are gathered just before they are boiled.

Old potatoes should stand in cold water for several hours; put them in immediately after they are peeled, as exposure to the air darkens them. Before putting on to boil, take out of the water and dry with a towel. New potatoes are best baked. If you wish to have potatoes mealy, do not let them stop boiling for an instant; and when they are done, turn the water off, and let them steam a few moments over the fire with the cover off. Or peel them, and put them in a pan over steam to cook. They will be mealy and white and look like large snow-balls. Green corn and peas should be prepared and cooked at once. Onions should be soaked in warm salt water, one hour before cooking, to remove the rank flavor. Never split onions, turnips or carrots, but cut them crosswise, as they thus cook tender much quicker.

In boiling vegetables there should be a tablespoonful of salt for each two quarts of water. Nearly all vegetables are eaten dressed with salt, pepper and butter, but sometimes a small piece of lean pork is boiled with them which seasons them sufficiently.

Egg plants should be picked when full grown,

but before they are ripe. A little sugar added to peas, beets, corn, squash, turnips, and pumpkin is an improvement, especially when the vegetables are not of prime quality. Sweet potatoes require longer to cook than the common variety. In gathering asparagus, never cut if off, but snap or break it; in this way you do not get the white woody part, which no boiling will make tender. Do the same way with rhubarb, taking it close to the ground and being careful it does not split.

Cabbage, potatoes, carrots, turnips, parsnips, onions and beets lose their flavor by being cooked with meat, as also does the meat. When vegetables are to be served with salt meat, the meat should be cooked first, and then removed and the vegetables cooked in the liquor, except in boiled dinner. A piece of red pepper, the size of the finger nail, dropped into vegetables when first beginning to cook, will add greatly in killing the unpleasant odor, or a small piece of bread crust will do the same service. This fact is worth remembering in cooking onions and vegetables.

When green peas have become old and yellow, they may be made tender and green by sprinkling in a pinch or two of pearlash while they are boiling. Old potatoes are improved in the same way.

Succulent vegetables, such a cabbages, and all sorts of greens, are best preserved in a cool, damp, and shady place. Potatoes, turnips carrots, and similar roots, intended to be stored up, should never, on any account, be cleaned from the earth adhering to them, till they are to be dressed.

(Detroit, 1881)

To Boil Asparagus

Clean the stalks of grit, wash in cold water and be sure to tie up the asparagus in bundles of fifteen or twenty when you to go boil them. Have the water on the full boil, in which there should be a good tablespoonful of salt; cook twenty minutes outside; drain thoroughly, steaming them slightly when they are cooked. Serve on toast, with a sauce of melted butter. Asparagus boiled plain and eaten cold, with a plain oil and vinegar dressing, is excellent. Or cut the asparagus, when boiled, into little bits, leaving out white end; make a gravy of the second water the asparagus is boiled in—the first should be poured off when nearly done and a second one poured on, if a gravy is made—a lump of butter, salt and pepper, thickened with a spoonful of flour, mixed up with cold water, if a thick gravy is liked.

(Detroit, 1881)

Vitamins, a twentieth-century discovery, were not in the Victorian vocabulary. The 1911 edition of Encyclopedia Britannica does not even mention the term. Consequently early cooks did not concern themselves with over boiling the vitamins out of vegetables.

We recommend cooking asparagus 5 to 7 minutes. Bring an inch of water to a boil, add the asparagus, and turn it down to simmer for 5 to 7 minutes so as to render it tender but not mushy. Or steam the stalks for 10 to 12 minutes.

Fried Asparagus

Boil the asparagus a couple of minutes, and then drain it; dip each piece in butter and fry it in hot fat. When done sprinkle with salt and serve hot.

(Detroit, 1881)

Our cooks in plying their art to please,
    Some new ways have discovered
To give mankind content and ease,
    By good things in the cupboard.
So Mother Hubbard's Modern Cupboard
    We offer to the nation,
We've proved its culinary hoard
    By close investigation.

So R. W. Snyder, a Battle Creek extract manufacturer, introduced the cookbook he gave away with each order for $1 worth of his products. The 170-page volume *Mother Hubbard's Modern Cupboard* published in Battle Creek in 1903 contained many recipes that used the locally produced breakfast cereals that had brought boom times to "The Cereal City," as well as the following recipe.

Asparagus in Ambush

Scrape out the inside of eight or nine rolls or plate biscuits (cut off tops to serve as covers). Set open in the oven to crisp. Heat two cups of milk, pour upon four beaten eggs; stir over the fire until it thickens, add one spoonful of butter rolled in flour. Put in the tops of two bunches of asparagus, boiled tender, chopped fine and seasoned. Fill the rolls with this mixture, put on the tops and serve hot.

(Battle Creek, 1903)

Asparagus Loaf

One large bunch asparagus, 5 eggs slightly beaten—save out yolk for sauce. 4 tablespoons flour, 4 tablespoons butter, 1 cup milk, 1 cup water that the asparagus was cooked in. 2 teaspoons salt (scant), pepper, 5 drops lemon extract. Cook asparagus, cut tips off, making ½ cup, cut up rest making 1 cup. Make white sauce, melt butter, add flour, mix well, add asparagus water and milk, salt and pepper. Stir until it boils. To half the white sauce add the cup of asparagus and the eggs. Turn into well buttered baking dish, set in pan of hot water, bake 45 minutes in moderate oven. Turn on platter and cover with the following sauce: Add the ½ cup of asparagus tips to the 1 cup of white sauce that has been left in the double boiler, the one egg yolk and lemon extract.

Marjorie Wolfenden Hopkins
(Higgins Lake, 1920)

Asparagus Loaf

Take a loaf of baker's bread, cut off the crust and scoop out the center, leaving the sides and bottom of loaf about one inch thick. Place in a hot oven until well browned. Cook two bunches of asparagus, cut in small pieces and add to one pint of cream sauce. Fill bread box, sprinkle with grated cheese and place in oven until cheese melts and is browned.

(Higgins Lake, 1920)

Asparagus à la Berti

Rub baking dish with onion, lay layer of asparagus tips and pieces of butter; repeat. Break eggs on top, season well with more butter and grated cheese. Sprinkle paprika and mustard over all and bake until eggs are set.

Mrs. F. Hill
(Hastings, 1920)

In 1945, the final year of the World War II, the Kalamazoo chapter of the Navy Mothers Club compiled a club cookbook. Inez M. Baker explained its purpose in verse:

The money that this book will bring
We'll use for many different things
To ease a pain, to fill a need,
For that's the "Navy Mother's" Creed
To bring some sunshine, love, and joy
To the heart of each brave Navy boy.

Navy mother May Knight, an employee of the Upjohn Company and one of the wittiest recipe writer's we've encountered, included directions for a very appropriate Navy dish.

Baked Beans

Soak 1 pound of beans in cold water overnight. Add enough more water to cover and cook slowly until the beans are tender. Place a good-sized, peeled whole onion in the bottom of your bean pot. Turn the beans into the pot. Pour boiling water over ¼ pound of salt pork and scrape the rind until white. Cut it in half-inch slices, but not clear through, only to the rind, and leave the pork showing on top of the beans. Mix ½ teaspoon of salt, 3 tablespoons of brown sugar, ⅓ cup of molasses and ¾ teaspoon of dry mustard. Add 1 cup of water and pour over the beans. Add enough more water to cover and bake in slow oven, 250–300°F., six to eight hours (it used to be all the day in the good brick ovens—all night too!) with the lid on, adding water to keep the beans just covered. Uncover during last half hour to brown the pork.

You must remember that there are about as many receipts for baked beans as there are beans to bake, so if you don't like mustard, don't blame me or anybody, but let the mustard go. And if you love molasses—and I do—put some more in the beans. It isn't going to hurt you or the bean pot, "far as I know." But whatever you do, don't leave out the salt pork. Try to get a piece striped: strips of fat and lean—you know. But get it and get it in among the beans, the top scored and scraped, just visible in the pot. Brown it well before it gets to the table. Its subtle flavor will permeate your beans to your everlasting praise, and the sweet savor of molasses will blend with the pork in a way that is unforgettable and, it may be, indescribable.

May Knight
(Kalamazoo, 1945)

Baked Pork and Beans

Soak 1 qt. beans in cold water over night. In morning put to cook in cold water, add a teaspoon soda to water, let them come to boiling point, drain, add freshly boiled water, simmer until you can blow skin off the beans, turn into colander, pour cold water through them. Pour boiling water over ¾ lb. salt pork, part fat, part lean, scrape the rind until white, cut in half-inch cuts, bury pork in beans in bean pot leaving only rind exposed. Add 1 teaspoon salt, 1 level tablespoon dry mustard, 2 tablespoons molasses to 1 cup hot water, mix well, pour over beans, add enough water to cover them. Bake from 6 to 8 hours in a moderate oven, keep covered with water until the last hour. Remove cover from beans toward the last so as to brown nicely.

Mrs. C. H. Ashby
(Kalamazoo, 1899)

Curried Beans

Boil 1 c. navy beans until soft, chop 1 onion, 1 apple and a carrot very fine; fry them in butter. Dredge over them 1 tsp. flour and curry powder mixed, and a seasoning of pepper and salt; add

BOSTON BAKED BEAN POTS.
Red Earthen Ware.

	Each.
2 quart, Covered and Handled	25
3 quart, Covered and Handled	35
4 quart, Covered and Handled	40
6 quart, Covered and Handled	50
8 quart, Covered and Handled	75

Traditional Boston baked bean pots could be bought new for as little as twenty-five cents in 1890 (Grand Rapids, 1890).

beans; mix well together; put them in a casserole; garnish top with strips of bacon. Bake in slow oven, and serve hot.

Mrs. A. E. Tompkins
(Kalamazoo, 1921)

Bean Loaf

Two c. cooked beans, 1½ c. bread crumbs, 1 c. cooked tomato, 1 small onion, 1 tsp. sage, salt and pepper; add cream or milk enough to make it soft. Put in a bread tin and cook 1 hour (moderate oven.)

Elizabeth Thomas
(Kalamazoo, 1921)

Scalloped Beans

Soak a pint of white beans over night in cold water. When ready to cook, put into an earthen baking dish, cover well with new milk, and bake in a slow oven for eight or nine hours, refilling the dish with milk as it boils away, and taking care that the beans do not at any time get dry enough to brown over the top till they are tender.

When nearly done, add salt to taste, and a half cup of cream. They may be allowed to bake till the milk is quite absorbed, and the beans dry, or may be served when rich with juice, according to taste. The beans may be parboiled in water for a half hour before beginning to bake, and the length of time thereby lessened. They should be well drained before adding the milk. Nut milk may be used if preferred.

(Battle Creek, 1910)

We recommend using domestic nuts; the wild ones won't hold still long enough to be milked.

Bean Turnover

Make a rich biscuit dough, roll thin, cut pieces size of a saucer, put 1 tablespoonful of cold baked beans on each dish, small piece of butter, fold over and press the edges together; bake brown and serve with butter sauce.

Annie Carpenter
(Union City, 1902)

Luncheon Dish

One can red kidney beans, 1 green pepper, chopped without seeds; 1 tbsp. cheese crumbs. Put together and heat until cheese is melted.

Eulalia Wallace Best
(Kalamazoo, 1921)

Beets

To cook them so that none of their color shall be lost, carefully wash them without breaking the skin or cutting off the roots or stalks, and plunge them in boiling salted water. Try them with a fork to see when tender; take out; drop in a pan of cold water and slip the skin off with the hands; slice those needed for present use, place in a dish, add salt, pepper and butter, set over boiling water to heat thoroughly, and serve hot with or without vinegar; put those which remain in a stone jar, whole, cover with vinegar, keep in a cool place, take out as wanted, slice and serve. A few pieces of horseradish put into the jar will prevent a white scum on the vinegar.

(Detroit, 1881)

Baked Beets

Beets are far better baked than boiled, though it takes a longer time to cook properly. French cooks bake them slowly six hours in a covered dish, the bottom of which is lined with well-moistened rye straw; however, they may be baked on the oven grate, like potatoes. Wipe dry after washing, and bake slowly. They are very nice served with a sauce made with equal quantities of lemon juice and whipped cream, with a little salt.

(Battle Creek, 1910)

Dressing for Beets

One tbs. butter, ⅓ c. vinegar, ½ c. sugar, 1 tbsp. cornstarch. Beat together, add 1 c. boiling water; cook until it thickens; add the cooked beets, sliced very thin, and serve hot.

Mrs. R. P. Beebe
(Kalamazoo, 1921)

Fried Cabbage

Cut the cabbage very fine, on a slaw cutter, if possible; salt and pepper, stir well, and let stand five minutes. Have an iron kettle smoking hot, drop one table-spoon lard into it, then the cabbage, stirring briskly until quite tender; send to table immediately. One half cup sweet cream, and three tablespoons vinegar—the vinegar added after the cream has been well stirred, and after taken from the stove, is an agreeable change. When properly done an invalid can eat it without injury, and there is no offensive odor from cooking.

Mrs. J. T. Liggett, Detroit
(Minneapolis, 1881)

Cabbage

Cut a cabbage as fine as you can slice it, boil in milk 30 minutes, and add butter, pepper and salt, with a little flour to thicken.

Mrs. Wm. Reynolds
(Muskegon, 1890)

Baked Cabbage

Baked cabbage is a nice side dish. Cut the cabbage in small pieces and boil till tender in salt and water; when cold chop it finely, add two beaten eggs, a little butter, pepper and salt, if it needs it, and two tablespoonfuls of cream; stir all vigorously, bake in a buttered pudding dish till it is brown on the top; serve hot.

(Grand Rapids, 1890)

Hot Slaw

Slice the cabbage as you would for cold slaw. Put in an iron spider and sprinkle with salt, cover with water and cover the spider tightly. When partly done, add piece of butter size of an egg, and a sprinkling of flour. Then cook until tender. Just before serving, take the yolk of one egg, beaten, one teaspoon mustard, one of sugar, and a little vinegar, mix all together and stir into the cabbage. Cook a minute to set the egg and serve.

Mrs. Chas. A. Peck
(Kalamazoo, 1906)

See the note about the iron spider on page 92.

Sauer Kraut

Make early in the light of the moon. Use just 1 pint of salt to a thirty-two gallon barrel of kraut, and you will not fail to have it first-class.

(Vermontville, 1906)

A colony of Congregationalists from Vermont settled in Eaton County in 1836 and, quite naturally, named their village Vermontville. Today Vermontville with its white, high-steepled Congregational Church very much resembles a typical New England town. In 1906 the Ladies' Christian Association of the Congregational Church compiled the *Twentieth Century Cook Book,* "a feast of good things." This recipe for sauerkraut harkens back to an old New England folk belief.

Fried Sauerkraut

Cut in small pieces 2 thin slices of salt pork, put in a frying pan with 1 qt. sauerkraut, set on the stove, cover and cook 30 minutes, stirring occasionally to prevent burning. Serve hot.

C. A. Zimmerman
(Union City, 1902)

Carrot Pudding

1 cup grated carrots, raw	½ cup currants
1 cup potatoes, raw	½ cup butter
1 teaspoon soda in potatoes	½ teaspoon cloves
1 cup flour (large)	1 do cinnamon
½ cup seeded raisins	¼ do nutmeg
	1 pinch of salt

Ida Watson
(Manistee, 1929)

The "do" in this recipe, means ditto, ie., 1 teaspoon of cinnamon and ¼ teaspoon nutmeg. Ms. Watson assumes you know the directions, since she lists only the ingredients. Add one beaten egg to this recipe and place the mixture in a buttered baking dish. Bake in a preheated 350° oven for 45 minutes.

Carrot Souffle

One quart of carrots, boil in salt water, drain and mash; add the yolks of four eggs, 1 tablespoon sugar; 1 cup cream, last the whites of eggs well beaten. Place in buttered baking dish and bake until firm.

(Manistee, 1929)

Cauliflower au Gratin

Boil cauliflower until done in boiling well salted water. Make a white sauce using the following recipe: Two tablespoonfuls butter, 2 tablespoonfuls flour, 1 cup milk, ½ teaspoon salt, a dash of red pepper. Melt with butter. When it is hot and beginning to brown, stir in the flour and cook together a few seconds, then slowly stir in the scalded milk. Drain the cauliflower, cut in pieces into a buttered baking dish, pour the warm white sauce over it and cover with a fourth of a cup of bread crumbs wet with melted butter. Cook until brown.

Mrs. T. J. Ramsdell
(Manistee, 1929)

Browned Cauliflower

Beat together two eggs, a little salt, four table-spoonfuls of sweet cream, and a small quantity of grated bread crumbs well moistened with a little milk, till of the consistency of batter. Steam the cauliflower until tender, separate it into small bunches, dip each top in the mixture, and place in nice order in a pudding dish; put in the oven and brown.

(Battle Creek, 1910)

Celery

Wash, trim and scrape the stalks, selecting those that are white and tender; crisp by leaving in ice-cold water until they are wanted for the table; arrange neatly in a celery-glass; pass between the oysters and the meat.

(Detroit, 1890)

A glass celery holder, resembling a wide brimmed base with handles, comprised an essential part of the Victorian table setting.

A decorative celery stand manufactured in 1873 (Wallingford, 1872).

Creamed Celery

Cut the celery in small pieces, cover with water and boil till tender, then drain. Add cream slightly thickened and bring to a boil.

Mrs. Hannah Trask Cornell
(Kalamazoo, 1899)

Baked Celery and Cheese

One quart sliced celery, cooked until tender, ¼ pound grated cheese, 1 pint soup stock. Place in your baking dish alternate layers of bread crumbs, celery and cheese, dusting each layer with salt and pepper. Pour over soup stock, add bread crumbs last and small bits of butter and bake thirty minutes in a brisk oven.

Jessie Dunham
(Kalamazoo, 1899)

Celery Fritters

Boil some thick but tender stalks of celery in salted water; when done dry them on a cloth, cut them in equal lengths about one and a half inches; fry them in batter to a golden color, sprinkling fine salt well over, and serve.

(Detroit, 1891)

Boiled Chestnuts

The large variety known as the Italian chestnut is best for this purpose. Remove the shells, drop into boiling water, and boil for ten minutes; take out, drop into cold water, and rub off the brown skins. Have some clean water boiling, turn the blanched nuts into it, and cook until they can be pierced with a fork. Drain thoroughly, put into a hot dish, dry in the oven for a few minutes, and serve. A cream sauce or tomato sauce may be served with them if liked.

(Battle Creek, 1910)

Mashed Chestnuts

Prepare and boil the chestnuts as in the preceding recipe. When tender, mash through a colander with a potato masher. Season with cream and salt if desired. Serve hot.

(Battle Creek, 1910)

Baked Chestnuts

Put Italian chestnuts in the shell on a perforated tin in a rather hot oven, and bake for ten minutes, or until tender. Remove the shells, and serve hot. If preferred, they can be roasted on a clean shovel, or on a corn-popper over a bed of glowing coals.

(Battle Creek, 1910)

Scalloped Corn

Take one can of corn; put a layer of corn in a baking dish, add butter, pepper and salt; then a very thin layer of powdered cracker, then another of corn, and so on. After putting in corn and crackers, pour two and one-half cupfuls of milk over the top. Bake for thirty-five minutes.

Flora Ruprecht, Menominee
(Chicago, 1898)

By 1898 canned vegetables were beginning to creep into Michigan recipes. Sweet corn does not grow well in the Upper Peninsula because of the short growing season, consequently commercially canned corn was probably Flora Ruprecht's only expedient.

Blue Grass Corn Pudding

For quart pan size: 12 ears corn; split corn down the grain (do not cut grains off cobb), then scrape; mix well with corn; 3 eggs well beaten, 1 lump butter, size egg, ½ teaspoonful of salt, just a little sugar, pepper to taste. 1 pint sweet milk. In medium hot oven, cook 25 minutes (till top of pudding is well brown). Serve as vegetable.

Roger Hanson Peters
(Kalamazoo, 1906)

Corn, To Fry

Cut corn from cob till there is about a quart of it and carefully pick out all bits of stalk or silk, beat 2 eggs very light, stir them into corn with 2 tablespoons of flour; salt and pepper, have some lard hot and drop in the corn tablespoonful at a time. Fry a light brown.

(Kalamazoo, 1899)

Succotash

Cut the corn from a dozen ears of corn, being careful not to cut into the cob. Boil one pint of Lima beans in three quarts of water two hours; boil also, the cobs, as they contain much saccharine matter, with the beans. Take out the cobs and put in the corn. Just before taking up, mix quarter of a pound of butter with two tablespoonfuls of flour, some salt and pepper. A cup of good cream is a great improvement. Let your corn boil only twenty minutes.

(Detroit, 1878)

Corn, For Winter Use

Cut the corn from the cob, raw, before it gets too hard; to each gallon of cut corn add 2 scant cups salt; pack tightly in a jar—don't be afraid of getting the jar too large—cover with a white cloth, put a heavy weight to keep the corn under the brine, which soon forms; now the most important part is to wash the cloth every morning for 2 weeks, or the corn will taste queerly; if the corn is too salty, freshen before cooking; this is as good as canned corn, and is much easier put up. Corn should be fresh in order to be good, and should be cooked as quickly as possible after being gathered, as it heats and loses much of its flavor.

(Detroit, 1890)

Remember: "wash the cloth every morning for 2 weeks, or the corn will taste queerly."

Fried Cucumbers

Pare, cut into lengthwise slices more than a quarter of an inch thick, and lay for half an hour in ice water; wipe each piece dry; sprinkle with pepper and salt, and dredge with flour; fry to a light brown in good dripping or butter; drain well and serve hot.

(Detroit, 1881)

Stewed Cucumbers

Cut the cucumbers fully ½ inch thick right through; put them in a sauce-pan, just covering them with hot water, and let them boil slowly for ¼ hour, or until tender, but not so as to break them; then drain them; you want now 1 pint good cream, and put your cream, with 1 teaspoon butter, in a sauce-pan, and when it is warm put in the cucumbers; season with a little salt and white pepper, cook 5 minutes, shaking the sauce-pan all the time; and serve hot; it is just as delicate as asparagus, and a very nice dish indeed.

(Detroit, 1890)

Baked Cucumbers

Peel good-sized green cucumbers, cut them into halves and scoop out the seeds; to each 6 allow 1 pint of finely chopped meat, to which add a table-spoonful of onion juice, a teaspoonful of salt, and a saltspoonful of pepper; fill this into the spaces from which you have taken the seeds; put the cucumbers together and tie or fasten them with a wooden skewer; stand them in a baking pan; put into the pan a teaspoonful of salt, 1 chopped onion, 2 peeled and chopped tomatoes, and ½ a cupful of

water or stock; bake for 1 hour, basting every 10 minutes; when done dish the cucumbers, strain the sauce in the pan over them and serve at once. The ordinary crooked-neck squash may be stuffed and baked in the same manner.

(Lansing, 1901)

Baked Cucumbers (Served with Chicken)

Six cucumbers. Make them boat shaped. Cook seeds and 1 tomato. Butter bread crumbs to thicken. To that add 3 slices of bacon cut in small pieces and fried. Add chopped celery and onions first and stuff cucumber. season with red pepper and salt. Put in pan, pour stock in water around. Cook 20 minutes. Serve with any sauce or without.

Marion Pigott
(Higgins Lake, 1920)

Roscommon County's Higgins Lake, named after early mapmaker Sylvester Higgins, had become a tourist mecca by the turn of the century. A local resort operator subdivided his property and platted the village of Higgins Lake in 1902. A group of local cottagers soon formed the Lakeside Association. Around 1920, ladies of the association compiled their own and their guests' best recipes and published a souvenir volume to "bring back a whiff of the pines, a memory of the sparkling sapphire blue of our lake, or of the moon climbing over tree tops and looking down on campfires where goodies are being prepared for the late feast." In addition to hundreds of recipes, the book also included views of many local scenes such as Harry Shiland's cottage "Itsuitsus."

Dandelions

Take 1 peck of dandelion leaves, wash in several waters, let lay in cold water ½ hour; put on to cook in boiling water; boil 10 minutes, pour off the water and cover with fresh boiling water with salt, boil 1 hour, drain and press out the water; put in a sauce-pan and set on the stove; season with butter, salt and pepper; take up in a hot dish, garnish with slices of hard-boiled eggs; serve with vinegar.

(Detroit, 1890)

Dandelions

Cook a piece of salt pork until tender. Wash thoroughly fresh tender dandelions, remove roots and cook until tender in the kettle with your pork.

(Manistee, 1929)

Egg Plant

Take a large sized egg plant, leave the stem and skin on and boil in a porcelain kettle until soft, taking up with a fork and spoon. Remove the skin and mash fine in a bowl, (not tin,) add a teaspoon of salt, plenty of pepper, a large spoonful of flour, (when it is cold,) a half teacupful of milk or cream and 3 eggs. This forms a nice batter. Have some butter and lard very hot and drop this batter from a spoon as you do fritters and brown nicely on each side.

(Muskegon, 1890)

Baked Egg Plant

Cut it into slices three-fourths of an inch thick and lay in salt water for an hour or more. Wipe the pieces dry and dip into beaten egg, then into bread crumbs or cracker dust; have the fat hot in your pan—just enough to prevent sticking—and put them in the oven until done. This will be found a better way than frying, and they are very light and delicious. Season to the taste before cooking.

(Detroit, 1881)

Baked Eggplant No. 2

Cut a slice from the top of a medium sized eggplant, leaving the stem; remove the inside of the larger portion, being careful not break the shell; chop fine 1 medium sized onion; brown in a little butter; add this, with 1 cup of canned tomatoes or 4 or 5 whole ones chopped, to the eggplant; season highly and cook for 10 minutes in sauce-pan; fill the shell, sprinkle bread crumbs over the top and bake for ½ an hour in a hot oven; cover with the top slice which has been heated. Serve on low dish garnished with parsley.

(Lansing, 1901)

Egg Plant Loaf

1 large egg plant pared and cooked until soft, then mash, add 2 eggs well beaten, butter size of hickory nut, chop ¼ pound lean fresh pork, season to taste, put in earthen dish or glass baking dish and put slices of pork on top. Bake ¾ hour, or until pork is nice and brown.

Mrs. H. G. Woodruff
(Higgins Lake, 1920)

Eggplant for Vegetarians

May be thrown into water and boiled for 10 minutes; cut into halves lengthwise, scoop out the center, chop fine, and mix with an equal quantity of bread crumbs; add 4 tablespoonfuls of nut butter, a level teaspoonful of salt and a dash of pepper; put this back into the shells, cover with bread crumbs and bake in a moderate oven for an hour.

(Lansing, 1901)

Greens

Cabbage plants, turnip or mustard tops, the roots and tops of young beets, cowslips, horse-radish, and dandelions, all make an excellent relish in the spring. When boiled enough they will sink to the bottom of the kettle. If pork is not objectionable, boil the greens with a ham bone; if it is, boil with lean corned beef, or in clear water. Salt a little and when done season with butter. Eat with vinegar.

(Battle Creek, 1910)

Beet Greens

Take the roots and leaves of the beets and wash them carefully, but do not separate the roots from the leaves; fill dinner pot half full of salted boiling water, add beets and boil from half to three-quarters of an hour; take out and drain in colander, pressing down with a large spoon so as to get out all the water. Dish and slice across until fine, and dress with a little butter, pepper and salt. Serve hot with vinegar. Some like to eat only the beet-root, in which case a little melted butter, with a little mustard and vinegar added, must be thrown over the hot slices of the root.

(Detroit, 1881)

First Prize Holland Lettuce

1 5 or 6 oz. head of
   lettuce
6 medium sized
   boiled potatoes
   (hot)
1 small onion

3 eggs
1 cup water
3 tbs. vinegar
2 thin slices of bacon
Pinch of salt

Dice and fry bacon until crisp. Then add water, salt and vinegar and when mixture boils drop in the eggs. As the eggs set cut through two or three times to break the yolks, and stir lightly. Continue cooking until eggs are firm. Remove from fire and allow to cool while breaking the hot potatoes into small pieces, with a fork. Do not mash. Then place the potatoes on top of shredded lettuce and onion, and pour the dressing directly onto the potatoes. Mix all together and serve at once. If desired, the bacon may be omitted and a rounding tablespoon of butter used instead. Served with bread and butter, fruit and your favorite beverage makes a complete meal.

Mrs. Lucille M. Krull
(Kalamazoo, 1935)

Hutspot

6 Onions
6 Carrots
8 Potatoes

½ cup Rich Milk
Butter

Dice and boil onions and carrots. Drain. Boil potatoes, drain and dry thoroughly, add onions and carrots and mash fine. Add salt and pepper, a good sized piece of butter and top milk. Stew all together until heated and serve.

(Holland, 1936)

This was a traditional dish served in every Dutch home on October 3rd, a national holiday in Holland corresponding to America's Thanksgiving Day. Its creamy orange and white texture makes it an attractive as well as tasty dish. The onions should be chopped very fine before cooking or left out entirely to suit your taste.

Kohl-Rabi

After the stems of the leaves have been cut off, the kohl-rabi should be washed and then pared to remove the outer skin. It is usually diced or sliced thin, and then cooked and dressed in any desirable way. Season according to taste. Also, kohl-rabi may be mashed, adding soy-bean milk as in mashed potatoes.

(Berrien Springs, 1941)

The following three macaroni dishes are using what we refer to today as spaghetti. Feel free to substitute your favorite pasta in these recipes.

Home-Made Macaroni

To four cupfuls of flour, add one egg well beaten, and enough water to make a dough that can be rolled. Roll thin on a bread board and cut in strips. Dry in the sun. The best arrangement for this purpose is a wooden frame to which a square of cheesecloth has been tightly tacked, upon which the macaroni may be laid in such a way as not to touch, and afterwards covered with cheesecloth to keep off the dust during the drying.

(Battle Creek, 1910)

Macaroni Loaf

Cook 1 pkg. macaroni, make tomato sauce as follows:

Mix 3 tsp. melted butter with 3 tbps. flour, add 2 c. strained tomatoes: cook until mixture thickens; season to taste with salt and pepper.

One tbsp. chopped onions, pour gradually into a beaten egg, cover bottom of baking dish with bread crumbs, fill pan with alternate layers of macaroni and tomato sauce. Bake in hot oven until brown.

Mrs. Shelly
(Kalamazoo, 1921)

Baked Macaroni and Olives

1 cup uncooked macaroni	*4 tablespoons tomato*
½ cup chopped ripe olives	*2 cups water in which the macaroni was cooked*
2 teaspoons chopped onion	*Salt and celery salt to taste*

Break the macaroni into ½ inch lengths, drop into boiling salted water, and cook until it is well done. Drain off the water. Cook in this water the onion and the chopped olives, for a few minutes. Then add the tomato and let boil 5 minutes. Combine the macaroni and the other ingredients. Turn into a baking dish, grate a few fresh bread crumbs over the top, and with a spoon press down so that they become moistened through. If this is too moist, add more crumbs or pour off some of the juice. Bake until a nice brown. Makes an excellent picnic dish.

(Berrien Springs, 1941)

Macaroni and Tomato

Put macaroni on stove, and boil ½ hour in boiling salt and water. Then drain and put in cold water for a short time. Cream 4 tbsp. of butter and 2 of flour and cook thoroughly; be careful not to burn it. Boil 1 qt. (or can) of tomatoes and strain, add soda the size of a pea, then add tomatoes to the butter and flour. Butter baking dish well and sprinkle with bread crumbs; put in layer of macaroni, then dressing and so on, adding a little salt and cayenne with each layer. Cover top with bread crumbs and bake.

Mrs. A. K. Edwards
(Kalamazoo, 1906)

Old-fashioned macaroni apparently was a harder variety that took longer to cook. Follow the directions appropriate for your particular brand.

Meat Loaf Vegetable Protein

One c. nut meats, 1 c. cooked rice, well drained; salt, pepper and chopped onion, 1 c. tomato pulp, do not have too wet; 1 egg. Bake in bread pan like a meat loaf; if too moist serve in side dish or in crust patties. This is a M. A. C. food demonstration recipe. Very good.

Mrs. S. H. V. H.
(Kalamazoo, 1921)

Michigan State University's former designation was the Michigan Agricultural College or M. A. C.

Mushrooms

Edible mushrooms have a pleasant smell and taste when raw; if peppery discard them or if the base of the stalk is greatly enlarged, is of bulbous shape, or sets in a distinct cup it is safer to pass them by. The puff-ball variety, i.e., the sort that when dry emits a brown powder fine as flour, when pressed by the foot, is always good, not poisonous. However, it must be picked when perfectly firm, solid and white as milk inside. These are better fried than those with gills as they absorb less butter. They grow to monstrous size, weighing from 1 to 15 pounds. Choose those of medium size, peel, cut in ½ inch slices, fry thoroughly in half batter and half cottolene until a rich brown. Serve hot. The slices may be cut of uniform size and the parts trimmed off used for stewing or catsup.

Mrs. Aiken
(Union City, 1902)

Cottolene was an early version of oleomargarine.

Baked Mushrooms

Peel the umbrella-shaped mushrooms, (if fresh enough to be wholesome they need no washing as they grow up in a night) flatten and lay in a pie tin, upper side down, with a piece of butter on each one, dust with salt and pepper, bake 20 minutes in a moderate oven, put on a hot plate, pour over the juice that cooks out and serve.

Mrs. Aiken
(Union City, 1902)

Stuffed Mushrooms

16 large fresh mushrooms	*1⅓ cups soft bread crumbs*
½ cup butter	*⅓ cup Parmesan cheese*
⅓ cup mushroom stems and caps chopped	*1 tbsp. parsley*
⅓ cup lean cooked ham	*1½ cups tomato sauce*
⅓ cup onion	*Salt, pepper and cayenne*

Wipe, peel and remove centers from mushrooms and put in a flat pan. Melt butter, add chopped mushroom stems and caps, ham and onion chopped fine and ⅓ cup soft bread crumbs. Stir and cook three min. Add 1 tbsp. grated Parmesan cheese, parsley chopped, tomato sauce to moisten (about ¾ cups) and season highly. Cover each mushroom with the mixture, surround with remaining sauce and cover with remaining crumbs and cheese mixed together. Twenty minutes before serving time, place in a hot oven (425 degrees) until heated through and slightly brown. Remove to serving places and put a little of the sauce on the side of each mushroom.

Mrs. Edw. Jones
(Kalamazoo, 1941)

Curried Mushrooms

Peel and remove the stems from a dish of full-grown mushrooms, sprinkle with salt, and add a very little butter; stew them gently in a little good gravy or stock; add 4 tablespoons cream, and 1 teaspoon curry powder, previously well mixed with 2 teaspoons wheat flour; mix carefully, and serve on a hot dish, with hot toast and hot plates attendant. The large horse-mushroom, when ½ or ¾ grown, and curried in this fashion, will be found to be delicious.

(Detroit, 1890)

The horse-mushroom or field mushroom, *Agaricus arvensis*, grows in fields under trees and in the borders of woods. We strongly suggest you make sure of your identification before eating any wild mushrooms.

To Pot Mushrooms

The small open mushrooms suit best for potting. Trim and rub them; put into a stew-pan 1 quart mushrooms, 3 ounces butter, 2 teaspoons salt and ½ teaspoon cayenne and mace mixed and stew for 10 or 15 minutes, or till the mushrooms are tender; take them carefully out and drain them perfectly on a sloping dish, and when cold press them into small pots, and pour clarified butter over them in which state they will keep for a week or two. If required to be longer preserved put writing paper over the butter and over that melted suet, which will effectually preserve them for many weeks, if kept in a dry, cool place.

(Detroit, 1890)

Noodles

One egg for each person served. Work in all the flour the egg will take, roll very thin, lay on piece of old table linen 1 hour, then roll up and cut very thin. Boil in salted water or any kind of soup. A delicious dish is made by frying the noodles after boiling in salted water, in browned butter, cooking quickly.

Mrs. John Snyder
(Charlotte, 1909)

Nut Loaf

To be served as a meat dish. Rub 1 cup cooked beans, 1 cup cooked peas and 1 cup soaked toast through colander. Add 1 cup chopped nuts, 1 cup cream, ½ teaspoon salt, pepper or sage. Bake 2 hours.

Mrs. Munger
(Hart, 1907)

The Ladies Aid Society of the First Baptist Church in Hart issued their cookbook in 1907. Alternate pages of the slim pamphlet carry local promotional matter. The ladies trusted that "the purchasers of the book will neither overlook the advertisements nor fail to patronize the advertisers." W. P. Roach and Co., producer of Hart brand canned goods, placed a large advertisement to further promote its well-known line of canned peas, corn, beans, berries, cherries, etc., all grown in Michigan.

Oatmeal

For Bone and Muscle; or, as Food and Drink for Laborers—Liebig has shown that oatmeal is almost as nutritious as the very best English beef, and that it is richer than wheaten bread in the elements that go to form bone and muscle. Prof. Forbes, of Edinburgh, during some 20 years, measured the breadth and height, and also tested the strength of both arms and loins of the students of the University—a very numerous class, and of various nationalities, drawn to Edinburgh by the fame of his teaching. He found that in height, breadth of chest and shoulders, and strength of arms and loins, the Belgians were at the bottom of the list, a little above them the French, very much higher the English, and highest of all the Scotch and Scotch-Irish, from Ulster, who, like the natives of Scotland, are fed in their early years with at least one meal a day of good milk and good oatmeal porridge.

As a Drink—Speaking of oatmeal an exchange remarks that a very good drink is made by putting about 2 spoonfuls of the meal into a tumbler of water. The western hunters and trappers consider it the best of drinks, as it is at once nourishing, stimulating and satisfying. It is popular in the Brooklyn navy yard, 2½ lbs. of oatmeal being put into a pail of moderately cold water. It is much better than any of the ordinary mixtures of vinegar and molasses with water, which farmers use in the haying and harvest field—*New York Mail.*

Remarks—I know the value of oatmeal as a

The famous Hart brand canned goods pioneered in making Michigan vegetables and fruit easily available throughout the year (Hart, 1907).

food; and I have not a doubt of its value as a drink; putting the meal to common water for the drinking, by laborers, when at work. My son and myself drank of it, as used by the laborers on the Brooklyn bridge, as we visited that structure, passing through there to the Centennial in 1876, and liked it very much; and the superintendent said he should not be willing to even try to do without it; though I think they only put 1 lb. to a pail of water. It would certainly be very nourishing with 2 tablespoonfuls of it to a glass of water, as spoken of by the exchange above, hálf the amount would meet my own ideas, as sufficient, even when the nourishment was especially needed.

(Ann Arbor, 1884)

Oatmeal Porridge, Scotch

An Englishwoman in the Germantown (Pa.) *Telegraph* gives the following instruction to make
Oatmeal Porridge—"Oatmeal porridge is especially suitable for children. It nourishes their bones and other tissues, and supplies them in a greater degree than most foods with the much needed element of phosphorus. If they grow weary of it, they can be tempted back with the bait of golden syrup, jam, or marmalade, to be eaten with the porridge. The Irish and Scotch make their porridge with water, and add cold milk, but the most agreeable and nutritive way is to make it entirely with milk, to use coarse oatmeal, and to see that it is not too thick." The following is a good receipt:
Bring a quart of milk to the boiling point in an enamel-lined sauce-pan, and drop in by degrees 8 oz. of coarse oatmeal; stir till it thickens, and then boil for half an hour. The mixture should not be too thick, and more milk can be added according to the taste.

Oatmeal Mush

The true way to make oatmeal mush is in a rice-kettle; but if you have it not, a porcelain lined one is next best; iron will do. If made in the rice or double kettle; simply water enough to cover the meal is enough; then cover the dish and cook till done, without fear of burning. To make in an open kettle, put in water sufficient to make the right quantity,

and bring to a boil; adding a little salt; then stir in coarse oatmeal until it is as thick as you wish to eat it; then slip back on the stove to simmer slowly for half an hour, or till done. Eaten with meat, or served with milk, milk or sugar, or cream, as desired.

(Ann Arbor, 1884)

Larry's father, a full-blooded Scot, raised his family of six strapping sons and one daughter to believe in the innate superiority of all things Scottish. He credits their good health to the oatmeal porridge they ate for breakfast every morning. The family however was sadly divided on one issue. Half followed the example of their mother, "a liberal," and put sugar on their porridge; the others salted theirs, the only correct way according to the Scotsman.

Botermelk Pap (Buttermilk Pop)

1 cup Barley	*3 quarts Buttermilk*
1½ quarts Water	*½ teaspoon Salt*

Boil barley in water slowly for about two hours. When water is cooked down add buttermilk, stirring until it boils—cook a few minutes, then add salt. Serve with syrup or sugar.

(Holland, 1936)

This could be served as a breakfast dish but was traditionally eaten at other meals in Dutch households.
Joseph Bert Smiley, one of Michigan's most eccentric rhymesters, offered his poetic opinion of onions in his first book, *Meditations of Samwell Wilkins,* published in his home town of Kalamazoo in 1886.

Onions

There is no perfume that I love so well
    As onions, fragrant onions.
Creation's most odoriferous smell
    Is onions, fragrant onions.
Nature is beautiful, calm, and bright.
From fruitful valley to lofty height.
She would show good sense if she'd only blight
    These onions, fragrant onions.

Sometimes when walking the street, you say,
  "Onions, fragrant onions!
"Somebody's cooking for dinner to-day
  "Onions, fragrant onions."
No flower's pure essence as sweet as they.
No fifty-cent odor could longer stay.
You can smell 'em a couple of blocks away.
  Onions, fragrant onions.

I wonder how Providence came to invent
  Onions, fragrant onions.
On what dire mission hath nature sent
  Onions, fragrant onions?
It seems too bad that an earth so fair
Should nourish and foster with so much care
A plant with a smell that will raise your hair—
  Onions, fragrant onions.

Onions

In peeling, if they are held under water, the eyes will not be affected. Boil them twenty minutes, add a pinch of soda, drain, add sweet milk and salt, and cook, twenty minutes more; take up, season to taste, and serve. Onions should be gashed to receive the seasoning.

(Battle Creek, 1890)

Larry, who dislikes raw onions, feels that all onions should be "gashed" and insisted on including the following statement by Mrs. John Harvey Kellogg.

The Onion

The onion belongs to a class of foods containing an acrid oil of a strongly irritating character, on which account it cannot be considered a wholesome food when eaten raw, as it so generally is. The essential oil is, however, quite volatile, so that when cooked, after being first parboiled in two or three waters, its irritating properties are largely removed. The varieties grown in warm climates are much milder and sweeter than those grown in colder countries. The onion is valuable for flavoring purposes. It may also be boiled and served whole with a cream sauce.

(Battle Creek, 1910)

Escalloped Onions

Boil till tender, chop and place in baking dish with alternate layers of bread crumbs; season with butter, pepper and salt, and nearly cover with milk; bake half an hour.

Mrs. Wm. Donker
(Grand Rapids, 1917)

"Green Onion Pie"

Wash and cut in inch pieces, using a part of the green, 4 bunches of green onions. Add water to just cover, boil for 8 minutes, drain and add 2½ or 3 cups cooked beef or pork left over, cut in small pieces. Add 1½ cup cold boiled potatoes sliced and gravy or hot water to cover, thicken slightly with flour if water is used. Season to taste.

Make biscuit dough, using: 2 cups flour, 2⅔ tsp. baking powder, ½ teaspoon salt. Sift and work in ⅓ cup shortening. Add all at once ⅔ cup sweet milk. Mix, pat about ½ inch thick on board, cut and place on onion and meat mixture. Bake in hot oven about 20 minutes. Serves 6 or 8 generously.

Mrs. John Beach
(Kalamazoo, 1935)

Spanish Onions (Fried)

Slice medium thickness, dip in egg and crumbs and fry in hot lard and butter. Add a very little water. Cover tightly that they may steam tender, and fry a rich brown.

(Niles, 1907)

With the preface, "cooking is a fine art, to which you must bring common sense and good judgment," the Ladies of Trinity Episcopal Church in Niles launched their collection of recipes, *Tried and True*, upon the market in 1907. It contains a variety of local advertisements including one by the Kompass and Stoll Co. of Niles, which enabled us to identify and date our kitchen cupboard.

Stuffed Onions

Parboil onions for one hour, remove top and scoop out insides. This part of the onions after being chopped fine is to be mixed thoroughly with an equal measure of cold cooked veal or chicken chopped fine, a quarter of teaspoonful of salt, half as much pepper, a spoonful of chopped parsley, a quarter of a cup of soft bread crumbs, a quarter of a cup of butter. Put a teaspoonful of the mixture in each hollow onion, then put in a French chestnut and three or four native chestnuts that have been boiled tender. Finish filling the onion with prepared mixture, bake slowly for an hour. Baste three or four times with butter melted in hot water. Fifteen minutes before the time for serving sprinkle with cracker crumbs and brown in oven.

(Higgins Lake, 1920)

Our eighty-one-year-old Kompass and Stoll "Hoosier cabinet" still serves as the center of our kitchen (Niles, 1907).

Stuffed Onion

Cook large white onions in boiling salted water until tender. Remove centers (beginning at stem ends) leave a wall ¼ inch thick. Chop onion removed and mix with round steak which has been ground fine, season with salt and pepper and mix thoroughly. Refill onion with mixture, sprinkle top with bread crumbs and butter. Arrange in baking dish. Add a little hot water and bake until meat is cooked.

(Hastings, 1921)

Crisp Parsley

This is used for garnishing dishes. Pick and wash young parsley, shake it in a cloth to dry it thoroughly, and spread it on a sheet of clean paper and put it in the oven. Turn the bunches frequently until they are quite crisp. Parsley is much more easily crisped than fried.

(Detroit, 1890)

To Fry Parsley

Wash the parsley and wipe dry; put in the frying-basket and plunge into boiling fat for ½ minute.

(Detroit, 1890)

Parsnips

Parsnips are not sufficiently appreciated, perhaps because of their too sweet taste; but this can be overcome to a palatable extent by judicious cookery; they are excellent when sliced, after boiling and warming in a sauce made by mixing flour, butter and milk over the fire and seasoning it with salt and pepper; as soon as warm they are served with a little chopped parsley and a squeeze of lemon juice. For parsnips fried brown in an old-fashioned iron pot with slices of salt pork and a seasoning of salt and pepper, many good words might be said.

(Detroit, 1881)

Parsnips

No. 1.—Peel, boil and mash, season with salt, pepper and butter to taste; serve hot.

No. 2.—Boil till tender, peel and cut into pieces about the size of a thumb and dip into a batter made of egg and flour salted, and fry in hot lard same as doughnuts.

No. 3.—Boil, peel and slice lengthwise in thin slices, and fry brown in butter or butter or lard; season to taste; serve hot.

E. C. L.
(Grand Rapids, 1890)

Escalloped Parsnips

Boil the parsnips tender in salted water with one medium sized red pepper. Drain off water and steam dry. Slice parsnips very fine. Put a layer of parsnips in a baking dish, dust over the layer rolled cracker crumbs and again layer of parsnips until baking dish is within 1 inch of being full. Put 1 teaspoon of brown sugar in 1 cup of sweet cream and pour over the parsnips. Bake 1 hour. Six medium sized parsnips will serve 8 to 10 people.

Mrs. Anna Walter, Marcellus
(Charlotte, 1909)

French Way of Cooking Pease, No. 2

Put some thin slices of bacon in a skillet and brown a little on both sides; then put in your pease, with 1 large onion quartered, 1 head lettuce, and a few sprigs parsley, tied up, water enough to cover them; salt and pepper (not much salt, as the bacon salts them); cook 1 hour; ten minutes before serving sprinkle a little flour to thicken the gravy; remove the bunch of lettuce and parsley.

(Detroit, 1890)

Peas in Turnip Cups

Select medium sized white turnips. Wash them thoroughly, and then hollow out the inside of each, leaving cup-shaped shells about ¼ inch thick. Cook these shells in boiling salted water until tender, but not tender enough to break into pieces, and remove from the water. Fill with hot peas, and pour a medium white sauce over them. Serve hot.

(Berrien Springs, 1941)

Scotch Pease Brose

Put 2 large tablespoons pea-meal into a bowl, add salt and a bit butter, then boiling water, making the brose stiff enough for the spoon to stand in, and serve immediately with 1 glass fresh milk.

(Detroit, 1890)

Brose is a traditional Scottish dish made by pouring boiling water or broth on various meals.

Escalloped Peanuts

One cup each of bread crumbs, chopped roasted peanuts and stewed tomatoes. Mix crumbs and nuts, season with salt, pepper and 2 tablespoons melted butter. Season tomato with butter, pepper and salt. On bottom of baking dish place layer of nut mixture, next add the tomato having the nut mixture on top. Bake in hot oven for 20 minutes.

Mrs. Grant Smith, Ludington
(Charlotte, 1909)

Green Peppers and Mushrooms

Wipe carefully and break into small pieces mushrooms; fry slightly in a tablespoonful of butter (there should be a cupful when cooked). Add half a cup of cream, three tablespoons of soft bread crumbs, half a teaspoon of salt, a dash of pepper and one beaten egg. Fill green peppers from which seeds have been removed and which have been parboiled in salted water. Place in fireproof serving dish and bake twenty minutes, basting occasionally with butter and water.

(Niles, 1907)

Potatoes

If cold ones are left they can rehabilitate themselves in favor by appearing chopped, moistened with white sauce or cream, and either fried in butter or baked quickly, with a covering of bread crumbs. Or steam-fried, that is sliced raw, put into a covered pan over the fire, with butter and seasoning, and kept covered until tender, with only enough stirring to prevent burning, they are capital. Larded, they have bits of fat ham or bacon inserted in them, and are baked tender. Note well that the more expeditiously a baked potato is cooked and eaten the better it will be.

(Detroit, 1881)

Lenda's Potatoes au Gratin

Cold boiled potatoes sliced rather thin, a quart of cream sauce, grated cheese, salt. Put in layers in baking dish, first potatoes, then cream sauce, then grated cheese, ending with cheese. Be generous with the cheese, and use a little paprika or cayenne on cheese layers. Bake 20 minutes.

M. H. P.
(Kalamazoo, 1906)

Potatoes—Baked with Bacon

Pare potatoes of uniform shape and size, and in one end make a hole large enough to slip in a piece of bacon rolled up, not larger than a lead pencil. Place in pan and put in oven, turning once or twice that the potatoes may be uniformly browned. Leave bacon in potato when served. It may be eaten or not

at choice. The bacon gives potato a delicious flavor and makes a nice change.

Mrs. W. H. Van Deman
(Kalamazoo, 1899)

This is an easy dish to prepare. Core the potatoes with an apple corer. Sausage can also be substituted for the bacon.

Baked Potatoes

One dozen medium sized potatoes, bake nicely, then cut off the top, scrape out the inside and put in a dish. Beat the whites of 6 eggs to a stiff froth, add half to the potatoes, also a cup of cream, salt and pepper. Beat up light and fill the skins, over the opening place a spoonful of the beaten whites, return to the oven until a light brown. Serve hot.

Mrs. Frank Wood
(Muskegon, 1890)

Potatoes Fried

Pare and slice the potatoes thin, cut them if you like in small fillets, about a quarter of an inch square and as long as the potato will admit; keep them in cold water till wanted, then drop them into boiling lard; when nearly done take them out with a skimmer and drain them, boil up the lard again, drop the potatoes back and fry till done; this operation causes the fillets to swell up and puff out; sprinkle with salt and serve very hot.

Mrs. J. Morgan Smith
(Grand Rapids, 1890)

Potato Loaves

These are very nice when eaten with roast beef, and are made of mashed potatoes prepared without milk, by mixing them with a quantity of very finely minced raw onions, powdered with pepper and salt; then beating up the whole with a little butter to bind it, and dividing it into small loaves of a conical form, and placing them under the meat to brown; that is, when it is so nearly done as to impart some of the gravy along with the fat.

(Detroit, 1881)

Long Branch Milk Potatoes

Take good, sound potatoes, cut them in slices (raw), and put the milk, according to the quantity you wish to make, in a pudding dish; then, after you have put the potatoes in the milk, put it in the oven for about twenty minutes; then take out and put potatoes, with the same milk, into a saucepan to boil until done. Season before putting them to boil.

(Detroit, 1881)

Potato Pie

Butter a shallow pie-dish rather thickly; line the edges with a good crust, and then fill the pie with mashed potatoes, seasoned with pepper, salt, and grated nutmeg, lay over them some marrow, together with small lumps of butter, hard-boiled eggs, blanched almonds, sliced dates, sliced lemon, and candied peel, cover the dish with pas-

A demure Victorian cook carries a pan of potatoes to her Majestic range equipped with a hot water heater (St. Louis, 1905).

try, and bake the pie in a well-heated oven for ½ hour or more, according to the size of the pie.

(Detroit, 1890)

Potato Puff

To each two cups of mashed potatoes add one tablespoonful of melted butter and beat to a cream; put with this two eggs whipped light, and a cup of milk, salting to taste. Beat all well; pour into a greased baking-dish and bake quickly to a light brown. Serve in the dish in which it was cooked.

(Detroit, 1881)

Don't worry if the mixture seems too milky, it will firm up while baking at 375° for 20 minutes, or until a golden brown.

Potato Roses

Pare carefully with a thin penknife some peeled potatoes round and round until all of each potato is pared to the center. Do not try to cut the slice too thin or they will break. Place in a wire basket and dip in boiling lard. They are a handsome garnish.

(Detroit, 1881)

Potato Sandwich

Form mashed potatoes into patties the thickness of ordinary crackers. Put into an oiled baking dish and bake until the under crust is nice and brown. While the patties are in the oven, put one cup of cream into a small pan; salt slightly, and when at the boiling point add two hard-boiled egg yolks, minced fine; then moisten a level teaspoonful of corn starch in cold water and stir rapidly into the cream. Remove the patties from the oven; place on a heated platter, alternately covering with the potato patties with the cream sauce, putting the brown side up. Garnish with parsley or lettuce leaves and serve while hot.

(Battle Creek, 1910)

119

Saratoga Chips

Peel good sized potatoes, slice them as evenly as possible, drop them into iced, or very cold water. Have a kettle of hot lard. Put a few at a time into a towel to dry the moisture out of them. Then drop into the hot lard. Stir occasionally; when light brown skim out; they will be crisp and not greasy. Sprinkle salt over while hot.

Mrs. L. J. Hale
(Kalamazoo, 1906)

Saratoga chips, originated at the fashionable New York resort, is the original name for potato chips.

Spaghetti—Italian Style

Take 3 moderately fat pork chops from the loin, fry slowly until very brown, add 1 can tomatoes, 1 medium onion, sliced, ½ clove of garlic; cover and simmer slowly until meat is in bits; put through a coarse sieve forcing meat through also. This will take from 3 to 4 hours to cook. For the spaghetti, have on the stove a kettle containing 4 qts. rapidly boiling water, slightly salted; break the spaghetti in 1½ inch pieces and drop in slowly so as not to stop the boiling; boil at a galloping rate until tender, from 20 to 35 minutes, according to brand and age; pour into a sieve and pour on abundance of cold water to prevent it sticking together; season the tomato mixture to taste with salt and pepper, add spaghetti; when very hot, turn into serving dish and sprinkle with grated parmesan cheese, or put in ramekins; sprinkle with cheese and brown in oven.

Mrs. Wm. E. Hill
(Kalamazoo, 1906)

Our Husband's Spaghetti

One-quarter pound bacon; 1 package spaghetti, about 7 to 9 ounce package; 2 good sized onions; 1 teacup grated cheese; 1 can, large can or

quart sealer tomatoes; ¼ can pimiento; ½ cup tomato catsup; ¼ cup chili sauce.

Cut bacon in fine strips like the teeth of a comb, put in frying pan, add onions, chopped fine. Cook to a nice brown, put package spaghetti in salted water, boil 15 minutes, then put in colander and run cold water over it. Place spaghetti in baking dish, add onions and bacon, mix thoroughly, add tomatoes, the fine chopped pimiento and ½ of the cheese, salt and pepper and a sprinkling of cayenne. Add the catsup and chili sauce. Mix thoroughly. If too dry add a can about a pint of tomato soup. Sprinkle the rest of the cheese over the top and bake for 1 to 2 hours. Fresh or canned mushrooms may be added to the above.

Frank Halsted
(Marine City, 1923)

Surprise Balls

Roll cold mashed potatoes into balls, and with a teaspoon press a hollow in the top. Chop fine some cold lean meat, season it with salt, pepper and gravy, and put 1 teaspoon of the meat into the hollow of the potato ball. Put a little milk or melted butter on top and brown in oven.

(Muskegon, 1912)

The ladies of the Social Department of the Muskegon Woman's Club included this recipe in their 1912 compilation. Don't add too much milk to the mashed potatoes, and make sure they have set in the refrigerator overnight. Otherwise you will have to arrange your surprise balls in cupcake tins as we did when we tried this recipe. We filled half of our two dozen surprise balls with 1½ cups canned corned beef spiced with one 1 teaspoon dill weed and ½ teaspoon celery seed and the other with canned peas. Bake for 45 minutes at 350°. If you use cupcake tins, oil them. Try inventing your own surprises.

Surprises

Boil one dozen potatoes; mash and add the beaten yolks of two eggs; pepper and salt to taste, and one tablespoon of butter. Drain off the liquor from a small teacup of canned peas. Form the potato into balls with a teaspoon of peas in the center. Dip it into beaten egg, then cracker crumbs. Fry in very hot lard.

(Saginaw, 1905)

Sweet Potatoes

Select those of uniform size; parboil them with the skins on; peel and lay in baking-pan. Bake until soft to the grasp, glazing with butter just before you take them up.

(Detroit, 1881)

Sweet Potato Balls

Cook sweet potatoes until done. Mash, and season with salt and pepper and butter. Form into balls. Hide one marshmallow inside each ball. Roll each potato ball in Post Toasties; brown in moderate oven, not over 15 minutes as too long heating melts the marshmallows.

Mrs. H. A. Fick
(Grayling, 1937)

There is an interesting story connected with the origins of Post Toasties, the popular cereal produced at Battle Creek's General Foods plant. Charles W. Post had become a millionaire through his successful marketing of Postum and Grape Nuts. In 1906 he launched his third product, Elijah's Manna. It was a thick corn flake packaged in a green and white container depicting a biblical prophet. Across the country, ministers thundered from the pulpit against sacrilegious advertising. Post, who had grown up in the Midwest Bible Belt, should have known better. The "grandfather of modern advertising" remedied his miscalculation in 1908 by marketing the same product under a label showing a young lady and her cat seated before a fireplace. Post's cereal, renamed Post Toasties, made an immediate hit with the public.

Sweet Potato Pumpkins

Boil 6 or 8 sweet potatoes until tender. Mash until no lumps remain. Season with salt, pepper and little nutmeg. Add enough cream to moisten. Add 2 tbsp. butter. Beat well. Shape mixture into small pumpkins and glaze by basting with butter and brown sugar melted in frying pan. Place in oven to brown. Add stems of green pepper. A cup of chopped nuts mixed with potato, adds to flavor. Also score down sides of the balls to look more like pumpkins.

Mrs. F. E. Leach
(Kalamazoo, 1941)

Sweet Potato Puffs

2 cups cold mashed sweet potatoes	2 tbsp. butter, melted
	Marshmallows
1 egg yolk	2 cups flaked cereal
½ tsp. salt	4 tbsp. butter, melted

Combine egg yolk, salt and two tablespoons butter, melted, with sweet potatoes. Divide into six portions. Flatten each portion, then place a marshmallow in center of each. Pull potato up around marsh-

Ella Kellogg of Battle Creek urged cooks to use the vegetable press as a universal utensil, ideal for mashing potatoes and other vegetables, straining sauces, gruel, and gravy, and pressing fruit (Battle Creek, 1910).

mallow leaving small opening in top. Crush flaked cereal very finely, and combine with four tablespoons melted butter. Roll sweet potato balls in buttered cereal flakes, then place on a buttered cookie sheet. Bake in hot oven, 10 to 15 minutes. Arrange on platter. Serve at once. Serves six. Marshmallows may be omitted.

Mrs. H. D. Cox
(Kalamazoo, 1941)

Dried Pumpkin

Pumpkin may be dried and kept for future use. The best way is first to cut and stew the pumpkin, then spread on plates, and dry quickly in the oven. Dried in this manner, it is easily softened, when needed, by soaking in a small quantity of water, and is considered nearly as good as that freshly stewed.

(Battle Creek, 1910)

Radishes

Prof. Blot says cut off the root and all the leaves, *but the center one,* or stalk. This should always be left on and eaten, as it contains an element which assists in the digestion of the radish. Split the radish up into stems, and leave whole at the top; serve in fresh ice water.

(Detroit, 1878)

Professor Pierre Blot, author of *What to Eat, and How to Cook It* (New York, 1863) and *Hand Book of Practical Cookery* (New York, 1867) was widely quoted in late nineteenth-century Michigan cookbooks.

Rice a la Chinaman

Mucha washee in cold water, clean of flour which make him sticky; have water boil ready, very fast, little salty; throw him in, rice can't burn, water shake him too much; boil quarter hour or little more; rub one rice 'tween thumb and finger; if all

rub away, rice done; put rice in pan with holes; hot water all run away; put rice back in saucepan, put little cup cold water on him, keep him covered awhile by the fire, then rice all ready, eat him up.

(Detroit, 1881)

Rice a la Creole

Put butter size of a pigeon's egg into a stewpan, and when hot mix in a small onion, minced, and cook until it assumes a pale-yellow color; put in the rice, uncooked; stir it over the fire until it has a yellow color also; then add a pint of stock. Boil slowly until the rice is tender, about half an hour. When about to serve, add one ounce of grated cheese, stirring for a few moments without letting it boil.

(Detroit, 1881)

Maryland Sauce for Rice

2 tablespoons butter	4 tablespoons brown sugar

Cream together and add yolks of two eggs, together with ½ cup milk or water and vanilla. Cook all together in double boiler until thick. Serve with boiled rice.

Mrs. Clayton W. Lawson
(Grand Rapids, 1917)

Baked Nut Rice
(A favorite recipe of Mrs. E. G. White)

2 cups cooked brown rice	2 dessert spoons finely chopped onion
1 cup peanut butter (consistency of thin cream)	1 teaspoon sage
	Salt to taste

The mixture should be quite thin. Bake in quick oven 20 to 30 minutes. This also makes a good filling for baked green peppers.

(Berrien Springs, 1941)

Mrs. Ellen G. White and her husband, James White, founded the Seventh Day Adventist Church. The story began when a New York State farmer, William Miller, predicted the exact day for the end of the world. In 1843, thousands of Millerites donned ascension robes, climbed hill tops, and awaited the Millennium. Following this "great disappointment," the Whites and other Millerite remnants continued to proselytize their distinctive beliefs. Sister White periodically went into trances where she received divine visions concerning church dogma. The Adventists relocated their printing house to Battle Creek in 1855, which subsequently became the church headquarters until 1902. In the early 1860s Sister White experienced a series of visions that decreed her followers be vegetarian. They continue as such to this day.

Spanish Rice

⅓ cup raw rice	2 T chopped green
1 cup hot water	pepper
2 cups tomatoes	2 T fat
1 cup grated cheese	Dash of paprika; salt
3 T chopped onion	to taste

Place mixture in a greased baking dish and bake one hour in a moderate oven.

Miss Bertha Pitsch, Byron Center
(Allegan, 1938)

Rutabagas

Pare and slice them, put into the chopping bowl, and chop into small pieces; stew in water until tender, let the water all dry out, then turn in cream or milk, and season to taste with salt, pepper, and butter. Let it boil up, and serve hot. They are also good mashed like potatoes, using no milk.

(Battle Creek, 1890)

Salsify or Vegetable Oysters

Wash thoroughly, scrape off skin with a knife, cut across in rather thin slices, stew until tender in water enough to cover them, with a piece of salt codfish for seasoning. Before sending to table, remove codfish, thicken with flour and butter rubbed together, toast slices of bread, put in dish, and then add the vegetable oyster. This method gives the flavor of oysters to the vegetable, and adds much to its delicacy. Or, after stewing until tender in clear water, mash, season with pepper and salt, and serve.

Mrs. Gov. J. J. Bagley, Michigan
(Minneapolis, 1881)

Recipes using the root of salsify or oyster plant, as it was called, are common in early Michigan cookbooks.

Frances Bagley contributed this distinctive recipe to the *Buckeye Cook Book* in 1881. Her husband, John Judson Bagley, born in 1832, grew up in Constantine and later made a fortune as a Detroit tobacco manufacturer. He served as Republican governor of Michigan from 1873–1877.

Salsify

In March and April salsify, or oyster plant, is a pleasant change from boiled turnips and cabbage, and can be prepared in various ways.

First way: Grate a bunch or two of salsify as you would horse-radish, add a raw egg beaten, and a little bread crumbs or flour, and fry in a frying-pan, as you would oysters. Parsnips prepared in this way, are extremely nice.

Second way: Cut your salsify into round lozenges, parboil; throw it into a frying-pan with a little butter, and heat through, but do not fry brown; turn over this enough soup stock, or the boilings from steak or other bone, to cover it; thicken with a little flour and butter braided together, add pepper and salt, and you have a nice dish.

(Detroit, 1878)

Fried Salsify

Stew the salsify as usual till very tender; then with the back of a spoon or a potato jammer mash it very fine. Beat up an egg, add a teacup of milk, a little flour, butter and seasoning of pepper and salt.

Make into little cakes, and fry to a light brown in boiling lard, first rolling in beaten eggs and then flour.

(Vermontville, 1906)

Potato "jammers" in use at this time were made of wood and shaped like a pestle.

Squash Soufflé

2 summer squash
2 eggs
2 rounded tbsp. flour
½ cup sugar

Salt and pepper to taste
Dash of nutmeg
1 cup rich milk

Pare squash and cut in small pieces. When boiled until tender, drain and mash with a piece of butter size of a large walnut. Add sugar, salt, pepper and nutmeg. Then add beaten yolks of eggs. Mix well and add flour and milk until smooth. Last, add beaten whites and pour in a well buttered casserole. Bake slowly about 45 minutes in a moderate oven.

(Kalamazoo, 1941)

Fried Tomatoes

Take ripe tomatoes sliced rather thick, dredge well with flour and fry on hot griddle well greased with lard and butter, add salt and pepper.

Mrs. E. A. Honey
(Kalamazoo, 1899)

This delicious dish is especially good using the small pulpy Italian tomatoes. We seasoned the flour with sweet basil, salt, and pepper. Make certain the butter is smoking hot.

Green Tomato Pie

Line a tin with puff paste and thinly sliced tomatoes, good handful of sugar, a little citric acid,

and sprinkle well with flour; cover with top crust and bake in a hot oven.

(Detroit, 1881)

Tomato Pudding

Fill an earthen pudding dish with alternate layers of stale bread and fresh tomatoes, peeled, sliced, and sprinkled lightly with sugar. Cover the dish and bake.

(Battle Creek, 1910)

Stuffed Tomatoes

Choose 12 large, round tomatoes; cut them off smooth at the stem end; take out the seeds and pulp; take 1 pound lean steak and 2 slices bacon; chop them fine, with the inside of the tomatoes; season with a finely-chopped onion, fried, 1 dessertspoon salt, ½ teaspoon white pepper, as much cayenne pepper as you can take on the end of a knife, and 1 tablespoon finely-chopped parsley; add 4 rolled crackers, and if too stiff, thin with stock, water or cold gravy; fill the tomatoes with this forcemeat, packing tight; sift cracker-crumbs over the top, and bake for 1 hour in moderate oven.

(Detroit, 1890)

Vegetable Pie—Potato Crust

Three tomatoes, 4 tbsp. fat, 1 large onion, 1 large carrot, 1 or 2 stalks celery, 1 can of peas, 3 tbsp. bread crumbs, 3 tsp. parsley, 1 c. gravy, ½ lb. boiled macaroni or rice. Melt fat in saucepan, mince onion, carrot, celery and cook in fat for 5 m. Add tomatoes, peas, parsley, macaroni and bread crumbs. Turn mixture into baking dish; cover with mashed potatoes, and bake about 30 m. in a hot oven.

Mabel Wedell
(Kalamazoo, 1921)

Vegetable Chop Suey

1 cup cooked beets　　*1 cup cooked string*
1 cup cooked turnips　　*beans*
1 cup cooked carrots　　*1 cup chopped onion*
　　　　　　　　　　　Salt, pepper

Two tablespoons vinegar, 1 tablespoon kitchen bouquet, 2 tablespoons butter, 1 cupful meat stock, 2 tablespoons flour, ¼ teaspoon mustard, 1 teaspoon sugar. Mix dry ingredients, add to melted butter. Blend and add liquid gradually. Cook until thick. Pour this hot mixture over first five ingredients and heat thoroughly.

(Grand Rapids, 1924)

Vegetarian Tamale in Stew-Pan

12 ears corn (1 can　　*1 teaspoon salt*
corn may be used)　　*1 onion*
4 cups water　　　　　*1 teaspoon vegetable*
1 can tomatoes　　　　*butter*

Grate the corn, and wet the cobs with the indicated water in order to take off all the juice. Combine with the liquid, and pass it through a sieve. Add the other ingredients, season with salt, and put all in the oven. Stir it well before serving.

(Berrien Springs, 1941)

Walnut or Peanut Butter Roast

2 cups of rolled walnut meats or peanut butter; 2 cups of bread crumbs; 1 cup milk; 2 eggs and a little salt, pepper and sage. Mix all together, mold in loaf shape. Place in a buttered baking pan, bake about twenty minutes. Garnish with celery, serve with the following sauce. 2 cups water; 1 of rolled walnuts or peanut butter, boil five minutes then add salt, blend in 1 tablespoonful of browned, flour and 1 of white stirred with a little water, put together and cook a few minutes.

Ida Snyder
(Homer, 1925)

French Batter for Frying Vegetables

Moisten a little flour with water, and add to it a small quantity of salt, 1 tablespoon olive oil, and 1½ spoons French brandy; beat up the mixture thoroughly, and, when you are ready to use it, beat into it the white of 1 egg previously beaten to a strong froth. This batter may be used for frying sweet *entremets*, in which case sugar must be used instead of salt.

(Detroit, 1890)

Meat

Electric refrigerators and freezers now found in virtually every U.S. kitchen have revolutionized many of our eating habits. The first General Electric "monitor top" refrigerators, with the motor and cooling grids on top, became available at a reasonable price in the late 1920s. Manufactured before the days of planned obsolescence, they were built to last generations. Our refrigerator, manufactured around 1932, still operates faithfully and has never needed repair. Prior to the advent of electric refrigeration, heavy wooden ice boxes with compartments for block ice and a drip pan offered some degree of cooling ability. Urban homemakers anxiously awaited the iceman to cometh with his horse-drawn ice wagon in summer months, as did children who were sometimes rewarded with slivers of ice picked from the huge cakes. In rural areas, some homemakers had their own icehouses, filled with lake ice harvested in the winter and packed between layers of sawdust, or they made do with a cool spring house. Needless to say, fresh meat could not be kept long in hot weather. Daily trips to the butcher were a necessity for most cooks.

General Remarks

Meat, to be in perfection, should be kept a number of days, when the weather will admit of it. Beef and mutton should be kept at least a week in cold weather and poultry three or four days. In the summer meat should be kept in a cool, airy place, away from the flies, and if there is any danger of its spoiling, a little salt should be rubbed over it. Or it may be kept sweet, even in very warm weather, by covering it lightly with bran and hanging it in a draught in a shady, cool room. Meat can also be preserved by washing the meat, drying it and laying in strong vinegar, or by being boiled in the vinegar, leaving it in until cold, and then setting aside in a cool cellar.

To thaw frozen meat, place it for a few hours in cold water, the ice which forms on the surface as it thaws being easily removed. If cooked before entirely thawed, it will be tough. Meat once frozen should not be allowed to thaw until just before cooking.

Boiling fresh meat is a science, for if not properly boiled it is tough and tasteless. To make fresh meat nutritious and to confine its rich juices, place it in a kettle of boiling water—pure soft water is best—placing it where it will slowly but constantly boil. Skim it well the first time it boils up, and keep the meat constantly turned and under the water, adding fresh hot water as it evaporates in boiling. Do not let the meat remain long in the water after it is done, as it injures it, and add salt when the meat is nearly done, as it extracts the juices of the meat if added too soon.

Salt meat should be put on in cold water so that it may freshen in cooking. Allow twenty-five minutes for the fresh and thirty-five for the salt meat; the time for boiling to be modified by the quality and quantity of the meat. A pod of red pepper in the water will prevent the unpleasant odor of boiling from filling the house.

The liquor in which any kind of meat is boiled makes a good soup when thickened and seasoned.

Baking meats is a very cheap and convenient way of dressing a dinner for a small family. Legs and loins of pork, legs of mutton, fillets of veal, and

126

Ice taken from the Detroit River was more appealing in 1881 than it would be in today's polluted environment (Polk, 1881).

many other joints will bake to great advantage, if the meat be good or rather fat; but if poor no baking will give satisfaction. Have the fire bright and the oven hot, wipe the meat dry with a towel, then, if not thoroughly clean, dash over cold water and quickly wipe dry. Have the pan hot when you put the meat in. If it is beef, put it in the hot pan and let it stand a half moment and then turn it over, thus searing both sides and preventing the juices from running so quickly. Do not put the salt and pepper on the meat, but put it in the pan with the water and then baste the meat every three or four minutes. You will find the meat will be thoroughly seasoned and will be much more juicy and tender, than by the old way of rubbing the salt on the meat; putting the salt direct on the meat draws the juice out and toughens it. The time for baking meat depends upon the state of the oven and kind of meat baked. Fifteen minutes to the pound and fifteen minutes longer is the rule for beef and mutton, and twenty minutes to the pound and twenty minutes longer for pork, lamb and veal, or a little less if wanted very rare. When done the roast should be a rich brown, and when cut the bright red juices should follow the knife of the carver; if purple, then it is raw, and unfit for food.

Broiling is the favorite method of cooking steaks and chops and is most acceptable for beef and mutton. Cleanliness in this mode of cooking is very essential. Keep the gridiron clean between the bars, and bright on the top; when it is hot wipe it well with a cloth just before you use it. It is best to oil the gridiron with suet, and, also, to heat it before putting the meat on. Chalk is sometimes rubbed on the gridiron, when fish is to be broiled. It is better to have a gridiron expressly for fish, otherwise, meat is often made to taste fishy.

Tough steak is made more tender by pounding or hacking with a dull knife, but a tender steak should never be cut, else the rich juices will be lost. Never salt or pepper steak before or while broiling, but if very lean, dip in melted butter. Steak should be placed over a hot, clear fire and turned often so that the inside may be seared at once to retain the juices. When done, which will require from five to ten minutes, according to thickness of steak, season with salt and pepper, and bits of butter; cover with a hot platter and serve at once. Use the best of butter for steak, and handle it with a small pair of broiling tongues, as a fork frees the juices. If fat drops on the coals below and there is danger of the meat tasting smoky, sprinkle a little salt on the coals and withdraw the gridiron for a moment. Have the meal all ready before broiling the steak and be diligently attentive to watch the moment anything is done. Never hasten the broiling of anything, lest you spoil it. Broiled meats must be brought to the table as hot as possible.

Frying is a very convenient mode of cookery. To make sure that the pan is quite clean, rub a little fat over it, and then make it warm, and wipe it out with a clean cloth. It is best to fry in lard not salted, and this is better than butter. Mutton and beef suet are good for frying. The real secret in frying is to know when the fat is of a proper heat—according to what you wish to fry. When the lard seems hot, try it by throwing in a bit of bread. To fry fish, the fire must be very clear, and the fat very hot. When taking up fried articles, drain off the fat on a wire sieve.

To roast meats or game before the fire, the first preparation is to have the spit properly cleansed. It is well, if possible, to wash them before they get

The first General Electric "monitor top" refrigerator began to revolutionize American kitchens in the 1920s (General Electric, 1927).

cold. When your meat is thin and tender, have a small, brisk fire. When you have a large joint to roast, make up a sound, strong fire, equally good in all parts. Set the meat, at first, some distance from the place where it is to roast, so as to have it heat through gradually, and then move it up to roast. Allow about fifteen minutes to the pound of most all kinds of meat in warm weather, but in winter twenty minutes. When the meat is nearly done, stir up the fire to brown it. The meat should be basted a good deal, especially the first part of the time. A pale brown is the proper color for a roast. When the meat is nearly done, the steam from it will be drawn towards the fire.

Parsley is the universal garnish for all kinds of cold meats, poultry, fish, etc. Horse-radish is a garnish for roast beef, and slices of lemon for roast veal and calf's head. Carrots in slices, for boiled beef, hot or cold. Red beet root sliced, for cold meat and boiled beef. Mint either with or without parsley for roast lamb, either hot or cold. Pickled gherkins, capers or boiled onions, for boiled meats and stews.

(Detroit, 1881)

It is interesting that in the above direction for broiling steak, there was a great concern that the meat not taste smoky, which we go to great lengths to achieve today.

BEEF

Roast Beef

Wash the joint and wipe it dry; then place it on a pan, with the fat and skin side up; put into a hot oven, and when the heat has started enough of the oil of the fat to baste with, open the oven, and drawing the pan toward you, take up a spoonful of the grease and pour over the meat for a few times, closing the door immediately; this should be repeated four or five times during the process of roasting. When nearly done sprinkle with salt, and baste. Have ready a warm platter, and when the meat is dished drain off the grease, carefully keeping back the rich, brown juice which has exuded from the meat.

This remaining gravy leave in the pan, placing it on the stove and adding about a gill of water, or soup stock, let it come to a boil and then pour it over the meat. If a made gravy is preferred, more water should be added and a little flour. Salt hardens and toughens meat, therefore in beef and mutton it should not be put on till it is cooked. It is also necessary to have the oven hot in order that the heat may quickly sear the surface, which will prevent the juice from escaping. It is obvious, if water is put in the pan, this quick searing cannot be effected; water cannot be raised above a certain temperature (its boiling point), while fat is susceptible of a much greater degree of heat, and, therefore, as a basting agent is preferable. Beef roasted before a fire has a flavor inexpressibly finer than that done in an oven.

(Detroit, 1878)

Beef a la Mode

Take the bone out of a small round of beef, cut some salt pork in strips, about the size of your two fingers, and the thickness of the beef; dip them in vinegar and roll them in the following seasoning: One grated nutmeg, one tablespoonful black pepper, one of ground cloves, one of allspice and two of salt; add parsley, thyme, sweet marjoram and summer savory; then cut openings about four inches apart all through the beef and insert them. Make a rich stuffing with bread crumb, etc., lay it over the top. Put the whole into a covered pan, pour over it half a pint of vinegar and let it stand in the oven for five hours. The addition of vegetables, one large onion, four carrots and two turnips, chopped fine, is a great improvement. Half an hour before serving skim off the fat, take up the round and vegetables, and add a little browned flour to the gravy; this is as delightful a dish as a turkey when it is no longer in season.

(Detroit, 1878)

We tried this using a three-pound round steak, cut thick. We used ½ teaspoon powdered (instead of grated) nutmeg, also ½ teaspoon each of parsley, thyme, sweet marjoram, and summer savory. One other small detail: unless you want your guests to be so puckered up they won't be able to talk, use 2 ounces of vinegar instead of the 8 ounces called for.

Boiled Beef with Parsley Sauce

Boil four pounds of beef with four cloves, one inch stick cinnamon, one-half teaspoon summer savory, two teaspoonfuls of salt, in two quarts of water till tender. Strain the liquor and thicken with two tablespoonfuls flour mixed in one-half cup of cold water; add one-quarter teaspoonful of pepper, one tablespoonful of minced parsley; pour over the beef on platter and serve.

Mrs. R. W. Boyd, Adrian
(Chicago, 1896)

This is an easy to prepare recipe that you can put on the stove and pay little attention to. We tried it with a beef roast. Bring the water and spices to a boil, add the beef roast, then turn the burner down so that it simmers for two hours. We used corn-starch instead of flour and added one beef bouillon cube to the sauce. Red wine could be substituted for the cold water mixed with flour.

Boiled Dinner

Put meat on, after washing well, in enough boil-ing water to just cover the meat; as soon as it boils, set kettle on the stove where it will boil very slowly; boil until almost tender then put in the vegetables, first skimming the meat well. Put in the cabbage first cut into quarters, turnips of medium size cut in halves, and potatoes. Parsnips and carrots may be added, or rutabagas in place of the turnips. Boil all together until thoroughly done, adding a little salt before taking from the kettle, in which there should be only just enough water to keep the meat from burning; take up vegetables in separate dishes and lastly the meat. A soup plate or saucer turned up-side down, is useful to place in bottom of kettle to keep meat from burning.

(Detroit, 1881)

Boiled Dinner

Put the corned beef in a large kettle of cold water early in the morning; boil and if it is very salty change the water; if intended for a twelve o'clock dinner, put in at ten o'clock a piece of salt pork, one or two pounds; at the same time wash beets very carefully and put them in; at eleven o'clock peel and cut into three or four pieces some turnips; divide a cabbage in four parts lengthwise; boil one-half hour and then put in some good sized peeled pota-toes. Beets will not injure the other vegetables if the skin is not broken or roots cut off; it is generally best to boil them separately. When they are done, take them up, peel them; take up the cabbage, drain it well and put in a vegetable dish. Serve the rest in separate dishes as there is hardly any platter large enough to hold all. Serve with horse-radish or some kind of bottled sauce.

E. C. L.
(Grand Rapids, 1890)

Hannah Barlow's Boiled Dinner

Select 8 lb. piece of corned beef with some fat on. Cover with cold water, changing water if too salty, skim carefully. Put meat over early, say 8 o'clock.

Our grandmothers always made a boiled Indian pudding.

Rule. Stir Indian meal into 1 qt. boiling milk making batter as thick as will pour. Add 2 well beaten eggs, 1 cup seeded raisins. Fill pudding bag three-quarters full, hang bag up and let swell for an hour. Put pudding in with meat for 3 hours, boil, turning several times. Prepare carefully cabbage, turnips, beets, carrots, pears, potatoes and any other vegetables you may fancy. Boil cabbage and turnips together with some of the liquor from meat pot to flavor. This will render meat fit to eat when cold. Boil beets and carrots by themselves. These vegetables usually require more than an hour's cooking; at the same time throw into the meat pot solid, just ripe pears, one to a person, ½ hour later the peeled potatoes. Meat, potatoes, pears and pudding all in one pot, with plenty of water. Always replenish the pot with boiling water.

The taking up and serving of a boiled dinner is the relish of the whole thing. Have vegetable dishes and large platter hot. Drain cabbage in colander, drain liquor from meat and place in center of plat-ter. Arrange around it well drained potatoes, pears, turnips. Cut beets and carrots in thin slices, pour over them hot vinegar seasoned with a little butter, sugar, salt and pepper. Drop the pudding quickly into cold water and turn on platter. Serve with rich cream and sugar or maple syrup.

(Hastings, 1921)

A pudding bag is a sack of tightly woven cloth in which a pudding is boiled. Puddings were originally boiled in a bag or cloth, but now more often steamed or baked.

Breaded Corned Beef

Chill canned corned beef, so that it will slice easily. Slice about ⅜ inch thick. Spread each side of each slice with prepared mustard. Dip in beaten egg, then in fine bread crumbs. Let stand 20 min. or longer to dry so that breading will stay on. This may be prepared several hours before serving time. Just before serving time, fry in deep fat until brown, drain and serve.

Mrs. H. D. Cox
(Kalamazoo, 1921)

Broiled Steak

If you have a tenderloin steak remove the tenderloin to broil by itself. Take the rest of the steak and trim off the gristle and bone, but leave a good deal of the fat. Chop rather fine. Form into pieces the shape and thickness of beefsteak, lay on a platter and press for a short time by setting another dish on top of them. Put on the gridiron and broil as other steak, lay on a platter when done, seasoning after cooking, not before, with salt, pepper and butter. Steak cooked in this way is always tender, always juicy, and in all ways very nice.

Mrs. Capt. Rossman
(Traverse City, 1900)

French Method of Broiling Steak

Have the steak about three-quarters of an inch thick; sprinkle lightly with pepper, dip it in olive oil and broil over a clear fire, turn it every two or three minutes until done to suit. Sprinkle with salt and

finely minced parsley and butter mixed together. Garnish with fried potatoes.

(Detroit, 1881)

German Way of Frying Beefsteak

Pound the cut steak a little, salt it and fry quickly with hot lard on both sides. Pour off the lard and place the steak on the dish. Put into the pan some fresh butter and fry in it some finely cut onions; pour this over the steak.

(Detroit, 1881)

Bubble and Squeak

Boil chop and fry, with a little butter, pepper and salt, some cabbage and lay on it slices of fried beef, lightly fried.

(Detroit, 1881)

Canned Beef

Have cans and covers sterilized. Cut beef in small pieces and pack as many in a quart can as will fit in nicely, put in a rounding teaspoonful of salt. Put on covers but not rubbers. Set in steam cooker and steam 3 hours longer if meat is tough. When done take out one can at a time, remove cover and put on a new rubber and seal as quickly as possible. The juice should nearly cover the meat but do not put in any water. Spare ribs, tenderloin and sausage may be canned in this way and keep nicely for summer use.

Laura Martin, Horseshoe Grange
(Cass County, 1917)

The Cass County Pomona Grange No. 20 headquartered in Cassopolis compiled a yearbook in 1917 that contained many recipes contributed by the area's rural homemakers. The Order of Patrons of Husbandry, a secret society formed to further the cause of farmers, was an important institution in Michigan. Membership was open to both men and women and meetings, held at the Grange Halls that once dotted the Michigan countryside, offered one of the few social activities for rural families during the late nineteenth century.

Chop Suey

Slice 6 medium sized onions, 1 c. diced celery, fry in butter; butter about size of an egg. When tender add 1 lb. of ground steak, well cooked; 1 pt. of hot water. Cook 1 c. of dry rice and add cooked rice to the other ingredients. Put in oven and bake 20 m. Season with salt and pepper.

Mrs. Geo. McElroy
(Kalamazoo, 1921)

It seems that everyone had their version of chop suey, except the Chinese, since it, like chile con carne, is a U.S. creation.

Daube

Take a round of beef, wipe it thoroughly with a clean, dry cloth. If possible do not wash it. Then have holes made in the meat and stuff with strips of fresh pork, or if not available, strips of fat bacon, a very tiny piece of garlic in each hole is an improvement. Many persons merely rub a little garlic in the hole. Rub a little salt and pepper on the meat, pour a cup of vinegar over and in cool weather let it stand in porcelain kettle or earthenware dish over night. The next day dredge with a little flour and fry on both sides till a very light brown in hot lard, then add a pint of hot water, two large onions stuffed with cloves, a little allspice, a little celery and carrots and a little catsup if desired. Cover the daube pot closely and let simmer slowly on back of stove for several hours, the time being dependent on amount of beef. The daube must be cooked very done. Just before taking up add a seasoning of wine or whiskey. Let cook a few minutes and remove from sauce. Have ready a meat jelly made from knuckles of veal cooked in water and seasoned with a little salt. Pour this over the daube when it is cooling until the bottom of the mold is filled. Preserve the rest of the jelly and pour in mold when the other has congealed. The reserved jelly

must be warmed again in order to pour. Fill the mold and place in ice box. It should all be congealed when ready to serve. When ready to serve remove from mold and garnish with slices of lemon or anything desired. (Gelatine can be used in place of veal knuckles; use two pkgs.)

(Higgins Lake, 1920)

The word daube comes from the French word daudi'ere, a covered casserole, hence daube pot.

Devils

These are made of rare cold beef, or of poultry legs; make a sauce of mustard, oil, Worcester sauce, pepper and salt; dip the meat or fowl into it piece by piece, and grill over a clear fire. Rib bones of cold roast beef are excellent in this way, and so, although not admissable in talking of meat cookery, are mackerel bones. Some cooks make devils by dipping the meat in curry sauce and grilling it, but the way first indicated is the best.

(Detroit, 1890)

Beef Steak Pie

One and one-half lbs. round steak, cut in small pieces; cook till done; 2 c. flour, 1 c. cold mashed potatoes, 2 tsp. baking powder, 1 of salt, use milk to make like biscuit dough, put meat and broth in a pan, place dough on top and bake.

Nellie Buoy
(Kalamazoo, 1921)

When we tried this it resulted in an unedible paste-like concoction. Perhaps ½ cup flour instead of 2 cups of flour would yield a more palatable result.

A Farmer's Dish

Peel and slice thin potatoes and onions (five potatoes to one small onion); take half a pound of sweet salt pork (in thin slices) to a pound of beef, mutton or veal; cut the meat in small pieces; take some nice bread dough and shorten a little; line the bottom of the stew-pan with slices of pork, then a layer of meat, potatoes and onions, dust over a little pepper and cover with a layer of crust; repeat this until the stewpot is full. The size of the pot will depend on the number in the family. Pour in sufficient water to cover, and finish with crust. Let it simmer until meat, vegetables, etc., are done, but do not let it boil hard. Serve hot.

(Detroit, 1881)

Beefsteak Fried

It is said that steak should never be fried, but it is not always convenient to broil it. The following always tastes well: Cut up the fat and suet cut off from steak, put in the pan and try out the fat, when smoking hot put in the steak, when browned on one side turn over and sprinkle with salt and pepper. Cook until about ⅔ done, put on a hot platter; put a very little hot water in the pan, salt a little, stir, and pour round the steak.

E. C. L.
(Grand Rapids, 1890)

This is an excellent way to prepare round steak. We always use a cast-iron skillet.

Dog in a Blanket

Four pounds nice round steak cut rather thick, cut in two and put one-half on your pan for baking with plenty of butter, salt and pepper; make a dressing of bread same as for turkey, spread on your meat, then place the other half on top the dressing, season as before; cover and bake from an hour and a half to two hours removing the pan toward the last.

Mrs. G. B. Allen
(Charlotte, 1893)

Where Mrs. Allen got the name for this dish is a mystery. We don't mind eating hot dogs and sometimes ask for a doggie bag, but unless we were sure of the restaurant, we would hesitate to order "Dog in a Blanket."

Frikadiller

1 lb. round steak (ground fine 3 times)	*1 egg*
	½ cup milk
Small piece of suet	*1 tablespoon flour*
Small onion	*Salt and pepper*

Add egg, milk, flour, salt and pepper. Mix thoroughly and mould into balls. Fry in butter.

Mrs. Henry Bauman
(Grayling, 1937)

Frizzled Beef

Shave dried beef very thin, put it in frying pan, add milk or water; when hot stir in a tablespoon of flour wet with cold water and 3 eggs, stir until thick and dish immediately.

Mrs. J. Morgan Smith
(Grand Rapids, 1890)

A lot of the fun of these old recipes comes from the unusual descriptive terms. Have you ever seen "frizzled beef" on a menu?

Frizzled Beef on Cream Toast

On ½ pound chipped dried beef pour 1 pint cold water to freshen it. Just as it comes to a boil turn it all off and add 1 pint of milk brought to the boiling point, 1 tablespoon butter, 1 tablespoon of cornstarch, boil 4 minutes. Put 1 tablespoon frizzled beef on each slice and serve hot.

Mrs. Worth Landon
(Niles, 1907)

Berlin Mock Roast Hare

One pound beef, 1 pound lean pork ground as for sausage; mix together with milk, salt and pepper and form into a long roll; cover the bottom of a baking pan with thin slices of bacon, lay the roast in the pan and with the finger make holes all through it and then put in strips of peppered bacon. Put a little water and ¼ cup sour cream in pan and bake in good oven one hour; baste often, season well.

(Union City, 1902)

Hash

Take pieces of meat left over from meals, put with a little water and boil until tender, chop fine; chop an equal quantity of cold boiled potatoes, put into a frying pan with the chopped meat, moisten with the water in which the meat was boiled, add a little butter, season with salt and pepper and cook thoroughly, stirring well; do not use too much water or the hash will be sloppy.

Mrs. C. H. L.
(Grand Rapids, 1890)

A Dish of Scraps

Take some cold potatoes, a few pieces of dry bread, some scraps of cold boiled or fried meat; chop it all quite fine in the chopping bowl; season with salt, pepper and sage; put in a piece of butter and cook it the same as hash. It is much better than potatoes alone warmed over.

Mrs. A. M. Fellows, Prairieville
(Ann Arbor, 1884)

Hassen Pfeffer

(From Bill Wooden)

Three lbs. round steak, cut 3 inches thick, cut in 2-inch squares, fry in butter, then drop into 2 qts.

of water, add ½ dozen bay leaves, ½ tsp. cloves, ½ tsp. allspice, ½ c. sugar, ½ c. vinegar, pepper and salt; boil until meat is very well done; make gravy from fat in frying pan and juice from meat; pour back over meat; serve with plain boiled mashed potatoes. Fine for a stag dinner.

Rabbit parboiled in soda and then cooked this way is excellent.

Mrs. S. H. V. H.
(Higgins Lake, 1920)

Where's the rabbit?

Kazoo Special

1 pkg. broad noodles	1 cup of fine cut celery
1 can or two cups tomatos	½ green pepper, (minced)
1½ lb. hamburg	⅓ cup bread crumbs
1 small onion, (cut fine)	

Cook noodles in boiling salted water until tender. Drain, fry hamburg quite well done. Place layer of noodles in buttered casserole, then hamburg, onion, celery and green pepper. Season and repeat. Pour over this one can or two cups of cooked tomatoes, sprinkle top with bread crumbs, dot with butter. Bake 45 minutes (350 deg. F.).

Mrs. H. S. Morrow
(Kalamazoo, 1935)

Meat Balls in Cabbage Jackets

Make raw chopped meat into balls; wrap each ball in a new cabbage leaf, tying with cord. Put in pan and brown carefully in butter; then add ½ cup boiling water, cover and cook 1 hour on slow fire. Add more water if needed.

Mrs. Van der Noot
(Detroit, 1915)

Meat Balls

Grind together 15¢ worth beef steak and 10¢ worth pork; 1 egg well beaten; salt; pepper; cracker crumbs to take up moisture, form in balls. Drop in boiling water. Boil 1 hour.

Bernice Daniels
(Homer, 1925)

In 1925 this would have been about 1½ pounds of beef steak and ¾ pound pork.

English Meat Pie

One pound round steak (or lamb,) one pint sweet milk, one cup flour, one egg, salt and pepper. Cut meat into dice; beat the egg very light. Add milk and a half teaspoon salt to the beaten egg. Pour this upon the flour gradually, beating very light and smooth. Put the meat into a buttered two-quart dish. Season well, and pour the batter over it. Bake an hour in a moderate oven, and serve hot.

(Ionia, 1912)

Sour Klopse (or Sour Meat Balls)

1 lb. of round steak or lean beef, with one-half lb. of pork ground fine together, 4 slices of stale bread, soaked in cold water, 1 egg, 2 good sized onions, 2 small bay leaf, few whole pepper kernels, scant half cup of vinegar not too strong, salt, pepper to taste, 1 qt. of water, flour for thickening, also sugar to taste.

Take a 2 qt. sauce pan, put in the qt. of water, slice in the onions, put in vinegar, put in bay leaf, pepper kernels and salt, let boil for a few minutes, now squeeze out the bread, add to your meat also the egg, pepper and salt to taste, mix this very thoroughly, then form into small meat balls, the size of a large walnut and drop in a few at a time into boiling liquid, lift out when done and put in another dish and continue until all are cooked. Now thicken the gravy, which is quite rich, add sugar to taste, and replace your cooked meat balls to repeat, if

more gravy is desired, add a little more water, vinegar seasoning to taste. This dish served with mashed potatoes or buttered vegetables or dish of apple sauce makes a menu fit for a king.

Mrs. E. G. Tracy
(Kalamazoo, 1935)

Swedish Meat Balls

Grind fine, 1 pound beef and ½ pound pork. Add 3 tablespoons minced onion, ½ teaspoon salt, ⅛ teaspoon pepper, 1 egg (beaten), 2 slices bread soaked in water, then squeezed dry, and 2 tablespoons flour, and ¼ teaspoon ginger for spice. Sift flour in carefully, add egg, bread and onion, pepper and salt.

Mix thoroughly; fry in hot fat till done. Keep hot on a platter until gravy is made. Add 4 tablespoons butter to fat in pan, blend 3 tablespoons flour, add balls, and let simmer. Before serving, add ½ cup cream.

Jane Welsh
(Grayling, 1937)

Meat Loaf

1 lb. hamburger (salt)	1 cup or more of
½ lb. pork sausage	bread crumbs
1 tsp. cinnamon	2 eggs
1 tsp. allspice	1 can tomato soup
1 onion	

Mix all ingredients, shape into loaf and bake.

Estabrook
(Parchment, 1935)

We baked this dish at 350° for 1½ hours. It was delicious, but needed some additional bread crumbs.

Mexican Hash

One-half box spaghetti, boil in salted water for 20 minutes and drain; ⅔ cup chopped onions; ½ pound hamburg steak; 2 cups tomatoes; which have been put through a collander; dash of cayenne pepper; salt. Cook all ingredients separately and mix together.

Mrs. Josephine Hulett
(Sunfield, 1915)

Noodle Ring

1 pkg. broad noodles	1½ cups diced,
1½ lb. ground round	cooked carrots
steak	1½ cups peas
1 onion	Butter

Fry meat loosely in skillet with onion until brown, add carrots and peas. Make the liquid which has been removed from the canned peas into a thin sauce and put with meat and vegetables. This must be of a consistency like chop suey.

Boil noodles in salt water until tender, drain and reheat in ½ cup butter, melted. Pour noodles onto large platter, pushing around edges to make ring. Pour meat and vegetable mixture onto center of platter and serve. Children love this.

Helen Kindleberger
(Parchment, 1935)

Beef Omelette

Four lbs. raw beef chopped fine, 4 rolled crackers, 4 eggs, piece butter size of an egg, season with pepper, salt and sage; make 2 loaves of this, roll them in crackers, and bake; slice when cold. Very good.

Miss Fanny McQuewan
(Grand Rapids, 1890)

Steak Smothered in Olives

Broil your favorite cut of steak. Season well and keep hot. Put a piece of butter in an agate dish and heat until it bubbles. Chop some olives until they

are minced fine. Put into the butter and pour over steak. Serve with baked potatoes.

Jane Mershon
(Higgins Lake, 1920)

Beefsteak with Oysters

For a large slice of steak 18 oysters will be required; wash and drain, heat one tablespoonful of butter, add nearly 1 pint of rich milk, when hot put in the oysters and let simmer only until they ruffle, thicken with flour to the consistency of cream, season with salt and paprika, turn over the steak as soon as it is broiled, buttered and placed on a hot platter.

(Union City, 1902)

Cornish Pasties

This recipe comes from its home among the miners of Cornwall. For a beef and potato pasty, make a paste as for pies (not quite as rich), and roll out the size of a tea plate, slightly thicker than for pie. Now slice a layer of potatoes on it, 1 onion, and a layer of finely cut raw steak. I use cheaper cuts for this. Season with pepper and salt, then fold together as you would a "turnover," and bake three-quarters of an hour in a slow oven. A turnip pasty is made in the same way only never combine turnips with onions or potatoes, simply turnips and beef. A beef pasty is composed of finely cut beef and parsley or an onion. Pasties may be eaten hot or cold and are therefore convenient where a hearty meal must be transported.

Mrs. Nichols
(Lansing, 1920)

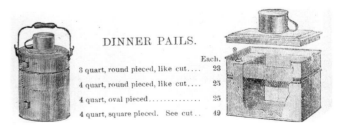

Ideal for keeping pasties warm, the bottom section of workingmen's dinner pails were filled with hot coffee (Grand Rapids, 1890).

Immigrants from Cornwall who flocked to the Upper Peninsula to work in the copper and iron mines in the nineteenth century brought the pasty or "tiddy oggie" with them from the old country. Carried deep within the mine in the morning, pasties could be eaten like sandwiches and made a convenient and hearty meal. There are many different variations found throughout the Upper Peninsula, including those that contain pork, ground beef, rutabagas, carrots, etc. The best we ever ate came from an Amish restaurant in the tough old lumbertown of Seney.

Cornish Pasties

Roll a not too rich pastry ¼ inch thick to fit a 7-inch plate. In the center place a heap of small cubes of baga, potato, carrots, onion and tender steak. Season to taste with salt, pepper and butter. Fold crust over, pinch edges. Place in pan, bake slowly one and one-half hours.

Mrs. Evangeline McDiarmid
Entre Nous Club
(Albion, 1940)

We have also experimented with miniature pasties about three inches long. They make a popular but very filling appetizer.

Planked Sirloin (a la Rathskeller)

Have a sirloin steak cut 2½ inches thick, and from heavy beef. Remove the bone, flank end and superfluous fat, wipe carefully, and place inside a hot, well-oiled hinged broiler. Cook 3 or 4 minutes over a bed of coals, turning the broiler every ten seconds, then set the broiler, resting on a dripping pan, in a hot oven to cook from 12 to 15 minutes. Have ready an oval hardwood plank, made hot in the oven, also hot mashed potato, cooked cauliflower, mushrooms, 4 small onions, and about ½ cup each of cooked string beans, flageolet (dried French beans), peas, carrot (cut in cubes or other shapes). Dispose the cooked steak in the center of the hot plank, fill in the space around the steak with a thin layer of mashed potato and pipe a border of potato around the plank ½ an inch from the edge. Set the onions at the 4 corners of the steak. Brush over the edges of the piping and the onions with the beaten yolk of an egg, and set the plank into the oven long enough to reheat the potato and brown the edges delicately. Mix the flageolet, carrots, peas, and string beans, season with pepper, salt and butter, and dispose these on one end of the plank between the steak and the piping on the edge. On the other end dispose cooked mushrooms (fresh or canned) hot and well seasoned. Lay flowerets of cooked cauliflower, well seasoned and hot, on the steak, and serve brown mushroom sauce in a boat. Cooked asparagus passed through a ring cut from a cooked carrot, may be pressed into the potato at the opposite ends of the steak (in the place of the cauliflower) and cubes of turnip or other vegetable may form a part of the macedoin. To serve, cut in strips through the tenderloin and portion above, and add to each plate the kinds of vegetables desired. If canned mushrooms are selected, reheat in boiling water, but without boiling. Saute fresh mushroom cups, after peeling, in butter, add a little stock, and let simmer about 20 minutes. They are then ready for serving on the steak and in the sauce. Brown mushroom sauce: Cook 1 tablespoonful each of bits of onion, carrot, a sprig of parsley, a sprig of thyme, and bit of bay leaf, in 2 tablespoonfuls of butter until browned, then add 3 tablespoonfuls of Thoman's Moss Rose flour, and stir until browned. Add gradually one cup of brown stock, and cook until smooth and boiling—then strain over ⅓ cup of mushrooms, cut in halves or pieces.

Janet McKenzie Hill
(Lansing, 1920)

Pressed Beef

Boil a shank of beef till it falls from the bone; remove every piece of bone; boil down a little longer, season with salt and pepper, pour into a form or put in a dish and press by putting a plate on top with a weight on top of plate.

E. C. L.
(Grand Rapids, 1890)

Savory Pyramids

May be made of pieces of beef, mutton, lamb, veal or pork. Beat 3 eggs light, then stir into them by degrees 6 tablespoons fine bread crumbs, 2 ozs.

butter slightly melted, 1 tablespoon finely minced parsley, 1 teaspoon mixed powdered herbs, one teaspoon grated lemon rind, 1 teaspoon pepper and salt, ¾ lb. of meat chopped fine, put in gravy to moisten the whole, mix thoroughly, form into pyramid shapes. Coat thickly with egg and bread crumbs, bake in greased tins, then serve with gravy.

Mrs. L. Kanits
(Muskegon, 1890)

This recipe yields individual-sized meat loaf volcanos.

Ragout of Beef

To six pounds of the round of beef take one-half dozen ripe tomatoes sliced, three onions sliced, one-half dozen cloves and a little whole black pepper; cut gashes into the meat, into which stuff one-half pound of salt pork cut into thin squares, place the meat upon the other ingredients and pour over them one-half cupful of vinegar and one cupful of water; cover tightly and bake in a moderate oven five hours, then when almost done salt to taste, strain the gravy through a colander and thicken with flour.

Miss Marie Leveque, Menominee
(Chicago, 1898)

Ravigote

2 pounds beef cut in inch squares	½ can peas
½ can tomatoes	3 or 4 okra (in season)
3 or 4 carrots cut in dice	⅓ cup tapioca
2 onions cut fine	5 allspice
	1 or 2 bay leaves
	Salt and pepper

Bake in casserole 3 to 5 hours, add water as necessary, or bake in fireless cooker 2 to 3 hours, add no water; or cook out of doors over open fire, add water when necessary and do not add tapioca till 20 minutes before serving. Cover tapioca with water and let soak while Ravigote is cooking.

Mrs. F. F. Sommers
(Higgins Lake, 1920)

"Irish Ravioli"

First make a noodle dough by mixing 1 egg, 3 tablespoons of water, ½ teaspoon of salt in flour enough to make a stiff dough, roll quite thin and cut in two inch squares.

One cup of ground (left over meat), one onion ground, mix with a little gravy (season to taste) put a little on each square of dough, fold over and pinch edges together. Put on a floured platter until ready to cook in following mixture: Two slices of bacon cut fine, two onions cut fine (fry a light brown), add 1 quart of tomatoes, 1 tablespoon of sugar, dash of red pepper, cloves, salt, and any left over gravy, let come to a boil and drop in Ravioli's, cook slowly for one-half hour. When done put on large platter and sprinkle with grated cheese. This with bread and butter is a delicious meal.

Mrs. Clark Rathbun, Otsego
(Kalamazoo, 1935)

Rolled Steak

Order a round steak less than an inch thick, have your butcher beat it well with the flat of the cleaver and cut it yourself across both ways with a sharp knife. Spread it thickly with a forcemeat made of salt pork and bread crumbs, season with pepper, salt and thyme, sweet marjoram and parsley, with a little finely minced onion. This done, roll up the steak as you would a piece of music and tie firmly into shape with a stout cord. Lay in a dripping pan half filled with boiling water, cover closely and cook 2 hours, turning two or three times. Serve with thickened gravy around it. Remove the strings, send to the table, and carve across the end.

Mrs. A. F. Temple
(Detroit, 1878)

We used a round steak about 2½ pounds in size. Getting our butcher to beat the steak with the flat of his cleaver proved difficult. As a matter of fact when we bought the meat the only one there was a young woman wrapping cuts of meat in styrofoam and cellophane. We trimmed the fat, cut the steak in two and beat it with a wooden meat mallet.

We substituted bacon for salt pork, two strips per roll, and eliminated additional salt because the bacon was salty enough. The forcemeat, actually a stuffing, consisted of:

½ cup bread crumbs	1 Tablespoon parsley
½ teaspoon thyme	1 Tablespoon minced onion
½ teaspoon mar-joram	pepper to taste

We prepared one steak with the above dressing sprinkled over the bacon strips and eliminated the bread crumbs from the other. We rolled the meat tightly, as Mrs. Temple would have rolled her sheet music in a leather carrying case, and tied it with kite string. Toothpicks work equally well.

For a "dripping pan" we used a small granite-ware roasting pan.

We cooked the steaks for 2 hours at 350°, turning them over 3 times. The drippings, thickened with flour and no additional spices, made a nice gravy.

We personally preferred the variant without the bread crumbs.

Sauerbraten with Potato Dumplings

4 lbs. pot roast beef	1 part vinegar to 3 of water
1 tsp. salt	1 Bay leaf
⅛ tsp. pepper	8 peppercorns
1 clove of garlic	1 sliced onion
2 cloves	

Chop a clove of garlic very fine with salt and pepper and beef suet cut from roast. Make 2 deep incisions on each side of meat—push garlic mixture in. Prepare enough vinegar and water to cover meat. Add seasonings. Let meat soak in this 48 hours, turning 4 times. When ready to cook brown on all sides. Add 1 cup soaking juice. Cook slowly for 3½ hours; add more juice if needed. Thicken gravy with flour or broken up ginger snaps. Prunes may be added the night before. Serve with potato dumplings.

Boil 6 potatoes in their jackets. Peel, run thru ricer. There should be 5 cupfuls. Mix them on pastry board with 1½ tsp. salt, ½ tsp. sugar, 1 egg, dash of nutmeg, and cloves. Add about 1 cupful of flour to make smooth dough with rolling pin. Shape in long roll about ½ inch thick, then cut in pieces 1½ inches long. Roll these finger lengths between the hands; drop in boiling salted water and cook 10 minutes. Drain and pour over them 4 tbsp. melted

butter in which 4 tbsp. bread crumbs have been browned.

Mrs. Geo. Wiegle
(Parchment, 1935)

Beefsteak with Sherry Sauce

Broil the steak in the usual way. Lay it in the chafing dish, and cover it with the sauce; after which, put on the cover, and let stand five minutes before serving.

Sauce

1 glass of sherry	2 tbsp. of butter, cut up in 1 tsp. of browned flour
Juice of ½ lemon	
1 tablespoon of cat-sup	½ teaspoonful of salt
	¼ teaspoon of pepper

Heat butter, catsup and lemon juice in a sauce pan; add seasoning, and wine; boil quickly, and pour over the steak.

Mrs. Edmund S. Rankin
(Kalamazoo, 1906)

Smothered Beef Stake

Take 1 large thin steak lay out smoothly and wipe dry; prepare a dressing with 1 cup of fine bread crumbs, ½ teaspoon salt, some pepper, tablespoon butter, ½ teaspoon sage, or use chopped onions and enough milk to moisten it; spread on the meat, roll up and tie carefully with stout string, put a few thin slices of pork in bottom of a kettle and fry till brown; put the roll of stake and also brown it on all sides, then add 1 pint of hot water and cook until tender, then thicken the gravy. The roll is to be carved crosswise.

(Vermontville, 1906)

Spanish Noodles

Twenty-five cents worth of hamburg, 2 green peppers, 3 onions. Grind, fry in butter until brown;

add 1 package cooked noodles and 1 can tomatoes. Bake about 10 m.

Mrs. Anna Schoonmaker
(Kalamazoo, 1921)

In 1921 a quarter bought about two pounds of hamburger.

Hot Tamales

Add to one quart of boiling water or soup stock, one tablespoon of salt, and enough corn meal to make a stiff mush. Cover and set aside. Soften clean corn husks by putting in hot water. Take two large red, dry chili peppers; remove seeds and pour hot water over peppers to soften. Toast the seeds in pan over the fire with six pepper corns. Add to softened chili pulp, and pound to a paste in a mortar. Add garlic and onions if desired and enough water to make a pint of liquid. Cut up a fat piece of raw beef or mutton into pieces an inch and a half or two inches long, and a spoonful of mush, flatten it out and put in center a teaspoon of chili sauce and one piece of cut meat, fold up, roll in corn husks and tie. Put in kettle and steam four hours. Serve hot.

(Greenville, 1910)

Tamale Pie

1 cup yellow corn meal	2 cups tomato soup or canned tomatoes
4 cups boiling water	6 ripe olives
1 teaspoon salt	Chili powder to taste
Cook into thick mush.	1 pound hamburger
1 medium onion	2 teaspoons salt
1 green pepper	Pepper
2 tablespoons butter	

Brown onion and green pepper in butter; add meat and seasonings. Cook until color changes, add tomatoes and simmer twenty minutes.

Line pan or casserole with mush, fill in with meat mixture and cover with mush. Bake twenty minutes.

Mrs. Hugh Gray
(Grand Rapids, 1935)

We enjoyed this interesting version of a tamale, and we suggest these variations. Line the bottom of the casserole dish with corn tortillas, add the bottom layer of mush and bake for ten minutes at 350°. Then fill with the meat mixture (we added additional salsa), add the top layer of mush, and bake at 350° for 25 minutes or until the top is browned. Shredded cheese on top is also good.

Michigan Tomales

1 cup mashed rice	1 pound chopped pork loin or steak
1 chopped onion	Salt and a little red pepper

Form in rolls like large sausages; wilt 8 or 9 cabbage leaves by boiling a few minutes; roll mixture loosely in the leaves, pin toothpicks through them to hold them together. Put in a pan, pour over a quart of tomatoes and water, enough to cover well. Steam or bake 1 hour.

Mrs. W. R. Townsend
(Grand Rapids, 1917)

This seems more like a German version of tamales. By World War II, a very similar recipe had become Victory Rolls.

Victory Rolls

1 lb. beef (ground)	2 eggs
1 lb. pork (ground)	salt and pepper to taste
1 onion, chopped fine	
3 tbsp. uncooked rice	1 cup milk

Mix all together, then roll and wrap in wilted cabbage leaves. Place in roaster, pour over top 1 can tomatoes, 1 can peas. Bake in oven for 2½ hours.

Mrs. Andrew Boers
(Kalamazoo, 1945)

Toad in the Puddle

One pound beefsteak cut size of dice, one dozen large potatoes sliced. Alternate layers of potatoes and meat, with small pieces of butter in each. Add one pint of milk and bake one and one-half hours.

Mrs. L. E. Towers
(Mattawan, 1906)

VEAL

Veal Birds

One and one-half pounds veal ¾ inch thick, pound till ¼ inch thick, cut in 2½ × 4 inch pieces. Take for dressing, ½ pound salt pork and remnants of veal chopped fine, 1 onion size of a walnut, chopped fine, 1 cup cracker crumbs, 1 egg, mix to a paste and spread on veal and roll, fastening with tooth picks. Roll them in flour and fry in butter ¾ of an hour. Just before taking from the fire, add ½ pint sweet cream and remove all the tooth picks except 2 for the legs, and then they are ready for the table.

Mrs. W. N. Moffet
(Kalamazoo, 1899)

Fricatelles

One pound of cold veal chopped very fine, add a little salt and plenty of pepper, 1 or 2 onions cut very fine, and a little parsley if liked. Soak some bread in water until soft, squeeze it dry in a towel and add as much in proportion as the meat. Chop the bread with the meat, and mix in 2 eggs. Make them up in patties, roll in bread crumbs and cook in hot lard as doughnuts. Serve with sliced lemon.

Mrs. Vestey
(Muskegon, 1890)

Baked Oranges with Veal

1 slice of veal steak 1
  inch thick
¼ cup of water
½ teaspoon of salt

2 tablespoons of flour
1 tablespoon of butter
1 bay leaf (small)
2 large oranges
¼ teaspoon of white
  pepper
Parsley

Dip veal in flour and put in a greased casserole. Dot over with bits of butter. Sprinkle with salt and butter and add bay leaf. Peel and quarter oranges, place around steak, add water and bake a golden brown, basting often. Serve on hot plates, alternating parsley and oranges. Make gravy with remainder of flour, seasoning and water as needed. Pour gravy over meat and serve.

Mrs. R. Howard Hall
(Grand Rapids, 1935)

Knuckle of Veal Ragout

Knuckle of veal, 1 onion, 1 head celery, 2 carrots, 1 tbsp. catsup, juice of lemon, 1 clove. Cut meat from knuckle of veal into small pieces, season with salt and pepper and dredge with flour. Fry in a little butter to a pale brown.

Chop meat bone in several places. Put meat and bone into a kettle, add celery, carrots and a few potatoes, diced if liked. Pour over about 2 c. hot water and simmer slowly for 2 hours. Take out meat and vegetables, strain to remove bone. Make a gravy, add catsup and lemon juice and boil for a minute; put back meat and vegetables and heat thoroughly.

Bertha G. Harrison
(Kalamazoo, 1921)

Leg of Veal

Veal should be cooked thoroughly and seasoned highly. A leg weighing 8 or 9 lbs. should roast 3 hours.

Take out bone, making several incisions. Fill with salt pork minced, salt and pepper, using about 1 lb. salt pork, adding about 3 tablespoons butter, roll and tie firmly. Place in pan, salt and pepper, dredging flour over it. Lay thin slices of salt pork over it, add 1 pt. water, basting often.

Mrs. Atkins' Society Veal
(Hastings, 1921)

Bacon makes a good substitute for salt pork.

Stewed Knuckle of Veal

Dedicated to the Rev. W. H. Osborn

Take a knuckle of veal;
You may buy it, not steal;
In a few pieces cut it.
In a stewing pan put it;
Salt, pepper, and mace
Must season this knuckle;
Then what's joined to a place—
With other herbs muckle,
And lettuce and beets.
With marigold meet.
Put no water at all
In a boiling hot kettle
And there let it be,
(Mark the doctrine I teach)
About—let me see—
Thrice as long as you preach.
So, skimming the fat off,
Say grace with your hat off.
Oh, then with what rapture
Will it fill Dean and Chapter!

(Battle Creek, 1903)

Rullipolse

One good sized veal flank cleaned thoroughly. Remove all tough gristle. Sprinkle with salt, pepper, and chopped onion. Cut flank in two pieces and roll each piece tight; sew and wind cord around to hold tight. Put in strong brine. Let stand three days, then boil until tender. Press 24 hours. Slice very thin and serve on rye bread.

Mrs. Oscar Hanson
(Grayling, 1937)

The original owner of our Grayling cookbook inserted a handwritten note to add "a little allspice" to the recipe for this traditional Scandinavian dish.

PORK

Baked Ham

Cover a ham with cold water and simmer gently just long enough to loosen the skin so that it can be pulled off; this will probably be from 2 to 3 hours, according to the size of the ham; when skimmed put it in a dripping pan in the oven; pour over it 2 teacupfuls of hot water, in which has been dissolved a teaspoonful of English mustard; bake slowly, basting with the liquid for 2 hours; then cover the ham all over to the depth of 1 inch with brown sugar, press it down firmly, and do not baste again until the sugar has formed a thick crust, which it will soon do in a very slow oven. Let it remain in the oven a full hour after covering with the sugar, until it becomes a rich golden brown. When done, drain from the liquor in the pan and put on a dish to cool; when it is cool, but not cold, press by turning another flat dish over it and a weight on that. The pressing makes it cut firmly for sandwiches or slicing.

Sister C. N. Tombaugh, Rodney
(Elgin, Il., 1907)

Sister Tombaugh of Rodney, Michigan, a hamlet in Mecosta County, submitted this excellent recipe for baked ham to the *Inglenook* magazine, a re-

A Michigan-bred porker of the pioneer period (Philadelphia, 1870).

ligious organ of the Dunker Church, published at Elgin, Illinois. In 1907, the Brethren Publishing House published a compilation of one thousand of the best *Inglenook* recipes.

Baked Ham

A ham weighing 10 or 12 pounds is preferable. Put in a kettle skin side down with cold water enough to cover. Add 1 cup N. O. molasses, 1 lemon cut in halves, ½ cup vinegar and grated half of nutmeg. Let boil from 20 minutes to half an hour, being sure that it does not boil more than the half hour. Take out of kettle, remove skin, and place in roaster. Mix 2 cups dark brown sugar with 1 cup fine cracker crumbs and dredge ham with it. Bake slowly for 3 hours. Very delicious.

Mary C. Miller, Kalamazoo
(Charlotte, 1909)

"N. O." is New Orleans.

Baked Virginia Ham in Milk

Slice of ham 1 inch thick, 1 teaspoon dry mustard, 2 teaspoons flour, 3 teaspoons granulated sugar, 1 pint sweet milk. Mix the above ingredients in the order given, sprinkle the same over ham, pour on milk. Bake one hour in moderate oven.

Mrs. Irvin T. Kumler
(Higgins Lake, 1920)

How to Bake a Ham

Prepare for baking a good smoked ham with some fat. Prepare a stiff dough, cover the ham with it and put it in the usual baking oven, fat side of the ham up, and bake four or five hours. Never mind how black or burnt looking the dough may be. When done, break off the dough with a hammer, clean off the ham and immerse for three weeks in a brine composed of 2 quarts of white wine and 3 quarts of hard cider; then hang it so it will drip for four or five days.

Ella Kellogg of Battle Creek thought zinc-covered tables such as this ideal for kitchen use. It was better they not have drawers, which were "too apt to become receptacles for a heterogeneous mass of rubbish" (Battle Creek, 1910).

This treatment will insure a delicious baked ham.

(Marine City, 1923)

Baked Ham

1 6 lb. ham	*1 egg*
3 cups rye flour	*1 pt. water*
1 qt. sweet cider	*1 cup brown sugar*

Soak and scrub ham thoroughly. Make a thick paste with rye flour and water. Spread all over the ham. Set on rack in pan or roaster and bake in hot oven until crust is hard, lower the heat bake average 6 lb. ham three hours.

Make hole in crust, pour in sweet cider or hot liquid from roaster, repeat again later on. One cup of sweet cider. Bake 1 hour longer, remove the crust and skin. Brush with beaten yolk of 1 egg, sprinkle with brown sugar and rye bread crumbs and brown.

Save the surplus crust to keep the ham moist.

Mrs. Clare Grigsby, Richland
(Kalamazoo, 1935)

Boiled Ham

Select a ham of convenient size, weighing 12 pounds, perhaps. Soak it over night in ice water, being sure that the water completely covers it and adding to the water a heaping teaspoonful baking soda, half a cupful of cider vinegar and tablespoonful of brown sugar. When ready to boil, drain from the water and place it fat-side down in a large granite kettle, cover it with water and add one scraped carrot cut in slices, a tablespoonful each of ground allspice and mace, a teaspoonful of celery salt, half a teaspoonful of white pepper, two tablespoonfuls of vinegar, one whole onion stuck with half a dozen cloves and one tart apple peeled and cut in quarters; bring slowly to the boiling point and then push to the back of the range where it will only simmer; allowing for a 12-lb. ham about 5 hours. When cooked remove from water, peel off the skin with a sharp knife, rub over quickly with thick maple syrup, sprinkle thickly with browned bread crumbs and crisp in a hot oven for 20 minutes; garnish the protruding bone with a decorative paper frill, arranging pickled beets and boiled vegetables cut in fancy forms as a border around the edge of the platter.

Gail Gardner
(Manistee, 1929)

Ham Banana Rolls

6 thin slices boiled ham	1 tsp. prepared mustard
1 tbsp. butter	6 firm bananas

Spread slices of ham with a mixture of butter and mustard. Wrap around peeled bananas and fasten with a toothpick. Place in a buttered shallow baking pan. Pour cheese sauce over bananas. Bake in a moderate oven 350 for 30 minutes. Serves 6.

Cheese Sauce

1½ tbsp. butter	¾ cup milk
1½ tbsp. flour	¼ # American cheese

Melt butter and add flour. Stir until smooth and add warm milk. Add grated cheese and cook until thick and smooth stirring constantly.

Mary Brown
(Lansing, 1941)

Ham Cake

Chop fine a pound and a half of ham. Boil a large slice of bread in half a pint of milk; beat it and the ham together, add an egg, put in a buttered dish and bake to a rich brown.

(Battle Creek, 1890)

Ham in Casserole

One slice ham cut thick, 1 small chopped onion, 1 bay leaf, 1 blade mace, 4 cloves, ½ teaspoon celery seed, 1 small sweet pepper, salt and pepper, cider. Brown the ham on both sides in hot frying pan, then lay it in a casserole, add the seasonings, the pepper and onion chopped. Pour over enough sweet cider to cover ham. Cover and bake slowly for 2½ or 3 hours. Serve hot with cider or tomato sauce.

Blanche Hay O'Reilly
(Higgins Lake, 1920)

Ham Puff

Scald 1 pt. of milk in double boiler, add ½ cup butter. When melted, add a smooth thickening made of 1 cup sifted flour, mixed with cold milk. Stir until smooth. Take from fire; let cool, then add the well beaten yolks of eight eggs. Then fold in the whites well beaten, salt, 1½ cups finely chopped ham. Bake in dish standing in a pan of water.

Mrs. W. H. Brown
(Kalamazoo, 1906)

This dish was to be the highlight of a televised old-fashioned cooking demonstration we did in our home. We followed the recipe closely, substituting corned beef for ham. We cooked it a few hours before the film crew arrived, intending to serve it for lunch. When we looked in the oven, it had puffed way above the top of the round casserole dish, and resembled a chef's hat in appearance. Larry insisted we cut the top off and brown what was left in the bowl. Twenty minutes after that operation, it had deflated to pancake size. On the second attempt we did not use enough of the mixture and it failed to rise. Nevertheless both batches tasted good.

We suggest reducing the recipe by half, pouring the mixture into a three-quart casserole dish, and baking it at 350° for 30 minutes and an additional 20 minutes at 300°. To render the flour mixture smooth, use equal parts flour and warmed, not scalded, milk.

Stuffed Ham

Soak the ham over night. The next morning take off the skin and lay it aside. Take some parsley, about four onions, celery and bay leaves, grind in meat grinder. To this add one teaspoonful of the following: Celery seed, spice, cloves, thyme, sage, allspice, red and black pepper, sugar and paprika, ½ teaspoonful mace and dry mustard, and the crumbs of about twelve large soda crackers, rolled and powdered fine. Mix this stuffing thoroughly, and with a long, sharp knife, make incision in the ham lengthwise, from the hock to the large end. Press the knife back and fill up the holes full with the stuffing. Put the skin back on the ham, place in oven and bake it slowly for several hours until very done. When the ham is done, take off the skin, rub the ham well with brown sugar over the top, and put back in the oven until brown. Serve cold. If desired stick whole cloves on top. Before rubbing the ham with sugar take out of pan it was baked and put into clean pan.

Ethel Alexander
(Higgins Lake, 1920)

Baked Pig

Take a pig six weeks old, nicely prepared, score it in squares and rub lard all over it. Scald two quarts of corn meal, make a stiff dough of it and bake. When brown, break it up, and add to it one-

fourth of a pound of butter, some pepper, and thyme. With this, fill the pig till plump, sew up, and place on its knees in the pan, with plenty of water. Baste frequently, turning as you would a turkey.

(Battle Creek, 1890)

Sucking Pig (to Roast)

The pig should be four weeks old. Make a dressing as follows: A cup of stale bread-crumbs, a heaping teaspoon of chopped suet, 1 tablespoon of chopped parsley, 1 teaspoon of powdered sage, 1 teaspoon of salt, ¼ of black pepper, 1 tablespoon of onion-juice, mix all well together. When ready put the stuffing in, sew the opening together, rub with melted butter. Roast from 2 hours to 2½. When done place on a dish with parsley, put in its mouth a small red apple. Serve hot with apple-sauce.

The Gravy

Put in the pan in which it was roasted 2 tablespoons of browned flour, stir till smooth, add one pint of boiling water; let boil up, take from the fire, add 4 tablespoons of sherry and serve.

(Battle Creek, 1903)

Pork Belly, Rolled and Boiled

Salt a belly of pork—young meat is the best—by mixing 1 saltspoon powdered saltpetre with 2 tablespoons common salt, sprinkle the mixture over the pork and let it lie for 3 days. When ready to dress the meat, wash it in cold water, and dry it with a cloth. Lay it, skin downwards, on the table, remove the bones and cover the inside with pickled gherkins cut into thin slices. Sprinkle over these a little powdered mace and pepper. Roll the meat tightly and bind securely with tape. Put it into a sauce-pan with 2 onions stuck with 6 cloves, 3 bay-leaves, 1 bunch parsley, and 1 sprig thyme. Bring the liquid slowly to a boil, skim carefully, draw it to the back of stove, and simmer gently till the meat is done enough. Put it between 2 dishes, lay a weight upon it and leave it until quite cold. The bandages should not be removed until the meat is ready to be served. Time to simmer, ½ hour per pound.

(Detroit, 1890)

Roast Pork with Apples

Put roast in the pan and season with salt, pepper and very little sage. Roast slowly. When about half done pour off all the fat and save for gravy. Pare the top half of some apples and put a piece of meat pie dough (same as made for pot pie dumplings) around the part that is pared, fasten on with tooth picks and place around the roast, one for each person to be served, and bake until meat and apples are done. Serve 1 apple to each person with slice of pork.

Mrs. S. H. Griffin
(Niles, 1907)

Pork Chops Fried with Apples, Very Fine

Put the fresh chops in the frying-pan, salt, pepper, and sage, if you like it, or any other sweet herb, to be scattered over, and fried; if not fat enough to make plenty of gravy, add butter or drippings. When the chops are nicely done, having sliced the apples, fry in the same dish, and when nicely browned put them over the chops or in a dish by themselves, as some may not like them, although the author, and probably most others, will be very fond of them. Use nice tart apples only. Chops of fresh pork, fried and seasoned the same way, are splendid, if nicely browned, even without the apples.

(Ann Arbor, 1884)

Balkenbrij

Cover one pound lean pork and one pound pork liver with water and cook until well done. Season with salt, pepper and cloves. When water is cooked down about half, chop meat fine, put back in juice and stir in enough Buckwheat flour to make

a stiff batter. Place in bread tins and when cold, slice and fry.

(Holland, 1936)

Pot Eten (Boiled Dinner)

Cook two pounds of very lean pork and one-half cup barley with water, for about 2½ hours. Add diced sweet apples or pears and 8 potatoes. Cook down, take out meat and mash.

(Holland, 1936)

Geldershems Pot

Boil 3 pounds spareribs until done, then remove from the liquid and add 12 potatoes cut in quarters, 6 carrots cut in small pieces and 2 large onions; season with salt to taste and let boil with a slow fire until done; mash lightly and serve.

Mrs. George Bilkert
(Kalamazoo, 1920)

Fried Salt Pork

Freshen the slices for 10 or 15 minutes in milk, setting the frying pan on the back of the stove where the heat is moderate; drain, roll in flour, fry crisp to a light brown, put on a platter, pour off the fat, leaving a scant tablespoonful in the pan; add ½ cup of cream; when it boils pour over the pork and serve. Let all who look disdainfully upon salt pork try this way of cooking.

(Union City, 1902)

Apples Stuffed with Sausage Meat

Scoop out the center of six good sized apples, leaving a thick shell and pulp from the core.

Chop this and mix with one cup of minced cooked sausage meat.

Refill the apples with mixture and bake in a medium hot oven until tender. Serve with baked or fried potatoes for luncheon or supper, or as a garnish for roast pork or chicken.

(Detroit, 1935)

Baked Apples with Vienna Sausage

Remove cores from sour apples and fill with vienna sausage, about three to each apple. Place in pan, add a little water, bake until apples are tender.

Mrs. Charles Gardner
(Homer, 1925)

Bologna Sausage—Fine, as Made in Germany

The London, England, *Farmer* claims to have obtained this from the classic land of sausages. I think it will be nice enough for the people of our country, as well as England and Germany. It is as follows: Lean beef, freed from gristle, is to be chopped up very fine and mixed with ⅓ or ½ its weight of lean pork similarly treated. To this mixture is added an equal bulk of fat bacon, cut in strips as thin as the back of a knife, and then chopped into pieces about the size of a pea. For every 12 lbs. of this mass are required ½ lb. of salt, 1 dr. of saltpeter, ⅓ lb. of powdered sugar, and 1 table-spoonful of whole white pepper. The block on which the meat is to be chopped should be previously rubbed over with garlic, but none of this must be mixed with the sausage mass. In filling the sausages the meat must be well crammed home with suitable appliances, as pressure with the hand alone is quite insufficient to keep out the air, which is sure to spoil the result. After hanging for 2 or 3 weeks to dry, the red color of the meat and the white bits of fat will be visible through the skin of the sausages, and then it is time to smoke them. By careful attention to these directions, sausages thus prepared will keep well for at least a year and a half, and the delicacy of their flavor increases as they get older. The great secret of their keeping qualities is to put in plenty of bacon.

Remarks—Where the word "bacon" is used here, and above "fat bacon," they mean simply fat pork, fresh, of course, the same as the beef must be, not "bacon," as we understand the word in the United States to mean cured and smoked sides—not at all—this is not it, but fresh, fat pork.

(Ann Arbor, 1884)

Bologna Sausage Americanized

Somebody has Americanized the above, as follows, but I don't know who; still, it will be nice for those who like cayenne (and, by the way, if we would all use more cayenne or red pepper, and less of the black, it would be the better for us); but I should try only 1 spoonful at first, and if more would be tolerated by the children (who, as a general thing dislike it very much), and only a small onion, increasing or lessening either, as found most agreeable:

"Lean pork, 6 lbs.; lean beef, 3 lbs.; beef suet, 2 lbs.; salt, 4 ozs. (I should say 6 ozs.); 6 table-spoonfuls of black pepper, 2 table-spoonfuls of cayenne pepper, 2 tea-spoonfuls of cloves, 1 of allspice, and 1 minced onion. Chop or grind the meat, and mix well the powdered spices through it. Pack in beef skins as you do those of pork, tie both ends tightly and lay them in strong brine. Let them remain one week, then change them into a new brine. Let them remain another week, frequently turning them. Then take them out, wipe them, and send them to be smoked; when smoked rub the surface well with sweet oil or butter and hang them in a dark, cool place."

Remarks—It strikes me that 1 table-spoonful of cayenne will be found enough for most persons, especially children, who are very fond of "Bologna."

(Ann Arbor, 1884)

Home Made Sausage

Twelve pounds of pork, 10 tbsp. salt, 4 of black pepper, 2 of ginger, 3 of light brown sugar, 4 of sage. Mix the seasoning thoroughly and rub on meat, then chop fine.

Mrs. S. H. V. H.
(Kalamazoo, 1921)

Peanut Sausage

Thoroughly mix to a cream, one level tablespoon peanut butter, with 2 tablespoons cold water, add 3 tablespoons grated bread crumbs, a

No respectable Victorian home was complete without a combination sausage stuffer and lard and fruit press manufactured by the Enterprise Manufacturing Company of Philadelphia (Philadelphia, 1906).

pinch of salt and a teaspoon of minced onion or powdered sage, mix well all together, form into small cakes and place in an oiled, heated frying pan till nicely browned, turn and brown on both sides, place on platter and garnish with sprigs of parsley. Serve with the following sauce: Melt a tablespoon butter in pan, sprinkle in a tablespoon of flour, stir until brown, add water to make consistency of cream, stirring constantly to prevent lumps, salt to taste.

A. C. B.
(Berrien Springs, 1923)

Sausage Loaf

2 pounds sausage
18 soda crackers
  (rolled)
3 eggs
2 teaspoons salt or
  less

Pepper
Pinch of cloves
Pinch of ginger
½ t cinnamon

Put in a salt sack tied tightly. Cover with boiling water. Boil 1½ hours.

Bertha Fox, Bradley
(Allegan, 1938)

Pork Scraffle

One and one-half lbs. shoulder of pork, 1 qt. cold water, 1 c. cornmeal, salt and pepper; cut pork in small pieces; cook until tender; remove any bone and measure the liquid remaining in the kettle; add enough water to bring it up to a quart; heat to a boiling point, and stir in the cornmeal; cook for two hours. The meat will break in shreds as the mixture cooks; turn into a greased pan, let get cold. When ready to use cut into ⅓ inch slices and fry.

Nellie Buoy
(Kalamazoo, 1921)

Barbecued Spareribs

3 lbs. spare ribs
1 cup water
1 cup catsup
⅛ tsp. red pepper
1 tsp. chili powder

Salt
Pepper
6 medium sized on-
  ions, sliced

Place a layer of spareribs in a roaster. Sprinkle with some of the spices, add a layer of onions, then a layer of ribs until all are used. Pour over the catsup and water and bake until brown and tender. When ready to serve, add a small can of mushrooms to the gravy.

Mrs. Paul Sangren
(Kalamazoo, 1941)

Sparerib Pie with Oysters

Saw or chop the rib into convenient pieces, boil until tender, season when nearly done; put into a pan, add 1 pint or more of oysters and 1 cupful of the liquor in which the rib was cooked, thicken the remainder for gravy to serve with the pie. Make a crust as for chicken pie, put over it while hot and bake until brown; it should take 30 minutes.

(Union City, 1902)

Pork Tenderloin with Sour Cream

Brown tenderloin on all sides, dredge in flour, salt and pepper. Put in roaster and cover with 1 cup sour cream. Add water and thicken for gravy.

(Higgins Lake, 1920)

Stuffed Pork Tenderloin

4 pork tenderloins	1 cup chopped apples
3 cups bread crumbs	½ tsp. cinnamon
½ cup water	2 tbsp. sugar
1 cup cooked prunes	4 tbsp. butter or drippings
1 tsp. salt	

Select tenderloins of equal length and weight. Split lengthwise and pound out as flat as possible. Fill and round out with well mixed stuffing. Place another tenderloin on top and fasten both ends and sides together. Dust slightly with flour, salt and pepper. Sear in hot oven 450 degrees 10 minutes; reduce to moderate heat, 350 degrees, and bake 1½ hours. Baste during last half with 1 pt. water. When baked remove from pan and strain liquid. Stir in 2 tbsp. flour in remaining fat. Add liquid slowly, and cook gently until smooth and clear. Serve with meat.

Mrs. Hubert Anderson
(Kalamazoo, 1941)

Tantalizing Pie

Filling—	1½ cups milk
1½ cups cooked ham, diced	¼ tsp. salt
1½ cups cooked pearl onions	⅛ tsp. pepper
1 cup cooked carrots, sliced	⅛ tsp. paprika
Sauce—	Cheese Pastry—
2 tbsp. Crisco	1 cup flour
2 tbsp. flour	¼ tsp. salt
	3 tbsp. Crisco
	⅓ cup grated cheese
	3 to 4 tbsp. cold water

Peas, potatoes or spinach may be used in place of onions or carrots. (2½ cupsful of cooked vegetables in all). Arrange alternate layers of vegetables and ham until 1½ qt. baking dish is filled. Pour over the following sauce:

Melt Crisco in sauce pan, stir in flour and smooth to paste. Slowly add milk, stirring constantly cook and stir until sauce boils, add seasonings.

Moisten rim of baking dish and cover top with Cheese Pastry. Sift flour and salt, cut in Crisco coarsely, stir in cheese, add only enough water to fold ingredients together. Roll out on lightly floured board. Fit pastry tightly over moistened rim of baking dish. Slash top. Bake in hot oven (425 degrees F.) about 25 minutes.

Mrs. Ray T. Linsley, Otsego
(Kalamazoo, 1935)

Tantalizing Pie won third prize in the *Kalamazoo Gazette*'s recipe contest in 1935. We cooked this in a casserole dish for 35 minutes at 350°. We suggest covering the bottom with the pastry also, which was very good. Eliminate ½ cup of milk or it won't thicken, and add one teaspoon of chicken bouillon instead of the salt.

Curing, Smoking, Keeping, Etc.— Curing Hams, Smoking, Etc., as Done in Pennsylvania.—Good for All Places and Kinds of Meat

The following is the plan pursued in Pennsylvania, where it is well known that they have the very nicest hams:

After the hams are nicely trimmed, lay them upon slanting boards, to carry off the dripping brine, and rub well with pure fine salt, working it into every part; then let them lay 48 hours. Then brush off the salt with a dry cloth or brush-broom, and have ready a mixture of powdered saltpeter, 1 teaspoon; brown sugar, 1 dessertspoon, or a small tablespoon, of red pepper; use 1 teaspoonful of the mixture for each ham or shoulder, and rub well into the fleshy parts; then pack in a tub or barrel, skin-side down always; put also a good sprinkling of nice, pure salt on the bottom, and between each layer, as packed. Let them stand thus 5 days; then cover with pickle made as follows:

To each pail of water required put 4 lbs. of pure, coarse salt; saltpeter, ¾ to 1½ ozs., and brown sugar, ¼ to 1½ lbs. The pickle should be made beforehand, so as to remove all skum arising, and to be cold when poured on. According to the size of the hams, let them lay 5, 6 or 7 weeks.

For Beef, 10 to 15 days only, according to size of pieces, in the same strength of pickle, and same treatment. Hang up a few days to dry nicely before smoking.

Remarks—It will be noticed that there is a margin given in the amount of saltpeter and the sugar; it is because some persons prefer more than others. The least amounts given would be enough for me. I will remark here, for all, that the smoking and putting away for summer use should always be done while the weather is yet too cold to allow a fly to be seen, so there need be no annoyance from them, nor from bugs, if packed according to direction.

The following for hams or beef is from a lady, a name-sake of mine, Jennie Chase, of Elsie, Mich., differing a little from the above in that she uses a little saleratus, which is said to prevent meat from becoming dry and hard. I will give it, as some of the ladies know more about such matters than their brothers or husbands. I do not know, however, that this one has either, for I have never seen her, but would be glad to, and thank her for not being ashamed to give her name with her information. She says:

Hams or Beef—Pickle for.—"For 200 lbs. of meat, use 14 lbs. of salt, 1½ lbs sugar, 6 oz. saltpeter, 2 oz. saleratus; dissolve by boiling in three pails of soft water; skim, and when cold, pour over your meat. Sprinkle a very little salt on when you put down your meat. As soon as the weather is warm, scald the brine, and add a little fresh salt."

Remarks—The plan of scalding on the approach of hot weather and adding a little more salt, is certainly desirable for keeping meat over summer in the pickle.

(Ann Arbor, 1884)

Saleratus is baking soda.

Frankfritters

1½ lbs. weiners	2 tbsp. lard
2 tbsp. mustard	1 cup flour
2 eggs	1 tsp. baking powder
½ cup milk	½ tsp. salt

Prick weiners and boil ten minutes. Cool. Split open enough to spread prepared mustard inside. Press together. Dip into batter and fry until brown.

Batter: Beat the eggs, add milk and melted lard. Then the sifted flour, salt and baking powder.

(Lansing, 1937)

LAMB and MUTTON

Breast of Lamb with Asparagus Tops

Remove the skin and part of the fat from a breast of lamb and cut it into neat pieces; dredge a little flour over them, and place them in a stew-pan with 1 ounce butter; let them remain until nicely browned; cover the meat with warm water, add 1 bunch parsley, 2 button onions; simmer until the meat is cooked; skim off the fat, take out the onions and parsley, and mince the latter finely; return it to the gravy with 1 pint of the tops of boiled asparagus, add salt and pepper, simmer a few minutes longer, and serve. Canned asparagus may be used when the fresh vegetable is out of season.

(Detroit, 1890)

Boudins

Take sufficient cold cooked mutton to make a pint when chopped. Cook together for a moment 2 tablespoons soft bread crumbs, ½ cup stock or water, add a tablespoon butter, the meat nicely seasoned with salt and pepper, and stir in 2 well beaten eggs. Fill into greased custard cups, stand in a pan of boiling water and cook in the oven for 15 or 20 minutes. Turn out on a platter and serve with a cream sauce.

Mrs. J. den Bleyker
(Kalamazoo, 1899)

Hungaria Meat Recipe

*2 pounds mutton from
  shoulder*
*1 pound mutton fat,
  preferably from the
  heart*

6 or 8 large tomatoes
6 or 8 large onions

Slice onions, tomatoes, mutton and mutton fat in pieces of equal size. Place on a spit, first a piece of mutton, then the mutton fat, then onion, then tomato, and continue in this order for the length of the spit.

Place spit over a large pan under grill; hot fire. Keep turning, and basting with:

½ cup water
1 tablespoon of salt

½ cup red wine

Serve with still Burgundy.

A good complement to this dish is grape-fruit salad and black coffee.

Given to Mrs. Homer Pace Ford in China by a Russian Woman.

(Grand Rapids, 1935)

Lamb Curry

Cut a pound of lean lamb into small cubes and wash it in two or three waters. Melt a tablespoonful of butter in a Berlin kettle and into this drop the meat with the water dripping from it. Now add the requisite amount of salt, a pinch of paprika, ¼ teaspoon tumeric and a finely-chopped, medium sized onion. Tightly cover the kettle and let the meat cook on a slow fire. Water will generate from the steam and this will help to cook the meat. When this water is exhausted, fry the meat over a brisk fire, as you would a pot roast, until it is a light brown. Then add 2 pts. of boiling water and cover it tightly. Cook until the water has boiled down to a pint. Then serve the curry on the rice.

(Charlotte, 1909)

A Berlin kettle is a tightly covered kettle with bulging sides.

Minced Lamb With Olives

Toast small pieces of bread and keep hot. Remove the skin and gristle from lamb and chop the meat. Add gravy to moisten, then add ½ cup of chopped green olives. Season with pepper and salt. After a thorough heating place on the toast. Arrange on a platter.

(Lansing, 1923)

"Toad-in-the-Hole"

Mix 1 pint flour and 1 egg with milk enough to make batter (like that for batter cakes) and a little salt; grease dish well with butter, put in lamb chops, add a little water with pepper and salt; pour batter over it and bake for one hour.

(Vermontville, 1906)

SAUCES and GRAVIES

Meats and Their Accompaniments

With roast beef: Tomato sauce, grated horse radish, mustard, cranberry sauce, pickles.

With roast pork: Apple sauce, cranberry sauce.

With roast veal: Tomato sauce, mushroom sauce, onion sauce and cranberry sauce. Horseradish and lemons are good.

With roast mutton: Currant jelly, caper sauce.

With boiled fowls: Bread sauce, onion sauce, lemon sauce, cranberry sauce, jellies, also cream sauce.

With roast lamb: Mint sauce.

(Manistee, 1929)

Asparagus Sauce

One dozen heads asparagus, 2 cups drawn butter, 2 eggs, the juice of ½ lemon, salt and white pepper; boil the tender heads in a very little salted water; drain and chop them; have ready 1 pint drawn butter, with 2 raw eggs beaten into it; add the asparagus and season, squeezing in the lemon-juice last; the butter must be hot, but do not cook after putting in the asparagus heads. This accompanies boiled fowls, stewed fillet of veal, or boiled mutton.

(Detroit, 1890)

Cauliflower Sauce

One small cauliflower, 3 tablespoons butter, cut in bits and rolled in flour, 1 onion, 1 small head celery, mace, pepper and salt, 1 cup water, 1 cup milk or cream; boil the cauliflower in 2 waters, changing when half done, and throwing away the first, reserve 1 teacup of the last; take out the cauliflower, drain and mince; cook in another sauce-pan the onion and celery, mincing them when tender; heat the reserved cup of water again in a saucepan and add the milk; when warm put in the cauliflower and onion, the butter and seasoning, coating the butter thickly with flour, boil until it thickens: good with corned beef or mutton.

(Detroit, 1890)

Cream of Celery Sauce

Cut 1 stalk or root of celery into small pieces. Cover with 1 pint cold water and boil until tender. Drain and measure liquid, add sufficient milk to it to make 1 cup. Put a tablespoon butter and 1 of flour in a sauce pan, when smooth add liquid, stir constantly until it boils, add ½ teaspoon salt and ¼ teaspoon pepper, then celery.

(Kalamazoo, 1899)

Celery Sauce

Fifteen large tomatoes, 5 large onions, 8 stalks of celery, 4 large green peppers, 1 red pepper, 10 tbsp. sugar, 2 tbsp. salt, 3½ c. vinegar 1 tsp. curry

powder. Drain everything; chop tomatoes separately; boil 1 hour.

Mrs. R. D. McKinney
(Kalamazoo, 1921)

Gravies

Is any one perplexed by gravy? Will the grease rise to the top, and the thickening fall to the bottom? Is good gravy on your table an accident rather than a result of thought and painstaking? If this is the case, and I know of one instance where it was so at one time, you will be glad to know that it is not hard to make good gravy.

The smoothness of gravy depends almost entirely upon the way in which the thickening is added. The broth of meat dripping, which is to be the foundation of the gravy, should be strained and skimmed clear of fat. It should then be returned to the stove and brought to a boil. Browned flour should *always* be used for gravy, except when a white sauce for fricasseed chicken, sweetbreads or something of that kind is desired. The flour should be wet up with cold water to a paste, the water being added little by little, until the mixture is about the consistency of very rich cream and *entirely* free from lumps. It should then be poured *slowly* into the boiling broth, stirring all the time. The addition of the cold liquid will, of course, break the boil for a moment or two. The stirring must be kept up until the gravy boils again and for about 3 minutes afterwards, or until the gravy reaches the requisite thickness. Close attention to these instructions should insure good gravy.

(Detroit, 1890)

How to Brown Flour

Sift 1 cup flour into a tin pie plate, and set it on the top of the stove; watch closely, stirring it frequently to see that it does not burn, and taking especial pains to prevent its sticking to the bottom of the pan. It should be of a fine brown, not at all blackened. Some housekeepers prefer browning it in the oven, but it cannot be watched as constantly there as when on the top of the range. It is well to prepare 1 or 2 cups browned flour at a time. It keeps perfectly in a tin box or glass preserve jar, and is then always ready for thickening. If this plan were more invariably followed, there would be fewer tables where a grayish yellow paste, thickened with uncooked flour, appears under the name of gravy.

(Detroit, 1890)

Hot Horseradish Sauce for Baked Ham

One-fourth c. horse radish, ¼ c. fine cracker crumbs, 1½ c. milk, 3 tbsp. butter, ½ tsp. salt, ⅛ tsp. pepper, 1 tbsp. vinegar, 2 tbsp. lemon juice, ½ tbsp. grated onion.

Process: Cook crumbs, horseradish and milk 20 m. in double boiler. Add seasoning, vinegar and lemon juice slowly, stirring constantly. Add grated onion, reheat and serve.

Mrs. J. A. Meulenberg
(Kalamazoo, 1921)

Horseradish Sauce

Mix one-quarter cup grated horseradish with one tablespoon strong vinegar; add one tablespoon sugar and a pinch of salt and pepper. Beat one-quarter cup of cream and mix with other ingredients. Serve cold with baked ham, cold meat, tongue, etc.

(Detroit, 1935)

Mint Sauce

One tablespoon chopped fresh mint; pour over a little hot water, steep a minute or two; take from stove and add ½ teacup vinegar, 2 tablespoons sugar; serve cold; let stand two or three hours before using.

Mrs. C. H. Leonard
(Grand Rapids, 1890)

Mushroom Sauce

One cup of milk, 1 can French mushrooms, 2 tablespoons of butter, 2 tablespoons of browned

flour, pepper and salt. Boil the milk, add butter and flour; lastly, add mushrooms.

Approved by Mrs. A. N. Lane
(Muskegon, 1890)

Mushroom Sauce

One cupful of soup stock, add to it the juice from a can of mushrooms, or better still, cook 1 pint of fresh ones, washed, peeled, cut into small pieces and stewed 15 minutes, using the liquor, to which add two level tablespoonfuls of flour and one of butter blended, stir in and when it thickens add mushrooms and ½ teaspoon lemon juice; serve with chicken, roast veal or fillet of beef.

(Union City, 1890)

Mushroom Sauce for Beefsteak

Take one can of mushrooms, drain and if large cut them up a little. Place in skillet with 1 tablespoonful of butter. Let fry to a light brown. Add 1½ cups of soup stock, if you have it. If not, use hot water, and three tablespoons of tomato catsup, salt and pepper to taste. Thicken a very little with flour. Let boil up thoroughly and serve.

Mrs. J. D. Munson
(Manistee, 1890)

Onion Sauce

Cut one large Spanish onion in small pieces, then add one cup of water and stew slowly until tender and most of the water is absorbed. Make a medium thick white sauce of one cup of cream and one cup of milk. Season well and be generous with the butter. Add the onion to the sauce and serve hot with roast beef.

Mrs. Eugene Richards
(Grand Rapids, 1935)

Pepper Sauce

Four dozen green peppers, five onions, one handful of garlic, three tablespoonfuls of grated horseradish, two quarts best cider vinegar, one quart of water. Put the whole into a kettle on the fire and boil until soft enough to mash in a sieve with a spoon, then add two tablespoonfuls of black pepper, one tablespoonful each of allspice powdered, mace pulverized, one-half tablespoonful of cloves pulverized and one tablespoonful of salt. Place the mixture on the fire and let boil ten minutes. Pass all the spices through a sieve before adding to the peppers.

(Detroit, 1881)

Shirley Sauce

Four quarts of tomatoes, four spoonfuls of salt, four of black pepper, one-half spoonful cayenne pepper, one-half of allspice, three spoonfuls of mustard, all simmered slowly in one quart of vinegar for three hours. Bottle when cold. Put one teaspoonful of olive oil in each bottle just before corking to preserve it.

(Detroit, 1881)

Sauce for Baked Ham

1 heaping tablespoon of dry mustard	2 tablespoons vinegar or ½ glass Sherry
1 glass currant jelly	2 egg yolks slightly beaten

Cook all together until they come to a boil. It can be served either hot or cold.

Mrs. Percy Owen
(Grand Rapids, 1935)

Raisin Sauce (For Baked Ham)

¾ cup seedless raisins	1 tablespoon butter
1 cup water	1 tablespoon vinegar

¾ cup sugar	1 teaspoon lemon juice
1 teaspoon cornstarch	½ teaspoon horse-radish
4 or 5 cloves	
Dash pepper	

Cover raisins with cold water, add cloves. Allow to simmer until raisins are tender. Combine dry ingredients. Add to mixture and stir until thickened slightly, add butter and remaining ingredients. Serve hot. Enough for six servings.

Mrs. T. H. Goodspeed
(Grand Rapids, 1935)

The following four recipes were intended to be served with pork.

Raisin Sauce

Cut half a pound of raisins and stew them in three teacups of water, into which has been stirred three tablespoonfuls of imperial grits and one salt-spoon of salt; let stew thirty-five or forty minutes, add half a teacup or six tablespoonfuls of sugar, and grate in half a nutmeg.

(Detroit, 1878)

Molasses Sauce

Half a pint of molasses, one pint of sugar, piece of butter the size of an egg, teaspoonful of ginger, half a teacup of water; let all boil and serve hot.

(Detroit, 1878)

Virginia Molasses Sauce

Moderately boil a pint of molasses from five to twenty minutes, according to its consistency, add three eggs well beaten, stir them, and continue to boil a few minutes longer; season with nutmeg and serve very hot.

(Detroit, 1878)

153

Maple Sugar Sauce

Make a rich syrup of one scant cup of water and one heaping cup of maple sugar; let boil from twenty to forty minutes. When ready to serve stir into the boiling sugar two tablespoonfuls of butter, braided with one teaspoon of flour.

(Detroit, 1878)

Sauces for the Table— Worcestershire Sauce

The *Druggists' Circular and Chemical Gazette* gives the following recipe for making Lee & Perrin's Worcestershire sauce, which is undoubtedly the most celebrated and popular sauce in the market. It is made in such large quantities that few, unless it be those manufacturing sauces, would undertake to make it: but it may be reduced (say by 15, or any less number, if one chooses) so as to bring it down to the wants of a family or neighborhood for the year. It is as follows: "White wine vinegar, 15 gals.; walnut and mushroom catsups, of each 10 gals.; Madeira wine, 5 gals.; Canton soy, 4 gals.; table salt, 25 lbs.; allspice and coriander seed, powdered, of each 1 lb.; mace and cinnamon, powdered, of each ½ lb.; assafoetida, 4 ozs. dissolved in brandy, 1 gal. Mix together and let stand 2 weeks. Then boil 20 lbs. of hog's liver in 10 gals. of water for 12 hours, renewing the waste water from time to time; then take out the liver, chop it fine and mix it with the water in which it was boiled, and work it through a sieve and mix it thoroughly with the strained liquor which has been standing two weeks; let settle for 24 hours and carefully pour off the clear liquor and bottle for use. Prime."

Remarks—I should think the last part, at least, would have to be filtered, or carefully strained again, to get rid of the sediment from the liver. If for sale, it had all better be filtered. And for me, I should prefer that the assafoetida be left out; yet in this amount, about 60 gals., its distinctive taste would not be noticed.

(Ann Arbor, 1884)

This recipe calls for 4 ozs. of assafoetida, or asefetida. Formerly used in medicine, it is the resin of various oriental plants. If you can't find asfetida, substitute a clove of garlic.

In 1907 the ladies of St. Mark's Episcopal Church in Coldwater published *Good Living and How to Attain It,* a revised edition of a cookbook first compiled by their membership in 1885. They dedicated the slim volume to "the young housewives of 1885 and 1907, who are striving with a laudable ambition to outstrip their mothers in the broad field of home rule."

Margaret L. Powers had written some choice advice on kitchen economy for the 1885 edition, which the ladies reprinted with some additional remarks under the heading "hashes." Margaret Cuyler Ledyard was born June 14, 1830, in Pultneyville, New York, and was educated at the Pittsfield, Massachusetts, Young Ladies Institute. In 1850 she married David Cooper Powers, a young physician. Five years later he hung out his shingle in Coldwater. He served as a surgeon with the famous artillery unit from Coldwater, the Loomis Battery, during the Civil War. After a lucrative medical practice of over thirty years, Dr. Powers died in 1887. Margaret Powers continued to exercise her sensible style of domestic economy at their large residence on Chicago Drive until her death sometime before 1916.

To the Young Housekeeper: Gathering up the Fragments Hashes and Other Made-Over Dishes

To Treat the Subjects at the head of this chapter successfully will require more than a few brief recipes for certain dishes of *Hash*. The needs of the *young* housekeeper will be consulted above every other one. We will make the contents of this division of "Our Cook Book" as helpful as possible to her.

To do justice to the question of "Made-Over Dishes" we will be obliged to go back to the original care of broken meats and every other kind of food, which is thrice a day removed from the family table.

In my old boarding school days in Pittsfield, Mass., it was required of every fifth young lady at the tables after dinner, before the dessert was brought on, to take care of the contents of five adjoining plates with the greatest neatness and good taste she was capable of—putting everything which was good for a second use nicely by itself on one plate and that suitable only for our four footed friends on another. The reason given for this by the wife of our Principal was, that a poor family depended entirely for their daily sustenance upon the crumbs from our table, "and," she said, "I find it utterly impossible to get it properly taken care of by my servants; and, young ladies, I think it most excellent training for you to do this that you may realize the difference between broken food nicely cared for, and, as you can imagine it would be, if swept off these plates *en masse* by a careless hand." Each girl served in turn at this duty, and no noise or sound of scraping of plates was expected to be heard in the dining-room.

I will venture to say that I am but one of hundreds of girls who were benefited through life by this very training, and I will try in this short chapter to pass it on to our own girls, whose boarding-school education was not received in practical New England.

The application of the principle to our private life does not assume the shape of "scraping of plates," which would have its objections, but it applies equally as well to the care of the contents of the general dishes of the table, which should never go to the pantry in the same dishes from which they were served.

It should be understood to begin with that the needs of the home that we have in view is the general average home of ease and comfort, but where the lady of the house is more or less conversant with her kitchen, and ought to know what is going on there, even if she is not obliged to "have a finger in the pie." To her who rests on flowery beds of ease and takes no thought for the morrow's breakfast of her family, the duty remains the same as mistress of a household—that some one shall be commissioned to prevent sinful waste of food, which once for all received Divine condemnation in the miracle of the loaves and fishes.

When you are buying your china then, Young Housekeeper, do not fail to lay in a supply of kitchen dishes for *scraps*—all sizes and kinds—plates, bowls, cups, saucers—some of them small enough to hold just a spoonful of something. It is the spoonful that tells in the throwing away and in the saving. In a snug little dish that *fits,* a spoonful looks much more valuable than in the bottom of a big vegetable dish, where it often looks hardly worth picking up; but scrape it all together nicely and it will grow in respectability with every stroke of your spoon. If you propose to have made-over

dishes often present on your table you must insist on these scrapdishes being utilized. Certain kinds of food harmonize, and delicious dishes are the products of a combination, and here is where the spoonful of this, and that, and the other, finds a place. It is the secret of far-famed French cookery.

Now as to Hashes, put out of your head at once the idea that you must go to the market and buy a particular kind of meat to make good hash. Given a certain amount of cold potato—baked, boiled, stewed or fried, with the addition of butter, salt and pepper—and you can have a good hash out of anything short of sawdust. Cold gravy is the first choice with which to moisten hash, then comes milk, but the absence of both of these and the presence of water instead, need not prove disastrous to your hash.

Some meats are better fitted to be hashed and served on toast instead of with potato. Of course all meats are nice served in this way, but cold ham of all kinds and broiled liver come under the above head. All hashed meat should be fine and free from strings of skin or bits of gristle, and when served on toast should be thickened a little so the meat and gravy will not separate and the watery gravy penetrate the toast. A dish of minced ham on toast garnished by a circle of poached eggs in perfect shape, will be very respectable even for dinner.

When you have mashed potato for dinner is the time for hash-balls. I distinguish between plain hash-balls and "croquets"; the latter are rich in their composition, and are cooked by being dropped in hot lard like doughnuts. *They* should always be served within a folded napkin laid on your dish to absorb the grease; but even then they are not a desirable dish for supper, if one expects to be at peace with his pillow through the night. Hash-balls, on the contrary, are hygienic for anybody in health—made simply of minced meat and gravy, if you have it, and mashed potato mixed with the hands, nicely seasoned, made into flat thin cakes and browned in the spider with as little grease as possible. Let me tell you here that nice beef drippings from a roast, or from the top of the kettle where a soup piece is cooked before any vegetables have been added, is the very best thing to use in browning anything in a spider. Butter scorches; always use as little as possible. Grease in excess in any dish is unwholesome and vulgar. Cold hash can be made over into these same patties.

Another dish from meat and mashed potato: Chop meat very fine: add to a pint or even less of that *one* boiled onion left from yesterday's dinner, mince it up with your knife and fork, season and mix well, never forgetting a little cold gravy if you have it; put in the bottom of a pudding dish and cover with mashed potato an inch deep or more. Bake half an hour for supper. Cold boiled onion is better for such uses than the raw: then you get what cook-books call "the suspicion of an onion."

The second day of a roast it generally comes to the table as a whole and cold. This day the gravy left of yesterday should not appear: it is not good with cold meat, and you need it for the third-day dish. All meats should be sliced very thin, and for this dish cold beef should be heated quickly as possible in the gravy and served. Muttons should be prepared two hours beforehand; remnants of mutton ham are best; add cold gravy, more water, butter, salt, pepper, and flour sifted from your dredger. Cover and let stand on the back of the stove, slowly stewing down; if in danger of getting too dry before needed add a little water. You will find this a very different dish from mutton simply warmed up.

Another good made-over dish of beef is from a piece used one day for a soup. We have always been taught to consider soup-meat unfit for further use, but recent scientific investigations disclose the fact that by cooking in water beef loses the salts and therefore becomes tasteless, but that the nourishment remains in the fiber, and beef-tea is now known to be stimulating but not nourishing. It will therefore be in accordance with the highest authority for me to tell you to get for a family of four or five, four pounds of lean beef from a good juicy round. Let it simmer all the morning in sufficient water to make soup for one dinner, with a pint or so to spare. This extra soup which will be left in the bottom of your tureen will be filled with rice, macaroni, tomato, or whatever you use in it, and flavored with onion. In this soup stew the next day your beef sliced (or a part of it). Cook it slowly for an hour or more, until the soup is of the right consistency for a gravy, and under all such stews fresh rolls or toasted soda biscuits find place. Any remainders of stews are particularly good for hashes.

You ask what is the proper proportion of meat and potato for a good hash. If you chance to have even less than a cup of minced meat you can make a good hash of it for a family of four or five, but if you have abundance you will find that one-third meat to two of potato is better than equal parts of each. If you consult the laws of hygiene in your family, veal will not often appear on your table—but even veal hash can be made safe for dyspeptics.

In the first place cook veal long and well; wet, underdone veal is rank poison. Chop it *very fine* and put it to stew in the gravy left from the roast.

Chop your potatoes less than usual, leaving it in dices, and use a larger proportion of it to the meat: add the potato to the minced veal and gravy which has been overseasoned to receive this addition, and you will have a savory hash with very little veal.

If you should go into your kitchen in search of something for hash and should find yourself in the distressing condition of Mother Hubbard, saving a bit of cold baked pork left from a dish of pork and beans (having a family who like baked beans but eschew the pork), you will probably be at your wit's end and give up your hash; but you take that same rejected remnant (I hope it isn't bigger than a Boston cracker), chop it fine, add salt, and put it on the stove in a spider by itself; as it cooks each particle will shrink by itself into little brown bits; add to this while piping hot enough finely-chopped potato for a dish for four or five people; stir it briskly till well mixed, and then let it brown a particle between the future stirrings and see if the result is not a hash that answers very well on occasion. Don't call it pork hash, "poverty hash" is better. It is very important to serve all hashes *hot*.

Corned-beef hash is well known, but the minced beef by itself, warmed up in cream or milk and butter, with a little flour sifted in, is very nice. Serve it on toast, or by itself, with baked potatoes.

The value of a dish of cold boiled rice—almost ever present in your pantry—is not generally appreciated. Rice as a food is most wholesome and nourishing, and it can be introduced into a great many dishes to advantage, besides appearing baked as a vegetable, and in its old and well-known role of puddings. Always put it into "Johnny-cake" or cornmeal griddlecakes. When you make mush to fry and your pudding has become a very thick gruel, then add cold boiled rice instead of more meal—it is much more delicate; and when made of white cornmeal it is still better. If you have a cup of codfish that was "picked up" and cooked in milk for breakfast, add half a cup of milk, some butter, and a cup or even more of cold boiled rice. When hot season and break in two or three eggs, stir quickly, and serve. To vary this dish, drop a spoonful of this mixture in a hot spider (one spoonful in a place), brown and turn, and you will have rice patties. Use baked rice often in the spring. For that purpose steam it first in salted water instead of milk, add butter, put in a pudding dish and bake half an hour on the grate of your oven, browning the top nicely. Teach your children to like rice in every shape.

Cold stewed corn, macaroni and tomatoes harmonize. Mix them just as they happen to be left, season nicely, put in a pudding dish (if you should have a few small ones to accommodate small quantities), and cover top with finely rolled crackers. Bake quickly not to dry it, as everything was previously cooked.

Cold stewed tomato is an addition to many dishes. If you have a cup of it in your pantry and the *menu* for your next meal includes lamb or mutton chops, take your tomato, heat and season well, and put it through your little gravy-strainer over the broiled chops after they are laid on the dish ready for the table. This is really too Frenchy and high-toned dish to properly come into the society of this chapter, but as it rescued a cup of remnants we will admit it. The scraping and polishing of the ribs of your chops we will omit for obvious reasons.

You young housekeepers will do well to remember that the great proportion of the cooking to be done in your kitchen will be simply for your own family. State occasions are far less important than your daily table, for on that hangs more or less your children's health, and, I might almost add, your husband's wealth. (You remember the old adage about the woman's spoon versus the man's shovel). Consequently any dish that is inviting to the taste and nourishing to the body is right and proper to set before your family and the accidental friend who may happen in. Try and have your family table always ready for this friend, for therein lies the truest hospitality. Never be ashamed of successful economics or be afraid to admit that a certain good dish on your table was made up of rescued scraps.

One of the very best cooks I ever interviewed for information was a dear old darkey who had cooked for high life in the South till after middle age, when she followed a member of her master's family to the North. She was celebrated for dishes peculiar to herself, and they were many of them these very made-over and mixed dishes. When I went to beg for "rules," she said: "Laws, honey, I don't have no rules: I jes puts things together that *tastes good.* You can come down and watch me all you want to; I'se cooked for grandees, from the Bishop down, and dey all likes my cookin', but I can't tell you jes how I does it." I found that the secret of all her cooking was to make things *taste good,* and if at any time you can improvise a good dish from what you may find in your pantry awaiting use or destruction, don't wait to look for authority in some cook-book but just mix and taste, and taste and mix, on the authority of a few general rules as to the eternal fitness of things, and ten to one your family will have set before them *something*—no matter if it has no name—better than you could have produced from following a high sounding recipe in some standard collection.

I fear this subject has already been voted tiresome, but if any of "our girls" who are just now entering on the trials and pleasures of a housekeeper's life find in this chapter on the homely art of kitchen economics any help or comfort the end will be gained.

Margaret L. Powers
Coldwater, March, 1885
(Coldwater, 1907)

Since the above was written twenty-one years have passed and now the advice contained therein is "of age," and should be able to speak for itself. The fundamental principles of the subject treated remain the same, but the popularity of mixed dishes has greatly increased during the passing of the years, and now the lady who can invent a dish containing the greatest variety of combinations that comes out a salad, a stew, or a sandwich, walks off with the prize. The rule of the old colored cook still hold good, "put things together as *tastes good.*"

When "Our Cook Book" was issued a sandwich was two slices of bread and one slice of cold boiled ham. Today, who is wise enough to tell what is in a sandwich? You only know it is good and ask no questions. And so apples and celery, nuts and eggs, olive oil, vinegar and sugar, lettuce leaves and jelly, all fraternize as a "happy family," and happy is the family who has among its members a skillful salad maker. We leave the same old homely chapter, aged twenty-one, because it is still needed in the kitchen of the young housekeepers of today, who will find that a family cannot subsist entirely on the mysterious and attractive salads and sandwiches.

The old-time kitchen economics are as valuable as ever, and they are as unchanging as the needs of the human race, which never fail to call for breakfast, dinner and supper, in the best shape and with the least waste possible.

So we hope the new generation of young housekeepers will be patient to still "mark, learn and inwardly digest" the advise given to a former generation.

Margaret L. Powers
(Coldwater, 1907)

Fowl and Fish

FOWL

Poultry

There are various ways of deciding about the age of poultry. If the bottom of the breast bone, which extends down between the legs, is soft, and gives easily, it is a sign of youth; if stiff, the poultry is old. If young, the legs are lighter, and the feet do not look so hard, stiff and worn.

There is more deception in geese than in any other kind of poultry. The above remarks are applied to them; but there are other signs more infallible. In a young goose, the cavity under the wings is very tender; it is a bad sign if you cannot, with very little trouble, push your finger directly into the flesh. There is another means by which you may decide whether a goose be tender, if it be frozen or not. Pass the head of a pin along the breast, or sides, and if the goose be young, the skin will rip, like fine paper under a knife.

Something may be judged concerning the age of a goose by the thickness of the web between the toes. When young, this is tender and transparent; it grows coarser and harder with time.

Do not feed poultry for twenty-four hours before killing; cut the throat or cut off the head with a very sharp knife or axe and allow it to hang head downward until the blood has ceased to drip. The thorough bleeding renders the meat white and wholesome. Scald well by dipping the fowl in and out of boiling water, taking care not to scald too much or the feathers will be hard to pluck. Pull the feathers from you and when the bird is carefully picked, remove all the fine feathers with a knife; singe, but not smoke, over blazing paper, place on a board and with a sharp knife cut off the legs a little below the knee; remove the oil-bag above the tail;

"He who snoozes loses" (Gems, 1880).

take out the crop, by making a slit at the front of the neck, taking care that everything pertaining to the crop is removed; cut the neck-bone off close to the body, leaving the skin a good length to be stuffed; cut around the rent, cut a slit three inches long from the tail upwards, being careful to cut only through the skin, put in the finger at the breast and detach all the intestines, taking care not to burst the gall-bag, for if broken, no washing can remove the bitter taint left on every spot it touches, put in the hand at the incision near the tail and draw out carefully all intestines; trim off the fat from the breast and at the lower incision; slip the gizzard and take out the outside and inside lining; wash the fowl thoroughly in cold water twice (or wipe carefully with a wet cloth and then with a dry), then hang up to drain, and it is ready for cooking.

Make the dressing, and fill the breast first, but not too full or it will burst in cooking; stuff the body rather fuller than the breast; sew up both openings with strong thread and sew the skin of the neck down upon the breast, not forgetting to remove the threads before sending to the table. Lay the points of the wings under the back and fasten them in that position with a skewer run through both wings or

158

tie down with a piece of twine; press the legs as closely toward the breast and sidebones as possible, and fasten with a skewer run through the body and both thighs, or tie with twine. After this is done, rub thoroughly with salt and pepper.

Chickens and turkeys are dressed and stuffed in the same manner. Those that are a little tough or old are greatly improved by a few moments' steaming before they are roasted or boiled. Roast chickens require twenty or thirty minutes, or till nicely browned. The giblets—liver, heart and gizzard— after being carefully washed and soaked in salt and water, are cooked and then minced fine and used for the gravy, or may be cooked and served with the fowl. When very young chickens are to be baked, or broiled, they should be cut open at the side of the backbone, pressed apart, cleaned as above directed, and placed on broiler or in dripping pan, with the meat side downward and butter them, or fowls may be larded in the same way as game or a tablespoonful of butter may be put in bits over the breast.

To roast; place in an oven rather hot at first, and then graduated to moderate heat until nearly done. To test this insert a fork between the thigh and body; if the juice is watery and not bloody it is done. Fowls are roasted upon dripping pans, with a wire rack or small rings placed on the bottom of pan. Some put fowls to roast in a dry pan, using the drippings for basting, and others put in a little water. In roasting a turkey allow twenty minutes to the pound and twenty minutes longer. If poultry cannot be served immediately it is done, it may be kept hot without drying up by placing over a kettle of boiling water and laying a dripping pan over it.

In broiling chickens, it is difficult to do the inside of the thickest pieces without scorching the outside. It is a good plan to parboil them about ten minutes in a spider or skillet, covered close to keep the steam in; then put them upon the gridiron, broil and butter; cover them with a plate, while on the gridiron. They may be basted with a very little of the water in which they were broiled; and if you like melted butter to pour upon the chicken, the remainder of the liquor will be good used for that purpose.

An hour is enough for common sized chicken to roast. A smart fire is better than a slow one; but they must be tended closely. Slices of bread, buttered, salted and peppered, put into the stomach (not the crop) are excellent.

Chickens should boil about an hour. If old, they should boil longer, in as little water as will cook them. Have the water hot unless wanted for soup and then put them in cold. Skim when it boils up first, and keep it just above the boiling point, but it must boil gently, not violently. A little vinegar added to the water in which fowls are boiled makes them more tender.

Many, in making meat or fish pies, line the bottom of the pan with crust, and place in the oven until well "set," then line the sides, fill, cover and bake; it is difficult to bake the crust on bottom of dish, unless this plan is followed. A still better plan is to use no bottom, lining only the sides of the pan.

The garnishes for turkey, chicken and duck, are slices of lemon, horseradish, fried sausages or force meat balls, parsley, fried oysters and thin slices of ham.

(Detroit, 1881)

Chicken à la Baltimore

Cut up a plump, year-old chicken, rub with one heaping teaspoon of salt and ¼ saltspoon of pepper, dip in flour egg and crumbs, place in a well-greased pan and bake in a hot oven until tender, basting several times. Arrange on a hot platter, pour over the cream sauce and garnish with parsley.

Cream Sauce

Melt 3 tablespoons butter, add three tablespoons flour and pour in gradually, while stirring constantly, two cupfuls of rich milk. Season with salt and pepper.

Mrs. Eugene Cook
(Kalamazoo, 1906)

Carrot Loaf

2 cups carrot ground fine (after cooking)	2 eggs beaten
1 cup (or more) bread crumbs	1 or 2 cups ground chicken

Salmon or other meat may be used.

Bake in greased loaf pan from 20 to 25 minutes.

Mrs. John Den Bleyker, Holland
(Allegan, 1938)

Chicken en Casserole

One chicken, 2 small onions, 2 small carrots, 2 or 3 stalks of celery, 1½ cups of stock, 1 tablespoon olive oil, 1½ teaspoons salt, dash of paprika. Cut the vegetables and cook in the olive oil until brown. Unless chicken is young it is best to fricassee before putting in casserole. When parboiled place chicken in casserole with 1½ cups of stock, the vegetables and olive oil, cover and cook until tender. When the chicken is young it can be prepared entirely in the casserole. When half done sprinkle with salt and paprika. Make gravy from liquor in casserole and pour again over chicken and serve in casserole.

Lucy Williams, Lapeer
(Charlotte, 1909)

We enjoyed this dish. We used chicken bouillon for the stock and eliminated the additional salt called for. Other vegetables such as mushrooms and zucchini can be added. Cook on top of the range slowly for two hours. We served this casserole with the following dumplings.

Dumplings for Meat

First have your meat or chicken cooked and tender, with not too much broth. Let the meat stick up out of the broth, as they will be lighter if not dropped into the broth, but around on the meat or chicken.

This "brown spray decorated" casserole dish with an "under glaze on white granite body" sold for $1.47 in 1890 (Grand Rapids, 1890).

Dumplings

One egg, ⅔ cupfull of sweet milk, a little salt, 2 teaspoons baking powder. Add enough flour to make as stiff as you can stir in easily, and drop over the meat or chicken. Cover and cook 20 minutes, not too fast. When done take up meat and dumplings and thicken any broth that is left and pour over dumplings.

Mrs. L. A. Carpenter
(Covert, 1903)

We found these dumplings to be light, tender, and tasty. Evaporated milk is a substitute for sweet milk. We used one heaping cup of flour and, after cooking the dumplings in the chicken broth, browned them in the oven for two minutes.

Stewed Chicken with Cauliflower

Wash and cut the chicken up as usual. Have water to cover, one teaspoon of salt, a shake or two of pepper, and, if the chicken is tough, put in a piece of baking soda, size of a pea. When it begins to boil skim carefully. Let the cauliflower lie in salt and water for half an hour. Then divide it and put in steamer over the chicken. When both are done take them out and place neatly on large, hot platter, and put in warming oven. Take two tablespoons of cornstarch, stir smooth in a little cold water; add this to the gravy in kettle, and a small lump of butter; if not salt enough add a trifle more. Stir five minutes until it thickens and tastes done, then pour it over the chicken and cauliflower.

Mrs. B. G. Wilbur, Hillsdale
(Chicago, 1896)

Chicken Cornucopias

Cut squares of cardboard 5 inches square and fold two corners together to form the cornucopia. Stick the edges together with mending tape and round off the corners. Make a pie crust and cut in 5½-inch square, flour the horns and fold the pastry squares around these, fastening together with cold water as in pies. Brush with milk. Bake in 450° F. oven until light brown. Before filling dip edges in egg white beaten slightly and then in chopped parsley that has been fairly well dried out. Fill with creamed chicken and mushroom, topping each with a whole mushroom surrounded with a strip of pimento.

Mrs. Bradford Apted
(Grand Rapids, 1935)

Creamed Chicken

2 cupfuls of cold chicken	*2 tablespoonfuls of butter*
1 cupful of chicken stock	*1 heaping tablespoonful of flour*
1 cupful of milk or cream	*Salt and pepper*

Cut the chicken into small pieces. Cook the butter and flour together in Chafing Dish; add the stock and milk or cream and stir all until smooth; put in the chicken, salt and pepper, and cook 3 minutes longer.

(Grand Rapids, 1917)

Our children thought this was great. We substituted bouillon for stock and margarine for butter, cooked it in a double boiler, and served it over biscuits.

Chicken Fricasseed, Upon Toast and Without

Cut up a chicken and put on to boil in a small quantity of water. Add a seasoning of salt and pepper, and onion if you like. Stew slowly (covered) until tender; then add rich milk, ½ pt. (cream is all the better), with a little butter; and if you have parsley, add a little of it chopped, just as ready to serve. Have the bread, which has been cut thin, nicely toasted and lightly buttered, arranged on a platter; then pour over the fricassee, and serve at once. Without the toast, it is the common fricassee.

Remarks—A young turkey, or a nicely dressed rabbit, treated in every way the same as the chicken, will also make a nice fricassee. But our chicken dishes would hardly be complete without a chicken currie, and perhaps, also, chicken with

green peas, both of which I have obtained from a book entitled "Indian Domestic Economy and Cookery," which I borrowed from a Mrs. Bronson, whose husband, Dr. Bronson, had spent over 40 years in India, as a missionary, but whose age and debility required him to return home, and he was then (1881) living at Eaton Rapids, Mich. Dr. Bronson was very anxious, if his health would allow, to return to his work; but being about 70 years old, I told him I thought he had done all that duty required of him in that far off country, and I doubted much if his health would ever allow his return. This lady was his third wife, a faithful and true helpmate in his work. I received several items of information from her in relation to the Indian customs, in cooking, etc., which helped me to understand the work above mentioned, much better than I otherwise would, their ways are so different from ours. These items I shall mention in the different places where needed, in the recipes I shall give from this work. They were married in India, where she had lived several years before their marriage. The book was printed in Madras, in 1853, at the "Christian Knowledge Society Press," and the copy she brought with her showed signs of having been much used. My acquaintance with her was, as some say, purely accidental, others, providential. I was standing in the door of the Frost House, Eaton Rapids, where I was stopping for the benefit of the mineral springs and rest, when Mrs. Bronson, in passing with a baby carriage, having twin babies in it, stopped to talk a few moments with the landlady, who, with some other ladies, were also standing about, when one of them knowing that Mrs. B. had recently come from India, asked her where the children were born, to which the answer was: "In Assam," when I at once became interested (as I had a cousin in that province of India), to know if they had met; when, on learning his name (Mason) they had been neighbors and co-workers for some years; hence my acquaintance with Mrs. B. and her husband, and I thus obtained access to the book from which I take the next recipe, and a few others which are credited as above indicated.

My cousin had then been in Assam about seven years, in the mission work. His health, and that of his wife, having already begun to fail considerably, so that during the following year (1882) he had to come home, more especially, however, on his wife's account, whose health continued to fail very fast, and although she seemed to recruit a little on her first arrival, or soon after, yet her health had been so undermined by her stay in India, she died within a few months after reaching her friends in

America. But, notwithstanding the lives of American women who go out as missionaries, are short in India, yet they generally are so devoted to their work, or to their husbands, they seldom make any complaint—they give themselves, and their lives, cheerfully, for the Master's cause. Let none fail, therefore, to do their duty, although it should call them to India.

(Ann Arbor, 1884)

Chicken Currie, With Rice, as Made in India

Cut the chicken into as many joints as possible. Take 1 onion and slice it finely and fry in a tablespoonful or more of *ghee* (the word used in India for butter, but drippings, or even lard, my informant, Mrs. Bronson, says is often used), sprinkling over the onion, 1 tea-spoonful of currie powder. When the onion is nicely browned put in the jointed chicken, and salt sufficient, and put on a tea-spoonful more of the currie powder, and fry until nicely browned; then pour on sufficient hot water (see in remarks that milk, or the milk of cocoanuts may be used) to cover the chicken, and stew (covered) until perfectly tender. [Some of the native cooks boil the chicken tender before frying in the currie, but my informant says this is not the best way.] Serve with plain boiled rice, either in separate dishes, or, preferably, put the boiled rice on the platter, pushing it out around the edge, then pour the currie into the middle, the whiteness of the rice making fine contrast with the browned currie.—*Indian Domestic Economy and Cookery.*

Remarks—Young mutton, lamb, veal, and fish, when cut into suitable pieces, Mrs. Bronson informs me, treated every way the same as chicken, makes an equally nice currie, and are more frequently used as such in India than chicken; but we Americans think there is nothing equal to chicken. This lady gives me the plan of cooking the rice in India, and the use of the water in which it is cooked, as follows:

To Boil the Rice India Fashion—Wash it through 3 or 4 waters. Have plenty of boiling water in a large kettle, put in the rice and boil very briskly until tender; then pour in a cup of cold water, and pour into a colander; when well drained, return to the kettle to steam a short time to dry out the surplus water;

"Go set the table Mary, an' let the cloth be white. / The hungry city children are comin' here to-night," wrote Michigan poet laureate Will Carleton in City Ballads, *published in 1886. A summer kitchen similar to the one illustrated here would have served well in making Dr. Chase's favorite chicken curry recipe (New York, 1886).*

then serve on the platter, or separate dish, as above.

The rice water poured off is, says this lady, the best kind of starch, and is used for that purpose by the washermen—men in India doing the washing wholly. What a blessed thing it would be for some of the over-worked women of our country if their husbands had to do the washing, instead of spending their time, and often the money their wives have earned by washing, for whiskey! How long shall it continue?

The Milk of Cocoanuts is often used in India, says our informant, and I think it would be very nice here, as well as there, instead of the water or milk in which, or with which, to cook the currie, whether it be chicken, veal, lamb, or fish; and they also scrape out the meat of the nut, having a tool for that purpose much like a scraper to remove letters from a box or barrel by shippers, except that the edge is rounding to fit the inside of the nut, and has sharp teeth like a saw, which makes the pulp fine and fit to mix into the gravy of the currie. Such a tool could be very easily made by an American blacksmith, taking him a cocoanut that he might get the shape for the toothed edge and knowing what it was to be used for.

At a subsequent time, while in Eaton Rapids, I was invited to take tea with Dr. Bronson, that I might partake of a currie prepared as above, by his wife and an Indian gentleman, who had been several years in the University at Ann Arbor, qualifying himself as a physician to go back to his country for the good of his countrymen. He understood Indian cookery, and between them they made a most excellent currie; and although it was pretty warm—I might say hot—with the currie powder, yet I liked it very much and should be glad to have a chance to eat of one every day in the week if not at every meal. It warmed up my stomach nicely, and it is said to be a cure of dyspepsia. If found too hot on the first trial to suit any one, use less currie powder next time, and you can soon work to suit the taste of any family. I believe it to be healthful, and they suit my taste exactly.

(Ann Arbor, 1884)

Chicken in Peas, as Cooked in India

Cut the chicken into joints, as for a fricassee or currie, and put into a sauce-pan with about a quart of young shelled peas, a spoonful or two of *ghee* (butter), a small sliced onion, and a nice sprig or two of parsley, and moisten more with drippings if thought best; put on the fire, dusting with a little flour, and stew (covered) until done; and add a little salt, and a little sugar, if relished, just before serving.—*Indian Domestic Economy and Cookery.*

(Ann Arbor, 1884)

Brown Fricasseed Chicken

Singe, draw and disjoint the chicken; put into a good sized sauce pan 2 tablespoons butter, when hot drop in the pieces of chicken, allow them to brown gradually, taking great care the butter does not burn. As soon as the pieces are browned, draw them to one side of the sauce pan, and add to the fat 2 tablespoons flour; mix and add 1 pint stock or water. Stir constantly until it begins to boil, moving the chicken around in the sauce. Add 1 slice of onion, 1 bay leaf, 1 tablespoon chopped carrot, 1 teaspoon salt, ¼ teaspoon pepper. Cover the sauce pan, push it to the back part of the stove, where the chicken may simmer gently till done. Dish the chicken, take the sauce from the fire, add to it the yolk of 1 egg, beaten with 2 tablespoons cream;

strain this over the chicken. Garnish with crescents of fried bread, dust over a little finely chopped parsley.

Mrs. F. B. Orcutt.
(Kalamazoo, 1899)

Fried Chicken

Cut up fowl and cook until tender but not to fall to pieces. Make a fritter batter of 1 egg, 1 cup milk, ¾ cup flour, 2 teaspoons baking powder. Dip the chicken in batter and fry in deep lard as you would doughnuts. Spring chickens may be cooked in same manner without previous cooking, but remain in hot fat a little longer. Delicious.

Annie H. Crabtree, South Haven
(Charlotte, 1909)

Chicken Italienne

½ cup olive oil	*2 cans tomatoes*
1 pkg. vermicelli	*2 cups water*
5 lb. chicken	*1 clove garlic*
1 box mushrooms	*Salt and pepper to*
2 green peppers	*taste*
1 large stalk celery	

Brown chicken in olive oil and put in a roaster or dutch oven and cook until tender. Dice celery, mushrooms, green pepper and onions, and sauté. Pour tomatoes and water over mushrooms and vegetables, add garlic, salt and pepper. Let simmer slowly while chicken is cooking. When chicken is almost done, pour tomato sauce over it and cook until chicken is done, which should be about 15 or 20 min. Serve Parmesan cheese with it.

Mrs. Harry Davisson
(Kalamazoo, 1941)

Kovski Cutlets

Slice thin cooked chicken breasts. Roll slices around butter balls flavored with a little onion juice.

Batter

Roll in batter
1 cup flour
½ teaspoon of salt
Pepper
½ cup cream

2 eggs well beaten
Mix flour, salt and pepper
Add cream and eggs

Drop in *deep very* hot fat. Fry till delicately brown.

Mrs. Hamer Pace Ford
(Grand Rapids, 1935)

Mrs. Hamer Pace Ford picked up this recipe on a world cruise during which she visited Russia. Most modern cookbooks refer to this dish as Chicken Kiev.

Left-over Chicken

Mince fine, add 1 pt. cream, butter, salt and pepper to taste; nutmeg, bread crumbs, 1 egg. Make in oval shape and fry like fritters. Make a white sauce, spiced to taste; throw over fine parsley or brown bread crumbs. Very nice.

Mrs. Alice Ibling
(Kalamazoo, 1921)

The nutmeg gave these ancestors to "Chicken McNuggets" an interesting flavor, but they turned out too mushy for our liking. Perhaps they would be better lightly breaded.

Chicken Pie

Cut up 2 tender chickens, cover with boiling water and cook until tender, covering closely; as water boils away add more, enough to make liquor for pie, and gravy to serve with it. Grease and trim the sides of a 4 qt. baking dish (or pan) with rich baking powder biscuit dough nearly half an inch thick; put in a few pieces of chicken, season with salt, pepper, and butter some bits or squares of dough, then more chicken, etc. Season also the liquor in which chicken was boiled, put in enough to make quite moist, cover with crust same thickness as above, cutting a hole the size of a silver dollar, in center of crust; through this more of the liquor can be added as the pie is baking, that it may have plenty of moisture. Bake 1 hour in a moderate oven. For gravy, add to the liquor left, 1 tablespoon butter rubbed with a little flour, season with salt and pepper, stirring in little by little; let boil up once and serve. Meat pie, especially veal pie, is delicious made in this way.

(Ann Arbor, 1872)

Chicken Pie

Stew tender 5 lbs. of chicken, add a cup of butter and 1 pt. of water and one of milk, thicken with a spoonful of flour, then take a qt. of flour, 3 teaspoons baking powder, mix with milk and take lard the size of an egg, roll ½ of the dough and line a 4 qt. baking tin or dish; the rest of the dough roll large and use a cup of butter, cut in little pieces and fold over and over, roll, and cover the dish after putting in the chicken; cut an artistic opening in the top crust.

Mrs. C. M. Hubbard
(Muskegon, 1890)

Chicken Pie

Cook chicken until it falls from bones. Put in baking dish with 2 tablespoons butter, 3 cups of

Turn-of-the-century cooks opted for roomy mutton-chop sleeves (New York, 1890).

stock and 1 cup milk, thickened with 3 tablespoons flour.

Place in oven while preparing crust.

Crust

2 cups flour	*2 teaspoons baking*
1 teaspoon salt	*powder*
	2 tablespoons butter

Rub through flour. Beat 1 egg, add 1 cup of milk, then the flour; stir to batter, spread over chicken and bake.

Mrs. Chas. S. Davies
(Grand Rapids, 1917)

Chicken and Ham Pie

Season sufficient slices of boiled ham, with pepper and salt, if needed, and put a layer upon the paste, which should be ½ inch thick; then a layer of chicken, which has been jointed and cooked till tender, upon the ham, and also the yolks of some hard-boiled eggs, sliced; a couple layers of each should properly fill the dish; putting in some gravy made with water in which the chicken was boiled, adding, if liked, ½ cup of tomatoes to the gravy; cover with another crust, and bake only to bake the crust; or it may be baked without the gravy, and I think this the better way, the gravy being made to dip upon the pie, and mashed potatoes, with which it is to be served. If no eggs and tomatoes, make it without, and still it will be very nice, if the meats have been cooked tender before putting into the pie.

(Ann Arbor, 1884)

We enjoyed this tasty dish on a cold winter's evening as the wind howled through the trees. We used Professor Blot's pie crust (see page 257). The bottom layer of crust should be baked for 10 minutes at 400° before adding the various layers. We added a 16 oz. can of peas to the layers and incorporated the juice from the peas into the gravy.

Pickled Fowl—Marinade

After removing the skin of a chicken, cut it in pieces and wash it in cold water, and clean and pre-

pare the giblets; cook these slowly for three or four hours in a pickle made of vinegar and chicken soup stock in equal parts, adding salt, pepper, parsley, onions. Then drain them, dip them in eggs well beaten, roll them in flour or fine cracker crumbs, fry them, and serve with garniture of parsley.

(Detroit, 1878)

Potted Chicken

Strip the meat from the bones of a cold, roast fowl; to every pound of meat allow ¼ pound butter, salt and cayenne pepper to taste, 1 teaspoon pounded mace, ½ a small nutmeg. Cut the meat into small pieces, pound it well with the butter, sprinkle in the spices gradually, and keep pounding until reduced to a perfectly smooth paste; pack it into small jars and cover with clarified butter, about ¼ inch thick. Two or 3 slices ham, minced and pounded with the above, will be an improvement. Keep in a dry place. A luncheon or breakfast dish.

Old fowls can be made very tender by putting into them, while boiling, a piece of soda as large as a bean.

(Detroit, 1890)

Larry, who has been a luncheon speaker at hundreds of Michigan organizations, and thereby considers himself an expert on chicken salad, insisted that we include the following variations.

Chicken Salad

Is eminently an American dish, and Detroit is quite celebrated for its delicious chicken salads. Our entertainments may not be as showy as in other western cities, but *our* caterers understand that the stale salads of a previous party can never be freshened. Mrs. Henderson makes a suggestion which we have found work very nicely, that she calls *"marinating the chicken."* Mix the celery and chicken together, and then stir well into them a mixture in the proportion of three tablespoonfuls of vinegar to one of oil and one (level) of salt, a pinch—the smallest pinch—of cayenne, about what would lie on the point of a penknife, and a teaspoonful of mixed mustard. Let the chicken stand in this mixture an hour or two; drain off what may be in the bottom of the bowl; ten or twenty minutes before serving pour over a mild mayonnaise. Little strips of anchovy rolled up are used with pickles, hard boiled eggs, and lettuce heads, or tender yellow celery tops to garnish.

We give as minute directions as possible for the various methods and tastes in mixing the dressing.

An eight-pound turkey, rubbed with fresh lemon, and boiled in well salted water (having two tablespoonfuls of raw rice in it), is used and preferred by many to a pair of chickens. The flavor is radically different, but quite delightful. Every one of the receipts given will make a nice salad, unless our scholars fall into the error of a well-meaning lady, who set her dish of salad into the hot oven for half an hour. The colder your salad is the crisper and fresher it will taste, and the thicker and better will be your dressing.

(Detroit, 1878)

Chicken Salad

Boil until tender two nice fowls; throw into the water a small handful of rice, which will make the meat white. When cold cut with a sharp knife into pieces about one quarter inch square; add one quart celery cut coarse, mix well together; boil six eggs very hard, take the yolks and stir with the bowl of a spoon, adding one gill of table oil or melted butter, until the consistency of cream, one teaspoonful of pepper, two tablespoonfuls mixed mustard, one teacup strong vinegar, one-half cup grated horse-radish, one-half cup sugar, one tablespoonful salt; beat well one-half hour before using; mix well with the chicken before serving. Ornament the top of the dish with the tops of the celery and the whites of the eggs.

(Detroit, 1878)

Chicken Salad

Boil three chickens until tender, salting to taste; when cold cut in small pieces and add twice the quantity of celery cut up with a knife but not chopped, and four cold-boiled eggs sliced and

thoroughly mixed through the other ingredients. For dressing, put on stove a sauce-pan with one pint vinegar and butter size of an egg; beat two or three eggs with two table-spoons mustard, one of black pepper, two of sugar, and a tea-spoon salt, and when thoroughly beaten together pour slowly into the vinegar until it thickens. Be careful not to cook too long or the egg will curdle. Remove, and when cold pour over salad. This may be prepared the day before, adding the dressing just before using. Add lemon juice to improve the flavor, and garnish the top with slices of lemon.

Mrs. C. E. Skinner, Battle Creek
(Minneapolis, 1881)

Chicken Salad (with Cabbage)

Boil tender two nice chickens, mince well the meat, removing every scrap of fat, gristle and skin; take the best part of a small cabbage, discarding all the pith and green leaves; chop fine—there should be less than a quart when chopped—chop half as much celery as cabbage and mix well with the chicken; then boil four eggs very hard, work the yolks to a paste with a wooden spoon; half gill of good sweet olive oil or one gill of melted butter; mix gradually with the egg until all is mixed; add one tablespoonful of finely ground best black pepper, two tablespoonfuls of mixed mustard stirred thoroughly into the paste, and add one teacup of vinegar and one tablespoonful of salt; mix all together half an hour before using. If liked add half a cup of grated horseradish.

(Detroit, 1881)

Chicken Salad

Take a chicken weighing about 3 lbs., boil tender; when cold, remove the bones, chop fine, using both dark and light meat; boil 4 eggs hard, rub the yolks fine with 2 teaspoons mustard and 1 teacup thick cream, salt and pepper to taste, chop the whites of the eggs, and as much celery as you have chicken; the last thing add 1 teacup of vinegar.

Mrs. C. C. Rood
(Grand Rapids, 1890)

Chicken Salad for Fifty

Six chickens, using only the white meat, second joints and the olives in backs. Four pounds sweet-breads, about a pound of pecan meats broken, 6 heads celery and what aspic jelly can be made from stock in which chicken was cooked. Cut up chicken about four hours before serving time, and pour over a marinade made in proportion of tablespoon oil to three of vinegar. When ready to mix, drain the chicken thoroughly and proceed as usual. The aspic should be cut in cubes and mixed lightly through, just at the last, reserving about a quarter of it for garnish. Use cooked mayonnaise made with butter and thinned with whipped cream.

Mrs. Chas. A. Peck
(Kalamazoo, 1906)

Smothered Chickens

Cut the chickens in the back, lay them flat in a dripping pan with one cup of water; let them stew in the oven until they begin to get tender, take them out and season with salt and pepper; rub together one and one-half tablespoonfuls of flour, one table-spoonful butter; spread all over the chicken; put back in the oven, baste well and when tender and nicely browned take out of the dripping pan; mix with the gravy in the pan one cup of thickened milk with a little flour; put on the stove and let it scald up well and pour over the chickens; parsley chopped fine is a nice addition to the gravy.

(Detroit, 1881)

Chicken (Spanish Stew)

Four lbs. chicken, 1 pt. can or 5 ripe tomatoes, 1 good sized red pepper (remove most of the seeds and chop), 1 medium sized onion minced, 1 table-spoon parsley minced, 1 can peas, 4 stalks celery, 1 can mushrooms, salt to taste, 1 qt. boiling water, potatoes sufficient for number of persons to be served.

Way of preparing—Clean and joint chicken, slice tomatoes, shred pepper (removing most of the seeds), mince onion and celery. Place chicken in stew pan with boiling water, add salt and cook until chicken is tender. Thicken the liquor slightly and add potatoes, when potatoes are nearly tender, add peas, parsley and mushrooms. Dish chicken in center of platter, with border of potatoes and pour remaining contents of stew over and serve hot.

Mrs. E. L. Bates, Pentwater
(Charlotte, 1909)

Chicken for Supper

Boil two chickens in as little water as possible, until the meat separates easily from the bones; pick it all off, cut it rather fine, and season it well with pepper and salt. Now put in a mold (a bowl or oval pan will answer) some slices of hard boiled eggs, then a layer of chicken, next more eggs, (always putting the best slices of egg at the sides and bottom of the mold, and the broken pieces through the chicken). Boil down the water in which the chicken was boiled, until there is a pint left, adding to it when done a large pinch of gelatine which has been dissolved in a little cold water. Season this gravy with butter, pepper and salt, and pour it over the chicken. It will sink through, forming a jelly around it. Let it stand on ice until perfectly cold; turn it out on a dish and garnish with bleached celery leaves. It is to be sliced at table. Delicious served with cucumber dressing.

Mrs. L. C. Chapin
(Kalamazoo, 1906)

We prepared this in a deep, depression-glass bowl. I turned it over on a bed of lettuce, and a few minutes later it released from the bowl. It made a very impressive and appetizing dish, ideal for a buffet. We recommended ½ envelope of gelatine be added to the liquid.

Chicken with Vegetable Dressing

Prepare fowl as for baking; boil whole for one hour with water half covering. Turn after forty-five minutes and immerse the part out of the water. Salt and pepper before starting to boil.

Prepare the stuffing with one quart bread

crumbs moistened with broth from fowl, season and add two eggs, one grated potato, one carrot, one onion and small parsnip if desired. Leaves from small bunch of celery, some parsley, one-half each red and green pepper, half a dozen leaves of spinach, shredded mushrooms, if desired (and a half pint of fresh oysters make it delicious, but may be omitted, if desired).

Mix vegetables into bread crumbs, add one heaping teaspoon baking powder, salt to season the vegetables, pepper to taste. Lift fowl from broth and fill with stuffing. Bake in moderate oven until tender and the vegetables are cooked.

(Detroit, 1935)

Roast Duck with Baked Apples

Take a young duck that weighs about four pounds; singe and wash quickly; wipe dry, and rub both the inside and outside of the fowl with the juice of half a lemon (reserve the other half for the pudding sauce); then fill with a dressing made of three cupfuls of light but stale bread crumbs, one large cookingspoonful of softened butter, one small onion minced fine, one large sour apple cut in rather thick slices, one teaspoonful of salt and one-fourth teaspoonful of pepper; mix all, place in the fowl, sew up and bake in a hot oven till tender, basting often. (Two or three very thin slices of bacon laid on any fowl when put in the roasting pan improves the flavor and color.) Serve with tart baked apples.

Miss Susan Sawyer Matron, State School, Coldwater
(Chicago, 1896)

Orange Sauce for Domestic Duck

Melt 4 tablespoons butter in sauce pan, add 4 tablespoons flour sifted with 1 teaspoon mustard, ½ teaspoon salt, and a few grains cayenne. Stir until smooth then add gradually 1 cup brown stock, stirring constantly, simmer 5 minutes, add ¼ glass currant jelly, continue stirring and simmer 5 minutes and add juice and grated rind of 2 sweet oranges. Bring quickly to a boiling point and serve

at once. Bits of orange rind may be cut in fancy shapes and added to sauce.

Nina Ramsey
(Higgins Lake, 1920)

Dressing for Geese or Ducks

Two ounces onions, one ounce green sage leaves, one ounce of pecans or walnuts, chopped fine; a sprig of fennel, thyme or a bay leaf; four ounces toasted bread crumbs (made by putting crusts in an oven and when thoroughly brown and dry grating them), one tablespoonful of butter, the yolk of one egg well beaten, a minced apple, one dozen raw oysters, one or two bird peppers, black pepper and salt to taste; a few mushrooms and a truffle or two, chopped fine, adds to the delicious flavor.

(Detroit, 1881)

Bird pepper is the small chilies of species capsicum from which ground cayenne is made, hence we would use ¼ teaspoon of cayenne pepper if bird pepper is not available.

Roast Goose

Parboil an hour or two to remove some of the strong flavor. There are many ways of stuffing. The apple stuffing may be used or one made as follows: Two medium-sized onions, boiled rapidly 10 minutes; chop fine, mince sage half the quantity of the onions, add two cups of bread-crumbs, pepper, and salt, introduce a little cayenne, and bind together with a beaten egg, adding a tablespoonful of hot water. Do not stuff closely but leave room for the stuffing to swell. Secure the openings carefully. Roast an hour and three quarters in a quick oven; baste very frequently. Fasten paper over the breast at first to prevent scorching. There should be at least 2 cupfuls of water in the dripping-pan. To make a rich brown gravy, pour off the fat from the pan gravy, add sufficient water, thicken with browned flour, season and let it boil. Previous to serving, a flavoring may be made if desired: 1 dessertspoon of prepared mustard, ¼ teaspoonful of

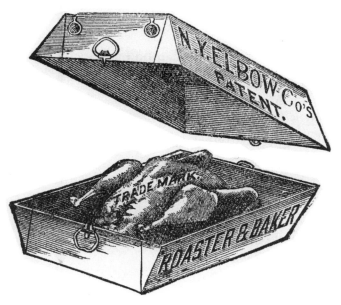

The "Delmonico" roaster and baker was made of "heavy Russian iron." It sold for $1.58 in the 10¾ inch by 16¼ inch size in 1890 (Grand Rapids, 1890).

cayenne, same of salt. Mix with 2 wineglassfuls of the gravy and the juice of half a lemon. Make hot, remove the threads from the fowl, and pour the flavoring into the opening for forcemeat. Serve with hot apple sauce. A giblet sauce or gravy may be made as for turkey, if preferred to the above.

(Battle Creek, 1903)

Boned Turkey

Get a turkey that has not been frozen—freezing makes it tear easily; see that every part is whole—one with a little break in the skin will not do; cut off the legs, in the joints, and the tips of the wings; do not draw the bird; place it on its breast, and with a small, sharp boning-knife, cut in a straight line through to the bone, from the neck down to that part of the bird where there is but little flesh, where it is all skin and fat; begin at the neck, and run the knife between the flesh and the bones until you come to the wing; then cut the ligaments that hold the bones together and the tendons that hold the flesh to the bones; with the thumb and forefinger, *press* the flesh from the smooth bone; when you come to the joint, carefully separate the ligaments and remove the bone; do not try to take the bone from the next joint, as that is not in the way when carving, and it gives a more natural shape to the bird; now begin at the wish-bone, and when that is free from the flesh, run the knife between the sides and the flesh, always using the fingers to press the meat from the smooth bones, as, for instance, the breast bone and lower part of the sides; work around the legs the same as you did around the wings, always using great care at the joints not to cut the skin; drawing out the leg-bones turns that part of the bird inside out; turn the bird over, and proceed in the same manner with the other side; when all is detached, carefully draw the skin from the breast-bone; then run the knife between the fat and bone at the rump, leaving the small bone in the extreme end, as it holds the skewers; carefully remove the flesh from the skeleton, and turn it right side out again; rub into it 2 tablespoons salt and a little pepper, and fill with dressing; sew up the back and neck, and then the vent; truss the same as if not boned; take a strong piece of cotton cloth and pin the bird firmly in it, drawing very tight at the legs, as this is the broadest place, and the shape will not be good unless this precaution be taken; steam 3 hours, and then place on a buttered tin sheet, which put in a baking-pan; baste well with butter, pepper, salt and flour; roast 1 hour, basting every 10 minutes, and twice with stock; when cold, remove the skewers and strings, and garnish with aspic jelly, cooked beets, and parsley. To carve: First cut off the wings, then about 2 thick slices from the neck, where it will be quite fat, and then cut in thin slices. Serve jelly with each plate.

Filling for a turkey weighing 8 pounds: The flesh of 1 chicken weighing 4 pounds, 1 pound clear veal, ½ pound clear salt pork, 1 small cup cracker-crumbs, 2 eggs, 1 cup broth, 2½ teaspoons salt, ½ teaspoon pepper, 1 teaspoon summer savory, 1 of sweet marjoram 1 of thyme, ½ teaspoon sage, and, if you like, 1 tablespoon capers, 1 quart oysters, and 2 tablespoons onion-juice; have the meat uncooked and free from any tough pieces; chop *very* fine; add seasoning, crackers, etc., mix thoroughly, and use; if oysters are used ½ pound of the veal must be omitted; where one cannot eat veal, use chicken instead; veal is recommended for its cheapness. Why people choose boned turkey, instead of a plain roast turkey or chicken is not plain, for the flavor is not so good; but at the times and places where boned birds are used, it is a very appropriate dish. That is, at suppers, lunches, and parties, where the guests are served standing, it is impracticable to provide anything that cannot be broken with a fork or spoon; therefore the advantage of a boned turkey, chicken, or bird is apparent. One turkey, weighing 8 pounds before being boned will serve 30 persons at a party, if there are also, say oysters, rolls, coffee, ices, cake and cream. If the supper is very elaborate, the turkey will answer for 1 of the dishes for 100 or more persons. If nothing more were gained in the boning of a bird, the knowledge of the anatomy, and the help this will give in carving, pay to bone 2 or 3 chickens. It is advisable to bone at least 2 fowls before trying a turkey, for if you spoil them there is nothing lost, as they make a stew or soup.

(Detroit, 1890)

Meat Jelly for Boned Turkey

Take oil from water (when cold) in which turkey was boiled, strain into a porcelain kettle, add 2 ounces of gelatine, 3 eggs with shells, a wine-glassful of sherry or Madeira; stir well. Add 1 quart of strained liquor, beat rapidly with an egg-beater, put on fire and stir till it boils; simmer 10 or 15 minutes, sprinkle with a pinch of turmeric, and strain as other jelly. Add lemon-juice to taste. When cold, break up and place over and around turkey. Cut in thick slices and fanciful shapes with paste cutter.

(Battle Creek, 1903)

Creamed Turkey or Chicken

2 cups turkey or
  chicken cut in small
  pieces
¼ cup butter
¼ cup mushrooms

¼ teaspoon salt and
  pepper
1 cup cream
Paprika

Serve on toast.

Effie Nelson, Seney
(Grand Marais, 1936)

Roast Turkey with Chestnut Stuffing and Sauce

Clean the turkey and lard the breast. Throw 50 large chestnuts into boiling water for a few minutes; then take them up, and rub off the thin, dark skin; cover them with boiling water, and simmer for 1 hour; take them up and mash fine. Chop 1 pound veal and ½ pound salt pork very fine; add ½ of the chestnuts to this, and add, also, ½ tablespoon pepper, 2 teaspoons salt, and 1 cup stock or water. Stuff the turkey with this; truss and roast; serve with a chestnut sauce. The remaining ½ of the chestnuts are for this sauce.

(Detroit, 1890)

Roast Turkey with Oyster Dressing

Clean a turkey and lay it in a dripping pan. Prepare a dressing of stale bread composed of 1 quart bread crumbs and 1 cup butter, water enough to moisten; add 2 dozen oysters, salt and pepper to suit the taste. Mix all and stuff the turkey with it. Sew up carefully. Put some water in the dripping pan; salt and a chunk of butter, set in the oven and bake until done, basting often. Never parboil a young turkey.

(Vermontville, 1906)

Dressing for Chicken or Turkey

Two cups of finely crumbed stale bread (baker's is best), half a cup of finely chopped beef suet, two

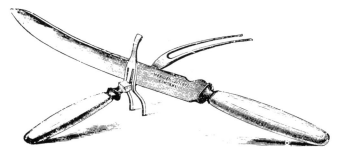

The Victorian head of the household might expect a carving set such as this beside his place setting.

170

tablespoonfuls chopped parsley (dried will do), one teaspoonful each of thyme and marjoram, a little shred lemon peel and grated nutmeg. Moisten with a beaten egg, salt and pepper to taste. This is sufficient for a chicken; it will take double the quantity for a turkey, and is equally good for veal. Or, take dry pieces of break or crackers, chop them fine, put in a small piece of butter or a little cream, with sage, pepper and salt, one egg and a small quantity of flour, moistened with milk.

(Detroit, 1878)

Almond Forcemeat

Beat up the yolks of 3 eggs with ¼ pint good cream, and flavor with a little nutmeg; blanch and pound in a mortar 3 ounces sweet almonds, using white of egg to moisten; add these with ¾ pound light bread crumbs, and 3 ounces butter broken into small bits, to the egg mixture; stir in, lastly, the whites of the eggs whisked to a solid froth, and fill either capon or turkey.

(Detroit, 1890)

Turkey Stuffing (Swedish Style)

Two cups of stale bread crumbs, three-fourths cup melted butter, one-half cup raisins, seeded and cut in pieces, one-half cup English walnuts, chopped fine, salt and pepper, sage, mix in the order given.

(Lansing, 1918)

We stuffed a large chicken with this dressing and prepared an extra panful. It enhanced the flavor of the bird, and not a morsel of stuffing survived a memorable Sunday dinner.

To Carve a Turkey

Place your turkey on its back; then insert the fork astride the breast bone. Place the knife cross-wise 1 inch from the wing towards the fork, cut then pry out and the wing will be unjointed. Place knife cross-wise on either side of the leg, cut down, place the point of your knife at the kneejoint, press out and the leg is unjointed at the hip. With the handle of your knife toward the neck, and the point towards the leg, slice four or more slices from the breast. Carve the opposite side of the body in the same manner. Place your knife cross-wise in front and close to the breast bone, cut down, and the wish bone is unjointed. Then place the knife, with the handle toward the neck in the breast, press down towards the leg, and pry out, this will leave the clavicle unjointed. Turn the turkey over and with a slight cut, separate the breast bones from the back, and lay them off on another plate. The fork is still remaining in the breast where it was first put. Enter the knife at the tail and cut forward, parallel with the back-bone, leaving the latter bone in its place, pry out and the bones are off.

(Ann Arbor, 1872)

Scalloped Turkey

Cut the meat from the bones of a cold turkey, remove the skin and gristle, and chop the meat fine; put on the bottom of a buttered dish a layer of cracker crumbs, moisten with milk, then spread a layer of the minced turkey with bits of the stuffing, pepper, salt and small pieces of butter; then another layer of crackers, and so on, until the dish is nearly full. Before putting on the upper crust pour in the gravy left from the turkey, cover with a crust of cracker crumbs soaked in milk, seasoned with salt, pepper, butter, and beaten up light with two eggs; spread it over the top and bake well.

(Detroit, 1881)

Sauces for Fowl

With roast turkey: Cranberry sauce, currant jelly.

With boiled turkey: Oyster sauce.

With venison or wild ducks: Cranberry sauce, currant jelly or currant jelly warmed with port wine.

With roast goose: Apple sauce, cranberry sauce, grape or currant jelly.

(Manistee, 1929)

FISH

Fish—The Ways of Cooking Them

Purchase those which are fresh, the fresher the better. The white kinds are the least nutritious, and the oily the most difficult of digestion. When fish are fresh and in season, the muscles are firm and they boil white; when out of season they boil bluish and flabby.

Most kinds of fish are best in cold weather. Mackerel are best in August, September and October, halibut in May and June. Oysters are good from September to April. Lobsters are best at the season when oysters are not good.

As soon as possible after the fish are caught, remove the scales and entrails, and scrape out every particle of blood and the white skin that lies along the backbone, being careful not to crush the fish. Rinse thoroughly in cold water, using only what is necessary for perfect cleanliness; drain, wipe dry and place on ice until ready to cook. To remove the earthy taste from fresh-water fish, sprinkle with salt and let it stand over night, or at least a few hours before cooking; rinse off, wipe dry, and, to completely take up all moisture, wrap in a dry napkin. Freshwater fish should never be soaked in water except when frozen, and then should be cooked immediately. Salt fish may be soaked over night, changing the water once or twice if very salt. To freshen fish, place it with the fleshy side down, so that the salt may go to the bottom, where it naturally settles.

Fish can be preserved for a long time by sprinkling with sugar, keeping the fish in a horizontal position, so that the sugar may penetrate as much as possible. Salmon thus treated has a more agreeable taste, and this method does not destroy the flavor of any fish if so treated. If you live remote from the seaport and cannot get fish hard and fresh, wet it with an egg (beaten) before you meal it, to prevent its breaking.

Fish should always be well done; baked or fried, it is most palatable, though some prefer it boiled. When one has no fish kettle (made purposely to boil the fish), wrap it in a cloth, lay in a circle on a plate and set it in the kettle. When done the fish may be lifted entirely out of the kettle without breaking,

and can then be removed to the platter. In boiling fish allow five to ten minutes to the pound, according to thickness, after putting it in the water. To test, pass a knife along a bone, and if done the flesh will separate easily. The addition of salt and vinegar to water in which fish is boiled seasons the fish and at the same time hardens the water, thus much improving the fish. In boiling fish always plunge it into boiling water and then let it simmer gently until done. In case of salmon, put into tepid water instead of hot, to preserve the rich color.

To fry fish, dip it in egg and bread crumbs, and use lard, not butter. Garnish with parsley, celery tops or lemon. Halibut is best cut in slices and fried or boiled. Bass are good any way. Salt shad and mackerel must be soaked over night for broiling. Sturgeons are best fried. Black and white fish are best broiled or fried. A broiled fish is done when the eyes turn white.

Cod frizzled, that is, cut in slices and wrapped round with greased paper, then placed in a covered pan just greased, and either put in the oven or on top of the stove and frizzled till done, is a very nice dish.

Mackerel merely steamed, with no sauce, eaten with vinegar, or oil and vinegar, is delicious.

Eels stewed in a plain sauce are nice, if not too fat. Make a sauce with hot butter, flour and warm water; add a little vinegar, some peppercorns and a clove, also a finely chopped onion. Place the eels, cut in pieces, in the sauce, cover and let simmer twenty minutes or so.

Cook halibut in white sauce. Make the sauce with hot butter, flour, warm milk; flavor with pepper, salt, and a little mace, add half a handful of chopped parsley, and put the piece of halibut in. Stew for half an hour and trim with lemon in serving.

Along the Atlantic coast there is a great variety of fish. The blue fish is excellent, boiled or baked, with a dressing of bread, butter and onions. Sea bass are boiled with egg sauce and garnished with

parsley. Salmon are baked, boiled and broiled, and smelts are cooked by dropping into boiling fat.

One of the most essential things in serving fish is to have everything hot and quickly dished, so that all may go to the table at once. Serve fresh fish with squash and green peas; salt fish with beets and carrots, salt pork and potatoes, and parsnips with either.

(Detroit, 1881)

How to Bone Fish

After cleaning fish, both inside and out, cut off the fins and cut around the head to backbone Be careful not to cut the bone. Loosen fish on both sides from the bone and with the left hand, or better, the forefinger and thumb, push gently down on backbone under meat, while holding head firmly in right hand. You will find that every bone, from head to tail, will be removed.

(Niles, 1907)

Norwegian Fish Balls

Remove flesh from 3 or 4 pound trout. Put through food chopper and add 2 beaten eggs, ½ cup milk, salt and pepper to taste, dash of nutmeg, ½ cup flour, and ½ teaspoon baking powder. Take the skin, bones and head of fish and boil in 2 quarts of salted water—add an onion if desired. Remove the bones and drop in the above mixture the size of an egg and boil 3 minutes. Remove and fry in butter until brown.

Mrs. Chas. Bleckiner
(Grand Marais, 1936)

William Donahey, originator of the famous Teenie Weenie cartoon characters, and his wife,

Mary, directed the compilation of *The Cooking Pots of Grand Marais* during the 1930s. They spent their summers in this picturesque Lake Superior resort village living in a giant pickle barrel converted into a cottage. The barrel now serves as the office of the Grand Marais Chamber of Commerce.

Black Bass

Skin and remove the backbone of the fish with a small sharp knife. Put on a paper two tablespoonsful of flour, and on a separate paper, some fine bread crumbs, salted and peppered. Dip each fillet of fish first in the flour, then in beaten egg and then in the crumbs, cooking in boiling lard five minutes. Lay on paper in the edge of the oven till ready to serve.

(Detroit, 1882)

Boiled Fish

Take a fresh water mackerel and tie in a clean cloth; boil three-quarters of an hour. While boiling make a gravy of three tablespoonfuls of flour, one large tablespoonful of butter; mix well together with a spoon, then pour a little boiling water, enough to wet it; stir, then set a pan on the stove, pour on the boiling water and boil five minutes, until as thick as you desire; put the fish on a platter and pour gravy over it.

(Detroit, 1881)

Oven Canned Fish

Thoroughly clean fish and wash well. Drain on a clean cloth. Cut up and pack in jars using plenty of salt. Place corrugated paste board in bottom of dripping pan and place jars on it. Put covers on lightly. Fill pan nearly full of water and set in hot oven. Bake for 3½ hours. Take from oven, put on scalded rubbers and replace covers as quickly as possible and seal tightly. Do not add any water to jar.

Mrs. Lawrence Phoenix
(Grand Marais, 1936)

Catfish

Take a large catfish and cut it up into pieces 2 inches in length and 1 inch thick. Beat up 3 eggs with a little salt and pepper and 1 teaspoon Worcestershire; dip the fish in the egg-batter, and roll in corn meal or bread crumbs. Fry a deep brown, garnish with lemon, parsley, or celery tops, and send to table with a cucumber salad.

(Detroit, 1890)

Caviar Jelly

One and one-half quarts of highly seasoned rich soup stock. To each quart add one level tablespoon of gelatine dissolved in a little cold water. Flavor. Have wet molds (rings) with pimentos in the bottom, cut in stars. When stock begins to thicken fold in two cans of caviar. Fill molds.

Egg Filling

Boil hard eight fresh eggs. Peel and chop. Mix with two stalks of celery chopped fine, a few minced sour pickles and two teaspoons of pearl onions. Mix all with highly seasoned mayonnaise and after jelly is unmolded fill center with egg salad and serve surrounded with shredded lettuce.

Mrs. John Byrne
(Grand Rapids, 1935)

Cusk à la Creme

One pint carefully picked cooked fish—whitefish preferred. Yolks of two eggs, one pint milk, one blade of mace, one bay leaf, one sprig parsley, small piece of onion, two tablespoonfuls flour and one of butter. Put milk in double boiler with mace, onion, parsley and bay leaf. Rub butter and flour together, stir into boiling milk, cook two minutes,

add salt and pepper to taste. Butter individual shells or a baking dish, put in a layer of the sauce, then a layer of fish, repeat till all is used having last layer of sauce. Sprinkle with bread crumbs and brown in the oven.

Mrs. D. L. Holbrook
(Union City, 1902)

To Fry Eels

Skin them, wash well, season with pepper and salt, roll each piece in fine Indian meal, fry in boiling lard, or egg them, and roll in cracker crumbs and fry. For sauce, use melted butter sharpened with lemon juice.

(Vermontville, 1906)

Fried Fish

All fish should be fried in the purest oil. This can be used over and over again by clarification; and, all things considered, oil is quite as economical as lard or dripping. Clean your pan, put therein sufficient oil to thoroughly and deeply immerse the fish. Permit this to boil, and it will attain so high a temperature that when a finger of bread is dipped into it and instantly drawn out, the bread has acquired a brown surface, or a piece of white paper dipped into it comes out dry, then—and not until then—your fish, already egged and bread-crumbed, is launched lightly on the surface of the oil, the boiling power of which will keep it afloat, and then, according to the thickness of the fish, from two to three minutes should be given to it; then turn it gently with flat tongs.

(Detroit, 1881)

Baked Halibut

Five lbs. fish, wash and wipe dry. Place in dripping pan with a few slices of salt port, fastened on with tooth picks. Bake about 1 hour. Baste with melted butter and water. When done stir into the gravy 1 tbsp. Worcestershire sauce and juice of 1 pour over all hot. This cooks the fish enough. Will keep several weeks.

M. M. G., Nahma
(Chicago, 1898)

Lakeside Fish

Take a good sized lake trout or whitefish about 5 pounds, cut off head and tail, open and take out bones, cut in halves, then in individual portions, about 5 or 6 to a side. Mix salt very generously in a pan of flour, roll fish in the flour and fry in griddle with bacon drippings, skin side up, until golden brown.

Mrs. Gaylord Smith
(Higgins Lake, 1920)

Fish Macaroni

Two pounds fish, ½ pound macaroni, 3 ounces finely grated cheese, 1 ounce butter, pepper and salt. Flake this fish carefully removing all skin and bones. Boil the macaroni in salted water until tender. Mix the fish, macaroni and grated cheese together, put in a well buttered dish, grate a little cheese over the top with bits of butter and bake ½ hour.

(Kalamazoo, 1899)

Fish Pie

Take a few pieces of bacon and place at the bottom of a pie dish. Cut up fresh cod or fresh haddock and place over it in layers, finishing with a couple of slices of bacon. Sprinkle in between a small finely chopped onion and parsley. Flavor with pepper and salt. Make a brown gravy by heating a piece of butter, stirring in a little flour, when brown adding some warm water and flavoring with a spoonful of sauce or brown catsup. Pour over fish. Now make crust, as for pot-pie, and place over. Bake gently and quickly, so as not to dry out the goodness of the fish. Prepare potatoes plain, steamed, or with parsley sauce.

(Detroit, 1881)

Dr. Alvin Chase of Ann Arbor thought such domestic scenes as women occupied with housework the "key to a happy house" (Ann Arbor, 1884).

lemon, season to taste and thicken. Serve on platter and garnish with slices of hard boiled egg.

Mrs. M. H. Deloof
(Kalamazoo, 1921)

Herring Salad

Take four Holland herrings, soak over night in soft water, remove skins and cut in three pieces crosswise. Place in a dish a layer of fish, then sliced onions, bay leaves, and lemon slices, a few whole cloves, and two black peppers. Boil vinegar and

175

Cornish Fish Pie

In Cornwall almost every kind of fish is put into a pie, well floured over with a little chopped parsley and onions, a little pepper and salt, some broth or water, and a nice short crust over it; there is a hole left in the crust at the top, and through this hole some cream is poured in just before serving.

(Detroit, 1881)

This is sort of a piscine version of the pasty.

Fish Réchauffé

The fish left over from dinner may, by this process, be made into a most palatable dish. Heat the fish in a frying-pan, removing the large bones if the fish is broken or has been cut, but if pan fish and whole do not break them. While heating, prepare the dressing. To one pound of fish allow one and one-half cupfuls of canned tomato, one level teaspoonful of salt, one egg (yolk), one-fourth teaspoonful of pepper. Stew the tomato until soft, strain through a coarse sieve to remove the ends, return to the stew-pan and add the salt and pepper. Beat the egg in two tablespoonfuls of cold water; when the tomato is boiling hot set the pan in a mild heat and add the yolk, stirring well. Do not boil the sauce after the egg is added, as it is likely to break. The heat should be just sufficient to cook the egg and thicken the tomato to the consistency of cream. Remove the fish to a platter, turn over it the sauce and serve.

Mrs. S. S. Wilson, Hudson
(Chicago, 1896)

Pekelharing (Pickled Herring)

Wash fish well as it comes out of the brine. Cut in pieces and put in jars and cover with a mixture of vinegar, sliced onions and spices.

(Holland, 1936)

Per-Fo Salmon Loaf

One can salmon with skin and bones removed—mince fine. Add the following mixture: Two beaten eggs, 2 level tablespoonfuls butter, 8 tablespoonfuls milk, 7 tablespoonfuls coarse Per-fo, salt and pepper to taste. Place in a greased can, cover and steam one hour.

Per-fo used in escalloped dishes is very fine; in fact, as a substitute, in whole or part, for cracker and bread crumbs, it is very superior, being much more healthful, and adding a rich, nutty flavor not to be obtained in the other. The up-to-date housewife and cook will find, constantly, some new use for Per-fo. It is her friend in many hours of need.

(Battle Creek, 1903)

Per-Fo, short for perfect food, was the product that Battle Creek grocer W. H. Hamilton invented during the great Battle Creek cereal boom in 1903. Like all but a few of the approximately eighty strange-sounding breakfast cereals that originated locally, Per-Fo soon disappeared from grocery shelves. The original "good old" corn flakes would make a good substitute in this recipe.

Grilled Sardines

One large can skinless sardines. Roll each fish in melted butter, season with cayenne pepper and salt, cover with finely chopped parsley. Wrap each fish in oiled paper and heat in the oven. Serve on rectangular slices of toast slightly larger than the fish.

Lucy Burrows Morley
(Higgins Lake, 1920)

Seafood Casserole

1½ lbs. fillet of haddock	*1 lb. mushrooms*
2 cans shrimp	*¼ lb. sharp cheese*
Rich white sauce	*Slices of cheese*

Boil haddock until tender. Sauté mushrooms in butter. Flake the haddock and in buttered baking dish; place one layer of haddock, one layer of shrimp and mushrooms. Dot each layer with butter. Season. Cover with rich white sauce and top with sliced cheese. Bake 40 min. at 350°. Serves 10.

Mrs. C. D. Brown
(Kalamazoo, 1941)

Planked Shad

Procure a hardwood plank, about an inch and a half thick. Split the shad as for broiling, put on the plank with skin down. Broil till done and rub it every once in a while with a little butter. The plank should be well seasoned and heated before putting the fish upon it. When done, dredge with salt and pepper. Put bits of butter over it. Serve on the plank with lemons cut in quarters and parsley.

(Saginaw, 1905)

We have tried various planked fish recipes using a 1½ or 2 inch piece of seasoned and split maple or oak cord wood. If you secure a plank from a lumberyard, make certain it has not been treated with chemical preservatives.

Shad Roe

Drop into boiling water, and cook gently for 20 minutes; then take from the fire and drain; butter a tin plate, and lay the drained roe upon it; dredge well with salt and pepper, and spread soft butter over it; then dredge thickly with flour; cook in the oven for ½ hour, basting frequently with salt, pepper, flour, butter and water.

(Detroit, 1890)

A Pretty Way to Serve Smelts

The French have a pretty manner of serving smelts; after frying them in the usual way, a little

skewer 4 inches long, silver-plated or of polished wire, is run through 2 or 3 of the smelts, running it carefully through the eyes; a slice of lemon is then put on top of each skewerful, which is served as a portion for 1 person.

(Detroit, 1890)

Baked Smelts

Wash and dry the smelts thoroughly in a cloth, and arrange them nicely in a flat baking dish. Cover them with fine bread crumbs and place little pieces of butter over them. Season and bake for fifteen minutes. Just before serving add a sprinkle of lemon juice, and garnish with fried parsley and cut lemon.

(Detroit, 1881)

Stuffed Rings of Fillet of Sole

This is truly a sea food dish not hard to prepare, although one would think so. With a little patience and the same amount of technique your efforts should be well rewarded. In the event you cannot purchase fillet of sole, haddock may be used if skimmed.

This is by no means a cheap dish, but for an occasional spread, your time, cost and talent should be well rewarded.

One and one-half pounds fillet of sole (no doubt they will be frozen) are needed.

When thawed out, cut in strips wide enough lengthwise to fit custard cup. Salt and pepper strips. Grease custard cups with butter. Overlap fillet strips a little, keeping thick end up, so as not to close the cup. Take the fish left and also any scraps, place on fire with 2 or 3 cups of water and cook 15 or 20 minutes. Strain off the broth.

The success of this recipe depends upon the sauce, which must be about one quart. The balance to be made up of cream. The consistency of the cream should be that of cream potatoes. Take enough butter and chicken fat and flour and build up white sauce, first using broth and then hot cream, cook until smooth, season well with salt and pepper and add 2 tablespoons of good sherry wine or cognac and stir in sauce. Take 1 can shrimp, 1 can lobster and 1 can crab meat which have been boned but not broken more than necessary, add any liquid from cans to white sauce. Take one-half of white sauce and add ½ teaspoon chives cut fine and 1 teaspoon chopped parsley. Pour sauce over contents from all cans, stirring gently but thoroughly. Now add 3 well beaten eggs. Taste to see if more salt, pepper or wine are needed. Now fill fish molds and place in baking pan with water, covering about one-half of mold. Cover molds with greased paper and bake in moderate oven until center is firm, but not hard. When done unmold on platter, garnish with half hard boiled eggs, hot ripe olives and water cress. The balance of sauce should be used to mask molds. Before masking, about 2 teaspoons of finely diced pimento, ½ teaspoon chives, 1 teaspoon parsley should be added to sauce.

Now you've gone to a lot of trouble, but if you like fish or fish mixtures this should please you.

Charles Bosma
Chef, Butterworth Hospital
(Grand Rapids, 1935)

Sturgeon

There are few people so poor that they will consent to eat sturgeon, yet this fish, if properly cooked, affords, it is said, a luxurious meal. Get a few slices, moderately thick, put them in a pot or pan of water, and parboil them to get rid of the oil; then roll in crumbs of cracker and egg, just as you would a veal cutlet, and fry. This makes a veal cutlet that beats the original by far, and you are sure that it is "full six weeks old," as the butcher always certifies in regard to the veal.

(Detroit, 1881)

Sturgeon were formerly caught in abundance in Lakes Michigan and Superior. Their roe was made into caviar, their air bladders into isinglass. The fish were kept alive in pens at fishing stations until orders were received to ship them to the city because of their enormous size. Sturgeon are now virtually extinct in the Great Lakes.

Stewed Fish

Cut a fish across in slices, an inch and a half thick, and sprinkle with salt; boil two sliced onions

until done; pour off water, season with pepper; add two teacups of hot water and a little parsley, and in this simmer the fish until thoroughly done. Serve hot. Good method for any fresh water fish.

(Detroit, 1881)

French Fish Stew

Take one onion, cut very fine, have lard quite hot in a good-sized stewpan, drop the onion in and let it fry brown, dust in two tablespoonfuls of flour; as soon as it is brown pour in boiling water. Season the gravy with salt, black and red pepper and a piece of garlic. Have a good-sized fish cut in half, put it in the stewpan, having enough gravy to cover it. Let it cook slowly, merely simmering, and keep well covered. When the fish is most done add a tumblerful of claret wine and a wineglassful of Madeira. Do not stir it—just shake until it mixes; let simmer a few minutes and it is ready to serve. Take the fish up as whole as possible and put on dish. Pour gravy over it and garnish with thin slices of lemon and sprigs of parsley and celery.

(Detroit, 1881)

La Bouille à Peche

Take different kinds of fish, as trout, white fish, or any small fish that may be at hand and a few well cleaned crabs. Place in a stewpan a diced onion, a piece of garlic, some parsley cut fine, a piece of orange peel, pepper, salt and spice, and water enough to cover the fish and a little oil. Let this mixture cook well, cut the fish in pieces, put it in, stir all well together and cook it over a fierce fire from fifteen to twenty minutes.

(Detroit, 1881)

Sweet-Sour Fish

4 pound pike, trout or   Tablespoon seeded
    other fish   raisins
½ cup vinegar   ½ teaspoon onion
½ cup brown sugar   juice
1 cup fish stock

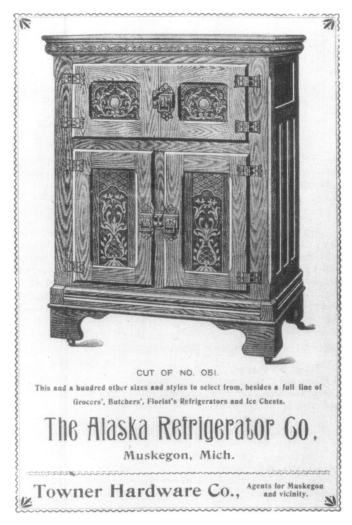

CUT OF NO. 051.

This and a hundred other sizes and styles to select from, besides a full line of
Grocers', Butchers', Florist's Refrigerators and Ice Chests.

The Alaska Refrigerator Co,
Muskegon, Mich.

Towner Hardware Co., Agents for Muskegon and vicinity.

If the ice man failed to cometh the food spoileth (Muskegon, 1899).

Clean, salt and slice the fish and allow to stand several hours. Boil the fish until the flesh drops away from the bone. Drain, reserving the liquid, and bone the fish. Mix and cook the other ingredients. Pour hot over the fish.

Serve cool.

(Grand Rapids, 1935)

Brook Trout

The general defect in cooking trout when they are fried, is the overcooking. Trout should never be done to a crisp. When overcooked you might as well

fry and eat chips—and one would taste just as well. Pork or bacon may do very well to cook trout with in camp, but it injures the flavor. The pork is not improved and the trout are worse, not better. If they have to be fried, use butter, or, what is better, sweet oil. Have the butter or oil quite hot, and do not cook too much. Try them with a fork. Put no egg or batter on them. They are better perfectly plain. If you want to broil them, wrap them up in a piece of glazed paper, which should be well buttered; sprinkle a very little salt and pepper on them; put them on a spring gridiron, such as oysters are broiled on, and turn the gridiron over from side to side; use lemons juice over them; you do not want parsley. A boiled trout is positively better than either a fried or a broiled trout, as it is a very delicate fish, and flaky, like salmon, and it ought not to be overcooked; use cold water, slightly salted, which bring up to the boil; serve with plain melted butter; brown butter is not an appropriate sauce. Baked trout are fairly good; dry the fish, do not split them; lay them on a baking dish, add a little butter, pepper and salt. It is the over-cooking which, nine times in ten, spoils this very fine fish.

(Detroit, 1881)

Baked Trout with Sauce

One trout or whitefish weighing six or seven pounds. Wash carefully, wipe dry. Take two cups of bread crumbs, moisten with cold water; chop one slice of onion and one-half stalk of celery very fine and add to the bread crumbs; season with one-quarter of a teaspoonful each of salt and pepper, one large tablespoonful of butter; cook ten minutes. Stuff the fish as full as possible, tie it together with white cord; put two tablespoonfuls of lard in a dripping pan, with hot water enough to keep from burning; rub the fish thoroughly with salt; cut fine, thin slices of salt pork, lay on the fish and bake one and a half hours. Make a sauce as follows: Two tablespoonfuls of browned flour, one-heaping tablespoonful of butter and one of cream; rub the flour and butter to a cream; add cream, one-fourth teaspoonful each of salt and pepper and six or seven capers; add boiling water until it is the right consistency; pour around fish; serve very hot.

Mrs. Gordon Beall, East Jordan
(Chicago, 1896)

Fried Trout

Do not cut the heads and tails off. After fish have been wiped dry and put away when they come from the stream, do not put them in water again. Keep them cold and do not bring them into the kitchen until you get ready to fry them for they should be hard and stiff when put into the frying pan and not allowed to get warm and limber.

Wipe them dry and clean. Put on plenty of salt and pepper and roll in flour or cornmeal.

Take your heaviest iron frying pan and put in it a few slices of pickled pork. Never use bacon. When the grease is very hot, put the fish in and never cover them. Do not let them burn on the bottom and turn them without breaking them. Let them cook quite a while so they will surely be well done, quite crisp. Remove them without grease. Sometimes it is better to lay them on a piece of brown paper for an instant to absorb the grease. Serve on a hot platter.

Be cooking the second frying-panful when the first goes on the table. Do not garnish the platter.

William B. Mershon
Sportsman, Saginaw
(Chicago, 1940)

William B. Mershon, one of Michigan's most famous sportsmen, was eighty-four years old when he submitted this recipe. His books, *The Passenger Pigeon* (1907) and *Recollections of My Fifty Years Hunting and Fishing* (1923), are highly sought after collector's items.

Brook Trout

Clean, but do not remove heads or tails, dust lightly with flour. Fry in a little fresh bacon fat for 10 minutes, keeping closely covered. Turn, remove cover, fry 10 minutes longer. Drain on paper before serving.

Mrs. Carey W. Dunton, Manistique
(Charlotte, 1909)

A Hearty Luncheon Dish

Pare and slice 6 medium sized potatoes, slice 3 small onions, sprinkle with flour, and alternate in a baking dish with a small can of tuna fish. Season with salt, pepper and butter. Pour over 1½ cups milk. Bake slowly.

Mrs. W. R. McKenzie
(Kalamazoo, 1921)

Tuna and Potato Casserole

2 cups sliced potatoes	1 chopped pimiento
1 small can tuna fish	1 chopped onion
1 small can mush-rooms	Salt and pepper to taste

Butter baking dish and place potatoes, then mixture of other ingredients, alternately. Cover with cracker crumbs and grated cheese and pour about 1½ cups milk over all. Bake one hour at 300 degrees. Serves 6.

Mrs. Alfred Moerdyke
(Kalamazoo, 1941)

Tuna Soufflé

1 cup celery	4 eggs
2 cups milk	1 small can tuna
¼ cup flour	2 tbsp. green peppers
2 tbsp. butter	1 pimiento
¼ tsp. salt	1 slice buttered bread
Few grains pepper	cut in cubes

Cook finely cut celery in milk until tender. Stir flour into melted butter, add salt, pepper and beaten egg yolks; then add milk and celery gradually, stirring constantly. Add fish, chopped green pepper and pimiento. Cool. Fold in stiffly beaten whites, pour into greased casserole. Place cubed bread on top and bake in moderate oven 350 degrees about 45 minutes. Serve with cottage cheese balls and slices of broiled pineapple.

Mrs. F. E. Leach
(Kalamazoo, 1941)

Fish Turbot

Steam large white fish or trout, until tender, pick it up fine with the fingers (so as to be sure to take out all the bones), mix with salt and pepper. Make a dressing of 1 pt. sweet milk, thicken with ¼ lb. flour, ¼ lb. butter, yolks of 2 eggs; put in a dish to bake (grease it with butter first) a layer of fish then one of dressing, continue this until the dish is full; put a little rolled cracker on top. Bake ¾ of an hour. 15 lbs of fish, made into Turbot will serve 50 people.

Mrs. H.
(Ann Arbor, 1872)

Turbot à la Creme

One pint milk, 1 pint cream, 4 tablespoons flour, 1 cup bread crumbs, and between 4 and 5 pounds of any kind of whitefish, cod, haddock or trout. Boil the fish, take out all bones, and shred very fine. Let the milk and cream, with a good sized onion, come to a boil, then stir in the flour; salt and pepper to taste. Remove the onion from the sauce after it is boiled. Butter a pan or dish, put in first a layer of sauce, then one of fish, and so on. Finish with sauce and sprinkle over it the bread or cracker crumbs. Bake an hour.

Mrs. J. Morgan Smith
(Grand Rapids, 1890)

Turbot

Four pounds fine white fish, steam until done, bone it. Take 1 quart milk, ¼ pound flour, little thyme or sage, salt and pepper, 3 slices of a large onion. Cook over a kettle of water until it comes to a thick cream, then add ¼ pound butter and 2 eggs; put in a large baking dish a layer of fish, salt and pepper, then the filling, until the dish is full, putting filling on top; sprinkle with bread crumbs, and cheese if preferred. Bake in a moderate oven ½ hour. One large dish will serve 15 or 20.

H. L. Kellogg
(Kalamazoo, 1906)

Baked Salt White Fish

Prepare as for boiling, lay four thin slices of bacon in a dripping pan and the fish on them skin down, pour over it a cup of cream and bake until nicely browned. This will be found an excellent way to cook salt fish.

Mrs. Addie Zimmerman
(Union City, 1902)

Baked Whitefish and Shad with Dressing

Clean, rinse and wipe dry with a napkin, a whitefish or any other good-sized fish, weighing 8 lbs. or more. Sprinkle salt and pepper inside and out; then fill with dressing, as for chicken or turkey, only having it pretty dry; sew up and lay on some sticks in the dripping pan; put in water and butter, dredging the fish with flour before putting in; and, if you have it and like it, put a few thin slices of fat pork on the fish—if no pork, then rub well with butter. Bake 1½ hours, basting frequently to avoid burning. Shad will be done the same, garnishing with a few pieces of lemon, sprigs of celery, or with lemon sauce.

(Ann Arbor, 1884)

Baked White Fish

Cleanse and bone a white fish weighing from 2 to 3 pounds. Stuff it with a dressing made as follows: One loaf of bread, ½ pint rich milk (part cream), 1 teacup butter. Salt and pepper to taste, and a little minced onion. Heat the milk enough to melt the butter and pour over crusty parts first, then add soft bread. Tie the fish with cord, and put it in baking pan with 1 small cup milk. Bake about ½ hour or until done. Before taking from pan, remove skin from upper side. Then flop the fish onto the hot platter and remove the skin from other side.

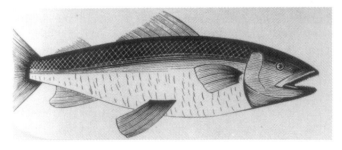

The most delectable fish in the world, the Great Lakes whitefish (Philadelphia, 1870).

Serve with melted butter poured over and garnish with parsley.

Mrs. C. A. Peck
(Kalamazoo, 1906)

Boiled White Fish

Taken from Mrs. A. W. Ferry's Cook Book, Mackinac, 1824.

The most delicate mode of cooking white fish:

Prepare the fish as for broiling, laying it open; put it into a dripping pan with the back down; nearly cover with water; to 1 fish 2 tablespoons salt; cover tightly and simmer (not boil) ½ hour. Dress with the gravy, a little butter and pepper, and garnish with hard boiled eggs.

Mrs. W. M. Ferry, Grand Haven
(Grand Rapids, 1890)

French explorers and missionaries, fur traders, and nineteenth-century tourists have penned exuberant descriptions of the joys of eating Michigan whitefish. To this day, many gourmets contend that nothing beats freshly caught whitefish for firmness and delicacy of flavor. In our experience, Lake Superior's cold waters breed the choicest whitefish.

Amanda Ferry's version of boiled whitefish from 1824 is the earliest printed Michigan recipe we have discovered and, through association, one of the most historic.

Following graduation from a theological college in New Jersey, twenty-six-year-old William Montague Ferry established a mission on Mackinac Island in 1822. The following year he returned to Massachusetts, married Amanda White, and brought her back to Mackinac Island. For ten years, they toiled to bring education and religion to the Indians and rugged fur traders who dwelt on the island. They were friends with Robert Stuart, Henry Rowe Schoolcraft, and other figures prominent in Michigan history. When his health failed in 1833, Ferry made an exploratory trip around Lake Michigan, and from the source of the Grand River at Grass Lake to its mouth. Based on what he saw, he determined that the splendid harbor at the mouth of the Grand River would be an ideal settlement site. Accordingly, in 1834 he became a co-proprietor of Grand Haven. Ferry returned to Mackinac Island for his family, and they pioneered the city that would become their permanent home.

His son, Thomas W. Ferry, was born on Mackinac Island in 1827. He carved out a prominent career in politics serving as U.S. Representative from 1865–67 and 1869–71 and U.S. Senator from 1871–1883. His older brother, William Montague Ferry, Jr., born on Mackinac Island in 1824, turned from a career in lumbering to politics in the 1850s. He served in a variety of positions, including mayor of Grand Rapids from 1876–78, before he moved to Utah where he distinguished himself in mining operations. His wife submitted Amanda Ferry's recipe for boiled whitefish to the cookbook published by the ladies of the Grand Rapids Congregational Church in 1873, which was reissued in revised form by H. Leonard & Sons Co. in 1890.

Baked White Fish

Select firm white fish. Carefully wash and wipe dry. Split down back and remove bones. Lay open in pan, skin down. Cover with cracker crumbs, 1 cup milk, butter, pepper and salt to taste. Baste often and serve with a good fish sauce.

(Grand Rapids, 1924)

Broiled Whitefish

It should be scaled, drawn and wiped dry with a cloth; water should not be allowed to touch it after being taken, and, like the blue-fish of the sea, the sooner cooked after being caught the better. Broil over a quick fire of live coals until a light brown; then bathe with good sweet butter and serve hot. Sauce: three tablespoonfuls of butter, red and black pepper to suit the taste, one-half cup each of tomato and walnut catsup, two teaspoonfuls mustard, salt to suit the taste; put all together in a saucepan and melt quickly.

(Detroit, 1881)

Broiled Whitefish

Get a 3 pound fish or larger, do not remove head nor tail. Split open and remove the bone. Lay the fish on a well greased piece of brown paper and trim paper exact size and shape of fish. Season with

Antebellum kitchen apparel was unglamorous but practical (Philadelphia, 1859).

salt and pepper and little dabs of butter, and while broiling baste often with a little hot water, butter and lemon juice. When cooked take hold of paper and pull the fish out to a hot platter. Do not remove paper. Garnish with ½ cup of melted butter stirred thick with chopped parsley and chives and a little lemon juice.

(Higgins Lake, 1920)

Deviled White Fish

Take a whitefish that weighs 2½ lbs. and boil 15 minutes, in salted water. Pick in small pieces, add 1 tablespoon butter, pinch cayenne, salt to taste, ½ pint milk, 1 tablespoon flour, wet and smooth in a little of the cold milk. Mix thoroughly, fill in patty

shells and sprinkle fine bread crumbs over top, put a lump of butter on each. Bake till brown.

Mrs. John Devlin
(Detroit, 1915)

Planked White Fish

Take a hardwood plank of well seasoned maple or oak about 1½ feet long, 10 or 12 inches wide and 2 inches thick. Pour boiling water over it before using, until heated through. Split the fish open, bone, season well, lay upon the plank and bake. If the fish seems too dry, slices of salt pork may be placed upon the fish while baking. The fish should be served on the plank which may be garnished with rock salt or sprigs of parsley. The plank gives a peculiar delicious flavor which distinguishes it from fish baked in the ordinary way. Before serving cover fish with maitre de hotel sauce.

Planks can be bought at the "Fair" in Chicago for, from fifteen cents up, according to size. They are oval in shape and very nice.

Mrs. Chas A. Peck
(Kalamazoo, 1906)

The Fair, named in honor of the World's Columbian Fair held in Chicago in 1893, was a large department store located at the corner of State, Adams, and Dearborn Streets.

Planked White Fish

The best size for planking is from 1½ to 2½ pounds. Clean, remove backbone, and spread open so that it will lay flat, skin side down on a buttered oak plank that has been heated until it sizzles. Season fish well with salt, cayenne, and spread lightly with a dressing made of fine cracker crumbs seasoned with a little sage and melted butter. Baste with melted butter frequently and bake from 30 to 45 minutes according to the size of the fish. After baking 30 minutes, arrange potato roses run through a pastry tube, brushed lightly with white of egg, around fish. Serve on plank, garnished with lemon quarters and sprigs of parsley.

Mrs. Carey W. Dunton, Manistique
(Charlotte, 1909)

How to Plank Fish

Clean and split a whitefish, pickerel, or pike, leaving on the head and tail. Spread on a proper oak plank. Make cuts in the fish from the back down toward the outer edge two inches apart from head to tail, cutting down to the ribs in each case and on both sides.

Then insert in the cuts strips of bacon and slices of apple about an eighth of an inch thick, slicing clear across the apple. Then cook in an oven as usual.

This will impart a delicious taste to the fish.

Frank F. Lodge. P. G. P.
(Marine City, 1923)

Planked Whitefish

Procure a medium-sized whitefish and split it down the back but do not cut the skin of the under side. Wipe it dry. Your plank, usually of hard maple about two inches thick, should be well buttered and placed in the oven to heat at a temperature of 375 degrees. When well heated, place the fish skin down on the plank. Butter, salt and a small amount of pepper should be spread on the flesh. Return to oven and when fish becomes flaky, add rosettes of potatoes, around edges, which should be brushed with beaten egg yolk. Hot cooked whole vegetables may also be added around the potatoes. Place more butter, minced parsley, and a bit of lemon juice on fish and serve on plank.

H. G. Salsinger
The Detroit News, Detroit
(Chicago, 1940)

Sauces for Fish

Dutch Sauce—For Fish
(Sauce Hollandaise)

One half teaspoonful of flour, two ounces of butter, four tablespoonfuls of vinegar—tarragon vinegar is best—yolk of two eggs, juice of half a lemon, salt to the taste. Put all the ingredients except the lemon juice into a stewpan. Set it over the fire and stir constantly until it heats (but not boils). Add the lemon.

(Detroit, 1878)

Drawn Butter

Take one-quarter of a pound of fresh butter, cut it up and mix with two teaspoonfuls of flour; when thoroughly mixed, put it into a saucepan and add to it four tablespoonfuls of cold water; set your stewpan over a slow fire and stir it continually one way; when the butter is entirely melted and begins to simmer, then let it rest until it boils up. This sauce may be greatly varied and called by a dozen names. 1st. By the addition of two tablespoonfuls of nasturtions, or pickled cucumber, or cauliflowers, these latter cut fine, or by two tablespoonfuls of capers. 2d. For Fish, anchovy paste or anchovy sauce may be added as desired, from one teaspoonful to one tablespoonful, or the inside of a lemon chopped fine, being careful to remove the seeds.

(Detroit, 1878)

"Nasturtions" in this recipe is a creative spelling of nasturtiums, not the houseplant, but any kind of cress, watercress, or garden cress.

Egg Sauce

Take yolks of two eggs boiled hard; mash them with a tablespoonful of mustard, a little pepper and salt, three tablespoonfuls of vinegar and three of salad oil. A tablespoonful of catsup improves this for some. This sauce is very nice for boiled fish.

(Detroit, 1881)

Egg Sauce for Fish

Mix together 2 tablespoons soft butter and 1 tablespoon flour. Stir this into 1 teacup hot milk and stir until it thickens. Season with pepper and salt, and just before serving stir carefully into this 3 hard boiled eggs cut into slices.

Mrs. Orson McKay
(Niles, 1907)

Fish Gravy

Is much improved by taking out some of the fat after the fish is fried, and putting in a little butter; the fat thus taken out will do to fry fish again, but it will not do for any kind of shortening. Shake a little flour into the hot fat, and pour in a little boiling water; stir it up well as it boils, a minute or so. Some think that a little vinegar adds to its taste.

(Detroit, 1881)

Fish Sauce

1 cup hot milk thick-
 ened with
1 tablespoon corn
 starch
1 teaspoon butter
1 egg

1 teaspoon anchovy,
 mushrooms or to-
 matoes or catsup
1 pinch of mace
1 pinch red pepper

Put egg in lastly and very carefully boil 1 minute.

(Grand Rapids, 1924)

Mustard Sauce

Melt three tablespoons butter, add one tea-spoon hot water, and three teaspoons prepared mustard. Serve while hot over fish.

(Detroit, 1935)

Parsley Sauce

After washing a bunch of parsley boil for 5 minutes in salt and water. Drain well and cut the leaves from the stalks and chop them fine. Have ready some melted butter and stir the parsley into it. A

pinch of cayenne is an addition. Serve with boiled fowls or fish.

(Charlotte, 1909)

Parsley Butter

1 teaspoon fine
 chopped parsley
1 tablespoon butter

1 teaspoon lemon
 juice
Salt and pepper

Cream the butter, add seasoning, lemon juice and chopped parsley. Spread this paste over hot broiled steak, lamb chops or broiled fish.

(Detroit, 1935)

Tartar Sauce

1 cup mayonnaise
 dressing
1 tablespoon chopped
 pickle
1 tablespoon chopped
 green olives

½ teaspoon chopped
 onion
1 tablespoon chopped
 capers
1½ tablespoons tarra-
 gon vinegar

Stir all ingredients together until well mixed. Chill and serve with cold fish, fried oysters, filet of sole, etc.

(Detroit, 1935)

SEAFOOD

Shell Fish—and the Many Ways of Cooking Them

Under the head of shell-fish are classed clams, crabs, lobsters, turtles and oysters. In choosing the latter, select those with firmly closed shells, else the oysters are not fresh. If fresh, the shell is firmly closed; when the shells of oysters are opened, they are dead and unfit for food. The small-shelled oysters, the Pyfleet, Colchester and Milford, are the finest in flavor. Larger kinds, called rock oysters, are generally considered only fit for stewing and sauces, though some persons prefer them to any other.

Always select the best of oysters, for it is impossible for even the best of cooks to make a first-rate dish out of even second-rate materials. It is just as impossible to make a first-class stew out of inferior oysters as it is to make a first-class fry. Stewing will, of course, reduce the size of all oysters more than frying; but those which are used in stews should be as large originally as those which are fried. Equally, for stews as for fries, select only those real prime oysters which are large, fresh and firm-fleshed, and which, though they will be made smaller by stewing, still remain plump and solid. More gratification and more nourishment will be obtained from three or four of the very best quality large oysters than from thirty or forty of the smaller and inferior quality which is generally served.

To pan oysters in their own juice, select a dozen of the freshest, largest and most highly flavored oysters, such as you would for a fry; have a small pan about one inch deep with a handle to it; open into this pan your dozen oysters, also the juice of the same and the juice of a dozen others; in this dish you are to put no water and no milk, only oyster juice, pure and simple; add one ounce best butter, a little of the best (for there are grades and adulteration even here) of black pepper and a pinch of salt; sprinkle on the top a small quantity of cracker dust; place on a quick fire; when the oysters begin to swell they are done; to cook to this stage will require about five minutes; do not turn out these oysters into another dish, but dish directly from the pan and while they are steaming hot.

A celebrated cook has discovered a way to have oyster flavor all the year round. Take fresh, large, plump oysters, beard them and place them in a vessel over the fire for a few moments in order to extract the juice, then put them to cool, and chop them very fine with powdered biscuit, mace, and finely minced lemon-peel; pound them until they become a paste; make them up into thin cakes, place them on a sheet of paper in a slow oven and let them bake until they become quite hard; pound them directly into powder, and place the powder in a dry tin box, well covered; keep in a dry place, and it will be very much appreciated when the true oyster flavor is imparted to fish, sauces and dishes. This makes a delicious sauce for fresh cod.

The ways of preparing oysters are many, but this method is not widely known: Take two dozen oysters and throw them in a large deep dish; then take a small bunch of parsley, chopped fine, a little lemonrind grated, half a nutmeg grated, and the crumbs of a stale French roll, also grated; let the latter be well incorporated, adding some cayenne. Have in readiness the yolks of three fresh eggs beaten up into a foam; dip each oyster separately into the eggs and roll them into the bread crumbs until they are all covered with a good coat. Put a quarter of a pound of butter in the oven, till it is melted, arrange the oysters in the pan, and turn them continually until they assume a perfect brown and crusty appearance. When fully cooked, serve them with some celery, salt and thin slices of Graham bread and butter.

(Detroit, 1881)

Clam Pie

Take a quantity of clams—if large, chop them; put in a saucepan and cook in their own liquor, or if necessary, add a little water; boil 3 or 4 medium-sized potatoes until done, then cut in slices; line a pudding-dish half way up its sides; turn a small cup bottom up in the middle of the dish to keep up the top crust; put in first a layer of clams and then a few potatoes, season with bits of butter and a little salt and pepper and dredge with flour; add another layer of clams, and so on until the dish is filled; add the liquor in which the clams were cooked and a little water if necessary; there should be as much liquid as for chicken or other meat pie; cover with top crust, cut places for steam to escape, and bake ¾ hour.

(Detroit, 1890)

Hot Crab

Pick the meat out of the crab, clear the shell from the head. Put the meat with a little salt, pepper, and nutmeg and butter, a few bread-crumbs and a little vinegar into the shell again. Place in the oven, let it heat through, remove and brown by holding a hot shovel over it or placing on the broiler in a gas range.

(Battle Creek, 1903)

The shovel referred to would have been the little device used to clean ashes out of the wood range.

Oysters on a Block of Ice

Having a perfectly clear and solid block of ice, weighing 10 or 15 pounds, a cavity is to be made in the top of it in either of 2 ways, the first is to carefully chip with an ice-pick; the other, to melt with heated bricks. If the latter be chosen, the ice must be put in a tub or large pan, and 1 of the bricks held upon the center of it until there is a slight depression, yet sufficient for the brick to rest in; when the first brick is cold, remove it, tip the block on one side to let off the water, and then use another brick; continue the operation till the cavity will hold as many oysters as are to be served; these should be kept 1 hour previous in a cool place, should be drained in a colander, and seasoned with salt, pepper and vinegar, after laying 2 folded napkins on a large platter, to prevent the block from slipping, cover the dish with parsley, so that only the ice is visible; stick a number of pinks, or of any small, bright flowers that do not wilt rapidly, into the parsley; pour oysters into the space on the top of the ice, and garnish with thin slices of lemon.

The oyster man cometh (Chicago, 1886).

This gives an elegant dish, and does away with the unsightly shells in which raw oysters are usually served. It is not expensive for the common oysters do as well as those of good size. Indeed, as many ladies dislike the large ones, here is an excellent substitute for serving in the shell, particularly as the oysters require no seasoning when once on the table. One quart is enough for a party of 10, but a block of the size given will hold 2 quarts.

(Detroit, 1890)

Oyster recipes appear in all the early cookbooks. Canned and fresh oysters were evidently easily procurable in Michigan at a reasonable price. Perhaps the many Michigan pioneers who migrated from New England brought with them a taste for oysters. We examined hundreds of nineteenth-century diary entries and found that oysters eclipsed turkey and ham as a favorite Christmas treat.

Canned Pickled Oysters

One hundred large oysters, one pint white wine vinegar, one dozen blades of mace, two dozen whole cloves, two dozen whole black peppers, one large red pepper broken into bits. Put oysters, liquor and all, into a porcelain kettle. Salt to the taste. Heat slowly until the oysters are very hot, but not boiling. Take them out with a perforated skimmer and set aside to cool. To the liquor which remains in the kettle add the vinegar and spices. Boil up fairly, and when the oysters are nearly cold, pour it over them scalding hot. Cover and put away in a cool place. Next day put them into glass cans with tight tops. If you open a can use up the contents as soon as possible.

(Detroit, 1881)

Pickled Oysters

Put the oysters over the fire in their own liquor and let them simmer; after they are plump skim them out into a stone pot, a layer of oysters sprinkled with whole mace, whole cloves and a little pepper. After all the oysters are in the pot cover them, alternating one cup of cold vinegar and one cup of hot oyster liquor. Cover slowly and let stand until next day.

Mrs. G. J. Diekema
(Holland, 1896)

Born in Holland, Michigan, in 1859, Gerrit J. Diekema earned degrees from Hope College and the University of Michigan before setting up a law practice in his hometown. He became active in politics and represented Ottawa County in the Michigan legislature from 1885–92 and served in the U.S. Congress from 1907–11. He is best remembered for his extraordinary oratorical abilities. His wife contributed this recipe to the cookbook published in 1896 by the Ladies' Aid Society of Holland's historic Hope Church.

Celeried Oysters

1 dozen large oysters
1 wineglassful sherry
1 tablespoonful
   minced celery

1 teaspoonful butter
Salt and pepper

Put the butter into the Chafing Dish, and when it is melted add the oysters and celery; season with salt and pepper; cook three minutes, add the sherry and cook two minutes; serve on toast.

(Grand Rapids, 1917)

Creamed Oysters

1 quart oysters

2 tablespoons of butter, browned in spider

Heat oysters in butter three minutes; add 3 tablespoons of cream, 1 tablespoon of flour, mixed with milk or water; beat yolks of 4 eggs and stir in eggs after you take from the stove. Serve on buttered toast or patties.

Mrs. L. J. Hale
(Kalamazoo, 1906)

Oysters Fried in Batter

Take one cup of sweet milk, one egg, a pinch of salt and flour enough to make a stiff batter; dip the oysters in the batter and fry one at a time, each one having a little batter on it.

(Detroit, 1881)

Oyster Fritters

Drain the liquor from the oysters, and to a cup of this add the same quantity of milk, three eggs, a little salt, and flour enough for a thin batter. Chop the oysters and stir into the batter. Have ready in the frying-pan a few spoonfuls of sweet lard, or half lard and half butter; heat very hot and drop the oyster batter in by the spoonful. Try a spoonful first to be sure the lard is hot enough and the fritter of the right consistency. Take from the pan as soon as they are done a light brown, and serve as soon as possible.

(Detroit, 1881)

Oyster Loaf

Cut a round piece, five inches across, from the top of a nicely baked round loaf of bread; remove the crumbs, leaving the crust half an inch thick; make a rich oyster stew and put it in the loaf in layers, sprinkled with bread crumbs; place the cover over the top, cover the loaf with the beaten yolk of an egg and put it in the oven to glaze. Serve very hot.

(Detroit, 1881)

Oyster Omelet

Twelve oysters, if large, double the number, if small; six eggs, one cup of milk, one tablespoonful of butter, chopped parsley, salt and pepper. Chop the oysters very fine; beat the yolks and whites of the eggs separately, as for nice cake, the whites until it stands in a heap. Put three tablespoonfuls of butter in a frying-pan, and heat while you are mixing the omelet. Stir the milk into a deep dish, with the yolks and seasoning. Next add the chopped oysters, heating them well as you add gradually. When thoroughly mixed, pour in melted butter, and finally whip in the whites as lightly as possible. Have the butter in the pan very hot, and pour in the mixture. Do not stir it, but when it begins to stiffen slip a broad-bladed knife around the sides, and cautiously under the omelet, that the butter may reach every part. As soon as the center is fairly set, and the bottom brown, turn out into a hot dish. Lay the dish bottom upward over the frying-pan, which must be turned upside down dexterously. This brings the brown side of the omelet uppermost. This is a delicious breakfast or supper omelet.

(Detroit, 1881)

Oyster Patties

Line some small patty pans with fine puff paste rolled thin, and to preserve their form when baked put a bit of bread in each, lay on the cover, trim the edges and place the patties in a brisk oven. Drain the oysters, put them in a saucepan, throw in a teaspoonful of flour with an ounce of butter, salt and spice to suit; stir the whole over a gentle fire two or three minutes, adding by slow degrees three spoonfuls of cream; then pour in the liquor of the oysters and let all boil for ten minutes. Raise the covers of the patties, take out the bread, fill them with oysters and sauce, replace the covers and serve hot.

(Detroit, 1881)

Oyster Pie

Two cans of oysters, or three pints of solid oysters, one quart of cream, one dozen rolled crackers, pepper, salt, etc. Stir all together and pour into a dish lined with thick puff paste, cover with an-

other paste and bake three-quarters of an hour. This is a delicious mode of cooking oysters.

(Detroit, 1878)

Escaloped Oysters, or Oyster Pie With Crackers

Oysters, 1½ qts.; crackers, sufficient; pepper, salt and a little mace. Directions—Drain the oysters as above; butter the dish and put a layer of the oysters over the bottom; then, the crackers being thin, butter one side lightly, and place a row of them around the dish in place of a crust; season the oysters, each layer as you go along, then sprinkle on some cracker-crumbs, else split crackers, buttered, does nicely in place of crumbs, and so fill the dish or until the oysters are all in, putting another tier of crackers up the side, if needed, as you fill up to the top of the first tier, and cover the top with a layer of buttered crackers, putting on the butter pretty freely on the top crackers, which melts down into the dish and makes a crispy cover or crust, without the trouble of making pastry.

Remarks—If this new plan is done carefully you will be pleased with the result. If not, you can take the old crusty, mushy way again; but I know you will not.

(Ann Arbor, 1884)

Oyster Pie

Line a deep dish that will hold rather more than a quart, with a good crust, nearly half an inch thick. Strain the liquor from a quart of oysters. Put in the bottom of the dish a layer of fine cracker or bread crumbs, then add the oysters with bits of butter and mace, a little pepper, salt, and a part of the liquor; enough to fill the dish about half full. Over the oysters put another layer of crumbs, and cover all with crust, leaving an opening in the top; ornament with leaves of pastry. Bake about one hour; browning gradually, and serve hot. If a teacup is turned down in the center of the pie, the liquor will be drawn under it and therefore not boil over. It also prevents the upper crust from falling in and becoming clammy.

(Battle Creek, 1890)

Oyster Pie

Make a rich biscuit crust as follows:

1 cup flour
1 scant half cup of
  butter

1 teaspoonful
  Brown's Brownie
  Baking Powder

Milk enough to make a soft crust which roll one inch thick and bake in a quick oven.

Cream one pint of fine oysters and while hot put between the layers of crust which are formed by splitting the same on coming from the oven. Serve hot with a dressing such as you used to cream the oysters.

Minnie Frances Brown
(Kalamazoo, 1906)

Little Pigs in Blankets

Season large oysters with pepper and salt, cut fat pork or bacon into thin slices, wrap one oyster in each slice and fasten with a little skewer (toothpicks are the best); cook long enough in a frying pan to crisp the bacon; place on small slices of buttered toast and serve.

Mrs. C. Stone, Menominee
(Chicago, 1898)

Philadelphia Fry

Take nice fat oysters, wipe dry, egg and crumb them, season to taste; then dip them in a very cold, thick mayonnaise, then into the egg crumbs again. Let stand a few minutes and fry in the chafing dish in the usual way.

Mrs. Spencer Carpenter, Menominee
(Chicago, 1898)

Roasted Oysters

Select the desired quantity of the freshest and best quality of large oysters, such as you would for the finest fry; wash the shells until they are as clean as polished marble; place them in a dripping-pan with the round shell down; put in a hot oven about twenty minutes; remove one of the shells (the round one) only when you come to eat them, placing on each a small piece of the freshest and sweetest of table butter, a dash of cayenne pepper and a few drops of a fresh, bright lemon.

(Detroit, 1881)

Spiced Oysters

For two hundred oysters, take one pint vinegar, one grated nutmeg, eight blades of whole mace, three dozen whole cloves, one teaspoonful salt, two teaspoonfuls whole allspice, and as much red pepper as will lie on the point of a knife; put the oysters, with their liquor, into a large earthen vessel; add vinegar and all other ingredients; stir well together and set over a slow fire; keep covered; stir them several times to the bottom; as soon as they are well scalded they are done; put into jars; if a larger quantity is made it can be kept for a long time; of course these are eaten cold.

(Detroit, 1881)

Stewed Oysters with Celery

In a large stew-pan put a pint of strong and clear broth, made of the choicest cuts of beef. Instead of milk and water, or milk even, as the prevailing practice is, use only the sweetest and richest of cream. Of this cream add one pint to the same quantity of best of beef broth. Also four ounces of the most excellent table butter, three teaspoonfuls of salt, two of white pepper, as much more of ground mace, and a teaspoonful of extract of celery. If the celery is to be had in stalk chop up fine and throw in. No more delicate or healthy flavor can be added to any stew, soup or broth than this exquisite vegetable. Now set to cooking, and while on the fire dredge in finely powdered cracker dust and

An oyster fork in the "olive" pattern popular in 1872 (Wallingford, 1872).

190

a little of the best corn starch flour, until thickened to your taste. Have ready parboiled (not in water, but in their own juice) fifty of the best quality of oysters in a hot tureen. Pour over these parboiled oysters the sauce compounded as above and serve while still scalding hot.

(Detroit, 1881)

Shredded Wheat Oyster, Meat or Vegetable Patties

Cut oblong cavity in top of biscuit, remove top carefully and all inside shreds, forming a shell. Sprinkle with salt and pepper, put small pieces of butter in bottom and fill the shell with drained, picked and washed oysters. Season with additional salt and pepper. Replace top of biscuit over oysters, then bits of butter on top. Place in a covered pan and bake in a moderate oven. Pour oyster liquor or cream sauce over it. Shell fish, vegetables, or meats may also be used.

(Grand Rapids, 1917)

Shrimps à la Creole

Take a pint of shelled shrimps, fresh or canned, place them in a sauce pan in which you have two ounces of butter, half of a small onion, thoroughly cooked and chopped fine, just enough to flavor the dish. Braise your shrimps in this preparation; add half a pint of canned tomatoes, seasoned highly with salt and chili pepper, add two tablespoonfuls of French peas; cook for ten minutes and serve in a chafing dish (excellent for a cool day); onions may be omitted.

Mrs. E. Peterson, Menominee
(Chicago, 1898)

Frogs, How to Cook

Somebody writes to the *Blade* how to cook frogs, and does it so nicely I will use his own words for it. He says: As potpies, stews and chowder they are a failure. The only legitimate way to cook a frog is to fry him brown in sweet table butter. As a pre-liminary he must be dipped in a batter of cracker dust, which should adhere closely when cooked, forming a dainty cracknel of a golden brown color, with a crisp tang to it when submitted to the teeth. The tender juices thus retained lose none of their delicate flavor, and the dainty morsel needs no condiments to give it an additional zest. Next to the pleasure of sitting on the borders of a frog-pond at eventide and listening to their sweet, melancholy ch-r-r-r-k is that of reviewing a plate heaped high with the mementoes of a finished feast—the bones of the "Frog that would a wooing go," and a goodly portion of his kindred.

Remarks—Having eaten them done thusly, I can say try them every chance you can get. They are splendid.

(Ann Arbor, 1884)

Frogs' Legs

First catch your frogs. Skin soon as possible. The hind legs are the only parts used. Fry a delicate brown in butter, season with a little salt and pepper, or dip in egg batter and fry.

(Grand Rapids, 1890)

Frogs and Tomatoes

Put the frog legs in boiling water; take them out and place them in cold water; prepare tomatoes as for a sauce; put in a frying-pan the frog-legs, with a piece of butter, and fry them gently. Serve the legs, nicely arranged in the tomato sauce. Garnish with toast, cut in lozenges.

(Detroit, 1881)

Restaurant Snapper

Put the snapper in boiling water about one minute; then lift out, take the skin and shell off and clean perfectly; then put in a pot with water sufficient to cover and boil until tender—salted, of course, to suit the taste; take out the snapper and leave the liquor on to boil. Mix one tablespoonful of butter and two of flour until smooth, season with mace, cayenne pepper and salt, put in the pot and let it come to a boil, put in the snapper and leave for a few minutes; add more or less flour, as you like it thick or thin, and some prefer a little wine.

(Detroit, 1881)

Terrapins, or Water Turtles

Land terrapins, it is hardly necessary to say, are uneatable, but the large turtle that frequents our mill-ponds and rivers can be converted into a relishable article of food. Plunge the turtle into a pot of boiling water, and let him lie there 5 minutes; you can then skin the under part easily, and pull off the horny parts of the feet; lay him for 10 minutes in cold salt and water; then put into more hot water salted, but not too much; boil until tender; the time will depend upon the size and age; take him out, drain and wipe dry; loosen the shell carefully, not to break the flesh; cut open also with care, lest you touch the gall-bag with the knife; remove this with the entrails and sand-bag; cut up all the rest of the animal into small bits; season with pepper, salt, 1 chopped onion, sweet herbs, and 1 teaspoon some spiced sauce, or 1 tablespoon catsup—walnut or mushroom; save the juice that runs from the meat, and put all together into a saucepan with a closely fitting top; stew gently 15 minutes, stirring occasionally, and add 1 large spoon butter, or 1 teaspoon browned flour wet in cold water, 1 glass brown sherry, and lastly, the beaten yolk of 1 egg, mixed with a little of the hot liquor, that it may not curdle; boil up once and turn into a covered dish. Send around green pickles and delicate slices of toast with it.

(Detroit, 1890)

Game

Pioneer Michigan was a hunter's paradise. Great herds of white-tailed deer bounded over the southern Michigan prairies and oak openings; rabbits, squirrels, and raccoons offered smaller targets for sharp-eyed frontiersmen. Black bears posed a threat to livestock and were soon all but eliminated. Feathered game included wild turkeys, quail, ruffled grouse, woodcocks, snipe, ducks, and geese. Enormous flocks of passenger pigeons darkened the sky for days on end during their migration season.

Game formed an important supplement to settler's diets and was a welcome relief from endless meals of salt pork. But as the Michigan Frontier pushed across the western Lower Peninsula and then to the north game rapidly vanished. There were no game laws or bag limits, and as settlers fought to carve homesteads out of the wilderness, few worried about the animal life they supplanted. In addition to the game harvested by settlers, expert hunters sometimes created small industries. When British author Harriet Martineau traveled across southern Michigan in 1836, she described a hunter west of Detroit who had shot a hundred deer the previous year and sold them for $3 a piece. Needless to say deer and other game animals were soon all but wiped out. By the 1890s, the sighting of a deer in southern Michigan made front-page news. Sportsmen soon established the tradition of traveling to the northern Lower Peninsula and the U.P. for their trophies.

Conservation-minded citizens and the Department of Natural Resources transplanted new populations of deer, turkeys, and other game animals in the 1930s and 1940s, and they have made a comeback. But for some species, like the passenger pigeon, it was too late.

We hope the following toothsome recipes appeal to those who meet with luck afield or who just enjoy the special taste of wild game.

Game—How to Cook It

Broiling is a favorite method of cooking game and all birds are exceedingly nice roasted, especially quails. Game is best if kept as long as possible, without tainting, before cooking, as it gives it the "gamy" flavor. When birds do become tainted, pick clean as soon as possible, and lay in milk, where they are completely covered, for twenty-four hours, when they will be sweet, fresh and ready for cooking.

Birds should be carefully dry-picked—removing all feathers that come off easily, plunged in a pot of boiling water, and skinned, drawn, wiped clean and all shot removed. Game should never be washed, unless absolutely necessary to assure cleanliness, and then must be washed quickly, using as little water as possible. The more plainly game is cooked, the finer the flavor. They require more heat than poultry, but cook quicker, and should be served smoking hot. White-meated game should be cooked to well-done; dark-meated game rare.

To lard game—After cleaning and washing, cut fat salt pork into thin, narrow strips; thread a larding needle with one of the strips, run the needle under the skin with a little of the flesh of the bird and draw the pork halfway through, so that the ends of the strips exposed will be of equal length. The strips should be about one inch apart. The larding destroys the flavor of the bird, and many prefer tying a piece of bacon on the breast instead, but the larding of birds renders them more juicy.

To roast game—Season with salt and pepper, place a lump of butter or port inside; truss, skewer and place in oven. The flavor is best preserved without dressing, but many prefer a plain bread dressing, or a few oysters placed inside. Or, put the fowl, with an onion, salt and hot water into a pan and baste for ten or fifteen minutes; change the pan; put in a slice of salt pork and baste with butter and pork drippings very often; just before serving dredge lightly with flour and baste. Ducks take from twenty-five to thirty-five minutes to roast, and woodcocks and snipe fifteen to twenty-five. Do not draw or take off the heads of either.

To broil—Split down the back; open and flatten the breast by covering with a cloth and pounding, season with pepper, and lay the inside first upon the gridiron. Turn as soon as browned, and when almost done, take off; place on a platter; sprinkle with salt and return to the gridiron. When done, place in a hot dish, butter both sides well, and serve at once. The time required is usually about twenty minutes. This is a very nice way to cook prairie chickens, partridges and quails, or you will find it a decided improvement to stuff them with sausage meat.

To roast them, they must be cleaned nicely, rinsed and dried and then filled with dressing, sewing them up nicely and binding down the legs and wings with cords. Put them in a steamer over hot water, and let them cook until just done. Then place them in a pan with a little butter, set them in the oven and baste them frequently with melted butter until of a nice brown. They ought to brown nicely in about fifteen minutes. Serve them on a platter with sprigs of parsley alternately with currant jelly.

Pigeons may be either roasted, potted or stewed. After they are thoroughly picked and cleaned, put a small piece of salt pork and a little ball of dressing into the body of every pigeon. The dressing should be made of one egg to one cracker, an equal quantity of suet, or butter, seasoned with sweet marjoram, or sage (if marjoram cannot be procured). Flour the pigeons well: lay them close together in the bottom of the pot; just cover them with water: throw in a bit of butter; and let them stew an hour and a quarter, if young; an hour and three-quarters if old. Some people turn off the liquor just before they are done, and brown the pigeons on the bottom of the pot; but this is very troublesome, as they are apt to break to pieces. Stewed pigeons are cooked in nearly the same way, with the omission of the stuffing. Being dry meat, they require a good deal of butter. Pigeons should be stuffed and roasted about fifteen minutes before a smart fire. Those who like birds just warmed through, would perhaps think less time necessary. It makes them nicer to butter them well just before you take them off the spit, and

sprinkle them with nicely pounded bread or cracker. All poultry should be basted and floured a few minutes before it is taken up.

The age of pigeons can be judged by the color of the legs. When young, they are of a pale, delicate brown; as they grow older, the color is deeper and redder.

If the wild flavor of larger birds, such as prairie chickens, is disliked, they may be soaked over night in salt water, or two or three hours in soda and water, or parboiled with an onion or two in the water for several hours, or a fresh lemon, stripped of the outer skin, may be put inside the game for a day or two, renewing the lemon every ten hours. This will absorb unpleasant flavors from nearly all game. Squirrels should be carefully skinned and laid in salt water a short time before cooking; if old, parboil. They are very savory if broiled, and are excellent made into a stew, or cooked with thin slices of bacon.

Venison is considered by many a very fine dish. The haunch, neck, shoulder and saddle should be roasted; the breast roasted or broiled, and the steaks broiled or fried with slices of bacon or salt pork. Venison requires more time for cooking than beefsteak.

The garnishes for small game are dried or roasted bread, slices of lemon, parsley and currant jelly; for larger game, such as wild ducks, cranberry sauce, apple sauce, sliced lemons, or sliced oranges and parsley.

(Detroit, 1881)

Bear Meat

Bear meat requires a longer time for cooking than almost any other kind. It requires parboiling, and should be cooked thoroughly. It may be roasted like pork or buffalo meat, or sliced into steaks and broiled or fried.

(Detroit, 1890)

Roast 'Possum

To roast a 'possum, first catch the 'possum. Dress it and soak in salt and water from 6 to 12 hours, then parboil in salt water for ½ to ¾ hour; if an old animal it requires longer boiling and roasting than a young one. Prepare a dressing the same as for a turkey or chicken, of which oysters may form an ingredient, as the dressing should be rich and savory; stuff, sew up and place in the baking-pan, the same as a turkey, with a little water. Place in the oven for 15 or 20 minutes; in the meantime partially boil some sweet potatoes; remove the pan from the oven, pour off the liquor in a dish in which it can be kept hot, and layer the sweet potatoes closely round the 'possum in the pan; cut some slices of bacon and lay them across the 'possum and on the potatoes; use the liquor that was turned off for 2 or 3 bastings, basting both the 'possum and the sweet potatoes, until it is all returned to the pan. Let bake for an hour or more, according to the age and size of the 'possum.

(Detroit, 1890)

Roast Hare or Rabbit

Have the hare skinned and well cleaned, stuff as you would a fowl, with a force-meat of bread crumbs, chopped fat pork, a little sweet marjoram, onion, pepper and salt, just moistened with hot water. Sew up the hare with fine cotton, tie the legs closely to the body in a kneeling position, lay in the dripping-pan, back uppermost, pour two cups of boiling water over it, cover with another pan and bake, closely covered—except when you baste it with butter and water—for three-quarters of an hour. Uncover, baste freely with the gravy until nicely browned; dredge with flour and anoint with butter until a fine froth appears on the surface. Take up the hare, put it on a hot dish and keep covered while you make the gravy. Strain and skim that left in the pan, season, thicken with browned flour, stir in a good spoonful of currant jelly and some chopped parsley, boil up, pour a few spoonfuls of it

A Sault Ste. Marie dealer advertised the product of the Michigan Stove Company, which had been established in Detroit in 1871 (Polk, 1881).

over the hare, and serve the rest in a gravy boat. Clip the threads and send the hare in with currant jelly around it.

(Detroit, 1881)

Roast Hare or Rabbit

A very close relationship exists between the hare and rabbit, the chief difference being in smaller size and shorter legs and ears of the latter. The manner of dressing and preparing each for the table, is therefore, pretty nearly the same. To prepare them for roasting, first skin, wash well in cold water and rinse thoroughly in lukewarm water. If a little musty from being emptied before they were hung up, afterwards neglected, rub the insides with vinegar and afterward remove all taint of the acid by a thorough washing in lukewarm water. After being well wiped with a soft cloth put in a dressing as usual, sew the animal up, truss it, and roast for half or three-quarters of an hour, until well-browned, basting it constantly with butter and dredging with flour, just before basting up.

To make a gravy, after the rabbits are roasted, pour nearly all the fat out of the pan, but do not pour the bottom or brown part of the drippings; put the pan over the fire, into it a heaping tablespoon flour and stir until the flour browns. Then stir in a pint of boiling water. Season the gravy with salt and pepper; let it boil for a moment, Send hot to the table in a tureen with the hot rabbits. Serve with currant jelly.

(Vermontville, 1906)

Rabbit Cutlets

Cut the different limbs into the size of cutlets; such as the shoulders cut in half; also the legs, with the ends of the bones chopped off, and pieces of the back, even to the half of the head. Have ready some breadcrumbs and the yolk of an egg beat up. Drop each cutlet into the egg, and then into the breadcrumbs, as for veal cutlets. Fry them a nice brown, and when you dish them pour round them some rich brown gravy, which may be flavored with tomato sauce, if approved, and put round them pieces of fried bacon, if liked.

(Ann Arbor, 1884)

Rabbit Friccasee

Joint 2 carefully dressed rabbits, and place in a large dish of cold water with a handful of salt. Soak for 2 hours. Remove and rinse with fresh water, cover the bottom of a kettle with strips of salt pork (about ¼ of a lb.). When it is fried brown, slice on it a large onion and toss till light brown. Now add the jointed rabbit and stir till all are seared over; then add 1 qt. of boiling water, 1 tsp. salt and a pinch of red pepper. Place on the back of the range and simmer gently for 2 hours, or until perfectly tender. Take up on a large buttered platter, thicken and strain the gravy to serve separately. Garnish with wedges of lemon and parsley. Serve with currant jelly. This is an excellent and economical dish in early winter when rabbits are in good condition.

Florence S. Wattles
(Kalamazoo, 1906)

Rabbit Pie

Cut up the rabbit, remove the breast bone and bone the legs. Put the rabbit, a few slices of ham, a few forcemeat balls, and 3 hard-boiled eggs, by

The kitchen cabinet featured in this Detroit department store advertisement included everything from a spice rack to a built-in flour sifter (Detroit, 1915).

turns, in layers, and season each with pepper, salt, 2 blades of pounded mace, and ½ tea-spoonful of grated nutmeg. Pour in ½ pt. water, cover with crust, and bake in a well-heated oven for 1½ hours. When done, pour in at the top, through the middle of the crust, a little good gravy, which may be made of the breast and leg bones, flavored with onion, herbs and spices.

(Ann Arbor, 1884)

Rabbit Pie

1 rabbit	1 cup of peas
2 cups cooked carrots	Biscuit dough
½ cups cooked celery	2 tbsp. bacon fat
3 onions chopped	

Heat bacon fat add onion cook light brown. Remove onions, browned pieces of rabbit which have been dipped in flour, cover with boiling water, simmer till soft, season with salt and pepper and one bay leaf. Remove rabbit, thicken broth to suit your own taste, cut meat from bones line a deep baking dish with rich biscuit dough rolled rather thin fill with alternate layers of meat, carrots, peas, celery and onions add broth cover top with biscuit dough, brush with cream. Bake in hot oven 450 degrees F., 10 minutes, continue baking in moderate oven (400 degrees F.) twenty minutes. This is a meal in itself and good for the whole family.

Mrs. S. B. Snyder, Fulton
(Kalamazoo, 1935)

Hasenfeffer

Cut up two rabbits and wash well, and then put them in an earthen kettle and pour over vinegar to cover them. Add: four sliced onions, four sticks celery, three bay leaves, six whole cloves, six whole peppers. Let it stand for four or five days. Then boil a piece of beef and use the stock to boil the rabbits in, and then when tender, roast one cup of bread crumbs and flour mixed in butter for thickening. Serve hot with mashed potatoes.

(Lansing, 1918)

Mrs. R. W. Camp's Rabbit Supreme

½ cup of vinegar
½ cup of water
1 tablespoon sugar
1 bay leaf
¼ teaspoon of cloves
¼ teaspoon of black
   pepper

⅛ teaspoon mace
1 teaspoon salt
1 medium sized rabbit
1 medium sized on-
   ion, sliced
½ pint of sour cream

Mix the water, vinegar, sugar and spices and simmer five minutes. Then set aside to cool. Wash the rabbit and cut into pieces for serving. Put in a deep bowl together with the sliced onion and pour over it the above cooled liquid. Be sure that the rabbit is well covered with the liquid. Cover bowl and set away in a cool place for at least three days. Freezing will not hurt it. When ready to cook place all in a heavy kettle or dutch oven and simmer gently until very tender. Add the sour cream and serve piping hot with dumplings or mashed potatoes. A pot roast of beef is delicious when treated in the same way.

Serves five to six persons.

(Grand Rapids, 1935)

Roast 'Coon

The raccoon should be first soaked in strong salt and water from 8 to 10 hours, and it is also desirable to have the carcass frozen. It should be parboiled from 1 to 1½ hours, and a dessertspoon of soda or saleratus should be put into the water. The time required for roasting, both in the case of the opossum and the raccoon, depends somewhat on circumstances, and the judgment of the cook must determine when they are ready for the table. Irish potatoes are a good accompaniment to the raccoon.

The season, both for the opossum and raccoon, is from about the 1st of November to the 1st of March.

(Detroit, 1890)

Broiled Squirrels

Clean and soak in cold water to draw out the blood; wipe dry and broil on a gridiron over a clear, hot fire, turning often; when done lay in a hot dish and dress with plenty of melted butter, pepper and salt, and let it lie between two hot dishes for five minutes before eating.

(Detroit, 1881)

Squirrel Soup

Wash and quarter three or four good sized squirrels; put them on, with a small teaspoon of salt, directly after breakfast, in a gallon of cold water. Cover the pot close and set it on the back part of the stove to simmer gently, not boil. Add vegetables just the same as you do in case of other meat soups in the summer season, but especially good will you find corn, Irish potatoes, tomatoes and Lima Beans. Strain the soup through a coarse cullender, when the meat has boiled to shreds so as to get rid of the squirrel's troublesome little bones. Then return to the pot, and after boiling a while longer, thicken with a piece of butter rubbed in flour. Celery salt and parsley leaves chopped up are also considered an improvement by many. Toast two slices of bread, cut them into slices one-half inch square, fry them in butter, put them into the bottom of your tureen, and then pour the soup boiling hot upon them. Very good.

(Vermontville, 1906)

The back burner of a wood-burning stove was the traditional place for soups to slowly simmer, but an electric crockpot on low makes a good modern expedient.

Squirrels in Casserole

Three squirrels, ½ pound chopped salt pork, 1 cupful onions, 1½ cupfuls sliced parboiled potatoes, 1 cupful green corn, 1 cupful lima beans, 4

197

quarts boiling water, 1 quart peeled cut tomatoes, 1 tablespoon sugar, 1 tablespoon salt, 4 heaping tablespoons butter, black and red pepper to taste. Clean, wash and joint the squirrels, lay them in salted water for thirty minutes. Put ingredients in casserole in the following order: First a layer of pork, then of onions, next of potatoes, follow with successive layers of corn cut from the cob, beans and the squirrels. Season each layer with salt, red and black pepper. Pour in the water, put on the cover, seal with a paste made of flour and water. Cook slowly for 3 hours. Then add tomatoes and sugar. Cook for an hour longer. Stir in the butter and flour mixed together, boil for five minutes and serve in the casserole.

(Higgins Lake, 1920)

Haunch of Venison

Wash all over with lukewarm vinegar and water, then rub well with butter or lard to soften the skin. Cover the top and sides with foolscap paper, well greased, and coat it with a paste of flour and water, half an inch thick. Lay over this a large sheet of thin wrapping paper and over this another of stout foolscap. Tie all down in place by greased pack-thread. The papers should also be thoroughly greased. Do this the day before needed to roast. About three hours before it will be needed, put into the dripping-pan, with two cups of boiling water in the bottom. Insert another pan over it to keep in the steam; be sure that the fire is good and leave it to itself for an hour. Then see that the paper is not scorching; wet it all over with hot water and a ladleful of gravy; cover it and let it alone for an hour and a half more. Remove the papers and paste, and test with a skewer in the thickest part. If it goes in readily, close the door and let it brown for half an hour. Baste freely four times with wine and butter, and at last dredge with flour and rub over with butter to make a froth. Take it up, put upon a hot dish. Skim the gravy left in the dripping-pan, strain it, thicken with browned flour, add two teaspoonfuls of currant jelly, a glass of wine, pepper and salt. Boil up for an instant, and serve in a gravy boat. Allow a quarter of an hour to the pound in roasting venison. The neck can be roasted in the same way as the haunch.

(Detroit, 1881)

Foolscap paper was ordinary writing or book paper that came in a sheet 13 × 16 inches. It drew its name from the watermark of a jester's or fool's cap used by early hand papermakers. Aluminum foil would provide a simpler modern alternative.

Venison Steaks

Cut them from the neck, season with pepper and salt; heat the gridiron hot and grease the bars before laying the steak on; broil them well; turn once, taking care to save as much gravy as possible. Serve hot with currant jelly on each piece.

(Detroit, 1881)

The gridiron described here would have been a specialized cast-iron pan shaped like a shallow frying pan but with an open lattice grid on the bottom.

Venison Ham

Trim the ham nicely and lard with thin slices of bacon, then soak five or six hours in the following pickle: One-half cup of olive oil, salt, spices, thyme, one onion cut in slices and one or two glasses of wine (red), turning it occasionally, then take out and roast before a bright fire, basting it with its pickle. It will take from one to two hours to cook.

(Detroit, 1881)

Venison

Venison should be roasted in the same manner as beef, always remembering that it must be served *rare* and *hot*. All the dishes and plates for serving must be hot, also. Currant or green grape jelly should be an accompaniment. In making the gravy after a roast, pour off all fat, and boil up in the stock four whole cloves, and a small slice of onion. Strain, and thicken with browned flour, creamed with butter. Boil one minute.

Venison is also very nice boiled, and then allowed to cook slowly until very tender and the water all cooked out. Turn frequently to prevent burning. Take up, and make a thick gravy in the kettle.

(Battle Creek, 1890)

Roast Venison

Choose a haunch with clear, bright and thick fat. Wash it in warm water and dry it well with a cloth. Cover it with a flour and water paste about ½ inch in thickness. Allow twenty minutes to each pound. About twenty minutes before it is done carefully remove the paste, dredge with flour and baste well with butter until a nice brown color. Serve with a good strong unflavored gravy and currant jelly.

Mrs. John Gray
(Kalamazoo, 1899)

Broiled Venison

Cut thin slices, mix stale crumbs of bread with pepper and salt, egg the slices, and dip into the seasoned bread; broil over a clear fire. Serve with a gravy sauce.

(Detroit, 1881)

Broiled Venison Steak

Salt and pepper	*½ tsp. allspice*
1 onion	*5 tbsp. butter or lard*
3 tsp flour	

Wipe steaks with a cloth wrung out of cold water. Place steak in hot buttered broiler and broil with a brisk fire. Turn every ten seconds for the first few minutes, then add salt and pepper to taste, cover with thin sliced onions and add allspice and 1 cup water or enough to cover steaks, let broil for ½ hour then add flour for thickening and serve hot. Broil slowly.

Mrs. Chester Taylor, Comstock
(Kalamazoo, 1935)

Venison Cutlets

Clean and trim slices of venison cut from loin. Sprinkle with salt and pepper, brush over with melted butter or olive oil and roll in soft stale bread crumbs. Place in broiler and broil five minutes; or saute with butter. Serve with Port wine sauce.

Helen A. Sebring
(Kalamazoo, 1906)

Mrs. Sarah Marshall Weaver compiled a cookbook under the auspices of the Michigan State Federation of Women's Clubs that was printed in Charlotte in 1909. Myrtle Koon Cherryman of Grand Rapids, author of a number of volumes of verse including *Songs of Sunshine* (1908) and *Mother Goose Meddlings* (1909), contributed a poetic introduction:

Here in the big bright kitchen called the earth,
    Ingredients are at hand
For us to use—of great and lesser worth—
    And if we understand
The proper ways of using them, and take
    A pleasure in the task,
We'll find the various viands that we make
    All that a king might ask. . . .

Club women from across the state sent in their favorite recipes. From the north country, where deer still roamed, came two recipes for venison.

To Fry Venison

Take the chops or steak, remove bone, pound, then scald until seared over. Then season, roll in flour and fry in drippings until brown on both sides.

Mrs. Henry Aldrich, Cadillac
(Charlotte, 1909)

Venison

Venison slices better if frozen. Slice extremely thin, roll in flour. Fry quickly in bacon fat and serve with crisp bacon. Must be well done. Venison is also delicious sliced thin and broiled and served with broiled bacon.

Mrs. Carey W. Dunton, Manistique
(Charlotte, 1909)

Jessie Marie De Both queried sportsmen across the country concerning their favorite recipes and published her findings in *Famous Sportsmen's Recipes*. Her compilation, published in Chicago in 1940, included a recipe from Federal Judge Arthur J. Tuttle of Detroit.

Roast Saddle of Venison

The saddle of the venison is a monstrous great roast cut right out of the back. It includes practically all of the back of the deer, and particularly that part which we call the tenderloin. If dinner is to be at seven o'clock, begin to barbecue the venison at four-thirty. Build a big wood fire out of logs and burn long enough so that there is not very much blaze to it but an immense amount of heat from the coals and the partially consumed wood.

Arrange a means by which the saddle of venison can be suspended in a perpendicular position right in front of the fireplace, close to the coals and the saddle hung right down in front of the coals, suspended by chains so that it can be turned around easily and practically all the time. Have the fire very hot at the outset so that the outside of the venison will be seared promptly to prevent the loss of the juices. From there on, keep the fire just good and hot and cook gradually for about two hours. Put a dripping pan under the venison and in this dripping pan prepare the sauce with which to baste the meat frequently—about once a minute.

Sauce

1 quart chili sauce	*1 tablespoon salt*
2 cups tart jelly (crab-apple)	*1 pound butter*
1 tablespoon black pepper	*1 pint cherry wine*

Melt all of the foregoing in the dripping pan and then into that pour the wine.

When the meat is done, let the sauce, that has dripped back into the pan during cooking, cool so that the tallow and grease from the venison may be removed as soon as it forms in a sheet on top of the sauce. Serve the remaining sauce with the meat.

Federal Judge Arthur Tuttle, Detroit
(Chicago, 1940)

Camp Way of Cooking Fowls

Kill the fowl (no matter what kind it may be) by cutting off the head; hang up by the feet till free from blood; then carefully remove all the entrails and crop; use no water in the operation, save upon your hands before commencing; be careful not to remove or disturb the feathers; stuff the fowl with ordinary stuffing; then wrap the body up in wet brown paper and roast in the ashes of the fire as you would potatoes till done. The time consumed in roasting will depend on the age and kind of fowl. There is no danger of burning, if properly attended to and better be overdone than rare. When you think the fowl sufficiently done, take out of the embers and unroll carefully; remove the feathers and skin together; place upon a large dish and carry to the table. A sweeter fowl was never eaten.

(Detroit, 1881)

To Cook Game Birds

Game birds should be dry picked, and not drawn until roasting. Wipe with damp cloth, but never let water touch game. Stuff with a celery stalk and an onion. This stuffing is not meant to be eaten but is for the purpose of neutralizing steam that will otherwise carry objectionable flavors through the shot holes into the meat. Put birds into an uncovered roaster into a cold oven set for temperature of 375° to 400° F. No basting is necessary.

Time Table for Cooking

Large ducks (such as Mallard), 50 to 60 minutes.
Pheasant, 60 minutes.
Small Ducks (Teal), 35 minutes.
Partridge, 40 minutes.
Woodcock and Snipe, 20 to 25 minutes.

Mrs. N. Rugee White
(Grand Rapids, 1935)

Ducks—To Bake Wild or Tame, to Avoid Their Naturally Strong Flavor

Directions—After having prepared them for stuffing, first parboil them for 1 hour, having an onion cut into 2 or 3 pieces, according to its size; put a piece inside of each duck while parboiling, which removes their strong flavor; then stuff with bread-crumb dressing, in which half of a common-sized onion, chopped fine, has been added for each duck. Bake in a hot oven, leaving the oven door ½ inch ajar to carry off the strong flavor which may be left. Baste often with water and butter kept on the stove for that purpose, as the water first put in is to be poured off, to get rid of the duck-oil, which at first comes out very freely and contains much of the rancid or strong flavor of the duck, which it is our design hereby to avoid. After this the water and butter may be put into the pan for basting and for the gravy. The object is to get rid of all the oil possible.

Another Plan—and some people like them better with wholly an onion dressing—is as follows: Peel and wash 4 medium-sized onions for each duck, slice them, and have some water in a sauce-pan, boiling as hard as may be, throw in the sliced onions (onions can be peeled and sliced under water without affecting the eyes), with a little salt, and boil for 1 minute only after they begin to boil, which removes the acrid oil, or strong taste of the onions; remove from the fire, pouring off the water and draining nicely (this should always be done in cooking onions, even as an onion stew in milk);

A blissful kitchen experience is marred by a feline reprobate (Ann Arbor, 1884).

chop the onions finely, and season with salt and pepper to taste and 1 tea-spoonful of powdered sage for each duck; stuff, and bake as above.

Remarks—This instruction was obtained of a boarding-house keeper, who had many years experience besides. I have had them tried several times myself and will say that for me I prefer at least half the dressing to be bread-crumbs, although the onion dressing alone, prepared as above, is very fine. If bread is used, of course butter is also to be added in all cases. Remember this, also, that in baking ducks, or any other wild game or poultry, they should be basted every 5 to 10 minutes while baking, if you desire them to be tender and sweet. Have plenty of water in the pan, with quite a bit of butter, for the purpose, and for the gravy after the oil has been poured or dipped off.

(Ann Arbor, 1884)

Ducks to Roast and Stuff With Potato Stuffing

The roasting to be the same as above; but for the stuffing, boil potatoes and mash them finely. Prepare 1 onion at least for each duck, as also above directed (by boiling 1 minute with a little salt and pouring off the water), then chopping fine and mixing with the potato sufficient for the number of ducks to be stuffed, seasoning with salt and pepper and a very little ½ tea-spoonful to a duck) of thyme, and when filled with this potato and onion mixture, roast as before directed; and as soon as the oil is got rid of, rub over with butter, dredge on a little flour, put in more hot water, and baste often. Put the giblets into the same pan, and when done chop fine, and put into the gravy.

(Ann Arbor, 1884)

Duck and Oyster Croquettes, or Balls, to Fry

Stuff a young and tender duck with oyster dressing (4 to 6, chopped, for a duck), roast, basting well to keep moist and from burning. When cold remove the bones and chop finely, and mix with the dressing, season with cayenne (if tolerated, else black pepper) and salt. Moisten with catsup and a well beaten egg, and stiffen properly with more bread or cracker crumbs, if needed. Make into croquettes, or balls, and brown nicely in hot butter or drippings. Put a sprig or two of parsley, if you have it, with each one, in serving.

(Ann Arbor, 1884)

Braised Grouse

Clean thoroughly, washing out the inside in soda and water, and then rinsing and wiping. Truss, but do not stuff the birds; tie them in shape. Cover the bottom of a saucepan with slices of fat salt pork; lay the grouse upon these; sprinkle minced onion and parsley over them with pepper, salt and a little sugar. Cover them with more pork, and pour in a large cup of soup stock, or other broth. Cover very closely; simmer one hour; turn the birds and cook—always covered—until tender. Dish the grouse, strain the gravy, thicken with browned flour, boil up and pour into a gravy boat. Partridges and wild pigeons may also be cooked in this way.

(Detroit, 1881)

Ruffed Grouse with Kraut

Use carefully plucked (never skinned) birds. Salt inside and out and roll in flour. Brown thoroughly in butter. Pad bottom of roaster, preferably of earthen-ware, with thick layer of sauerkraut. Place birds, on their backs, in roaster. Cover breasts with bacon strips. Pack birds lightly in generous covering of kraut and roast in hot oven from two and a quarter to two and a half hours.

(Chicago, 1940)

Harold Titus of Traverse City submitted this recipe to *Famous Sportsmen's Recipes* in 1940. His hobby, Titus wrote, was the "pursuit of anything—legally permissible—which swims and flies, with particular emphasis on trout and ruffed grouse." Titus returned to the Grand Traverse region where he

had been born and raised following a stint in the army during World War I. When not hunting or fishing, he wrote a number of novels set in the area he loved so well, including *Timber* (1922), about the logging industry, *The Beloved Pawn* (1923), about Beaver Island, and a historical novel concerning the Mackinac Island fur trade, *Black Feather* (1936).

A Nice Way to Cook Pigeons

Stuff the birds with a rich bread dressing; place compactly in an iron or earthen dish; season with salt, pepper and butter (or if you like best thin slices of salt pork over the top), dredge thickly with flour and nearly cover them with water. Then put over a closely fitting plate or cover, and place the dish in a moderate oven, from two to four or even five hours, according to the age of the birds. If the birds are *old* and *tough* this is the best way they can be cooked, and they may be made perfectly tender and much sweeter than by any other process. If the gravy is insufficient add a little water before dishing.

(Detroit, 1878)

The pigeons referred to in this recipe undoubtedly were wild pigeons or passenger pigeons. Coincidently, 1878, the year in which the *Home Messenger Book of Tested Receipts* was published in Detroit, marked the last major pigeon nesting in Michigan. The beech forests of Michigan were the final refuge of the wild pigeons that once nested by the billions in the eastern and midwestern states. A social bird unable to exist in small numbers, passenger pigeons nested so thickly, as many as one hundred to a branch, that they destroyed entire forests by breaking down the foliage. Wherever they nested, local citizens shot, netted, and knocked the squabs out of the trees by the thousands. Some entrepreneurs made lucrative professions out of pigeon hunting, shipping them by the barrel to eastern markets. In one region of Michigan alone more than three million birds were slain in one season. People's greed and the destruction of the forest habitats eventually accomplished their extinction. By the 1890s pigeons were rarely seen. In 1914 the last representative of species died in a Cincinnati zoo.

Commercially raised pigeons and other wild varieties such as mourning doves remained prize dishes after the passenger pigeons were gone.

Broiled Pigeons

Split them down the back, spread open, season with pepper and salt and broil over a quick, clear fire.

(Detroit, 1881)

Roast Pigeons

Wipe them quite dry; truss them, and season them inside with pepper and salt, and put a piece of butter the size of a walnut in each. Put them down to a sharp fire and baste them all the time they are cooking. They will take about half an hour. Garnish them with fried parsley, and serve with a tureen of bread sauce.

(Detroit, 1881)

Roast Pigeons

Pigeons lose their flavor by being kept more than one day after being killed. They may be prepared and roasted or broiled the same as chicken; they will require from twenty to thirty minutes cooking. Make a gravy of the giblets or not; season with pepper and salt, and add a little flour and butter.

(Vermontville, 1906)

Even though the passenger pigeons are extinct, these various recipes for pigeons can be applied to other wild game such as quail and partridge as well as cornish game hens and chicken.

Stewed Pigeons

Put the pigeons into a pot with a cup of water to keep them from burning, and a tablespoonful of butter for each one. Shut the lid down tightly and subject to a slow heat until they are of a nice dark brown. Once in a great while turn them, and see that each is well set with the liquor. Take them out and cover in a warm place—a colander set over a pan of hot water is best—while you make the gravy. Chop the giblets of the pigeons very fine, with a little onion and parsley. Put into the gravy, pepper and salt, boil up and thicken with browned flour. Return the pigeons to the pot, cover again tightly, and cook slowly until tender. If there should not be liquor enough in the pot to make the gravy, add boiling water before the giblets go in.

(Detroit, 1881)

Pigeons

Dress and stuff them as you do chickens, cut a thin slice of salt pork and tie around each, place in the dripper and baste often while baking. Cook young birds from 2 to 3 hours. If old longer time.

Mrs. F. B. Peck
(Muskegon, 1890)

Pigeon Pie

6 pigeons
6 strips bacon
1 tablespoon flour

1 tablespoon butter
2 cups soup-stock
3 onions, quartered

Have the pigeons cleaned and place in a glass baking dish or casserole with a strip of bacon on each bird. Bake for five minutes in a very hot oven.

Brown the flour in the butter in a saucepan, add the soup stock, salt and pepper and bring to boiling point. Add the onions and set the pigeons in this gravy. Simmer for one hour and then replace the pigeons and the gravy in the baking dish, cover with a baking powder or pie dough, with incisions for the steam to escape. Bake in the hot oven for another fifteen minutes and serve in the baking dish.

(Detroit, 1935)

To Pot Birds

Prepare them as for roasting. Fill each with a dressing made as follows: Allow for each bird of the size of a pigeon one-half of a hard boiled egg, chopped fine, a tablespoonful of bread crumbs, a teaspoonful of chopped pork; season the bird with pepper and salt; stuff them, lay them in a kettle that has a tight cover. Place over the birds a few slices of pork, add a pint of water, dredge over them a little flour, cover and put them in a hot oven. Let them cook until tender, then add a little cream and butter. If the sauce is too thin, thicken with flour. One pint of water sufficient for twelve birds.

(Detroit, 1878)

Prairie Chickens, Partridges and Quail

Clean nicely, using a little soda in the water in which they are washed; rinse them and drain, and fill with dressing, sewing them up nicely, and binding down the legs and wings with cord. Put them in a steamer and let them cook ten minutes. Then put them in a pan with a little butter, set them in the oven and baste frequently, until of a nice brown. They ought to brown in about thirty-five minutes. Serve them in a platter with sprigs of parsley alternated with currant jelly.

(Detroit, 1878)

The correct presentation of partridge and quail specified that the bird's head be tucked under its wing (Townsend, 1894).

Broiled Partridge or Quail

Split the bird down the back. Wipe with a damp towel. Season with salt and pepper, rub thickly with soft butter, and dredge with flour. Broil partridge 20 minutes, quail ten minutes, over hot fire. Serve on buttered toast, garnishing with parsley.

Mrs. Robert Eddy, Bay City
(Kalamazoo, 1906)

Partridge is synonymous with ruffed grouse.

Roast Partridge

Clean and wash the bird. Lard the breast and legs. Run a small skewer into the legs and through the tail. Tie firmly with twine. Dredge with salt, and rub the breast with soft butter; then dredge thickly with flour. Put a small onion into the body of the bird. Roast in a quick oven twenty minutes, if to be rare; if wished better done thirty minutes. When done place on a hot platter on which has been spread bread sauce. Garnish with parsley.

(Kalamazoo, 1906)

Broiled Quail

Pick and draw the birds. Wipe inside and out with a damp cloth, then rub with salt and pepper. Over the breast of each bird skewer a thin slice of bacon. Place the birds on the rack in the broiler pan with a cup of boiling water. Baste very frequently, turning the birds to brown them alike all over. Have ready a square of toast for each bird, dip the squares lightly in the drippings, place on a platter with a bird on each square of toast, garnish with parsley and serve very hot.

Mrs. Geo. Pierson
(Kalamazoo, 1899)

Fried Quails

Pick and clean, cut in the middle of back, fry in butter to a nice brown, salt and pepper; now put in an earthen or porcelain lined dish, one tablespoonful of nice butter and the same of flour; stir on a slow fire until butter is dissolved, then pour in slowly two-thirds glass of water and the same quantity of wine, salt and pepper; put in your birds that are nicely fried, simmer slowly one-quarter of an hour; toast some thin slices of bread (one toast to each bird); put in the dish you wish to serve, laying the birds on top; pour the gravy over all; serve very hot.

(Detroit, 1881)

Quails Roasted with Ham

Clean, truss and stuff as usual. Cover the entire bird with thin slices of ham or salt pork, binding all with buttered pack-thread. Roast three-quarters of an hour, basting with butter and water three times, then with the dripping. When done dish with the ham laid about the body of the bird. Skim the gravy, thicken with browned flour mixed in a little cold water, pepper and salt. Boil up once and pour over the bird.

(Detroit, 1881)

Reed Birds

Roast them on the little wire that accompanies the roaster; turn and baste frequently, and season with pepper and salt, or boil in a crust like dumplings.

(Detroit, 1881)

It seems incredible but reed birds are the little black and white songsters called bobolinks. They were called reed birds because they nest in marshes where reeds grow.

Woodcock

Tie the legs, skin the head and neck, turn the beak under the wing and tie it, tie a piece of bacon over it, and immerse in hot fat for two or three minutes. Serve on toast. Or split them through the back and broil, basting with butter and serving on toast. They may also be roasted whole before the fire for fifteen or twenty minutes.

(Detroit, 1881)

Game Pie

To be eaten cold: Bone partridges, ducks or other game; stuff with forcemeat; allow one peeled raw truffle to each small bird, two or more to ducks, etc. Prepare the crust, place a few slices of veal and a thick layer of forcemeat on the bottom, lay in the game, cover with thin slices of bacon, and put on upper crust. Bake four hours. Stew the giblets with some ham, the bones, some shallots, a little mace,

The rush bird or bobolink was a highly prized delicacy in nineteenth-century Michigan (Battle Creek, 1890).

205

thyme and parsley, in two quarts of stock until reduced to one pint; strain and pour into the pie when cold. Let it stand twenty-four hours before cutting. It will keep weeks after cutting, if the fat is not disturbed.

(Detroit, 1881)

Game Soup

Two rabbits, one-half pound of lean lamb, two medium-sized onions, one pound of lean beef; fried bread; butter for frying; pepper, salt and two stalks of white celery cut into inch lengths; three quarts of water. Joint the game neatly; cut the lamb and onions into small pieces, and fry all in butter to a light brown. Put into a soup-pot with the beef; cut into strips and add a little pepper. Pour on the water; heat slowly and stew gently two hours. Take out the pieces and cover in a bowl; cook the soup an hour longer; strain, cool, drop in the celery and simmer ten minutes. Pour upon fried bread in the tureen.

(Detroit, 1881)

SAUCES

Sauce for Wild Duck

Stuff ducks with boiled wild rice and chopped nuts and serve with the following sauce: Yolks of 3 eggs, 1 tablespoon butter, ½ teaspoon Tarragon vinegar, ½ teaspoon lemon, a dash each of cloves, allspice, salt and pepper. Heat, but do not let boil or sauce will curdle.

(Higgins Lake, 1920)

Hot Sauce for Wild Duck

½ cup of currant jelly
Juice of two lemons
Butter the size of an egg

3 tablespoons of Worcestershire sauce

Melt jelly in double boiler and add other ingredients.

Mrs. N. Rugee White
(Grand Rapids, 1935)

Cold Sauce for Wild Duck

Combine horseradish, apple sauce and whipped cream to taste.

Mrs. N. Rugee White
(Grand Rapids, 1935)

Bread Sauce for Partridge

First roll a pint of dry bread crumbs and pass half of them through a sieve. Put a small onion into two cups of milk and when it boils remove the onion and add the cup of sifted crumbs. Take from fire and stir in a heaping teaspoon of butter, salt, pepper and nutmeg to taste. Put a little butter into a saute pan and when hot add the cup of coarse crumbs, adding cayenne and letting them brown. To serve, pour over the slice of bird some of the sauce and add on top some of the dry crumbs.

Mrs. N. Rugee White
(Grand Rapids, 1935)

Bread Sauce

Place 1 sliced onion and 6 pepper-corns in ½ pint milk, over boiling water, until onion is perfectly soft; pour it on ½ pint bread-crumbs without crust, and leave it covered for 1 hour; beat it smooth, add pinch salt, and 2 tablespoons butter rubbed in a little flour; add enough sweet cream or milk to make it the proper consistency, and boil a few minutes; it must be thin enough to pour; serve with duck or any kind of game.

(Detroit, 1890)

Bread Sauce for Game

2 cupfuls of milk
1 cupful of dried
   bread crumbs
¼ of an onion

2 tablespoonfuls of
   butter
Dash of salt and pep-
   per

Dry the bread in a warm oven, and roll into rather coarse crumbs. Sift; and put the fine crumbs which come through, about ⅓ of a cupful, on to boil with the milk and onion. Boil ten minutes, and add a tablespoonful of butter and the seasoning. Skim out the onion. Fry the coarse crumbs a light brown in the remaining butter. Stir over a hot fire two minutes; take care not to burn. Cover breasts of birds with these and serve sauce poured around the birds.

(Kalamazoo, 1906)

Port Wine Sauce for Game

½ tumbler of currant
   jelly
½ tumbler of port
   wine
½ tumbler of stock

½ teaspoonful of salt
2 tablespoonfuls of
   lemon juice
4 cloves and a speck
   of cayenne

Simmer the cloves and stock together half an hour. Strain on the other ingredients, and let all melt together. Part of the gravy from the game may be added to it.

(Kalamazoo, 1906)

Within the Beast

Turn-of-the-century Chicago meat packers claimed that they used everything but the squeal; this applied equally to Michigan kitchens. Following the dictum "waste not, want not," housewives used just about every imaginable portion of a butchered animal. Some specialties, such as head cheese, tongue, and liver, continue to be popular with less squeamish diners, other types of innards are rarely encountered at the meat market. We've included a variety of early Michigan recipes for internal organs because they are uncommon in modern cookbooks.

Brain Cutlets

Well wash the brains and soak them in cold water till white. Parboil them till tender in a small saucepan for about a quarter of an hour; then thoroughly drain them, and place them on a board. Divide them, into small pieces with a knife. Dip each piece into flour, and then roll them in egg and bread crumbs, and fry them in butter or well-clarified drippings. Serve very hot with gravy. Another way of doing brains is to prepare them as above, and then stew them gently in rich stock, like stewed sweetbread. They are also nice plainly boiled, and served with parsley and butter sauce.

(Vermontville, 1906)

Scrambled Eggs with Calves' Brains

To a pair of calves' brains use 3 or 4 eggs. Scald the brains by letting them stand in scalding water for six to eight minutes. Trim them into ½-inch dices. Put them in a sauté-pan with a tablespoon of butter and cook them until they look white. Then add the beaten eggs and stir them all together, using a fork, until the eggs are cooked. Add ½ teaspoon of salt and ¼ teaspoon of pepper.

(Grand Rapids, 1935)

Head Cheese

Boil the forehead, ears and feet and nice scraps trimmed from the hams of a fresh pig, until the meat will almost drop from the bones, put it in a large chopping bowl, and season with pepper, salt, sage and summer savory. Chop it rather coarsely; put it back into the same kettle it was boiled in, with just enough of the liquor in which it was boiled to prevent its burning; warm it through thoroughly, mixing it well together. Now pour it into a strong muslin bag, press the bag between two flat surfaces, with a heavy weight on top; when cold and solid it can be cut in slices. Good cold or warmed up in vinegar.

(Vermontville, 1906)

Pork Brawn

Take a small pig's head with the tongue, and 2 pig's feet. Clean and wash them, sprinkle 2 tablespoons salt over them, and let them drain until the following day; dry them with a soft cloth and rub into them a powder made of 6 ounces common salt, 6 ounces moist sugar, ¾ ounce saltpetre, and ¾ ounce black pepper. Dry the powder well, and rub it into every part of the head, tongue, ears and feet; turn them over and rub them again every day for 10 days. Wash the pickle from them, cut off the ears, and boil the feet and ears 1½ hours; then put in the head and tongue, cover with cold water, and boil until the meat will leave the bones. Take them up, drain, cut the meat into small pieces; first remove all bones and skin the tongue. Season the mince with 1 teaspoon white pepper, 3 saltspoons powdered mace, 1 saltspoon each of powdered nutmeg and cayenne. Stir all well together, press the meat while warm into a brawn-tin, and lay a heavy weight on the lid. Put in a cool place until the following day; dip the mold in boiling water, turn the brawn out, and serve with vinegar and mustard.

(Detroit, 1890)

Brawn is the English name for headcheese. A brawn-tin is a mold for headcheese. A good substitute for a brawn-tin is a coffee can.

Scotch Haggis

Take the stomach of a sheep, wash it well, and let is soak for several hours in cold salt and water, then turn it inside out, put it into boiling water to scald, scrape it quickly with a knife, and let it remain in water until wanted; clean a sheep's pluck thoroughly; pierce the heart and the liver in several places, to let the blood run out, and boil the liver and lights for 1½ hours; when they have boiled ¼ hour, put them into fresh water, and, during the last ½ hour, let the rest of the pluck be boiled with them; trim away the skins and any discolored parts there may be, grate ½ the liver, and mince all the rest very finely; add 1 pound finely-shred suet, 2 chopped onions, ½ pint oatmeal, or, if preferred, ½ pound oatcakes, toasted and crumbled, 2 teaspoons salt, and 1 of pepper, ½ a nutmeg, grated, and 1 grain cayenne; moisten with ½ pint good gravy and the juice of 1 small lemon, and put the mixture into the bag already prepared for it; be careful to leave room for swelling, sew it securely, and plunge it into boiling water; it will require 3 hours' gentle boiling; prick it with a needle every now and then, especially during the first half hour, to let the air out. A haggis should be sent to table as hot as possible, and neither sauce nor gravy should be served with it. The above is sufficient for 8 or 10 persons.

(Detroit, 1890)

This is the Scotch national dish that inspired rapturous poetry by Robert Burns. The pluck is the heart, liver, lungs, and windpipe of a butchered animal. The lights are the lungs.

Stuffed Heart

Wash thoroughly inside and out. Let stand in clear cold water for 1 hour. Drain and dry. Make a stuffing as follows: ¾ cup of bread crumbs; 2 tablespoonfuls minced bacon; 1 tablespoonful minced onion; ¼ teaspoonful of salt and pepper. Put bacon in a frying pan, when fat begins to try out, add bread crumbs and stir lightly. Make the bread a light straw color. Do not at any time let the bacon become smoking hot. Remove from the stove, add seasoning. Fill the heart with mixture, sew up and tie in a cheese cloth. Put in rapidly boiling salt water for 1 hour. Remove from water, take off cloth. Dredge with flour and roast an hour in a moderate oven.

Mrs. J. R. Bartholomew
(Homer, 1925)

Stuffed Heart

Take a beef's or sheep's or veal's heart, wash deeply and thoroughly so as to remove all blood, make the two cells into one by cutting through the partition with a long, sharp knife, being careful not to cut through to the outside; make a stuffing of bread crumbs same as for roast turkey, fill the cavity, cover with greased paper or cloth to secure the stuffing, and bake in a deep pan with plenty of water, for two hours or longer, basting and turning often, as the upper part particularly is apt to get dry. While heart is roasting, put the valves or "deaf ears" which must be cut off after washing, into a sauce-pan, with pint of cold water and a sliced onion, Let simmer slowly one hour; melt in same sauce-pan a tablespoon of butter, add a tablespoon flour then the strained liquor from valves, and serve as gravy.

(Vermontville, 1906)

French Beef Kidney

Slice the kidney rather thin, after having stripped off the skin and removed the fat; season it with pepper salt and grated nutmeg, and sprinkle over it plenty of minced parsley and eschallots chopped very small. Fry the slices over a brisk fire, and when nicely browned on both sides stir amongst them a teaspoonful of flour, and pour in by degrees a cup of gravy and a glass of white wine. Bring the sauce to the point of boiling, add a morsel of fresh butter and tablespoonful of lemon juice, and pour the whole into a hot dish garnished with fried bread.

(Detroit, 1881)

Steak or Kidney Pie

If kidney, split and soak it, and season that or the meat. Make a paste with suet, flour and milk; roll, and line a basin with it; put the kidney or steaks in—both may be used—cover with paste, and pinch round the edge; cover with a cloth and boil a considerable time; if the pudding is large boil three hours. Make some gravy with bones or gristle. After taking to the table, cut out a small piece of the crust and pour in the gravy.

(Detroit, 1881)

Liver Loaf

1 pound beef liver	1 tablespoon lemon
½ pound pork sausage	juice
	1 teaspoon salt
1 medium sized onion	⅛ teaspoon pepper
1 cup dry bread	1 teaspoon celery salt
crumbs	2 beaten eggs
1 teaspoon Worcestershire sauce	½ cup stock
	4 slices bacon

Cover liver with hot water, simmer five minutes. Drain liquid and reserve for stock. Grind liver and onion, using medium blade. Add remaining ingredients and put in loaf pan about 5½ × 10½ inches. Top with bacon strips. Bake in moderate oven 350 degrees 45 minutes. Serves eight. Very good sliced cold.

Romaine McIntire
(Lansing, 1941)

Home Made Liver Wurst

Ingredients:—Liver, fat pork, lean pork, cooked oat meal and seasoning.

Proportions:—Liver 25 percent of the entire amount used. Fat pork, 10 percent of the entire amount used. Lean pork, 15 percent of entire amount used. Cooked oatmeal 50 percent of entire amount used.

Seasoning:—Season to taste with salt and pepper. And here is the secret of wurst: Use ground cloves with the seasoning. For ten pounds of wurst I use about 1 level tablespoonful of ground cloves. Heart, tongue and kidneys can be used in the lean meat. The meat should be chopped, not ground so that the finished product is coarse and chunky and not smooth and salvy. The oatmeal should be cooked dryer than oatmeal used for breakfast cereal. Use regular oatmeal, not quick cook.

Put all ingredients into a large mixing bowl and mix thoroughly. Then pack into bread tins or other convenient dishes so it can be sliced. This is excellent for sandwiches, or for the supper meal dish. Wurst is delicious when fried.

I wish I had a little wurst handy so the judges could sample it. It is a great favorite for those who have tried it and very different from the wurst we buy at meat counters.

Mrs. Ed Blue
(Kalamazoo, 1935)

Sweetbreads, the thymus and pancreas glands, usually of a calf, were considered a great delicacy in Victorian days and can still be obtained, at a high price, in certain restaurants. The thymus was known as throat or neck sweetbread and the pancreas as stomach sweetbread. You won't find sweetbreads at the meat counter, but your butcher may be able to order them for you.

To Clean Sweetbreads

Carefully pull off all the tough and fibrous skin. Place them in a dish of cold water for ten minutes or more, and then they are ready to be boiled. They must always be boiled twenty minutes, no matter what the mode of cooking is to be.

(Kalamazoo, 1906)

Sweetbreads Broiled

Parboil, rub them well with butter, and broil on a clean gridiron; turn frequently, and now and then roll over on a plate containing some hot melted butter. This will prevent them from getting too dry and hard. Season to taste and serve very hot.

(Detroit, 1881)

Creamed Sweetbreads

Let the sweetbreads stand in cold water one hour, then remove all surplus skin or fat, cover with boiling salted water, add a slice of onion, one-half bay leaf, a sprig of parsley, and small piece of celery, cover and let simmer thirty minutes. Drain and throw into cold water until cool, when cold pick into small pieces, rejecting all skin, at serving time place in the chafing dish two level tablespoonfuls each of butter and flour—for each pint of sweetbreads—paste together until smooth, then add one cupful of rich milk, and stir constantly until it bubbles, add salt and pepper to taste, then the sweetbreads, stir until hot and serve at once from chafing dish.

Mrs. W. Rea, Menominee
(Chicago, 1898)

Fried Sweetbreads

Wash very carefully and dry with a linen cloth. Lard, with narrow strips of fat salt pork set closely

COOK WITH GAS

The money and worry saved and the increased cleanliness of **Gas** over all other fuels ought to be sufficient to induce any thinking woman to

COOK WITH GAS

NILES GAS LIGHT COMPANY

The age of gas not only made cookery easier but freed the kitchen from the dirt and ashes that accompanied the use of the wood stove (Niles, 1907).

together. Lay the sweetbreads in a clean, hot frying-pan, which has been well buttered, and cook to a fine brown, turning frequently until the pork is crisp.

(Detroit, 1881)

Fried Sweet Breads

Remove from sweet breads all skin and fat, shape them in suitable pieces to fry. Plunge them into boiling water for about two minutes, remove from water, drain and dry them with a cloth. Dip each piece into a dish of beaten egg, roll in grated bread crumbs, sprinkle with salt and pepper, and fry in butter. Serve with mushrooms cooked in cream, or with green peas, or plain with a few pieces of lemon.

Mrs. V. T. Barker
(Kalamazoo, 1899)

Sweetbreads Manitou

Over par-boiled blanched sweetbreads, served in individual shell baking dishes is poured a delicious sauce made from 1 pint of chicken or veal stock thickened with a tablespoon each of butter and flour, and cooked until smooth with 4 egg yolks, beaten with a cup of cream, and seasoned with salt, pepper, a dash of lemon juice and chopped parsley. These are baked delicately brown.

(Higgins Lake, 1920)

Sweetbreads Roasted

Parboil and put into cold water for fifteen minutes; change to more cold water for five minutes longer; wipe perfectly dry, lay them in a dripping-pan and roast, basting with butter and water until they begin to brown; then withdraw them for an instant, roll in beaten egg, then in cracker crumbs, and return to the fire for ten minutes longer, basting meanwhile twice with melted butter. Keep hot in a dish while you add to the dripping half a cup of hot water, some chopped parsley, a teaspoonful of browned flour and the juice of half a lemon. Pour over the sweetbreads and serve at once.

(Detroit, 1881)

Sweetbread Salad

One pound sweetbreads, peeled, cooked and broken in small pieces, 1 can French peas, 1 can button mushrooms broken in small pieces, put together with plenty of mayonnaise dressing.

Mrs. Louise T. Harrison
(Kalamazoo, 1899)

Sweet Bread Salad

In preparing salad for six persons cook one pair of sweetbreads in water to which is added a slice of onion and a half teaspoonful of salt. After simmering for twenty minutes drop in cold water until chilled, dry and dice with a silver knife. Pare two cucumbers, dice them and let drain. Whip one cupful of thick sweet cream to a solid froth. Gradually beat in two tablespoonfuls of lemon juice, adding salt and cayenne to season and one tablespoonful of thick mayonnaise. Mix meat, cucumbers and half of the dressing, using the remainder of the latter for garnishing. Serve in cups made of blanched lettuce leaves. Pass cheese straws with the salad.

M. H. P.
(Kalamazoo, 1906)

Sweetbread Salad

Cook sweetbreads in the usual way; and continue to boil them fifteen minutes, then cool and slice them. Wash for each pair of sweetbreads, a head of lettuce in plenty of cold water, and dry on a clean towel. Arrange the lettuce on a salad dish, put the sweetbreads in it and pour a cream dressing over them. Serve the salad as soon as it is made.

Mrs. Ed. Ranons, Powers
(Chicago, 1898)

Sweetbread and Cucumber Salad

Prepare a small pair of sweetbreads in the usual way. When very cold remove the membranes, cut into dice, and place on ice. When ready to serve, peel and slice two cucumbers into very thin slices, mix with the sweetbreads and pour over the mixture a cupful of mayonnaise, or some other rich salad dressing.

Mrs. E. Louis Ellis, Nahma
(Chicago, 1898)

Sweetbread Salad

One pair sweetbreads boiled in salt and water, 6 eggs boiled hard, 1 can French peas from which the liquor has been drained. Cut sweetbreads and eggs into dice, add peas and mix with sufficient salad dressing. A convenient salad to make when celery is out of season.

Mrs. W. H. Van Deman
(Kalamazoo, 1899)

Sweetbread and Walnut Salad

Soak the sweetbreads, boil them till tender and remove the membrane. One pound sweetbreads, 1 bunch celery, ½ pound English walnuts. Mince the sweetbreads, crisp celery in ice water and cut in ½ inch pieces. Boil walnuts in a little salted water, and throw in cold water to harden; mix thoroughly, cover with mayonnaise and serve on crisp lettuce leaves.

Mrs. F. A. Taylor
(Kalamazoo, 1899)

Tongue Sandwiches

Boil a good sized tongue four or five hours, not letting the water boil hard, but keep it on a simmer, leave it in the pot until the water is cold, then skin it, and when ready to make the sandwiches cut it as thin as wafers, using a sharp, thin-bladed knife; rub a small quantity of mustard into a large slice of sweet butter and cut slices of bread as thin as they can be shaved; spread them with the prepared butter and lay the slices of tongue between two slices of bread; then cut the slices in halves.

(Detroit, 1881)

Tongue Fingers

Chop ½ pound of cold cooked salt tongue very fine, rub to a paste, add 2 tablespoons olive oil, 2

of lemon juice, a dash of cayenne and a few drops onion juice. Spread between thin slices of buttered bread.

(Kalamazoo, 1899)

Tomato Sauce

To serve with hot boiled tongue:

1 pt. stewed tomatoes	1 tablespoon of butter
1 sliced onion	1 tablespoon of flour
1 bay leaf	Salt and pepper
1 sprig of parsley	

Cook tomatoes, onion, bay leaf and parsley 15 minutes, then strain. Melt butter, add flour and while cooking, add tomatoes slowly. Cook until smooth and glossy.

If tomatoes are very acid, add a speck of soda.

Mrs. A. K. Edwards
(Kalamazoo, 1906)

Perfect Mock Turtle Soup

Endeavor to have the head and the broth ready for the soup, the day before it is to be eaten. It will take eight hours to prepare it properly.

	Hours
Cleaning and soaking the head	1
To parboil it to cut up	1
Cooling, nearly	1
Making the broth and finishing the soup	5
	8

Get a calf's head with the skin on (the fresher the better); take out the brains, wash the head several times in cold water, let it soak for about an hour in spring water, then lay it in a stewpan, and cover it with cold water, and half a gallon over; as it becomes warm, a great deal of scum will rise, which must be immediately removed; let it boil gently for one hour, take it up, and, when almost cold, cut the head into pieces about an inch and a half by an inch and a quarter, and the tongue into mouthfuls, or rather make a side dish of the tongue and brains.

When the head is taken out, put in the stock

meat (about five pounds of knuckle of veal), and as much beef; add to the stock all the trimmings and bones of the head, skim it well, and then cover it close and let it boil five hours (reserve a couple of quarts of this to make gravy sauces); then strain it off and let it stand till the next morning; then take off the fat, set a large stewpan on the fire with half a pound of good fresh butter, twelve ounces of onions sliced, and four ounces of green sage; chop it a little; let these fry one hour; then rub in half a pound of flour, and by degrees add your broth till it is the thickness of cream; season it with a quarter of an ounce of ground allspice and half an ounce of black pepper ground very fine, salt to your taste, and the rind of one lemon peeled very thin; let it simmer very gently for one hour and a half, then strain it through a hair sieve; do not rub your soup to get it through the sieve, or it will make it grouty; if it does not run through easily, knock your wooden spoon against the side of your sieve; put it in a clean stewpan with the head, and season it by adding to each gallon of soup two tablespoonfuls of tarragon vinegar and two tablespoonfuls of lemon juice; let it simmer gently till the meat is tender; this may take from half an hour to an hour; take care it is not overdone; stir it frequently to prevent the meat sticking to the bottom of the stewpan, and when the meat is quite tender the soup is ready.

A head weighing twenty pounds, and ten pounds of stock meat, will make ten quarts of excellent soup, besides the two quarts of stock you have put by for made dishes.

Obs.—If there is more meat on the head than you wish to put in the soup, prepare it for a pie, and, with the addition of a calf's foot boiled tender, it will make an excellent ragout pie; season it with zest and a little minced onion, put in half a teacupful of stock, cover it with puff paste, and bake it one hour; when the soup comes from table, if there is a deal of meat and no soup, put it into a pie-dish, season it a little, and add some little stock to it; then cover it with paste, bake it one hour, and you have a good mock turtle pie.

To season the Soup—To each gallon put four tablespoonfuls of lemon-juice, two of mushroom catsup, and one teaspoonful of mace, a teaspoonful of curry powder, or a quarter of a drachm of cayenne, and the peel of a lemon pared as thin as possible, let it simmer for five minutes more, take out the lemon peel, add the yolks of four hard boiled eggs, and the soup is ready for the tureen.

While the soup is doing, prepare for each tureen a dozen and a half of mock turtle forcemeat balls, and put them into the tureen. Brain balls, or cakes, are a very elegant addition, and are made by boiling the brains for ten minutes, then putting them in cold water and cutting them into pieces about as big as a large nutmeg; take savory or lemon thyme dried and finely powdered, nutmeg grated, and pepper and salt, and pound them all together; beat up an egg, dip the brains in it, and then roll them in this mixture, and make as much of it as possible stick to them; dip them in the egg again, and then in finely-grated and sifted bread crumbs; fry them in hot fat, and send them up as a side dish.

A veal sweet-bread, not too much done or it will break, cut into pieces the same size as you cut the calf's head, and put in the soup, just to get warm before it goes to table, is a superb "*bonne bouche*"; and pickled tongue, stewed till very tender, and cut into mouthfuls, is a favorite addition. We order the meat to be cut into mouthfuls, that it may be eaten with a spoon; the knife and fork have no business in a soupplate.

N. B.—In helping this soup, the distributer of it should serve out the meat, force-meat and gravy, in equal parts; however trifling or needless this remark may appear, the writer has often suffered from the want of such a hint being given to the soup-server, who has sometimes sent a plate of mere gravy without meat, at others, of meat without gravy, and sometimes scarcely anything but force-meat balls.

Obs.—This is a delicious soup, within the reach of those who "eat to live"; but if it had been composed expressly for those who only "live to eat," I do not know how it could have been made more agreeable; as it is, the lover of good eating will "wish his throat a mile long, and every inch of it a palate."

(Detroit, 1878)

Bread, Rolls, Pancakes, and Waffles

BREAD

❖

Bread

Remarks—If the simple word "bread" only, is spoken, it is always understood to mean white, or bread made from wheat flour. Other kinds always have a descriptive attachment, as Graham, Indian, brown, Boston brown, corn, etc. Two things are especially essential in good bread—lightness and sweetness. If bread is heavy—not light and porous—or if it is sour, it is only fit for the pigs. And it is important to know that good bread cannot be made out of poor flour. In the following these points are nicely explained, together with full and complete instructions in the three necessary processes of making good bread—making sponge, kneading, and baking.

How to Make Good Bread—A loaf of perfect bread, white, light, sweet, tender, and elastic, with a golden brown crust, is a proof of high civilization; and is so indispensable a basis of all good eating that the name "lady," or "loaf-giver," applied to the Saxon (English, as now understood, for England was overrun and conquered by the people of Saxony, in northern Germany, in an early day, so that now, to say a "Saxon," or of the Saxon race, refers to the English, descended from them, more often than to the people of Saxony itself—and especially Anglo-Saxon always means English) matron, may well be held in honor by wife or maiden. But do all the gracious ladies who preside in our country homes see such loaves set forth as daily bread?

Inexperienced housekeepers and amateur cooks will find it a good general rule to attempt at the beginning only a few things, and learn to do those perfectly. And these should be, not the elaborate dishes of special occasions, but the plain every-day things. Where can one better begin than with bread? The eager patronage of the overcrowded, carelessly served, high-priced Vienna bakery at the Centennial gave evidence that Americans appreciate good bread and good coffee, and had, perhaps, some effect in stimulating an effort for a better home supply. To make and to be able to teach others to make bread of this high character is an accomplishment worth at least as much practice as a *sonata* (a piece of music); and the work is excellent as a gymnastic exercise. With good digestion, honest personal pride, and the grateful admiration of the family circle as rewards, surely no girl or woman who aspires to responsibilities and joys of home, will shrink from the labor of learning to make bread.

The whole art and science of bread-making is no mean study. The *why* as well as the *how*, should be aimed at, although exact knowledge or science,

"What queen her subjects with more anxious eyes / Can watch, than she her emptyings, as they rise? / What conquest gives what warrior more delight / Then she has, when her baking comes out right?" (New York, 1881).

even in bread-making, is not so simple a matter as some might fancy. Varying conditions, even the temperature of the kitchen, work confusion in the phenomena of a batch of bread as surely as in the delicate experiments of a Tyndall or a Huxley. Fortunately, an exhaustive knowledge is not essential to practical success. Skillful manipulation will come with experience, and I have taught the actual art to a succession of uneducated cooks so that, with a little supervision, they satisfactorily supplied an exacting family. But the mistress, the house-mother, who must give intelligent direction, will not be satisfied without going to the root of the matter. Let her not rest upon her laurels without making sure that her table is constantly supplied with such delicious loaves of "the staff of life" as, with the fragrant, highly-flavored butter of May or June, shall make a fit repast even for the good women whose hand have prepared them.

Good Flour Essential—The first requisite to good bread is good flour (and *sifted*, to enliven it and make it mix more readily). If the very best seems too expensive, make up the difference in cost by eating less cake. With really delicious bread you will do this naturally, and almost unconsciously.

The Yeast, to Make—In the country, where fresh yeast from breweries is out of the question, the first process must be making yeast; and it is well to begin there, and know every step of your way. The commercial yeast cakes must form a basis; from them it is easy to make the potato yeast, which is perhaps the simplest and best of several good forms of soft yeast. Dry yeast cake used directly will not make bread of the first quality. For the yeast, soak *three yeast cakes* in a cup of tepid water, while *six* or *eight* fair-sized potatoes are boiling. When they are perfectly soft, put the potatoes, with a quart of water in which they were boiled, through a colander, and add a teaspoonful of salt and two of sugar. When tepid, add the yeast cakes, rubbed with a spoon to a smooth paste, and place the whole in a stone jar, and keep the contents at blood heat for twelve hours, when a lively effervescence should have taken place. The yeast will be in perfect condition the next day, and will remain good for ten days or more if kept in a cool cellar in a closely covered jar.

Setting the Sponge—Many New England housekeepers make a great mistake in setting their sponge over night. One secret of good bread is that every stage of the process must be complete and rapid. Every moment of waiting means deterioration. At the precise moment *when the sponge is*

fully light the bread should be kneaded, and the process of rising ought not to require more than *three hours* at most. Set your sponge, then, as early in the morning as you like, by taking in the bowl or basin kept for the purpose (and you will soon learn just how high in it the sponge should rise) two quarts of *sifted* flour. Make a hole in the middle with the stirring spoon; pour in half a pint of the soft yeast, first thoroughly stirring it from the bottom, then mixing with the flour; add tepid water, stirring constantly, until a smooth, stiff batter is formed, which stir and beat vigorously with the spoon for at least five minutes after it is perfectly mixed. Cover lightly, and set in a warm place until thoroughly light, almost foaming; but be sure not to delay kneading until it begins to subside.

Kneading—Sift the flour, say 6 qts., in a pan, make a hole in the middle, pour in the sponge; add a pinch of salt, and, dexterously mingle the flour with the soft sponge by the hand, gradually add a quart of warm milk or warm water, quickly incorporating the whole into a smooth, even mass. Cover the kneading-board with flour, place upon it the dough, which must not be soft enough to stick or stiff enough to make much resistance to pressure, and knead vigorously and long. Half an hour's energetic kneading is not too much for a family baking. By that time the bread should be elastic, free from stickiness, and disposed to rise in blisters. Cover with a soft bread-cloth folded to four thicknesses, and set it where a temperature of about blood-heat will be maintained.

In two hours it should have risen to fully twice its volume. Place it again upon the board; divide with the hands (which may be floured, or, better, buttered) a portion of the size which you wish for your loaves, remembering that it will rise again half as much more; lightly mold it into a smooth, shapely loaf, with as little handling as possible, and place in a well-greased pan. Set the loaves back in their warm corner for half an hour, when they should be very light and show signs of cracking. Bake at once in a hot oven, with a steady heat, from 45 minutes to 1 hour, according to the size of the loaves. Take immediately from the pans and wrap in soft, fresh linen until cold.

Biscuit From Some of the Dough—A portion of the dough will make a pan of delicious biscuits by adding a piece of butter as large as an egg to sufficient dough for a small loaf, mixing it lightly but thoroughly, and molding into small round balls, set a little distance apart in the pan. They will soon close up the space, and should rise to twice their first height. The swift, sure touch which makes the work easy, rapid, and confident, will come with practice; but the necessary practice may come only with patience and determination.

To Make Bread Crust Soft and Delicate—Take a cup of cream off the pan, and put it into your bread when you are about molding it, and it will cause the crust to be very soft and delicate.

Remarks—Knowing this to contain good sound sense, from the fact that I know the Vienna bread has a softer and more delicate crust than common bread, I mention it, believing that one reason, at least, for this is that the Vienna bread is made richer with milk than the common, as you will notice, by comparison. Bread should not be made too thin and soft, in kneading, nor too stiff and hard; but of such a consistence that when you press the doubled hand upon the mass of dough the depression will quickly rise up again to nearly its former shape. Let beginners be a little careful in all the foregoing points of instruction, and the author has no fears in guaranteeing a bread that they, even, shall not be ashamed of. If bread, or rather the sponge, becomes sour from being set over night (although it is conceded not to be best to set it over night), or from neglect to knead it at the right time (when just fully light), dissolve a teaspoonful of soda (baking soda is always meant) in a little warm milk or water and work it in, which will correct it. If there is danger at any time, in baking, of burning, or over baking, cover the bread with thick brown paper or a folded newspaper, until the loaf is done through; and if too hot at the bottom to endanger burning, put the oven grate, or a few nails or bits of iron, under the pan, which will prevent it from burning by the admission of air under it. By observing these points you are always safe.

(Ann Arbor, 1884)

Bread—Proper Temperature of the Oven

The objects to be attained in the baking of bread are to break up the starch and gluten cells of the flour so as to make them easily digestible, to destroy the yeast plant, and render permanent the cells formed by the action of the carbonic acid gas. To accomplish well these ends, the loaf must be surrounded by a temperature ranging from 400° to 600°. The oven should be one in which the heat is equal in all parts, and which can be kept at a steady, uniform heat. Old-fashioned brick ovens were su-

perior in this respect to most modern ranges. The fire for baking bread should be of sufficient strength to keep the oven heated for at least an hour. If the oven has a tendency to become too hot upon the bottom, a thin, open grate, broiler, or toasting rack, should be placed underneath the tins to allow a circulation of air and avoid danger of burning. If the heat be insufficient, fermentation will not cease until the bread has become sour; the cells will be imperfectly fixed or entirely collapsed; too little of the moisture will have evaporated, and the result will be a soft, wet, and pasty or sour loaf. If the heat be too great, the bread will be baked before it has perfectly risen, or a thick, burned crust will be produced, forming a non-conducting covering to the loaf, which will prevent the heat from permeating the interior, and thus the loaf will have an overdone exterior, but will be raw and doughy within. If, however, the temperature of the oven be just right, the loaf will continue for a little time to enlarge, owing to the expansion of the carbonic acid gas, the conversion of the water into steam, and the vaporizing of the alcohol, which rises in a gaseous form and is driven off by the heat; a nicely browned crust will be formed over the surface, the result of the rapid evaporation of water from the surface and consequent consolidation of the dough of this portion of the loaf, and a chemical change caused by the action of the heat upon the starch by which it is converted into dextrine, finally assuming a brown color due to the production of a substance known to the chemist as *assama*.

Bread is often spoiled in the baking. The dough may be made of the best of flour and yeast, mixed and kneaded in the most perfect manner, and may have risen to the proper degree of lightness before going to the oven, yet if the oven is either too hot or not hot enough, the bread will be of an inferior quality.

Without an oven thermometer, there is no accurate means of determining the temperature of the oven; but housekeepers resort to various means to form a judgment about it. The baker's old-fashioned method is to throw a handful of flour on the oven bottom. If it blackens without igniting, the heat is deemed sufficient. Since the object for which the heat is desired is to cook the flour, not to burn it, it might be supposed that this would indicate too high a temperature; but the flour within the loaf to be baked is combined with a certain amount of moisture, the vaporation of which lowers the temperature of the bread considerably below that of the surrounding heated atmosphere. The temperature of the inner portion of the loaf cannot

Ella Kellogg of Battle Creek advocated unfermented bread, which this woman is making, as a healthier product (Battle Creek, 1910).

exceed 212° so long as it continues moist. Bread might be perfectly cooked at this temperature by steam, but it would lack that most digestible portion of the loaf, the crust.

A common way of ascertaining if the heat of the oven is sufficient, is to hold the bare arm inside it for a few seconds. If the arm cannot be held within while thirty is counted, it is too hot to begin with. The following test is more accurate: For rolls, the oven should be hot enough to brown a teaspoonful of flour in *one* minute, and for loaves in *five* minutes.

The temperature should be high enough to arrest the fermentation, which it would do at a point considerably below the boiling point of water, and at the same time to form a shell or crust, which will so support the dough as to prevent it from sinking or collapsing when the evolution of carbonic acid gas shall cease; but it should not be hot enough to brown the crust within ten or fifteen minutes. The heat should increase for the first fifteen minutes, remain steady for the next fifteen minutes, and may then gradually decrease during the remainder of the baking. If by any mischance the oven be so hot as to brown the crust too soon, cover the loaf with a clean paper for a few minutes. Be careful that no draught reaches the bread while baking; open the oven door very seldom, and not at all for the first ten minutes. If it is necessary to turn the loaf, try to do so without bringing it to the air. From three fourths of an hour to an hour is usually a sufficient length of time to bake an ordinary sized loaf. Be careful not to remove the bread from the oven until perfectly done. It is better to allow it to bake ten minutes too long than not long enough. The crust of bread, when done, should be equally browned all over.

The common test for well-baked bread is to tap it on the bottom with the finger; if it is light and well done, it will sound hollow; heavy bread will have a dull sound. A thoroughly baked loaf will not burn the hand when lifted upon it from the pan.

(Battle Creek, 1910)

The majority of contributors in this book not only assumed that you knew how hot your oven should be and how long to cook the recipe, but that you would routinely oil and flour your pans. We've had a few disasters when we failed to perform this step in our baking. To play it safe, always oil and flour your tins or pans, unless otherwise specified.

The ingredient saleratus, called for in many of these recipes, is common baking soda.

Apple Bread

Take one pound of fresh, juicy apples, peel, core, and stew them to a pulp. Use a porcelain kettle, or a stone jar, placed inside a kettle of boiling water. Sift the apples, and mix with two pounds of the best flour; add half a cup of yeast, and enough water to make a fine smooth dough; put it in a pan, and let it stand in a warm place for at least twelve hours, to rise. Form into long loaves, and bake in a quick oven.

(Battle Creek, 1890)

A "quick" oven is equivalent to 400°.

Banana All-Bran Nut Bread

¼ cup shortening	*½ tsp. soda*
½ cup sugar	*½ cup chopped nuts*
1 egg well beaten	*½ cup mashed ba-*
1 cup All-Bran	*nanas*
1½ cups flour	*2 tbsp. water*
2 tsp. baking powder	*1 tsp. vanilla*
½ tsp. salt	

Cream shortening and sugar. Add egg and all-bran. Sift flour with baking powder, salt and soda. Mix nuts with flour and add alternately with bananas to which water has been added. Stir in vanilla, pour in greased loaf pan. Let stand 30 min. and bake in mod. oven 1 hour. Let cool before cutting. Makes 1 loaf 8½ × 4½". (This is better the next day after baking.)

Mrs. D. G. Parent
Mrs. W. J. Berry
(Kalamazoo, 1941)

Brown Bread

2 tablespoons of molasses	⅔ cup of wheat flour
2 tablespoons of brown sugar	2 small cups graham flour
1 cup of sour milk	1 teaspoon of soda
	1 teaspoon of salt

Steam two and one-half hours or bake one-half hour.

Mrs. J. B. Kindleberger
(Parchment, 1926)

Mrs. Kindleberger's recipe for brown bread is delicious. It yields a very heavy loaf that is good with pea or bean soup. The quantities called for result in a small loaf. Bake at 350° for 30 minutes.

Yankee Brown Bread

For each good sized loaf being made, take 1½ pts. corn meal, and pour boiling water upon it, to scald it properly; let stand until only blood warm, then put about 1 qt. of rye flour upon the meal, and pour in a good bowl of emptyings, with a little saleratus dissolved in a gill of water, kneading in more flour, to make of the consistence of common bread. If you raise it with yeast, put a little salt in the meal, but if you raise it with salt-risings, or emptyings which I prefer, no more salt is needed.

Form into loaves, and let them set an hour and a half, or until light; in a cool place, in summer, and on the hearth, or under the stove, in winter; then bake about two hours. Make the dough fully as stiff as for wheat bread, or a little harder; for if made too soft it does not rise good. The old style was to use only one-third rye flour, but it does not wear if made that way; or, in other words, most persons get tired of it when mostly corn meal, but I never do when mostly rye flour.

Let all persons bear in mind that bread should never be eaten the day on which it is baked, and *positively* must this be observed by *dyspeptics*. Hotels never ought to be without this bread, nor families who care for health.

(Ann Arbor, 1864)

A recipe for salt risings or emptyings will be found later in this chapter (see pp. 223–25). Saleratus is common baking soda.

Brown Bread

One cup sour milk, ½ cup sweet milk, ½ cup molasses, 1 cup corn meal, 1¼ cups graham flour, 1 teaspoon soda, 1 level teaspoon salt, a handful of raisins. Mix all together, leaving raisins whole and

A perfect loaf of bread as presented by a stylishly dressed Victorian cook (Chicago, 1909).

placing on top after bread is in the tin. Steam 3 hours and bake 15 minutes.

Estella I. Kneeland, Traverse City
(Charlotte, 1909)

Diet Bread

For "Eat and Grow Thin" or Diabetic Diet:

1½ cups gluten flour
3 cups bran
½ gr. (or more) Sac-
   charin dissolved in
   2 cups water or
   skim milk

1 egg
1 teaspoon salt
1½ teaspoons soda
3 teaspoons baking
   powder

Bake in two small loaves. Do not keep with other bread. Wrap in waxed paper or napkin. For diabetic diet, 1 teaspoon butter can be added and whole milk substituted for skim milk.

(Higgins Lake, 1920)

Gluten flour is a low-starch product prepared especially for diabetics.

Dutch Bread

Very nice to eat at breakfast with coffee, at tea, or for lunch. One pint warm milk, a little salt, scant half cup butter, scant half cup sugar, even teaspoon cinnamon, ½ cup English currants, ½ cake compressed yeast, cream, butter and sugar together; stir in cinnamon and add the warm milk, then the yeast dissolved in a little warm milk, then mold in all the flour needed to make a stiff dough; let this rise till light; then mold out into loaves and put in bread tins to rise; then bake. Mold all the flour to be used at the first kneading; when the sponge for white bread has risen, the sugar, butter, spice, currants, etc., may be stirred into some of it, and put to rise, but the first way makes the best.

Mrs. Frank Leonard
(Grand Rapids, 1890)

Graham Biscuit

Take one quart sour milk, half a cup of cream, one teaspoon soda, a little salt; make a dough stiff enough to keep in the shape of biscuit, and bake longer than wheat biscuit.

Rye biscuit are nice made in the same way.

(Battle Creek, 1890)

Graham Bread, No. 1

Take a pint of the sponge raised from railroad emptyings or ordinary "salt-rising," one tablespoonful of sugar or molasses, enough unbolted flour to make a two-quart basin half full, a little salt. Add just enough water or milk to make as stiff a dough as you can stir with a large spoon, and then let it rise until your dish is full. Bake one hour. When done, cover it up in the dish and let it steam. If you wish it to be extra good, add a beaten egg, and a tablespoonful of melted butter.

(Battle Creek, 1890)

A recipe for salt risings or emptyings will be found later in this chapter. Unbolted flour is a heavy, coarse flour that is usually not sifted.

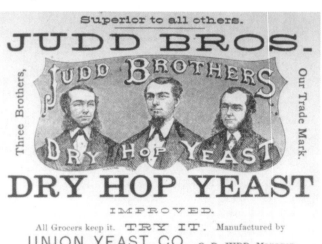

The hirsute Judd Brothers of Detroit did the Smith Brothers of cough drop fame one better (Polk, 1881).

Graham Bread, No. 3

One pint of sour milk, one egg, one small tablespoonful of soda, one-half cup molasses, one quart Graham flour; beat thoroughly, and bake one hour.

(Battle Creek, 1890)

The memory of Sylvester Graham, an American health-food reformer active in the antebellum period, is perpetuated in the flour he popularized. It is whole wheat flour.

Graham Bread

1 egg	1 cup flour
2 T sugar	1 cup graham flour
2 T molasses	1 t soda
2 T shortening	Salt
1½ cups buttermilk	Raisins if you like

Mrs. Arthur Esseltine, Otsego
(Allegan, 1938)

Grape-Nut Bread

½ cup sugar	4 cups flour
1 cup grape nuts	1 teaspoon baking
2 cups sour milk	powder
(Soak 20 minutes)	1 teaspoon soda
2 tablespoons short-ening	1 teaspoon salt

Mix and let stand 30 minutes. Bake in a moderate oven for 1 hour.

Mrs. H. A. Fick
(Grayling, 1937)

Grape Nuts, a product introduced by Charles W. Post in 1898, was actually a version of Dr. John Harvey Kellogg's health-food invention granola. Post's clever advertising made him a millionaire by 1901. Early packages of Grape Nuts contained a miniature volume, *The Road to Wellville*, which set forth Post's distinctive philosophy of healthful eating and right living.

Hop-Yeast Bread

One tea-cup yeast, three pints warm water; make a thin sponge at tea time, cover and let it remain two hours or until very light. By adding the water to the flour first and having the sponge quite warm, it is never necessary to put the sponge over hot water or in an oven to make it rise. Knead into a loaf before going to bed; in the morning mold into three loaves, spreading a little lard between as they are put in the pan. When light, bake one hour, having oven quite hot when the bread is put in, and very moderate when it is done. (Bread made in this way is never sour or heavy.) To have fine, light biscuit, add shortening at night, and in the morning make into biscuit and bake for breakfast. By this recipe bread is baked before the stove is cold from breakfast, and out of the way for other baking.

To cool bread there should be a board for the purpose. An oaken board, covered with heavy white flannel, is the best; over this spread a fresh linen bread-cloth, and lay the bread on it right side up, with nothing over it except a very thin cover to keep off the flies. It should be placed immediately in the fresh air or wind to cool; when cool, place immediately in a tin box or stone jar, and cover closely. Bread cooled in this way will have a soft crust, and be filled with pure air.

Mrs. J. T. Liggett, Detroit
(Minneapolis, 1881)

In Morning Bread

Two tablespoons flour, 1 tablespoon salt, 1 tablespoon sugar. Pour over this 1 pint boiling water and when cool, add 1 yeast cake soaked in warm water. Set in a warm place to rise. At noon boil 4 medium sized potatoes, mash thoroughly and when cool add them with 1 quart of the water in which they were boiled to the first mixture, and let rise over night. In the morning add flour and 1 tablespoon lard, knead well, let rise and knead into

This fashionable gas range sported a carryover from the wood burning era: a warming oven (Kalamazoo, 1906).

loaves and rise again. Bake 45 minutes in a moderate oven.

Mrs. E. L. Winslow
(Kalamazoo, 1899)

Mollie's Bread

Nearly 1 qt. tepid water, flour sifter (holding little more than 1 qt.) twice full, 1 spoon salt, 1 or ½ cake compressed yeast dissolved in ½ cup warm water, stir into batter, in center of flour—leave over night. In the morning *mix thoroughly, add as little flour* as will answer, let rise, then mix *as before,* put in tins, let rise again and bake. Keeps moist a long time.

(Ann Arbor, 1872)

Mother's Bread

In the morning take a quart bowl that is sweet and clean, put in an even teaspoonful of salt, sugar,

soda and ginger, one teacupful of coarse flour. Turn boiling water on and stir until a thick batter is made; then cover and set back until they become lukewarm; now look at them; if they have become set, like pudding, add a little warm water and stir until thin; put in a good warm place, and keep warm until they fill the bowl full. The yeast or risings are now ready for use, and there will be enough to bake with three times.

Early in the morning get the bread pan and fill two-thirds full of flour, well sifted; make a hollow in the center, throw in a small tablespoonful of salt. Pour in a pint of boiling water, stirring it into the flour; then half a pint of milk; add hot water enough to make a pint, then another pint of water, the right temperature to make the sponge cool enough to not scald and kill the life of the yeast and yet leave it real warm; now stir in one-third of your yeast; cover with dry flour; then cover with your bread board or another pan and let rise; mold into loaves; let rise again and bake in a brisk oven. The quicker bread bakes and not burn, the nicer the flavor. This amount will make three good sized loaves. If the oven is just the right heat when it goes in, it will bake in twenty minutes. If it has to stay in over thirty minutes it will lose its best flavor. Be sure and bake a nice brown.

(Detroit, 1881)

Pan American Exposition Bread

Cream one-half cup butter in warm crock, slowly add one cup sugar, beat to a cream, beat yolks of three eggs and one teaspoon vanilla, sift one and a-half cups flour with two teaspoons baking powder and six tablespoons cocoa, three-fourths cup milk, last put in beaten whites of three eggs. Bake in three layers.

(Vermontville, 1906)

This bread sounds more like a cake, similar to a three layer cake. The Pan-American Exposition, held in Buffalo, New York, in 1901, was second in grandeur only to the World's Columbian Exposition of 1893. But the assassination of President McKinley, which occurred as he visited the exposition, brought a somber note to the festivities.

Peanut Butter Bread

Two c. flour, ½ c. peanut butter, 2 eggs, 1 c. sweet milk, ½ c. sugar, 1 tsp. salt, 2 hp. tsp. Royal baking powder. Sift flour, sugar, baking powder and salt in a large bowl; add peanut butter; mix thoroughly. Beat eggs, add milk, then add to flour mixture. Mix well and bake in a moderate oven 30 m.

Mrs. J. A. Meulenberg
(Kalamazoo, 1921)

Potato Bread

Boil 6 or 8 good sized potatoes, mash fine while hot, then add 1 qt. sweet milk, ½ cup of white sugar, a good pinch of salt, ⅓ of a cup of good yeast; have ready a pan of sifted flour, make a hole in the middle, stir in the ingredients; do this about 6 o'clock, and if it gets light before you retire at night, stir it down, sprinkle flour over the top and let it stand until morning, then mix it down again, and when light the third time, knead into loaves. Try this, and if your yeast is good you will never have poor bread.—Mrs. S. T. Dolph, McBride, Mich.

Remarks—It will not be amiss to say here, that new potatoes are of no value in bread making. Only those that are fully ripe can be used.

About Setting Sponge Over Night—It will be observed that the above recipe for potato bread, . . . directs to set the sponge over night; but those who may use them, must act upon their own judgment as to doing so, or in beginning in the morning, depending upon its being cold winter weather, warmth of the room, etc.; and also depending upon whether they can give it their watchful care during the day, or until the sponge is risen and the whole process completed and the bread baked, thus avoiding all possibility of souring, as it often does if set over night; for, although to a certain extent, by the use of soda, this condition is corrected, yet, after once souring, the bread will never be as good as if kneaded and baked at just the right time, *i.e.,* as soon as light in each process, not having stood to overwork in either case.

(Ann Arbor, 1884)

Potato Bread with Whole-Wheat Flour

Take a half gill of liquid yeast made as for Boiled Potato Yeast No. 2, and add milk, sterilized and cooled to lukewarm, to make a pint. Add one cup of well-mashed, mealy potato and one cup of white flour, or enough to make a rather thick batter. Beat thoroughly, cover, and set to rise. When well risen, add sufficient whole-wheat flour to knead. The quantity will vary somewhat with the brand of flour used, but about four and one-fourth cupfuls will in general be needed. Knead well, let it rise in mass and again in the loaf, and bake.

(Battle Creek, 1910)

See page 237 for Boiled Potato Yeast No. 2.

Pulled Bread

Remove a loaf from the oven when about half baked, and lightly pull the partially set dough into pieces of irregular shape, about half the size of one's fist. Do not smooth or mold the pieces; the rougher the shape the better. Place them on perforated tins, and bake in a slow oven until browned and crisp throughout.

(Battle Creek, 1910)

Railroad Emptyings

One quart of coarse flour, into which stir thoroughly one teaspoonful of soda, one of ginger, one of sugar, one of salt; pour boiling water upon it, stir until thin enough for yeast, and set it in a warm place to rise. When light put away in a cool place.

When you wish to bake, take four large spoonfuls of sweet milk, soda the size of a large pea, and add one teacupful of hot water; when cool, add a tablespoonful of the yeast, and thicken with flour. If put in a warm place it will be light in an hour, and ready to be made into sponge. The emptyings made of flour will last two or three weeks, if kept cool.

(Battle Creek, 1890)

Rolled Oats Bread (2 Loaves)

Four cupsful boiling water; 2 cupsful rolled oats; 2 teaspoonsful salt; 1 tablespoonful butter; 2 tablespoonsful sugar. Put boiling water in double cooker; add salt and stir in rolled oats. Cook from 1 to 2 hours (or steam 3 hours). Remove from fire and let cool until luke-warm. Let ½ yeast cake dissolve in a little luke-warm water. When the rolled oat mixture has cooled add sugar and butter, and sufficient wheat flour (either pastry or bread flour) to make a firm dough. Dust molding board with flour plentifully, and turn out dough and knead from 15 to 20 minutes. Let rise over night in moderately warm place. In the morning knead down and let rise until twice its bulk; knead again sufficiently to form into loaves and let rise until twice their bulk. Bake 1 hour in moderately hot oven. This is excellent for sick people or those troubled with indigestion.

Mrs. D. S. Zach
(Flint, 1912)

Railroad emptyings, evidently a variation of "milk emptin's," were commonly used on the Michigan frontier when yeast was not available. Salt risings were a similar substitute.

Caroline Kirkland, a cultured lady from New York, moved with her family to the frontier settlement of Pinckney in 1837. She satirized the coarse manners of the pioneers and the privations of backwoods life in her book *A New Home: Who'll Follow*, published in 1839. Pinckney residents recognized themselves in her thinly veiled characters and made her life even more unpleasant. She returned to New York in 1843. Her volume contains a humorous description of bread-making on the Michigan frontier.

When every body is buying land and scarce any body cultivating it, one must not expect to find living either good or cheap; but, I confess, I was surprised at the dearth of comforts which we observed every where. Neither milk, eggs, nor vegetables were to be had, and those who could not live on hard salt ham, stewed dried apples, and bread raised with "salt risin'," would necessarily run some risk of starvation.

One word as to this and similar modes of making bread, so much practised throughout this country. It is my opinion that the sin of bewitching snow-white flour by means of either of those abominations, "salt risin',"

"milk emptin's," "bran 'east," or any of their odious compounds, ought to be classed with the turning of grain into whiskey, and both made indictable offences. To those who know of no other means of producing the requisite sponginess in bread than the wholesome hop-yeast of the brewer, I may be allowed to explain the mode to which I have alluded with such hearty reprobation. Here follows the recipe:

To make milk emptin's. Take quantum suf. of good sweet milk—add a teaspoon full of salt, and some water, and set the mixture in a warm place till it ferments, then mix your bread with it; and if you are lucky enough to catch it just in the right moment before the fermentation reaches the putrescent stage, you may make tolerably good rolls, but if you are five minutes too late, you will have to open your doors and windows while your bread is baking.—Verbam sap.

"Salt risin'" is made with water slightly salted and fermented like the other; and becomes putrid rather sooner; and "bran 'east" is on the same plan. The consequences of letting these mixtures stand too long will become known to those whom it may concern, when they shall travel through the remoter parts of Michigan; so I shall not dwell upon them here—but I offer my counsel to such of my friends as may be removing westward, to bring with them some form of portable yeast (the old fashioned dried cakes which mothers and aunts can furnish, are as good as any)—and also full instructions for perpetuating the same; and to plant hops as soon as they get a corner to plant them in.

"And may they better reek the rede,
Than ever did th' adviser."

Salt-Rising Bread, How to Make

Knowing my propensities for gathering valuable recipes, a gentleman friend said to me one day: "Doctor, the finest bread I ever ate in my life was at Mrs. J. A. Marks' in Detroit. I wish I had asked her for the recipe, especially for you." As my friend seemed so enthusiastic over the elegant bread eaten at the table of Mrs. Marks I took her name and address and wrote her, asking for the recipe. Here it is in her own words: "Early in the evening I scald 2 table-spoonfuls of corn-meal, a pinch of salt and 1 of sugar, with milk enough to make a mush; then set in a warm place till morning; then scald a teaspoonful of sugar, 1 of salt and ⅓ as much soda with a pint of boiling water; then add cold water till lukewarm, and thicken to a thick batter with flour, then add the mush made the night before and stir briskly for a minute or two. Put in a close vessel in a kettle of warm water, not too hot. When light, mix stiff, add a little shortening, and mold into loaves. It will soon rise and will not require as long to bake as yeast bread—25 to 30 minutes in a good oven. Great care is required to keep the sponge of a uniform heat (the water should be about as warm as the hand will bear). The finest patent process flour is not as good as a little coarser grade—I prefer Knickerbocker—for this kind of bread. All dishes used in making should be perfectly clean and sweet, scalding them, out with saleratus or lime-water."

(Ann Arbor, 1884)

Salt-Rising Bread No. 3

Take a pint of warm water—about 90 degrees—(if too hot it will not rise) in a perfectly clean bowl and stir up a thick batter with flour, adding a teaspoon of salt; a thorough beating of the batter is necessary. Set in a pan of warm water and keep it at the same temperature, and it will begin to rise in two to four hours; the rising is much more sure if coarse flour or shorts is used in the place of fine flour. When the rising is nearly light enough, take a pint of milk and a pint of boiling water (a little soda added prevents its souring); mix the sponge in a bread pan, and when cooled to about milk warm stir in the rising; the sponge thus made will be light in two to four hours with good warmth; the dough does not require as much kneading as yeast raised dough.

E. C. L.
(Grand Rapids, 1890)

"Shorts" is a term used for a cheap grade of flour which contains the germ, fine bran, and a small amount of flour.

Superior Raised Johnny Cake

One quart of sifted corn meal, three tablespoonfuls of hop yeast, and enough water to make a batter. Let it rise two hours, and then add one tablespoonful of shortening, one-fourth tablespoonful of soda; mix well, and bake in a thin cake in a quick oven.

(Battle Creek, 1890)

Tryabita Bread

One pint milk, or milk and water, lukewarm; 1 teaspoonful of sugar and 1 of salt; 1 compressed yeast cake dissolved in ¼ cup of water. Stir this into 1½ pints of Tryabita Food and 1½ pints of spring wheat flour, thoroughly mixed, adding more flour if necessary, so that it will make a stiff dough that will knead without sticking to the board. After it has been thoroughly kneaded, grease your bread-raising pan with a piece of sweet lard about the size of an egg, put in dough and let it raise until three times its size; then take it out and put it upon the board and fold down; place back into greased bread-pan and let raise again, and fold down the second time. Divide the dough into two equal parts, put into tins and raise to twice its size. Bake in oven from 30 to 40 minutes.

Tryabita bread may truly be called the "Staff of Life" as it contains all the nourishing qualities to make bone and muscle and feed the nerves. These qualities are nearly all lacking in ordinary white bread.

(Battle Creek, 1903)

You need not look on your grocery shelves for Tryabita Food. It hasn't been manufactured since around 1903. Tryabita, the brainchild of a mysterious entrepreneur from Chicago, Dr. V. C. Price, was produced at the tiny village of Yorkville on Gull Lake in Kalamazoo County. Price attempted to capitalize on Battle Creek's "Cereal City" boom as well as Kalamazoo's reputation as the "Celery City." He dreamed up a combination of the two, a hot cereal-flavored breakfast food. Despite widespread advertising, including mention in *Mother Hubbard's Modern Cupboard* (Battle Creek, 1903) and endorsements by the University of Michigan's sports programs, his company folded within a year.

Cream of wheat, or farina, and a little celery seed might work as a substitute for Tryabita.

Water Bread

Dissolve a tablespoonful of sugar in a pint of boiling water. When lukewarm, add one fourth of a cupful of liquid yeast, and sufficient flour to make a batter thick enough to drop from the spoon. Beat vigorously for ten minutes, turn into a clean, well-scalded bread bowl, cover (wrapping in a blanket if in cold weather), and let it rise over night. In the morning, when well risen, add flour to knead. Knead well for half an hour, cover, and let it become light in mass. When light, shape into loaves, allow it to rise again, and bake.

(Battle Creek, 1910)

Whole-Wheat Bread

Take one pint of warm water, one teaspoonful of sugar, one level quart of whole-wheat flour, one and one fourth level pints of any good spring wheat flour, three tablespoonfuls of soft yeast or one half a cake of compressed yeast, dissolved in three tablespoonfuls of *cold* water. Put the yeast and sugar into the warm water, add the white flour, beating well. Wrap in a thick blanket and let rise until foamy. When light, add one half teaspoonful of salt, if desired, and the whole-wheat flour, *warm*. The dough should be *very stiff*. Knead well for twenty minutes, and return to the bowl (which has been washed and oiled). When risen to double its size, form into two loaves, place in brick-shaped pans, and let rise until very light. Then put into a *very hot* oven. After ten or fifteen minutes, lower the temperature of the oven, and bake from three fourths to one and one fourth hours, according to the heat of the oven.

(Battle Creek, 1910)

Whole-Wheat Bread No. 2

Scald one pint of unskimmed milk; when lukewarm, add one half cup of liquid yeast, or one fourth cake of compressed yeast, dissolved in one half cup of warm water, and a pint of Pillsbury's best white flour. Beat this batter thoroughly, and allow it to rise. When well risen, add three and two thirds cups of wheat berry flour. Knead thoroughly, and allow it to become light in mass; then shape into two loaves, allow it to rise again, and bake.

(Battle Creek, 1910)

ROLLS, BISCUITS, BUNS, and GEMS

Beaten Biscuit

Of course I'll gladly give de rule
   I meks beat biscuit by,
Dough I ain't sure dat you will mek
   Dat bread de same as I.

'Case cookin's like religion is—
   Some's 'lected an' some ain't,
An' rules don't no more mek a cook
   Dan sermons mek a saint.

Well, 'bout de 'grediances required
   I needn't mention dem;
Of course, you knows of flour an' things
   How much to put, an' when;

But soon as you is got dat dough
   Mixed up all smoove an' neat,
Den's when youh genius gwine to show
   To get dem biscuit beat!

Two hundred licks is what I gives
   For home-folks, never fewer,
An' if I'm 'spectin' company in,
   I gives five hundred sure!

From Bandanna Ballads, by Miss Howard Weeden
(Saginaw, 1905)

Buckwheat Cakes

Soak 5 or 6 slices of stale bread in 2 qts. boiling water. Add a large tps. of salt. When cool, add 1 yeast foam cake, which has been soaked in ½ c. tepid water, and stir very thick with buckwheat flour. Do this in the morning and let rise until the next morning, when they are ready to use. Take out what you need for breakfast and dilute with milk in which you have dissolved ½ tsp. soda. Add a little more salt. If you do not bake all you take out, put back in the large batter and stir down. Keep in a cool place until used up. The longer they stand the better they are. You may have to increase the soda allowance toward the last.

Mrs. Geo. P. Hopkins
(Kalamazoo, 1921)

Bunns

Three cups milk, 1 cup sugar, 1 cup yeast, 2 eggs; let it rise over night; add in the morning 1 cup butter, 1 cup sugar, ½ nutmeg, 1 teaspoon soda; make as thick as biscuit, let it rise again very light, then roll the dough and cut out the size of a teacup, and lay in pans by the fire while the oven is heating, bake; when nearly done, glaze with molasses and milk.

Mrs. E. E. Judd
(Grand Rapids, 1890)

Nutmegs, the pit of the fruit of a tropical tree, were traditionally sold whole and each cook grated them in a special tool. One half of a nutmeg should equal about ½ teaspoon of the powdered nutmeg which is now more readily available. Connecticut, incidentally, draws its nickname, the Nutmeg State, from the itinerant Connecticut peddlers who duped the public with wooden nutmegs.

Bicycle Buns

Over one pint of finely sifted wheat flour pour one-half pint of boiling water; stir into it one table-spoonful of butter, one-quarter teaspoonful of salt, two-thirds of a cup of sugar and one-half cup of softened butter. When all are thoroughly mixed add one-half cake of compressed yeast, which has been dissolved in one-half cup of lukewarm water. Set this sponge to rise over night; in the morning knead and roll out the dough to about one-half inch in thickness, cut with round cooky cutter, then with case-knife cut strips toward the center, making "wheels;" connect two of the buns with small strip of dough, making imitations of bicycles; brush over with melted butter, let rise and bake in moderate oven thirty minutes. If carefully prepared these buns are an ornament to the table, as well as being very toothsome.

Mrs. R. W. Boyd, Adrian
(Chicago, 1896)

Safety bicycles replaced the high-wheeled "bone breakers" in the 1880s. The Gay Nineties witnessed a bicycle mania as men and women took to the streets by the millions. Anybody who was anybody got a "wheel." Bicyclist groups first promoted a good-roads movement in Michigan, and many young inventors who cut their mechanical teeth on bicycles went on to design horseless carriages.

Mrs. Boyd calls for the use of a case-knife in her bicycle buns recipe. It is a regular table knife.

Bacon Muffins

2 cups flour	⅓ cup broiled bacon, well drained (about 6 slices)
2 tsp. Calumet baking powder	
½ tsp. salt	1 egg
1 tbsp. sugar	1 cup milk
	¼ cup bacon fat, melted

Add bacon to sifted dry ingredients. Bacon should be cut in ½ inch squares. Beat egg until light, blend in milk and add to flour mixture. Start to mix then add bacon fat. Do not stir any more than necessary. Fill greased muffin pans ⅔ full. Bake 20–25 min. at 400°. Makes 16 small muffins.

Mrs. H. D. Cox
(Kalamazoo, 1941)

Buttermilk Scones

One pound sifted flour, saltspoon of salt, three ounces of butter rubbed into the flour, heaping teaspoonful of baking powder. Mix the whole into a light paste with buttermilk, roll out a quarter of an inch thick, cut in three-cornered pieces and bake a nice brown. These are delicious cut open and toasted for breakfast.

Mrs. W. Birchby, Holland
(Chicago, 1896)

Biscuits (Using No Wheat)

Most of these biscuits are not as light and fluffy as wheat biscuits but are still a desirable and edible product.

Barley Biscuit

1¼ cups liquid	6 teaspoons baking
4 cups barley flour	powder
3 tablespoons fat	1 teaspoon salt

(Kalamazoo, 1918)

Mix all ingredients and bake at 350° for 20 minutes.

During World War I, patriotic citizens reduced their consumption of wheat to increase food for the doughboys. Students of the "Cookery Department" of Western State Normal (later to become Western Michigan University) tested a number of recipes using wheat substitutes in 1918.

Light Biscuit

With one quart of boiled milk when nearly cold, mix flour to form a thick sponge, add half a cup of good hop yeast, beat fifteen minutes. Let it rise four or five hours, or over night; then add two-thirds of a cup of shortening (butter and lard, half and half), two tablespoonfuls of sugar, and a little salt, stirring in the flour with a large wooden spoon until the dough cleaves from the spoon. Roll out to an inch or less in thickness; mold into cakes and let them stand in a warm place till thoroughly light. Bake in a quick oven. These are old-fashioned and excellent.

(Detroit, 1878)

Raised Biscuit

These may be made from dough prepared by any of the recipes for bread. They will be more ten-der if made with milk, and if the dough is prepared expressly for biscuits, one third cream may be used. When the dough has been thoroughly kneaded the last time, divide into small, equal-sized pieces. A quantity of dough sufficient for one loaf of bread should be divided into twelve or sixteen such portions. Shape into smooth, round biscuits, fit closely into a shallow pan, and let them rise until very light. Biscuit should be allowed to become lighter than bread before putting in the oven, since, being so much smaller, fermentation is arrested much sooner, and they do not rise as much in the oven as does bread.

(Battle Creek, 1910)

Corn Bread or Breakfast Corn Cake

Some years ago business called me to pass through Toledo several times, and I staid over night, each time, at the Island House, where I found so much better corn bread at the breakfast table than I had ever eaten—according to my custom when traveling and finding some dish extra nice—I obtained the recipe, through influence of the waiter girl, as "mail carrier," (paying a price equal to the price of this book,) who wrote it out for me in my diary while I ate my breakfast; here it is: One quart of corn meal, 1 cup of flour, or a little less; 1 tablespoonful of baking powder; milk, to wet; beating in 1 or 2 eggs, a little sugar and salt; put into a dripping pan, and put, at once, into a hot oven, but do not dry it up by over-baking.

Remarks—I think I have eaten of it more than 100 times since, but I have never seen corn cake to excel it. It should be 1 to 1½ inches thick when baked.

(Ann Arbor, 1884)

Togus or Steamed Corn Bread

3 cups sweet milk	1 cup sugar and mo-
1 cup sour milk	lasses
3 cups Indian meal	1 teaspoon soda
1 cup flour	1 teaspoon salt

Steam 3 hours and bake 1 hour.

Mrs. Inez Austin
(Grand Rapids, 1917)

Indian meal, named for the original maize or "Indian corn" growers, is corn meal.

Corn Meal Puffs

Scale 4 tablespoons white corn meal and while hot add 2 tablespoons butter and 2 eggs well beaten. When cool 2 teacups milk, 8 tablespoons wheat flour, a little salt. Bake in patty pans in quick oven.

Mrs. Wm. Tomlinson
(Kalamazoo, 1899)

Corn Dodgers

Two cups of flour, 1 cup of corn meal, 1 egg, 2 tablespoons of lard, 2 cups of sour milk, 1 teaspoon soda, salt; beat well and bake either in one tin or in gem tins.

Mrs. C. C. Rood
(Grand Rapids, 1890)

For the Cracknels, or Scotch Bannocks, to Keep a Year

Take the finest oatmeal and stir in barely enough water to wet it thorough; add a pinch of salt; let it stand for 10 minutes to swell; then roll it out a quarter of an inch in thickness, first flouring the board and rolling pin with wheaten flour; cut it with a biscuit cutter, and bake in a moderate oven; these cakes will burn quickly and only require to be of the lightest brown. If put in a close jar they will keep for several months. In the Highlands they preserve their bannocks in the barrels of oatmeal and keep them a year or so.

(Ann Arbor, 1884)

Crumpets

Mix together thoroughly while dry one quart sifted flour, two heaping teaspoonfuls baking powder, a little salt, then add two tablespoonfuls melted butter and sweet milk enough to make a thin dough. Bake quickly in muffin rings or patty pans.

(Detroit, 1891)

London Crumpets

Sift together one and one-half pints flour, one-half teaspoonful salt, one teaspoonful sugar, and two teaspoonfuls baking powder; add one beaten egg, a scant pint of milk and cream in equal parts, a little ground cinnamon or a teaspoonful extract of cinnamon; half fill greased muffin rings, place on a hot, well-greased griddle. Bake on one side only. Serve hot with cottage cheese.

(Detroit, 1891)

Elvira's Muffins

One egg, 1 spoon melted butter, 1 spoon sugar, 1 cup sweet milk, 2 cups flour, 2 teaspoons baking powder (heaping), bake in muffin rings, or gem tins.

(Ann Arbor, 1872)

Golden Manna Puffs

Two eggs, ½ teaspoon of salt, 1½ cups of milk, 1½ cups of flour, ½ cup of Golden Manna. Beat briskly for 2 minutes. Bake in gem irons previously oiled and heated.

(Battle Creek, 1903)

Golden Manna, another short-lived product of the Battle Creek cereal boom of the first decade of the twentieth century, was devised by a local real estate dealer. Benjamin F. Morgan advertised his yellow meal to be "Battle Creek's best builder of blood, bone, body, brawn and brain." Bunkum should also have been added to Golden Manna's alliterative slogan. With each purchase, consumers got a ticket for a free trip in Morgan's new three-seater automobile, which turned out to be a leisurely ride out to his newly platted subdivision for the sales pitch. Cornflakes make a more obtainable substitute.

Graham Gems, No. 1

One pint sour milk, half a teaspoon of soda, same of salt, flour to make a stiff batter. Have your gem-pans very hot, butter them, and drop-in the batter, and bake fifteen or twenty minutes in a quick oven.

(Battle Creek, 1890)

A "quick" oven is equivalent to 400°.

Graham Gems. No. 2

Mix one tablespoonful of baking powder with one pint Graham flour, one cup fine flour, and two tablespoonfuls of lard or butter. Use either sweet milk or water for wetting, stirring as stiff as possible. Bake quickly in hot, well-buttered gem pans.

(Battle Creek, 1890)

Graham Gems

I have been watching your papers to see if they gave any recipe for graham gems as good as mine.

No. 2 Iron Gem Pan, each...... 25c.

Gems, usually made of coarse unleavened flour, were baked in shallow cast-iron pans (Grand Rapids, 1890).

I have seen none. Take 1½ good pt. of graham flour, 1 pt. of sweet milk, mix them well together, beat the whites of 2 large eggs to a stiff foam, add yolks, beat well, heat gem pans hot, grease, have oven pretty hot, mix eggs in the last thing, carefully and quickly, as soon as they are beaten. Bake from 7 to 10 minutes.

Mrs. M. P. Bush, Saline, Mich.
Detroit Post and Tribune
(Ann Arbor, 1884)

Kringler

*1 cup butter   1 cup sweet cream
2 cups flour*

Mix butter and flour well; then add cream until the right consistency to roll. Roll about ⅛th of an inch; spread with sugar. Cut in strips ¼ inch by 10 inches, and shape like a pretzel. Bake in hot oven.

Olga Nielsen
(Grayling, 1937)

This is a traditional Scandinavian delicacy with Michigan variations.

Mobile Rolls

To 1 cup yeast dissolved in a cup of warm water, add 1 mealy Irish potato mashed fine and 1 pint milk. Rub 1 tablespoon lard in 1 quart flour, 1 teaspoon salt, 1 tablespoon sugar and add yeast and milk. Set at night. In morning work till dough blisters. If kept hot will be ready to bake in 1 hour.

Mrs. E. J. Schettler
(Kalamazoo, 1899)

Old-Time Rusk

Scald one pint milk, add to it half cup butter, one and one-half cups sugar, flour enough to make stiff batter, and one yeast cake dissolved in a gill of warm water; set away covered over night. In the morning break into this two eggs and one teaspoon cinnamon, one teaspoon salt, and flour enough to knead soft; handle as little as possible. Grease the top, cover, and let rise. When light roll out about half inch thick, cut with biscuit cutter, place in pans, and allow them to get very light. Just before putting in the oven paint each one with equal parts of milk and yolk of eggs and thickened with sugar.

F. L. Ball
(Coldwater, 1907)

Olive Rolls

2 cakes yeast
½–1 cup finely
  chopped olives
3 tablespoons honey
1 pint luke warm
  water

2½ cups whole wheat
  flour
½ cup soy bean flour
3–4 cups unbleached
  flour
1 teaspoon salt

Combine all ingredients, making a stiff dough. Let rise, make into rolls. When light, bake 35 minutes.

(Berrien Springs, 1941)

Peanut Butter Muffins

One-third c. of peanut butter, ¼ c. of sugar, ½ tsp. salt, 4 tsp. baking powder, ¾ c. milk, 1 egg, 1½ c. flour. Cream the peanut butter; add sugar gradually; add beaten egg; add milk and dry ingredients. Bake in moderate oven 20 m.

Mrs. C. M. Brown
(Kalamazoo, 1921)

These make nice breakfast rolls, and children love them. We used crunchy peanut butter. Bake at 350° for 20 minutes. The recipe yields eight muffins.

Rice Muffins

One c. cold rice, 1 c. sweet milk, 2 eggs, 1 tsp. salt, 1 tsp. sugar, 1 tbsp. butter, 1 tsp. baking powder; flour to make a stiff batter.

Mrs. W. M. Milham
(Kalamazoo, 1921)

Rolls

Well kneaded and risen bread dough is made into a variety of small forms termed rolls, by rolling with the hands or with a rolling-pin, and afterward cutting or folding into any shape desired, the particular manner by which they are folded and shaped giving to the rolls their characteristic names. Dough prepared with rich milk or part cream makes the best rolls. It may be divided into small, irregular portions, about one inch in thickness, and shaped by taking each piece separately in the left hand, then with the thumb and first finger of the right hand, slightly stretch one of the points of the piece and draw it over the left thumb toward the center of the roll, holding it there with the left thumb. Turn the dough and repeat the operation until you have been all around the dough, and each point has been drawn in; then place on the pan to rise. Allow the rolls to become very light, and bake. Rolls prepared in this manner are termed *Imperial Rolls*, and if the folding has been properly done, when well baked they will be composed of a succession of light layers, which can be readily separated.

French Rolls may be made by shaping each portion of dough into small oval rolls quite tapering at each end, allowing them to become light, and baking far enough apart so that one will not touch another.

If, when the dough is light and ready to shape, it be rolled on the board until about one eighth of an inch in thickness, and cut into five-inch squares, then divided through the center into triangles, rolled up, beginning with the wide side, and placed in the pan to rise in semicircular shape, the rolls are called *Crescents*.

(Battle Creek, 1910)

Rye Muffins

One and one-half c. sifted rye flour, ½ c. white flour, 1 tsp. melted butter, 1 beaten egg, 1 c. milk, ½ tsp. salt, 4 tsp. baking powder. Bake in moderate oven.

Mrs. C. W. Keyser
(Kalamazoo, 1921)

Sour Milk Biscuit Dough

Can be used as a shortcake meat pie or however one sees fit to use it.

6 cups flour
4 rounding tea-
    spoons baking
    powder

2 level teaspoons
    soda, if milk is
    very sour; if not,
    1½ teaspoons
1 heaping teaspoon
    salt

Put all in sifter and sift. Then mix in 2 heaping tablespoons of shortening as for pie crust. Add enough sour milk to make a soft dough and handle as little as possible.

Mrs. Wm. Hildebrand, Shelbyville
(Allegan, 1938)

Southern Spoon Bread

Heat 1 pt. fresh milk to nearly boiling. Gradually stir in ½ c. cornmeal and cook until it is like mush. Add ½ tsp. of baking powder and 1 tsp. salt; add the yolks of 3 eggs (well beaten); fold in the stiffly beaten whites; pour into greased pan. Bake ½ hour slowly. Serve with butter from the dish in which it was baked.

Mrs. G. E. Miller
(Kalamazoo, 1921)

Squash Buns

1 cake Fleischman's
    yeast
1 cup milk
1 cup mashed squash

1 tsp. salt
1 cup warm water
½ cup shortening
1½ qts. flour

Soften yeast in water, add milk which has been scalded and cooled to lukewarm. Add squash, sugar, salt, butter and flour. Mix to soft dough. Knead ten minutes, using no more flour than necessary—about ⅔ cup. Set in a greased bowl, cover and let stand until light. Put on floured board. Roll in a sheet, nearly an inch thick, and cut with a bis-

cuit cutter. Set buns close together in a greased baking pan, brushing the surfaces with melted butter or fat or put in greased muffin tins. When light, bake at 425 deg. about twenty to twenty-five minutes.

Mrs. Jas. Roosevelt
(Parchment, 1935)

Squash Muffins

One-half cup sifted squash, 1 cup milk, ½ cup sugar, 2 cups flour, 1 egg, 1 teaspoon baking powder.

Mrs. C. B. Williams
(Kalamazoo, 1899)

Sunday Morning Muffins

Sift together 2 c. flour, 1 c. sugar, 2 tsp. baking powder, ½ tsp. salt, and add 1 c. washed, seedless raisins. Beat together 2 eggs, 1 c. milk or water and ¼ c. oil, or other shortening. Add this mixture to dry ingredients, beat as for cake, and bake in muffin tins in a moderate oven. Serve with butter.

Mrs. H. C. Jackson
(Kalamazoo, 1921)

Wheaten Scones (Scotch)

Take from your bread *dough*, when light in the morning before it has been kneaded, bits of dough the size of your fist; roll each one out thin (less than half an inch in thickness and the size of a breakfast plate in circumference), lay it on a *hot* but *dry* griddle—no grease whatever must be used; let it bake on one side, then turn and bake on the other; have a napkin warmed and lay the scone in it, covering, while a second scone is baking; when you have three baked fold your napkin close over them and send to table piping hot. Tear them open and butter. They are very nice.

(Detroit, 1878)

PANCAKES and WAFFLES

Buckwheat Griddle Cakes, in Rhyme

For ordinary buckwheat cakes, we will give one in rhyme, from one of the muses of the Detroit *Free Press*, which may be relied upon as safe to follow:

If you fine buckwheat cakes would make
One quart of buckwheat flour take;
Four table-spoonfuls then of yeast;
Of salt one tea-spoonful at least;
One handful Indian meal and two
Good table-spoonfuls of real New
Orleans molasses, then enough
Warm water to make of the stuff
A batter thin. Beat very well;
Set it to rise where warmth do dwell.
If in the morning, it should be
The least bit sour, stir in free
A very little soda that

Is first dissolved in water hot,
Mix in an earthen crock, and leave
Each morn a cupful in to give
A sponge for the next night, so you
Need not get fresh yeast to renew.

In weather cold this plan may be
Pursued ten days successfully,
Providing you add every night
Flour, salt, molasses, meal in right
Proportions, beating as before,
And setting it to rise once more.
When baking make of generous size
Your cakes; and if they'd take the prize
They must be light and nicely browned,
Then by your husband you'll be crowned
Queen of the kitchen; but you'll bake,
And he will, man-like, "take the cake."

Remarks—When buckwheat cakes are made without molasses, as is often done, if a small spoonful of molasses is added, each morning, to the cake batter, they will take a much nicer brown, being careful, however, not to burn them.

(Ann Arbor, 1884)

Corn Fritters

One can corn, 1 c. flour, 1 tsp. baking powder, 2 tsp. salt, ¼ tsp. paprika, 2 eggs; add dry ingredients to corn; add yolks of eggs, beaten until thick; fold in whites of eggs, beaten stiff. Cook in frying pan in hot lard. Drain on paper. Serve with syrup.

Mrs. Marguerite Brown
(Kalamazoo, 1921)

Grape-Nuts Cream Fritters

One quart of milk, 6 ounces of sugar, 1 cup of Grape-Nuts, 1 tablespoonful of butter, 1 pinch of salt, yolks of 6 eggs, 6 ounces of flour and cornstarch mixed. Boil milk with butter and salt in it, mix the sugar with the starch and flour, beat into the boiling milk, add the Grape-Nuts that have been slightly moistened. Let boil slowly about 10 minutes, stir in the yolks and take off the fire. Flavor with lemon or vanilla. Put into buttered pan and let

Syrup cups featured a special built-in spout that retained the dribblings within the container (Wallingford, 1872).

233

get cold, cut in slices, roll in eggs, then in cracker-meal, fry in smoking hot lard. Serve with syrup.

(Battle Creek, 1903)

Fritters, Plain—Quick

Sweet milk, 1 pt.; 4 eggs; salt 1 teaspoonful; baking powder, 1 table-spoonful; flour. Directions—Beat the eggs well, stir in salt and milk; then put the baking powder into 2 or 3 cups of flour and stir in, using as much more flour as will stir in well; drop into hot lard. To be eaten with maple syrup, or syrup made by dissolving granulated sugar.

(Ann Arbor, 1884)

Orange Fritters

Take 3, or as many large smooth oranges as needed, take off the peel and the white skin also, then slice them, crosswise, ¼ inch thick, pick the seeds out, and dip the slices in a thick batter made according to the foregoing recipe; fry nicely, placing them in layers, on a plate, as fried, sifting sugar over each layer. Serve hot.

(Ann Arbor, 1884)

Cornmeal Mush (Hasty Pudding)

When the water is boiling, salt it and scatter the meal in by the handful, stirring constantly. Make it a thick, smooth batter, and at the last; stir in a good handful of flour, this binds it and makes it better for frying. It is a good way to pour into a greased bread pan and bake awhile. Cut in slices when cold, and fry in hot lard or butter to a nice brown.

E. C. L.
(Grand Rapids, 1890)

Corn Meal Slap Jacks

Mix 1 pint sour milk with two-thirds parts corn meal and one-third part of flour to a batter. Add 1

beaten egg, 1 teaspoon of melted butter, 1 level teaspoon of soda and a pinch of salt and mix thoroughly. Fry on a hot griddle.

Rev. J. C. Hageman
(Portland, 1910)

Kissingen Phannekuchen

One cup of flour, one pint of milk, one table-spoonful of sugar, piece of butter the size of a walnut (a heaping teaspoonful); scald the milk, butter and flour together. After the batter is cold stir in the yolks of eight eggs, and just before cooking add the whites beaten very light. Put into a frying or omelet pan a tablespoonful of butter; let it boil up, pour in one-sixth of this mixture, and let it fry as you do an omelet; fold over from each side of the pan and double in the middle, as you do an omelet. In Germany they sprinkle sugar over before folding up. We prefer sifting the powdered sugar on after it is folded. Raspberry jam is served with phanne-kuchen. We prefer it without.

(Detroit, 1878)

Rice Griddle Cakes

One and one-half pint solid cold boiled rice, soaked over night in 1 pint of water, or milk, 1 quart milk added in the morning, 1 quart flour, 2 eggs well beaten, ½ teaspoon saleratus dissolved in a little hot water, 1 teaspoon salt; bake on a griddle.

Mrs. Fuller
(Grand Rapids, 1890)

Saleratus is common baking soda.

Squash Pancakes

Wash the squash, remove the seeds, and then grate the squash. To one grated squash weighing about ½ pound, add ½ cup water, ½ cup flour, one egg, and a little salt. Mix thoroughly and drop on a

234

Elongated cast-iron griddles came in handy for flapjacks as well as fried fish (Grand Rapids, 1890).

well greased skillet with a spoon. This will make between fifteen and twenty medium sized pancakes. Sprinkle these pancakes with a little sugar before serving.

(Detroit, 1935)

Strawberry Pancakes

Separate the yolks and whites of 3 eggs. Mix the yolks with 2 cups milk, add ¼ of a teaspoonful of salt and a heaping cup of flour. Mix into a smooth batter and strain through a sieve. Beat the whites to a stiff froth, add slowly while beating constantly the batter to the whites. Place a medium sized frying pan with ½ tablespoonful of butter and same of lard over the fire. When hot pour in sufficient batter to cover the pan. Bake till light brown on the under side. Then turn the cake and bake on the other side. When done slip the pancake into a hot dish. Have 1 quart of well cleaned strawberries mashed with a fork and sweetened with ½ cupful of sugar. Cover the pancake with a layer of strawberries. Continue to bake the remaining batter the same way, place a layer of berries over each pancake as soon as it is removed from the pan. This recipe will make four thin pancakes.

J. A. P.
(Covert, 1903)

Waffles

A pint bowlful of sour cream or buttermilk, a pint bowl heaped of sifted flour, three eggs, and a teaspoonful of soda stirred well into a tablespoonful of hot water and then with the milk and half a teaspoonful of salt.

(Traverse City, 1900)

Bread Waffles

Crusts and pieces can be put in a pitcher and milk poured over them; when needed, add more milk, and a little flour, to make the right consistency; add enough soda to make sweet; salt, and make waffles, or pancakes.

(Detroit, 1881)

NO BURNING FINGERS!   ALWAYS READY FOR USE!

THE MOST COMPLETE

ROUND WAFFLE IRON IN THE MARKET.

WILL FIT No. 8 OR 9 STOVE.

This waffle iron cost ninety-eight cents in 1890 (Grand Rapids, 1890).

235

German Waffles

Half a pound of butter stirred to a cream, the yolks of five eggs stirred into half a pound of flour, half a pint of milk gradually stirred in, and lastly the whites of the eggs beaten to a stiff froth. Bake in well buttered waffle-irons, as usual. This recipe furnishes very rich, delicious cakes.

(Detroit, 1890)

Raised Waffles

One quart flour, 1 pint sweet, lukewarm milk, 2 eggs, 1 tablespoon melted butter, 1 teaspoon salt ½ teacup yeast or ½ cake compressed yeast.

Put the waffle iron on the stove, when one side is hot grease it and turn it, when the other is hot grease it and fill two-thirds full of batter. Serve hot with butter and pulverised sugar or syrup.

E. C. L.
(Grand Rapids, 1890)

Cast-iron waffle irons that were heated one side at a time on the cooking range were a standard utensil in Victorian kitchens.

Rice Waffles

One cupful cold boiled rice, one cupful of milk and two tablespoonfuls of butter, beat this mixture well, then add two well beaten eggs, a pinch of salt, one-half teaspoonful of soda, stir in flour enough to make a thin batter, adding a teaspoonful of cream of tartar, beat vigorously and bake in hot well greased waffle irons.

Mrs. Spencer Carpenter, Menominee
(Chicago, 1898)

Southern Waffles

Sift 1 pint of flour with 1 teaspoon of salt and add 1 pint thick sour milk; 1 tablespoonful of sour cream is an improvement. Beat long and hard till very smooth; then add 2 tablespoons of melted lard, and 1 well-beaten egg and beat again. Just before frying, add 1 teaspoon of soda, dissolved in warm water; the irons should be very hot and well greased. Serve with maple syrup.

Florence S. Wattles
(Kalamazoo, 1906)

Hop Yeast

Boil one dozen common-sized potatoes in two quarts of water, with a handful of hops, which should be closely tied in a linen bag before putting in the water. When done, pour off the water, mash the potatoes fine, and mix with the liquid. When cool, add half a pint of good yeast, or two dry yeast cakes. When light, place in a jug, or covered jar, and set in the cellar. A teacupful will be sufficient for an ordinary baking.

(Battle Creek, 1890)

Raw Potato Yeast

Mix one fourth of a cup of flour, the same of white sugar, and a teaspoonful of salt to a paste with a little water. Pare three medium-sized, fresh, and sound potatoes, and grate them as rapidly as possible into the paste; mix all quickly together with a silver spoon, then pour three pints of boiling water slowly over the mixture, stirring well at the same time. If this does not rupture the starch cells of the flour and potatoes so that the mixture becomes thickened to the consistency of starch, turn it into a granite-ware kettle and boil up for a minute, stirring well to keep it from sticking and burning. If it becomes too much thickened, add a little more boiling water. It is impossible to give the exact amount of water, since the quality of the flour will vary, and likewise the size of the potatoes; but three pints is an approximate proportion. Strain the mixture through a fine colander into an earthen bread bowl, and let it cool. When lukewarm, add one cup of good, lively yeast. Cover with a napkin, and keep in a moderately warm place for several hours, or until it ceases to ferment. As it begins to ferment, stir it well occasionally, and when well fermented, turn into a clean glass or earthen jar. The next morning cover closely, and put in the cellar or refrigerator, not, however, in contact with the ice. It is best to reserve enough for the first baking in some smaller jar, so that the larger portion need not be opened so soon. Always shake the yeast before using.

(Battle Creek, 1910)

Raw Potato Yeast No. 2

This is made in the same manner as the preceding, with this exception, that one fourth of a cup of loose hops tied in a clean muslin bag, is boiled in the water for five minutes before pouring it into the potato and flour mixture. Many think the addition of the hops aids in keeping the yeast sweet for a longer period. But potato yeast may be kept sweet for two weeks without hops, if well cared for, and is preferred by those who dislike the peculiar flavor of the bread made from hop yeast.

(Battle Creek, 1910)

Boiled Potato Yeast

Peel four large potatoes, and put them to boil in two quarts of cold water. Tie two loose handfuls of hops securely in a piece of muslin, and place in the water to boil with the potatoes. When the potatoes are tender, remove them with a perforated skimmer, leaving the water still boiling. Mash them, and work in four tablespoonfuls of flour and two of

sugar. Over this mixture pour gradually the boiling hop infusion, stirring constantly, that it may form a smooth paste, and set it aside to cool. When lukewarm, add a gill of lively yeast, and proceed as in the preceding recipe.

(Battle Creek, 1910)

Boiled Potato Yeast No. 2

Take one heaping cupful of smoothly mashed, mealy potato. (Tie a bunch of hops, about the size of a hickorynut, in a piece of cheese-cloth, and boil in the water with the potatoes. The yeast will be lighter if the potatoes are boiled with the skins on and pealed just before washing.) Add to it one teaspoonful of salt, three teaspoonfuls of sugar, three fourths of a cup of water in which the potatoes and hops were boiled, and one cake of Yeast Foam, dissolved in one fourth of a cup of warm water, or one half cup of the *hop* water and one half cup of lively yeast. Turn into a glass can, and keep moderately warm until full of bubbles, then put in a cool place.

(Battle Creek, 1910)

Raisin Yeast

Cover a cup of raisins with water, and keep warm until fermentation takes place. Then prepare a solution of starch and water as directed in any of the foregoing recipes, using this fermenting liquor in the place of seed yeast.

(Battle Creek, 1910)

Cakes, Pies, and Other Sweets

We used to think that senior citizens developed an increased liking for desserts as their sense of taste diminished. But after studying historic Michigan cookbooks, we are convinced that a sweet tooth is part of our national heritage. Victorians considered no meal, including breakfast, complete without one or as many as six distinct desserts. Cakes, pies, puddings, and candy comprise the largest categories of recipes found in early Michigan cookbooks. Everyone, it seems, had a "prize-winning" specialty. Then too, the more vigorous life-style pursued by working men and homemakers in the preautomated era allowed a higher caloric intake. More sedentary vocations have lessened the need for calories but apparently not dulled the love of sweets. Many of the following treats, however, are worth jogging an extra mile for each morning. Few early recipes call for cake, bread, or muffin pans to be oiled and floured because the writers assumed any cook would know this. To play it safe, oil and flour all pans when baking, unless otherwise specified. Saleratus, an ingredient called for in many of these recipes, is common baking soda.

tinge, and will not stick to the hand while kneading it.

The same rule holds good of all groceries. It is poor economy to buy cheap, coarse sugar. A barrel of pure, clear, granulated sugar will last longer, and therefore in the end be cheaper, than any of the moist cheap browns, or coffee sugars. The pulverized sugar that is considered the only kind to use on fruit and for making cake is tasteless, disagreeable, and so strongly suggestive of adulteration that it requires courage to attempt to use it. Cake can be made just as light with granulated as with pulverized sugar, and far more palatable.

In getting ready to make cake the first step is to see that the fire in the range or stove is in good order—burning clearly, and enough of it to last till the

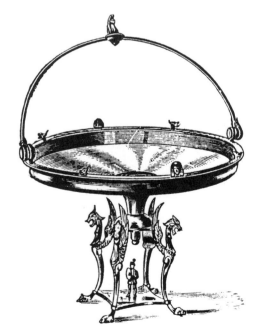

This elaborately decorated silver-plated cake basket resembled a similar device used to receive visitors' calling cards (Wallingford, 1872).

CAKES

❖

Cake—How to Make It

As good a test of flour as can be had at sight is to take up a handful and squeeze it tight; if good, when the hand is unclasped the lines on the palm of the hand will be plainly defined on the ball of flour. Good flour, when made into dough, will never be a clear blue-white, but of a creamy, yellowish

238

cake is baked; adding coal or wood while the baking is in progress is very injurious to whatever is cooking. Shake all the ashes out, add all the fuel needed, and then there will be sufficient time for it to burn clearly while the cake is being put together. Be sure that no door is opened or window raised, that is in such direction from the stove that the wind or sun will come across it. No oven will bake well when the wind or sun can strike upon it; the wind will cool the oven, and the sun deaden the coal and make it look white.

A marble slab is excellent, particularly for pastry, and will never grow rough, like wood, by use. But, next to that, a large smooth moldingboard is desirable, even when nothing is to be molded or rolled out. It helps to keep all flour, sugar, etc., from the floor and table while cooking, and is easily taken to the sink for cleaning, with all the soiled dishes upon it, and that also saves steps and time.

For cake let the flour dry near the fire while the other ingredients are being collected. Then sift it, and if cream of tartar or baking powder is desired, sift that with the flour. Roll the sugar to avoid lumps (granulated sugar never lumps), and then weigh or measure the desired quantity, putting it in a clean dish or bowl on the table. For cake or pastry, the butter should be washed in ice-cold water the night before using, squeezed hard in a clean cloth, and put into ice-water, and set on ice till needed. Raisins should also be stoned the night before; and currants washed, picked over, rubbed dry in a clean cloth, then spread on a broad dish or platter till needed. The citron, when required, should be cut in very thin slices, all covered up closely, and set on the ice. By attending to these preliminaries the evening before making cake, the morning work is much expedited.

When ready for immediate work, gather all these things compactly on the table, butter the pans, or line with white paper well buttered. Use butter, not lard or drippings, for this, or the under crust will taste unpleasantly. Cake is not as likely to burn at the bottom when the pans are lined with buttered paper. Keep clean brown paper to cover the top, if there is any danger of scorching. The cheap white unglazed paper on which newspapers are printed answers every purpose for lining cake pans, is more economical than letter paper, and safer, as writing paper has often some poisonous substance like arsenic employed in finishing it.

Eggs used for cake should be put into cold water in summer while the preliminary work is going on. Then break each one in a cup separately to be sure it is good. If it proves so, turn it into the

bowl they are to be beaten in, break the next into the cup, and so on till all are broken. If broken, without this precaution, into the bowl they are to be beaten in, there is the risk of breaking one poor one and so ruining the whole. Have nutmegs grated and allspice measured on hand.

First beat butter and sugar together till white and creamy; then the eggs, whites and yolks beaten separately always, for the whites require much longer time to be beaten perfectly. Strain the yolks after beating, and add to them the well-beaten sugar and butter. Next add the spices. Stir the flour gradually before using the sweet or sour milk needed. If soda or cream tartar are to be used, the latter should be sifted with the flour (also, as above stated, when only baking powder is called for). Dissolve soda in cool water or milk, never in anything hot, as heat destroys the best part of it. Put in the soda after the milk has been added and well beaten with all the other ingredients.

If prepared flour is used, neither soda nor cream of tartar can be employed. The currants, citrons or raisins must be well floured, but use for this the flour measured out for the cake, else the cake will be too stiff. Beat up the latter very light before adding the fruit, as it should be beaten gently and not long after that is added. The whites, beaten very stiff, are to be put in the last thing. After that very little beating is allowed—only what is necessary to incorporate the fruit and whites of eggs thoroughly with all the other ingredients. When beating the whites do not stop, after once having begun, till they are very stiff, else they will "go back," and can never be brought up light again.

In making raised cake all fruit must be well rolled in flour left out for that purpose, and not be added to the cake till just ready to put into the oven. It must not then be beaten in, but spread over the top lightly and pressed in a little way, else the fruit will all sink to the bottom and be worthless.

(Detroit, 1881)

Cakes—General Directions

Measure everything carefully. Powdered sugar makes a lighter cake. Flour differs in thickening qualities. You have used too much flour when the cake rises, cracks and remains so. Use lard to grease the cake pans; butter sticks and burns easily. The oven can wait for the cake, but the cake can *never* wait for the oven. Cakes without butter require a quick oven; with butter a moderate oven. If your cake browns as soon as you put it in the oven, it is too hot; cover the cake with paper and cool the oven. Never move the cake or shake the oven before the center is set. Don't take a cake out unless surely done. Run a broom splint through the center, if no dough adheres it is done. Or put your ear to the cake, if it ticks loudly put it back; if very faint it is done. When done, turn out gently on a cloth or sieve to cool. Never melt or warm the butter. Add to all cakes ¼ teaspoonful of salt.

(Grand Rapids, 1890)

Angels' Food

Break the whites of eleven eggs into a large cake bowl and beat stiff; add gradually one and one-half tumblerfuls of granulated sugar which has been sifted eight times; then one tumblerful of flour which has been sifted five times; the fifth time sift in one teaspoonful of cream of tartar, then add one teaspoonful of vanilla. Keep stirring while you turn it into the pan. Bake from forty to fifty minutes in a moderate oven and in a pan that has never been greased.

Many think angel's food an expensive cake, but when it is considered how cheap eggs are at this season of the year—while butter is high—it is one of the most economical cakes that can be made. Five of the yolks left should be used for the gold cake and those that remain can be scrambled for breakfast the next morning, or used in a baked custard.

Mrs. R. G. Wilbur, Hillsdale
(Chicago, 1896)

Angel Food

Whites of nine large eggs or ten smaller ones, one and one-fourth cupfuls sugar, one cupful flour, one-half teaspoonful cream tartar; after sifting flour four or five times, measure and set aside one cup. Then roll, sift, and measure one and one-fourth cupfuls sugar. Beat whites of eggs about half, then add cream tartar and beat very stiff. Stir in sugar,

then flour very lightly and flavor to taste. Do not grease pan. Moderate oven.

Mrs. A. C. Van Raalte
(Holland, 1896)

Rev. Albertus C. Van Raalte led a group of 100 penniless Dutch peasants who had fled religious persecution in the Netherlands into the western Michigan wilderness in 1847. Despite a heavy death rate during the first season due to starvation, inadequate housing, and disease, the theocratic colony he founded survived as the city of Holland. Van Raalte's wife supplied this recipe to the cookbook published in 1896 by the Ladies Aid Society of the Hope Church, which her husband founded.

Apple Cake

Two eggs, whites and yolks beaten separately, one and a half teacupfuls of sugar, scant three-quarters of a teacupful of butter, half a cup of sweet milk, three cups of flour, one teaspoonful of cream of tartar, sifted in the flour, half a teaspoonful of soda in the milk. Bake in jelly tins or cut for dressing.

Dressing for same

Three good-sized sour apples grated, the juice and grated rind of one lemon, one egg, beaten, one cup of sugar. Cook all together, three minutes, and spread between the layers.

(Detroit, 1878)

Hollandsch Appel Koek
(Dutch Apple Cake)

2 cups Flour	*1 Egg*
2 teaspoons Baking Powder	*¾ cups Milk*
½ teaspoon Salt	*¼ cup Lard*

Mix ingredients.

Fill deep pie tin with sliced apples, sprinkle with sugar and cinnamon.

Cover with above mixture and bake 25 minutes.

Sauce for Cake

1 cup Brown Sugar   1 tablespoon Butter
1 tablespoon Flour

Mix above ingredients with two cups hot water and boil two minutes.

(Holland, 1936)

Black Cake

1 pound flour   3 pounds currants
  (browned)   ½ pound citron
1½ pounds brown   1 cup molasses
  sugar   4 tablespoons rose-
1¼ pounds butter   water
3 pounds raisins   10 eggs

Season with cloves, cinnamon and mace, to taste. Better have too little, than too much.

Mrs. L. Currey, Detroit
(Chicago, 1886)

Blackberry-Jam Cake

Rub to a cream one-half of a cupful of butter, gradually add one cupful of sugar, the yolks of three eggs and the whites of two (reserve the other white for frosting), one-half a cupful of sour milk or thin cream, one-half teaspoonful of soda, one level teaspoonful each of cinnamon and allspice, two scant cupfuls of sifted flour and one cupful of thick blackberry jam or preserves.

Miss Susan Sawyer
(Chicago, 1896)

Butternut Cake

One cup of butter, 2 cups of sugar, 1 cup of sweet milk, 3 cups well sifted flour, 4 eggs, whites beaten separately, 1 teaspoon of cream of tartar, 1 teaspoon of soda, 1 teacup of butternut meats, 1 cup of chopped raisins.

Mrs. C. H. Hackley
(Muskegon, 1890)

You will probably have to harvest your own butternuts. They resemble an elongated walnut and are highly esteemed for their taste.

Camp-Meeting Cake

One cupful of sugar, half a cupful of butter, half a cupful of milk, two eggs, two teaspoonfuls of baking powder, two cups flour. Sprinkle with sugar before putting in the oven.

(Battle Creek, 1890)

Camp-meetings, during which shouting Methodist preachers beat the bible for days, formed an important social function as well as means for getting religion on the Michigan frontier.

A Cherry Birthday Cake

For any child so happy as to be born in cherry time, his mother may make a cake (any cake will do) with a filling of cherries, sweetened and stewed thick, and an icing may be colored with cherry juice. Save some of the finest cherries, a cluster with stems, and dip them first in the white of an egg, then in pulverized sugar, and let them dry. Then lay these lovely white frosted cherries on top the pink cake.

(Traverse City, 1900)

What could be more appropriate for a Michigan cookbook than cherry cake from Traverse City, "the Cherry Capital of the World."

Chocolate Cake

2 cups pulverized   4 eggs
  sugar   1 cup flour
½ cake chocolate,   1 teaspoon vanilla
  grated

Cook the chocolate to a smooth paste in a very little milk. Beat the yolks of eggs and sugar to a cream, add the chocolate, the flour by degrees, the vanilla, and the beaten whites. Bake in a square shallow pan. Frost with white frosting. This cake cut in 2 inch squares with white sponge cake makes a very pretty appearance in a cake-basket.

Mrs. J. P. Howlett, Niles
(Chicago, 1886)

Chocolate Cream Cake

Whites of five eggs, 2 cups sugar, ¾ cup butter, 1 cup sweet milk, 3 cups flour, 2 teaspoons baking powder.

White Icing—1½ cups sugar, ½ cup milk. Boil hard without stirring until it ropes from spoon; beat until it becomes thick and when cool spread on cake.

Dark Icing—1 cup sugar, 1 cup grated chocolate, ½ cup milk. Boil until thick then take off stove and add 1 teaspoon vanilla and a piece of butter the size of a hickorynut. When almost cold spread very carefully over the white icing.

Mrs. O. E. Latham
(Kalamazoo, 1899)

Hoosier cabinets worked quite well in the Wolverine State (Hart, 1907).

Chocolate Cream Cake

One cup sugar, butter size of a goose egg, (cream together); 2 eggs (whites beaten separately), ¾ cup milk, 2 squares Baker's chocolate, 1 teaspoon vanilla, 2 scant cups flour, 2 teaspoons baking powder.

Filling: Cover top with marshmallows which have been pulled apart. The heat of the cake will dissolve them. Then make a chocolate frosting and spread over the marshmallows.

Mrs. W. M. Van Peenen
(Kalamazoo, 1920)

Chocolate Nouget Cake

One-fourth cup butter, 1½ cups powdered sugar, 1 egg, 1 cup milk, 2 cups flour, 3 teaspoons baking powder, ½ teaspoon vanilla, 2 squares chocolate, melted, ⅓ cup powdered sugar, ⅔ cup almonds blanched and shredded. Cream the butter, add gradually 1½ cups sugar and egg unbeaten; when well mixed add ⅔ of the cup of milk, flour mixed and sifted with the baking powder and the vanilla. To melted chocolate add ⅓ cup powdered sugar, place on the range and add gradually the remaining milk and stir until smooth; cool slightly and add to cake mixture. Bake 15 or 20 minutes in round layer pans. Put between layers and on top White Mountain Cream sprinkled with the almonds.

White Mountain Cream (boiled frosting)—1 cup sugar, ⅓ cup boiling water, boil until it hairs, white of 1 egg, ½ teaspoon vanilla.

Mrs. J. J. Morse
(Kalamazoo, 1899)

Cocoa Cake

One-half cup butter, ¾ cup milk, 1 cup sugar, 6 tablespoons cocoa, 3 eggs, 2 teaspoons baking powder, ½ teacup sifted pastry flour, 1 teaspoon vanilla. Cream the butter in a warm dish until soft, but not melted, stir in the sugar gradually, beaten well, then the beaten yolks of the eggs, also the vanilla, sift the baking powder and cocoa with half cup flour and stir this in the mixture first, then alternate the milk and flour, using enough flour to make a mixture stiff enough to drop with a spoon. Beat vigorously, then fold in the stiffly beaten white of the eggs. Bake in a loaf in a moderately hot oven thirty-five minutes, according to the size and shape of the pan. Cake mixture should be a little stiffer than for jems or layer cake. Never beat the cake after the whites are added.

Test for baking. It is baked enough when, first, it shrinks from the pan; second, touching it on the top it springs back; third, no singing sound.

(Vermontville, 1906)

Crystal Falls Cake

Three eggs beaten very light; 1 cupful sugar; beat well; add 1 cupful walnut meats broken; 1 cupful dates; 1½ cupsful flour; 1 teaspoonful baking powder; 1 teaspoonful vanilla; pinch of salt. Will be very stiff and need to be spread on with a knife; cut in squares, and dip in powdered sugar.

Mrs. Rumford
(Flint, 1912)

Dark Cake

Brown sugar, 2 cups; molasses, 1 cup; butter, 1 cup; raisins, chopped, 2 cups; sour milk, 1 cup; saleratus, 2 tea-spoonfuls; 3 eggs; flour, 5 cups; cloves and cinnamon, of each, 1 table-spoonful; allspice, 1 tea-spoonful; 1 small nutmeg, all well beaten.

Remarks—Mrs. C. B. Greely, of Alpena, Mich., says: This makes two good sized loaves. Is splendid! Don't get too much butter in, take large cups of flour, etc.

(Ann Arbor, 1884)

Date Cake

Yolks of 12 eggs and 1 pound powdered sugar beaten together, a little over ½ bar Baker's chocolate grated, grated rind and juice of 1 lemon, 1

Hunter's sifter could do just about anything but interest the operator in her work (Cincinnati, 1884).

teaspoon allspice, 1 teaspoon cinnamon, 1 cup chopped dates, 5 cents worth chopped almonds, 1 cup cracker meal, (this is bought in packages). Add the beaten whites the last thing before the vanilla.

Louise M. Haynes
(Kalamazoo, 1899)

In 1899, 5 cents worth of chopped almonds equalled 2 ounces.

Delicious Cake

One cup flour, 1 cup sugar, 1 teaspoon baking powder, sifted three times; butter size of an egg melted in a cup, then break 2 eggs into a cup and fill with milk; pour into sifted flour and sugar, add flavoring and beat well. Bake in loaf as for layer cake. Do not think that it will be just as good if the flour and sugar are not sifted three times, for it will not.

Mrs. C. Ver Cies
(Kalamazoo, 1920)

Spare the sifter and spoil the cake!

Economy Cake

Boil together three minutes the following: 1 c. brown sugar, 1 c. seeded, or seedless, raisins, 1 c.

water, ⅓ c. shortening, 1 tsp. nutmeg, cinnamon, cloves and salt, each; when cold add 1 tsp. soda dissolved in warm water, 2 c. flour containing tsp. baking powder, bake in slow oven.

Grace H. Peck
(Kalamazoo, 1921)

Fanny's Molasses Cake

One cupful of molasses, one egg, two-thirds of a cupful of sour cream, one teaspoonful of ginger, one-half teaspoon of soda, flour to make not very stiff. Eat warm with butter.

(Battle Creek, 1890)

New England Fire Cakes

Make a pie crust not quite as rich as for puff paste. Cut off small pieces and roll out to about the size of a breakfast plate and as nearly round as possible. Have a griddle over the fire. Grease and place one cake on it and bake a nice brown. Turn it when done on one side and brown nicely on the other. When done put on a plate and butter it well. Spread a layer of preserved strawberries or raspberries on it. Have ready another cake and bake. Pile one upon the other and butter and spread layers of preserves until all the pastry you have made is cooked. Serve quite hot. Cut down through all the layers. It is an old-fashioned New England cake and in olden times was cooked in iron spiders propped up before the kitchen fire; hence its name. It is a very nice shortcake to be eaten hot for luncheon or supper.

Miss Helen Brown, Hudson
(Chicago, 1896)

French Loaf Cake—Plain

Sugar, 2 cups; butter, ½ cup; sweet milk, 1 cup; flour, 3 cups; 3 eggs; baking powder, 3 teaspoonfuls. Directions—Cream the sugar and butter together with the hand; beat the eggs well and stir in; then add the milk; stir the baking powder into the sifted flour and mix in thoroughly, and bake in a moderate oven two fair-sized cakes.

Remarks—Flavoring of any kind may be used; but the first time I ate of it was at my own table, made by one of my married daughters, without flavoring. If flavoring is used, of course it is not plain, and it certainly is very nice with any flavoring.

(Ann Arbor, 1884)

Food for the Gods

Whites of 6 eggs beaten stiff, 2 cups sugar, 6 tablespoons cracker crumbs, 2 teaspoons baking powder, 1 cup chopped English walnuts, 1 cup cut dates. Bake in slow oven ½ hour. Serve with whipped cream.

Cora Tullis Reed, Benton Harbor
(Charlotte, 1909)

Fruit Cake

Three-fourths lb. butter, 1 lb. brown sugar, 8 eggs, 2 lbs. raisins, 2 lbs. currants, 1 lb. citron chopped fine, ½ c. molasses, 1 tsp. cloves, 1 tsp. cinnamon, 4 cups flour, 2 teaspoons baking powder, 1 wine glass sherry, 1 wine glass brandy.

Mrs. E. Ranch
(Kalamazoo, 1921)

Drop Fruit Cakes

One and one-half c. brown sugar, 1 scant c. lard, 3 well beaten eggs, 3 tbsp. hot water, ½ c. sour milk or cream, 1 tsp. soda, 1 tsp. vanila, 1 hp. tsp. cinnamon, ½ tsp. cloves, 2¼ c. flour, 1 c. raisins, 1 c. walnut meats.

Mrs. Beerstecher
(Kalamazoo, 1921)

Black Fruit Cake

Four pounds raisins, 3 pounds currants, 1 pound citron, 1 pound almonds, 1 pound sugar, 1 ¼ pound butter, 1 pound flour, 16 eggs, 2 wine glasses liquid, 1 cup molasses, spices to taste. Cream butter and sugar, add yolks beaten, wash currants in 3 or 4 waters, dry well and rub in flour, also raisins. Put in cake with molasses, liquid, spices, add a little salt, last the whites of 16 eggs well beaten. Put in cake pan thin layer of the dough, then almonds blanched and cut in thin pieces. A layer of dough and thin pieces of citron. Cover the dough well with citron and almonds, and do so up to the top of the pan. Bake 3 or 4 hours in a slow oven.

Mrs. A. B. Williams
(Higgins Lake, 1920)

White Fruit Cake

One and one-half cups pulverized sugar, ⅔ cup of butter, 1 cup of milk, 3½ cups flour, 1 cup seeded raisins, 2 teaspoons of baking powder, whites of 4 eggs, flavor to taste.

Mrs. L. C. G.
(Muskegon, 1890)

In our experience, the only Victorian cookbooks that rivaled Dr. Chase's Ann Arbor compendiums in popularity were the many editions of the *White House Cook Book*. Hugo Ziemann, "at one time caterer for that Prince Napoleon who was killed fighting the Zulus in Africa," and Mrs. F. L. Gillette, who had "made a life long and thorough study of cookery and housekeeping," collaborated to produce the first edition in 1887. Ziemann went on to further culinary laurels, including the laying of a "famous spread to which the chiefs of the warring factions of the Republican convention sat down in June, 1888, and from which they arose with asperities softened, difference harmonized and victory organized." Anyone who could so soften Republican asperities deserved a place in the White House, which Ziemann apparently got as chief steward.

We don't know what happened to Mrs. Gillette, but the cookbook she co-authored went through many large editions. Each time a new First Lady oversaw White House domestic economy, her visage graced the frontispiece of a new edition of the *White House Cook Book*. Portraits of Frances Folson Cleveland, Ida Saxton McKinley, Edith Bohling Wilson, and other First Ladies gazed benevolently at the millions of their countrywomen who purchased the oversized volumes. Republican and

Hugo Ziemann and his celebrated white house kitchen (White House, 1925).

Democratic administrations came and went, Ida McKinley's husband fell to an assassin's bullet, a roughriding cowboy took his place, and two wars were fought, but the pages of the *White House Cook Book* seemed frozen in time. The publishers were not about to ruin a lucrative item with unnecessary revisions. Finally in 1925, when Grace Goodhue Coolidge, wife of "silent Cal," assumed her place of honor in the cookbook, a new editor, Mrs. Mary E. Dague, made a few amendments. Among them, she finally credited the following recipe, which had appeared in the cookbook for decades, to Mrs. S. A. Camp of Grand Rapids.

Fruit Cake by Measure (excellent)

One and one half cupfuls of butter, three cupfuls of dark brown sugar, six eggs, whites and yolks beaten separately, one pound of raisins, seeded, one of currants, washed and dried, and half a pound of citron cut in thin strips; also half a cupful of cooking molasses and half a cupful of sour milk. Stir the butter and sugar to a cream, add to that half a grated nutmeg, one tablespoonful of mace, add the molasses and sourmilk. Stir all well; then put in the beaten yolks of eggs, two tablespoons lemon juice, two tablespoons cold strong coffee; stir again all thoroughly, and add four cupfuls of sifted flour alternately with the beaten whites of eggs. Now dissolve a level teaspoonful of soda and stir in thoroughly. Mix the fruit together and stir into it two heaping tablespoonfuls of flour; then stir it in the cake. Butter two common-sized cake pans carefully, line them with letter paper well buttered, and bake in a moderate oven two hours. After it is baked, let cool in the pan. Afterward put it into a tight can, or let it remain in the pans and cover tightly. Best recipe of all.

Mrs. S. A. Camp, Grand Rapids
(White House, 1925)

Hickory Nut Cake

Two cups sugar, ⅔ cup butter, 3 eggs, 3 cups Silver Leaf flour, 2 teaspoons Christie's Perfect Baking Powder, 1 cup nut meats chopped fine.

Mrs. Geo. Huff, Ironwood
(Muskegon, 1899)

Jam Cake

One cup white sugar; ½ cup shortening; 3 eggs; 3 tablespoonfuls of sour milk; 1 teaspoonful of soda; 1 teaspoonful allspice, cinnamon, nutmeg; 1 cup of jam; 1½ cups flour. Bake in layers; put together with any frosting.

Mrs. English
(Flint, 1912)

Roll Jelly Cake

One cup sugar, 3 eggs, 3 tablespoons boiling water, 1½ cups French's White Lily flour, 2 teaspoons baking powder. Bake in dripping pan, spread with jelly and roll up in napkin.

Mrs. Dr. Drake
(Hastings, 1921)

Iron Mountain Cake

One cup sugar, ⅔ cup milk, ½ cup butter, 2 eggs, yolks and whites beaten separately, 2 cups

French's White Lily flour, 1 heaping teaspoon baking powder, 1 teaspoon vanilla. Makes 1 qt. loaf.

(Hastings, 1921)

King George Cake

One c. white sugar, ¾ c. butter, 1 c. molasses, 3 eggs, 1 c. sour milk, 1 tsp. soda dissolved in the milk, ½ nutmeg, 1 tsp. cinnamon, small tsp. cloves, 3 c. flour, ½ lb. raisins cut up.

Mrs. W. G. Bray
(Kalamazoo, 1921)

Lemon Honey Cake

Two cups of sugar, two-thirds of a cup of butter, one cup of sweet milk, one cup of corn starch, three cups of flour, three teaspoonfuls of baking powder; rub the butter and sugar to a cream, then add the milk, lastly the whites of eight eggs beaten to a stiff froth, then the corn starch and flour to which has been added the baking powder; bake in jelly tins.

Lemon Honey for same

Take one pound of loaf sugar, the yolks of eight eggs with two whole ones, juice of six lemons, grated rind of two, quarter of a pound of butter. Put the sugar, lemons and butter in a saucepan, melt over a gentle fire; when all are dissolved stir in the eggs which have been well beaten; stir rapidly until it is as thick as honey. Spread this between the layers of cake. Set aside the remainder in a closely covered vessel for future use.

(Detroit, 1878)

Lunch Cake

Beat thoroughly 2 cups butter and 2 cups sugar; add 2 cups egg well beaten, 1½ pints flour sifted with 1 heaping teaspoon baking powder, 1 gill wine, 1 teaspoon each extract rose, cinnamon, and nutmeg; mix into a smooth batter and bake in a moderate oven 1 hour; when cold, ice with white icing.

(Detroit, 1890)

M'Kinley Drop Cake

Two eggs, 2 cups "C" sugar, 1 cup lard and butter mixed, 1 cup molasses, 1½ cups sour milk, 2 teaspoons soda, 3 teaspoons ginger, flour to make a thick batter. Drop in pan in small spoonsful.

(Vermontville, 1906)

"C" sugar was a grade of cane sugar similar to our present brown sugar.

Marsh Mallow Cake

One cupful of sugar, one-half pound of butter, one-half cupful of milk, two cupfuls of flour, one teaspoonful of cream of tartar, one-half teaspoonful of soda, whites of six eggs, cream the butter and sugar, sift the soda and cream of tartar with the flour; add the eggs lastly, beaten to a stiff froth, and one teaspoonful of Pistach extract. Bake in layers and put together with a boiled frosting. On each layer and on the top place marshmallows which have been split in two; press them into the frosting while it is warm and put them around the edge as thickly as possible.

Miss Kitty Emery, Muskegon
(Chicago, 1898)

Pistach, or properly pistache, is the flavoring of the pistachio nut.

National Cake

White part—Cream together 1 cup white sugar and ½ cup of butter, then add ½ cup of sweet milk, the beaten whites of 4 eggs, ½ cup of corn starch, 1 cup of flour into which has been mixed 1 tea-spoonful of cream tartar and ½ tea-spoonful of soda. Flavor with lemon extract.

Blue part—Cream together 1 cup of blue sugar a ½ cup of butter, then add ½ cup of sweet milk, the beaten whites of 4 eggs and 2 cups of flour, in which mix 1 tea-spoonful of cream of tartar and ½ tea-spoonful of soda. No flavor.

Red part—Cream together 1 cup of red sugar and ½ cup of butter, then add ½ cup of sweet milk, the beaten whites of 4 eggs and 2 cups of flour, in which mix ½ tea-spoonful of cream of tartar and ½ tea-spoonful of soda. No flavor. Place in a bake pan, first the red, then the white, and last the blue. Bake in a moderate oven.

(Ann Arbor, 1884)

The perfect cake for the Fourth of July. Instead of using colored sugars in the cake, try food coloring.

Minnehaha Cake No. 1

Two cups sugar, ½ cup butter, 3 cups flour, 1 cup milk, 3 teaspoons baking powder. Filling—Two cups sugar, 4 or 5 teaspoons boiling water, boil till it threads from the spoon, have ready the beaten whites of 2 eggs, pour the boiling liquid over the eggs, beating till cool, then add 1 cup of English walnuts broken fine and 1 cup of small raisins, spread between layer and on top of cake.

M. S. Ionia
(Muskegon, 1890)

Cheap Minnehaha Cake

One cup sugar, piece of butter the size of an egg, yolks of 2 eggs, 1 cup milk or water, 2 cups flour, 2 teaspoons cream of tartar, 1 of soda. Bake this in 3 or 4 tins according to their size.

For the Layers—One and one-half cups sugar in a basin, put on a little water, let boil till it ropes; have the whites of the eggs beaten to a stiff froth and add. Have a cup of raisins chopped fine, add them, stirring briskly so it will not cook in lumps. Spread between the layers and on top. Try it.

(Detroit, 1890)

According to Jessup Whitehead's classic, *The Steward's Handbook*, first published in 1887, sugar threads (called ropes or hairs) at 230°. Whitehead's test, which seems a sure way to burn your fingers, is to "dip the handle of a teaspoon into the boiling sugar, draw it between your finger and thumb, close your finger and thumb together and gently part them, when, if you perceive a threadlike appearance between them, it has passed into this degree." Perhaps Victorian cooks had fire-hardened their hands through the routine procedure of testing the heat of the oven by counting how many seconds they could keep their arm in it. Modern cooks might prefer to test the hairing quality of molten sugar by letting it run from a spoon.

Nut Cake

⅔ cups sugar
1 egg
⅔ cup milk
1 tablespoon butter
1⅔ cups flour
3 teaspoons baking
   powder

1 cup nut meats
   chopped fine and
   sprinkled with flour
1 teaspoon vanilla
1 teaspoon lemon

M. C., Bad Axe
(Freeport IL, 1915)

Oatmeal Cake

One-half c. sugar, 1 c. sour milk with 1 tsp. soda, 2½ c. ground oatmeal, 1 c. raisins, spices to taste, salt, 1 egg, butter size of walnut, ½ tsp. baking powder.

Mrs. Lucy Knappen
(Kalamazoo, 1921)

Old-fashioned Loaf Cake

Three pounds (three quarts sifted and well heaped) flour, one and a fourth pounds (a rounded pint of soft) butter, one and three-fourth pounds (one quart) sugar, five gills new milk, half pint yeast, three eggs, two pounds raisins, tea-spoon soda, gill of brandy or wine, or a fourth pint of molasses, two tea-spoons cinnamon and two of nutmeg. Scald the milk, cool to blood warm, add the yeast, then the flour, to which all the butter and half the sugar have been added; then mix together, and let rise until light. It is better to set this sponge over night, and in the morning add the other ingredients (flouring raisins), and let rise again. When light, fill baking-pans and let rise again. Bake in a moderate

oven. This recipe makes three *large* loaves, and is a standard, economical loaf-cake.

Mrs. Ex-Gov. John J. Bagley
(Minneapolis, 1881)

The year Mrs. Bagley submitted this recipe turned out tragically. Her husband, John Judson Bagley, had served as governor of Michigan from 1873 to 1877. In 1881 he ran as a candidate for the U.S. Senate but came one vote shy of receiving the caucus Republican nomination. He died suddenly on December 27, 1881, at the age of forty-nine, leaving Mrs. Bagley and seven children.

Orange Cake

Two cups of sugar; two cups of flour; one-half cup of cold water; one and one-half tea spoonfuls baking powder; three whole eggs and yolks of two. Bake in layers.

Filling—Beat the whites of two eggs with sugar enough to make a good frosting; add the grated rind and juice of one orange; when nearly cold spread on the cakes and stack.

Lou McDeid
(Mendon, 1890)

We made this as a sheet cake in an 8 × 13 inch pan. Bake it at 350° for 25 minutes. The filling tends to be thin, so use a small orange. The cake is delectable with a texture similar to pound cake.

Orange Jelly Cake

Jelly—The grated rind and all the pulp of 1 orange except the white skin, add 1 cup water, 1 cup sugar, 2 tablespoons flour with a little of the water; then cook together. When cold spread between the layers of the cake. If wished, grate in a little sour apple.

Cake—4 eggs (leave out white of 1 egg to frost with), 1 cup sugar, 1 cup flour, 1½ teaspoons baking powder, butter size of an egg, 3 tablespoons sweet milk; flavor to taste.

Mrs. C. H. Leonard
(Grand Rapids, 1890)

Keystone Peach Cake

Separate 10 eggs, add to the yolks 1 lb. powdered sugar, and with No. 2 beater beat until very, very light, about 1 minute. Now with No. 1 beater beat the whites to stiff froth, add them carefully to the yolks, mix gently by giving the machine a backward and forward motion; and now add gradually, continuing this motion, a ½ lb. sifted flour. Line a large, shallow pan with greased paper, turn in the mixture and bake in a quick oven 15 minutes. While the cake is baking prepare the following filling: Put ½ pint milk on to boil in a farina boiler; beat 1½ tablespoons cornstarch, 2 tablespoons sugar and 3 eggs together until very light (use small beater); add this to the boiling milk and stir continually until it thickens; take from the fire and stand away to cool. When the cake is done, turn it carefully from the pan, bottom upwards, and spread it, while warm, with the filling. Cut the cake in halves; place over one half, and in the filling, mellow peaches, pared and divided into quarters. Now fold the bottoms together, thus having two layers of cake with a thick layer of filling and peaches between. Cover the top with halves of peaches, dust thickly with powdered sugar, and serve with cream. Delicious.

Mrs. Rorer
(Grand Rapids, 1890)

A farina boiler is a double boiler.

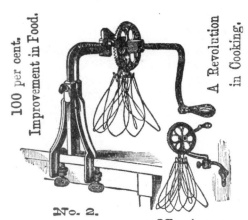

Keystone culinary beaters, available in two models, promised to "reduce the work of an hour to a few minutes" (Grand Rapids, 1890).

Pecan Cake

1 pound sifted flour	*1 teaspoon baking powder*
1 pound sugar	
1 ½ pound raisins	*1 nutmeg grated*
½ pound butter	*6 eggs*
1½ quarts shelled pecans	*1 glass whiskey*

Flour fruit with part in measure flour and bake two hours in moderate oven.

This recipe was sent to Mrs. Bessie Ketcham Gaylord by Angelique Alexander Tray, Ethel and Connie Alexander.

(Higgins Lake, 1920)

Pork Cake

Grind a pound of salt pork fine and pour over it a pint of boiling coffee. Stir until the pork is well blended with the coffee. Then add two cups of brown sugar, two cups of New Orleans molasses, a teaspoonful each of cinnamon, cloves, and allspice, all ground; 1 grated nutmeg, 2 heaping teaspoonfuls of baking soda, a pound each of seedless raisins and cleaned currants, and half a pound of shredded citron (the fruit mixed and well dredged with flour) and eight cups of sifted flour. Mix well and bake slowly for an hour and a half.

Mrs. F. A. Stebbins
(Manistee, 1929)

Prince of Wales Cake

Yolks of 3 eggs and white of 1, 1 cup brown sugar, ½ cup butter, ½ cup molasses, 1 cup sour milk, 1 teaspoon each, of soda and cinnamon, ½ teaspoon each of cloves, nutmeg and baking powder, 2½ cups flour. This amount will make three layers.

Filling—Two cups sugar, ½ cup water. Boil until it "hairs." Pour slowly into the well beaten whites of 2 eggs. Reserve part of this for the frosting of the upper layer, while into the rest stir well 1 cup chopped raisins for the filling between layers.

Mrs. George E. Foote, Kalamazoo
(Charlotte, 1909)

Prune Cake

Two-thirds cup butter, 1 cup flour, 1 cup sugar, 1 teaspoon soda in 2 tablespoons prune juice, ½ teaspoon each cinnamon, cloves and nutmeg.

Cream butter and sugar and add well beaten egg. Add prunes stoned and cut. Add sifted flour and spices, add soda in prune juice. Bake in 2 layer in moderate oven about 20 minutes. Put together with whipped cream to which has been added chopped almonds, cherries or pineapple.

Mrs. P. P. Schnorbach
(Manistee, 1929)

Queen's Cake

Two cups sugar, 1 cup butter, 2½ cups flour, 3 cups fruit, 3 eggs, 1 nutmeg, ½ cup wine, ½ cup cream, 1 teaspoon soda, ½ teaspoon alum.

Mrs. P. C. Davis
(Kalamazoo, 1899)

Scripture Cake

Four and a half cups of I Kings IX, 22; 1½ cups of Judges V, 25 (last clause); 2 cups of Jeremiah VI, 20 (sugar); 2 cups of I Samuel XXX, 12 (raisins); 2 cups of Nahum III, 12; 1 cup of Numbers XXIII, 12; season to taste of II Chronicles IX, 9; ½ cup of Judges IV, 5 (last clause); the whites of 5 of Job IV, 6; a pinch of Leviticus II, 13; 2 tablespoons of Amos IV, 5 (baking powder); Follow Solomon's prescription for making a good boy, Proverbs XXIII, 14, and you will have a good cake.

(Vermontville, 1906)

This is a recipe found in many early cookbooks compiled by church guilds. Larry remembers his grandmother making it. It is similar to a Spanish bar or spice cake. Consult the King James Version of the Bible to unravel the puzzle.

Shrewsbury Cakes

Two cupfuls of butter, 1 pt. of white sugar, 3 pts. of flour, 4 eggs, half a teaspoonful of mace. Roll thin, cut into small cakes and bake in a quick oven. Not a particle more of the flour than is given above must be used. The cake should be made in a rather cool room, and they cannot be made in very warm weather. They can be kept a long time, and are delicious.

Mrs. H. D. Baker
(Muskegon, 1890)

Snow Cake

Half tea-cup butter, one of sugar, one and a half of flour, half cup sweet milk, whites of four eggs, tea-spoon baking powder; flavor with lemon.

Mrs. Wm. Patrick, Midland
(Minneapolis, 1881)

Spice Layer Cake

Four eggs, reserving the whites of 2 if small, the white of 1 if large, 2 cups brown sugar, ½ cup butter, ½ cup sour milk, 1 teaspoon soda, 1 teaspoon cinnamon, ½ teaspoon of cloves, 2 scant cups of flour. Bake in 3 layers.

Raisin filling—One cup raisins, seeded, chopped and stirred into boiled icing, for which the whites of 2 eggs, if small, are to be reserved as before said. Use 2 scant cups of sugar to 2 small eggs, 1 cup to one large egg. This is a delicious cake.

Estella I. Kneeland, Traverse City
(Charlotte, 1909)

Layer-Coffee Spice Cake

One-third cup shortening and 1 cup sugar, beat until smooth; 2 egg yolks beaten light; two-thirds cup strong coffee, cold; 2 cups flour; 3 teaspoons baking powder; salt; 1 teaspoon cinnamon; ½ teaspoon cloves; ¼ teaspoon allspice; add last beaten whites of eggs. Mocha frosting and filling—1½ tablespoons butter; 2½ cups confectionary sugar; 2½ tablespoons cocoa, 4 tablespoons coffee; ¼ tsp. salt.

Mrs. Agnes Murray
(Manistee, 1929)

Mrs. Chase's Sponge Cake

Sugar, 1 cup; 4 eggs; sweet milk, 3 tablespoonfuls; flour, 2 cups; baking powder, 2 teaspoonfuls; salt, 1 pinch; orange or lemon extract (home-made), 2 tea-spoonfuls. Directions—Beat the eggs, then beat in the sugar, add the milk, salt and flavor; and, having mixed the baking powder into the flour, sift it in, beat all together and bake in a quick oven.

Remarks—This will make 2 cakes if baked in the round tin, or 1 in the square. I have eaten of this many times with great satisfaction, and expect the same in eating of the one which, I am just informed, is ready for tea. Sponge cake is credited with being the most healthful of any form of cake, for the reason that, as a general thing, no butter or other shortening is used, although of late, some people are beginning to introduce them; but, for myself, I am very fond of one of the above, coming warm from the oven at tea-time, having some very nice butter to eat with it. Those who are dyspeptic had better forego this luxury.

(Ann Arbor, 1884)

Mother's Sponge Cake

One scant cup granulated sugar, 3 eggs beaten very light, ⅓ cup milk, ½ teaspoon soda, ½ teaspoon cream tartar, or 1 teaspoon baking powder, 1 cup flour, vanilla.

Winnifred Weaver Dodge
(Charlotte, 1909)

Strawberry Cake

One scant cup powdered sugar, 1 heaping cup flour, one tablespoon butter, 2 or 3 tablespoons sweet cream, 3 eggs beaten separately, 3 teaspoons baking powder. Cream butter and sugar, add the beaten yolks, the cream, flour, and lastly the whites of eggs. Bake in two cakes, put crushed berries between. Ice the top, placing whole strawberries here and there. Serve with sugar and cream.

Mrs. Louise G. Harrison, Detroit
(Kalamazoo, 1899)

Tomato Soup Cake

1 cup sugar	¼ tsp. salt
2 tbsp. shortening	1 can tomato soup
1 tsp. cinnamon	1½ cup flour
1 tsp. nutmeg	1 cup raisins
1 tsp. soda	½ cup nut meats

Cream shortening, add sugar, then tomato soup, then flour, cinnamon, nutmeg, salt and soda. Then add raisins and nut meats and bake in loaf about 50 minutes in moderate oven, 350°

Mrs. E. G. McMahon
(Kalamazoo, 1945)

The tomato soup gives the cake a rich dark color. Double the recipe if you want a two-layer cake. See Mrs. Harry Fawley's recipe for the frosting (page 255).

Kartoffel Torte (German Potato Cake)

Pass through a ricer or sieve enough cold boiled potatoes to make 2 cupsful. Chop fine enough blanched almonds to make 1 cup. Sift together 3 times; 2 cups of flour, 2 level teaspoons baking powder, 1 scant teaspoon salt, 1 teaspoon cinnamon, ½ teaspoon cloves. Cream 1 cup butter and gradually beat in 2 cups sugar and 1 cup sweet chocolate grated. Then add the beaten yolks of 4 eggs, ¾ cup milk, the potatoes, flour and almonds, and lastly the beaten whites of the 4 eggs. Bake in large tube cake pan, in moderate oven for 1 hour. When cold, cover with chocolate icing.

L. K. W.
(Charlotte, 1909)

Two-Minute Cake

Two eggs broken in cup, fill cup with sweet milk, 1½ c. flour, 1 c. sugar, 2 tsp. baking powder, sift sugar, flour and baking powder together, add 5 tbsp. melted butter last. Flavor with vanilla, beat well.

Mrs. G. P. Truesdale
(Kalamazoo, 1921)

U. of M. Cake

One cup sugar, ½ cup butter, 1 cup milk, 2 eggs, 2 teaspoons baking powder, 2 cups flour, using cornstarch, Thoman's Moss Rose flour and corn flour, ⅓ of each. Bake in square tin.

(Lansing, 1920)

What a nasty thing to put in a Lansing cookbook!

Walnut Cake

Scant ½ cup butter, 1 cup of powdered sugar, ½ cup sweet milk 2½ cups flour, 2 full teaspoons baking powder, scant half teaspoon of bitter almond extract, 1 cup coarsely broken English walnut meats, 1 cup seedless raisins, whites of 4 eggs. Cream butter and sugar, add flavoring, milk, flour after being sifted with baking powder several times, beat briskly one minute, add eggs beaten to a stiff froth, mix well. Lastly add fruit which should be floured. Bake in a tin with opening in center if possible; bake slowly in an oven previously well heated.

Mrs. Fred Loveless
(Muskegon, 1890)

Watermelon Cake

I. White sugar, 2 cups; butter and sweet milk, each ⅔ cup; whites of 5 eggs; flour, 3 cups; baking powder, 1 tea-spoonful. Directions—Beat the eggs, sugar, butter and milk together; put the baking powder into the flour before sifting it in, and mix.

II. Red sugar (kept by confectioners), 1 cup; butter and sweet milk, each ½ cup; flour, 2 cups; baking powder, 1 tea-spoonful; whites of five eggs: raisins (nice large ones), ½ lb. Directions—Beat together in the same order as the first, cut the raisins into halves, the longest way, and mix in last; then put some of the first into the pan, hollowing it in the center to receive all of the second or red part, if it is sufficiently stiff to allow it, piling it up in the round form as neatly as possible, to represent the red core of the melon; then cover with the balance of the white, so you have a white outside and a red core, like a watermelon, if neatly done.

(Ann Arbor, 1884)

This is a fun cake. We made it for an anniversary party. Bake this cake at 350° for 45 min and turn oven down to 325° for 15 min. We baked the cake in a large, ovenproof bowl so that it came out round like a watermelon. We put green food coloring in the frosting and used red food coloring instead of red sugar in the batter. Like many of the nineteenth-century cake recipes we have tried, it had a heavy, grainy texture and a delicious taste. Check with a toothpick to make sure the center is done.

Weary Willy Cake

One cup sugar, 1 cup flour, 1 heaping teaspoon baking powder, sift together; 2 eggs broken into cup, fill cup with sweet milk, 2 squares chocolate melted with 2 tablespoons butter, add eggs and milk to dry ingredients, then add chocolate and butter; bake slowly in 2 layers filling and frosting; 2 cups powdered sugar, 2 large tablespoons butter, 1 teaspoon milk, 4 teaspoons cocoa, 4 tablespoons boiling water or coffee, beat until creamy and then spread between layers and on top.

Mrs. F. W. White
(Manistee, 1890)

Wedding Cake

2 coffee cups sugar
1½ coffee cups butter
4 coffee cups flour
10 eggs
1 pint New Orleans molasses
6 pounds raisins
4 pounds currants
3 pounds citron

1 quart brandy
1 teacupful cinnamon
8 nutmegs
1 tablespoonful extract bitter almonds
1 tablespoonful extract lemon
½ teaspoon soda
(Original)

Mix everything together and bake at 325° for an hour. Too many slices of this and it would be a short wedding!

Mrs. J. B. Daniels
(Kalamazoo, 1906)

Upside Down Cake

Three tablespoons butter, melt and add 1 cup brown sugar, 3 eggs (well beaten), 1 scant cup white sugar, 1 cup flour, alternate with 3 tablespoons pineapple juice, 1½ teaspoons baking powder in flour. Cover sugar (brown) and butter with slices of pineapple; pour batter over it and bake. When done, turn upside down. Serve with whipped cream.

Mrs. Harold Rasmusson
(Grayling, 1937)

Zucker Kuchen (Sugar Cake)

Take bread dough, as large as a good-sized leaf; one pint of milk, a small cup of butter, two handfuls of sugar, and a teaspoonful of cinnamon. Mix the butter in the milk, on the stove; make a hole in the dough, put in the sugar, two eggs and the cinnamon; then add the warm milk and butter, mix well, add flour enough to make a light dough; let it rise again. Roll it out one and one-half inches thick, put in a dripping-pan; beat light one egg and spread it over the top; lay on pieces of butter, rais-

ins and chopped almonds, and sifted sugar on the top. Bake in a hot oven fifteen or sixteen minutes.

(Detroit, 1878)

Frostings and Fillings

Butternut Filling

To whites of 2 eggs, add ½ cup chopped butternuts, and 1 cup of sugar. Whip the whites and sugar first, then add the nuts. Spread between the layers.

(Kalamazoo, 1906)

Chocolate Frosting

Two whites of eggs; beat to a stiff froth. Add 1½ cups pulverized sugar, 6 tablespoons grated chocolate. ½ tablespoon essence of vanilla.

Mrs. J. P. Howlett, Niles
(Chicago, 1886)

Fig Filling

1 lb. figs, chopped fine
2 tumblers sugar

1 pint wine

Cook in double boiler till thick, like jelly. This is enough for two cakes of 3 layers each.

Mary H. Peck
(Kalamazoo, 1906)

Hickorynut Filling

One coffee cup milk, 1 tablespoon flour, 2 tablespoons sugar, yolks of 4 eggs. Heat the milk and sugar in a double boiler, add flour mixed with a little cold milk, then the well beaten yolks. After taking from stove stir in 1 cup hickorynut meats chopped fine and 1 teaspoon vanilla.

Mrs. A. S. White
(Kalamazoo, 1899)

Filling with Hickorynuts for Layer Cake

One cup sour cream, one-half cup of granulated sugar cooked until it strings, stir in 1 cup of rolled hickorynuts.

(Vermontville, 1906)

Lemon Jelly for Cake

A cup of sugar, 1 tablespoon of butter, grated rind and juice of one lemon, 1 sour apple grated. A heaping teaspoon of flour put with the sugar, a half cup of boiling water and let boil about 5 minutes. Just before taking from the stove stir in one beaten egg.

Mrs. Geo. D. Smith
(Muskegon, 1890)

Maple Icing

1 tablespoon hot coffee	Few drops of vanilla
3 tablespoons maple syrup	Confectioner's sugar

Mix together coffee, syrup and vanilla and beat in confectioner's sugar till stiff enough to spread.

(Detroit, 1935)

Meringue Paste

Whites 10 eggs, 1 lb. powdered sugar, 2 teaspoons flavoring. Have everything cold and dry, put eggs in deep bowl to whip, using whisk made of bunch of wires, beat until you can turn the bowl up side down, add sugar and flavoring all at once. Spread it on cake and sift a little powdered sugar over it, set in the oven 10 or 15 minutes.

John Rorig
D. Christie & Co.
(Muskegon, 1890)

D. Christie & Company was a grocery store located on W. Western Avenue in Muskegon. It specialized in wholesale and retail oysters as well as the manufacture of baking powder.

Marshmallow Filling

Two cups sugar, 1 cup water; let boil three minutes; then add 10 cents worth of marshmallow, cut up in small pieces, let this cook till it hairs, stirring constantly, turn this into a dish into which has been beaten the white of 1 egg, beat all together until thick, and then add 10 cents worth of shelled almonds (but not blanched), and then spread on cake. Delicious.

(Vermontville, 1906)

In 1906, 10 cents worth of marshmallows equaled 1 pound and 10 cents worth of almonds equaled 4 ounces.

Peanut Butter Boiled Icing

One-fourth c. peanut butter, 1 c. sugar, ½ c. water, butter, 1 egg white. Combine sugar and water and boil gently until a thread is formed when the spoon is lifted from the cooking mixture. Pour this syrup in a fine stream on the egg white, which should be beaten stiff, and then add the peanut butter. Place over hot water and cook for a few moments until the icing is a little dry around the edge, when it is ready to be beaten until thickened and used on any plain cake.

Miss Aileen Thomas
(Kalamazoo, 1921)

Frosting for Tomato Soup Cake

One package Phil. cream cheese, mix with 2 tablespoons powdered sugar; add 1 tablespoon melted butter, add 2 more tablespoons powdered sugar, 1 teaspoon vanilla. Mix well and spread on top of cake when cake is cool.

Mrs. Harry Fawley
(Kalamazoo, 1945)

Walnut Caramel Frosting

One pound of light brown sugar, one cupful of cream, small cupful of butter, boil twenty minutes, add half a pound of finely chopped nut meats, one teaspoonful of vanilla. Stir till cool and right thickness to spread.

Mrs. C. E. Scott, Escanaba
(Chicago, 1898)

A Cheap Flavoring

An inexpensive but good flavoring for cake and puddings is made as follows: Put seven green peach leaves in a cup, and pour on them two tablespoonfuls of boiling water, cover tightly for a few moments. Allow two teaspoonfuls for one cake.

(Battle Creek, 1890)

PIES and TARTS

Crusts and Pastries

Puff Paste, Pies and Tartlets

Use the best of fresh lard for pastry, or the crust will be bitter, tough, and anything but flaky. The best way to secure good lard is to take the leaf and try out the lard, and then you are sure of having the genuine article. Keep a board or marble slab purposely for pastry, and see that it is never used for any other purpose except to mold bread or pastry upon. A good way to avoid wasting flour each time you use your kneading board is to brush it carefully off the board into a small sieve; sift out the flour, it will be good to use again.

An economical pie crust is made by allowing one cup of flour and a large spoonful of lard to each covered pie of ordinary size. Sift the flour and take out a handful for rolling out; add a pinch of salt for each pie; put your lard into the flour in lumps as large as an almond, but do not rub, as every lump will make it flaky; work in as much cold water as will make a dough just soft enough to roll easily; handle as little as possible to form an oblong roll of dough, and cut into as many slices as you need tops and bottoms; lay the cut side on the board and roll just large enough to cover your platter neatly; roll top crust very thin and bake well in a quick oven, and you will surely have good pie crust, even in warm weather. For meat pies use less shortening and put in a little yeast powder; roll top crust of meat pies half an inch thick, and line sides only of the pan.

The real puff paste for tarts or pies is made in this way: Before beginning operations, select the coolest possible place in which to work, use a marble slab, if possible, when rolling out the paste for pies, and work quickly, handling as little as possible. To a pound of flour a pound of butter is generally supposed necessary, but a half a pound of shortening to a pound of flour is quite as good, and much more healthful. Again, if considered necessary, the shortening may be half lard or good dripping, and the other half only butter, with half teaspoonful of salt added. Mix half the butter (or other shortening), with the flour as finely as possible, till it is no coarser than oatmeal; wet it up with iced water until about the consistency of the butter to be used; then roll out smooth, spread with some of the remaining butter, sprinkle with flour and fold three times and set away on ice, or if in winter, in a cold but not freezing place, for fifteen minutes. Repeat this process three times, then line a pie-pan with a lower crust, brown it lightly in the oven before putting in the fruit or custard, then add the top crust and bake in a moderately quick oven.

All crust will be more flaky if laid on ice a short time before using. Lard for pastry may be used as hard as it can be cut with a knife, and it will be better than if left stand to warm. It needs only to be cut through the flour, *not* rubbed.

Pie crust without lard can be made by taking rich buttermilk, soda, and a little salt, and mixing just as soft as it can be mixed and hold together; have plenty of flour on the molding board and rolling-pin; then make and bake as other pies, or rather in a slow oven, and when the pie is taken from the oven do not cover it up. In this way a dyspeptic can indulge in the luxury of a pie.

Pot-pie crusts with baking powder are made in this wise: Take one quart of flour, three teaspoonfuls of baking powder, a piece of butter as large as a hen's egg, well rubbed in the flour; mix just hard enough to handle; use either sweet milk or water to mix with; then, twenty minutes before you take up your dinner, pull your dough in pieces about as large as two hen's eggs and put in your kettle; cover and keep boiling briskly. Use buttermilk or sour milk for pot-pie crust when it can be procured. These are the proper proportions: One quart of flour, a little piece of butter rubbed in the flour, salt and a teaspoonful of saleratus or soda dissolved in enough sour milk to make a dough just hard enough to handle; then, as in the other kind, pull in pieces and put in your pie. Allow twenty minutes to cook. Do not raise the cover of your kettle more than once while it is cooking. When making the crust for a pot-pie there is danger, as every cook knows, of the crust falling when it is cooked in the kettle with the meat or chicken. If instead of doing this you put the crust on a plate and steam it for three-quarters of an hour, it will not be heavy. Be sure to have plenty of water in the kettle, so that you will not have to take the steamer off in order to put more in. Make the crust just as you do baking powder biscuit. When the meat is cooked and the gravy made, drop the crust into the gravy and leave it there a minute or two.

In warm weather, if the crust can not be used immediately after making, put in the ice-box until ready to use, and roll always with a well-floured rolling-pin. To prevent the juice from soaking into the under-crust, beat an egg well and with a soft cloth rub the crust before filling the pies. In the upper crust make air-holes, or the crust will break. These are best made with the point of the spoon or with a pastry-cutter, and may be drawn a little apart when placed over the pie. Use tin pie-plates, as the crust does not bake well in earthen ones, and do not fill with fruit until ready to place in the oven. When using juicy fruit, such as currants, gooseberries, sprinkle a little corn starch and sugar over the fruit after it is in the pie, and immediately put on the top crust and bake. Just before putting on the upper crust wet the rim of the lower, with water, and press the two crusts firmly together; this will prevent the pie bursting. Bake pies in a moderate oven, having the most heat at the bottom, or the lower crust will be clammy and raw. Remove fruit pies immediately from the tins, or the crust will become wet and ruin the pie.

A superior paste for mince pies or tarts is made by rubbing into a quart of the best flour one-third of a pound of sweet lard. Chop it in with a broad knife; wet up with ice-water; roll out very thin and cover with dabs of butter, also of the best; fold into a tight roll; flatten with a few strokes of the rolling-pin, and roll out into a sheet as thin as the first; baste again with the butter; roll up and out into a third sheet hardly thicker than drawing paper; a third time dot with butter and fold up closely. Having used as much butter for this purpose as you have lard, set aside your roll for an hour on ice, or in a very cold place; then roll out, line your pie-plates with the paste, fill with mince meat, put strips across them in squares or triangles, and bake in a steady but not dull heat.

Sweetened tart paste is very nice for tartlets, and is much used for the delicate tarts, as lemon or orange. For these, use one pound each of loaf sugar, flour and butter; mix thoroughly, then beat well with the rolling-pin (without rolling), for half an hour, folding it up and beating it out again; then roll out the pieces in any shape you wish for the tarts. In rolling the crust use the rolling-pin as lightly as possible, and take care that the pressure is even. For fruit tarts the crust is baked with the fruit in them but for jelly the crusts are baked first and then filled with the jelly.

(Detroit, 1881)

The finest quality lard was traditionally "tried" or rendered from the layer of fat surrounding the bowels and kidneys of hogs and was known as leaf lard. Manufacturers, however, marketed cheaper types of lard containing fat from other animals as well as adulterations such as cotton seed oil. That is why Dr. Chase advises us to try our own leaf lard.

Pastry, or Crust, No. 1, for Minced and All Other Pies

As it is of the utmost importance to have a light and flaky crust for minced pies, as well as all others, I will give two or three plans of making. The first is the celebrated Soyer's Receipt given by

"She was as pretty as a pie" (St. Louis, 1900).

"Shirly Dare," in the *Blade Household;* and, although it is some labor to make it, it will pay to follow it whenever a very nice, flaky crust is desirable. It is as follows:

"To every quart of sifted flour allow the yolk of 1 egg, the juice of 1 lemon, 1 saltspoonful of salt, and 1 lb. of fresh butter. Make a hole in the flour, in which put the beaten egg, the lemon and salt, and mix the whole with *ice water* (*very cold* water will do) into a soft paste. Roll it out, put the butter, which should have all the buttermilk thoroughly worked out of it, on the paste, and fold the edges over so as to cover it. Roll it out to the thickness of a quarter of an inch; fold over one-third and roll, fold over the other third and roll, always rolling one way. Place it with the ends toward you, repeat the turns and rolls as before twice. Flour a baking sheet, put the paste in it on ice or in some very cool place half an hour, roll twice more as before; chill again for a quarter of an hour; give it two more rolls and it is ready for use.

"This is very rich paste, and may be made with *half* the quantity of butter only, chopped fine in the flour, rolled and chilled, forming a very light puff paste that will rise an inch, and be flaky throughout."

Remarks—The object of chilling the pastry, by putting it upon ice or into a cold place, is to keep the butter cold, so it shall not be absorbed into the crust, but keep its buttery form, which makes it flaky, by keeping the dough in layers, while the many foldings and rolling out makes them thin like flakes of snow. But it is only in *hot* weather that this chilling becomes necessary, and not then, unless you desire it to be flaky. In making pie by the last paragraph above, using only ½ lb. of butter to 1 qt. of flour, for common use, the lemon juice, and egg too, may be left out, using the salt however. Still the yolk of an egg gives some richness, but more especially a richness of *color*. And even *half* lard, or "drippings" may be used, as indicated at the close of the 1st receipt below, and be good enough for all common purposes, using the egg, or not, as you choose.

It has always seemed to me, however, that pie-crust ought to have soda or baking-powder in it to make it light; and to be certain about it, I have just called on one of our best bakers in the city and asked him about it. He tells me that some bakers keep flour, sifted with baking-powder or soda, ready for use; and, in making crust, they take one-fourth of the amount of flour to be used from that having the baking-powder or soda in it, to make the crust rise a little, and help to prevent any soggyness from using a juicy pie-mixture; but he says it depends more upon the heat on the bottom, or rather from the want of a proper heat at the bottom of many stoves. With the uniform heat of the bottom of a baker's brick-oven they have no trouble, generally, in baking the bottom crust so it is done, and hence not soggy. To do this in a stove-oven, move the pie occasionally to another part of the oven, where the heat has not been absorbed or used up in heating the plate or tin—in other words, see that the bottom of the oven is kept as hot as it ought to be, and you have no soggy or under-done crusts. Pies, not to be eaten the day they are baked, should be baked harder than those for immediate use, to prevent the absorption of the juice of the pie or dampness from the air.

(Ann Arbor, 1884)

Prof. Blot's Receipt for Pie-Crust

One pound of flour, wet with water; then stir in one pound of butter, cut in small pieces, and roll out.

(Detroit, 1878)

Dr. John Harvey Kellogg of Battle Creek, an indefatigable advocate of food reform, thought pies unhealthy and American housewives "slaves of the rolling pin" (Battle Creek, 1910).

Prof. Pierre Blot's recipe yields an excellent pie crust. We recommend that you blend the butter or margarine with the flour before adding ¼ cup of ice-cold water.

Plain, but Good Family Pie-Crust

One pound of flour, half a pound butter, mix thoroughly with a knife or spoon. Pour in very cold water, just enough to form a dough for rolling out; flour the board and rolling pin, using a knife to handle the dough (the warmth of the hand makes it heavy); roll out the size of one plate at a time, so as to work it as little as possible. Bake in a quick oven.

(Detroit, 1878)

Pie Crust

Five cups sifted flour, 1 cup lard, a little salt, ½ cup ice water (or very cold water). Put the salt in the flour, take a knife or spatula and use to mix the shortening with the flour, when it is well cut up add the water gradually, keep chopping the mixture; do not knead it with the hands, sprinkle some flour on the moulding board; use if possible a porcelain or glass rolling pin, so it will be cold (they can be had at Leonard's), flour it well, take enough paste to make one crust and roll it out, cover the bottom and sides of the pie plate; to make the upper crust, roll it out and spread lightly with soft butter or lard, sprinkle with flour, roll up and repeat twice; slash it for the escape of steam; put the material in the pie, put on the upper crust and pinch the edges of the crusts together.

Mrs. C. H. Leonard
(Grand Rapids, 1890)

Mrs. Leonard could not resist doing a little advertising for her husband's department store in this recipe she submitted to *The Grand Rapids Cook Book* published by the firm in 1890.

Graham Pie Crust

Sift half teaspoon of baking powder into a pint of Graham flour, add enough thick, sweet cream to form a paste to roll. If sour cream be used, add saleratus to place of baking powder. Milk with butter may be used in place of cream.

Mrs. A. C. Firman
(Muskegon, 1890)

Granola Crust

For certain pies requiring an under crust only, the prepared granola manufactured by the Sanitarium Food Co. makes a superior crust. For one medium-sized pie, take three fourths of a cup of granola, mix, if desired, a little salt with it, and pour over it quickly from one fourth to one third of a cup

Rolling pins were handy for pie crust but notoriously lethal for husbands (Grand Rapids, 1890).

of rich milk or thin cream, just enough to moisten it slightly. If too moist, the crust will be soggy. Turn immediately into the pie tin, and spread and press evenly with a spoon over the bottom and sides of the tin. A teaspoon is best for the sides, and pressing the finger against the other side of the edge, as you are pressing with the spoon, makes the edge firmer. Do not allow the crust to come over the edge of the tin. Fill with fruit pulp prepared from nicely stewed dried apple, apricot, peach, or prune, or with a lemon filling prepared as directed for lemon pie. Stewed cranberries, grape, or peach may be rubbed through a colander, thickened if necessary with a little cornstarch, and baked in a granola crust. A cream pie may be baked in this crust if the filling be first cooked. After filling, bake ten or fifteen minutes in a quick oven.

(Battle Creek, 1910)

Dr. John Harvey Kellogg had invented granola, peanut butter, and corn flakes as health foods for patients at his fashionable Battle Creek Sanitarium (he also invented that word). His brother, William Keith Kellogg, served as his faithful henchman for over twenty years, but the brothers feuded over marketing strategy for corn flakes. W. K. Kellogg acquired control of the Kellogg's Toasted Corn Flake Company in 1906, and henceforth the name on the label was his. Dr. Kellogg continued to produce and market health foods at his Sanitarium Food Company. Ella Kellogg, quite naturally, advertised her husband's products in her cookbook.

Oatmeal Pie Crust

Scald two parts of oatmeal with one part of hot water. Roll thin. It bakes very quickly, so that fruit which requires much cooking must be cooked before making into the pie. This remark, however, applies only to pies which are baked with an upper crust. This crust is very tender, and possesses all

the desirable qualities of shortened pie crusts, with none of their deleterious properties.

(Battle Creek, 1876)

Pea Pie-Crust, No. 3

Stew the split peas as for dinner. Strain through a colander or coarse sieve. Then add equal parts good wheat meal (sifted Graham will do nicely) and fine corn meal sufficient to make a soft dough. Knead well for fifteen minutes, adding mixed meal enough to make a moderately stiff dough, then roll out and use as any other pie-crust. As it cooks very quickly, it is not best to put in for a filling, any fruit that requires long cooking.

Remarks—This is undoubtedly of German origin, as they make great use of the split pea soup, etc. But you may be assured of its healthfulness, for the Germans, with their plain cookery and hard labor manage to be healthy and long-lived people.

(Ann Arbor, 1884)

Puff Paste

Take 2 lbs. of fine winter wheat flour, ½ teaspoonful of salt and the juice of one lemon, mix with cold water into the consistency of firm butter, do not knead too much, dust your board with flour and roll out the paste into a square ½ inch thick. Mould out into a square cake 2 lbs. of good butter, which has had all the salt washed out, and place in the middle of the sheet of paste. Then fold each side over it and roll out in an oblong so as to equally spread the butter between the paste, fold this into three and roll out so that what were before the sides of the sheet may now become the ends; repeat this, folding and rolling three times more. Wrap in a cloth and put in the ice box or any cold place until next day. Then roll and fold three times more and cut out with a sharp, thin cutter, and bake in a hot oven, be sure and dust off all the dry flour from the surface of the paste before folding, and keep the hands also free. The scraps must not be used for patties, because the grain of the paste will be lost.

Harry Fox
(Muskegon, 1890)

Pie-Crust Glaze

In making any pie which has a juicy mixture, the juice soaks into the crust, making it soggy and unfit to eat; to prevent this:

Beat an egg well; and with a brush or bit of cloth, wet the crust of the pie with the beaten egg, just before you put in the pie mixture.

For pies which have a top crust also, wet the top with the same before baking, which gives it a beautiful yellow brown. It gives beauty also to biscuit, ginger cakes, and is just the thing for rusk, by putting in a little sugar.

(Ann Arbor, 1864)

Pies and Tartlets

Apple Pie

Take two good-sized apples, stew them and sweeten; grate in the rind of one lemon, and stir together with the yolk of one egg. Put a paste in the bottom only, and bake till done. Then take the white of the egg and beat it up with sugar; put on top and put back in oven a few minutes.

(Detroit, 1881)

English Apple Pie (No pastry)

2 very large mellow apples	1 teaspoon white sugar
1 cup sifted flour	1/4 teaspoon nutmeg
1/2 cup brown sugar	1 teaspoon lemon juice
Butter size of an egg	

Mix well the brown sugar, flour and butter (dry). Grease deep baking dish; put in all the apples sliced very thin, add an extra piece of butter about size of English walnut sliced thin and placed over apples; sprinkle over this white sugar. Add teaspoon water, nutmeg and lemon juice. Place on top of pie the dry mixture (sugar, butter and flour). Cover contents thoroughly. Bake in moderate oven 30 minutes. Serve hot or cold with whipped cream.

(Detroit, 1935)

Apple Custard Pie— The Nicest Pie Ever Eaten

Peel sour apples and stew until soft and not much water left in them; then rub them through a cullender—beat 3 eggs for each pie to be baked; and put in at the rate of 1 cup of butter and 1 of sugar for 3 pies; season with nutmeg.

My wife has more recently made them with only 1 egg to each pie, with only half of a cup of butter and sugar each, to 4 or 5 pies; but the amount of sugar must be governed somewhat by the acidity of the apples.

Bake as pumpkin pies, which they resemble in appearance; and between them and apple pies in taste; very nice indeed. We find them equally nice with dried apples by making them a little more juicy.

(Ann Arbor, 1864)

Apple Custard Pie

Scald the milk and let it cool. Grate some sweet apples. Take two-thirds of a cup of powdered sugar, four well-beaten eggs, one cup of milk, one-fourth of a nutmeg. Line an earthen pie-dish with a rich crust and let it bake. Then fill with the custard and let it bake for half an hour. To be eaten cold.

(Detroit, 1881)

Butter and Sugar Pie

The pastry does not need to be quite as rich as for other pies. Line a tin with pastry, take a piece of butter the size of an egg, cut up into small pieces, scatter around in the tin and add the following mixture: Three-fourths cupfuls of sugar, two eggs, beaten light, eight tablespoonfuls of sweet cream (milk can be used), a little nutmeg. Bake with two crusts.

Mrs. C. E. Scott, Escanaba
(Chicago, 1898)

Butterscotch Pie

1 tablespoon butter, browned	2 tablespoons flour, mix with a little milk
1½ cups brown sugar	2 cups milk
	1 egg

Mix ingredients together, cook in double boiler until it thickens. When cooled pour into pie tin lined with baked pie crust. Cover with well beaten white of egg. Brown in oven.

Mrs. Chas. Ellenger
(Grand Rapids, 1917)

Carrot Pie

One cup cooked, mashed carrot, 2 tablespoonfuls sugar, 1 of Little Wonder flour, pinch of salt, cinnamon and ginger, 2 eggs. Make in one crust, also add milk.

Mrs. Bannister
(Holland, 1908)

This dessert has an excellent taste, very similar to a rich pumpkin pie. Rather than mashing the carrots, which leaves too much fibrous material, we recommend that you purée the cooked carrots in a blender or food processor. Spice as you would a pumpkin pie.

Cherry Pie

If you have cherries, stew up a quart, with 1 cup of sugar mixed in with ¼ cup of flour and a pinch of salt. Cook it all until the cherries are soft and the juice thickened. Flavor with ½ teaspoon of almond; if you like it. You may need more sugar. A cherry can be as sour as a deacon with a bunion.

Make up your best pastry and bake it and fill the shells, big one for the Fourth or little ones for a picnic.

May Knight
(Kalamazoo, 1945)

Cherry Whang

Line pie tin with rich crust, fill it with cherries, 1 cup sugar, take 1 cup sweet cream and stir in 1 tablespoon flour, pour this over cherries and bake.

Frosting. Whites of 3 eggs beaten to a stiff froth, add 2 tablespoons sugar. Spread on pies; set in oven; brown lightly.

(Vermontville, 1906)

Mock Cherry Pie

Cover the bottom of a pie plate with paste, reserving enough for upper crust. For filling use 1 cup cranberries cut in halves; ½ cup raisins, seeded and cut in pieces; ¾ cup sugar; 1 tablespoonful

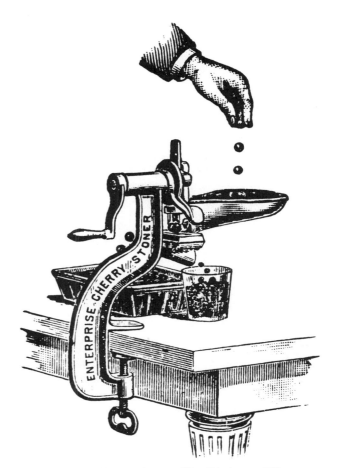

Hand-cranked cherry stoners like this turn-of-the-century model are still the best way to pit delicious Michigan cherries (Philadelphia, 1906).

flour; butter the size of a walnut. Bake 30 minutes in moderate oven.

Mrs. Eberhard
(Flint, 1912)

Mock Cherry Pie

One cupful of cranberries; cut into each one with a knife (this keeps them from bursting and cooking to pieces), one cupful of sugar, one-half cupful of water and one tablespoonful of flour wet in a little of the water. Stir all together and bake between two crusts. The pie should be baked early in the day, or before the roast is in the oven, as the steam and smoke will ruin pie crust.

Mrs. Olive P. Abbott, Reading
(Chicago, 1896)

Chess Pie

One c. dates, cut fine; ½ c. sugar; 1 c. raisins. ¾ c. milk; 2 eggs, ½ c. nut meats. Mix dates, raisins, egg yolks, sugar and milk and cook until thick. If necessary add a little cornstarch. After removing from fire add the nut meats. Put in baked pie shell and cover with meringue, made from egg whites.

Mrs. C. G. Wenzel
(Kalamazoo, 1921)

Chocolate Pie

Beat the yolks of 2 eggs with ½ cup sugar, add 2 oz. of sweet chocolate and 1 cup of milk. Line a pie plate with pastry and bake and when half done pour in the mixture and finish baking. When cooled slightly beat the whites of the eggs and spread over the top and brown lightly.

Janette Newton
(Hart, 1907)

Chocolate Cream Pie

Beat to a cream half a cupful of butter and a cupful and a quarter of powdered sugar. Add two well beaten eggs, two tablespoonfuls of wine, half a cupful of milk, a cupful and a half of sifted flour, with which has been mixed one teaspoonful and a half of baking powder. Bake this in four well buttered tin plates for fifteen minutes in a moderate oven. Put half a pint of milk in the double boiler on the fire. Beat together the yolks of two eggs, three teaspoonfuls of powdered sugar and a level tablespoonful of flour. Stir this into the boiling milk, beating well. Add a pinch of salt, stirring often for fifteen minutes. Flavor with vanilla. Put two of the cakes on large plates, spread the cream over them and lay the other two cakes on top. Beat the whites of the two eggs to a stiff froth. Then beat into them one cupful of powdered sugar, one teaspoonful of vanilla, one ounce Baker's chocolate. Add to it two tablespoonfuls of boiling water, and when smooth and glossy, stir this into the beaten whites and sugar. Set away for a few hours.

Ella Taylor, Menominee
(Chicago, 1898)

Cranberry and Raisin Pie

Two c. cranberries; 1 c. raisins; 2 c. water; 1 c. sugar; 1 tbsp. butter. Put together in saucepan the cranberries, raisins, water and sugar. Cook slowly till thick, being careful that they do not burn. Add a little butter, and vanilla flavoring, if desired. Bake in open crust.

Ethel Clay
(Kalamazoo, 1921)

Cranberry Tart Pie

Stew cranberries, allowing 1 pint sugar and 1 pint water to a quart of berries. Line a pie plate with paste; fill with stewed berries. Put narrow strips of pie crust across the top. A quart of berries make 2 good pies.

Mrs. C. H. L.
(Grand Rapids, 1890)

Philadelphia Cream Cheese Pie Crust

½ cup butter	1 pkg. Philadelphia
1 cup flour	Cream cheese
	Pinch salt

Combine for pie crust, roll out, line pie tin and bake. Fill with the following when cool:

Raisin Filling

1 cup sour cream	Pinch of salt and cin-
1 cup brown sugar	namon
1 cup raisins	1 teaspoon vanilla
Yolks of three eggs	1 large tablespoon
3 teaspoons corn	butter
starch	

Combine and cook in double boiler; cool and fill pie crust. Make meringue of the three egg whites.

Mrs. John Galster, Petoskey
(Grayling, 1937)

Crumb Pie

One cup molasses, 1 cup water, spice to suit taste, 1 teaspoon soda, for crumbs, 1 cup sugar, 1 cup lard and butter, 4 cups flour, mix in crumbs and bake in four pans.

(Vermontville, 1906)

Grape Pie

Pulp the grapes and reserve the skins. Cook the seed pulp until soft and press through a sieve. Add the skins and measure out 1 cupful for each pie. Add 1 cupful of sugar blended with 2 tablespoonfuls of flour and ⅛ teaspoonful of salt. Cook slightly; or the filling may be left uncooked and poured into a pastry lined pan. Beat together 1 egg and 2 tablespoonfuls of thick cream, then pour over the top of the grape filling. Arrange strips of pastry in criss-cross fashion over the pie and bake in a hot oven of 450 degrees for 15 minutes or until it begins to brown then reduce the heat to 325 degrees and continue baking for 25 minutes.

Mrs. J. A. Trutsch
(Allegan, 1938)

Filling for Grape Pie

One egg, beaten well; 1 c. sugar; 2 tbsp. flour; small piece of butter; 1½ c. grapes. Take seeds out of grapes, use peelings and meats. Put between two crusts and bake.

Mrs. H. Martinson
(Kalamazoo, 1921)

Lemon Pie

Grate the rind (yellow part only) of one lemon and add the juice; grate a raw potato, the size of a lemon; one cup of white sugar; one cup of cold water; one tea-spoonful of corn starch. Mix all well and boil a minute or two. Have your crust prepared and pour in this mixture and bake. If one wishes, the yolk of an egg can be added to the mixture; the white of the egg used to frost the top of the pie.

A. E. Savage
(Mendon, 1890)

Lemon Pie

Take four tablespoonfuls of lemon juice (one large lemon or two small ones will yield about this quantity), the grated yellow portion only of the rind of half a lemon, and two thirds of a cup of sugar. Beat the lemon juice and sugar together. Braid two level tablespoonfuls of cornstarch with as little water as possible, and pour over it, stirring constantly, one half pint of boiling water, to thicken the starch. Add the lemon and sugar to the starch, and let it cool; then stir in the yolks of two eggs and half the white of one, well beaten together. Beat thoroughly, pour into a deep crust, and bake. When done, cover with the remaining whites of tne eggs, beaten with one and a half tablespoonfuls of sugar, and brown lightly in the oven.

(Battle Creek, 1910)

Lemon Pie

One lemon, grate the rind
Squeeze in juice
One cup sugar
Butter, size of walnut
Three eggs, save whites of two for meringue
2 tablespoons cornstarch

Beat all together. Add 1 cup of hot water, cook over boiling water.

Place in baked pie shell, over which place whites beaten. Brown in hot oven.

Mrs. R. W. Ridlen, Dunningville
(Allegan, 1938)

Lemon and Raisin Pie

One cup sugar, 1 lemon, 1 heaping tablespoon cornstarch, butter size of walnut, 1 cup cold water. Line a pie tin with rich pie crust, peel the lemon, being careful to remove all the white part of the skin, slice very thin and place in a layer in the crust, with ½ cup raisins scattered over. Mix the sugar and cornstarch together and sprinkle in, cut the butter into small bits and scatter over, and just before putting the top crust on put in a cup of cold water. Do not gash the top until it is partly baked and begins to look flaky.

Mrs. John D. Sumner
(Kalamazoo, 1899)

Maple Sugar Pie

One and one-half cups of scraped maple sugar laid in a crust slightly sprinkled with flour. Then drop bits of butter over top. Add to this ⅔ cup of

Michigan pioneers learned sugar-making techniques from the native Ottawa and Chippewa (Battle Creek, 1886).

thick sweet cream, a little more flour, and top crust. Bake.

Mrs. Ira H. Benjamin
(Detroit, 1923)

Minced Pies, No. 1

Boil a fresh beef's tongue (or very nice tender beef in equal amount, about 3 lbs), remove the skin and roots (any remains of the wind-pipe, blood vessels, etc.) and chop it very fine, when cold; add 1 lb of chopped suet; 2 lbs of stoned raisins; 2 lbs of English currants; 2 lbs of citron, cut in fine pieces; 6 cloves, powdered (½ teaspoonful powdered cloves); 2 teaspoonsful of cinnamon; ½ teaspoonful of powdered mace; 1 pt. of brandy; 1 pt. of wine, or cider; 2 lbs of sugar; mix well and put into a stone jar and cover well. This will keep some time. When making the pies, chop some tart apples very fine, and to 1 lb of the prepared meat put 2 bowls of the apple; add more sugar if taste requires it, and sweet cider to make the pies juicy, but not thin; mix and warm the ingredients before putting into pie plates. Always bake with an upper and under crust, made as follows:

Crust—Lard, butter and water, each 1 cup; flour, 4 cups.

Remarks—To which I would add, the yolk of an egg and and a little salt. As a general thing, I do not think so much brandy and wine are used, and although I do not object to eating, occasionally, of such a pie, yet, as many persons do, they can leave them out, substituting boiled cider—3 to 1—in the place of the brandy or wine; or pure alcohol, ½ pt., would be as strong in spirit, and cost less than half as much, while the difference in taste would not be observed. Each person can now suit themselves and be alone responsible. I will guarantee this much, however, no one will be led into habits of drink from the amount of spirit they will get in a piece of pie thus made—possibly one-fourth of a teaspoonful. Nearly all receipts for minced pies contain wine or brandy; they can be used or left out, as any one shall choose, by using the cider more freely.

(Ann Arbor, 1884)

Orange Pie

One large or 2 small oranges, grate part of the rind and squeeze the juice, 3 eggs beaten separately. Stir the yolks with 1 cup of sugar, 1 cup milk, add the orange and whites last. Bake with under crust.

Mrs. Robt. Easton
(Muskegon, 1890)

Orange Cream Pie

One large orange and ½ of a lemon, 1 cup sugar, butter, size of a walnut, 2 tablespoons corn starch, 4 eggs, ½ cup milk. Put milk and 1 cup boiling water in double boiler, then grate the yellow part of orange, squeeze juice into a bowl and lemon juice also, then put the orange and lemon in an-other bowl and pour 1 cup boiling water over and let stand until you beat the 4 yolks and whites of 1 with the butter, sugar and starch, then add the juice and grated rind and the water from the orange and lemon, a pinch of salt, then pour into the boiling milk and water, stirring all the time until well cooked. Bake shell, put in mixture and add whites of eggs whipped stiff with a little orange flavor and powdered sugar to top off pie. Brown in oven.

(Vermontville, 1906)

One-Crust Peach Pie

Pare and remove the stones from ripe, nice flavored peaches; stew till soft in the smallest quantity of water possible without burning. Rub through a colander, or beat smooth with a large spoon. Add sugar as required. Bake with one crust. If the peach sauce is evaporated until quite dry, it is very nice baked in a granola crust. When done, meringue with the whites of two eggs whipped stiff with two tablespoonfuls of sugar. The flavor is improved by adding by degrees to the egg while whipping, a tablespoonful of lemon juice. Return to the oven and brown lightly. Serve cold.

Canned peaches or stewed dried peaches may be used in place of the fresh ones. In using the dried peaches, carefully examine and wash; soak them over night in cold water, and stew them in the same water until soft enough to rub through the colander. For each pie, add two tablespoonfuls of sweet cream, and sufficient sugar to sweeten; too much sugar destroys the flavor of the fruit. Evaporated peaches, soaked over night and stewed carefully until tender, then removed from the syrup, which may be sweetened and boiled until thick and rich and afterward turned over the peaches, makes a delicious pie. Bake in one crust, with or without a meringue.

(Battle Creek, 1910)

Dried Peach Pie

Stew peaches until tender, mash fine and add for two pies ½ teacup sweet cream, 1 teacup sugar, bake with two crusts, or omit cream and add ½ teacup boiling water and butter size of hickorynut.

(Vermontville, 1906)

Pecan Pie

3 eggs	¼ cup soft butter
½ cup sugar	2 tbsp. flour
1 cup light Karo syrup	½ cup broken pecans

Mix flour and sugar. Beat eggs lightly and add butter, sugar and pinch of salt, syrup and pecans. Mix well and pour into unbaked shell. Bake 400 degrees for 10 minutes and 350 degrees for 50 minutes.

Mrs. R. F. Ware
(Kalamazoo, 1941)

Pineapple Pie

1 can sliced pineapple	1 egg
1 cup sugar	1 rounding table-
1 rounding teaspoon butter	spoon corn starch

Dice pineapple and pour with juice into sauce pan. Add butter and sugar. Boil five minutes. Add corn starch to beaten egg and stir until well mixed. At the end of five minutes add to hot mixture and stir constantly until thick. Cool slightly and bake between two crusts.

Mrs. J. W. Thaler, Caledonia
(Allegan, 1938)

Pumpkin Pie

Stewed pumpkin, 1 heaping pint; 6 eggs; flour, 6 table-spoonfuls; butter, size of an egg; sugar, 1½ cups; cinnamon, 2 level teaspoonfuls; ginger, ½ tea-spoonful; ½ a grated nutmeg. Directions—Rub the pumpkin through a colander, adding the butter, sugar and spices, and make hot, then the beaten eggs and flour; mix smoothly together, and while hot put into the dish, having a thick crust to receive it, and bake in a moderate oven.—*Henry Crane, Frost House, Eaton Rapids, Mich.*

Remarks—This makes a thick, salvy pie, very nice. If fearful of a soggy crust, bake it before putting in the pie mixture. If a pint of milk was added,

it would be more like the old-fashioned pumpkin-custard pie, softer and not quite so rich, unless an additional egg or two, with an extra cup of sugar is put in. If milk is plenty, and pumpkin scarce, take this latter plan.

(Ann Arbor, 1884)

Pumpkin Pie

1 cup stewed pumpkin	Butter the size of a walnut
1 coffee cup milk	½ teaspoon cinnamon
1 or 2 eggs	¼ teaspoon cloves
⅔ cup sugar	¼ teaspoon ginger

If 1 egg is used add 1 heaping tablespoon flour.

Mrs. E. E. Keyes
(Parchment, 1926)

Pie Plant or Rhubarb Pie

Peel a bunch of pie plant, put it into your chopping-bowl and chop into pieces the size of your little finger nail; grate the rind and squeeze the juice of a lemon over this, add sugar to taste; put this into a pie dish lined with paste, and cut strips of paste and lay them across the top, and bake. Or

"The golden pumpkin, nugget of the field" (New York, 1881).

pour the chopped pie plant into a porcelain-lined basin and give it a good scald with the sugar. Bake with under and upper crust.

(Detroit, 1878)

Rhubarb Pie

Peel the stalks. Cut into ½ inch pieces. Pour boiling water over and let remain until cold. This takes the bitter sour from the rhubarb, thus saving much sugar. When cool, strew lavishly with sugar, a little butter and a sprinkling of flour. Half an orange improves the flavor. Bake with 2 crusts.

Grandma Graves, Ypsilanti
(Chicago, 1886)

Pie-plant Pie

Mix ½ teacup white sugar and 1 heaping teaspoon flour together, sprinkle over the bottom crust, then add the pie-plant cut up fine; sprinkle over this another half teaspoon sugar and heaping teaspoon flour; bake fully ¾ hour in a slow oven. Or stew the pie-plant, sweeten, add grated rind of one lemon and yolks of 2 eggs, and bake and frost like lemon pie.

(Vermontville, 1906)

Rhubarb Cream Pie

Put on to boil 2 cups finely cut rhubarb; ½ cup sugar and 2 tablespoons water.
Cream together:

2 egg yolks	*Pinch of salt*
2 T flour	*1 cup milk*
½ cup sugar	

Add to the boiling rhubarb and boil until it thickens. Put in baked pie crust and egg whites over the top and put in oven to brown.

Mrs. J. Overbeek, Hamilton
(Allegan, 1938)

Shoepack Pie

Mix ½ cup of flour with as much sugar. Add 1½ cups of boiling water and bring to a boil again. Then add half a cup of molasses, the same amount of vinegar, and 1 lemon, juice and grated rind. Stir well.

Next put in half a cup of seedless raisins and 2 tablespoons of butter. Stir well, then let this cool. Line a pie pan with rich pastry and pour in the filling. Bake in a real hot oven for 15 minutes, then reduce the heat to make a moderate oven and bake until the filling is set.

Robert H. Rayburn
Sportsman,
Alpena
(Chicago, 1940)

This is a strange name for a pie. Shoepacks were the moccasin-type footgear worn by the French *courier de bois*, not a very appealing image for a dessert.

Shoo Fly Pie

Line a pie pan with crust, put 3 tablespoons syrup in a cup, ½ teaspoon soda and pour 2 tablespoons boiling water over this, stir well and put in crust; have ready 1 heaping cup flour, ½ cup brown sugar, butter size of egg, all rubbed well together with the hands, then sprinkle over the molasses, but don't stir it. Bake like any ordinary pie.

(Vermontville, 1906)

Silver Pie

Peel and grate one large white potato into a deep plate; add the juice and grated rind of one lemon, the beaten white of one egg, one teacupful of white sugar and one cup of cold water. Stir well together and pour into a nice under-crust and bake. When done have ready the beaten whites of two eggs well beaten, half a teacupful of white sugar and a few drops of lemon, all thoroughly beaten. Put this mixture on the top of the pie evenly and return to the oven to stiffen a few moments. When sent to the table just cold lay a teaspoonful of jelly on the center of each piece, to ornament, if you wish.

Miss Helen Brown, Hudson
(Chicago, 1896)

Squash Pies

Cut the squash in pieces and steam or boil until thoroughly done. Then remove from the shell and mash fine. To one quart of stewed and sifted squash add one quart of milk, three eggs, one cup of sugar, and a teaspoonful of salt; spice to taste.

(Detroit, 1881)

Squash Pie

Two cups boiled squash, 3 eggs, ¾ cup sugar, 2 tablespoons molasses, 1 tablespoon melted butter, 1 tablespoon ginger, 1 teaspoon cinnamon, 2 cups milk, a little salt. Instead of ginger, nutmeg and vanilla may be used.

Mrs. N. Chase
(Kalamazoo, 1899)

Sweet Potato Pie

Boil potatoes until soft; peel, mash and put through a sieve. To ¼ lb. potato, add 1 pt. sweet milk, 3 tablespoonfuls melted butter, 4 eggs, 1 glass wine, sugar and nutmeg to taste.

Rose B. Nisbet
(Kalamazoo, 1906)

Southern Tomato Pie

For one pie peel and slice green tomatoes, add 4 tablespoons sugar, flavor with nutmeg or cinnamon, nutmeg is the best. Bake with two crusts slowly. This tastes very much like green apple pie.

(Vermontville, 1906)

Transparent Pie

Three cups white sugar, ¾ cup butter, 4 well-beaten eggs, mix well together and bake with lower crust. The above will make two pies.

(Vermontville, 1906)

Vinegar Pies

One and a half cups good vinegar, one cup of water, lump of butter size of an egg, sugar enough to sweeten to the taste; flavor with lemon, put in stew-pan on stove; take five eggs, beat the yolks with one cup of water and two heaping teaspoonfuls of flour; when the vinegar comes to a boil put in the eggs and flour, stirring till well cooked; have ready crust for four pies, put in the filling and bake; beat the whites with two spoonfuls of white sugar to a froth, spread on the pies when done, and color in the oven.

(Detroit, 1881)

Vinegar Pie

1½ cup water	4 T cornstarch
½ cup vinegar (cider)	2 egg yolks
1 cup sugar	1 t lemon extract

Put water and vinegar on to boil. Mix sugar, cornstarch and egg yolks to a smooth paste with a little cold water and add to boiling water and vinegar. When cooked add butter and lemon extract. Pour in a baked pie shell. Beat the whites of two eggs and spread on top and set in oven to brown slightly.

Mrs. Charles Booyinga, Charlotte
(Allegan, 1938)

Banbury Tart

One-fourth lb. figs, 1 cup seeded raisins, 1 cup water, 1½ cups sugar, 1 orange, rind and juice, 1 lemon, rind and juice, 1 cup nutmeats. Chop fine figs, raisins, rinds, and nutmeats, cook all until thick, then let cool. It is better if made the day before using. Roll rich pie crust thin and cut with biscuit cutter. Place 1 tablespoon of mixture on one side of the crust, fold over, bake a light brown and roll in powdered sugar. Delicious to serve with coffee.

Mrs. C. S. Allison, Owosso
(Charlotte, 1909)

Cheese Turn-Overs

2 packages cream cheese	*½ pound butter*

Mix well. Knead in 2 cups sifted flour. Let stand in cold place several hours or over night. Roll out thin. Cut in squares. Put jam in center and turn over. Bake about 15 minutes.

(Detroit, 1935)

Cranberry Tarts

Roll rich paste one-eighth inch thick; cut in three-inch squares, put 1 or 2 tsp. cranberry sauce, to which raisins and butter has been added, on one side of square; moisten edges with water; fold in triangle shape. Crimp the edges and prick over top with fork. Bake same as pies. Sprinkle with fine sugar. Serve hot with cheese.

(Kalamazoo, 1921)

COOKIES

Bachelor Buttons

Rub 2 ounces butter into 5 ounces flour; add 5 ounces white-sugar, and 1 beaten egg; flavor; roll into small balls with the hands; sprinkle with sugar. Bake on tins covered with buttered paper.

(Detroit, 1890)

Bill Cookies

Bill Cookies,—and rightly they are named,
　If they are gone in a jiffy no one can be blamed,
Take one cup of sugar, a half cup of lard;
　Cream these together, add 2 eggs and beat
　　hard,
One scant teaspoon of soda, now put in a cup,
　Add a mite of hot water, and now 'twill foam up;
Sift 3 cups of flour and place in a bowl,
　Mix smoothly and swiftly, and then neatly roll;
If dough is too soft, a little flour add,
　I'll assure better cookies your husband ne'er
　　had.

Mrs. Josie Morris
(Berrien Springs, 1923)

Aunt Charlotte's Cookies

Three cups sugar, 3 eggs, 1½ cup butter, 1½ cup sour cream, 1½ teaspoon soda, nutmeg, salt. Mix soft. Will make 60 large soft cookies.

Winnifred Weaver Dodge
(Charlotte, 1909)

Chocolate Cookies

One-half teaspoon soda dissolved in ½ cup milk; ½ cup melted butter; 1 cup sugar; 1½ cups flour; pinch of salt; 2 squares chocolate melted; yolks of 2 eggs; then well beaten whites of 2; ½ cup dates; ½ cup raisins; ½ cup nuts; cut fine.

Frosting: 1 cup pulverized sugar; 3 teaspoons cocoa; 3 tablespoons boiling coffee or milk; 1 teaspoon butter; vanilla. Beat and spread.

Zoe Ramsdell
(Manistee, 1929)

Clove Cookies

Two cups brown sugar, 1 cup butter, 2 teaspoons cloves, 2 eggs, 1 teaspoons soda in a little hot water, and flour enough to roll out.

Mrs. John A. Pieters, Fennville
(Charlotte, 1909)

Cocoanut Kisses

2 cups corn flakes   Whites of 2 eggs
1 cup sugar   ½ teaspoon vanilla
1 cup cocoanut

Mix cornflakes, sugar, cocoanut, and add two stiffly beaten whites of eggs. Add vanilla and bake in a slow oven.

(Kalamazoo, 1918)

Cookies of 1812

One pint of sugar, one teacup of butter, four eggs, two tablespoons of sweet milk, one-half teaspoon of soda, one teaspoon of cream of tartar, one-half nutmeg, one teaspoon of vanilla, one pint of flour. Roll the sugar (granulated) until quite fine; add the butter and cream them. Stir in the milk gradually, and beat the eggs separately, and then put together and beat again. Add to the mixture butter, sugar and milk, and lastly the flour and soda, which has been dissolved in a little warm water. After these have been well mixed add the nutmeg and vanilla. Beat all well together, and add enough flour to handle well in rolling and cutting out. Bake in a moderate oven a delicate brown. These keep well.

Helen Brown, Hudson
(Chicago, 1896)

Cornflake Kisses

3 cups cornflakes   ¼ teaspoon salt
1 cup dry chipped co-   ½ teaspoon vanilla
  coanut   ½ cup corn syrup
2 eggs   ½ cup sugar

Stir together all the ingredients and drop on buttered baking sheets. Use the equivalent of a heaping tablespoon for each "kiss." Bake for half an hour in a moderate oven.

(Detroit, 1935)

White Crullers

One quart flour, 1 cup powdered sugar, 3 teaspoons druggist cream of tartar and 1½ teaspoons soda. Sift all together twice, then add butter the size of a small hickorynut, little nutmeg, add milk, mix very soft.

Mrs. Charles S. Dayton
(Kalamazoo, 1899)

Deerfield Cookies

Nine cups of flour, 2 cups of butter, 4 cups of sugar, 3 eggs, ½ teaspoonful soda, cinnamon, caraway seed; roll thin.

Mrs. L. D. Putnam
(Grand Rapids, 1890)

Fruit Cookies

One cup granulated sugar, ½ cup sour milk, ½ cup butter, 1 cup currants, ½ teaspoon soda, flour to make soft dough. Flavor to taste (almond preferred).

Martha Diekema Kollen, Holland
(Charlotte, 1909)

Fruit Cookies

One and one-half cups sugar, 1 cup butter worked to a cream, add three eggs well beaten, ½ cup molasses, 1 teaspoon soda dissolved in a little cold water, 1 cup raisins seeded and chopped, 1 cup currants, 1 teaspoon all kinds of spices, flour to roll.

Ida A. Gilmore, Kalamazoo
(Charlotte, 1909)

Our Old Ginger Cookie Receipt

Two cups black molasses, 2 cups New Orleans molasses, 2 cups brown sugar, 2 cups shortening, 1½ cups water, 4 tablespoons ginger, 4 table-spoonsful of soda, alum the size of 2 hickory nuts pulverized. Will make 6 gallons of cookies.

Mrs. P. P. Misner
(Muskegon, 1890)

Ginger Cookies

One cupful of molasses, one cupful of sugar, three-fourths cupful of lard—fill the cup with water, two tablespoonfuls of ginger, one tablespoonful of soda, one teaspoonful of salt; mix all together, place on stove and let come to a boil, let it cool just enough to mix with the hands, add flour to roll thin easily.

Mrs. Dr. O'Keef, Menominee
(Chicago, 1898)

Nelley's Ginger Snaps

One cup molasses, 1 cup brown sugar, 1 cup shortening, (part butter, part lard). Boil in a basin 10 minutes; cool, then put in 1 teaspoon soda dissolved in about 2 tablespoons hot water, 1 teaspoon ginger; stir in enough flour to make stiff; roll thin and bake.

(Ann Arbor, 1872)

Culinary secrets were traditionally passed on from mother to daughter (Chicago, 1909).

Ginger Snaps

1 cup New Orleans molasses	1 teaspoon soda
1 cup brown sugar	1 well beaten egg
1 cup butter or lard. Boil 20 minutes; then add	1 tablespoon ginger
	Flour to make it very stiff

After it is well kneaded, cut off a small piece to roll out, and put the balance where it will keep warm until needed. It should be so stiff that it will be necessary to keep it quite warm in order to roll out smoothly.

Mrs. J. P. Howlett, Niles
(Chicago, 1886)

Gum Drop Cookies

2 cups light brown sugar	½ cup nut meats (broken)

4 eggs (lightly beaten)
Butter (size of walnut)
2 tablespoons water
2 cups flour
½ teaspoon salt

1 cup small gum drops (cut in pieces)
1 teaspoon cinnamon

Mix. Spread on cookie sheet. Bake slowly. Cut in squares. Frost or roll in powdered sugar.

Mrs. H. A. Fick
(Grayling, 1937)

Happy Thought Cookies

One c. sugar, ½ c. butter, 1 egg, 1 tsp. soda, 2½ c. flour, caraway seed. Mix soft and use as little flour to roll out as possible.

Mrs. C. C. High
(Kalamazoo, 1921)

Jumbles

One and a half cups white sugar, three-fourths cup butter, three eggs, three table-spoons sweet milk, half tea-spoon soda and one of cream tartar; mix with sufficient flour to roll; roll and sprinkle with sugar; cut out and bake.

Mrs. Mollie Pilcher, Jackson
(Minneapolis, 1881)

Macaroons

Pour boiling water on ½ lb. almond meats, take the skins off and throw into cold water for a few moments, take out and pound to a smooth paste, adding 1 tablespoon essence lemon, add 1 pound pulverized sugar, whites of 3 eggs, and work the paste well together, dip the hands in water and roll the mixture into balls size of a nutmeg, lay on buttered paper an inch apart, when done dip the hands in water and pass gently over the macaroons making the surface smooth, set in a slow oven ¾ hour.

E. C. L.
(Grand Rapids, 1890)

Cocoanut Macaroons No. 1

One lb. of cocoanut, fine or granulated, shred will do, 1½ lbs. powdered sugar, whites of 7 eggs well beaten, 2 oz. corn starch, ½ oz. flour; mix well together, for at least half an hour, let lay for 2 or 3 hours, finely dust a sheet of paper, with rice flour, or corn starch and drop the dough in pieces about the size of half dollars; bake in a fair oven, damp the paper on the back and the cakes will come off, if they will not without.

Harry Fox
(Muskegon, 1890)

Cornflake Macaroons

Two eggs, 1 cup sugar, 1 cup cocoanut, 2 cups corn flakes, a little salt, ½ teaspoon Quaker vanilla. Drop on buttered tin. Bake 10 minutes.

Mrs. Cora A. Stoffer
(Lansing, 1923)

Maple Syrup Drop Cookies

Two eggs; 1 cup sugar; 1 cup maple syrup; ½ cup hot water; ½ cup lard; 2 teaspoons soda; 1 teaspoon cinnamon; 1 teaspoon ginger; 4 cups flour; salt. Add nuts or raisins if desired.

Mrs. Cora Hildinger
(Sunfield, 1915)

Molasses Snaps

One cup butter and lard mixed, 1 cup sugar, 1 cup molasses, 2 teaspoons soda, 4 teaspoons vinegar. Dissolve soda in vinegar, flour enough to roll easily very thin and bake in hot oven.

M. F. S.
(Muskegon, 1890)

My Mother's Cookie Recipe

Four eggs, three cups brown sugar, one and one-half cups shortening, one-quarter nutmeg grated, one level teaspoonful of soda and one-half teacup cold water. Mix eggs, sugar and shortening. (Shortening should be butter and pork drippings) thoroughly together, then add the other ingredients and flour enough to make a soft dough. Roll thin and bake quick. These cookies will keep several weeks and not get stale as some cream cookies do.

Mrs. C. French
(Muskegon, 1906)

St. Nikolaas Koekjes
(Santa Claus Cookies)

1 cup Butter	½ teaspoon Nutmeg
1 cup Lard	½ teaspoon Cloves
2 cups Sugar	½ cup Sour Cream
4 cups Flour	with
4 teaspoons Cinna-	½ teaspoon Soda
mon	½ cup Nut Meats

Mix ingredients and knead into loaf. Set away overnight. Cut in slices and bake in moderate oven.

(Holland, 1936)

Nut Jumbles

One cup butter, 1 heaping cup sugar, 2 eggs, cream together. One scant cup milk, 4 cups flour, 2 heaping teaspoons baking powder, 1 dessert spoon vanilla extract. Roll soft, adding a little flour if needed. One-half glass pecans or hickorynut meats broken and rolled lightly into dough before cutting with biscuit cutter. Bake in quick oven.

Mrs. Henrietta V. Larned
(Kalamazoo, 1899)

Mrs. MacCrath's Oat Meal Cookies

Four cups oatmeal, 2 cups French's White Lily flour, 1 cup lard and butter, mixed; 2 cups brown sugar, 1 teaspoon salt, 1 level teaspoon soda, ½ cup boiling water, 1 cup raisins, 1 cup nuts. Mix oatmeal and flour thoroughly. Add sugar and last the boiling water.

(Hasting, 1921)

Oatmeal Jam-Jams (Eggless)

2 cups flour	½ tsp. salt
2 cups rolled oats	½ tsp. cinnamon
1 cup drippings	1 tsp. soda
1 cup sugar	sour milk

Rub all ingredients together with the exception of the soda, which should be dissolved in enough sour milk to hold other ingredients together. Roll thin. Have ready 1 pound of figs or dates cooked soft with one cup sugar and a little water. Cut cakes into shapes and put a spoonful of figs on top then put another cake on and press edges firmly together and bake in hot oven. These are delicious.

Mrs. R. VanderSalm
(Kalamazoo, 1945)

Rocks

One and one-half cups brown sugar, 1 cup butter, ½ cup cold water, ½ cup molasses, 4 eggs, 1 pound English walnut meats, cut fine; drop in buttered pan with spoon, 1 pound raisins (chopped), 1 teaspoon soda in flour, 1 teaspoon vanilla, ½ teaspoon salt, flour enough to make rather stiff.

Fannie Collins
(Manistee, 1929)

Debby's Soft Cookies

Very small ½ cup butter, 1½ cups sugar, 1 egg, ⅔ cup sweet milk, 3 teaspoons baking powder, very little nutmeg, (or lemon extract); stir butter and sugar to a cream then add other ingredients, not too much flour, mix very soft, roll out, (not too thin,) cut in strips, roll in sugar and flour; braid so as to form a round, and bake: or cut round, and put raisins in center. These are very nice.

(Ann Arbor, 1872)

Wheaties Patties

Melt a bar of Nestle's Sweet Chocolate in a double boiler. Remove from fire and add 1 teaspoon vanilla and enough Wheaties to make thick mixture. Drop by spoonfuls onto waxed paper.

Jean Peterson
(Grayling, 1937)

PUDDINGS

Nowadays we think of pudding as a soft creamy mixture, but the term as used in early recipes has a much broader meaning. Dishes labeled pudding are usually sweet, but not always, and vary in consistency from something resembling yogurt to what we would call a cake.

Steaming in an enclosed box or cannister made of sheet metal was a favorite method of cooking puddings. Water was placed in the bottom of the steamer, and it was set on the range.

Puddings

In these days, when puddings are always "steamed in a mold," the temperature of the water is not a matter of such vital importance. We confess to being old-fashioned enough to prefer a pudding boiled in a bag. Take a half a yard of nice, new "Russia Duck," or strong, unbleached drilling, or sail cloth, sew together so as to form a sausage; turn it inside out, dip it in boiling water, and rub it into a pan of flour, turn the bag so that the flour is on the inside, tie up one end tightly, and pour the pudding into the other, leave room for it to swell; tie the other end. Put a plate in your pot, have the water boiling, and keep it boiling for three hours after you have plunged your pudding in. The flavor of a bag pudding is greatly superior to that of a mold.

Baking a pudding is a more simple process, but let us warn our students not to bake it to death. A bread or any custard pudding *should shake in the middle* when it is done. A rice pudding should be lightly baked; an Indian meal pudding will bear much longer baking. The boiled lemon pudding requires a mold as it is so delicate.

(Detroit, 1878)

Apple Pudding

1 cup of flour	*1 egg*
½ cup sugar	*1 teaspoon baking*
½ cup milk	*powder*
2 spoons melted butter	

Turn this batter over sliced apples, and bake 1 hour. Serve with cream.

Mrs. George McDonald
(Kalamazoo, 1906)

Scotch Pie

Pare and slice enough in apples to nearly fill a deep pie plate, and cover with the following batter: 1½ cups flour, 2 tablespoons melted butter, 1½ teaspoons baking powder, salt, moisten with enough sweet milk so that it will spread nicely, and turn over the apples. Bake a rich brown and until the apples are tender; turn out, crust down,

sweeten, add a generous amount of butter and nutmeg as for any apple pie. Serve with sweetened cream.

Mrs. Merriman
(Kalamazoo, 1899)

As our contribution to a family Thanksgiving dinner, we decided to experiment with both variations of this sort of upside-down apple cake. The first attempt at the apple pudding proved disastrous. We did not use enough sliced apples, and since Mrs. McDonald had not mentioned it, we failed to grease the pie tin. The apples burned and stuck to the bottom.

The next effort turned out better. We lightly greased and floured the pie tin and peeled and thinly sliced six medium-sized apples. The apples were not tart, so over each layer we sprinkled lemon juice and a light dusting of cinnamon and sugar. We sifted the dry ingredients, added ¼ tsp. salt, beat the egg and 2 tablespoons melted butter and mixed until smooth. After spooning the batter over the apples, bake the pie for 35–40 minutes at 350° until the top is golden brown.

Slice it as you would a pie and turn each piece over. Top with whipped cream or ice cream. The Scotch Pie was less like a cake and more the texture of a Scottish scone. We noticed that the apple pudding disappeared much sooner at Thanksgiving.

A Simple Apple Pudding

Pare and slice, thin, enough tart cooking apples to make an inch layer in a granite pie pan. Sift together 1½ cups flour, 3 level teaspoons baking powder, and a pinch of salt. Rub into this 1 tablespoon lard and ½ tablespoon butter. Mix to a stiff batter, with sweet milk, and spread over apples. Bake until apples are soft and turn out on a plate, with apple on top. Sprinkle thick with sugar, and serve either with cream or a boiled sauce.

Mrs. E. A. Balyeat
(Kalamazoo, 1906)

Baking-Day Pudding

On baking day, take 1½ cups dough, work in a little shortening, place in a basin. Let it get light

These two girls are peeling Michigan apples beside a Detroit-made Garland range (undated trade card).

and steam 1 hour. If the basin has no tube, put an inverted cup in the center. Eat with vanilla sauce.

Grandma Graves, Ypsilanti
(Chicago, 1886)

Irish Moss Blanc Mange

Put ½ cup Irish moss in a qt. of sweet milk, after washing carefully. Let it set over a pan of hot water for 30 minutes, flavor, then strain and mould. To be eaten with cream and sugar.

Mrs. L. L. Trott
(Muskegon, 1890)

Irish moss or carrageen is a dark purple seaweed found on the coast of Northern Europe. It was dried and commonly used as a gelling agent in cookery.

Bread Custard Pudding

Take one cup of finely powdered bread crumbs, one half cup of sugar, one quart of milk, and the beaten yolks of three eggs and whites of two. Mix the bread and milk, and when well softened, add the beaten yolks, sugar, and lastly the well-beaten whites; beat all together thoroughly, season with a little grated lemon rind; place the pudding dish in the oven in a pan of hot water, and bake till firm and lightly brown. Take from the oven, cover the top with a layer of apple marmalade made without sugar, or with some tart fruit jelly; add to this a meringue made of the white of the remaining egg and a tablespoonful of sugar, beaten to a stiff froth, and place in the oven a moment to brown lightly.

Fresh fruit, strawberries, raspberries, chopped peaches, currants, cherries, or shredded oranges are equally as good as the marmalade or jelly for the top dressing, and may be used to vary this pudding in a number of different ways. Canned fruits, if well drained from juice, especially apricots and peaches, are excellent for this purpose. A cocoanut custard pudding may be made of the above by flavoring the milk before using, with two tablespoonfuls of desiccated cocoanut. Another variety still may be made by adding to the first recipe half a cup of Zante currants and the same of seedless raisins, or a half cup of finely shredded, tender citron.

(Battle Creek, 1910)

Bread and Butter Pudding

Cut about a pound of good light bread into thin slices, and butter as for eating, lay them in a pudding dish, and stew seeded raisins between each layer. Beat six eggs with four large spoonfuls of sugar, mix with three pints of sweet milk and a grated nutmeg; turn the whole over the bread, let it stand until half of the milk is absorbed, then bake. This will make a large, excellent pudding.

(Battle Creek, 1890)

Buckeye Pudding

1 cup raisins	2½ cups flour
1½ cup molasses	Dessert-spoon soda—
1 cup warm water	yolks 2 eggs

Steam 2 hours. Silver sauce.

Mrs. Oliver P. Arnold, White Pigeon
(Chicago, 1886)

Buttermilk Pop

Boil one quart of fresh buttermilk; beat one egg, a pinch of salt and a heaping tablespoonful of flour together, and pour into the boiling milk. Stir briskly and boil for two or three minutes, and serve while warm with sugar, or, better still, maple syrup. Although this is an old-fashioned and homely dish, eaten and relished by our grandparents before cornstarch, sea moss farina, dessicated cocoanut and other similar delicacies were ever heard of, it is perhaps as nutritious as any of them, and often far more easily obtained.

(Detroit, 1881)

Caramel Pudding

2 cups milk, heated	¾ cup sugar
1 cup granulated sugar, browned	1 cup milk
½ cup flour	1 egg and pinch of salt

Stir granulated sugar together until dissolved. Mix together.

Cook together until it thickens and when cool add ½ cup walnut meats. Serve with whipped cream.

Mrs. Frank Hachmuth
(Grand Rapids, 1917)

Carrot Pudding

Take two cups of carrots, boiled tender and rubbed through a colander, one pint of milk, two thirds of a cup of sugar, and two well-beaten eggs. Flavor with vanilla, and having beaten all well together, turn into an earthen pudding dish; set the dish in a pan of hot water, and place in the oven. Bake only till set custard sets.

(Battle Creek, 1903)

Cherry Pudding

One c. sugar; 1 c. sour milk; 1 tsp. salt; butter the size of an egg; 1 tsp. soda; flour to thicken as for loaf cake.

Cherry Part: 1 pt. cherries, with juice; 1¼ c. sugar; 2 c. boiling water; butter the size of an egg. Stir all together when sugar is dissolved; pour over batter and bake from ½ to ¾ of an hour.

Mrs. J. Monroe Maus
(Kalamazoo, 1921)

Chestnut Pudding

Peel off the shells, cover the kernels with water, and boil till their skins readily peel off. Then pound them in a mortar, and to every cup of chestnuts add 3 cups of chopped apple, 1 of chopped raisins, ½ cup of sugar, and 1 qt. of water. Mix thoroughly, and bake until the apple is tender—about ½ hour. Serve cold with sweet sauce.

Remarks—Whoever loves chestnuts (and who does not) will like the flavor of this pudding. Take out a chestnut from the boiling water, and drop it into cold water a moment, and if the dark skin will rub off with the thumb and finger (which is called blanching), they have boiled enough.

(Ann Arbor, 1884)

Corn Meal Pudding

Heat a quart of milk lacking two thirds of a cupful, to boiling. Moisten nine tablespoonfuls of nice granulated corn meal with the two thirds of a cup of milk, and stir gradually into the boiling milk. Let it boil up until set, turn into a double boiler, and cook for an hour. Then add a tablespoonful of thick sweet cream, one half a cup of molasses or sugar, a quart of cold milk, a little salt if desired, and lastly, two well-beaten eggs. Mix thoroughly. Pour into a pudding dish and bake one hour. A cup of currants or seeded raisins may be used to give variety.

(Battle Creek, 1910)

Cottage Pudding

Butter size of black
*   walnut*
1 egg
1 tablespoon sugar

½ cup milk
Flour like cake dough
Heaping teaspoon
*   baking powder*

Butter cups, and put in 1 tablespoon canned raspberries; add dough, and steam 20 minutes; serve with raspberry sauce.

Mrs. George McDonald
(Kalamazoo, 1906)

Delicate Pudding

One-half cup rice in 3 pints milk, cook over water until soft. Beat 5 eggs, leaving out 2 whites, 1 coffee cup sugar and one of cocoanut, stir into the rice and milk and bake in oven. Take out as soon as custard is formed, do not wait for it to set, frost with the two whites and 6 tablespoons sugar and brown in oven. Can leave out the cocoanut and flavor with vanilla or lemon.

Mrs. I. D. Bixby
(Kalamazoo, 1899)

Easter Egg Pudding

Bake half pint of rich and rather thick boiled custard. Pour it into a glass dish and leave it. While it is cooling, beat the whites of three eggs to a very stiff froth with four ounces of powdered sugar. Divide this into three parts. Color one brown with coffee, one pink with cochineal, cranberry juice, or melted currant jelly, and leave the third one white. Have ready a saucepan full of boiling water. Draw this to the side of the stove; dip a dessert spoon into this, and heat it; then lift up a spoonful of the egg froth and shape it into the form of an egg. Now plunge the spoon into the water, and the meringue will float off. Proceed thus until all the mixture is made into "eggs." Allow them to cook on the water for six or seven minutes, after which carefully lift them out on a skimmer; let them drain for a moment and pile them artistically on the custard. Be careful not to let the water boil up after the meringue is put in or the eggs will break.

(Ionia, 1912)

English Plum Pudding (Very Rich)

Six ounces of suet chopped fine, six ounces Malaga raisins stoned, eight ounces of currants, well washed and dried, three ounces of bread crumbs, three ounces of flour, three eggs, four ounces of sugar, small one-half pint of milk, a very little mace, one-sixth of a nutmeg, one teaspoonful of cinnamon, one-half teaspoonful of salt, one-half pound of citron cut up fine; dip a pudding bag in boiling water, flour well and turn; put the batter in, tie, leaving a little room to swell, put in a kettle of boiling water and boil steadily for six hours, filling up the kettle with boiling water as required to keep the pudding well covered with the boiling water. When done, plunge the bag into cold water and the pudding will come out of the bag nicely; pour brandy over the pudding and carry to the table burning. Serve with brandy sauce. This pudding may be made weeks before using and is as good when warmed over.

Mrs. C. E. Scott, Escanaba
(Chicago, 1898)

Dr. Chase enlivened his *Last Receipt Book and Household Physician* with a good sea story he had clipped from the *Detroit Free Press:*

English Plum Pudding

It was about the stormiest voyage I ever see. We left the Hook on November 5, 1839, in a regular blow, and struck worse weather off the Banks (New Foundland), and it grew dirtier every mile we made. The old man was kind of gruff and anxious like, and wasn't easy to manage. This ain't no Christmas story, and ain't got no moral to it. I was second mate and knowed the captain pretty well, but he wasn't sociable, and the nearer we got to land according to our dead reckoning (for we hadn't been able to take an observation) the more cross-grained he got. I was eating my supper on the 24th, when the steward he comes in, and says he, "Captain, plum pudding to-morrow, as usual, sir?" It wouldn't be polite in me to give what that captain replied, but the steward he didn't mind. All that night and next day, the 25th of December, it was a howling storm, and the captain he kept the deck. About 8 o'clock Christmas day dinner was ready, and a precious hard time it was to get that dinner from the galley to the cabin on account of the green seas that swept over the ship. The old man, after a bit, came down, and says he, "Where's the puddin'?" The steward he come in just then as pale as a ghost, and says he showing an empty dish: "Washed overboard, sir." It ain't necessary to repeat what that there captain said. Kind of how it looked as if the old man had wanted to give himself some heart with that pudding, and now there wasn't none. I disremember whether it wasn't a passenger as said "that, providing we only reached port safe, in such a gale puddings was of no consequence." I guess the old man most bit his head off for interfering with the ship's regulations. Just then the cook he came into the cabin with a dish in his hand, saying: "There is another pudding. I halved 'em," and he sot a good-sized pudding down on the table. Then the old man kind of unbent and went for that pudding and cut it in big hunks, helping the passenger last, with a kind of triumphant look. He hadn't swallowed more than a single bit than the first mate he comes running down, and says he: "Lizard Light on the starboard bow, and weather brightening up." "How does she head?" "East by north." "Then give her full three points more northerly, sir, and the Lord be praised." And the captain, he swallowed his pudding in three gulps, and was on deck, just saying, "I knowed the pudding would fetch it," and he left us. We was in Liverpool three days after that, though a ship that started the day before us from New York was never heard of. This here is the receipt for that there pudding:

Take six ounces of suet, mind you skin it and cut it up fine. Just you use the same quantity of raisins, taking out the stones, and the same of currants: always wash your currants and dry them in a cloth. Have a stale loaf of bread, and crumble, say three ounces of it. You will want about the same of sifted flour. Break three eggs, yolks and all, but don't beat them much. Have a teaspoonful of ground cinnamon and grate half a nutmeg. Don't forget a teaspoon of salt. You will require with all this a half pint of milk—we kept a cow on board of ship in those days—say to that four ounces of white sugar. In old days angelica root candied was used; it's gone out of fashion now. [Angelica grows all over the United States, as well as Europe, has a peculiar flavor, and was, at least, once believed to be a very valuable medicine, but used more, of late, merely for the agreeable flavor it imparts to other medicines.] Put that in—if you have it—not a big piece, and slice it thin. You can't do well without half an ounce of candied citron. Now mix all this up together, adding the milk last in which you put half a glass of brandy. Take a piece of linen, big enough to double over, put it in boiling water, squeeze out all the water, and flour it; turn out your mixture in that cloth, and tie it up tight; good cooks sew up their pudding bags. It can't be squeezed too much, for a loosely tied pudding is a soggy thing, because it won't cook dry. Put in 5 qts. of boiling water, and let it boil 6 hours steady, covering it up. Watch it, and if the water gives out, add more boiling water. This is a real English plum pudding, with no nonsense about it.

(Ann Arbor, 1884)

Eve's Pudding—Mrs. T.'s

If you want a good pudding, mind what you are
  taught;
Take of eggs six in number when bought for a
  groat;
The fruit with which Eve her husband did cozen,
Well pared and well chopped at least half a dozen;
Six ounces of bread—let Moll eat the crust,

And crumble the rest as fine as the dust;
Six ounces of sugar won't make it too sweet;
Some salt and some nutmeg will make it
  complete;
Three hours let it boil without any flutter,
But Adam won't like it without sauce or butter.

(Detroit, 1878)

Boiled Huckleberry Pudding

Measure ¾ pt. of sifted flour; add to it 1 teaspoon baking powder, ½ salt spoon of salt. Sift thoroughly together. Stir a well beaten egg into ½ pt. milk, and stir this gradually into flour, making a smooth batter. Then stir in 1½ cups of berries; turn into a buttered mould, and steam, in enough boiling water to partly cover the mould, for 1 hour. Serve with hard or liquid sauce.

Mrs. A. K. Edwards
(Kalamazoo, 1906)

Huckleberry Pudding

One cup molasses, 1 egg, 1 teaspoon cloves, 1 teaspoon salt, scant teaspoon cinnamon, small teaspoon soda in a tablespoon hot water, flour to make as thick as pound cake, 1 quart huckleberries with a little flour dusted over them. Steam 1½ hours. Liquid sauce the best.

Mrs. T. Sherwood
(Kalamazoo, 1899)

Hunters' Pudding, Boiled—
Will Keep for Months

Flour, suet finely chopped, raisins chopped, and English currants, each, 1 lb; sugar, ¼ lb.; the outer rind of a lemon, grated; 6 berries of pimento (all-spice) finely powdered; salt, ¼ tea-spoonful; when well mixed add 4 well beaten eggs, a ½ pt. of brandy, and 1 or 2 table-spoonfuls of milk to reduce it to a thick batter; boil in a cloth 9 hours, and serve with brandy sauce. This pudding may be kept for 6 months after boiling, if closely tied up; it will

279

be required to be boiled 1 hour when it is to be used.—*Farm and Fireside.*

Remarks—This, for hunters going out upon a long expedition, would a very desirable relish to take along. There is not a doubt as to its keeping qualities, as it contains no fermentive principles; and the fruit and brandy are both anti-ferments, while the long boiling is also done to kill any possible tendency to fermentation. I should, however, boil it in a tin can, having a suitable tight-fitting cover, if intended for long keeping, on the principle of air-tight canning, as well as to be safe from insects, and convenience in carrying. Do not think, however, but what it would be very nice for present use with only 4 or 5 hours boiling, using the sauce freely, as it is made so dry for the purpose of long keeping.

(Ann Arbor, 1884)

Indian Pudding, No. 1, Baked

This pudding was made at the Cataract House, Niagara Falls, by Mrs. Polk, for thirty-six successive seasons: One quart of milk put on to boil; 1 cup of meal, stirred up with about a cup of cold milk; a piece of butter, about the size of an egg, stirred into the hot milk, and let boil; beat 6 eggs, or less, with 1 cup of powdered sugar, and add a teaspoonful of ginger and nutmeg; then stir the whole together, and have it thick enough to pour into the dish, buttered. Bake in a quick oven.

Sauce for Same—One cup powdered sugar; ½ cup butter, beaten to a cream. Flavor with nutmeg and a little wine or brandy, to taste.

Remarks—Myself and family spent several days at the above hotel, in 1874, where we were so well pleased with this pudding—as has always been my custom, in my travels, if I found some particularly nice dish upon the table—I made an effort (through the waiter) to obtain the recipe, and, by "oiling the machinery," at both ends of the route—paying waiter and cook—I succeeded. I have given it word for word as dictated by Mrs. Polk (colored), who was highly gratified because we were so much pleased with her pudding, assuring us she "had made it in the same house for thirty-six seasons, without missing one." The family having made it many times since, I can, therefore, assure every one "it is genuine," and very nice indeed. Coarse meal is considered better than fine for baked puddings; and if the milk is rich by stirring in the cream so much the

better. They are made without eggs, molasses taking the place of sugar.

(Ann Arbor, 1884)

Korn-Krisp Pudding

Two cups Korn-Krisp. 2 cups milk (sweet), 2 eggs, ½ cup of sugar. Season to taste with vanilla or other flavoring, and add raisins or currants if desired. Bake in a moderate oven 25 minutes.

(Battle Creek, 1903)

Two young mechanics from Kalamazoo, Frank and George Fuller, shifted their operations to Battle Creek to take advantage of the big breakfast cereal boom of 1903. They came up with a clever name, Korn Krisp, but left too much oil in the malt-flavored flakes. The cereal grew moldy on grocery shelves. They returned to Kalamazoo to tinker with automobiles and eventually establish Fuller Brothers, famous manufacturer of truck transmissions. We've found corn flakes a fine substitute for Korn Krisp.

Orange Pudding

Peel and slice 4 large oranges, lay them in your pudding dish and sprinkle over them 1 cup of sugar. Beat the yolks of 3 eggs, ½ cup of sugar, 2 table-spoonfuls of corn starch, and pour into a quart of boiling milk; let this boil and thicken; then let it cool a little, before pouring it over the oranges. Beat the whites of the eggs and pour over the top. Set it in the oven to brown slightly.

Mrs. R. McK., Jackson, Mich.
Farm and Fireside
(Ann Arbor, 1884)

"Pain Perdu"

Cut break thick—cut off crusts, soak 2 hours in 1 pint milk with 1 egg, fry in deep lard.

Sauce—One cup butter and 2 cups fine sugar, mix to a cream, heat over boiling water, add ¾ cup wine heated, stirring well. An egg may be added before the wine.

Mrs. Wm. Tomlinson
(Kalamazoo, 1899)

Pop Corn Pudding

Take a scant pint of the pop corn which is ground and put up in boxes, or if not available, freshly popped corn, rolled fine, is just as good. Add to it three cups of new milk, one half cup of sugar, two whole eggs and the yolk of another, well beaten. Bake in a pudding dish placed inside another filled with hot water, till the custard is set. Cover with a meringue made of the remaining white of egg, a teaspoonful of sugar, and a sprinkling of the pop corn.

(Battle Creek, 1919)

Puff Pudding

Sift one pint of flour, and two teaspoonfuls of baking powder; rub into a tablespoonful of butter and one beaten egg, add enough milk to make a drop dough. Put into a steamer six well buttered cups, drop a spoonful of dough into each cup, then a spoonful of fruit, apples, peaches or berries. Cover with dough (no sugar in it.) Steam thirty minutes.

Sauce—Beat two eggs with half a cupful of butter, one cupful of sugar, add a cupful of boiling milk and a cupful of the fruit juice.

Anna Hall, Nahma
(Chicago, 1898)

Sailor's Duff

One-half cup molasses, 2 tablespoons sugar, 2 tablespoons melted butter, 1½ cups sifted flour, 1 teaspoon soda in ½ cup boiling water, 1 egg, pinch of salt. Steam 1 hour—This serves 7 persons. Sauce:—½ cup powdered sugar, 1 egg beaten thor-

oughly; just before serving add ½ pint of cream whipped.

Mrs. J. M. Petersen
(Manistee, 1929)

We'll bet you thought a sailor's duff was something he sat on.

St. James' Stale Bread Pudding

Grate a stale loaf of bread (*i.e.,* 2 or 3 days old) into crumbs; pour over them 1 pt. of boiling milk; let stand 1 hour; then beat to a pulp; then beat, sugar, 1½ cups, to a cream with 4 eggs, and butter, 2 table-spoonfuls; grate in the yellow of a lemon, and a bit of nutmeg, and a pinch of cinnamon, if liked; beat all well together, and pour into a pudding dish lined with nice puff paste, and bake about 1 hour. The juice of the lemon to be used in making whatever sauce you prefer.

Remarks—The author feels very sure you will ask St. James to call again. Bread, buttered well on each side, may be substituted for the puff paste to line the dish.

(Ann Arbor, 1884)

School Days' Pudding

One quart bowl of Indian meal, a little salt, a tablespoonful of ginger. Moisten thoroughly with cold water, tie in a cloth, and boil two hours.

Sauce—One pint of molasses, a small teacupful of water, one teaspoonful of ginger, two heaping tablespoonfuls of butter; heat together, and pour hot over each slice.

(Battle Creek, 1890)

Stewed Fruit Pudding

Take a deep, square or oblong granite-ware or earthen dish; cut strips of stale bread uniformly an inch in width and three fourths of an inch in thickness, and place them in the mold with spaces between them equal to their width. Or, fit the strips

281

around the bottom of a round, earthen pudding dish, like the spokes of a wheel, with an open space between each and in the center. Have ready some hot stewed or canned fruit, sweetened to taste; whortleberries are best, but apricots, cherries, currants, strawberries, and gooseberries may all be used. Separate the juice from the berries by turning them into a colander. Fill the interstices between the bread with hot fruit, using just as little juice as possible. Cover with another layer, this time placing the strips of bread over the fruit in the first layer, and leaving the spaces for fruit over the bread in the first layer. Fill the dish with these layers of fruit and bread, and when full, pour over all the hot fruit juice. Put a plate with a weight on it on the top to press it firmly. Dip off any juice that may be pressed out, and set the pudding in the refrigerator to cool and press. When cold, it will turn out whole, and can be cut in slices and served with whipped cream or cocoanut sauce.

(Battle Creek, 1910)

Whortleberries are blueberries.

Sweet Potato Pone

Take four large sweet potatoes, peel and grate them, then add two cups of water or milk, a lump of butter the size of an egg, melted, three eggs well beaten, a teaspoonful each of allspice and cinnamon, one and a half teaspoonfuls of ginger, and half a nutmeg, grated; mix all the ingredients well, butter a pudding-pan, pour in your pone, and bake in a moderate oven.

(Detroit, 1884)

Sweet Potato Pudding

Grate six medium-sized, raw sweet potatoes. Add two quarts of cold sweet cider, one cup of grated cocoanut, and an equal quantity of raisins. Thicken with graham flour, beat the batter well, and bake in a moderate oven.

(Battle Creek, 1876)

Whortleberry Pudding

One pound sugar, half pound butter, three-fourths pound flour, five eggs and one quart berries. Beat butter and sugar to a cream; add the flour, sifted, alternately with the eggs, whipped to a froth; the berries last rolled in flour. Bake in a buttered cake dish.

(Detroit, 1881)

Yorkshire Pudding, English

Sweet milk, 1½ pts.; flour, 7 tablespoonfuls (as you lift them out of the sifted flour); a little salt. Directions—Put the flour into a basin with the salt and sufficient of the milk to make a stiff, smooth batter (that is, to be no lumps); then stir in two well-beaten eggs and the remainder of the milk; beat all well together, and pour into a shallow tin which has been previously rubbed with butter. Bake for 1 hour; then place it under the meat for ½ an hour to catch a little of the gravy as it flows from the roasting beef. (This is the English way, where they "spit" the beef in roasting. See remarks below for the American way, and also about serving on a napkin.) Cut the pudding into square pieces and serve on a hot folded napkin with hot roast beef.—*Warne's Model Cookery*, London, Eng.

Remarks—The plan of putting the pudding under the roasting beef, where they roast it upon spits (a pointed bar of iron, or several of them, to roast before a fire), as our grandmothers used to roast a goose, turkey or spare-rib, was a very convenient way of moistening the top of the pudding with the rich juices of the beef; but in place of that we, here in America, have the pudding 10 or 15 minutes longer in the oven, but baste it frequently during this time, with the meat drippings: make this pudding only when you are roasting beef; and we serve it upon the plates with the beef, and not upon napkins, which makes too much washing for our wives and daughters. In England, with plenty of "servants," they care not for this extra work. "A hot oven, a well beaten batter, and serving quickly are the secrets of a Yorkshire pudding," to which the author will add, also a rich meat gravy.

(Ann Arbor, 1884)

Pudding Sauces

Mrs. John S. Newberry contributed the following recipe to *The Spicy Recipe Book,* compiled by the Young Ladies Missionary Society of the Jefferson Avenue Presbyterian Church of Detroit in 1882. Her husband achieved cartographic immortality that same year as he lent his name to a small Upper Peninsula logging village that ultimately became the county seat of Luce County. Newberry, a Detroit lawyer and railroad manufacturer and promoter, built the Mackinaw and Marquette Railroad through the Upper Peninsula, completed in 1881. The Newberry's son, Truman Handy Newberry, distinguished himself as Secretary of the Navy under Theodore Roosevelt and as U.S. Senator from 1912–22.

Pudding Sauce

One and one half cups of powdered sugar, two and one third cups of butter, stirred to a cream; then add two tablespoonsful of vanilla. Just before serving add half a wineglass of boiling water and beat to a froth.

Mrs. John S. Newberry
(Detroit, 1882)

Bath Lemon Sauce

One cup of sugar, half a cup of butter, stirred to a light cream; add the yolks of two eggs, then pour over this half a pint of boiling water and the juice of one lemon; then the whites of the eggs well beaten.

(Detroit, 1878)

The Eyre Sauce

Stew together for fifteen minutes half a pound of sugar, a piece of butter as large as an egg, and one pint of water; beat the yolks of three eggs; remove the pan from the fire and pour several spoonfuls of its contents into the beaten egg, stirring

briskly; then pour all into a pan, place it over a slow fire and stir till it thickens; season with extract of nectarine (Burnet's) or vanilla.

(Detroit, 1878)

Fairy or Nun's Butter

One tablespoonful of butter and three of powdered sugar stirred together till very light; grate a little nutmeg over the top.

(Detroit, 1878)

Foaming Sauce

One cup of sugar, one cup of butter, two eggs; beat the yolks with the sugar and the juice, and grated rind of one lemon; beat the white by itself, when it is stiff, mix it with the sugar and yolks. *The minute before* it is sent to the table, stir in rapidly a teacup of boiling water.

(Detroit, 1878)

German Foam Sauce

Select a German pudding dish with dasher, or use a Dover egg beater; into this put the yolks of five eggs, two dessertspoonfuls of raspberry vinegar and three of water, three-fourths of a cup of sugar; add lemon peel; stir to a foam by whipping it with a Dover egg-beater; then place over the heater till it boils, stirring constantly; to be prime it should be prepared after the dinner is served; there should be nothing but foam.

(Detroit, 1878)

Hard Sauce

Take two cups of powdered sugar; add half a cup of butter slightly warmed, so that the two can be worked up together. When they are well mixed,

283

beat a grating of nutmeg and the juice of a lemon. Whip smooth and light, mound neatly on a dish and set in the cold to harden.

(Detroit, 1881)

Heidelberg Sauce

Take of the mace compound [below] five table-spoons, sugar three tablespoons, one scant tea-cupful of water, one teaspoonful of flour, one tea-spoonful of butter; put all on the fire and stew to a glaze.

(Detroit, 1878)

Mace Compound

To take the place of "sherry wine" in puddings and sauces. Soak half an ounce of mace eight hours in one teacup of lemon juice, add half a tea-cup of boiling water and scald twenty minutes.

(Detroit, 1878)

Maple Sugar Sauce

Melt over a slow fire, in a small teacup of water, half a pound of maple sugar; let it simmer, remov-ing all scum; add four tablespoonfuls of butter mixed with a level tablespoonful of flour and one of grated nutmeg; boil for a few moments and serve. Or make a "hard sauce" of one tablespoonful of butter to two of sugar.

(Detroit, 1881)

Pudding Sauce

Three tablespoonfuls of white sugar, one even of flour, a piece of butter the size of a hen's egg, stirred to a cream. Stir in gradually two tablespoon-fuls of mace compound [above], add a teacup of boiling water. Then set into a kettle of boiling

water, stirring it constantly, until the flour is cooked.

(Detroit, 1878)

Pudding Sauce

Add to a coffeecup of boiling milk, one table-spoonful of flour, wetted with two of cold milk, have ready a teacup of sugar, and half a teacup of butter, thoroughly stirred together, and when the flour and milk have boiled two or three minutes, add the sugar and butter; stir well but do not boil, flavor with lemon or vanilla.

(Detroit, 1878)

Rappahannock Cold Sauce for Eight Persons

One heaping tablespoonful of butter creamed till very light, adding sugar till as thick as you can stir; then add two tablespoonfuls of very rich milk or thin cream, a dozen pounded almonds or a tea-spoonful of extract of almonds and a little grated nutmeg.

(Detroit, 1878)

Southern Pudding Sauce

One cupful of cream from morning's milk, two cupfuls of sugar, one egg well beaten, one table-spoonful of butter, one teaspoonful of corn starch. Boil all together till it is a thick syrup, take off the fire and add grated nutmeg and a teaspoonful of ext. of nectarine.

(Detroit, 1878)

Sauce for Sponge Pudding

Two cups of sugar, one cup of butter, yolks of two eggs beaten to a cream; heat over the kettle top, add the beaten whites. Flavor to your taste.

(Detroit, 1878)

Virginia Cold Sauce

Whites of five eggs beaten to a stiff froth; sweeten to taste; pour in some *hot* melted butter, stirring well; season with almond or lemon.

(Detroit, 1878)

DOUGHNUTS, SHORTCAKES, and MISCELLANEOUS SWEETS

Aebelskiver No. 1

Take one-half compressed yeast and dissolve in a little warm water with one teaspoonful sugar. Take a quart of milk and warm it a little. Mix enough flour in to make a smooth batter. Beat the yolks of 4 eggs into all this and let it rise to almost double the amount. Then beat the 4 egg whites and 2 teaspoonfuls of melted butter and add a little salt to it and bake in an iron cup griddle. Serve with jelly or coat with pulverized sugar.

Your Danish Friend
(Grayling, 1937)

Aebelskiver No. 2

Take 4 eggs; beat yolks and whites separately. Take 2 cups of buttermilk and a half teaspoonful soda. Stir the soda into the milk and add a little salt. Take enough flour to make a smooth batter. Then stir in the whites of the eggs and 2 tablespoonfuls of melted butter. Bake in an iron cup griddle.

Your Danish Friend
(Grayling, 1937)

A cast-iron cup griddle, sometimes called an aebelskiver pan, resembles a circular muffin tin with a handle.

Apple Loaf

Fill a quart baking dish with alternate layers of thinly sliced apples and sugar; add half a teacupful of water, cover with a saucer, held in place by a weight. Bake slowly three hours. Let it stand until cold, and turn it out. It will be a rounded loaf of clear red slices, imbedded in a firm jelly.

Use ⅔ cup of apples for this recipe.

(Battle Creek, 1890)

Apple Omelet

Six large pippins or other tart apples, one tablespoonful of butter, three eggs, six tablespoonfuls of white sugar, nutmeg to the taste, and one teaspoonful of rosewater; pare, core and stew the apples, as for sauce; beat them very smooth while hot, adding butter, sugar and flavoring; when quite cold add the eggs, beaten separately very light; put in the whites last and pour into a deep bake dish previously warmed and well buttered. Bake in a moderate oven until it is delicately browned. Eat warm—not hot.

(Detroit, 1881)

Apple Sandwich

Mix half a cup of sugar with the grated yellow rind of half a lemon. Stir half a cup of cream into a quart of soft bread crumbs; prepare three pints of sliced apples, sprinkled with the sugar; fill a pudding dish with alternate layers of moistened crumbs and sliced apples, finishing with a thick layer of crumbs. Unless the apples are very juicy, add half a cup of cold water, and unless quite tart, have mixed with the water the juice of half a lemon. Cover and bake about one hour. Remove the cover toward the last, that the top may brown lightly. Serve with cream. Berries or other acid fruits may be used in place of apples, and almond cream substituted for cream.

(Battle Creek, 1910)

Apple Sandwich No. 2

Prepare and stew some apples as for sauce, allowing them to become quite dry; flavor with lemon, pineapple, quince, or any desired flavor. Moisten slices of zwieback in hot cream as for toast. Spread a slice with the apple mixture, cover with a second slice of the moistened zwieback, then cut in squares and serve, with or without a dressing of mock cream. If desired to have the sandwiches particularly dainty, cut the bread from which the zwieback is prepared in rounds, triangles, or stars before toasting.

(Battle Creek, 1910)

Blueberry Muffins

1 quart box berries
1½ cups sweet milk
1 cup sugar
2 eggs

1 tablespoonful of
    melted butter
A little salt

Flour enough to make quite a thick muffin batter. Bake in a very hot oven.

Miss Helen Snook
(Kalamazoo, 1906)

Blueberry Tea Cake

3 cups of fresh blue-
    berries
2 tablespoons of but-
    ter
1 cup of sugar
1 cup of sweet milk

2½ cups of flour
2 teaspoons of baking
    powder
And 2 eggs beaten
    very light

Mrs. A. C. Wortley
(Kalamazoo, 1906)

Brown Betty

One-third bread and ⅔ apple. Crumb the bread fine and chop the apples; 2 cups brown sugar, ½

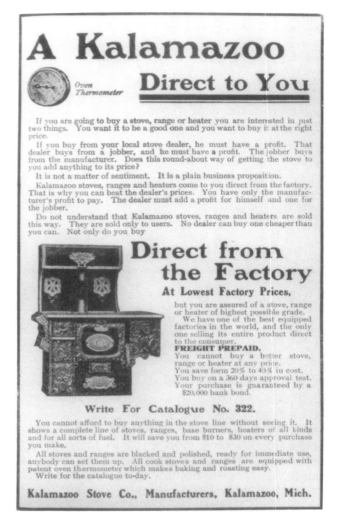

The Kalamazoo Stove Company established in 1901 made the city famous with its aggressive merchandising that bypassed the middleman (Adrian, 1905).

cup butter, 2 teaspoons cinnamon, a little nutmeg. Mix thoroughly and spread over the apples and bread. Bake very brown.

Mrs. C. B. Mann
(Muskegon, 1890)

Cape Ann Berry Cake

Four cups sugar, 1 cup butter, 1 quart sweet milk, 1 tablespoon salt, 2 teaspoons baking powder, 5 pints whortleberries or other berries, flour to form a thick batter; to be baked in a dripper; cut in squares for the table and serve with butter for tea.

Mrs. Wm. M. Ferry, Grand Haven
(Grand Rapids, 1890)

Drop Cakes

1 small cup sugar
1 rounded table-
　spoonful butter
1½ cups flour (small)
½ cup milk

1 teaspoonful baking
　powder
Yolks of three eggs
Flavor to taste

Cream well the butter and sugar.

Mrs. Ralph McCoy
(Kalamazoo, 1906)

We suppose you bake this, but Mrs. McCoy didn't say.

Huckleberry Cobbler

2 cups huckleberries
½ cup honey
2 cups bread crumbs

2 tablespoons nut but-
　ter

Oil the casserole; put alternate layers of huckleberries, honey, nut butter and crumbs. The top layer should be crumbs. Bake, covered in moderate oven for 20 minutes, remove cover and bake until crumbs are a delicate brown.

(Berrien Springs, 1941)

Orange Bread

Peelings of two
　oranges
2 eggs
1½ cups sugar
2 cups milk

½ t salt
½ cup butter
2 t baking powder
3 to 4 cups flour

Cut peelings fine, add ½ cup of water and boil until tender, add ½ cup sugar, cool then take butter, sugar and salt, beat well, add eggs beaten, milk, part of sifted flour, drench peelings with flour then put together, add baking powder, beat until more solid than cake; grease two loaf pans, put your dough into them and let rise 20 minutes. Bake in moderate oven about 30 minutes. Delicious for sandwiches the next day.

Mrs. Melvin Barlow, Millgrove
(Allegan, 1938)

Patent Tea Cake

Sift 2 teaspoons cream tartar and 2 tablespoons white sugar into 1 quart of flour, beat 2 eggs, add after mixing a piece of butter the size of an egg. Mix all with a pint of milk, and the last thing a teaspoon of soda dissolved in a little milk; bake in muffin rings.

Mrs. S. L. Withey
(Grand Rapids, 1890)

Peach Flummery

One pint of ripe peaches, stewed in one pint of water until soft. Add one cup sugar, three tablespoonfuls cornstarch dissolved in a little water. Cook five minutes, turn in molds. When cold serve with sweetened cream.

Mrs. J. A. Mabbs
(Holland, 1908)

"The peach—rich alto of the orchard's tune," according to Will Carleton, thrived along Lake Michigan's shores (New York, 1881).

287

Plumb Cobler

Take 1 quart flour, 4 tablespoons melted lard, ½ teaspoon salt, 2 teaspoons baking powder; mixed as for biscuits, with either sweet milk or water, roll thin and line pudding-dish or dripping-pan, nine by eighteen inches; mix 3 tablespoons flour and 2 of sugar together and sprinkle over the crust; then pour in 3 pints canned damson plumbs and sprinkle over them 1 coffee-cup sugar; wet edges with a little flour and water mixed, put on upper crust, press the two edges together, make two openings by cutting two incisions at right angles an inch in length, and bake in a quick oven half an hour. Peaches, apples of any kind of fresh or canned fruit, can be made in the same way.

(Vermontville, 1906)

Prune Whip

Twenty prunes stewed until juice is gone, then stone and cut up fine. Whites of 6 eggs beaten light, 6 tablespoons sugar added with prunes and beaten light. Put in moderate oven a short time until it puffs up. Eat with whipped cream.

Miss Mary Priest
(Kalamazoo, 1890)

Short Bread—The True Scotch Receipt

Four pounds of flour, two and a half pounds of butter, one and one-quarter pounds of sugar, one wine-glass of rose water, one-half pound of caraway comfits and one-half pound of citron. Rub the butter and sugar to a cream, add the rose water and then the flour, roll out to rather less than half an inch in thickness and strew over the top the candy comfits and the citron cut in thin pieces the size of your thumb nail, pass your rolling-pin over this and then cut out into squares and diamonds with a paste-jigger, and bake in a dripping-pan; it will keep nice and fresh two or three months. This receipt has been in an old Scotch family for more than three-quarters of a century, and has always

been the New Year's cake in the old-fashioned Knickerbocker visitations on that day. The candy and citron make it a very handsome-looking cake, as well as delightful in flavor.

(Detroit, 1878)

A paste-jigger is a pastry cutter with a round revolving blade.

Shortcake

Make biscuits, using plenty of shortening; make a little larger than ordinary; when baked, split and butter the biscuits while hot. Take fresh fruit and crush, and add enough sugar to make plenty of juice; spread between biscuits and over top. Serve with whipped cream. This shortcake has become quite popular on account of its convenience.

Mrs. H. J. Quay
(Flint, 1912)

Corn-Meal Short-Cake

One cup Indian meal, and ½ cup flour, sifted into a bowl with ½ teaspoon soda, and same of salt. Sift three times.

One tablespoon butter, 1 tablespoon lard, 1 tablespoon sugar, 2 eggs, 1 cup thick sour milk. Cream sugar, butter and lard, add yolks beaten light, then milk, then mingled flour and meal, lastly beaten whites. Bake in shallow pan.

Mrs. C. M. Chamberlin, Kalamazoo
(Charlotte, 1909)

Pumpkin Shortcake, With Graham Flour

"Stewed and strained pumpkin or squash, 'C' oatmeal porridge and water, each 1 cup. Beat these up together, and then stir in 3 cups of Graham flour. Mix thoroughly, spread ½ an inch thick on a baking-tin, and bake half an hour in a good oven. Cover for 10 minutes, and serve warm or cold."

Remarks—Our readers will see by the quotation marks (" ") that this is not my own, nor do I known who to credit it to. But I have given it for the sake of a few explanations, or remarks, which, I think, will be for the general good; and first, you will see that a porridge is called for made from "C" oatmeal; what does the "C" mean here? It means the grade of fineness of the meal, as known to dealers, the same as "A" coffee sugar means the best— "C" coffee sugar is not quite so good. While with the oatmeal it means not quite so coarse a meal as "A" would be. For Scotch cake the finest kind is used, and, I should think, would be the best to make into a porridge. Second, some persons never use oatmeal porridge; then, unless people will use a little of good common sense, they, or persons living where they cannot get oatmeal, could never have those nice short cakes; but by using, or calling up this common sense, and reasoning a little, they may say, "now I have not got the oatmeal, nor can I get it; but I will take milk in its place; and even, if no milk, I will take water, and by adding a little butter, lard or drippings, I will have just as good a cake"— and so they would. Now, please judge, in the same manner, in all cases, where such difficulties may of necessity arise, then these remarks will have their intended effect. I will add this word, only, additional, those who don't know anything more than simply to always confine themselves to, or follow a recipe, or receipt, as generally called, (never changing it at all) will never amount to much, to themselves, or to the world. The above recipe says "pumpkin, or squash"—everybody ought to know that squash will make the richer cake.

(Ann Arbor, 1884)

Strawberry Shortcake, Old Way

Mix as for biscuit, roll about 1 inch thick, and bake. When done, have the strawberries mixed with sugared cream: split the cake with a sharp knife, spread lightly with butter the lower half, then put in a thick layer of the fruit, replacing the top, and covering the top also. Some persons then replace in the oven for a few minutes; but this, I think, make it more like pie than fresh berry shortcake. Other berries or pieplant may be used, but pieplant must be stewed and no cream used.

(Ann Arbor, 1884)

Taffy Biscuits

One quart flour, 1 rounding tablespoon butter, 3 teaspoons baking powder, 1 level teaspoon salt, a little less than 1 pint milk, mix and roll out dough ½ inch thick. Spread with the following mixture: ¼ cup butter, ¾ cup brown sugar, mix well together and spread on biscuit dough, roll up firmly and slice in layers 1 inch thick, bake. Handle little; soft dough and quick fire insure success.

Fay Ashby
(Kalamazoo, 1899)

Pumpkin Indian Loaf

Scald one quart of corn meal, and stir in one pint of stewed and sifted pumpkin; add one teaspoonful of salt, and one gill of molasses; mix to a stiff batter, and bake in a deep dish.

(Battle Creek, 1890)

Ginger Bread

Two eggs, one cupful of molasses, one cupful of sugar, two-thirds cupful of shortening, one cupful of sour milk, three cupfuls of flour, one-half teaspoonful each of different spices, a little salt, two teaspoonfuls of soda.

Mrs. W. A. Armstrong, Menominee
(Chicago, 1898)

Babalaars

Three cups brown sugar, 1 cup water, 3 tablespoons of vinegar, 2 tablespoons molasses, 1 tablespoon butter, pinch of salt. Boil until it becomes brittle when dropped in cold water. Pour into buttered dripping pan and when cold pull until hard, and cut into small pieces.

Mrs. John L. Hollander
(Kalamazoo, 1920)

Elephants' Ears

Beat 3 eggs, add pinch of salt and small table-spoon milk. Mix very stiff with flour. Pinch off a piece about the size of a walnut, roll out very thin, fry in deep, hot fat. Serve hot with maple syrup.

Mrs. C. P. Savigny
(Detroit, 1915)

Jolly Boys

One cup of sour milk, half a level teaspoonful of soda (dissolve soda in a little of the sour milk with a pinch of salt), one egg beaten light, one or two tablespoonfuls (think the children will like two), of molasses. Mix rye meal with the milk, to the con-sistency of a thin batter, and then add Indian meal until the batter becomes a stiff one. Last of all stir in the egg. Drop from tablespoon (about half a spoonful at a time), into a kettle of boiling drip-pings or lard, and brown as you would crullers or fried cakes. If they are rightly made they will pop over themselves when done on one side, in a light and bouyant manner, and that's why they are called "jolly boys."

(Detroit, 1881)

David Stott's flour undoubtedly drew its name from the excitement produced by the Columbian World's Exposi-tion of 1893 (Detroit, 1915).

Kleiner

¾ cup sugar	*1 teaspoon ground*
¾ cup butter	*cardemon seed*
3 eggs	*9 tablespoons sweet*
	cream
	Flour (enough to roll)

Mix sugar and butter well. Then add cardemon seed, cream and flour. Roll out and cut in strips 1 by 4 inches. Slit in center lengthwise; then twist. Fry in lard as fried-cakes.

Margrethe Nielsen
(Grayling, 1937)

Oliebollen (Fat Balls)

3 cups Potato Water	*1 Egg*
½ cup Sugar	*2 Compressed Yeast*
1 teaspoon Salt	*Cakes*
¼ cup Lard or Butter	*6 or 7 cups Flour*
1 cup Currants	*1 cup Raisins*

Mix all ingredients into soft dough. Let rise. Make small balls about dessert spoonful. Drop in deep hot fat and fry until brown. Serve with brown sugar.

(Holland, 1936)

Vat-Bollen

Scald 1 quart of milk, let cool, when luke warm add ¾ cake compressed yeast cake dissolved in a little water, add small ½ cup sugar, 1 teaspoon salt, ¾ cup raisins, 1 or 2 eggs, flour enough to make a soft batter, let rise and stir once or twice; let rise again. Fry in hot lard, slowly. Dip spoon in cold water each time to prevent sticking.

Mrs. De Koning
(Kalamazoo, 1920)

Olie Koeken, or Dutch Doughnuts

Three quarts of flour, 1 package of seedless raisins, 1 cup of granulated sugar, 1 tablespoon of salt, 1 tablespoonful of grated nutmeg, 2 tablespoons of melted lard, 1 compressed yeast cake; soak yeast cake in a cup of water until light. Mix all together in a large bowl, add enough water to make a soft batter and let rise until light. Drop by spoonfuls in hot lard and fry until brown.

Mrs. J. L. Lage
(Kalamazoo, 1920)

Orange Fritters

Take 3, or as many large smooth oranges, as needed, take off the peel and the white skin also, then slice them, crosswise, ¼ inch thick, pick the seeds out, and dip the slices in a thick batter, fry nicely, placing them in layers, on a plate, as fried, sifting sugar over each layer. Serve hot.

(Ann Arbor, 1884)

Pumpkin Fritters

One pint of flour, one of buttermilk, half a teaspoonful of salt, one of soda, half a cupful each of molasses and stewed pumpkin, two eggs. Fry quickly in plenty of lard. Serve hot with sugar and cream.

(Battle Creek, 1890)

Apple Dumplings

Pare and core without quartering 12 large apples. Make a crust of 4 cups flour, 3 teaspoons baking powder, ½ cup butter; rub butter well into flour, mix with milk as for biscuit, cover each apple with the dough and put in a buttered tin, pour boiling water over them and bake. Serve with cream and sugar.

Mrs. W. W. Barcus
(Muskegon, 1890)

Cherry Dumplings

Take one cup of prepared flour, or use baking powder and flour same as for biscuits; two heaping tablespoonfuls of lard, two cups fresh milk, a little salt, two cups of stoned cherries, and one-half cup of sugar. Rub the lard into the salted flour, wet up with the milk; roll into a sheet a quarter of an inch thick, and cut into squares. Put two tablespoonfuls of cherries into the center of each; sugar them; turn up the edges of the paste and pinch them together. Lay the joined edges downward, upon a floured baking-pan and bake half an hour or until browned. Eat hot with a good sauce.

(Detroit, 1881)

Huckleberry Dumplings

One quart flour, three teaspoonfuls baking powder, one tablespoonful lard worked into the flour, one cup milk. Roll out and cut larger than biscuit; put in the berries and turn the edges closely. Steam or boil in a closely covered kettle fifteen minutes. Eat with melted sauce.

(Detroit, 1881)

The huckleberry is commonly known as the blueberry.

Plum Dumplings

Sift two teaspoons baking powder with 1 quart flour, use sweet milk to make stiff batter. Put 1 quart plums in a kettle and cover with water well sweetened, drop the dough in the kettle with the plums and boil until done.

(Vermontville, 1906)

Raspberry Dumplings

Make a puff paste and roll it out. Spread raspberry jam (any other is just as good), and make it into dumplings. Boil them an hour; pour melted butter into a dish and strew sugar over it for sauce.

(Detroit, 1881)

COLD DESSERTS

If you have never enjoyed homemade ice cream, you owe it to yourself to try some. It takes a good deal of work to crank the handle of the ice cream freezer, but it's worth it. Larry has pleasant childhood memories of his father making ice cream. Salt was poured on the ice to make it colder, and the whole family took turns cranking. Their favorite flavor was caramel, made from burnt sugar. The one-gallon bucket of ice cream always disappeared too soon.

Ice Creams

We have lived so much in the country that years ago we gave our mind to the simplification of making ice cream. We like a patent freezer; almost all are good, especially those that have not too much machinery, but we can make mighty good cream with a tall four-quart tin pail and an ordinary wooden bucket. Any of the receipts given are good. All cream is the richest—the flour, milk and whites of eggs with part cream is the next—the frozen custard is thoroughly digestible and an excellent and economical receipt. To freeze ice cream or water ices quickly and well: Have your cream or custard on the ice for two or three hours before you are ready to use it; flavor and sweeten the former when you are prepared to freeze it. Take a fifteen pound lump of ice, put it into an old bag or coffee sack, have at your hand three pints of course salt; then take the flat of the axe or a mallet, or, if you have neither, and are a woman, a great deal may be accomplished with a flat-iron, pound the ice *fine*, empty it out of the bag into an old dishpan or tub, pour over the salt, take your short-handled stove shovel or a scoop, mix all thoroughly and fill round the ice cream freezer after it has been properly placed in the tub; then pour in your cream.

(Detroit, 1878)

Ice Cream

Three pints sweet cream, one quart of new milk, one pint of powdered sugar; put in a freezer till thoroughly chilled through, then add the whites of two eggs beaten light, and freeze.

(Detroit, 1878)

Ice Cream, No. 2

Boil two quarts of milk, into which stir a pint of cold milk that has had four level tablespoonfuls of arrowroot mixed smoothly into it, then scald, but not boil; when cold, add two quarts of cream, a tablespoonful of vanilla or other flavoring, and two pounds (or pints) of sugar; put in the freezer and whip till well chilled, then add the whites of six eggs beaten to a stiff froth.

(Detroit, 1878)

Ice Cream

(These recipes come with the Gooch Triple Motion Freezer.)

Vanilla Ice Cream—To each quart of cream add ¼ of 1 vanilla bean previously cut into small pieces and boiled in a small quantity of cream or milk and strained. If preferred, substitute 1 tablespoon of vanilla extract. Sweeten very sweet and freeze.

Lemon Ice Cream—To each quart of cream add the juice and grated rind of one lemon, or a teaspoonful of lemon extract. Sweeten very sweet and freeze.

Pine Apple Ice Cream—To each quart of cream add the juice of ¼ of a good sized pineapple, which should be previously cut up, sprinkled with sugar and strained. Sweeten very sweet and freeze.

Strawberry or Raspberry Ice Cream—The same as vanilla, substitute the fruit, which should be first mashed and strained through a fine net.

Vanilla Ice Cream (cheap)—To each quart of rich milk add 2 eggs, well beaten, and a teaspoonful of corn starch; sweeten very sweet, cook it well without boiling. When cold stir in a teaspoonful of vanilla extract and freeze.

THE PEERLESS
GOOCH
ICE CREAM FREEZER.
SIMPLE, CHEAP AND PERFECT.

With crank,	3 quart, each	....	2 25
"	"	4	"	"	....	2 75
"	"	6	"	"	....	3 50
"	"	8	"	"	....	4 50
"	"	10	"	"	....	6 00
"	wheel,	14	"	"	....	10 00
"	"	18	"	"	....	12 50
"	"	21	"	"	....	15 00
"	"	25	"	"	....	17 50
"	"	32	"	"	....	20 00
"	"	42	"	"	....	22 50

Home ice cream freezers like the Gooch required lots of cranking but produced an unexcelled product (Grand Rapids, 1890).

Orange Water Ice—To each quart of water add the juice of 3 or more oranges, 1 lb. of sugar, the grated rind of 1 orange, an ½ a lemon grated fine; also the juice of 1 lemon to every 4 quarts of water. Strain carefully into the can and freeze the same as ice cream.

Lemon Water Ice—Make a rich, sweet lemonade and freeze. This may be much improved by adding the well beaten whites of 6 eggs to each quart of lemonade.

Raspberry or Strawberry Water Ice—Simmer 1 quart of fruit a little with 1 lb. of sugar, and strain. When cool stir into 1 quart of water and freeze. The well beaten whites of 6 eggs to each quart of water will much improve it.

Strawberry or Other Fruit Iced Custard—Make a quart of rich, boiled custard; when cold pour it on a quart of ripe fruit. Mash, pass through a sieve, sweeten and freeze.

(Grand Rapids, 1890)

Burnt Cream

One qt. milk, 4 tablespoons cornstarch, 1¼ lbs. brown sugar, ½ cup walnuts. Put milk to boil, when hot add cornstarch blended with a little cold milk, stir till it thickens. Burn the sugar in an iron pan until it is deep brown, pour into the cornstarch, add the walnuts broken up. Pour into a mould and set away to chill. Serve with cream.

Clara B. Arthur, Detroit
President, Michigan Equal Suffrage Association
(Charlotte, 1909)

Cantaloupe Frappe

Soak one tablespoonful of Knox's gelatine in one-quarter cupful of cold water, then set cup in pan of boiling water until it is dissolved. Cut in halves two large cantaloupes (more if family is large), scrape the pulp from same after removing the seeds (not using any of the rind), put the pulp through potato ricer, which will keep out all the stringy parts; add to the pulp one pinch of salt, four tablespoonfuls of powdered sugar, one gill of sherry wine. Add to this the dissolved gelatine. When cold, turn into a freezer and freeze slowly; when ready for the table, pack back into the cantaloupe rind and serve. The cantaloupes must be ripe and of fine flavor.

Mrs. Lizzie Carpenter, Menominee
(Chicago, 1898)

Caramel Ice Cream

One generous pint milk, 1 cup sugar, scant ½ cup flour, 2 eggs. Let milk come to a boil, beat sugar, eggs and flour together, stir into milk and cook 20 minutes. Put 1 small cup sugar in frying pan, stir over fire until sugar turns liquid and begins to smoke, add this to above mixture and cool. When cold add 1 quart cream and strain into freezer.

Mrs. Frank Henderson
(Kalamazoo, 1899)

Hamburg Cream

Juice of one large lemon; one cup sugar; five eggs. Add the lemon juice and sugar to the well beaten yolks of five eggs. Put in double boiler and stir often. When thick add to the stiffly beaten egg whites. Put in serving glasses and place on ice. Serves eight.

Mrs. John H. Rademaker
(Manistee, 1929)

Lemon Custard

Beat the yolks of eight eggs till they are white, add pint boiling water, the rinds of two lemons grated, and the juice sweetened to taste; stir this on the fire till it thickens, then add a large glass of rich wine, and one-half glass brandy; give the whole a good boil, and put in glasses. To be eaten cold. Or, put the thin yellow rind of two lemons, with the juice of three, and sugar to taste, into one pint of warm water. As lemons vary in size and juiciness, the exact quantity of sugar can not be given. Ordinary lemons requires three gills. It will be safe to begin with that quantity, more may be added if required. Beat the whites to a stiff froth, then the yolks; then beat both together, pour in gradually while beating the other ingredients; put all in a pail, set in a pot of boiling water, and stir until thick as boiled custard; strain it in a deep dish; when cool place on ice. Serve in glasses.

Mrs. Belle R. Liggett, Detroit
(Minneapolis, 1881)

Lemon Ice

2 small cups granu-
  lated sugar

Juice of 3 lemons,
  squeezed into the
  sugar

Stir well. When ready to turn into the freezer, add 1 quart of morning's milk.

Mrs. W. S. Dewing
(Kalamazoo, 1906)

Lemon Jelly

Soak one box gelatine in warm water two hours. Two cups sugar; put on stove and just let come to a boil. Add juice of six lemons and the gelatine. Let this mixture just come to a boil and dissolve, then take from the stove and add sliced bananas. Put on ice one-half day, or in the cellar one whole day.

Mrs. W. J. Hickmott
(Mendon, 1890)

Maple Ice

Three cups maple syrup, yolks of 12 eggs, 2½ quarts cream; beat yolks into cold syrup, bring to boiling point, stirring constantly; let cool, whip cream and add to syrup when perfectly cold, pack in ice and salt for 7 or 8 hours. If cream will not whip, this will make a delicious plain maple cream. Cook syrup and eggs as above and add cream and freeze. Sufficient for one gallon.

(Vermontville, 1906)

Maple Sauce for Ice Cream

One cup maple syrup boiled till it hairs, white of 1 egg beaten, fold into hot syrup; when cold add ½ cup of cream whipped.

Mrs. H. B. Pierson
(Manistee, 1929)

Currant Sherbet

One pint of sugar, one quart of water, one pint of currant juice, the juice of a lemon. Boil water and sugar together half an hour, add lemon and currant juice to this and let cool and freeze.

Mrs. L. S. Boughton, Battle Creek
(Chicago, 1896)

Milk Sherbet

The juice of four lemons, the grated rind of one lemon, the juice of two oranges and one pint of sugar, one quart of water, one quart of sweet milk. When half frozen add the whites of two eggs, well beaten, add the milk last, just at you place the mixture in the freezer.

Mrs. Lizzie Carpenter, Menominee
(Chicago, 1898)

Rice Blanc Mange

Pick over and wash a scant half cupful of rice; put in double boiler with 3 cups of milk and a pinch of salt; cook until very soft, then, add two rather scant tablespoons of granulated gelatine, which has been soaked in four tablespoons of cold water; stir gently, and add good ½ cup powdered sugar. Set aside until cold, and beginning to thicken; then add ¼ cup of sherry, 1 teaspoon vanilla and 1 cup cream, whipped stiff. Turn into wetted moulds until firm. When ready to serve, unmould and garnish with candied cherries. Serve with whipped cream.

Mrs. Wm. E. Hill
(Kalamazoo, 1906)

Sea-Moss Blanc-Mange

Wash 2 tablespoons sea-moss from druggist in water with small pinch soda, rinse twice, put into a granite kettle and add 1 quart new milk, let it boil ½ minute, stirring constantly. Strain through cheese-cloth and pour into moulds. When it has hardened turn into saucers and serve with pulverized sugar and rich cream. A teaspoon of jelly or sun-dried fruit at side of dish is delicious. Even invalids may take this nutritious delicacy.

Mrs. Frank Cornell
(Kalamazoo, 1899)

Sea moss is the same as Irish moss or carrageen, used as a gelling agent.

Charlotte Russe, No. 1

Sweeten and flavor to taste one quart of fresh cream; whip it to a froth with a Dover egg-beater or wire spoon. Break up half an ounce of Cooper's isinglass into half a pint of cold water; let soak one hour, then set it over a boiling teakettle, or on the stove, to dissolve. When thoroughly dissolved and cooled, pour it into the cream, stirring it until it be-

gins to thicken. Line a mold with lady's-fingers and pour in the mixture.

(Detroit, 1878)

The Dover egg-beater is the familiar hand-operated whirling machine first patented and popularized by the Dover Manufacturing Company in the 1870s. See pages 74–75 for a note on isinglass.

Sabyon

3 eggs well beaten	*¾ cup boiling water*
½ cup sugar	*¼ cup Sherry wine*
2 teaspoons corn- *starch*	*3 tablespoons Brandy* *1 cup cream*

Beat eggs, sugar and cornstarch together, add boiling water slowly, put in double boiler and cook until thick. When cold add Sherry, Brandy and cream whipped stiffly and sweetened. Serve in punch glasses with lady fingers.

Mrs. Dudley E. Waters
(Grand Rapids, 1935)

Sultana Roll

Scald one pint of milk, add one cupful of sugar and a tablespoonful of flour mixed together, one egg beaten light, cook twenty minutes, add one pinch of salt, strain and cool. Add one quart of whipped cream; flavor with vanilla and almond extract, lightly color with leaf green, if desired, and freeze. When frozen, line a mould with the cream and sprinkle with sultana raisins which have been soaked several hours in brandy. Fill the center of

The famous Dover eggbeater was one of many labor-saving devices that made life a little easier (Chicago, 1901).

the mould with one pint of cream whipped to a stiff dry froth, sweetened with one-half cupful of powdered sugar and flavored with one teaspoonful of vanilla. Cover the mould. Pack in salt and ice and let stand several hours. Serve with claret sauce as follows: Put one cupful of sugar and one-fourth cupful of water in a saucepan on the stove; stir until sugar dissolves, then boil until it thickens slightly and add four tablespoonfuls of claret.

Floride Ruprecht, Menominee
(Chicago, 1898)

Snow Custard (Winter Receipt)

For a three-pint mold put one-half box of gelatine in a bowl, soak it one hour with one pint of cold water, then add one pint of boiling water, stir until dissolved; then put to cool; sweeten with three-quarters of a pound of sugar and flavor with the juice of three lemons. Whip the whites of four eggs to a stiff froth; add them to the gelatine when it begins to stiffen or set; then whip the whole to a light froth, and when all begins to stiffen pour it into a mold. Take the four yolks of the eggs and make a rich custard, flavor it with the rind of one lemon and pour round. This pudding will keep for a day or two. This receipt is excellent in cold weather or where you can use plenty of ice.

(Detroit, 1878)

Snow Custard (Summer Receipt)

Soak one-half a box of gelatine one hour in half a pint of cold water; add half a pint of boiling water, three-quarters of a pound of powdered sugar. Beat the whites of three eggs, add gradually the gelatine and sugar, when it begins to set then the juice of three lemons, grated rind of one; beat constantly, *hard* and *fast*, from half an hour to an hour; or until it is about as stiff as pancake batter; put it in the dish in which it is to be served, and set in a cold place or on ice; make the yolks into a soft custard, with a pint of milk, flavoring with the rind of the lemon. This pudding is good the second day, eaten with strawberries or canned fruit.

(Detroit, 1878)

CANDY

Dentists quite frequently inserted advertisements somewhere near this section in the early cookbooks.

Confectionery

Candy Making

The first step is the reduction of sugar to a syrup, which is done by adding water to sugar in the proportion of a pint and a half of water to three and a half pounds of sugar. Put in a marbelized saucepan, and when it has boiled ten minutes begin to try it; have a bowl of water, snow, or piece of ice near, and drop the syrup from the end of the spoon. While it falls to the bottom and you can make it into a softish ball, it is ready to take off; if allowed to stay on until it snaps it will be too hard. If this is the case, add a little water and boil again, being sure this time not to let it get too brittle. A pinch of cream of tartar is useful in checking a tendency for the syrup to go to sugar. When the sugar is boiled just right, set off to cool, and when you can bear your finger in it pull into sticks, or into one solid mass like that bought at the confectioners. Flat sticks are formed by pouring the candy into long, flat pans, and when cooling, crease the mass, which will readily break into sticks when cold. If the hands are slightly greased the candy will not stick to the hands.

In making molasses candy, get the best molasses (not syrup) and add to a quart of molasses one pound of white sugar. The sugar makes it whiter and more brittle. Boil this until it will snap like glass when dropped into water, and then add a teaspoonful of vinegar and a pinch of soda; stir well in, as the soda whitens the candy, and the vinegar checks a tendency to graining. Remove from the stove, cool a moment and pour into greased platters. Set out to cool, and with a knife keep the edges turned in so that all will be cool and ready to pull at the same time. When making nut candies, use the same mixture before it gets quite to the brittle point; have the meats in shallow tins and pour the candy over

Advertisements like this frequently appeared amidst candy recipes in early Michigan cookbooks (Muskegon, 1899).

them. Before quite cold, slash with the knife so that it will break into oblong pieces or squares.

(Detroit, 1881)

Candy, made of Corn Syrup

Two cups granulated sugar, ½ cup corn syrup, ½ cup boiling water, whites of 2 eggs, 1 cup nuts, flavor to taste. Cook sugar, corn syrup and boiling water until it hardens in water. Cool five minutes then add beaten whites of eggs, nuts and flavoring and beat as long as possible then turn on buttered tins. When cold, cut in squares.

Miss Cora Campbell, Reading
(Charlotte, 1909)

Chocolate Caramels

Boil one quart of good New Orleans molasses until it hardens, when tested by cooling a little of it in water. Just before removal from the fire, add four ounces of chocolate finely and uniformly grated. Pour a thin layer into tin trays slightly greased, and when the surface of the candy has become hardened a little, mark with a knife into squares. These may be flavored, but the natural flavor of the chocolate and molasses is generally preferred without addition.

(Detroit, 1881)

Crackerjack

Pop corn, not putting on much lard or butter, make a syrup of 2 cups sugar, 1 cup baking molas-

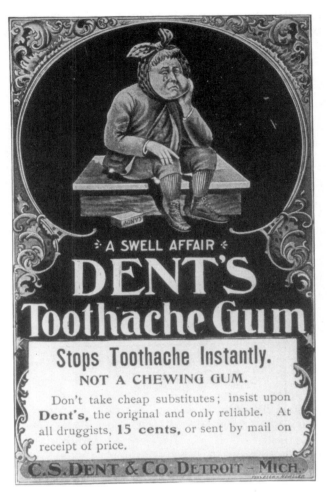

Too many gumdrops brought a dose of Dent's (Pearson's, 1900).

ses, butter the size of an egg. Flavor. Pour over popped corn slowly, stirring constantly, and be sure to put enough syrup so it will stick together good, take out of pan you are stirring it in and pack in a greased pan. Let cool before cutting.

(Vermontville, 1906)

January Thaw

2 cups brown sugar   1 cup nuts
½ cup milk   Butter size of a walnut

Put sugar and milk in a saucepan and let it dissolve slowly; add butter and let boil until it forms a ball when dropped into cold water. Remove from stove, add the chopped nuts and beat well. Turn into a buttered pan and, when cool, cut in squares.

(Manistee, 1929)

Lemon Drops

Pour clear lemon juice upon powdered sugar and boil till a thick syrup; then drop upon plates in drops singly and put to dry in a warm place.

Or, pour four ounces of lemon juice upon one pound of loaf sugar with the same amount of rose water as of lemon juice; boil to a thick syrup, add grated lemon peel and proceed as in the first recipe.

(Detroit, 1878)

Clear Drops and Lollypops

1½ cupfuls of sugar
⅓ cupful of light corn
   syrup
⅛ teaspoonful of
   cream of tartar
¾ cupful of water
10 drops of flavoring
   oil coloring matter

Without stirring, boil the sugar, corn syrup, cream of tartar and water together, cooking slowly to 310° F. Take from the fire, add the flavoring oil and the coloring matter. Then shape into lollypops, spice or fruit drops or molded candies.

(Manistee, 1929)

Maple Candy

Four cups brown sugar, 1 cup rich milk or cream, butter size of an egg, 2 tablespoons vanilla, 2 cups chopped nuts. Let sugar and milk boil five minutes, add butter. When melted take off the fire, add vanilla and nuts, beat well till the bubbles have disappeared, pour into greased tins; when cool trace in squares. Very good.

(Vermontville, 1906)

"Don't cry over spilt milk" or taffy either (Freeport, IL, 1915).

Maple Fudge

For Maple fudge, first get the genuine maple sugar, no imitation or half-and-half preparation, and grind it through a mill; this will make it light, and it will not pack in the cup. Take three cups of the ground sugar, one full cup milk and a piece of butter as large as a small egg, mix all together and set over a hot fire. Cook till boils away from the sides of the kettle, beating all the time. Then pour into a pan and beat until cold.

(Ionia, 1912)

Mexican Candy

Two c. pecan nuts, 2 c. sugar, 2 c. water. Boil all together until it hairs. Beat until it sugars and drop on buttered paper.

Mrs. W. M. Milham
(Kalamazoo, 1921)

Candied Orange or Lemon Peel

Save orange or lemon peel in halves or quarters; weigh and soak in strong salt water for 24 hours; then rinse, drain and put on to boil in water for 10 minutes. Drain again, and boil in a syrup, using 1 lb. sugar to 1 lb. of peel. When the peel looks clear, remove it from the syrup, laying each piece on a platter. Boil the syrup as thick as possible, and pour it into the hollows of the peel. Allow it to remain on the platter until dry, then roll in white sugar and pack in glass jars.

Miss Maizie Beamer
(Flint, 1912)

Penoche

Two and one-half cups brown sugar, ½ cup cream, butter size of an egg, boil until it will form a ball in cold water, add ½ cup chopped walnuts, ½ cup chopped almonds, 1 teaspoon vanilla. Beat well and pour in buttered tins. Cut in squares before cool.

Belle Colton, Rockford
(Charlotte, 1909)

Potato Candy

One cup mashed potatoes; 2 lbs. pulverized sugar. Mix potatoes and sugar together and flavor. Make into shape as for chocolate creams, and let stand awhile, and then melt chocolate and dip them in. These are good without the chocolate with nut meats on top.

Mrs. Burleson
(Flint, 1912)

Shellbark Candy

2 cups white sugar   *2 tablespoons vinegar*
Scant half cup water   *Butter size of walnut*

Mix thoroughly before putting on the fire; do not stir while cooking; test with cold water. Butter the pans, put in nuts, and pour the candy on them. Cream candy is made the same way, only without the nuts, and when a little cool, pull it.

Blanche Hull
(Kalamazoo, 1906)

Shellbarks are nuts from the shagbark or shellbark hickory tree.

Walnut Candy

The meats of hickory nuts, English walnuts, or black walnuts may be used according to preference in that regard. After removal from the shells in as large pieces as practicable, they are to be placed on the bottoms of tins, previously greased, to the depth of about a half inch. Next, boil two pounds brown sugar, a half pint of water and one gill of good molasses until a portion of the mass hardens when cooled. Pour the hot candy on the meats and allow it to remain until hard.

(Detroit, 1881)

FRUIT DESSERTS

Fruit

Fruit should be carefully selected and only that which is perfect and ripe be served on the table. Grapes and oranges surrounding a pineapple make a pretty center piece. The best oranges are the Florida and Havana. A rough reddish skin covers the sweetest oranges, while the light yellow thin skin covers those more acid and juicy. Fine grained pears are best for eating, the California and Bartletts taking the lead. The little Delaware grape is the sweetest and mixed with the California Concords and Malagas, makes a dish beautiful in coloring and rich in flavor. Of pineapples the best flavor is secured by slicing them thin and letting them stand a few hours thickly sprinkled with sugar. Lady fingers served with pineapples makes a nice dessert. In raisins the loose Muscatels and layer raisins take the precedence, served with nuts or candy. Hickory nuts, filberts, almonds, English walnuts, American walnuts and Brazil nuts, are very satisfactory served with raisins, as they require but little trouble to get out the meats, and should be cracked before being served on the table—with the exception of soft-shell almonds, which may be brought on with raisins, and cracked with nut-crackers at the table.

In preparing small fruits for the table avoid washing them if possible, though if they are gritty and bought at the market, instead of being raised in one's own garden, it is advisable to wash them in cold soft water, a few at a time in the hand, until they look clean, and then hull them, so that they may be handled as little as possible. After being hulled, put a layer carefully in a dish, then sprinkle over them sugar, and so on until the dish is filled; set away in a cool place until ready to serve. Never drain berries in a colander nor stir them with a spoon. When berries are very large, or with large stems—as currants and strawberries—they are neither stemmed or hulled, but pulverized sugar is passed and the fruit is taken by the stem, dipped into the sugar and eaten.

(Detroit, 1881)

We suggest you disregard the advice concerning not washing fruit.

Baked Apples

Pare and core without quartering, 12 apples; put them in a tin with a small piece of butter on each apple, sprinkle ½ cup of sugar over them, add ½ cup water and bake in the hot oven.

Mrs. W. W. Barcus
(Muskegon, 1890)

Apples

Take large firm apples, peel and core, boil in a syrup of sugar and water until tender, take from syrup and cool, spread the outside of apple with jam and stick almonds all around the apple as the jam will hold them. Almonds must be blanched and put in milk for an hour. Fill the center with whipped

cream and put a cherry or preserved strawberry on top of the cream. Serve with more cream.

(Higgins Lake, 1920)

Baked Apples Stuffed with Prunes

Select fine-flavored, tart apples, wipe, core and pare half way. Fill cavities with stewed prunes cut in pieces, pour around the apples a hot sugar syrup, bake until tender in a hot oven, basting often with the syrup. Serve cold on a salad plate with a tbsp. of whipped cream at the side of the apple. Take 5 pieces of the prunes cut in the shape of leaves and form a daisy on the whipped cream using a Maraschino cherry for the center.

Genevieve Menlenberg
(Kalamazoo, 1921)

Painted Ladies

Remove the eyes and stalks from some nice round-looking apples that will cook well, and peel them very evenly to preserve their shape. Place them in a shallow stewpan large enough to hold them in one layer. Dissolve loaf sugar in sufficient water to completely cover the apples, allowing four ounces of sugar to each pint of water; add a few cloves and a little lemon peel and stick cinnamon. Cover the stewpan and simmer the apples very gently, or they will break before being cooked thoroughly. When done, and they are cool enough, lift them carefully to a glass dish, and with a small brush tint them delicately on one side with a little liquid cochineal or melted red currant jelly; strain the syrup, return it to the stewpan and boil it rapidly until reduced to one-third of a pint. When cold stir to it the juice of half a lemon, and pour it round but not over the apples.

(Detroit, 1881)

Scalloped Apples

| *2 cupfuls soft bread crumbs* | *3 cupfuls apples, cut fine* |

*2 tablespoons nut but-
ter*   *½ cupful honey
                   ¼ cupful water*

Blend thoroughly, and bake about 20 minutes or until apples are cooked. Serve hot.

(Berrien Springs, 1941)

Banana Puffs

Take as many bananas as there are persons to serve. Roll in sugar and cinnamon, then roll each banana in thin pie crust. Bake in hot oven 15 minutes. Serve with whipped cream or lemon sauce. Puffs may be served hot or cold.

(Detroit, 1935)

Baked Bananas with Sauce

Bake bananas in skins for about 15 minutes, or until soft; then peel and while hot pour over them this sauce:

To ½ cup sultana raisins, soaked in 1 cup of water, add ½ cup granulated sugar and cook in double boiler until raisins are well swelled; then add 1 heaping teaspoon cornstarch dissolved in a little cold water. Just before removing from stove add 2 tablespoons fruit juice. This is to be served with meat course.

Mrs. Frank Kennedy
(Detroit, 1915)

Frozen Beets

If you want a real delicacy, try this: Boil the amount of sugar beets required. When boiled peel, slice and cover with vinegar. Allow them to freeze over night. Serve with the ice slightly melted, and you will be surprised to find they have imbibed the flavor of rare old wine.

(Greenville, 1910)

Canned Citron

To each pound of citron add ⅔ cup sugar and ⅓ water. Make a syrup of the sugar and water and boil till clear; put the citron in and boil till the citron becomes almost transparent, usually about 2 hours. About 15 minutes before the citron is done, add a little ginger root and a few slices of lemon. When it is cooled, the citron juice should be about as thick as syrup. Another way is to add a few raisins and the lemon instead of the ginger and lemon. About ¼ cup of raisins is enough to each pound of citron. Just enough to flavor.

(Muskegon, 1899)

Baked Dates

1 pound stoned dates   1¼ cups whole milk

Put dates in buttered baking dish, breaking them apart and cutting or chopping lightly, so they are not in large pieces. Pour on milk, which should come to top but not entirely cover them. Let stand at least six hours, over night is better, and bake in slow oven three quarters of an hour. Serve either hot or cold, with whipped cream. Chopped nuts may be scattered on top before or after baking, but are not necessary.

Mrs. William Donahey
(Grand Marais, 1936)

Gooseberry Fool

Take green gooseberries; to every pint of pulp add one pint of milk, or one-half pint of cream and one-half pint of milk; sugar to taste. Cut the tops and tails of the gooseberries; put them in a jar with two tablespoonfuls of water and a little moist sugar. Set this jar in a saucepan of boiling water, and let it boil until the fruit is soft enough to mash. When done enough beat it to a pulp, work this pulp through a colander, and stir to every pint the above proportions of milk, or equal quantities of cream and milk. Ascertain if the mixture is sweet enough, and put in plenty of sugar, or it will not be eatable;

and in mixing the milk and gooseberries, add the former very gradually to these. This, although a very old-fashioned and homely dish, is, when well made, very delicious, and a very suitable dish for children.

(Detroit, 1881)

Gooseberry Trifle

Scald the fruit, press it through a sieve, and add sugar to taste. Make a thick layer of this at the bottom of the dish. Mix a pint of milk, a pint of cream, and the yolks of two eggs; scald it over the fire, stirring it well; add a small quantity of sugar, and let it get cold. Then lay it over the gooseberries with a spoon, and put on the whole a whip made the day before.

(Detroit, 1881)

A whip is a whipped cream.

Fried Grape-Nuts and Bananas

Six bananas, 2 eggs, ½ cup milk, 1 tablespoonful of sugar, 1½ cups of Grape-Nuts. Peel bananas, beat eggs well, and add milk and sugar, roll bananas in flour, then in the eggs, then in Grape-Nuts. Fry in hot lard till light brown. Serve with sugar, syrup, or sprinkle with powdered sugar.

(Battle Creek, 1903)

Orange Hash

Orange hash is a new fancy dessert, consisting of oranges, bananas, lemons, apples, raisins and pine-apples cut into little bits and served with nutmeg and sugar. The manner of serving is as peculiar as the dish. A hole is cut in the stem end of an orange, large enough to admit a spoon, and after the inside is scooped out the orange is filled with the hash, a little champagne or other wine is poured in and the whole is frozen.

(Detroit, 1890)

Orange Straws

Carefully remove the peel from a dozen Havana oranges and trim out every particle of the white part, leaving only the yellow rind. Cut this into strips the width of a straw. Boil half a pint of sugar in half a pint of water until it hairs, add the orange straws and boil five minutes, remove from the fire and stir with a silver spoon till the syrup grains like sugar and clings to the straws; spread them on a coarse sieve, sift off the loose sugar, separate the straws when cold and store between layers of waxed paper. These will be found excellent for puddings and fancy dishes.

Mrs. Will Armstrong, Menominee
(Chicago, 1898)

Leonard refrigerators were one of the many wooden products that won Grand Rapids fame as The Furniture City (Grand Rapids, 1890).

302

Orange and Strawberries

Place a layer of strawberries in a deep dish, cover thickly with pulverized sugar, then a layer of sliced oranges and so on until all are used; pour over them orange juice, using three oranges to each quart of berries, let stand for an hour in a Leonard Refrigerator before serving.

Mrs. C. H. Leonard
(Grand Rapids, 1890)

Mrs. Leonard might not have agreed, but other brands of refrigerators would have worked quite nicely.

Fried Peaches

(Nice for a luncheon side dish)

Pare and halve good sized peaches, place in frying pan with pit side up, in each of which place a small piece of butter, cover and simmer until tender, brown slightly, remove cover, sprinkle generously with sugar. After sugar has melted to syrup it is ready to serve.

Mrs. S. T. Metzger
(Greenville, 1915)

Pumpkin Chips

Cut the pumpkin into lengthwise strips about two inches wide. Take nine lemons, squeeze the juice from them, cut the rind into small strips and boil them until tender, weigh six pounds sugar for the same weight of pumpkin; at night sprinkle half the sugar over the chips and over that pour the lemon juice. Next morning put in the kettle with rest of the sugar and lemon rind, add one cup of water, and boil until clear and rich.

Mrs. Homer G. Barber
(Coldwater, 1907)

Red Rice, a Danish Dish

Take ripe, red currants, 1½ pts.; very ripe raspberries, 1 pt.; water, 1 qt.; rice flour, 1 cup; sugar to taste, according to the acidity of the currants. Directions—Stew the currants until the juice flows freely, add the raspberries, just before the currants are ready to strain; then return to the sauce pan, add the sugar; then the rice flour, stirring smoothly, and pour into molds; and when cold turn out upon a glass dish. Thicken with cream and sugar if desired. It may be made with red currant jelly, and raspberry jelly, in place of the fruits, out of their season.

(Ann Arbor, 1884)

Beverages

Recipe for Quarreling

Steep a root of sassafras in a pint of water and bottle. When your husband comes in to quarrel, fill your mouth with this solution and hold until he goes away. A sure cure.

(Flint, 1912)

This works equally well in the quarrelsome husband's mouth. Root beer is a good modern substitute for steeped sassafrass root, but if the quarreling continues you may want to use something stronger.

Coffee, Tea and Chocolate

Coffee is more heating and stimulating than tea. The former excites the pulse, the latter quiets it. Coffee may act as a laxative; tea diminishes the action of the bowels and promotes perspiration. Coffee may produce headache; tea frequently relieves it. Both have power to sustain under fatigue and privation, coffee being particularly active in this direction. Hunger is better borne by their aid. Tea disposes to mental cheerfulness and activity, clears the brain, and diminishes the tendency to sleep. Coffee produce simple wakefulness. If used to excess, they both produce tremor, palpitation, anxiety and deranged vision, and seriously impair digestion. Coffee is heating in warm weather and warming in cold. They are both to be recommended, because they introduce a part of the necessary amount of water needed, because they act as gentle stimulants, and because the milk and sugar added to make them agreeable, furnishes nutriment to the body.

Cocoa possesses in milder degree the properties of tea or coffee, but it differs from them in possessing much higher nutritive powers.

With regard to the quality of coffee, the best is the cheapest. Burn it at home, in small quantities, taking care in using a close roaster, never to fill it more than half. Turn the roaster, slowly at first, more rapidly as the process advances, keeping up a lively fire. Burn it until of a light chestnut color. Keep it in close canisters or bottles. Grind it as wanted. Boil it in a vessel only half full, to prevent boiling over, in proportion of one and a half ounces to a pint of water. Put in a few hartshorn shavings or isinglass, if you will, but if the coffee is taken off the fire while boiling, and set on again, alternately, until nothing remains on the top but a clear bubble, and then some poured out to clear the pipe and poured back again, it will be as fine as if cleared artificially. Long boiling does not make coffee stronger, but destroys its color and makes it turbid. In making coffee the broader the bottom of the pot and the smaller the top the better it will prove.

Various are the methods of preparing this "beverage of Arabia"; but it will be found, after all, that there is no surer way of having coffee clear and strong than by pursuing the plan here given: Beat up an egg (two for a large pot) and mix it well with the coffee till you have formed a ball; fill the pot with cold water, allowing room enough to put in the ingredients; let it simmer very gently for an hour, but do not think of stirring it, on any account. Just before it is required, put the pot on the fire and warm it well; but, as you value the true aroma, take care that it does not boil. Pour off gently, and you will have as pure and as strong an extract of the Indian berry as you can desire. Use white sugar candy, in powder, in preference to sugar. Cream, if attainable; if not, boiled milk.

A celebrated cook gives this receipt for making

a good cup of coffee: Use Java and Mocha mixed. For each tablespoonful of coffee use nearly a pint of boiling water. Beat the coffee up with the white of an egg and half a tablespoonful of cold water. Pour the boiling water over this and allow it to boil once. Take it from the fire and then replace long enough to come to the boiling point.

A Frenchman roasts coffee, grinds it to a flour, moistens it slightly, mixes it with twice its weight of sugar, and then presses it into tablets. One of these tablets can be dissolved at any time.

Be careful in the choice of coffee pot and keep it clean. A carelessly kept coffee pot will impart a rank flavor to the strongest infusion of the best Java. Wash the coffee pot thoroughly every day and twice a week boil borax and water in it for fifteen minutes.

(Detroit, 1881)

Hartshorn is the antler of a deer and isinglass comes from the bladder of a sturgeon. These were both used as thickening agents in recipes. We suggest gelatin as an alternative.

Good Coffee

Put a quart of boiling water into the coffee pot, wet up a cup of ground coffee with the white of an egg, add the eggshell and a little cold water; put this into the boiling hot water and boil fast ten minutes; then add a half cup cold water and set it before the hearth or table to settle for five minutes; pour it off carefully into the metal or china coffee pot or urn.

(Detroit, 1881)

Vienna Coffee

With very little extra trouble mornings coffee can be greatly improved. Beat the white of an egg

to a stiff froth, mix with an equal quantity of whipped cream and use in coffee instead of cream; put in cream first, then coffee and lastly this mixture.

(Detroit, 1881)

Imperial Coffee

If intended for two persons, take four rounding teaspoonfuls of coffee tied up in a piece of Swiss muslin (leave plenty of room for expansion); pour on two cups of bubbling, boiling water, cover close and set back on the range about ten minutes. Break one egg in a large coffee cup, give it a good whip with an egg-beater, divide it half in each cup, add the usual quantity of sugar, pour on the hot coffee,

The village water pump refreshed both man and beast to say nothing of little boys (Battle Creek, 1886).

add warm milk and one spoonful of cream, and with the golden foam standing one inch above the rim of the cup you will think it too pretty to drink, and when you taste it will think you never knew how good coffee was before.

(Detroit, 1881)

Iced Coffee

Make more coffee than usual at breakfast time and stronger. Add one-third as much hot milk as you have coffee and set away. When cold, put upon ice. Serve as dessert, with cracked ice in each tumbler.

(Detroit, 1881)

Tea

Many say that tea is very hurtful, but we all know it causes cheerfulness, clearness of mind—and is a welcome accessory to every table. It should be banished from the breakfast table, as not being so nourishing as coffee, and at the early meal we know how necessary it is to have nourishing food. To a few people it is hurtful, therefore they should use but a moderate quantity.

Tea is recommended for the following cases: After a full meal, when the system is oppressed; for the corpulent and the old; for hot climates, and especially for those who, living there, eat freely, or drink milk or alcohol; in cases of suspended animation; for soldiers and others marching in hot climates; for them, by promoting evaporation and cooling the body, it prevents in a degree the effects of too much food as of too great heat.

A judicious mixture of several kinds of tea is often advisable. An excellent mixture which combines cheapness with fineness of flavor, is composed of one pound of Congo tea with a quarter of a pound each of Assam and Orange Pekoe. The usual mixture of black and green tea is four quarters of black and one of green.

In order to draw tea properly, be sure and have soft water; in order to avoid the limy taste often in water boiled in tea kettle, put a clean oyster shell in the kettle, which will always keep it in good order by attracting all particles that may be impregnated in

the water. If tea is infused in soft water it will be found to have the best color and to draw best. It is a mistake to make tea strong, if the full flavor is desired. Professional tea-tasters use but a single pinch to a cup of boiling water. In China and Russia, where tea is made to perfection, it is very weak, boiling water being poured upon a few leaves, the decoction covered a few minutes, and then drank hot and clear. Two minutes is long enough for tea to stand, and it should never be boiled, or the fine aroma will be thrown off by evaporation, leaving as flavor only the bitter tannic acid extracted by boiling. If hard water must be used in making tea, a little carbonate of soda put into the tea-pot, will both increase the strength of the tea and make it more nutritious, the alkali dissolving the gluten to some extent.

A silver tea-urn is a matter of economy, for it may be kept boiling with a much smaller quantity of spirits of wine than when a varnished or bronzed urn is used. A good cup of tea is made by putting the tea in the tea-pot and then put in the oven or near the fire where it can get very hot, and the pot then filled with boiling-hot water. The result will be a delicious cup of tea much superior to that drawn in the ordinary way.

Never make tea in any other way than a highly-polished urn, for it is a chemical fact that metal retains the heat longer than earthenware, and the better it is polished, the more complete will the liquid be kept hot and the essence of the tea be extracted. See that the water is really boiling. Tea retains its flavor better if kept in little tin canisters instead of a caddy.

A French chemist asserts that if tea be ground like coffee, immediately before hot water is poured upon it, it will yield nearly double the amount of its exhilarating qualities.

Tastes differ regarding the flavor of teas. A good mixture in point of flavor (and what we use ourselves) is two-fifths black, two-fifths green and one-fifth gunpowder, all being, of course, of superior quality.

(Detroit, 1881)

Iced Tea

The tea should be made in the morning, very strong, and not allowed to steep long. Keep in the ice-box till the meal is ready and then put in a small quantity of cracked ice. Very few understand the art of making iced tea, but pour the scalding hot tea on a goblet of ice lumped in, and as the ice melts the tea is weak, insipid, and a libel on its name. Iced coffee is very nice made in the same way. Too much ice is detrimental to health and often causes gastric fever; so beware of it when in a heated state, or do not drink of it in large quantities.

(Detroit, 1881)

Coffee

Allow 1 teaspoon of coffee for each person to be served and one for the pot. Moisten with the white of an egg and sufficient water to make a thick paste. Add as many cups of boiling water as spoonfuls of coffee used. Boil three minutes. Pour a little to free the spout of grounds and return it to the pot. Let stand on stove where it will keep hot, but not boil, 10 minutes before serving. For after dinner coffee use more coffee to the same amount of liquid.

"COM"
(Kalamazoo, 1920)

To Make a Small Pot of Coffee

Mix 1 c. ground coffee with 1 egg, slightly beaten; to ⅓ of this amount add ⅓ c. cold water; turn into coffee pot; add 1 pt. boiling water and boil three minutes. Keep remaining coffee closely covered in a cool place, to use two successive mornings.

(Kalamazoo, 1921)

Beverages

The use of beverages in quantities with food at mealtime is prejudicial to digestion, because they delay the action of the gastric juice upon solid foods. The practice of washing down food by copious draughts of water, tea, or coffee is detrimental, not only because it introduces large quantities of fluid into the stomach, which must be absorbed before digestion can begin, but also because it offers temptation to careless and imperfect mastication, while tea and coffee also serve as a vehicle for an excessive use of sugar, thus becoming a potent cause of indigestion and dyspepsia. It is best to drink but sparingly, if at all, at mealtimes. Consideration should also be given to the nature of the beverage, since many in common use are far from wholesome. Very cold fluids, like iced water, iced tea, and iced milk, are harmful, because they cool the contents of the stomach to a degree at which digestion is checked. If drunk at all, they should be taken only in small sips and retained in the mouth until partly warmed.

Tea is often spoken of as the "cup that cheers but not inebriates." "The cup that may cheer yet does injury" would be nearer the truth, for there is every evidence to prove that this common beverage is exceedingly harmful, and that the evils of its excessive use are second only to those of tobacco and alcohol. Tea contains two harmful substances, theine and tannin,—from three to six per cent of the former and more than one fourth its weight of the latter. Theine is a poison belonging to the same class of poisonous alkaloids, and is closely allied to cocaine. It is a much more powerful poison than alcohol, producing death in less then one hundredth part the deadly dose of alcohol; and when taken in any but the smallest doses, it produces all the symptoms of intoxication. Tannin is an astringent exercising a powerful effect in delaying salivary and stomach digestion, thus becoming one of the most common causes of digestive disorders. It is also a matter of frequent observation that sleeplessness, palpitation of the heart, and various disorders of the nervous system frequently follow the prolonged use of tea. Both theine and tannin are more abundant in green than in black tea.

The dependence of the habitual tea-drinker upon the beverage, and the sense of loss experienced when deprived of it, are among the strongest proofs of its evil effects, and should be warnings against its use. No such physical discomfort is experienced when deprived of any article of ordinary food. The use of tea makes one feel bright and fresh when really exhausted; but like all other stimulants, it is by exciting vital action above the normal without supplying extra force to support the extra expenditure. The fact that a person feels tired is evidence that the system demands rest, that his body is worn and needs repair; but the relief experienced after a cup of tea is not recuperation. Instead, it indicates that his nerves are paralyzed so that they are insensible to fatigue.

Some people suppose the manner of preparing

tea has much to do with its deleterious effects, and that by infusion for two or three minutes only, the evils resulting from the tannin will be greatly lessened. This, however, is a delusion, if the same amount of tea be used proportionate to the water; for tannin in its free state, the condition in which it is found in tea is one of the most readily soluble of substances; and tea infused for two minutes is likely to hold nearly as much tannin in solution as that infused for a longer period.

Tea is not a food, and can in no wise take the place of food, as so many people attempt to make it, without detriment to health in every respect.

Coffee, cocoa, and chocolate rank in the same category with tea, as beverages which are more or less harmful. Coffee contains caffein, a principle identical with theine and a modified form of tannin, though in less quantity than tea. Cocoa and chocolate contain substances similar to theine and equally harmful, though usually present in much less proportion than in tea.

Custom has made the use of these beverages so common that most people seldom stop to inquire into their nature. Doubtless the question arises in many minds, If these beverages contain such poisons, why do they not more commonly produce fatal results?—Because a tolerance of the poison is established in the system by use, as in the case of tobacco and other narcotics and stimulants; but that the poisons surely though insidiously are doing their work is attested by the prevalence of numerous disorders of the digestive and nervous systems, directly attributable to the use of these beverages.

Both tea and coffee are largely adulterated with other harmful substances, thus adding another reason why their use should be discarded. It is stated on good authority that it is almost impossible to obtain unadulterated ground coffee.

In view of all these facts, it certainly seems wisest if a beverage is considered essential, to make use of one less harmful. Hot milk, hot water, hot lemonade, caramel coffee, or some of the various grain coffees are all excellent substitutes for tea and coffee, if a hot drink is desired.

(Battle Creek, 1910)

Ella Kellogg echoed the advice her husband, Dr. John Harvey Kellogg, reiterated in his many medical treatises. Coffee and tea were banned from the table at his health spa, the Battle Creek Sanitarium. Instead, guests were treated to a caramel cereal coffee he had invented or lemon oatmeal gruel. Around the turn of the century, Dr. Kellogg introduced Kaffir tea, made from a species of South African grass. Julian Street, a traveling journalist with a sense of humor, visited the "San" in 1914 and wrote: "It looked like tea and would probably taste like it too, if they didn't let the Kaffirs steep so long. But they should use only fresh, young tender Kafirs, the old ones get too strong; they have too much bouquet. The one they used in my tea may have been slightly spoiled. I tasted him all afternoon."

Tea and Coffee for Children

Tea and coffee dietary for children is as bad in its effects as its use is universal. Dr. Ferguson found that children so fed only grow four pounds per annum between the ages of thirteen and sixteen; while those that got milk night and morning grew fifteen pounds each year. The deteriorated physiques of tea-and-coffee-fed children, as seen in their lessened power to resist disease, is notorious among the medical men of factory districts.

Selected
(Muskegon, 1890)

Before the advent of indoor plumbing, water coolers saved a trip to the hand pump (Grand Rapids, 1890).

Substitutes for Coffee

As a matter of economy, equal parts of rye or barley may be mixed with coffee, and browned for use. Another substitute highly recommended is sweet potatoes. Take the small ones unfit for market, wash clean, cut in pieces about one-fourth inch in diameter, and dry in the oven. When thoroughly dry, put away in a box or tin can. Brown and grind the same as coffee, with which mix in equal parts.

(Battle Creek, 1890)

Crust Coffee

Tea and coffee are both injurious to children, yet when it is on the table it is difficult to deny them. The following will be found a wholesome and pleasant drink. Take a large crust of brown or white bread, dry thoroughly in the oven, allowing it to become very brown at the last. Pour boiling water over it, and let it boil two minutes. Strain, return the coffee to the fire, add sugar and milk to taste, let it boil up again, and serve.

(Battle Creek, 1890)

Acorn Coffee

Select plump, round, sweet acorns. Shell, and brown in an oven; then grind in a coffee-mill, and use as ordinary coffee.

(Battle Creek, 1910)

This would only work with acorns from certain species of oak trees, as some are extremely bitter.

Beet Coffee

Wash best beets thoroughly, but do not scrape; slice, and brown in a moderate oven, taking care

not to burn. When brown, break in small pieces and steep the same as ordinary coffee.

(Battle Creek, 1910)

Slippery-Elm Tea

Break the bark into bits, pour boiling water over it, cover, and let it infuse until cold. Sweeten, ice, and take for summer disorders, or add lemon-juice and drink for a bad cold.

Put 1 teaspoon powdered slippery-elm into a tumbler, pour cold water upon it, and season with lemon and sugar.

(Detroit, 1890)

Slippery-elm, the inner bark of *Almus fulva*, was used medically to soothe inflamed mucus membranes.

Celery Juice

Wash and clean desired amount of celery. Press juice from stalks and season to taste. Serve warm or cold.

(Berrien Springs, 1941)

The Leonard Company's "octagon tea pot," ideal for slippery-elm tea, featured a hammered tin bottom (Grand Rapids, 1890).

Samuel J. Dunkley, a turn-of-the-century Kalamazoo entrepreneur, bottled up celery juice, added a healthy measure of alcohol, and marketed Celerytone as a sexual tonic.

A Delicious Summer Drink

In one quart of hot water, dissolve four pounds of granulated sugar and one tea spoonful ginger; dissolve one quarter pound of tartaric acid in one pint of cold water and add to the sugar and ginger. Beat the whites of six eggs and stir in when the mixture is cold. Flavor with winter green essence. Put two table spoonfuls of this syrup into a glass and fill the glass nearly full of water. Stir into this one-fourth of tea spoonful soda and drink as it foams. The syrup will keep any length of time if well corked.

Mrs. A. H. Estes
(Mendon, 1890)

A coterie of Mendon ladies who called themselves the Idlers put together an eight-page compilation published by the *Mendon Globe* in 1890. Mrs. A. H. Estes contributed this recipe to *The Idlers Cook Book.*

Fruit Punch

Make three pounds of granulated sugar into syrup for a foundation. Wash and squeeze juice from 1 dozen lemons and 3 oranges, and strain into the foundation. Cut up the rinds, add the strained out pulp and cover with boiling water. Let stand 10 or 15 minutes. Strain and add to foundation. Add 3 or 4 quarts of grape juice according to richness desired. This should make from 2½ to 3 gallons.

Ella G. Simmons, Owosso
(Charlotte, 1909)

Real Grape Juice

Wash grapes and remove from stems. Have jars and tops sterilized and use new rubbers. Fill quart

jars half full of grapes. Add ½ cup sugar. Fill jar with boiling water and seal at once. Let stand for 6 or 8 weeks before using.

Edith Bayley
(Kalamazoo, 1933)

Lemonade

Slice the lemons, peeled or not, as you choose, into a pitcher, then add the sugar, and mash them thoroughly together; add pure cold water to taste. Or, if you have a lemon squeezer, extract and strain one pint of lemon juice, add three pints of water, and a generous pint of sugar. Stir till sugar is dissolved. It should be very cold, and a slice of lemon should be on the top of each glass.

Hot lemonade is highly recommended for a cold. The juice of one lemon, a tablespoonful of sugar, and a cupful of boiling water makes a glass. Drink as hot as can be swallowed, just before retiring.

(Battle Creek, 1890)

Lemonade No. 2

Roll the lemon, to make the juice flow more readily, press the juice into an earthen or glass dish; take all the pulp from the peel and boil five minutes, strain this water and the juice together, and put one pound of white sugar to a pint of juice. Boil ten minutes. Bottle this, and your lemonade can be made at any time. One tablespoonful to a glass of water is sufficient. By the addition of one-

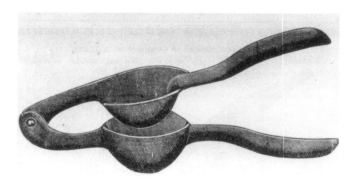

These early lemon squeezers almost guaranteed a squirt in the eye (Grand Rapids, 1890).

half teaspoonful of soda, you will have a sparkling drink.

(Battle Creek, 1890)

Simon Pure Lemonade

Take thin-skinned lemons; roll them on the table until very soft; slice very thin with a sharp knife into a large pitcher, averaging one lemon to a person, thus allowing them two glasses apiece. Put in the pitcher with the sliced lemon a cup of white sugar to five lemons (or more if you want it sweeter) and pound all well together with a potato masher; put in a lump of ice; let it stand a few minutes and fill the pitcher with ice water. This makes lemonade that is lemonade, and the peel in the pitcher is delicious.

(Detroit, 1891)

Lemonade

Use three large or four medium-sized lemons for each quart of water, and from six to eight tablespoonfuls of sugar. Rub or squeeze the lemons till soft. Cut a slice or two from each, and extract the juice with a lemon drill; strain the juice through a fine wire strainer to remove the seeds and bits of pulp, and pour it over the sugar. Add the slices of lemon, and pour over all a very little boiling water to thoroughly dissolve the sugar; let it stand ten or fifteen minutes, then add the necessary quantity of cold water, and serve. Or rub the sugar over the outside of the lemons to flavor it, and make it into a syrup by adding sufficient boiling water to dissolve it. Extract and strain the lemon juice, add the prepared syrup and the requisite quantity of cold water, and serve.

(Battle Creek, 1910)

Liberty Punch

To 1 quart of grape juice add the juice of 2 lemons and 4 oranges, 2 cups of sugar, 1 quart water.

Let chill on ice. Serve with red cherries and white grapes.

Mrs. Lillian Lewis
(Kalamazoo, 1933)

Mint Ginger

2 cups ginger ale
1/4 cup lemon juice
1/2 cup powdered sugar
3 slices lemon

1/2 cup fresh mint leaves
2 cups orange juice
6 sprigs fresh mint

Rub mint leaves and sugar together until well mixed, and add lemon juice and orange juice. Allow to stand at least 15 minutes in a cold place. Strain, add ginger ale and pour into glasses a third full of crushed ice. Garnish each glass with a sprig of mint and a half slice of lemon.

Mrs. Hubert Anderson
(Kalamazoo, 1941)

Raspberry Flip

One quart raspberry juice, 1 quart peach juice, 2 cups grated pineapple and juice, 2 quarts water, 2 cups sugar. Mix altogether and serve very cold.

(Holland, 1925)

Raspberry Vinegar

Fill a stone jar with ripe raspberries, cover with the purest and strongest vinegar, let stand for a week, pour the whole through a sieve or strainer crushing out all the juice of the berries; to each pint of this add one and one-half pounds lump sugar and let it boil long enough to dissolve, removing scum which may rise, then remove from fire; let cool, bottle and cork tightly. Two tablespoons of this vinegar stirred into a tumbler of iced water makes a delicious drink, or a little soda may be added.

(Charlotte, 1893)

The ladies of the First Congregational Church in Charlotte found their original *Charlotte Cook Book* so popular that they published an enlarged second edition in 1893. They prefaced their 153-page volume with a bit of advice that still applies: "Cooking is a fine art, to which you must bring common sense and judgment."

Root Beer

Boil together one pint of dandelion roots, one of spruce sprigs, one-fourth pint of burdock roots, half a pint of molasses, two tablespoonfuls of ginger. Strain, and when cold, add one-third of a cupful of yeast, and stir thoroughly. It will be ready for use in twenty-four hours. This is *not* a stimulating drink, but is excellent for the blood, and may be used freely.

(Battle Creek, 1890)

Rhubarb Cocktail

2 cups rhubarb   1 cup sugar
1 cup water

Cook in double boiler. Drain through sieve. Mix with equal amount of ginger ale and serve.

Mrs. Jessie Buskirk
(Kalamazoo, 1941)

Unfermented Wines

The juice of grapes, blackberries, raspberries, etc., pressed out without mashing the seeds, adding 1 pint water, and ½ lb. sugar for each pint of the juice; then boil a few minutes, skimming if any sediment or scum rises, and bottling while hot, corking tightly, cutting off the corks, and dipping the tops into wax, and keeping in a dry, cool place, gives a wine that no one would object to, if iced when drank. It is nourishing, satisfying to the thirst, and not intoxicating, because there has been no fermentation. Made of grapes, this wine is in every way suitable for communion.

(Detroit, 1890)

Before we get into the "good stuff," we think it proper to peruse Dr. Chase's temperance lecture.

Spirits

"Spiritual Facts—That whis-key is the *key* by which many gain entrance into our prisons and almshouses.

That *brandy brands* the noses of all those who cannot govern their appetite.

That *punch* is the cause of many *un*friendly *punches*.

That *ale* causes many *ailings,* while *beer brings* to the *bier.*

That *wine* causes many to take a *winding* way home.

That *cham*-pagne is the source of many *real* pains.

That *gin slings* have "*slewed*" more than *slings of old.*"

(Ann Arbor, 1864)

Cottage Beer

Take 1 peck good wheat bran and put it into 10 gallons water with 3 handfuls good hops, and boil the whole together until the bran and hops sink to the bottom. Then strain it through a hair sieve or a thin cloth into a cooler, and when it is about lukewarm add 2 quarts molasses. As soon as the molas-

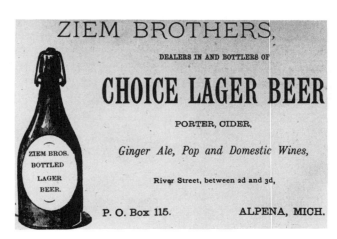

Alpena and most other Michigan communities enjoyed locally produced beer until the Prohibition era (Polk, 1881).

312

ses is melted, pour the whole into a 10-gallon cask, with 2 tablespoons yeast. When the fermentation has subsided, bung up the cask, and in 4 days it will be fit to use.

(Detroit, 1890)

Lemon Beer

Nine lbs. sugar, 3 nutmegs, 6 ozs. cream tartar, 6 lemons, 3 pts. yeast, 10 gallons water; put 4 gals. water to the sugar and boil it, put in 3 eggs well beaten to cleanse it before it boils, then skim it carefully, turn the remaining part of the water into a firkin, slice in the lemons, grate in the nutmegs, put in the cream tartar, the boiling sugar and then the yeast, stir, let stand 12 hours and bottle up.

Mrs. E. E. Judd
(Grand Rapids, 1890)

A firkin is a small wooden barrel holding about nine gallons.

Lemon Ginger Beer

Ingredients: Two and a half pounds loaf sugar, one and a half ounces of bruised ginger, one ounce of cream of tartar, the rind and juice of two lemons, three gallons of boiling water, two large table-spoonfuls of thick and fresh brewer's yeast. Mode: Peel the lemons, squeeze the juice, strain it, and put the peel and juice in a large earthen pan with the bruised ginger, cream of tartar and loaf sugar. Pour over these ingredients three gallons of boiling water, let it stand until just warm, when add the yeast, which should be perfectly fresh. Stir the contents of the pan well and let them remain near the fire all night, covering the pan with a cloth. The next day skim off the yeast and pour the liquor carefully into another vessel, leaving the sediment; then bottle immediately and tie the corks down, and in three days the ginger beer will be fit for use. For some tastes the above proportion of sugar may be found rather too large, when it may be diminished, but the beer will not keep so long good.

To Make a Small Quantity Quickly—Over three-quarters of a pound of loaf sugar, one and a quarter ounces of sliced ginger, and the peel of a lemon, pour a gallon of boiling water; when lukewarm, add

GEORGE GETTER,

PROPRIETOR OF

EAGLE BREWERY

—AND—

BOTTLING   WORKS.

Brewer of Ale, Porter & Lager Beer

COLDWATER, MICH.

Brewery wagons, which dispersed kegs to the numerous taverns found in nineteenth-century Michigan communities, were a common sight (Polk, 1881).

a spoonful of yeast and the juice of a lemon. This last is a most convenient receipt, when only a small quantity for some particular occasion is required, and is as quickly made and not much trouble to prepare. The yeast should be in one night.

(Detroit, 1881)

Maple Beer

To four gallons boiling water put one quart maple syrup and one tablespoonful essence of spruce; when about milk-warm add one pint yeast, and when fermented bottle it. In three days it is a good drink.

(Detroit, 1881)

"Milk-warm" is the temperature of milk when it leaves the cow's udder, in "udder" words, about 98°.

Root Beer

For each gallon of water to be used, take hops, burdock, yellow dock, sarsaparilla, dandelion, and spikenard roots, bruised, of each ½ oz.; boil about 20 minutes, and strain while hot, add 8 or 10 drops of oils of spruce and sassafras mixed in equal proportions, when cool enough not to scald your hand, put in 2 or 3 table-spoons of yeast; molasses ⅔ of a pint, or white sugar ½ lb. gives it about the right sweetness.

Keep these proportions for as many gallons as you wish to make. You can use more or less of the roots to suit your taste after trying it; it is best to get the dry roots, or dig them and let them get dry, and of course you can add any other root known to possess medicinal properties desired in the beer. After all is mixed, let it stand in a jar with a cloth thrown over it, to work about two hours, then bottle and set in a cool place. This is a nice way to take alternatives, without taking medicine. And families ought to make it every Spring, and drink freely of it for several weeks, and thereby save, perhaps, several dollars in doctors' bills.

(Ann Arbor, 1864)

Spruce or Aromatic Beer

For 3 gals. water put in 1 qt. and ½ pt. of molasses, 3 eggs well beaten, yeast 1 gill. Into 2 qts. of the water boiling hot put 50 drops of any oil you wish the flavor of; or mix 1 oz. each, oils sassafras, spruce and wintergreen, then use 50 drops of the mixed oils.

Mix all, and strain; let it stand two hours, then bottle, bearing in mind that yeast must not be put in when the fluid would scald the hand. Boiling water cuts oil for beers, equal to alcohol.

(Ann Arbor, 1864)

Spruce Beer

Hops two ounces, sassafras, in chips, two ounces, water ten gallons. Boil half an hour, strain, and add brown sugar seven pounds, essence of spruce one ounce, essence of ginger one ounce, pimento, ground, one-half ounce. Put the whole in a cask and let cool, then add one-half pint of yeast, let stand twenty-four hours, fine and bottle it.

(Detroit, 1881)

Fine is an old term meaning to refine or clarify.

Currant Wine

For every gallon of water take one gallon of currants off the stalks, bruise well and let them stand

over night. Next morning wash them well with the hands and strain through a fine sieve. To every gallon of the liquor add four pounds of sugar. Rinse the cask well with brandy and strain the liquor again when putting in, by which you will see whether the sugar is dissolved. Lay the bung lightly on and stop it up in ten days.

(Detroit, 1881)

If you bung her down too tight too soon she'll blow.

Dandelion Wine No. 2

One quart of dandelion blossoms, pour over them 4 quarts boiling water, let stand over night and then strain.

Slice in 3 oranges and 3 lemons and let stand 24 hours. Squeeze out, then add 3 pounds of white sugar and 3 tablespoons yeast.

Sarah A. Balch, Kalamazoo
(Charlotte, 1909)

Elderberry Wine

Strip the berries from the stem and put into crock, add water enough to cover. Let stand in a warm place to sour, then strain. To each gallon of juice add three cups of sugar. Set on stove and boil twenty minutes. Skim and bottle while hot.

Mrs. Quay
(Flint, 1912)

Understandably, it is unusual to find recipes for alcoholic beverages in cookbooks compiled by church groups. Nevertheless, the Ladies Aid of the Oak Park Methodist Episcopal Church of Flint included in their 1912 cookbook Mrs. Quay's recipe for elderberry wine, which has been known to turn out very potent.

Ginger Wine

Boil twenty ponds of sugar in seven gallons of water for half an hour skimming it well; then put

314

nine ounces of bruised ginger in a portion of the liquor, and mix all together. When nearly cold put nine pounds of raisins chopped very small, into a wine gallon cask; add four lemons, sliced, after taking out the seeds, and pour the liquor over all, with one half-pint of yeast. Leave the cask open for three weeks, keeping it filled up with some of the reserved liquor, and bottle it in from six to nine months.

(Detroit, 1881)

Mulled Wine

Into one pint of water, put two ounces of stick cinnamon, and let it simmer fifteen minutes. Pour in one quart of claret, sweeten to taste, and heat, all together, boiling hot, then strain. Serve hot in small glasses.

Mrs. A. C. Wortley
(Kalamazoo, 1906)

Rhubarb, or English Patent Wine

An agreeable and healthful wine is made from the expressed juice of the garden rhubarb.

To each gal. of juice, add 1 gal. of soft water in which 7 lbs. of brown sugar has been dissolved; fill a keg or a barrel with this proportion, leaving the bung out, and keep it filled with sweetened water as it works over until clear; then bung down or bottle as you desire.

These stalks will furnish about three-fourths their weight in juice, or from sixteen hundred to two thousand gallons of wine to each acre of well cultivated plants. Fill the barrels and let them stand until spring, and bottle, as any wine will be better in glass or stone.

(Ann Arbor, 1864)

Ripe Gooseberry Wine

Put ripe and well picked red gooseberries into a tub or pan, bruise the fruit well and leave it uncovered for twenty-four hours. Squeeze the juice from the pulp through a fine sieve or canvas bag. Put the

This wine caster with etched-glass decanters sold for thirty dollars in 1872 (Wallingford, 1872).

residue of each squeezing into a vessel, pour upon it one-half gallon of boiling water for each gallon of fruit and stir well for a quarter of an hour. Let it stand for twelve hours; squeeze the pulp through the bag and add the liquor to the juice of the fruit obtained. Add two and a half pounds of sugar to each gallon of the liquor and stir it well. Let it stand to ferment. When it has done fermenting, draw it off and add three-quarters of a pint of brandy to each gallon. Let it stand to settle for four or five weeks, then draw it off carefully into a cask that will just hold it; keep it in a cool cellar for twelve months or more, when it may be bottled. Choose a dry, clear, cold day for bottling. This ought to be a splendid wine in two years.

(Detroit, 1881)

Tomato Wine

Express the juice from clean, ripe tomatoes, and to each gallon of it, (without any water), put brown sugar 4 lbs.

Put in the sugar immediately, or before fermentation begins—this ought to be done in making any fruit wine. Something of the character of a cheese press, hoop and cloth, is the best plan to squeeze out the juice of tomatoes or other fruits. Let the wine stand in a keg or barrel for two or three months; then draw off into bottles, carefully avoiding the sediment. It makes a most delightful wine, having all the beauties of flavor belonging to the tomato, and I have no doubt all its medicinal properties also, either as a tonic in disease, or as a beverage for those who are in the habit of using intoxicating beverages, and if such persons would have the good sense to make some wine of this kind, and use it instead of rot-gut whiskey, there would not be one-hundredth part of the "snakes in the boot" that now curse our land. It must be tasted to be appreciated. I have it now, which is three years old, worth more than much pretended wine which is sold for three or four shillings a pint.

(Ann Arbor, 1864)

Blackberry Cordial

Add 1 pound white sugar to 3 pounds ripe blackberries; let it stand 12 hours, then press out the juice, straining it; add ⅓ brandy or rum; put 1 teaspoon powdered allspice to each quart of cordial. It is not fit to use at once.

(Detroit, 1890)

Judging from the following two recipes Anna Wortley contributed to *New Crumbs of Comfort*, she must have been a lively hostess. Based on a compilation originally published by the Ladies of St. Luke's Episcopal Church in Kalamazoo in 1888, the third edition of 1906 was revised and enlarged to replace the previous copies that had "in most instances become completely worn out through daily use."

Cherry Bounce

1 gal. of whiskey
9 qts. of sour, red cherries

3 lbs. of granulated sugar

Wash and stem the cherries; put them in a jug, including the pits. Add the sugar, then the whiskey.

Let stand for a few weeks, when it will be ready for use. As you use it, leave the cherries in the jug, until the whiskey is all drained off.

Mrs. A. C. Wortley
(Kalamazoo, 1906)

Ginger Cordial

5 lbs of ripe, red currants, after they have been washed and picked from the stems
3 ozs. of broken Jamaica ginger root

4 lemons, sliced and seeded, leaving the peel on
1 gallon of whiskey

Crush the currants in a stone jar; add the broken ginger root, lemons and whiskey. Let them stand three weeks, stirring frequently. Cover the jar with muslin, and put a plate over it. At the end of three weeks, strain twice through a flannel bag, and add 4 pounds of granulated sugar. When sugar is dissolved, bottle and seal.

Mrs. A. C. Wortley
(Kalamazoo, 1906)

The following two recipes appeared in a cookbook compiled by the Marine City Eastern Star Relief Board in 1923, the depth of Prohibition. Evidently the folks in Marine City, across the river from Canada where liquor still flowed, continued to enjoy their cocktails.

Lakeside Beach Thirst Quencher

Take a tall lemonade or cold tea glass; fill ⅓ with cracked ice. To each glass use the juice of ¼ lemon and ¼ orange; 1 wine glass full of Vermouth. Fill the glass up with ginger ale and serve.

Loganberry syrup of juice, grape juice or home made wine may be used if you have no Vermouth.

Frank Halsted, P. G. P.
(Marine City, 1923)

Roshon Special
(A Nectar Fit for the Gods)

Two quarts ice cream; 3 pints gingerale; 1 pint home made wine; Vermouth or other liquor.

Have the ice cream in a 6 quart or larger freezer and leave it packed in the ice. With a good, stiff paddle or wooden spoon, stir in the ginger ale, adding a little at a time. When all thoroughly mixed and smooth, add the wine or liquor and serve in drinking glasses with the dinner. Raspberry vinegar or any sharp acid fruit juice may be used instead of the wine.

Harvey Roshon
(Marine City, 1923)

Flavoring Extracts, Fruit-Juices, Etc.

The following directions for the preparation at home of extracts, etc., may be relied upon. Of flavoring extracts put up for the general market, almond and peach are seldom pure, and are sometimes even poisonous. The other kinds are less liable to be adulterated.

To prepare vanilla, take 1 ounce fresh vanilla beans, cut fine and rub thoroughly with 2 ounces granulated sugar, put in a pint bottle, and pour over it 4 ounces pure water, and 10 ounces 95 per cent. deodorized alcohol. Set in a warm place, and shake occasionally for 14 days.

To prepare lemon, cut in small pieces the rinds of 2 lemons, put in a 4-ounce bottle, and fill with deodorized strong alcohol, set in a warm place for 1 week; then put 2 drachms fresh oil lemon, 4 ounces deodorized strong alcohol, and the juice of ½ lemon, in a bottle of sufficient size to hold all; then strain in the tincture of lemon-peel.

To make orange extract, use the rind and oil of orange, as directed for lemon.

To make rose extract, put 1 ounce red rose leaves in 1 pint deodorized alcohol, let stand 8 days; press out the liquid from the leaves, and add it to ½ drachm otto of roses.

Oils must be fresh and pure, or the extract will have a turpentine taste; and always use deodorized alcohol.

For fruit juices, select clean, ripe fruit, press out juice, and strain it through flannel; to each pint juice, add 6 ounces pure granulated sugar; put in a porcelain kettle, bring to boiling point, and bottle while hot, in 2 or 4 ounce bottles.

(Detroit, 1890)

Otto, or attar, of roses is a fragrant volatile oil obtained from the distillation of rose petals. It is also known as rose oil.

Measuring Tables, Oven Temperatures, Hints, and Suggestions

Sprinkled among the culinary recipes in early cookbooks are often found tidbits of domestic wisdom ranging from medical advice and common-sense philosophy to directions for creating substitutes for expensive "store-bought" articles. We have included a selection of what appear the most useful and interesting. Some we have applied in our own household with excellent results, but we would urge caution on others such as the application of gasoline on your carpet as a moth repellent.

Housekeepers' Helpful Standard

With wisdom fraught, not such as books, but such as patience taught.

4 saltspoonfuls of liquid equal 1 teaspoonful.
4 teaspoonfuls of liquid equal 1 tablespoonful.
3 teaspoonfuls of dry material equal 1 tablespoonful.
4 tablespoonfuls of liquid equal 1 wineglass, 1 gill or ¼ cupful.
16 tablespoonfuls of liquid equal 1 cupful.
8 heaping tablespoonfuls of dry material equal 1 cupful.
2 gills equal 1 cupful or ½ pint.
4 cupfuls of liquid equal 1 quart.
4 cupfuls of flour equal 1 quart.
2 cupfuls of solid butter equal 1 pound.
2 cupfuls of granulated sugar equal 1 pound.
1 pint of milk or water equals 1 pound.
1 pint of chopped meat solidly packed equals 1 pound.
   Butter the size of an egg, ¼ of a cupful.
1 teaspoonful Wyandotte soda to one pint of sour milk.
1 teaspoonful of salt to 1 quart of soup stock.

1 teaspoonful of salt to 2 quarts of flour.
   A "speck" of cayenne pepper is what can be taken upon the point of a penknife, or ¼ of a saltspoon.
   A pinch of salt, or spice, is about a saltspoonful, or ¼ teaspoonful.
   This seasoning is for moderate tastes.

(Lansing, 1923)

Weights and Measures

1 quart flour weighs	1 lb.
1 quart Indian meal weighs	1 lb. 2 oz.
1 quart soft butter weighs	1 lb. 1 oz.
1 quart lump sugar weighs	1 lb.
1 quart powdered sugar weighs	1 lb. 1 oz.
1 quart best brown sugar weighs	1 lb. 2 oz.
10 eggs average	1 lb.
2 cups sifted flour weighs	1 lb.
1 pint sifted flour weighs	1 lb.
2 tablespoonfuls of liquid weighs	1 oz.
1 gill weighs	4 oz.
1 pint weighs	16 oz.

One drachm is ⅛ of an ounce.

(Lansing, 1923)

Table of Weights and Measures

1 gill is 4 ounces.
4 teaspoons liquid is 1 tablespoon.
4 tablespoons liquid is 1 wine glass or ½ gill.
8 tablespoons liquid is 1 teacup.

2 tablespoons flour is 1 ounce.
1 heaping tablespoon sugar is 1 ounce.
12 tablespoons dry material is 1 teacup.
1 tablespoon butter is 1 ounce.
1 heaping tablespoon flour is ½ ounce.
1 teacup liquid is 2 gills or ½ pint.
1 teacup butter is ½ pound.
1 heaping teacup flour is ¼ pound.
2 teacups granulated sugar is 1 pound.
2 heaping teacups pulverized sugar is 1 pound.
1 quart flour is 1 pound.
10 eggs equal 1 pound.
Butter the size of a walnut is 1 ounce.
Butter the size of an egg is 2 ounces.

(Kalamazoo, 1899)

Oven Temperatures and Terms

Slow oven	250°
Medium Oven	300°
Hot Oven	350°
Quick Oven	400°
Very Hot Oven	450°
Broil	500°
Roast	600°

Canned Goods and Preserves

Right Time for Canning Different Fruits and Vegetables

Cherries—June 15th to July 1st.
Currants—June 10th to July 1st.
Strawberries—June 10th to July 1st.
Raspberries—June 1st to July 25th.
Blueberries—July 1st to August 5th.
Blackberries—July 15th to August 25th.
Pineapples—May 10th to July 1st.
Peaches—August 5th to October 15th.
Pears—August 20th to October 15th.
Apricots and Plums—August 10th to September 10th.
Apples—October 20th to November 20th.
Quinces—September 10th to October 25th.
Asparagus—May 15th to July 1st.

Peas—May 25th to July 1st.
Tomatoes—August 15th to October 1st.
Corn—August 15th to October 15th.
Beans—September 20th to October 20th.
Lima Beans—August 20th to October 15th.
Rhubarb—May 15th to July 1st.
Cauliflower—September 15th to October 25th.

(Marine City, 1930)

To Mothers

And now a word to mothers—those of you who do your own work. Women who keep servants may skip this chapter. Save yourself. *Save yourself.*

Save Yourself

In the first place, sit all you can. Sit down to prepare the vegetables for dinner. Sit down to wash the dishes. Sit down to scour the knives and rub up the silver. Sit down to take up the ashes. Sit down to the ironing-board and smooth the plain pieces. And here, before I forget it, let me say, get your steel knives plated and save yourself about six hours' time each month. Once plated, they will keep bright, with ordinary washing and wiping, three or four years. Nothing will spot them. Vinegar or acid of any kind has no effect. It is called Stannil Plating. The cost is one dollar per dozen knives. It is an investment that pays a very large interest.

When you wash your dishes—being sure they are well washed—pour hot water over them, and turn them upside down on a cloth laid on the table, in a basket, or, better still, get a dish-drainer, cover them up with a cloth or newspaper, and go about your other work. They will be clean and dry when you are ready to put them away.

Now, about ironing. If your husband's night-shirt is smoothed in front and folded artistically, who is to know whether the back has been ironed or not? I'll venture to say that he will not, unless you tell him. The same with your own night-dresses; and the children's drawers! Little romps, they soil them in less time than it takes to do them up. Let

Miscellaneous Household Hints

319

the gathers go. Iron the bottoms of the legs smoothly, and that is enough. You can iron six or eight pairs in this way, while, otherwise, you would be working at two pairs.

Learn to slight where it will do to slight. Some garments must not be slighted in the least. Aprons and dresses should be done the very best that one knows how.

Sheets may be folded smoothly and have a weight put upon them; or, take one at a time, and lay it under the ironing-sheet and iron over it for awhile. Then fold and put away, and take another, until all are done.

It is not absolutely necessary to iron skirts, except for twelve or fifteen inches above the bottom.

Bear in mind, these are hints to those only, who need them. But there is enough in life that has to be done, without vexing our souls and wearing out our bodies over work that is not essential either to the happiness or well-being of our fellows.

(Chicago, 1886)

To Clean the Cupboard

When cleaning dining room cupboard, move the dishes from one shelf to a light table on castors. Wheel the table to the kitchen, wash or wipe dishes, place on table again, and wheel back to the cupboard. This will save many steps.

Lois Thomas, Schoolcraft
(Charlotte, 1909)

Hints

Have shelf just over the door at the bottom of the stairs, for the things that are waiting to be carried up.

Always sit down to wash the dishes. Have trays for the dishes bound for different places, and place them on the proper trays when wiped. (Use trays in the same way when clearing the table.) Wipe all grease off of dishes with bits of paper or old cloth. Try a dishcloth of quilted mosquito netting. Remember, "it takes a lady to wash dishes."

Caroline Bartlett Crane, Kalamazoo
(Charlotte, 1909)

A frenetic social reformer, Caroline Bartlett Crane became minister of the People's Church in Kalamazoo in 1890. She pioneered the city's first kindergarten and manual training classes. She also led clean streets crusades across the nation and advocated inspection of slaughterhouses. In 1924 Crane published *Everyman's House*, a description of a model home she had designed to make the life of the average housewife easier. Among other innovations, she advocated that a large window be placed over the sink so that women might enjoy a view and that the nursery be situated adjacent to the kitchen to save mothers from needless walking.

To Keep a Teakettle Clean

Keep an oyster shell in your teakettle and you will not be troubled with a crust forming on the bottom or sides.

(Niles, 1907)

To Prevent Jars from Breaking

When putting up fruit, set the jars on a folded cloth wet with cold water, then fill with the boiling fruit, putting it in slowly, at first; I have never known a jar to break, thus.

(Muskegon, 1890)

To Keep Silver Bright

A little milk added to the water in which silver is washed, will help to keep it bright.

(Flint, 1912)

Discolored Cups

Salt and vinegar will remove stains from discolored cups.

(Lansing, 1923)

Hints

Glass should be washed in cold water, which gives it a brighter and clearer look than when cleaned with warm water.

A simple and very efficient disinfectant to pour down a sink is a small quantity of charcoal, mixed with clean water. A little charcoal put into the water containing cut flowers will keep the water fresh for some time.

(Lansing, 1901)

To Clean Cut Glass

To clean cut glass carafes, vases, etc., rinse with a teaspoon of salt dissolved in a half cup of vinegar.

(Charlotte, 1909)

To Polish Metal

Salt wet with strong vinegar, rub well and then wash with soap suds and wipe dry.

One teaspoon corn starch in 1 pt. of salt will keep it dry, just try it.

Mrs. J. J. Hoyt
(Muskegon, 1890)

To Clean Tinware

After thoroughly washing in hot soap suds and wiped dry, then apply dry flour and rub with newspaper.

(Vermontville, 1906)

To Clean Zinc

One tablespoonful sulphuric acid in a saucer of water applied with a rag tied on a stick; then rub well with clean cloths; after rub over with a rag wet in kerosene and rub off with a clean cloth. Be careful not to breathe the fumes, or get it on your hands.

(Muskegon, 1890)

To Clean Piano Keys

Clean the keys of your piano with a soft cloth dipped in alcohol. This will keep the ivory from turning yellow.

Josephine M. Gould, Owosso
(Charlotte, 1909)

Stove Hints

Use a blackboard eraser for polishing the kitchen stove. It will save the fingers and give the stove a good polish.

If soot falls upon the carpet, cover it thickly with dry salt. It can then be swept up and will leave no stain.

Use old newspapers to polish stoves. Much better than a cloth.

(Flint, 1912)

White Spots on Furniture

Hold a hot iron a few inches above the spots, raising and lowering it several times, not to "draw" the varnish, until the spots disappear. Or, rub with a flannel wrung out of alcohol, and when dry, with one dampened with kerosene.

Elnora Chamberlin, Hartford
(Charlotte, 1909)

Hinges

Rub hinges with a feather dipped in oil and they will not creak.

(Lansing, 1901)

To Fill Holes in Plaster

Tear old newspapers into small bits, cover with water and cook until it forms a thin paste and apply with a small wooden paddle, pressing it in well. Let it harden twenty-four hours before you paper. This is as satisfactory as plastering, and has the additional advantage of being easily applied by a woman, if the men folks are busy. It is equally good for filling cracks in the floor or woodwork.

(Charlotte, 1909)

To Remove Glass

Panes of glass may be easily removed by the application of soft soap for a few hours. However hard the putty may be, this recipe rarely fails.

(Lansing, 1901)

To Wash Windows

Two tablespoons turpentine in water.

(Vermontville, 1906)

Raw Potato and Oil Paintings

To clean an oil painting without injury, cut a raw potato in half and rub quickly over the surface, after which polish with a silk handkerchief to remove dust or dirt.

Marguerite Phillips
(Charlotte, 1909)

Sing

Sing about your work, 'twill keep you cheerful, and thus preserve your youth and beauty which is the best preserves for your family.

(Flint, 1912)

Carpet Beating

"Here's to the housewife that's thrifty!" Beat a carpet on the wrong side first and then more gently on the right side. Beware of sharp jointed beaters, which quickly tear well-worn places.

(Charlotte, 1909)

Carpet Moths

To protect carpet from moths, sponge with a mixture of equal parts gasoline and water, and a little salt.

(Flint, 1912)

To Remove Kerosene Spots

Kerosene when spilled on a carpet can be readily removed by putting on Indian meal, then brushing out when it has lain a few hours. It may need more than one application if much has been spilled, but it will all come out by repeated application.

(Vermontville, 1906)

" Use a Wire Beater."

One of the few domestic chores that was "man's work" was rug beating (New York, 1908).

Morning Hours

The writer once asked Mrs. L. H. Stone of revered memory, how she managed to accomplish so many things—literary work, acquiring several languages, taking classes abroad for study, to say nothing of unlimited correspondence with and for clubs. Her answer was as unassuming and direct as possible, "I get up early in the morning, from girlhood I have loved to see the sunrise."

Thus while many were sleeping away what to her were the most delightful hours of the day, she was acquiring knowledge to scatter it broadcast for the enrichment of womanhood. She had learned well the lesson that the morning hours are most fruitful of results and mental growth.

Irma T. Jones, Detroit
(Charlotte, 1909)

The Use of Borax

The washerwomen of Holland and Belgium, so proverbially clean, and who get their linen so beautifully white, use fine borax for washing powder instead of soda, in the proportion of a large handful of borax powder to ten gallons of water. They save soap nearly one-half. All the large washing establishments adopt the same mode. For laces, cambrics, etc., an extra quantity of the powder is used; and for crinolines (requiring to made stiff) a stronger solution is necessary. Borax, being a neutral salt, does not in the slightest degree injure the

This washing machine was powered by elbow grease (Muskegon, 1899).

texture of linen. Its effect is to soften the hardest water, and therefore it should be kept on the toilet table. As a way of cleaning the hair, nothing is better than a solution of borax in water. It leaves the scalp in a most cleanly condition, and the hair is just sufficiently stiffened to retain its place. This stiffness, however, can be readily removed, if objectionable, by washing with water. Borax is also an excellent dentrifice; dissolved in water, it is one of the best tooth-washes. In hot countries it is used, in combination with tartaric acid and bicarbonate of soda, as a cooling beverage.

(Detroit, 1878)

A Laundress' Recipe for Doing up Shirts

Take 2 oz. fine, white gum arabic powder, put into a pitcher and pour on a pint or more of water, cover and let it stand all night: in the morning pour it carefully from the dregs into a clean bottle, cork it and keep it for use, a tablespoon of gum water stirred into a pint of starch made in the usual manner, will give to lawns either white or printed, a look of newness, when nothing else can restore them.

(Muskegon, 1890)

The Morning Glory Cleanser

To whiten linen or cotton that has become yellow: Take a handful of large sized Morning Glory leaves, wash them, place them in a dish, pour boiling water over them, cover tightly; when cool, add the water from the leaves to the water in which the clothes are to be boiled. Historical family recipe used in "ye olden times."

Mrs. A. G. Stevens
(Coldwater, 1907)

To Wash Blankets

One bar kitchen soap cut and dissolved in hot water, 2 tablespoons pulverized borax: fold blankets and soak over night or for several hours; don't rub unless there are spots. Squeeze and douse, and pull from one hand to the other. Rinse in 2 or 3 luke warm waters, and hang in a hot sun without wringing.

(Muskegon, 1890)

Pleasure at Home

Nothing is such a temptation to husband and father to find pleasure elsewhere, as the absence of it in the home.

(Flint, 1912)

To Remove Fruit Stain and Iron Rust

Put the clothes from the boiling suds on to the grass, cover the spots with cream of tartar, and let them dry. Take them up, and boil again. If the spots still show, repeat the process.

(Battle Creek, 1890)

To Remove Rust

To remove rust from white garments, soak them thoroughly in butter milk. It will remove the rust and make white as snow.

(Vermontville, 1906)

To Remove Iron Rust

The juice of lemon and salt placed on the spot, and the fabric placed in the sun, will remove the rust. Shining through glass its rays are stronger. I hang mine in a window.

(Muskegon, 1890)

Tea Stains

On your napkins and tablecloths may be removed by plunging them into fairly strong ammonia water.

(Lansing, 1901)

Perfume for Clothing

Take equal parts of cinnamon, cloves, nutmeg, caraway seed ground fine; one-third amount orris root. Mix and put into a small bag and place in the drawer among the clothing. This gives the clothing a fine perfume, and is also a protection from moths.

(Flint, 1912)

Hot Soapstones for Flatirons

The perfect treasure in one northern Michigan home was so interested in her work that she read the various household magazines her mistress placed in her hands. One of the suggestions, which saved her many steps, was the use of a hot soapstone as a flatiron stand. "And it saves gas, too!" she was heard to remark.

Clara Bates, Traverse City
(Charlotte, 1909)

"Clean a Small Section."

In between meals there was the floor to clean (New York, 1908).

To Make Toilet Soap

Six pounds of salsoda, three pounds of un-slacked lime, four gallons of soft water, seven pounds of grease. Put the water, lime, and salsoda into a kettle, and boil until dissolved; then let it stand until it settles. Pour out the liquid, throwing away the dregs; add the grease to the liquid and boil with the consistency of honey. Perfume as you please, and color with vermillion.

(Battle Creek, 1890)

To Make Hard Soap

Put into an iron kettle five pounds each of un-slacked lime and soda, and three gallons of soft water. Let soak over night; in the morning, pour off the water, then add three and one-half pounds of grease, boil till thick, turn into a pan until cool, and then cut into bars.

(Battle Creek, 1890)

How to Set a Table and Serve a Meal

Many books have been written on the subjects of table setting and the serving of meals, but they are usually too elaborate for the use of an average family, where one, or at most, two maids are kept. This article will endeavor to embody a few general rules applicable alike to the "general girl," and the maid whose work is what is known as "second work."

In setting a table, one's first care should be, that the husher cloth is smoothly and tightly drawn over the table—it is best to pin it box-like over the corners; or on a round table it should be fastened by tapes, tying diagonally opposite corners to-gether. (By far the best "husher" is the asbestos pad which can be procured in both square and round shapes, with as many separate additional leaves as one cares for). Then be sure the cloth is fresh, smoothly laid and straight. If carving cloths are used, see that their folds are straight with the folds of the table cloth.

Lay the silver straight, placing knives with sharp edge towards the plate, bowls of spoons and tines of forks should be turned up. All silver is laid in the order in which it is to be used, starting from the out-side; forks at the left and knives and spoons at the right. Water and wine glasses at the right of plate, bread and butter plates and napkins at the left. Carvers and silver for serving should be laid out on a side table, to be placed on the table as needed. Also dessert plates.

The other appointments of the table vary some-what in individual households, as to arrangement, and are not amenable to any fixed rule.

In serving an ordinary family dinner of three or four courses, the soup may be served in the kitchen and placed on the table before announcing the meal. After the soup is removed, the hot plates should be brought in, and set before the one who carves, then bring the meat, then vegetables. Bread, relishes, etc., should be ready in pantry for passing.

Remember, plates should be handed and re-moved from the right side. Dishes passed, are of-fered at the left side. In clearing this course remove first the plates, taking one at a time; place it on small tray, and except at formal dinners, the small vegetable dish, if any, may be placed quietly upon the large plate, taking butter plate in other hand. Repeat this for each person, then remove vege-tables, bread, etc., removing meat platter last. A salad, if served at table, is usually placed before the mistress. Observe same directions in handling and removing, as with other courses, remembering at all times *never* to reach across in front of a person for any purpose. As, when taking a plate from the right, step around to left side to remove butter plate. After the salad course is removed, clear the table of everything except the dessert silver and centerpiece, using tray for all small articles such as salts and peppers, unused silver, etc. With a plate and scraper, carefully remove all crumbs. (At lunch-eon, when bare table is used with doylies, use a folded napkin instead of scraper). Then serve the dessert.

All dining room service should be as noiseless as possible and the clatter of dishes in the pantry avoided.

A good waitress does not need to be reminded to replenish glasses or pass anything a second time; she will be watchful and relieve the mistress of all care in those matters, especially if there be guests at table.

A waitress must always present a neat appear-ance. Even the general maid, who cooks her meal as well as serves it, can, by a little care and fore-thought, always have a fresh white apron and a tidy neck and wrist dressing. To that end, half sleeves with elastic at wrists and elbows, and large bib aprons for kitchen use, save many soiled cuffs and spotted aprons.

M. H. P.
(Kalamazoo, 1906)

Things that May be Eaten with the Fingers

Olives, which should never be handled with a fork; asparagus, when served whole; lettuce, which can be thus dipped in the dressing; celery which may properly be placed on the tablecloth beside the plate; strawberries, when served with the stems on; fruits, cheese, potato chips, bread, toast, tarts, small cakes, etc.

Don't say a word to mar the happiness of those you love at meal time. Better not eat at all than after being scolded.

Dr. Geisel
(Charlotte, 1909)

A B Supper

In front of the building where the supper is to be held post the following notice:

B on Hand to the B supper, Wednesday evening, at 6:30.

An appropriate menu would be:

Baked Beans	Brown Bread
Beet Pickles	Buns
Baked Beef	Blanc Mange
Bachelor's Buttons	Blackberry Jam
Blueberry Pie	Butternuts
Bananas	Berry Sherbet
Brazil-nuts	

On the table beside each plate place a card with a sketch of a bee on it, and a simple motto, like: Be earnest; Be wise; Be kind; Be good.

After supper play games, using only words commencing with B, like "My ship is coming in"; "With what is she loaded?" and then follows a list, "beans," "books," "bowls," etc., all around the circle of players.

The "Parson's Cat" is another game, the adjectives describing the cat beginning with B.

Selected
(Charlotte, 1909)

Quantities Required to Serve Supper to Twelve People

Three doz. tea rolls
Three medium sized spring chickens
Five lbs. of fish, escalloped
One doz. tea patties
Two small glasses of jelly
One doz. peach pickles
Two qts. ice cream

A Victorian etiquette guide included a depiction of all conceivable bad manners at one boisterous table. The numbers identified respective faux pas:
  1. Tips back his chair
  2. Eats with his mouth too full
  3. Feeds a dog at the table
  4. Holds his knife improperly
  5. Engages in violent argument
  6. Lounges upon the table
  7. Brings a cross child to the table
  8. Drinks from the saucer and laps with his tongue the last drop from the plate
  9. Comes to the table in his shirt sleeves and puts his feet beside his chair
  10. Picks his teeth with his fingers
  11. Scratches her head and is frequently, unnecessarily getting up from the table (Chicago, 1890).

The table as it ought to be (Chicago, 1890).

Three boxes of strawberries, or three pts. of pre-
serves.
One medium sized cake.

(Kalamazoo, 1906)

Picnic Lunch for Twenty-Five

Six doz. sandwiches
Two chickens, pressed
Twenty-five hard boiled eggs
One qt. cucumber pickles
One-half gal. salad
1 gal. ice cream
Two medium sized cakes
One-half lb. salted almonds

(Kalamazoo, 1906)

Utensils Necessary in the Kitchen of a Small Family

Wooden Ware

Kitchen Table; Wash Bench; Wash Tubs (two sizes); Wash Board; Skirt Board; Bosom Board; Bread Board; Towel Roll; Potato Masher; Wooden Spoons; Clothes Stick; Flour Barrel Cover; Flour Sieve; Chopping Bowl; Soap Bowl; Pails; Lemon Squeezer; Clothes Wringer; Clothes Bars; Clothes Pins; Clothes Baskets; Mop; Wood Boxes.

Tin Ware

Boiler for Clothes; Bread Pan; two Dish Pans; Preserving Pan; four Milk Pans; two Quart Basins; two Pint Basins; two quart covered Tin Pails; one four-quart covered Tin Pail; Sauce Pans with covers, two sizes; two Tin Cups, with handles; four Jelly Molds (half-pint); two Pint Molds for rice, blanc mange, etc.; one Skimmer; two Dippers, different sizes; two Funnels (one for jug and one for cruets); one quart measure, also, pint, half-pint and gill measures (they should be broad and low as they are more easily kept clean), two Scoops; Bread Pan; two round Jelly Cake Pans, and two long Pie Pans; Coffee Pot; Tea Steeper; Colander; Steamer; Horse-radish Grater; Nutmeg Grater; small Salt Sieve; Hair Sieve for straining jelly; Dover's Egg Beater; Cake Turner; Cake Cutter; Apple Corer; Potato Cutter; one dozen Muffin Rings; Soap Shaker; Ice Filter; Flour Dredge; Tea Canister; Coffee Canister; Cake, Bread, Cracker, and Cheese Boxes; Crumb Tray; Dust Pan.

Iron Ware

Range; Pot with steamer to fit; Soup Kettle; Preserving Kettle (porcelain); Tea Kettle; large and small Frying Pans; Dripping Pans; Gem Pans; Iron Spoons of different sizes; Gridiron; Griddle; Waffle Iron; Toasting Rack; Meat Fork; Jagging Iron; Can opener; Coffee Mill; Flat Irons; Hammer; Tack Hammer; Screw Driver; Ice Pick.

Stone Ware

Crocks of various sizes; Bowls holding six quarts, four quarts, two quarts, and pint bowls; six Earthen Baking Dishes, different sizes.

Brushes

Table Brush: Two Dust Brushes; two Scrub Brushes; one Blacking Brush for stove; Shoe Brush; Hearth Brush; Brooms.

(Detroit, 1881)

Baking Powder

Six oz. tartaric acid, 8 oz. of best baking soda and 1 qt. of sifted flour; stir well together and sift 5 or 6 times through a fine sieve. Always procure the materials from a good druggist, by so doing you have for 40 cts. what would cost $1 from a grocer. Keep well corked, and use the same quantity as of any other baking powder.

(Muskegon, 1890)

Remember

A spoonful of *butter melted*, is more than a spoonful of *melted butter*. Take care to note which is called for.

(Kalamazoo, 1906)

Heat the Bowl

When butter is too hard to cream easily, heat the bowl slightly instead of warming the butter.

(Lansing, 1923)

To Detect Oleomargerine

Grease a piece of clean writing paper with the suspected butter; burn the greased paper; when half consumed blow it out. If the smoking paper smells like a blown-out candle, or, in other words, smells of tallow, the butter is impure.

C. H. L.
(Grand Rapids, 1890)

Hints for Bread and Cake

Much of heavy cake and bread is the result of the oven door being banged in closing. It should be closed as gently as possible.

Take cake to the door and beat hard a moment before putting it in tins to bake. Air makes it lighter.

(Flint, 1912)

Icing the Cake

To keep icing from running off a cake sift flour lightly over top of cake before icing.

(Charlotte, 1909)

Oven Temperatures

Test the oven for baking with a piece of white paper. If it turns it a light yellow in 5 minutes, it is ready for sponge cake; if a dark yellow in 5 minutes, it is ready for cup cake. Cake should not be moved in the oven till it has risen its full height. When it feels firm to the touch, shrinks from the pan and a straw inserted comes out clean, the cake is done.

(Kalamazoo, 1906)

Too Much Salt

Brown sugar is an antidote to salt; if soup or gravy becomes too salty, stir in a little brown sugar and it will become palatable again.

(Niles, 1907)

To Preserve Eggs

To each pail of water add one quart fresh slacked lime and one pint common salt, mix well; fill a barrel half full of this fluid; put your eggs in it any time after June and they will keep for months.

(Vermontville, 1906)

Item

Fresh fish rubbed with half a lemon before boiling or frying will hasten their cooking and also removes any earth or oily taste.

Mrs. F. B. Peck
(Muskegon, 1890)

"The general arrangement of the table set for a party of twelve persons. The plates are often left off, and furnished by the waiter afterwards" (Chicago, 1890).

Be Prepared

Always have flour ready when frying, to throw on fire, in case, lard should burn.

(Kalamazoo, 1906)

Dried Fruit

To keep dried fruit from becoming wormy— after being prepared, as it should always be before putting away, by scalding—as you put it in sacks scatter amongst it pieces of sassafras bark from the root. Tie closely: it will keep for years.

(Detroit, 1881)

Fruit Cooking, Suitable Vessels for

In cooking any acid fruit (and most of them are of an acid nature), tin, brass, or porcelain vessels are the best; never cook them in glazed earthen, on account of the lead in the glazing, nor in copper

without especial care to brighten it with brick-dust and flannel, and to pour out as soon as done.

(Ann Arbor, 1884)

Garlic

Garlic requires to be used most judiciously, or it will spoil whatever is cooked with it; if used carefully, however, it will impart a most delicious flavor to salads and sauces, but it is so strong that, for many dishes, all that is necessary is to rub the dish which is to be sent to table sharply round with a slice of it; or, better still, to rub it on a crust of bread, and put the bread into the soup, etc., for a few minutes. A very general prejudice exists against garlic, probably on account of its being used in the same way as an onion. If it is desired to diminish the strength of the flavor, this may be done by boiling the garlic in 2 or 3 waters.

(Detroit, 1890)

Keeping Grapes in Winter

Who does not enjoy a bunch of luscious grapes in mid-winter? Either of the following recipes will be found valuable to lovers of this delicious fruit:

Use full, ripe and perfect bunches. If there are any defective ones, pick them off. Seal the end cut from the vine with sealing wax or melted resin, so that the sap may not escape, and to exclude the air. Let them stand one day after sealing, to see that it is well done; if not, they will shrivel up. Then pack in dry sawdust. The bottom of the box should be covered with sawdust, then put the grapes in carefully, not crowding them, and cover with sawdust. Then put in more grapes, and proceed until the box is full; cover, and put in a cool, dry place.

Or, prepare the grapes as above, then hang them by twine to sticks, placed across the edge of a wooden box—a lean cheese box will answer—that is deep enough for the bunches not to touch the bottom. Hang the bunches close together, but do not let them touch. Then take dry sawdust and pour into the boxes, working it with a small rod among the bunches so that they may be perfectly enveloped, cover the box first with a sheet of newspaper,

329

then put on the box cover. Put in a cool place. Ten pounds may be put in a cheese box.

(Battle Creek, 1890)

Seasoning Food, Sweet Herbs for—How to Raise, When to Cut and Dry, and How to Preserve their Flavor, etc.

It is a mistaken idea that nicely flavored dishes are expensive. If purchased the herbs cost but a trifle per oz., and if raised at home it costs only a trifle to buy the seeds for them. The principal kinds used are sage, summer savory, thyme, parsley, sweet basil and sweet marjoram, tarragon, mint, mace, cloves, celery seed and onions. The mints grow readily along small streams and the others may be raised in boxes, even in the window or garden, wherever the sun will shine upon them. Sage need not be gathered till the last of September or first of October; summer savory, thyme and marjoram in July and August; basil in August and September; tarragon and parsley in June or July, or just before flowering; mints for winter use, when fully matured, in June and July. All should be gathered on a dry, sunny day and dried in the shade, and best if carefully dried in an open, moderate oven, or else hung up close by a stove to dry quickly. And when very dry is the time to powder and sift them, and then to bottle and cork tightly or keep in airtight cans, which saves their flavor perfectly.

Remarks—The reason why French dishes are superior to other cooking is that they are seasoned with a variety of herbs or spices, or both; and the flavor, although indistinct (*i.e.*, no one thing overbalancing another) from the variety used in a single dish; yet they are remarkably fine in themselves.

(Ann Arbor, 1884)

To Keep Lemons

Lemons can be kept a long time by placing them in a jar of cold water and changing water every week. Place a plate on top to keep the lemons under water.

(Niles, 1907)

This elaborate silver-plated napkin ring sold for $1.20 at the H. Leonard's and Sons store in Grand Rapids in 1890 (Grand Rapids, 1890).

A Workingman's Lunch

Should always be served hot. Good health and long life depend upon it. To accomplish this result, pack the lunch in one of our square dinner pails and pack with it a pocket stove supplied with a teaspoonful of alcohol. At noon the man can warm his dinner.

(Grand Rapids, 1890)

Vinegar in Boiling Meat

In boiling meat, a tablespoonful of vinegar will hasten the cooking.

(Flint, 1912)

To Prevent Scorching

Salt spread on the oven bottom under a baking pan will prevent scorching; asbestos mats are also good.

(Kalamazoo, 1906)

Burned Cooking

When your cooking has been scorched, lift the vessel holding the food quickly from the fire, and stand it in a pan of water for a few minutes, and the scorched taste will entirely disappear.

(Flint, 1912)

Meat

Tough meat may be made tender by laying it a few minutes in vinegar water.

(Flint, 1912)

To Prevent Curdling Milk

A pinch of soda stirred into milk that is boiled, will keep it from curdling.

(Flint, 1912)

To Cook Mushrooms

When cooking mushrooms, use a silver spoon for it. If any impure qualities be present, the spoon will be blackened and the mushrooms should be thrown away.

(Lansing, 1901)

Oatmeal Mush

Oatmeal mush is one of the most wholesome articles of food.

(Grand Rapids, 1890)

Onions

Onions absorb poison more quickly than any other kind of food. It is unsafe therefore to use onions which have been kept for any length of time, especially after they are cut.

(Lansing, 1901)

Peaches—To Peel

In peeling small peaches with a knife, too much of the peach is wasted; but by having a wire-cage, similar to those made for popping corn; fill the cage with peaches and dip it into boiling water, for a moment, then into cold water for a moment and empty out, going on in the same way for all you wish to peel. This toughens the skin and enables you to strip it off, saving much in labor, as also the waste of peach. Why not, as well as tomatoes?

(Ann Arbor, 1864)

To Prevent Soggy Pie Crust

Brush the bottom crust of a fruit pie with the white of egg and it will not be soggy.

(Kalamazoo, 1906)

Pie Shells

Bake pie shells on a pie pan turned upside down.

(Flint, 1912)

An Easy Way To Prepare Pineapple

Cut off end of pineapple, cut through lengthwise, take out core, then you can easily dip the pineapple from shell with a spoon. This process is much easier than peeling and cutting out the eyes of the pineapple.

(Charlotte, 1909)

To Bake Potatoes

To hasten the baking of potatoes I let them stand a few minutes in hot water, after washing them clean.

(Manistee, 1930)

To Mash Potatoes

Potatoes should steam dry before mashing.

(Grand Rapids, 1890)

To Cook Rice

Rice will cook in 20 minutes. Always have water boiling before adding rice.

(Kalamazoo, 1906)

Picnic Sandwiches

Our favorite picnic sandwiches are made of bread and butter spread with mayonnaise, with thin slices of onion between.

Caroline Bartlett Crane, Kalamazoo
(Charlotte, 1909)

Meat Trimmings

The frugal housewife does not leave the trimmings from her meats at the market, but has them sent home for soup stock.

(Niles, 1907)

Celery for Soup

If you relish celery in soup and live where it cannot be obtained the year around, dry the celery leaves as you get them and put them away in a fruit jar. When preparing soup, tie a few of the leaves in a cloth and drop it into the kettle. You will find that the soup will have even more of the taste of celery than when using the stalk.

(Marine City 1923)

Vanilla Extract

Get 3 fresh vanilla beans of a druggist, break them in small pieces and put them in ½ pt. of alcohol. It will be fit for use in a few months. Select beans 6 or 7 inches long; vanilla improves with age.

(Muskegon, 1890)

Home Remedies

To drive away ants or cockroaches, sprinkle mule team borax plentifully in places infested.

May Stocking Knaggs, Bay City
(Charlotte, 1909)

Ant Trap

Procure a large sponge, wash it well and press it dry which will leave the cells open, then sprinkle it with fine white sugar, and place it near where the ants are troublesome. The ants will soon collect upon the sponge, dip the sponge in boiling water; it may be set over and over again.

(Muskegon, 1890)

Cure for Alcoholism

In the morning before breakfast, an orange should be eaten, one about 9 o'clock, one before dinner, one before supper and one before retiring; continue one week. The second week 4 oranges per day will be sufficient, the third week 3 and the fourth week the tippler won't be able to bear the smell of alcohol. Try it.

(Vermontville, 1906)

Take Fire Out of Burns

Pour hot water on a lump of white lime; strain off the water, and add linseed oil, shake well in a bottle and apply at once. This should be kept in every house for an emergency.

(Vermontville, 1906)

Castor Oil Cookies

A sure way to give castor oil is to add two table-spoonsful of the oil to a batch of nine cookies, and one teaspoonful of ground cinnamon. Bake and keep the secret to yourself.

(Flint, 1912)

Choking Remedy

Blowing forcibly into the ear gives great assistance in coughing up anything which a person has imperfectly swallowed and which threatens to choke him.

(Lansing, 1901)

A Fragrant and Always With You Disinfectant

Scatter ground cinnamon slowly on a shovelful of hot coals.

(Charlotte, 1909)

Remedy for Convulsions

Dr. M. Hammond gives it is his experience that in convulsions of children, to turn them upon the left side will cut short, like magic, the convulsions. Epileptics treated in the same way are always promptly relieved.

(Vermontville, 1906)

Envelopes for Drinking Cups

It seems almost unnecessary to caution people against drinking from public cups on trains and boats, yet this is a common practice, even in states where travelers flock because of tuberculosis. Always carry with you a few new envelopes and cut these in two diagonally, making triangular drinking cups which can be used once and thrown away.

Mabel Bates Williams, Traverse City
(Charlotte, 1909)

To Keep Flowers Fresh

Keep flowers fresh by adding a pinch of salt or soda to the water.

(Lansing, 1923)

Freckle Remover

To remove freckles, put a teaspoonful of salt in the wash basin, when washing, and see how soon they will fade.

(Flint, 1912)

To Beautify the Hair

Put 1 ounce pulverized sulphur into 1 quart rain water, shake well every few hours, then pour liquid off and saturate the scalp every morning. Cures dandruff and falling out of hair.

(Vermontville, 1906)

To Stop Hoccoughs

Put a few drops of good, cider vinegar on a lump of sugar. Let dissolve in mouth.

(Vermontville, 1906)

To Keep Flies from Horses

Take two or three handsfull of green walnut leaves, pour over two or three quarts of soft cold water; let stand one night, pour in a kettle and boil fifteen minutes. When cold, wet a sponge and before the horse goes out of the stable, let those parts which are most irritated be washed over with the liquid.

(Vermontville, 1906)

Uses of the Lemon

In the spring, when people are apt to feel poorly, the eating of a lemon every day before breakfast, will be found beneficial. It should be kept up for at least a week. Lemon juice is excellent for relieving headache. The juice of two lemons, mixed

Essential tools for messy eaters, the crumb tray and brush were used between courses (Townsend, 1894).

with the white of an egg and a cup of sugar, will often check a cough. Slices of lemon also make a pretty garnish for cold meats, prepared fish, etc.

(Battle Creek, 1890)

To Drive Away Mice

Put camphor into places which they frequent. It will completely drive them away.

(Lansing, 1901)

Misery Sauce

Take 1 set of feelings (parboiled),
1 lb. envy,
1 lb. egotism,
1 qt. tears,
1 tsp. being misunderstood,
2 qts. selfishness.

Mix the feelings as fine as possible; stir in the envy thoroughly, then add the egotism, which must be very strong, as much of the success of the sauce depends upon a woman's never thinking of any one but herself. Put in the tears, drop by drop, to spread them out as much as possible, and mix in the flavor of misunderstanding, while things are hot. Saturate the mixture thoroughly with selfishness, and set away in the mind to ferment. Those who enjoy being unhappy, should always keep this in the house. It can be applied like a salad dressing, to any kind of circumstances, and enough of it can be concocted at a moment's notice to last a month.

One thing about misery sauce is this: That it will not *keep* in fresh air and sunshine.

Mrs. Jane L. Shaw
(Kalamazoo, 1906)

Mosquitos

To rid a room of mosquitos burn a piece of gum camphor about the size of a walnut on a plate. To prevent their bites, bathe hands and face in water in which you have dissolved enough salt to make it taste slightly salty.

(Lansing, 1901)

Nose Bleed

Lemon juice and vinegar are excellent means of arresting flow of blood from a large artery which is wounded. Snuffing a little lemon juice or vinegar is good for nose bleed, or a small syringe may be used.

(Muskegon, 1890)

To Stop Nose Bleeding

Place a penny between the upper lip and teeth; hold there a few minutes. Never fails.

(Kalamazoo, 1906)

Nose Bleed Remedy

The best remedy for nose bleeding consists in a vigorous motion of the jaws, as in the act of mastication.

(Lansing, 1901)

To Get Rid of Odors

Dried orange peel allowed to smoulder on a piece of red hot iron or on an old shovel will kill any bad odor in existence and leave a fragrant one instead.

(Kalamazoo, 1906)

We tried this on our pot bellied stove, "Hot Blast Florence," and it filled the room with a pleasant sweet scent.

Margie's Potato Starch

Grate a quantity of raw potatoes, put in a coarse bag, and wash until starch is removed, then let settle and drain water off. When nearly dry, pulverize and it will be ready for use. Superior to any other powder for chafing or bed-sore or children's use.

Mrs. John C. Sharp
(Charlotte, 1909)

Sure Cure for Snake Bite

I have seen many people bitten, but have never known a case proving fatal where this remedy was used. Procure the yolk of an egg and mix with enough salt to make a good, thick poultice, put the poultice on the bite and bandage tightly. Watch the solution and when it is full of poison it will change color and should be renewed.

(Vermontville, 1906)

Vomiting

Excessive vomiting, or nausea, can be relieved by a little cayenne pepper, about what will go on a 10-cent piece, in half a glass of milk. Drink nothing cold.

(Lansing, 1901)

For Excessive Vomiting

Try two teaspoons whiskey, one teaspoon water, one teaspoon ground cinnamon.

Adelaide Goodrich, Hillsdale
(Charlotte, 1909)

Those who sample the historic recipes contained in this volume will be spared from the above complaint.

To Purify Water

To purify water, add powdered alum to the water in the proportion of a teaspoonful to every 4 gallons. Stir this briskly round and round and it will have the effect of precipitating any impurities to the bottom of the water and leave the rest pure and clean.

(Lansing, 1901)

Sources

Adrian, 1905: *Confidential Trade Catalogue of the Michigan State Grange . . .* Adrian: Times Printing Co., 1905.

Albion, 1940: Calhoun County Federation of Women's Clubs. *Favorite Recipes.* Golden Jubilee ed. Albion: Art Craft Press, 1940.

Allegan, 1938: *Your Cook Book.* Allegan: Allegan News, [1938].

Ann Arbor, 1864: Chase, A. W. *Dr. Chase's Recipes. . . .* Ann Arbor: A. W. Chase, 1864.

Ann Arbor, 1872: Chase, A. W. *Dr. Chase's . . . Second Receipt Book. . . .* Ann Arbor: Chase Publishing Co., 1872.

Ann Arbor, 1884: Chase, A. W. *Dr. Chase's Third Last and Complete Receipt Book. . . .* Detroit: E. B. Dickerson & Co., 1884.

Battle Creek, 1875: *The Household Manual. . . .* Battle Creek: Office of the Health Reformer, 1875.

Battle Creek, 1879: Kellogg, John Harvey, *Dyspepsia, Its Causes, Prevention and Cure.* Battle Creek: Good Health Publishing Co., 1879.

Battle Creek, 1886: *Chips and Sticks with Pictures.* Battle Creek: The J. E. White Publishing Co., 1886.

Battle Creek, 1890: Sabin, Ransom. *The Home Treasure. . . .* Battle Creek: Wm. C. Gage & Son, 1890.

Battle Creek, 1890 II: Ladies of the Independent Congregational Church. *The Battle Creek Cook Book.* Battle Creek: Review & Herald, 1890.

Battle Creek, 1903: *Mother Hubbard's Modern Cupboard.* Battle Creek: R. W. Snyder, [1903].

Battle Creek, 1910: Kellogg, Ella Eaton. *Science in the Kitchen.* rev. and enlarged ed. Battle Creek: Good Health Publishing Co., 1910.

Berrien Springs, 1923: Ladies Aid of the United Brethren Church. *A Feast of Good Things.* n.p., [1923].

Berrien Springs, 1941: Whitfield, Mildred G., Hornbacher, Maria, and Pearson, Ruth. *The Fine Art of Cooking.* Berrien Springs: White Brothers, [1941].

Cass County, 1917: Pomona Grange No. 20. *Year Book.* n.p., 1917.

Charlotte, 1893: Ladies of the First Congregational Church. *The Charlotte Cook Book.* 2d ed. Charlotte: Perry & McGrath, Book and Job Printers, 1893.

Charlotte, 1909: *Michigan State Federation Cook Book.* [Charlotte: Perry, Nies & Co., 1909].

Chicago, 1877: Taylor, Benjamin F. *Songs of Yesterday.* Chicago: S. C. Griggs & Co., 1877.

Chicago, 1886: Owens, Frances E. *Mrs. Owens' Cook Book. . . .* Chicago: Owens Publishing Co., 1886.

Chicago, 1890: Hill, Thomas E. *Hills Manual of Social and Business Forms . . .* Chicago: Hill Standard Cook Co., 1890.

Chicago, 1896: *The Chicago Record Cook Book.* Chicago: Chicago Record, [1896].

Chicago, 1898: Ellis, Mary. *Ellis Cook Book. . . .* 2d ed. Chicago: H. J. Faithorn & Co., 1898.

Chicago, 1901: Sears Roebuck and Company. *Sears Roebuck and Company Catalogue.* Chicago: n.p., 1901.

Chicago, 1909: *The Cook's Book.* Chicago: Jaques Manufacturing Co., 1909.

Chicago, 1940: De Both, Jessie Marie. *Famous Sportsmen's Recipes for Fish, Game, Fowl and Fixin's.* Chicago: n.p., 1940.

Cincinnati, 1884: *The Hunter Sifter Cook Book . . .* Cincinnati: Hunter Sifter Manufacturing Co., 1884.

Cleveland, 1894: Standard Lighting Company. Trade Card. Cleveland: n.p., 1894.

Coldwater, 1907: Ladies of St. Mark's Church of Coldwater. *Good Living and How to Attain It.* Coldwater: G. E. Kleindinst, 1907.

Covert, 1903: Ladies of Covert. *Souvenir Cook Book.* n.p., 1903.

Detroit, 1878: Stewart, Isabella G. D., Sill, Sally B., and Duffield, Mary B. *The Home Messenger Book of Tested Receipts.* 2d ed. Detroit: E. B. Smith & Co., 1878.

Detroit, 1881: Goff, Mary Perrin. *The Household of the Detroit Free Press.* Detroit: Detroit Free Press Publishing Co., [1881].

Detroit, 1882: Young Ladies Missionary Society of the Jefferson Ave. Presbyterian Church. *The Spicy Recipe Book.* Detroit: Gulley Printing House, 1882.

Detroit, 1890: Ellsworth, Mrs. M. W. *The Queen of the Household.* Detroit: Ellsworth & Brey, 1890.

Detroit, 1891: *Our Home Cyclopedia: Cookery and Housekeeping.* Detroit: Mercantile Publishing Co., 1891.

Detroit, 1915: Woman's Association of Brewster Congregational Church, Detroit. *Book of Recipes.* n.p., [ca. 1915].

Detroit, 1923: Missionary Committee, Woman's Association, North Woodward Avenue Congregational Church, Detroit. *Favorite Recipes.* n.p., [1923].

Detroit, 1935: *A Book of Practical Recipes for the Housewife.* Detroit: Detroit Times, [1935].

Detroit, 1939: Drayton Ave. Presbyterian Church. *Selected Recipes.* Ferndale: [ca. 1939].

Elgin, IL, 1907: *The Inglenook Cook Book.* Elgin, IL: Brethren Publishing House, 1907.

Fennville, 1924: The Woman's Club, Fennville. *The Fennville Cook Book.* Grand Rapids: Caslon Press, 1924.

Flint, 1912: The Ladies' Aid Published for the Benefit of the Oak Park Methodist Episcopal Church, Flint. [Gaylord: Herald & Times], 1912.

Freeport, IL, 1915: *F. W. McNess' Cook Book and Health Hints.* Freeport, IL: n.p., 1915.

Gems, 1880: *Beautiful Gems of Poetry.* n.p.: n.p., [1880].

General Electric, 1927: Bradley, Mrs. Alice. *Electric Refrigerator Menus and Recipes . . .* Cleveland: General Electric, 1927.

Grand Marais, 1936: Grand Marais Women's Club. *The Cooking Pots of Grand Marais.* Grand Marais: n.p., [ca. 1936].

Grand Rapids, 1890: *The Grand Rapids Cook Book.* Grand Rapids: Eaton Lyon & Allen Printing Co., [ca. 1890].

Grand Rapids, 1902: Tuesday Ten of Park Congregational Church, Grand Rapids. *Tuesday Ten Cook Book.* 2d ed. n.p., 1902.

Grand Rapids, 1924: Ladies' Aid Society, Trinity Community Church. *The Trinity Community Church Cook Book.* Grand Rapids: n.p., 1924.

Grand Rapids, 1935: Cathedral League of St. Mark's Church, Grand Rapids. *The Cathedral League Cook Book.* [Grand Rapids: DeVries Ptg. Co.], 1935.

Grandville, 1920: First Congregational Church, Grandville. *A Cook Book of Reliable Recipes.* . . . Camden, NJ: B. H. Stone, ca. 1920.

Grayling, 1937: Ladies' of the Michelson Memorial Church Aid Society, Grayling. *Grayling Cook Book.* n.p., [1937].

Greenville, 1910: Ladies' Aid Society of the Baptist Church, Greenville. *Dainty Dishes.* n.p., [ca. 1910].

Greenville, 1915: *Cook Book by the Ladies' Aid Society of the First Congregational Church of Greenville.* n.p., [ca. 1915].

Hammond, IN, 1913: Rhodes, Susie Root, and Hopkins, Grace Porter. *The Economy Administration Cook Book.* Hammond, IN: W. B. Conkey Co., [1913].

Hart, 1907: *Cook Book Issued by the Ladies Aid Society of the First Baptist Church, Hart, Michigan.* Hart: Journal Press, 1907.

Hastings, 1921: Ladies of Emmanuel Church, Hastings. *A Feast of Good Things.* . . . 5th ed. Hastings: Hastings Printing Co., 1921.

Higgins Lake, 1920: *Back to the Kitchen with Lakeside Cooks.* [Higgins Lake, ca. 1920].

Holland, 1896: Ladies Aid Society of Hope Church, Holland. *Receipt Book.* Holland: John O. Kanters, 1896.

Holland, 1908: Ladies' Aid Society of the Methodist Episcopal Church, Holland. *The Ever-Ready Cook Book.* [Holland: W. H. Bingham], 1908.

Holland, 1925: Ladies of the Eunice Aid Society, Holland. *Holland's Choicest Cooking Recipes.* n.p., 1925.

Holland, 1936: Dieters, Mrs. Rena. *Hollandsche Kookerij Boek.* Holland: Steketee-Van Huis, [1936].

Homer, 1925: Second Division of the Ladies Aid Society of the Presbyterian Church. *Homer Cook Book.* n.p., 1925.

Ionia, 1912: *Women's Exchange Cook Book.* Ionia: Daily Standard, 1912.

Kalamazoo, 1899: Ladies of the First Presbyterian Church, Kalamazoo. *A Friend in Need.* . . . Kalamazoo: Ihling Bros. & Everard, 1899.

Kalamazoo, 1906: Ladies of St. Luke's Church, Kalamazoo. *New Crumbs of Comfort.* Kalamazoo: Kalamazoo Publishing Co., 1906.

Kalamazoo, 1918: *Wheat Substitutes. Recipes Tested by Students of Cookery Department, Western State Normal, Kalamazoo, Michigan.* n.p., [ca. 1918].

Kalamazoo, 1920: Ladies' Aid Society of the Second Reformed Church, Kalamazoo. *Cook Book.* n.p., [ca. 1920].

Kalamazoo, 1921: Ladies of Corinthian Chapter No. 123 Order of the Eastern Star. *Book of Recipes.* Kalamazoo: n.p., [1921].

Kalamazoo, 1930: Mayflower Guild of the First Congregational Church, Kalamazoo. *Cook Book.* [Kalamazoo: Dalm Printing Co.], 1930.

Kalamazoo, 1933: Women of the Yo-Mar Class of the First Baptist Church, Kalamazoo. *Five Hundred Favorite Recipes of Kalamazoo Women.* Kalamazoo: n.p., 1933.

Kalamazoo, 1935: *Prize Winning and Selected Recipes from the Kalamazoo Gazette Saturday Recipe Pages. November 1934–May 1935.* [Kalamazoo: Kalamazoo Gazette, 1935].

Kalamazoo, 1941: Mayflower Guild of the First Congregational Church, Kalamazoo. *Cook Book,* Kalamazoo: Ihling Bros. & Everard Co., 1941.

Kalamazoo, 1945: Kalamazoo Navy Mothers Club No. 366. *Cook Book.* Kalamazoo: [Dalm Printing Co.], 1945.

Lansing, 1901: Pilgrim Congregational Church, Lansing. *The Pilgrim Cook Book.* 2d ed. Lansing: Wynkoop, Hallenbeck Crawford Co., 1901.

Lansing, 1918: Ladies Aid Society of the Methodist Protestant Church, Main Street, Lansing. *Victory Cook Book.* n.p., [1918].

Lansing, 1920: Women's Guild of St. Paul's Episcopal Church, Lansing. *Favorite Recipes.* n.p., 1920.

Lansing, 1923: Benevolent Committee of Arbutus Chapter No. 45 Order of the Eastern Star. *Arbutus Cook Book.* [Lansing: n.p.], 1923.

Lansing, 1937: Amity Chapter No. 490 Order of the Eastern Star, Lansing. *The Mixing Bowl.* Lansing: n.p., [1937].

Lansing, 1941: *The Social Study Club of Lansing, Michigan, Cook Book.* Lansing: Maurice Polack, Inc., 1941.

Manistee, 1929: *Congregational Cook Book, First Congregational Church, Manistee, Michigan.* Manistee: [J. H. Shults Co.], 1929.

Marine City, 1923: Order of the Eastern Star. *Relief Fund Cook Book.* [Marine City]: n.p., [1923].

Mattawan, 1906: W.H.W.V. of the Congregational Church. *The Reliable Economical Cook Book.* Mattawan: n.p., 1906.

Mendon, 1890: *Idlers Cook Book.* Mendon: Mendon Globe Print, 1890.

Minneapolis, 1881: *Buckeye Cookery.* . . . Minneapolis: Buckeye Publishing Co., 1881.

Muskegon, 1890: Ladies' Society of the First Baptist Church, Muskegon. *The Muskegon Cook Book of Tested Receipts.* Muskegon: Wantz & Manning, 1890.

Muskegon, 1899: Ladies of the Wood Avenue M.E. Church, Muskegon. *Tried and True.* . . . n.p., 1899.

Muskegon, 1912: Social Department of the Muskegon Women's Club. *Cook Book.* Muskegon: Dana Printing Co., 1912.

New York, 1881: Carleton, Will. *Farm Festivals.* New York: Harper & Brothers, 1881.

New York, 1886: Carleton, Will. *City Ballads.* New York: Harper & Brothers, 1886.

New York, 1890: *Wehman's Cook Book* . . . New York: Henry J. Wehman Publisher, [1890].

New York, 1908: Morse, Sidney. *Household Discoveries and Mrs. Curtis's Cook Book.* New York: The Success Company, 1908.

Niles, 1907: Ladies of Trinity Church, Niles. *Tried and True.* . . . Elkhart, IN: Mennonite Publishing Co., 1907.

Parchment, 1926: Parent Teacher Association. *Parchment Cook Book.* Kalamazoo: n.p., 1926.

Parchment, 1935: Ladies Society, Parchment. *The Four Hundred.* n.p., [1935].

Pearson's Magazine, 1900: *Pearson's Magazine,* May, [1900].

Philadelphia, 1859: A Practical Housekeeper. *The American Practical Cookery Book.* Philadelphia, G. G. Evans, 1859.

Philadelphia, 1870: *The Specimen Book of Collins and McLeester.* Philadelphia: Collins and McLeester, [1870].

Philadelphia, 1906: Johnson, Helen Louise. *The Enterprising*

Housekeeper . . . Philadelphia: Enterprising Manufacturing Co., 1906.

Polk, 1881: *State Gazetteer.* Detroit: R. L. Polk Co., 1881.

Portland, 1910: Tomy, Reva Crane. *The Portland Observer Cook Book.* Portland: Portland Observer, [ca. 1910].

Saginaw, 1905: Young Woman's Auxiliary to the Woman's Hospital Association, Saginaw. *Twelve Menus.* 2d ed. Saginaw: Seemann & Peters, 1905.

St. Louis, 1905: Majestic Manufacturing Company. *Majestic Range Cook Book.* St. Louis: n.p., 1905.

Sunfield, 1915: *Eastern Star Cook Book.* Sunfield: Sunfield Sentinel, [ca. 1915].

Townsend, 1894: Townsend, Mrs. Grace. *Dining Room and Kitchen . . .* n.p.: Home Publishing Co., [1894].

Traverse City, 1900: *The Herald Century Cook Book.* Traverse City: Herald Print, 1900.

Union City, 1902: Ladies of the First Congregational Church of Union City. *The Union City Cook Book.* n.p., [ca. 1902].

Vermontville, 1906: Ladies' Christian Association of the Congregational Church, Vermontville. *Twentieth Century Cook Book.* n.p., 1906.

Wallingford, 1872: Simpson, Hall, Miller & Company. *Catalogue of Improved Electro Plated Ware.* Wallingford, CT: [Wallingford Printing Co., 1872].

White House, 1925: Ziemann, Hugo, and Gillette, Mrs. F. L. *The White House Cook Book.* Akron: Saalfield, 1925.

Historical Index

Index

Index

Larry and Priscilla Massie are a husband and wife team specializing in Michigan history. Larry holds the B.A., M.A., and Specialist of Arts degrees in history from Western Michigan University. He has co-authored with Peter Schmitt *Kalamazoo: The Place Behind the Products* and *Battle Creek: The Place Behind the Products.* His other publications include *From Frontier Folk to Factory Smoke: Michigan's First Century of Historical Fiction; Voyages into Michigan's Past; Copper Trails and Iron Rails: More Voyages into Michigan's Past;* and *Warm Friends and Wooden Shoes: A Pictorial History of the Holland Area.*

Priscilla, born in Kalamazoo in 1955, traces her Michigan ancestry to Michel Campau, one of the one hundred Frenchmen who founded Detroit with Cadillac in 1701. Her research, photographic, word processing, and culinary skills allow the Massies to participate in a wide range of Michigan history projects.

The Massies live in the Allegan State Forest in a century-old schoolhouse filled with their research library of thirty thousand volumes and their collection of historic artifacts from Michigan's past.

The manuscript was edited by G. Aimée Ergas. The book was designed by Joanne Elkin Kinney. The typeface is Benguiat Book and the display face is Benguiat Medium Condensed. The book is printed on 60-lb. Finch Opaque and is bound in Kivar 9 cover paper.

Manufactured in the United States of America.